NEW THEOREMS,

TABLES, AND DIAGRAMS,

FOR THE

COMPUTATION OF EARTH-WORK.

DESIGNED FOR THE USE OF

ENGINEERS IN PRELIMINARY AND FINAL ESTIMATES,
OF STUDENTS IN ENGINEERING,
AND OF CONTRACTORS AND OTHER NON-PROFESSIONAL COMPUTERS.

IN TWO PARTS, WITH AN APPENDIX.

PART I.—A PRACTICAL TREATISE;

PART II.—A THEORETICAL TREATISE;

AND

THE APPENDIX.

CONTAINING NOTES TO THE RULES AND EXAMPLES OF PART I.; EXPLANATIONS OF THE CONSTRUCTION OF SCALES, TABLES, AND DIAGRAMS, AND A TREATISE UPON EQUIVALENT SQUARE BASES AND EQUIVALENT LEVEL HEIGHTS.

THE WHOLE ILLUSTRATED BY

NUMEROUS ORIGINAL ENGRAVINGS,

COMPRISING EXPLANATORY CUTS FOR DEFINITIONS AND PROBLEMS,
STEREOMETRIC SCALES AND DIAGRAMS,

AND A SERIES OF

LITHOGRAPHIC DRAWINGS FROM MODELS;

SHOWING ALL THE COMBINATIONS OF SOLID FORMS WHICH OCCUR IN RAILROAD EXCAVATIONS AND EMBANKMENTS.

BY

JOHN WARNER, A.M.

MINING AND MECHANICAL ENGINEER; AUTHOR OF STUDIES IN ORGANIC MORPHOLOGY.

PHILADELPHIA:
J. B. LIPPINCOTT & CO.
1861.

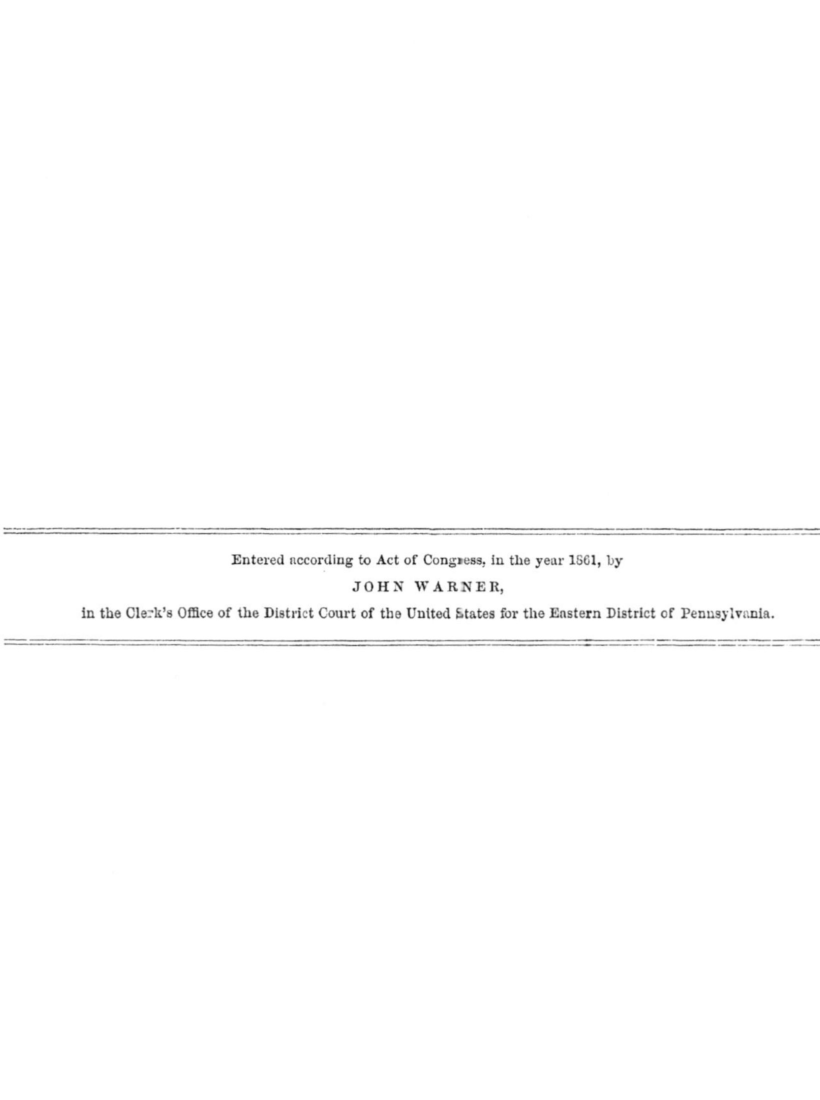

PREFACE.

THE main object of this work is to present both a theoretical and practical solution of some of the most important problems of earth-work. The rules given are, however, applicable to other computations of solidity for solids having the same form as those of earth-work; but cubic yards must be converted into other measure when required.

It will doubtless be conceded that there is yet room for improvement in the theory of our subject; and that previous treatises do not satisfy the wants of computers, is evident from the demand so constantly heard for "*something practical.*" This indicates that a system is yet desired which, though sufficient for the ordinary practice of engineering, does not require of the computer either unusual mathematical knowledge or extraordinary patience.

It has appeared to the writer that such a system followed by a theoretical treatise, would constitute a work suitable both as a text-book for students and as a manual for computers. Such a work we believe to be needed, and to produce it has been our principal aim. In attempting this, the author has endeavored, both by study and by oral consultation, to ascertain the wants of the practical man, and to reconcile them with the theoretical exigencies of the subject.

No method of earth-work computations is likely to be generally adopted which does not reduce them to an operation of routine. To this end, uniformity is necessary in the processes of calculation. This the author has sought to attain by founding those processes, as far as possible, on a few ideas easily understood and remembered. One of them is the use of the sum and difference of end dimensions.

The manner and the object of the arrangement of the work will be obvious without a minute explanation here. In general, we have endeavored to make the several parts available either separately or collectively, according to the wants of the reader. A portion of the First Part is put in small type,—most of which may be passed over if desired; and we have also avoided, as far as practicable, the use of algebraic signs and the phraseology of mathematical enunciation. Some further remarks upon the work and its subject will be found in the Introduction.

It is believed that the rules and explanations of the First Part will also enable non-professional computers to perform the most necessary calculations, and that the work will thus meet the wants of a large class of persons to whom its subject has hitherto appeared difficult or inaccessible.

We have endeavored, in the prosecution of the work, to remember that most readers will judge it by the standard of utility rather than of novelty. We desire, however, to say that it is considered to be in no proper sense a compilation, or a mere amplification of known methods, but as fairly original as any performance of the kind which does not lay claim to absolute novelty. The mathematical investigations are original, and, it is believed, are mostly new in method, results, and practical application. The tables as a body, and, for the most part, individually, are also thought to be new. They are adapted to the author's formulæ; they were all computed by him,* and faithfully revised with the assistance of an experienced proof-reader, and, it is believed, they may be relied on.

The Subdivision of Sections has been but slightly noticed by former writers, yet the want of explicit rules for it is daily felt. Our treatment of this subject is original, and we have much increased the size of the work by devoting the necessary space to it, believing that a brief disposition of it would be unsatisfactory.

Several gentlemen are especially entitled to the author's thanks for assistance and encouragement. Professors Vethake and Franck, of the Polytechnic College of Pennsylvania, and Professor Kirkwood, of Indiana University, have examined considerable portions of the work in proof or in manuscript; and Messrs. Ellwood Morris and N. F. Jones, civil engineers, have also rendered assistance. Whilst the author was employed under the direction of Mr. Jones, that gentleman kindly assumed a task from which his position as chief engineer might have exempted him: he tested the author's system by actual computations, and devoted much time to assist in perfecting it. The author is assured that in profiting, to the best of his ability, by the suggestions of these able gentlemen, he has acquired an additional claim to public favor.

THE AUTHOR.

PHILADELPHIA, May, 1861.

---

* With two exceptions. Messrs. Uriah Hunt & Son have kindly granted the use of Table XXVI. from their last edition (1860) of Gummere's Surveying; and Table A is a table of Natural Tangents.

CONTENTS.

INTRODUCTION.

PART I.—PRACTICAL TREATISE.

CHAPTER I.

PRELIMINARY DEFINITION AND DESCRIPTION—SUBDIVISION OF SECTIONS.

PRELIMINARY DEFINITION AND DESCRIPTION.

SUBDIVISION OF SECTIONS.

CHAPTER II.

AUXILIARY CONSTRUCTIONS—DETERMINATION OF VARIETIES AND PREPARATION OF ELEMENTS BY CONSTRUCTION AND BY TABULATION.

CHAPTER III.

COMPUTATION OF EXCAVATION AND EMBANKMENT BY TRANSVERSE GROUND-SLOPES.

Computation by Scale.

CHAPTER IV.

COMPUTATION OF EXCAVATION AND EMBANKMENT BY CENTRE AND SIDE HEIGHTS.

STRAIGHT WORK.

CHAPTER V.

THE TABLES AND THEIR USE.

PART II.—THEORETICAL TREATISE.

AUXILIARY CONSTRUCTIONS AND CALCULATIONS.

COMPUTATION OF SOLIDITY.

Straight Work.

APPENDIX.

NOTES TO THE RULES AND EXAMPLES OF PART I.

CATALOGUE OF FORMULÆ AND CONSTRUCTION OF THE TABLES.

DISCUSSION OF GRAPHICAL PROCESSES.

CONSTRUCTION OF SCALES.

BASES OF EQUIVALENT SQUARE PRISMS.

CONVERSION OF SLOPES.

INTRODUCTION.

The author's employment in the practical duties of computation engaged him in the special studies which have resulted in the production of this work, —commenced several years since. The completion of it has been delayed by business and by the prosecution and publication of other researches. In May, 1858, it was submitted to the Pottsville Scientific Association. Since then additions have been made, and the text has been in a good measure re-written. The first printed notice of the work is contained in the Annual of Scientific Discovery, for 1859, page 196. In the summer of 1859, a portion of the work, containing rules and tables for computation by centre and side heights, and also scales and the sub-section diagram, was distributed, in pamphlet form, among the author's friends.

The time employed upon the original labors of the work left inadequate leisure for the collection of historical materials; and of those now presented, a considerable portion were not known, or if known, but slightly regarded, until the work had been nearly completed. The writer therefore hopes to be excused if interesting historical facts or meritorious works have been overlooked.

As far as the writer is informed by British authorities, the study of rules for earthwork computations began to engage special attention about the commencement of railway-enterprises in England, some thirty-five years ago.

Among British authors who have furnished tables, or who have otherwise labored on the subject in question, may be mentioned Macneil, Bidder, Huntingdon, Hughes, Bashforth, Sibley, Rutherford, Law, Lowe, and Baker. This list is from Baker's works.* He appears to have labored with zeal and success. Macneil's works are frequently cited.

Of the writings of our own countrymen, those of Mr. Morris deserve especial attention, as well for their valuable information and suggestions as for their early historical place in our engineering literature. This writer, by original research, revived the discussion of the prismoidal formula, showed its importance in earthwork computations, and noticed its applicability to solids included under curved surfaces.† Professor Gillespie has shown its application to the hyperbolic paraboloid;‡ and Mr. Chauncey Wright has recently much promoted our knowledge of the subject by his papers on the Prismoidal Formula.§

* Rudimentary Treatise on Land Engineering, by T. Baker, C.E. London, 1850, p. 188. Also Baker's Railway Engineering. The critical student should not omit to consult Baker's works.

† Journal of Franklin Institute, vol. xxv., 2d series, pp. 25, 387, and vol. xxiii., 3d series, p. 240.

‡ Journal of Franklin Institute, vol. xxxiv., third series, p. 372.

§ Mathematical Monthly, vol. i., No. 1, p. 21, and No. 2, p. 53.

It was, however, previously known, but not generally taught in text-books of Mensuration or of Engineering, that the formula holds for various solids contained under ruled or other curved surfaces. Up to the time of his paper, two methods (says Mr. Morris) had come into general use. They are thus defined by him as adapted to dimensions given in feet:*

1. *Arithmetical Average.*—Multiply the sum of the end areas by their distance apart, and divide the product by 6 and by 9; the result will give, approximately, the number of cubic yards in the given length of excavation or embankment.

2. *Geometrical Average.*—Multiply the sum of the end areas and the square root of their product, by the distance apart, and divide the product by 9 and by 9. The result will be, nearly, the number of cubic yards in the given length of excavation or embankment.

We may here digress for a moment from our notice of this paper, to record the prismoidal rule, and to give some historical references pertaining to it.

3. The *Prismoidal Rule.* Add together the end areas and four times the area of the mid cross-section. Multiply the sum thus found by the distance between the end areas, and divide by 6, by 9, and by 3. The result will be the number of cubic yards in the given length of excavation or embankment as nearly, in our opinion, as by any general rule known.

Cardan finds the frustum of a pyramid, or of a cone, by computing the whole solid; and also the redundant part, and then subtracting the latter.† Hutton gives for this problem the rule of geometrical average before cited,‡ but subsequently applies the prismoidal formula to the mensuration of prismoids and cylindroids.§ He afterwards extends it to the hyperbolic conoid,|| and finally to the frusta of solids generated by the revolution of conic sections about their axes.¶ Bonnycastle follows Hutton in several of these applications,** and refers to Simpson for the demonstration in regard to the prismoid,††—the earliest notice we have found.

The methods for the quadrature of curves, which began with Newton's theorem of interpolation, seem to have led to more comprehensive formulæ for the mensuration of solids.‡‡ Montucla gives an interesting review of the labors of Newton, Cotes, and Simpson, in relation to the quadrature of curves by equidistant ordinates;§§ but at present I am unable to refer to other authorities than those already cited, for the extension of this method to solids. The

* Journal of Franklin Institute, vol. xxv., second series, p. 23.

† "In pyramide autem curta sciemus magnitudinem totius pyramidis, et partis defficientis, unde detracta parte defficiente à tota pyramide, remanebit pyramis curta."—*Cardani Opera*, vol. iv. p. 133.

‡ Treatise of Mensuration, 1770, page 159.

§ Ibid. p. 163.

|| Ibid. p. 389.

¶ Ibid. p. 456.

** An Introduction to Mensuration and Practical Geometry; 3d edition, London, 1791, pp. 135, 141, 178, and note, p. 180.

†† Doctrine and Application of Fluxions. London, 1750, p. 178.

‡‡ Hutton, pp. 458 to 468, and Gregory's Mathematics for Practical Men. London, 1848, p. 133. The later editions of Hutton and Simpson do not, as far as we have examined, contain much new matter on these subjects.

§§ Histoire des Recherches sur la Quadrature du Cercle. Paris, 1831, p. 176. When only three ordinates are taken, the series of Cotes and of Simpson reduce to the prismoidal formula. The notes of the author and of the editor refer to numerous original sources; among others, to an extensive series of memoirs, by MM. Kramp and Bérard: their formulæ appear to us similar to those of Cotes and Stirling.—(Harmonia Mensurarum, 1722, 2d part, p. 33; Phil. Trans., vol. xxx., 1720, p. 1063.) A report to the French Academy upon the method of M. Bérard (1817) may be found in vol. VIII.

incorrectness of No. 1 and No. 2, tried by No. 3 as a standard, is shown by Mr. Morris in numerous examples. Both Baker and Macneil, we believe, have also examined the errors of these methods.*

Mr. Morris has suggested the general application of the prismoidal rule, and has given instructions for its employment in practice. To find the area of the mid-section, which is here required, is, however, not always an easy operation; and this may be a principal reason why his method has not prevailed. Whatever be the objections to it, it is, if I do not err, the only general one yet proposed applicable to all ground, and with any number of end level-heights and their corresponding distances out.

Subsequent to Mr. Morris, among American engineers, Mr. Trautwine, and, after him, Mr. Lyons, are well known for their various publications upon Earthwork.† Mr. Henck is also prominent among recent American authors who have published methods of earthwork computation.‡ His rules appear to us in general original, ingenious, and accurate. We have not, however, found them, as a system, gaining the favor which they seem to deserve. The works of Messrs. Trautwine and Lyons are devoted to the method of computation by transverse ground-slopes. To the former we are indebted for the introduction of this method. As far as whole-section work is concerned, both writers proceed upon the principle of finding centre-heights which, under level ground, would contain the same area as the heights of the given cross-sections under sloping ground. Mr. Trautwine obtains these heights by the aid of diagrams. Mr. Lyons finds them from a table. The heights, being found by either method, are used to enter a table adapted to level ground.

The Transverse-Slope method has acquired considerable popularity, especially for preliminary estimates. This appears to depend on the fact that it possesses several of the requisites of a *practical system*, such as, in the Preface, we have said is still desired by computers. As regards the labor of observation upon the field, the method employs only a few data, which can be collected with facility and despatch. It also permits simple modes of computation. Hence an approximate result is obtained with comparatively small labor, both on the field and in the office. These remarks apply to what we have termed whole-section work. The subdivision of sections is part of the work of computation; for it must be remembered that to subdivide sections *upon the field* would scarcely consist with the expedition required in preliminary surveys.

A large portion of the present work is devoted to the method of transverse slopes. The writer has endeavored to supply a code of rules for the subdivision of sections in the office, and to increase by original methods the comprehensiveness and the practical facilities of the whole system.

---

of Gergonne's Annales. The method is considered useful, and its publication is recommended, by the examiners Ampère and Poinsot. In some of Mr. Wright's formulæ, by adding in pairs the areas of parallel sections equidistant from the mid-area, the coefficients of Cotes and Stirling are reproduced. Mr. Wright shows the degree of approximation attainable by his formulæ.

* See also a paper by Professor Gillespie, Journal of Franklin Institute, vol. xxxvii., third series, p. 11.

† A New Method of Calculating the Cubic Contents of Excavations and Embankments. By John C. Trautwine. Also, for the same, Journal of Franklin Institute, vol. xxii., third series, pp. 1 and 80. Earthwork Tables, by M. E. Lyons, C.E. Printed by J. Knabb, Reading, Pa., 1855.

‡ Field-Book for Railroad Engineers, by John B. Henck, A.M., Civil Engineer. New York, 1854.

It is doubtful whether sub-section work can be treated in such a manner as to reconcile entirely theoretical and practical requirements. The rules given in Art. 36, and the modes of computation adopted in these cases, are intended as a practical disposition of the subject by giving a running estimate. It may not, however, be out of place to offer here some remarks on the detailed computation of sub-sections. Our methods of finding abscissas are accurate and consistent with our hypothesis concerning the surface, provided the true width of roadbed be taken. The surface-slope of neutral cross-sections, or of other sections where the slope may be required, may be approximately* found by assuming the variation of slope to be proportional to the distance passed over in the direction of the roadbed, (Art. 53.) The means would therefore be provided for finding the dimensions of each solid of a subdivided section. Those solids which take the form of prismoids might then be treated by the rules for whole-section work. The other solids might be treated as pyramids and truncated pyramids.

The use, in computation, of solids not representing real excavation or embankment may doubtless be of advantage. The writer has, in the main text, confined himself to a single one,—viz., the Redundant Prism. This being always subtractive, and easily imagined, the employment of it can rarely lead to error. The observance of algebraic signs requires care and thought, even with trained computers; but the use of these signs cannot be entirely dispensed with. Where several quantities, each of which may be positive or negative, are to be combined,—either quantitatively or characteristically, or in both ways at once,—the attainment of correct results may necessarily be somewhat difficult and tedious. This applies especially to the purely tabular treatment of sub-sections; but neither these difficulties nor the necessary labor of research, it seems to us, would have justified the omission of the tabular processes given in small type in the latter part of Chapter II.

We have intimated that the direct use of the mid-section has so far complicated the rules given by Mr. Morris as to cause them to be neglected. The direct use of the mid-area may be avoided by confining the problem to the case where the same number of level-heights are taken at each end of the work, and equidistant on their respective cross-sections. Our rule for proceeding by this method is given in Art. 4 of the Appendix. It has not been presented as the principal rule for irregular cross-sections. The method given in Art. 124, Part I., employs but one redundant solid; more than five heights are seldom required on a cross-section; the mode of computation consists in repeating a process previously understood, does not require equidistant heights, and may be extended to various polygonal cross-sections. We have therefore preferred it as a rule of routine. The method of equidistant heights is, however, easily applicable when both of the surfaces which terminate the heights, or ordinates, are irregular. Besides this, auxiliary solids may be employed, (as explained in the Appendix,) and by this means many diverse and irregular forms of cross-sections may be treated.† The rule will frequently be useful in the estimation of excavations for borrowing. Another useful

* Or accurately by construction or by calculation. (Arts. 52, p. 28, and 3, p. 277.)

† The use of auxiliary solids may, indeed, be avoided by putting the external heights $= 0$; but every angle of the cross-section must be upon an ordinate. When the process is not strictly practicable, an empirical modification of cross-sections (Art. 93) may permit this spacing of ordinates.

application may be mentioned, not connected with the special object of this work,—viz., the computation of the cubic contents of *coal-veins*. The width of the cross-section will, according to general usage in such measurements, correspond to the *distance across the strike*, (or height of breast, as it is termed in our coal-regions;) the heights will be the *thickness of the vein* taken at regular intervals, and the *length* will be measured in the *direction of the strike*.

A few new technical terms have been introduced. This will be sufficiently justified, if it shall be found to serve a useful purpose. The scales and diagrams designed to assist calculation, although carefully executed, are intended rather for illustration than for actual use. The author is prepared to issue them in form and variety adapted to the wants of computers, should they be required separate from the volume. The lithographic plates, showing the subdivision of sections, were taken from models made expressly for this purpose.* These plates, or stereoscopic views of similar models, will also be furnished separately if necessary.

We shall now offer some remarks upon the necessity of adopting a standard ground-surface. The writer is of opinion that in most estimates a considerable sacrifice of accuracy has been, and is likely to be, made for the sake of expedition. It is evident that there must be some limit to the collection of data and the labor of computation. Therefore the surface cannot be treated as a network of indefinitely small surfaces, discontinuous or heterogeneous, belonging to a polyhedral solid. Hence there must be some sacrifice of theoretical accuracy: the question is, how much? This question, as far as I know, has never been either definitely proposed or answered. To reply to it strictly would require the mathematical definition of theoretical accuracy; that is, the determination of a surface or of an assemblage of surfaces which, with a given number of heights, distances out, and lengths, (co-ordinates,) would include a solidity most nearly approximating that which it is desired to compute. Some of the usages of engineering would restrict the inquiries suggested by the general question,—as, for instance, that of taking levels only on two cross-sections forming the end-planes of a piece of work.

A desideratum yet to be attained seems, therefore, to be the following. That there should be established and adopted a surface whose contained solid sufficiently approximates the actual content, and at the same time permits a ready computation of solidity from a moderate number of data.

The writer has not undertaken to decide what this standard surface should be: he has adopted that of an hyperbolic paraboloid generated by the surface-line of the cross-section, modified upon curves, by assuming curvilinear directrices, and, having made this choice, has merely shown what data his rules require, and has there left this subject.†

---

* The working drawings for these models were executed, after the author's designs, by E. T. Quilitch, Esq., Engineer to the Forest Improvement Company. To Professor J. P. Lesley, of the University of Penna., I am indebted for the suggestion of showing the contour-lines by horizontal strata. My thanks are due to both gentlemen for these and other friendly offices requiring time and attention.

At the time of making these models I was acquainted with the *cono-cuneus* of Wallis only by a brief citation, and was not aware of Mr. Pett's treatment of that solid. The passages cited in the note on page 288 also escaped notice until too late for other recognition.

† By diversifying the mode of generation of ruled surfaces, a satisfactory imitation of most of the

For the purpose of exhibiting the most usual characteristic dimensions of railroad excavation and embankment, and also of showing that these are all embraced in the author's tables for transverse slopes, it may be proper to give, in tabular form, a list furnished him by an engineer of experience and ability.*

"*Widths of Base and Ratio of Side-Slopes desirable to be included in a series of Tables for computing Excavation and Embankment.*

Kind of Work.	Material.	Single-Track Bases.	Double-Track Bases.	Side-Slopes.
Excavation.	Earth.	16 feet.	26 feet.	2 to 1, $1\frac{1}{2}$ to 1, $1\frac{1}{4}$ to 1, 1 to 1.
		18 feet.	28 feet.	2 to 1, $1\frac{1}{2}$ to 1, $1\frac{1}{4}$ to 1, 1 to 1.
		20 feet.	30 feet.	2 to 1, $1\frac{1}{2}$ to 1, $1\frac{1}{4}$ to 1, 1 to 1.
	Rock.	14 feet.	24 feet.	$\frac{1}{3}$ to 1, $\frac{1}{4}$ to 1.
		16 feet.	26 feet.	$\frac{1}{3}$ to 1, $\frac{1}{4}$ to 1.
		18 feet.	28 feet.	$\frac{1}{3}$ to 1, $\frac{1}{4}$ to 1.
Embankment.	Characteristic dimensions alike for all material.	12 feet.	22 feet.	$1\frac{1}{2}$ to 1.
		14 feet.	24 feet.	$1\frac{1}{2}$ to 1.
		16 feet.	26 feet.	$1\frac{1}{2}$ to 1.

"Making in all forty-two varieties."

These forty-two varieties may all be computed by aid of Tables XV., XVI., and XVII. Several of these varieties, however, are not of very frequent occurrence. If, therefore, it were proposed to compute a tolerably complete set of tables similar to VII. and VIII., or, for whole sections alone, similar to XIV., the work would be altogether practicable. In the first case, the number of tables would be double that of the selected side-slopes; in the second, the same as the number of selected varieties.

---

solids of earthwork could probably be obtained. (Note, p. 288.) The following notices and citations may perhaps be interesting and suggestive in this connection.

The *cono-cuneus* is a solid shaped like a cone at the base and like a wedge at the vertex. It was invented by Mr. Pett, a Naval Architect, who submitted it to Wallis in the belief that the curves resulting from its section might be useful in ship-building. To exhibit these curves, the inventor cut the *cono-cuneus* from a block made of slabs glued together. Afterwards he dissolved the glue and obtained the slabs cut in the curved forms desired. Wallis devotes considerable attention to the geometrical delineation of these curves. His memoir appears to contain one of the earlier steps in the generalization of ruled surfaces,—a subject, it would seem, not familiar to mathematicians in his time; for, in giving his reasons for undertaking the treatment of his subject, he says, "Quod eo potius suscepi, quoniam hoc solidum est de novo excogitatum, quod nescio an quisquam prior considerandum proposuerit. Atque exemplo sit, aliis ejusmodi solidis considerandis, siquando postulaverit occasio." The delineations given by Wallis appear interesting in relation to the progress of Descriptive Geometry. Ruled surfaces continue to be much discussed, and are important in the arts. The solids devised by Gregory St. Vincent in his attempted quadrature of the circle, appear to me suggestive of a general investigation of ruled surfaces. These are the principal references of this kind which I have been able to collect.— *Wallisii Opera*, vol. ii. p. 681; 1662. *M. Tinseau, Mémoires présentés à l'Académie par divers savans*, Tome ix. p. 625; 1780. *P. Gregorii A Sto Vincentio Opus*, 1647; also, p. 82 of *Montucla's Histoire*, &c., before cited.

*Ellwood Morris. September 9, 1856.

NEW

THEOREMS, TABLES, AND DIAGRAMS

FOR THE

COMPUTATION OF EARTHWORK.

PART I.—PRACTICAL TREATISE.

COMPUTATION BY TRANSVERSE GROUND-SLOPES, AND BY CENTRE AND SIDE HEIGHTS.

CHAPTER I.

PRELIMINARY DEFINITION AND DESCRIPTION—SUBDIVISION OF SECTIONS.

1. DATA are the given dimensions upon which computations are founded.

(1.) *Arbitrary Data* are determined by expediency alone. Such are the width of roadbed and rate of side-slope. (See the Table, page 14.)

(2.) *Observed Data* are obtained by measurement or observation upon the field.

2. ELEMENTS. Earthwork computations may be facilitated by deriving from the data other quantities proper for the purposes of calculation. Quantities thus prepared are called *elements.*

In some cases the quantities necessary for computation are not directly given among the data, and must be found by auxiliary processes. For example, when a section is to be subdivided, (Art. 29,) the lengths of the different parts must be found, in order to compute the solidity.

3. PREPARATION OF ELEMENTS BY CONSTRUCTION* AND CALCULATION. The derivation of elements from the original data may be performed either by construction or calculation, or by both conjointly. In Chapter II. we shall treat at length of the preparation of elements.

---

* Construction, or the drawing of mathematical figures, requires a knowledge of the use of the scale and graduated arc, and the method of drawing angles, parallel lines, and perpendiculars. The reader who is unprepared in this respect should consult some suitable work upon Mensuration, or on Practical Geometry.

4. Sections. Regular lengths of ground staked out for excavation or embankment, or the quantities of work enclosed, are called *sections*. We shall understand by a section, any given length of ground marked out for excavation or embankment. The length of a section is supposed to be taken *horizontally*. It is generally one hundred feet. To facilitate the computation of the solid contents of sections is the principal object of this work.

We shall treat of two methods of computation,—viz., by Transverse Slopes, in Chapter III., and by Centre and Side Heights, in Chapter IV. The meaning of these terms will duly appear. The present and the following chapter, as their titles import, will be devoted to preliminary subjects.

5. Bounding Surfaces of Sections. The solid to be excavated or embanked in a section is contained by six surfaces,—viz.: By the natural, or ground surface; by the plane of the roadbed;* by the two sloping side-planes; and by two vertical and parallel end-planes. On *curves*, the side-walls are curved, and the end-planes converge. Unless otherwise understood, straight work is meant.

6. The Ground-Surface. It is not known what kind of mathematical surface most nearly resembles the actual surface of the ground. It is usual to assume the surface to be either a plane or a warped surface. The ground-surface is frequently called simply *the surface*.

7. Plane Ground-Surface. The ground-surface is seldom a true plane, but it may frequently be as well represented by a plane as by any other surface of easy definition.

8. Warped Ground-Surface. When the ground is not supposed to be a plane, it is assumed to be a warped surface.

Fig. 1.

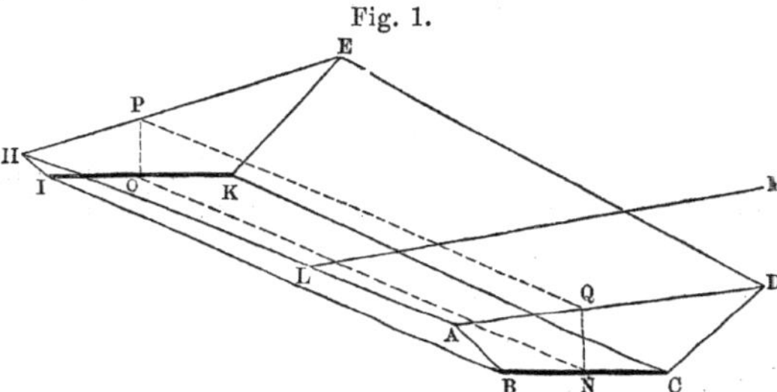

Suppose A B C D E H I K (Fig. 1) to represent a section of excavation. B C K I is the roadbed. BAHI and CDEK are the side-planes. ABCD, HIKE are the end-planes. ADEH is the surface of the ground. A warped surface is supposed to be generated by the motion of a straight line L M parallel to the end-plane A B C D, and guided by the straight side-lines A H, D E. Such a surface is called, in Geometry, an *hyperbolic paraboloid*. Surfaces generated by a straight line moving parallel to a fixed plane, as in this case, are also called *ruled* surfaces.

Since a ruler applied to a flat table may be slid over its surface in the manner described, a plane may be considered as a variety of the paraboloid.

Ruled surfaces, therefore, have this advantage,—that they include, under a simple definition, both plane and curved ground.

* We shall speak only of railroad-work, leaving the reader to make the proper application of our rules to other computations.

9. Particular Kind of Warped Surface. When the work of a section is all excavation or all embankment, we suppose the lines A H, D E to join the corners of the section, as in Fig. 1. But when a section contains both excavation and embankment, it may simplify the calculation to suppose A H, D E to be parallel to a vertical plane N M R L (Fig. 2) passing through the centre of the roadbed.

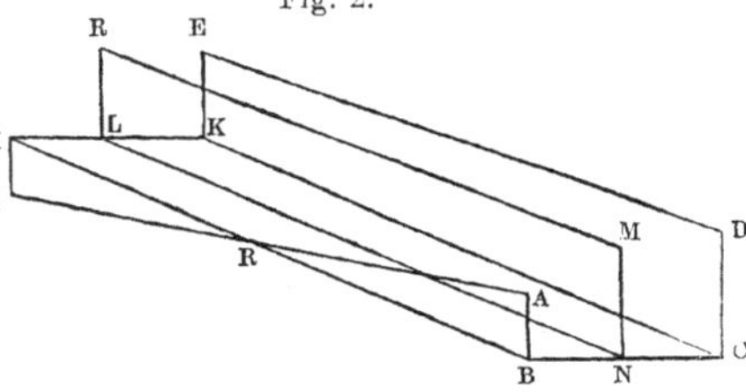

Fig. 2.

It will also be convenient to suppose A H and D E to lie respectively in the vertical planes B A H I, C D E K which pass through the sides B I, C K of the roadbed. (For illustrations, see Plates and Description, page 316.)

10. Median Plane. The vertical plane N M R L is called the *median plane.*

11. Marginal Planes and Heights. B A H I, C D E K are called *marginal planes.* B A, C D, K E, I H are called *marginal heights.*

12. Median Surface-Line. The line P Q, in which the median plane intersects the surface, is called the *median surface-line.* (See now Fig. 1.)

13. Stations. Upon the field, the ends P, Q of a section are marked by stakes which are numbered. In a continuous line of railroad, the first stake is numbered 0, the second 1, and so on as far as required. No. 1 will then designate the first section, No. 2 the second, and thus continuously.

14. Profile. A profile contains such a figure as N O P Q, for a single section, or for a continuous series of sections. Profiles drawn on the median plane are called *median profiles.* Profiles drawn on the marginal planes are called *marginal profiles.* N O P Q (Fig. 1) is a median profile, A H I B (Fig. 2) a marginal profile.

15. Directrices. Each of the lines D E, A H is called a *directrix,* because it directs the motion of the line supposed to generate the surface. In Fig. 1 these lines may properly also be called *external surface-lines,* because they there form the external boundaries of the surface.

16. Ground-Trace. A trace is the line of intersection of two surfaces. The *ground-trace* is the line which the surface of the ground would mark upon the plane of the roadbed if both were continued so as to meet. In the case of warped surfaces, the ground-trace is a curved line called an *hyperbola.* When the ground-surface is a plane, the trace is a straight line.

17. Grade-Level. The roadbed is considered to be level in a direction transverse to the length of the road; but in the direction of the length the roadbed frequently has a vertical rise or fall, which is called *grade.* Grade is measured by the number of feet, rise or fall, per mile. *Grade-level,* at any point, is the height which the roadbed-plane there has compared with a standard level-plane called the *datum-plane.* This is a plane which is imagined to pass through some one known fixed point.

18. GRADE-LINE is generally understood to mean a line of considerable extent, marked at every one hundred feet, or other regular interval, and following the grade of a proposed roadbed. Such lines assist preliminary exploration.

19. NAMES OF EARTHWORK SOLIDS. When all the bounding surfaces are planes, these solids are either prisms, prismoids, pyramids, truncated pyramids, or wedges. A B C D E K (Fig. 3) is a triangular prism. In a prism, the ends ABC, DEK are of equal size and similar shape. B L M C D E N O is also a prism. If the ends were unequal in size or dissimilar in shape, the solid would properly be called a *prismoid.* A B C D (Fig. 4) is a triangular *pyramid.* If the point of the pyramid be cut off by the plane K L M, the part A B C M L K is a *truncated pyramid.* Fig. 5 represents a *wedge-shaped* mass. It is a prismoid, in which one of the end-surfaces dwindles nearly or quite to a line or sharp edge.

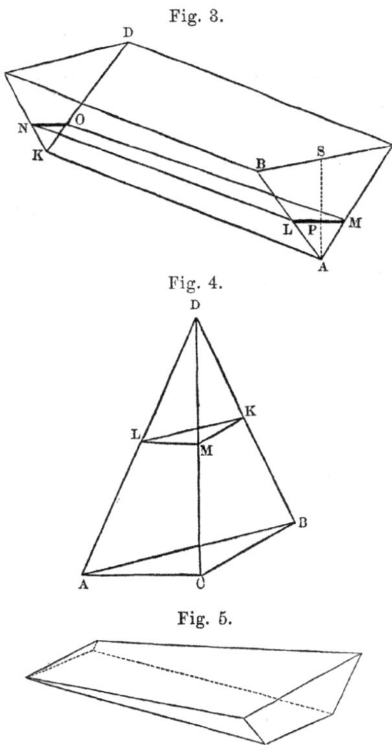

Fig. 3. Fig. 4. Fig. 5.

When the ground-surface or the side-walls are curved, earthwork solids will still resemble the geometrical figures mentioned; but the same names cannot be strictly applied. They may, however, by a license of language, be employed, provided they clearly indicate what is meant.

20. EXTENSION OF ILLUSTRATION. The general form is the same for embankment as for excavation; but if the eye be accustomed to consider only excavation, embankment will appear as inverted excavation,—and *vice versa.* The reader must, when necessary, endeavor to extend the illustrations afforded by the diagrams, by imagining the inversion.

21. REDUNDANT PRISM is the prism A L M O N K (Fig. 3) lying below the roadbed in excavation and above it in embankment. If this be subtracted from the solid A B C D E K, there is left the prismoid B L M C D E N O, which is the solid to be excavated or embanked. Hence, as the content of the redundant prism is easily found, it frequently assists computation to calculate the content of the solid A B C D E K, and then subtract the redundant prism.

22. CENTRE-HEIGHT is the vertical distance P S, (Fig. 3,) measured on the median plane, from the roadbed to the surface. S A is called the *Augmented Centre-Height*. It is equal to P S augmented by PA, the height of the redundant prism. Centre-heights may be taken anywhere between the ends of a section, but are understood to be taken at the ends, unless otherwise stated. They may be called *end-heights*, also, when taken at the ends. Centre-heights are said to be *plus* when they are above the roadbed, or in excavation, and *minus* when they are below, or in embankment.

23. PLUS AND MINUS SIGNS. These signs are borrowed from Algebra. +(*plus*) indicates addition, or an additive quantity. — (*minus*) indicates subtraction, or a subtractive quantity. When applied in Geometry, or in Algebra combined with Geometry, plus and minus are also used as relative terms, indicating *opposite directions*. When direction is taken into account, distances are measured from a common point of beginning, called the *Origin*. Plus is called the *positive sign*, and minus, the *negative sign*.*

24. DISTANCE OUT is the distance from the median plane to the outside corners of an excavation or embankment. AD or E C (Fig. 6) is the distance out on the right. A M or K B is the distance out on the left. Distances out, when necessary, may be taken to points intermediate between B or C and the centre-line AE. The point where B C meets the roadbed P Q is called the *grade-point* of the cross-section, and its distance out the distance out of the grade-point.

Fig. 6.

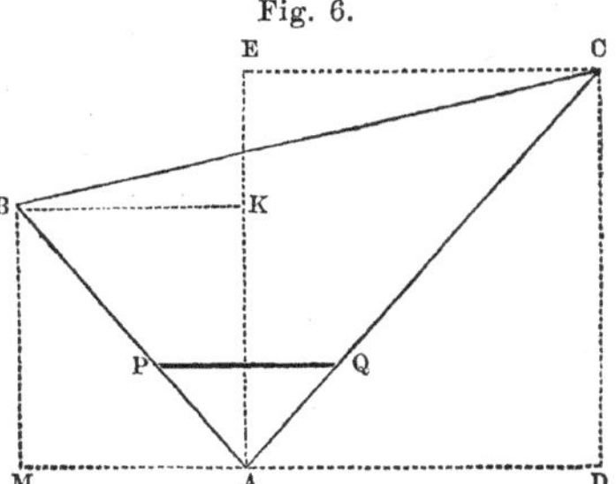

25. SIDE-SLOPE is the inclination of the side A C or A B (Fig. 6) to the roadbed P Q, or to the horizontal line M D. It is generally the same on both sides. Side-slope is measured by comparing horizontal with vertical distance. If a point be supposed to move along A C from A toward C, so that it departs horizontally from A E one and a half feet in the same time that it rises or falls vertically one foot from A D, the side-slope is said to be *one and one-half to one*.

26. TRANSVERSE GROUND-SLOPE is the inclination of the line B C (Fig. 6) to the horizontal line M D. It is for brevity called *ground-slope*, *surface-slope*, *cross-slope*, *top or bottom slope*, or simply *slope*, when this term is not ambiguous. This slope is measured, by a *slope-instrument*, in degrees of the quadrant.

Similar and Opposite Slopes.—The slopes may or may not incline toward the same side of the roadbed. If they incline toward the same side, they are called *similar;* if they incline toward opposite sides, they are called *opposite*.

---

* A reference to treatises on Algebra and Algebraic Geometry will afford the student a fuller explanation of the meaning of positive and negative signs.

27. Cross-Sections are the plane figures formed by cutting earthwork solids transversely. B C Q P (Fig. 6) is a cross-section. When the surface-line B C is a single straight line, the form and area of a cross-section depend upon four quantities,—viz., the *width of roadbed*, the *centre-height*, the *side-slope*, and the *surface-slope*. When the surface-line is not straight, instead of using the surface-slope to draw the cross-section, the heights and the distances out of certain points in the surface-line are employed. In the cross-section A B C D E H K L A, (Fig. 7,) besides the centre-height H M, the heights C N, D O, E Q, K S, L T, and also the distances out of the points C, D, E, K, L, would be used to draw the figure. C N and L T are called *side-heights.*

Fig. 7.

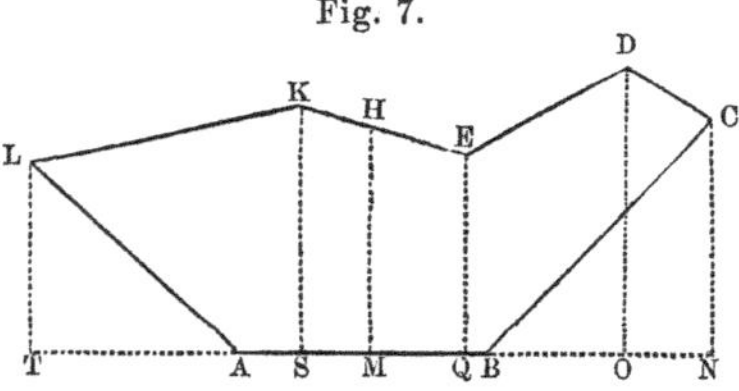

28. Full, Partial, and Neutral Cross-Sections. When the cross-section is wholly in excavation or wholly in embankment, it is said to be *full.* Fig. 8.

Fig. 8.

When the cross-section is partially in excavation and partially in embankment, it is said to be *partial.* Fig. 9.

Fig. 9.

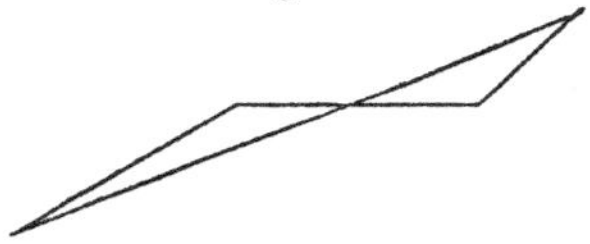

Excavation and embankment may be called full or partial, according as the cross-section of the work is full or partial. When the surface-line just touches the edge of the roadbed, the cross-section is said to be *neutral.* Fig. 10.

Fig. 10.

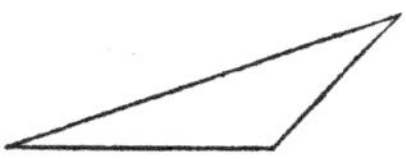

Neutral cross-sections may with propriety also be regarded as *full,* because they really fill out the whole figure; but occasionally it may be convenient to have a special designation for them.

Work having a neutral cross-section in all parts might without impropriety be called neutral; but such work requires no distinctive appellation. The solid in such work is a prism. It may be computed either as full work or as partial work.

Subdivision of Sections.

29. Subdivision of Sections is so dividing them as to show the form and dimensions of the component excavation and embankment solids. Subdivision is necessary whenever a partial cross-section can be made at any part of the work. Otherwise, it is not necessary. If there be a partial cross-section, it will be shown by the methods indicated in Articles 34, 47, and 54.

30. Three Cases include all the varieties of work, whether full or partial, which can occur in any section. These cases are distinguished by the nature of the end cross-sections. The end cross-sections of any piece of work must be either alike or different. Like cross-sections may be either *full* or *partial.* Hence, there are three combinations of cross-sections,—viz.: Case I., both full. Case II., one full, and the other partial. Case III., both partial.

31. Twelve Varieties, four to each case, belong to these cases. This results from combining, for each case, the *sign* (plus or minus) of the centre-height, with *similar* or *opposite* surface-slopes. Four combinations of signs and slopes are possible. It may facilitate the study of the subject to view the neutral section as a full one, with a *small but visible side.* By this means the prismoids (F, f, on the Plates) may be imagined to exist, if wanting, but to be evanescent. In this way the twelve varieties will include all the combinations. End-heights equal to 0 may have either sign prefixed.

32. Sub-Varieties. If the neutral cross-section be kept distinct, we must, in order to a strict classification, either make use of this section in characterizing the cases, or introduce it among the characteristics of sub-varieties. The complete discussion would probably exceed the limits of practical expediency.

33. General Scheme. The cases and their varieties are exhibited in the following general scheme. (See Plates I., II., III.)

GENERAL SCHEME,

FOR ALL VARIETIES OF FULL AND PARTIAL WORK IN A SECTION.

Case I.

Cross-Section Full at Both Ends.

Signs of Centre-Heights.	Direction of Slopes.	Number of Diagram.	Enumeration and Description of Component Solids.
Like.	Similar.	No. 1.	One prismoid F.
	Opposite.	No. 2.	One prismoid F.
Unlike.	Similar.	No. 3.	One prismoid F, and one pyramid P. One prismoid f, and one pyramid p.
	Opposite.	No. 4.	One prismoid F, and one pyramid P. One prismoid f, and one pyramid p.

Case II.

Cross-Section Full at One End, Partial at the Other.

Signs of Centre-Heights.	Direction of Slopes.	Number of Diagram.	Enumeration and Description of Component Solids.
Like.	Similar.	No. 5.	One prismoid F, one truncated pyramid T, and one pyramid P.
	Opposite.	No. 6.	One prismoid F, one truncated pyramid T, and one pyramid P.
Unlike.	Similar.	No. 7.	One prismoid F, one truncated pyramid T, and one pyramid P.
	Opposite.	No. 8.	One prismoid F, one truncated pyramid T, and one pyramid P.

Case III.

Cross-Section Partial at Both Ends.

Signs of Centre-Heights.	Direction of Slopes.	Number of Diagram.	Enumeration and Description of Component Solids.
Like.	Similar.	No. 9.	Two truncated pyramids T and t.
	Opposite.	No. 10.	One prismoid F, and two truncated pyramids T and t. Two pyramids P and p.
Unlike.	Similar.	No. 11.	Two truncated pyramids T and t.
	Opposite.	No. 12.	One prismoid F, and two truncated pyramids T and t. Two pyramids P and p.

This scheme is adapted to a mean roadbed. It may be studied by first observing, on all the diagrams belonging to each case, the characteristic end cross-sections of that case. Then examine, in the scheme, the repetition of the four combinations of centre heights and slopes, and follow it on the diagrams. Finally, apply to its proper diagram the description of each variety given in the scheme, and observe the component solids. Solids are separated by neutral cross-sections, because a solid continues of the same kind as long as its cross-section does, and the cross-section becomes neutral at the point where it changes its character.

34. Application of the General Scheme. The scheme shows that unlike signs of the end-heights always require subdivision of the section. When the signs are alike, the necessity for subdivision must be examined, by observing whether one of the end cross-sections is partial.* If there be a partial cross-section, it will be shown by construction, (Art. 47;) also, by observing (Table III.) whether either end-height be less than the height of the neutral cross-section.

35. Determination of the Variety. If subdivision be necessary, assume a mean roadbed, and find the abscissas of the neutral cross-section. (Art. 50 or 52.) The abscissas being marked on the diagram, (Fig. 16,) together with the surface-slopes, the computer may sketch the ground-trace through the ends of the abscissas and through the grade-points of the end cross-sections. If desirable, the side-slopes may be added, in order to give relief to the diagram. Then consult the drawings illustrative of the *Case* to which the section belongs, and determine its *variety*.

36. Union of several Component Solids and Reduction to a Plane Surface. Having found the variety, we endeavor to find a single solid with a plane surface, which shall be approximately equal, in the case of excavation and embankment respectively, to the sum of the component solids. This is done as follows for the several cases of the General Scheme:—

Case I. *Solids reduced to Prismoids.*—Nos. 1 and 2 are whole sections, requiring no reduction: they are prismoids.

Nos. 3 and 4. The median grade-point is on the division-line between the pyramids P and p. Assume that if these pyramids were cut off at this point, the apex of each would contain material enough to fill out the basal portion to a neutral cross-section. Thus a single prismoid would be formed with a full cross-section at one end, neutral at the other, and consisting of F or f and the basal part of P or p. The length of it is the abscissa of the median grade-point. (Arts. 9 and 51.) The greater end-height is given;

* A little exercise of memory will assist us in judging whether it is worth while to draw cross-sections or to refer to Table III. in order to find whether there can be a partial cross-section. The widths for double track are: excavation, 28 feet; embankment, 24 feet. 28 feet roadbed and 35° surface-slope give, by Table III., say 10 feet for height of neutral cross-section; and 24 feet and 18°, say 4 feet. Hence, in general, no height in excavation over 10 feet, and none in embankment over 4 feet, require examination. This method of judging can be applied according to circumstances.

the lesser is the height of the neutral cross-section. For the surface-slope, assume a mean slope.

CASE II. *Solids reduced to Prismoids and Pyramids.*—Nos. 5, 6, 7, 8. Assume, in a manner similar to the previous, that if T be cut *in half*, the prismoid F would be filled out to a neutral cross-section. The dimensions then are, greater end-height given; lesser, the height of neutral cross-section; length, the length of whole section *less half* the abscissa of P T. Assume a mean surface-slope.

If T should predominate over F, then F and T together may be taken as a truncated pyramid having its end-heights given. The length, the whole length of the section. Assume a mean slope, as before.

The pyramid P may take the surface-slope of its base. Its length is shown by the abscissa. It needs no further remark here.

CASE III. *Solids reduced to Truncated Pyramids or to Prisms and to Pyramids.* Nos. 9 and 11. Assume a mean slope, and these become truncated pyramids. They retain their original heights and length.

Nos. 10 and 12. The parts T, F, and t may be taken together as a prism. It is assumed equal to a prism erected upon a triangle having a mean base between the widths shown at the ends of the section. Its length, that of the section; the slope, the *half-sum* of the given slopes.

The pyramids P and p may be treated in a similar manner. Assume them equal to a pyramid of mean base and a slope equal to the half-sum of the given slopes; the length equal to the united length of P and p.

In No. 10, the end-heights, being of the same sign, show to what kind of work—whether excavation or embankment—the parts T, F, and t belong.

In No. 12, from whichever end the section be regarded, the longer marginal abscissa, counting from that end, shows the character of the work. The work will be of that kind in which the longer abscissa is contained.

Curved Sections.—(See Arts. 5, 105, 120, 128.)—The rules for curved solids require the length to be measured on the circle of alignment; but it is nearly correct to find the length as if for straight work, which gives the length somewhat too short.*

It is usual and generally sufficient—at least for preliminary estimates—to disregard curvature and compute as if for straight work. For pyramids and truncated pyramids, it is a better approximation to modify the process for straight work, thus:—Find the *marginal radius*, by increasing or diminishing the *radius* of *alignment* by the half-width of roadbed; multiply the length for straight work by the marginal radius belonging to the solid, and divide by the radius of alignment to find a corrected length. (Approximately, the curved marginal length.)

As these solids are not greatly distorted, the plates illustrative of straight solids will suffice.

37. WEDGES AND WEDGE-SHAPED MASSES.—True wedges rarely occur. Solids which may be so termed have one end-height practically inconsiderable, and a nearly level surface-slope. We may sometimes assume the surface-slope to be level, or 0°, and one end-height nothing. The sum and difference of the end-heights are then the same,—viz., equal to the greater end-height.

---

*By employing the marginal radius, and the distances out counted from the margin, we might proceed as in Arts. 107, 122. (See § 2, Art. 7, p. 286.)

CHAPTER II.

AUXILIARY CONSTRUCTIONS—DETERMINATION OF VARIETIES AND PREPARATION OF ELEMENTS BY CONSTRUCTION AND BY TABULATION.

Auxiliary Constructions.

38. Drawing Profiles. The method of doing this is sufficiently indicated by the figures NOPQ (Art. 8) and AHIB, (Art. 9.) The lines PQ, AH, DE (Fig. 1) are all drawn straight. In reality, PQ would be curved in such surfaces as are described in Art. 8; but this is not regarded in drawing profiles. It is usual, when a continuous profile is constructed for numerous sections, to draw the heights OP, NQ upon a larger scale than the length NO, in order to economize space. For computing solidities, the scale for the heights should be sufficiently large to permit the estimation of tenths of feet. The scale for the length should permit the estimation of single feet.

39. Reduction of Oblique to Direct Length. The length of a section is supposed to be measured in a direction perpendicular to the parallel planes of the end cross-sections. Generally, it is taken on the median surface-line. This makes the direction perpendicular to the end planes, as far as any deviation to the right or left is concerned. But in most cases there is a vertical deviation on account of the rising or falling of the surface lengthwise of the section. This vertical deviation is not generally regarded; the length is supposed to have been measured horizontally upon the field, by taking care to hold the measuring-chain in a horizontal position. The chain cannot be held, with ordinary care, strictly horizontal, but sufficiently so for practical purposes. Cases may arise, however, where the length is known to have been measured so obliquely as to require correction. The direct length for a measured length of 100 feet and a horizontal or vertical deviation of 10 feet will be $99\frac{1}{2}$ feet; and for other lengths in proportion, with the same rate of deviation.

40. Finding the Direct Length by Construction. Let AB (Fig. 11) be the measured length. Take C in the middle of AB, and from C describe a portion BD of a circle. Then, taking in the dividers a length equal to the vertical rise from A to B, place a point of the dividers in B, and describe an arc ED meeting the first arc in D. Join AD. AD is the horizontal length. If there be no deviation to the right or left, this is the direct length required. If there be any deviation right or left, repeat the process. Take H in the middle of AD, and from H describe a portion DK of a circle. Then, taking in the dividers a length equal to the horizontal deviation in measuring from A to B, place a point of the dividers in D, and describe

Fig. 11.

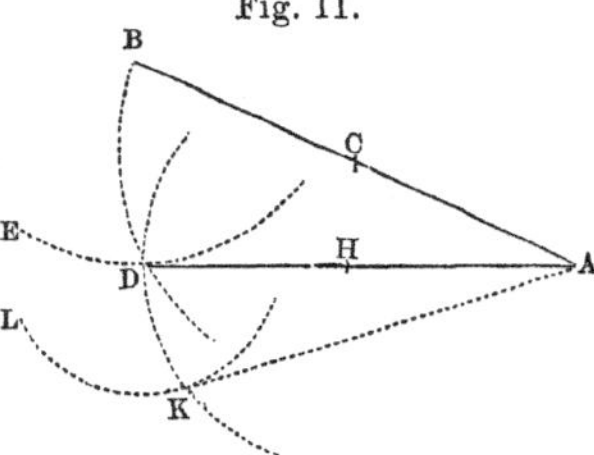

an arc L K meeting D K in K. Join A K. A K is the direct length, reduced both for vertical and horizontal deviation.

Explanation.—By a known property of the circle, if B and D be joined, B D A is a right angle: hence B D is the vertical height in a vertical position, and A D is the horizontal length corresponding to the sloping length A B. In the same manner D K, if joined, would represent the end cross-section, perpendicular to the median line. A K would be the direct length corresponding to the oblique length A D.

41. To Draw the Side-Slope when the Rate of Slope is given. Suppose the rate of slope to be $1\frac{1}{2}$ to 1. Let A B represent part of the roadbed upon the cross-section. B is the side of the roadbed. Prolong A B and make B C, by any convenient scale of equal parts, equal $1\frac{1}{2}$. Draw C D perpendicular to A C and equal 1. Join B D. B D is the side-slope required.

Fig. 12.

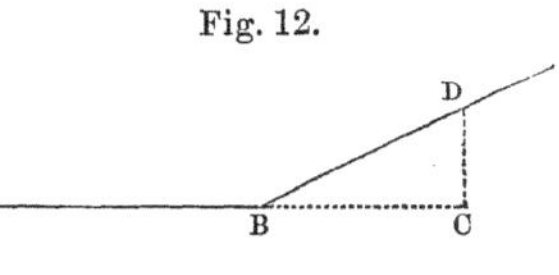

42. To Draw a Cross-Section, the necessary data are the width of roadbed, the rate of side-slope, the centre-height, and either the side-heights or the surface-slope.

(1.) *When the side-heights are given.** Make A B equal to the width of roadbed. Draw the centre line C D perpendicular to A B, and take C E and C K equal to the respective side-heights. Through E and K, parallel to A B, draw E N, K M to intersect the side-slopes, taking care to transport thus the heights C E, C K each to its proper side. Make C D equal to the centre-height, and join D M, D N. A B M D N is the cross-section required.

Fig. 13.

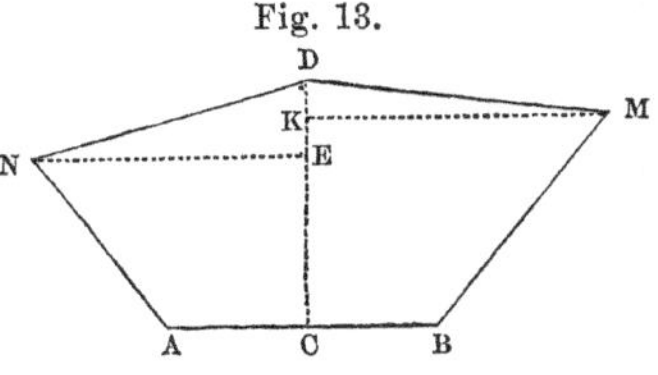

(2.) *When the surface-slope is given.* We shall suppose the roadbed, the side-slopes, and the centre-line drawn in the same manner as when the side-heights are given; and that these lines, so drawn, are ready for use upon a diagram or an engraving as in Fig. 14. Upon the centre-line C E is a scale of equal parts, counting from C toward E. Through H, the intersection of the side-slopes, passes the diameter I L parallel to A B. From this diameter are reckoned the graduated arcs I K, L M. To construct the cross-section, draw, or suppose to be drawn, the radius H N, making the angle N H L of the same magnitude as the given surface-slope, and the direction from N to H to correspond with that of the surface. Then, through the point D, indicating upon the scale the given

Fig. 14.

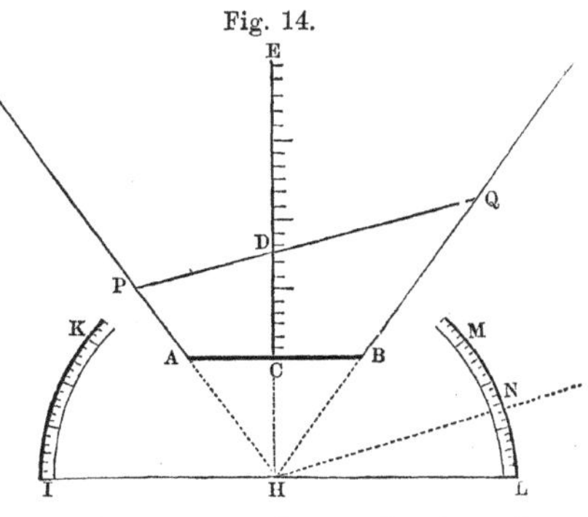

* When the surface-slope is not given, the known points on the surface must be found by giving to each its proper height and distance out. Art. 27.

centre-height, draw PQ parallel to HN. ABQP is the cross-section required. The distance HC is called the augment for the centre-height. Twice this distance is the augment for the sum of the end-heights. It is given in Table II. The augmented height HD may be measured upon the scale CE.

43. To find the Augmented Centre-Height and the Surface-Slope of the Mid Cross-Section. Draw the surface-slopes PQ, RS (Fig. 15) at their respective end-heights, as in Art. 42. Take T half-way between P and R, and U half-way between Q and S. ABUT is the mid cross-section. The augmented centre-height HV and the surface-slope TU can be measured upon a diagram, as in Art. 42.

Fig. 15.

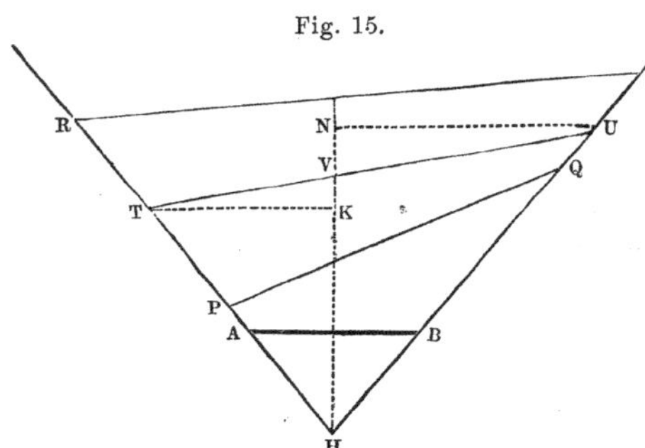

44. To find the Distances Out of the Mid-Section. Having drawn TU, (Fig. 15,) as in Art. 43, draw TK and UN parallel to AB. TK and UN are the distances out of the mid-section, and can be measured on a scale. If the cross-section be not full, one of the distances, as UN, will be found in the manner described. The other will become the distance out of the grade-point. (Art. 48.) It is evident that the distance out of the mid cross-section is equal to the half-sum of the end-distances out on the same side.

45. Cross-Sections Drawn on the Plane of the Roadbed. Let ABCD (Fig. 16) represent the roadbed, the sides of which may be divided into feet. At each end are graduated arcs whose centres are H and K. The cross-section at each end may be drawn in the manner described in Art. 42, observing that *plus* centre-heights count in the direction KE, and *minus* heights in the direction HL; also observing the proper directions of the surface-slopes. They are here supposed to be *opposite*. The side-slopes, if desired, may be drawn through the corners A, B, C, D of the roadbed. Cross-sections will thus show their dimensions as accurately as if drawn separately from the roadbed, and may be perfectly understood. If this mode of representation appear strange, the reader need only imagine the plane of the cross-section turned upon AR or CS,

Fig. 16.

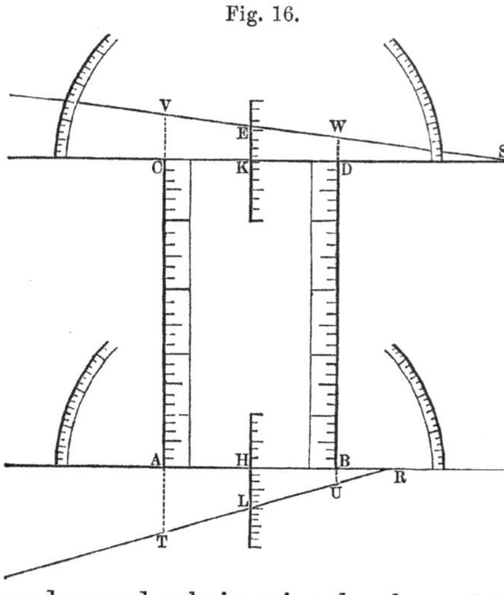

upward or downward, as may be required, at right angles to the plane of the roadbed. The distances out of the grade-points R and S will remain unchanged.

46. To find the Marginal Heights at the Ends of a Section. Draw, as above, (Fig. 16,) the surface-slopes T R, VS. A T, B U, CV, DW represent the marginal heights, and may be measured on one of the scales of the diagram.

47. To find the Centre-Height of the Neutral Cross-Section. Draw the surface-slope, in its proper direction, through the corner of the road-bed. The height may be read off from the central scale. (Fig. 16.) This dimension is the tabular quantity of Table III.

48. To find the Distance Out of the Grade-Point. Apply HR or KS to the scale. This distance is the tabular quantity of Table V. Added to or subtracted from the half-width of roadbed, as may be required, it gives the base.

49. To find the Base of a Sub-Section. When R and S (Fig. 16) fall within the roadbed, the bases A R and C S require to be measured. The sum and the difference of the bases at the ends of a section are elements for computing solidity. They are easily found after measuring the bases. The sum and difference of marginal heights (Art. 46) may be used instead, with suitable rules.

50. To find the Abscissa of the Neutral Cross-Section. To simplify this subject, we shall adopt a *mean roadbed.* There can then never be more than two marginal grade-points belonging to the same section. Let A B C D (Fig. 17) represent the roadbed, and A T, B U, CV, DW the marginal heights found, as in Fig. 16. By considering the mode of generation of the ground-surface, as described in Art. 9, it is plain that the abscissas required are those of the *grade-point of the directrix.* In the present example, because the marginal heights B U, DW are both of the *same sign,* there can be no such grade-point within the section on the marginal plane through B U and D W. Take, therefore, the plane through A T and CV. Let A T C V (Fig. 18) represent the side view of the side AC, Fig. 17. Care must be taken to observe the *plus* and *minus* signs in drawing A T, C V. Join TV, and P will be the grade-point of the directrix, because AC represents the plane of the roadbed, and TV is the directrix. The abscissa A P or C P may be measured on the side-scale of Fig. 16. Instead of drawing a separate diagram, as here shown, the operation may be performed at once, on the side-scale A C of Fig. 16. It will only be necessary there to transfer A T in the direction A H, and C V in

Fig. 17.

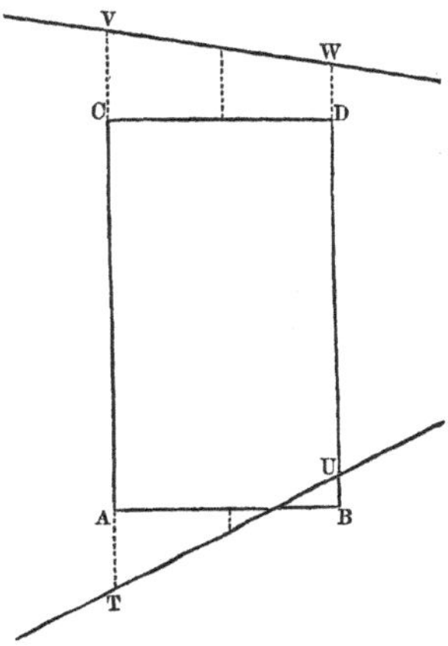

Fig. 18.

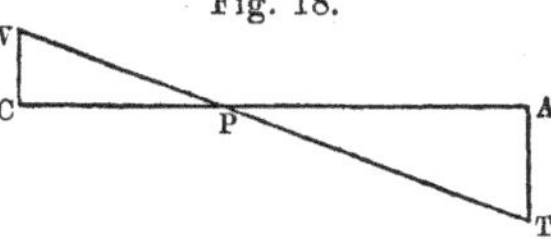

the opposite direction. The point P will then fall on the scale, and the abscissa can be at once read. The inner-side lines of Fig. 16 may, if desired, be drawn to represent embankment-width. The abscissa for each width of roadbed may be thus determined by separate operations. The abscissa is required in the subdivision of sections. (Art. 29.)

51. TO FIND THE ABSCISSA OF THE MEDIAN GRADE-POINT. If, in Fig. 18, A T, C V represent the end centre-heights, A T V C is the median plane, and T V the median surface-line. A P and C P are the abscissas required. It is plain that the finding of the abscissas in this manner is equivalent to drawing the marginal and median profiles. In Fig. 2, Art. 9, R is the marginal grade-point, and B R is the abscissa of the neutral cross-section.

52. A METHOD FOR FINDING ABSCISSAS WHEN THE GROUND-SURFACE IS A PLANE. We have seen (Art. 8) that a plane surface may be generated by means of directrices, in the same manner as a curved surface. The above methods for finding abscissas therefore apply to plane as well as to curved surfaces. But we know (Art. 16) that when the surface is plane the *ground-trace* is a straight line. Hence, any two points of the ground-trace being found, we have only to join those points in order to find the trace itself, which will show the abscissas. Let A B C D (Fig. 19) be the roadbed. Draw the surface-slopes L R and E S, and find the grade-points R and S of the end cross-sections, as in Fig. 16, Art. 45. S R will be the *ground-trace*, and will show the abscissas A P, B X upon the graduated sides of the diagram. If two widths of roadbed be drawn, the abscissas of the marginal grade-points will be shown for each. Draw the centre-line of the roadbed, H K. H M is the abscissa of the median grade-point.

Fig. 19.

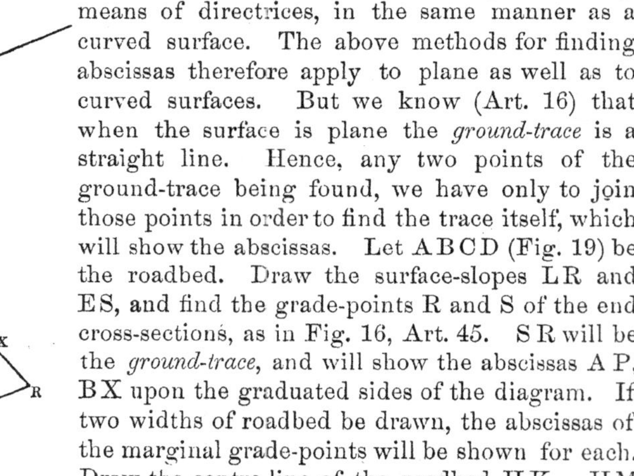

Warped Surfaces.—(Plates I., II., III., IV.)—The curved ground-trace may be drawn: 1st, by finding (Art. 50) a series of abscissas at different distances out; 2d, by drawing two marginal profiles for any roadbed: by means of these the marginal heights may be found for a series of cross-sections, and the surface-slopes drawn, (Art. 45.) Either method will determine a series of grade-points which are points of the ground-trace.

53. TO FIND THE TOTAL VARIATION OF SURFACE-SLOPE AND THE MEAN SLOPE. The total variation is the variation occurring in passing from end to end of a section.

Let A B C D (Figs. 20, 21) represent the roadbed, and H I and K L the respective surface-slopes: the end cross-sections are supposed to be perpendicular to the roadbed, as in Fig. 16. In Fig. 20, the slopes are *similar;* in Fig. 21, they are *opposite.* Draw, in both figures, M N parallel to H I, and P N parallel to A B or C D. P N M is then equal to the slope of H I. In Fig. 20, K N P is the slope of K L, and K N M is the *variation of slope.* This is here equal to the *difference* between KNP and MNP, the two end-slopes. In Fig. 21, LNP is the slope of KL, and LNM is the *variation* of slope. This is here

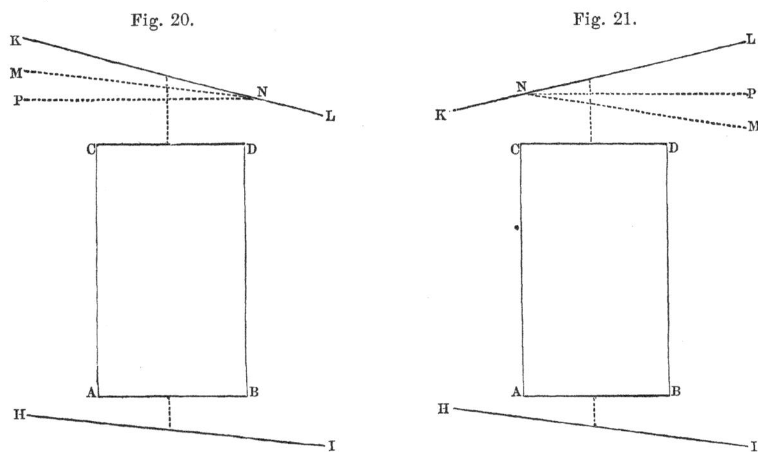

Fig. 20. Fig. 21.

equal to the *sum* of MNP and LNP, the two end-slopes. Hence, to find the total variation,—

I. *When the end-slopes are similar*, take their *difference*.

II. *When the end-slopes are opposite*, take their *sum*.

According to the method of Art. 9, the slope increases or diminishes approximately in proportion to the distance passed over. Hence, in order to find the *mean slope*, approximately equal to that of the mid cross-section,—

III. *When the slopes are similar*, take their *half-sum*.

IV. *When the slopes are opposite*, subtract the half-sum from the greater slope, or from either, if the slopes are equal.

Determination of Varieties and Preparation of Elements by Construction.

54. Determination of Varieties. For this purpose, and for subsequent use, the most thorough method is to prepare a continuous series of cross-sections for all consecutive sections to be computed. It will not be necessary to draw the side-slopes. By such a series of diagrams, all the characteristics of the varieties in question will be exhibited, and may be applied according to the General Scheme, Art. 33.

Plate V. exhibits a series of cross-sections for twelve consecutive sections. The numbers of the stations, the centre-heights, and the variety of each section are marked. These cross-sections are drawn to a mean roadbed. The nature of the cross-sections can then be sufficiently ascertained. Their marginal heights suffice for determining abscissas by profiles, (Plate VI.) But for computing solidity, the true heights and bases should be taken. (Art. 56.)

If the labor of drawing consecutive cross-sections be too great, then cross-sections may be drawn whenever there is reason to suppose the section will require subdivision. In judging of this, we may proceed as follows:—

1st. Observe the signs of the end-heights: unlike signs require subdivision. If no subdivision be indicated by the diversity of signs, then consider, 2d, Whether there be a partial cross-section. This is done by comparing the centre-height with the height of the neutral cross-section. On the scale (Fig. 22) the centre-heights occupy the central space. On each side, under the respective heads of Excavation and Embankment, are placed the heights of neutral cross-sections, which are severally designated by the degree of slope to which each belongs. The heights of the neutral cross sections may also be found by construction, (Art. 47,) or may be taken from Table III. This comparison should in strictness be made for every cross-section which is not obviously a full one; if it be not made, the computer relies upon his judgment for determining whether the cross-section be full or partial. The comparison may be made for a number of sections, and those requiring subdivision marked for subsequent investigation. In what follows, the roadbed and side-slope are supposed to be given.

Fig. 22.

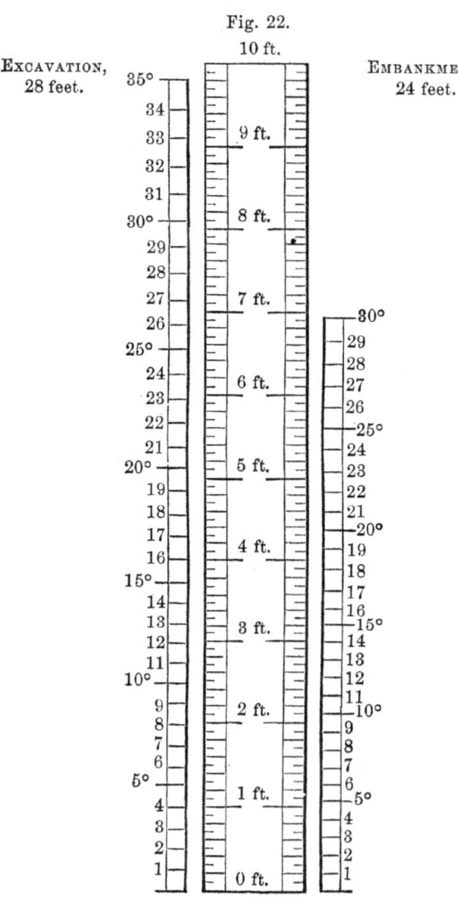

Preparation of Elements.

55. For Whole Sections. The mean slope, when required, or the slope of the mid-section, can be found by the methods described in Articles 53 and 43. Plate VIII. shows the kind of diagram suitable for measuring slopes and heights. As a mean slope has been adopted for the reduced solids, (Art. 36,) we need not hereafter enumerate the finding of slopes.

For whole-section work, the other elements required are the sum of the augmented end-heights, or the sum of the heights A S (Fig. 3) at each end; also the difference of the heights, and the length.

The sum of the heights may be obtained by the aid of a diagram similar to that of Plate VIII., or by any equivalent construction. The difference is found by subtracting the lesser given height from the greater. When a section requires no subdivision, its length is given. When a portion of a subdivided section takes by reduction the form of a whole section, the length will be either the median abscissa, or a marginal abscissa with half the remaining length of the section: the equivalent of this latter is found by subtracting half the length of a pyramid from the length of the section. The abscissas required will be found by drawing marginal and median profiles. (Arts. 50 and 51, or by Art. 52.)

56. FOR SUB-SECTIONS. The elements are the sum and difference of end-widths or bases, or the sum and difference of marginal heights, and the length of the work.

The bases and the marginal heights will be shown by drawing cross-sections: hence their respective sum and difference are easily found. It must be remembered that the bases or the heights, whichever be employed, must be taken for that width of roadbed to which they belong; that is, if the work be excavation, for excavation width, and *vice versa*. The base and the marginal height of the apex of a pyramid are both nothing: hence the sum is equal to the difference, both for heights and bases. The pyramid in sub-section work is therefore comparable to the wedge in whole-section work. (Art. 37.)

57. LENGTH OF SUB-SECTIONS. If the slopes be similar and both cross-sections partial, the length is given. (Varieties 9 and 11.) Otherwise, there will be one pyramid, except for varieties 3 and 4, which reduce to whole-section work; and varieties 10 and 12, which are less frequent forms, and which contain two pyramids, whose united lengths are taken. The lengths of all pyramids will be discovered by drawing marginal profiles. If these profiles be drawn upon the true margin of each section, they will exhibit the true abscissas. If the profiles be drawn upon the margin of a mean roadbed, they will show the approximate lengths of the abscissas. Plate VI. shows continuous marginal and median profiles for the cross-sections drawn on Plate V. The median profile will show the abscissa which is taken for the length in varieties 3 and 4.

58. CROSS-SECTIONS AND PROFILES UPON A PREPARED DIAGRAM. The study of Articles 45, 50, and 52 will show how cross-sections and profiles may be drawn upon diagrams similar to that of Plate VII. The operations of construction may, if the computer please, be supplied by the use of tables. We shall here notice some of the more simple tabular processes.

59. CONJOINT USE OF DIAGRAMS AND TABLES. The augmented sum of the end-heights for whole sections may be conveniently formed by adding together the two end-heights and the augment from Table II.

Example.—Width of roadbed, 28.5 feet; side-slope, $1\frac{1}{2}$ to 1; end-heights, 7.4 and 9.1. Required the augmented sum of the heights and the difference of the heights.

First end-height	7.4	difference, 1.7.
Second end-height	9.1	
Augment from Table II.	19.0	
	35.5	augmented sum of end-heights.

The augment, and the redundant prism, which is also required, may, for convenience, be recorded upon the diagram of Plate VII.

Marginal heights found by construction may be used to find abscissas, by Table IV. This dispenses with the necessity of drawing the marginal profiles. The median abscissa may also be found by the same table. The work of construction may, therefore, be reduced to drawing the cross-sections only.

Determination of Varieties and Preparation of Elements by Tabulation.

60. The Tabular Method of determining varieties and preparing the elements consists in tabulating the cross-sections and the marginal and median profiles. The method applies to single or to continuous sections. The operations for continuous sections may either be performed for each section consecutively, or similar processes may be simultaneously conducted, for a number of sections.

61. Determination of Variety is performed by tabulating the cross-sections for a mean width of roadbed. The nature of the cross-section is ascertained by observing whether the end-height be greater or less than the height of the neutral cross-section from Table III.

In the central column of the annexed scheme, (page 33,) opposite to the number designating the station, set down the end-height of that station; and, above the height, write the degree and direction of surface-slope. Upon the right and left of each centre-height of the section, set down the augment belonging to the roadbed and the degree of slope. The nature of each cross-section will now appear; and, as the signs of the end-heights and the directions of the slopes are recorded, the variety of the section can be made out according to the General Scheme. Write the variety in the proper column, opposite to the station designating the number of the section.

62. Preparation of Elements. The next thing is to take out the abscissas, when necessary. Varieties 1, 2, 9, and 11 do not require any abscissa to be found. Varieties 3 and 4 require the median abscissa. Varieties 5, 6, 7, and 8 require one marginal abscissa. Varieties 10 and 12 require both marginal abscissas.

63. Finding the Marginal Heights and their Differences. These are necessary in order to find the marginal abscissas. Prefix the sign + to the augment on the right-hand side of the centre-height of the first station of the first section, and the sign — to the same augment on the left of the same height. Then, regarding well the signs, add the centre-height successively to the augment on each side of it, and carry out the results on their respective sides to the column of Marginal Heights. Perform the same thing at the next station, observing to make the augment on the right + only in case the slope here is similar to the first slope. If the slopes are opposite, put — on the right and + on the left.

Having now the marginal heights at each end of the section, subtract, on the right and left respectively, the lower height from the upper, and set the result in the column of Differences, opposite the first station of the section.

64. Difference of Centre-Heights. This, when required for finding the median abscissa, is the *numerical sum* of the heights. It is to be recorded, in its proper column, opposite the first station of the section.

65. Finding the Abscissas.—These are found by Table IV. The marginal height and the difference accompanying it, which are set opposite the first station of the section, are the numbers to be used in entering the table. That abscissa which is not required in Varieties 5, 6, 7, 8 is either negative, or greater than the length of the section. Negative abscissas result when the height and difference are of unlike sign. If the height is greater than the difference, the abscissa exceeds the length of the section.

66. Succeeding Consecutive Sections. The next section is disposed of precisely in the same way. It must be observed that both its slopes are to be compared, as directed, (Art. 63,) with the first slope of the first section, and the signs of the augment treated accordingly. The last marginal heights of a previous section are the first of the next consecutive section.

Tabulation of Cross-Sections and Profiles for a Mean Roadbed 26 *feet.*

Station.	Distance.	Marginal Abscissa	Difference of M. H.	Marginal Height.	Augment.	Centre-Height & Slope.	Augment.	Marginal Height.	Difference of M. H.	Marginal Abscissa	Variety.	Difference of C. H.	Median Abscissa
						17° L							
0	100	23	—11.0	—2.5	—4.0	+1.5	+4.0	+5.5	+2.0				
						11° R							
1	100		+3.1	+8.5	+2.5	+6.0	—2.5	+3.5	+7.1	49	6		
						19° R							
2	100		+4.6	+5.4	+4.5	+0.9	—4.5	—3.6	+1.6		5		
						13° R							
3	100		—1.7	+0.8	+3.0	—2.2	—3.0	—5.2	—11.3	46	11		
						8° L							
4	100		+11.1	+2.5	—1.8	+4.3	+1.8	+6.1	+9.1		8	10.1	43
						12° L							
5	100		+4.4	—8.6	—2.8	—5.8	+2.8	—3.0	+7.2		3		
						6° L							
6	100		—8.3	—13.0	—1.4	—11.6	+1.4	—10.2	+1.5		1		
						15° R							
7	100		—6.7	—4.7	+3.5	—8.2	—3.5	—11.7	—17.9		2	12.3	67
						9° L							
8	100	23	+8.6	+2.0	—2.1	+4.1	+2.1	+6.2	+3.4		4		
						20° L							
9	100	55	—12.1	—6.6	—4.7	—1.9	+4.7	+2.8	+5.7	49	7		
						18° R							
10	100		—0.9	+5.5	+4.2	+1.3	—4.2	—2.9	—1.9		12		
						16° R							
11	100	59	+10.8	+6.4	+3.7	+2.7	—3.7	—1.0	—6.6	15	9		
						21° L							
12	100			—4.4	—5.0	+0.6	+5.0	+5.6			10		

67. Arbitrary Assumption of the Direction of Slope. In the above processes, the direction of the first slope of the series is assumed to be from the right downward towards the left. If this be the case, then the marginal abscissas on the right side of the scheme belong to the right side of the roadbed, and the others to the left. If the direction of slope be not as assumed, then the abscissas in the right-hand column belong to the left-hand side of the road. If it were desired to make the position of the abscissas on the scheme correspond with their true position, then the augments set down at the first station of the first section must have + prefixed on that side corresponding to the high side of the slope, and — on the other. For the following sections, the sign of the augment will be + on the same side as at first, whenever the slope is in the same direction.

The signs of the marginal heights as thus found agree with the centre-heights in signification

A positive height shows excavation, and a negative height shows embankment. Difference of sign in marginal heights set opposite to any station indicates a partial cross-section at that station. Difference of sign in heights at opposite ends of a section, and on the same side, shows that there is a marginal grade-point on that side.

68. DOUBLE TABULATION. In the same way, it is possible to tabulate for two widths of roadbed, taking care to put the positive augment, as before, on the same side of the scheme when the slope is in the same direction as at first. The number of columns may be increased; but it is probably better to adopt a separate scheme for each width of roadbed. The operation requires more care than the previous one, but has, in theory, the advantage of giving the true length of abscissa. In practice, however, it is sufficient if a tolerably good approximation can be easily obtained.

69. MARGINAL HEIGHTS AND BASES UNDER PLANE GROUND. One object of the preceding tabulation was to find the abscissas. For this purpose it was necessary to find the marginal heights correctly, observing the surface-slope at each end of the section. The length being found, we assume a plane surface for the reduced solids, in computing the solidity of sub-sections. The height of neutral cross-section is, therefore, now the same at both ends in calculating the marginal heights, (Arts. 46, 49:) the distance out of the grade-point is also the same at each end, for the same height. These augments corresponding now to the same surface-slope at both ends of the work, convenient methods of finding the sums and differences for bases and for heights may be derived.

70. SUM AND DIFFERENCE OF BASES. It is the sum and difference of the bases which are required for computing solidity.

RULE.

Enter Table V. with the algebraic sum of the end-heights, and apply the tabular number thus found, according to the sign of the sum, to the width of excavation-roadbed, and with contrary sign to the width of embankment-roadbed.* The result in each case is the sum of the bases: no sign need be prefixed to the result.

Enter Table V. with the algebraic difference of the end-heights. The tabular number is the difference of the bases, both for excavation and embankment. Only the numerical value of the difference of heights is required in entering the table: no sign need be prefixed to the tabular number.

The remark concerning the sign applies, in both cases, to the use of the result in computation of solidity. If an error has been made in forming the sum or difference of the bases, the sign of the result, if observed, may lead to the discovery of the error.

Example 1.—End-heights, +2.1 and —1.0. Surface-slope, 20°. Roadbed, 28 feet for excavation; 24 feet for embankment.

$\left.\begin{matrix}+2.1\\-1.0\end{matrix}\right\}$ 3.1 difference. Gives difference of bases 8.5

+1.1 sum. Gives tabular number	+3.0	The same with sign changed	—3.0
Roadbeds	28.0	. . . .	24.0
Sums of bases: Excavation . .	31.0	Embankment . . .	21.0

In this manner the sum and the difference of the bases may be found for varieties 9, 10, 11, and 12 of the General Scheme.

Example 2.—End-heights, +4.37† and —3.9. Surface-slope, 20°. Roadbed, 28 feet for excavation; 24 feet for embankment.

---

* This is equivalent to inverting the embankment; in which case the height belonging to the work then in question would be counted plus, as it is for excavation.

† This height is taken to the second decimal merely to show more exactly the operation of the tables.

$\left.\begin{array}{r}+4.37\\-3.90\end{array}\right\}$ 8.27 difference. Gives difference of bases 22.7

+0.47 sum. Gives tabular number +1.3 The same with sign changed —1.3
Roadbeds . . . . . . 28.0 . . . . 24.0

Sums of bases: Excavation . . 29.3 Embankment . . . 22.7

These dimensions correspond to a case wherein one of the end-heights (+4.37) belongs to the neutral cross-section through the point of a pyramid whose base has the end-height —3.9. We perceive, therefore, that pyramids can be worked by this rule. Pyramids, however, generally occur in one of the varieties of Case II. of the General Scheme. As the sum of the bases is not then wanted for that portion of the work which is not of the same kind as the pyramid, it will be sufficient to find the tabular number by entering the table with the centre-height at the base of the pyramid. Apply the number, as for sums of bases, to the half-width of roadbed. The result is the base of the pyramid, which is both sum and difference, since the base of the point is nothing.

Example 3.—End-heights, each +1.6. Surface-slope, 10°. Roadbed, 18 feet for excavation; embankment, none.

$\left.\begin{array}{r}+1.6\\+1.6\end{array}\right\}$ 0.0 difference. Gives difference of bases 0.0

+3.2 sum. Gives tabular number, say 18.0
Excavation-roadbed 18.0

Sum of bases 36.0

The cross-section is neutral at each end of the work. Had we not known this, we should have been led to inquire, and to perceive it, upon taking 14 feet for the width of embankment. On changing the sign of the tabular number 18, we should have derived the negative sum of bases, —4. But this result would have been absurd, because the base is, in the formula from which the rule is derived, considered essentially positive.

71. Sum and Difference of End-Heights. The method of finding the augmented sum and the difference of end-heights for whole sections is sufficiently explained in Art. 59.

RULE.

For Sub-Sections.—The augment of the end-height is the height of the neutral cross-section. This converts the end-height into the marginal height. The augment for the sum of the heights is therefore the double tabular number from Table III.* The rule is similar to that for the bases.

For the Sum.—Take double the augment from Table III., giving it the sign *plus*. For excavation, add the algebraic sum of the end-heights to the double augment; and, for embankment, add the sum with its sign changed to the double augment.

For the Difference.—Take the algebraic difference of the end-heights, both for excavation and embankment.

No sign need be prefixed to the result, either for the sum or the difference.

EXAMPLES.

Example 1.—The same as in Art. 70.

$\left.\begin{array}{r}+2.1\\-1.0\end{array}\right\}$ 3.1 difference for excavation and embankment.

+1.1 sum. The same with sign changed . . . . —1.1
+10.2 augment for excavation. Augment for embankment . . . +8.7

11.3 sum for excavation. Sum for embankment 7.6

In this manner the augmented sum and the difference of heights may be found, after reduction, (Art. 36,) for varieties 9, 10, 11, and 12 of the General Scheme.

* The enunciation of a general rule for both whole and sub sections might have been rendered more simple in this respect if Table III. had been made to contain the double augment. It is, however, sometimes desirable to make use of the single augment, as in Art. 61, and following.

Example 2.—The same as in Art. 70.

$\left.\begin{matrix}-3.90\\+4.37\end{matrix}\right\}$ 8.27 difference, for excavation and embankment.

+0.47	sum.	The same with sign changed . .	—0.47
+10.20	augment for excavation.	Augment for embankment . . .	+8.74
10.67	sum for excavation.	Sum for embankment	+8.27

If the given end-heights should happen to belong to a pyramid, this would be shown by the sum being found equal to the difference, as is here the case for embankment. To find the sum and difference for a pyramid, when known to be one, we have simply to find the marginal height of the base according to Art. 63. Thus, in the above, —3.90 added to —4.37 gives —8.27. The negative sign shows embankment.

Example 3.—The same as in Art. 70.

$\left.\begin{matrix}+1.6\\+1.6\end{matrix}\right\}$ 0.0 difference, for excavation and embankment.

+3.2	sum.	The same with sign changed . . .	—3.2
+3.2	augment for excavation.	Augment for embankment . . .	+2.5
6.4	sum for excavation.	Sum for embankment	—0.7

The augmented sum for embankment, found by taking a 14 feet roadbed, is —0.7. Although the negative sign belongs to embankment, it is assumed to be temporarily changed in our rule: therefore the sum derived shows an absurd result. It is so, because the work is all excavation.

The following problems relating to cross-sections, unless otherwise specified, are restricted to full cross-sections.

72. To find the Distance Out. The distance out may be measured either upon the sloping ground-surface or upon a horizontal plane. The horizontal distance is understood to be meant when not otherwise stated or sufficiently indicated. The methods of computation are similar for both. The distance out of the mid cross-section is the mean of the end distances out.

RULE.*

Find the common logarithm of double the augmented centre-height of the cross-section. To this add the tabular logarithm from Table XIX. or XX. for the given side and surface slope. The result is the logarithm of the distance out, which will be for horizontal distance from Table XIX. and for sloping distance from Table XX. For the use of Table XVIII., see Art. 131.

Example 1.—The centre-height from the roadbed is 28.7; the surface-slope, 18°; roadbed, 24; side-slope, 1½ to 1. Required the horizontal distances out. (See Art. 6, Appendix.)

57.4 double centre-height.
16.0 augment from Table II.

73.4 double augmented centre-height; logarithm	1.86570
Opposite 18°, under 1½ to 1, Table XIX.	0.16527
Logarithm of 107.39+, the long distance out, ...	2.03097
73.4 double augmented centre-height; logarithm	1.86570
Opposite 18°, under 1½ to 1, Table XIX.	—1.70264
Logarithm of 37.01+, the short distance out, ...	1.56834

Example 2.—Suppose the previous cross-section to be at one end of a piece of work, and the following at the other. Centre-height from roadbed, 14.5; surface-slope, 12°, and in the same direction as before. Required the distances out at this end. (See Art. 6, Appendix.)

---

*A provisional selection has been made in printing the tables to which this rule applies. In the author's manuscript they were coextensive with Tables XVI. and XVII. See Note on p. 39.

45 double augmented centre-height; logarithm	1.65321
Opposite 12°, under $1\frac{1}{2}$ to 1, Table XIX.	0.04181
Logarithm of 49.55, the long distance out, ...	1.69502

45 double augmented centre-height; logarithm	1.65321
Opposite 12°, under $1\frac{1}{2}$ to 1, Table XIX.	—1.75487
Logarithm of 25.59+, the short distance out, ...	1.40808

Example 3.—What is the long sloping distance in the cross-section given in the first example?

73.4 double augmented centre-height; logarithm	1.86570
Opposite 18°, under $1\frac{1}{2}$ to 1, Table XX.	0.18706
Logarithm of 112.92, the long sloping distance, ...	2.05276

73. To find the Distances Out of the Mid Cross-Section for a Plane Surface. The sum of the end-heights being now double the height of the mid cross-section, the distances out can be found by employing the augmented sum of the end-heights.

Example.—What are the distances out of the mid cross-section of the piece of work whose end-heights from the roadbed are 28.7 and 14.5, the surface-slope 15°, side-slope $1\frac{1}{2}$ to 1, and the roadbed 24? (See Example 1, Arts. 86, and 107.)

59.2 augmented sum of heights; logarithm	1.77232
Opposite 15°, under $1\frac{1}{2}$ to 1, Table XIX.	0.09830
Logarithm of 74.24, the long distance out, ...	1.87062

59.2 augmented sum of heights; logarithm	1.77232
Opposite 15°, under $1\frac{1}{2}$ to 1, Table XIX.	—1.72834
Logarithm of 31.67, the short distance out, ...	1.50066

74. Level Side-Slope and Distance Out of Triangular Cross-Sections. It should be remembered that these distances out, both for Tables XIX. and XX., count to the meeting of the side and surface slopes. When the side-slope is level, the two slopes will meet on a horizontal line through the intersection of the side-slopes. There can then be but one set of distances out,—the logarithms, for these are given in the level columns on each side of the tables. By means of these tables, for any of the given side-slopes, the distances out of a triangle can be found. Let A B C be a triangle, in which the angles are given, and the vertical height D E; also the distance A D. Produce the side C A and the height D E to meet in K. Consider A D as the half-width of roadbed, and E K the augmented centre-height. Then the distances out K N and E C can be found as above.

Fig. 23.

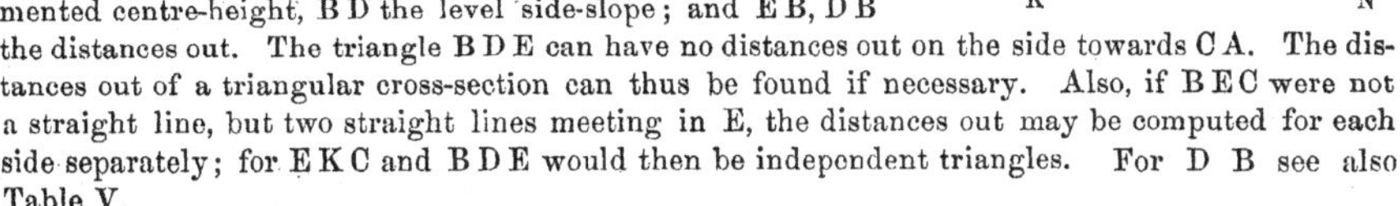

In the triangle B D E, D E may be regarded as an augmented centre-height, B D the level side-slope; and E B, D B the distances out. The triangle B D E can have no distances out on the side towards C A. The distances out of a triangular cross-section can thus be found if necessary. Also, if B E C were not a straight line, but two straight lines meeting in E, the distances out may be computed for each side separately; for E K C and B D E would then be independent triangles. For D B see also Table V.

75. To find the Augmented Height of the Mid Cross-Section. The distances out at the ends are supposed to be known; if not given, they may be found by the rule, (Art. 72.) The rule applies to all such surfaces as are described in Art. 8.

RULE.

Multiply the sum of the distances out on one side by the sum of those on the other, and divide the product by the sum of all the distances out. Divide again by the rate of side-slope.

Example 1.—Take the work of which the dimensions of the end cross-sections are as in examples 1 and 2, Art. 72, observing that the long distances out belong on the same side, because the slopes are similar. (See Note and Example 1, Art. 104.)

Logarithm of 156.94, the sum of long distances, ...	2.19573
Logarithm of 62.6, the sum of short distances, ...	1.79657
Logarithm of product of sums	3.99230
Logarithm of 219.54, the sum of all the distances, ...	2.34151
Logarithm of product divided by sum of all the distances . . .	1.65079
Logarithm of $1\frac{1}{2}$, the rate of side-slope	0.17609
Logarithm of 29.83+, the mid-height, ...	1.47470

Example 2.—Take the same end-dimensions, but suppose the surface-slopes to be opposite; the distances out will then be paired differently. (See Note and Example 2, Art. 104.)

Logarithm of 132.98, sum of first pair of distances, ...	2.12379
Logarithm of 86.56, sum of second pair of distances, ...	1.93732
Logarithm of product of sums	4.06111
Logarithm of 219.54, the sum of all the distances, ...	2.34151
Logarithm of product divided by sum of all the distances	1.71960
Logarithm of $1\frac{1}{2}$, the rate of side-slope, ...	0.17609
Logarithm of 34.96, the mid-height, ...	1.54351

76. To find the Augmented Centre-Height of a Cross-Section whose Distances Out are given. Divide twice the product of the distances out by their sum, and divide again by the rate of the side-slope. This is equivalent to supposing two equal end cross-sections, and then proceeding as above to find the mid-height.

Example 1.—The distances out are 57.84 and 11.42; side-slope, $1\frac{1}{2}$ to 1. Required the centre-height from the intersection of the side-slopes. (See Art. 7, Appendix.)

57.84 multiplied by 11.42, and by 2, gives	1321.07
And 1321.07 divided by 69.26, the sum of the distance, gives . . .	19.07
And 19.07 divided by $1\frac{1}{2}$ gives the centre-height	12.71

Example 2.—The distances out are 81.80 and 12.54; side-slope, $1\frac{1}{2}$ to 1. Required the centre-height from the intersection of the side-slopes. (See Art. 7, Appendix.)

81.80 multiplied by 12.54, and by 2, gives	2051.54
And 2051.54 divided by 94.34, the sum of the distance, gives . . .	21.74
And 21.74 divided by $1\frac{1}{2}$ gives the centre-height	14.49

77. To find the Augmented Side-Height when the Distance Out is given. Divide the distance out by the rate of side-slope.

Example.—Take the end cross-sections of Art. 72, with slopes opposed, so that the sum of distances out on one side is 132.98; the distance out of the mid-section on that side will be one-half this number =66.49. In like manner, the other distance out will be the half of 86.56 = 43.28.

66.49 divided by $1\frac{1}{2}$, the rate of side-slope, gives height . . .	44.33
43.28 divided by $1\frac{1}{2}$, the rate of side-slope, gives height . . .	28.85

78. To find Twice the Difference of the Side-Heights. Divide twice the difference of the distances out by the rate of side-slope. It is evident from the preceding that, for the mid-section, it is only necessary to subtract the sum of end distances out on one side from the sum of those on the other and divide the remainder by the rate of side-slope.

Example.—Take the previous example. (See Art. 7, Appendix.)

86.56 from 132.98 leaves 46.42
And 46.42 divided by 1½ gives twice the difference 30.95

79. To find the Surface-Slope of a Cross-Section. Divide the difference of the side-heights by the sum of the distances out. The result is the tangent of the surface-slope to radius = 1. It is the same thing to divide twice the difference of the side-heights by twice the sum of the distances out. Hence, having computed the end distances out according to Art. 72, we may find twice the difference of the mid-section side-heights by Art. 78; after which the tangent of the surface-slope of that cross-section may be computed as here directed. The sum of all the distances out is equal to twice the sum of the distances out of the mid cross-section.

Having computed the tangent, find the surface-slope in Table A, page 123.

Example.—Take the work given in the examples Arts. 77 and 78. (See Example 2, Art. 104.)

Twice the difference 30.95 divided by 219.54, the sum of all the distances, gives .141.

In Table A, opposite to the tangent .141, is found the degree of slope 8°, the surface-slope of the mid cross-section.

Note.—The division necessary to find the tangent may be approximately performed by Table IV. Divide both dividend and divisor by 10 or by 100, so that the new divisor shall not exceed 20; and take it to the nearest tenth. Take the new dividend to two or three figures; then find the new divisor in the side column of Table IV., and proceed as directed for that Table in Art. 131. Remove the decimal point of the result two places to the left.

Thus, in the above example, the new dividend becomes, say .31, and the new divisor 2.2; which gives .141 by Table IV., after removal of the decimal point.

Note to Art. 72, p. 36.

Staking out by the method of transverse slopes is not generally practised. The Slope Distance may, however, be occasionally required for this or other purposes not included in the main design of this work. Tables XVIII. and XX. will meet such demands for various slopes, and serve as samples of tables proper for this purpose.

CHAPTER III.

COMPUTATION OF EXCAVATION AND EMBANKMENT BY TRANSVERSE GROUND-SLOPES.

Straight Work and Plane Ground-Surface.

80. Three Different Methods of Computation. We shall treat the computation of solidity in three different ways, which, for the sake of distinction, may be designated,—1st, the method by Tables of Cubical Content; 2d, by Scale; 3d, by Logarithms. These methods are essentially the same: they differ in the manner of applying the same principles to computation from the same elements. But, though the methods are different in some of their parts, the similarity of fundamental processes can be observed.

81. Necessary References. In studying this chapter, the reader should refer, as occasion may require, to the preceding chapters and to the general and special remarks upon the tables in Chapter V. He is now presumed to be acquainted with the constructive methods alluded to in Articles 54 to 59, and with previous auxiliary processes. After giving the data of our examples, we shall assume the elements to have been found by construction. Such allusion will be made to finding elements by calculation as will assist the student desirous of pursuing that subject.

82. Cubical Content Proportional to the Length of the Work. In treating of the computation of solidity, it may be well to call attention to this principle, which is applicable to all our problems. (See Art. 129.) It is therefore unnecessary to complicate our examples by assuming lengths differing from the standard of 100 feet. The subdivision of sections will, incidentally, give illustration of such cases. Unless otherwise specified, the length will be supposed to be 100 feet.

83. Transverse Ground-Slope in Whole Degrees. The transverse slope is to be understood as given or derived in whole degrees. When a given slope or a slope derived by taking the mean is not in whole degrees, it will suffice in general to take the nearest degree. Where half-degrees occur, the computer will decide whether to take the greater or lesser whole number. By taking the greater slope, a larger content is in general obtained. By taking alternately the larger and smaller slope for successive sections, there is a probability of ultimate balancing of errors. Where the end-heights are great and the slope considerable, interpolation may be necessary, and can be made approximately by proportional parts for a fraction of a degree. (See page 79.) We have found no simple method for exact interpolation.

84. Preliminaries Necessary to Computation. The preliminary operations may be advantageously rehearsed in this place. They are as follows:—

First Operation. — Variety and Dimensions of a Section.—The first operation is to ascertain the *variety* to which the section belongs in the General Scheme. If the section requires subdivision, the dimensions of the component solids must be found, and the solids reduced to a plane surface.

Second Operation.—Preparation of Elements.—From the dimensions of the section, if whole, or from the dimensions of its component solids after reduction, find the elements required by the General Rule hereafter given. There are four kinds of elements,—viz., for whole and for sub sections, both in excavation and in embankment. These should be properly classified in recording them. It is also well to find—in Tables I. and II.—and to record the redundant prism and the whole-section augment for the widths of excavation and embankment respectively belonging to the work in hand.

Third Operation.—Computation.—According to the rate of side-slope and the nature of the work, as to whole or sub sections, find the proper tables,—VII., VIII., IX., X., XI., XII., XIII., XV., XVI., or XVII.

Computation by Tables of Cubical Content.

GENERAL RULE.

85. With the augmented sum of centre-heights, or with the sum of the bases, enter the table, and, under the degree of surface-slope, take out a first term.

With the difference of the heights or of the bases (according as the first term was found by heights or bases) enter the same table under the surface-slope; and take one-third of the tabular quantity thus found for a second term or correction.

Add the correction to the first term for the true content in sub-sections, and for the true content of the whole prismoid between the surface and intersection of side-slopes in whole sections. Subtract the redundant prism (Art. 21) in order to find the residual prismoid.

Only the heights are used for whole sections: heights or bases for sub-sections.

86. EXAMPLES IN WHOLE AND SUB SECTIONS.

Whole Sections.

Example 1.—Prismoid. First end-height, —28.7; second end-height, —14.5; surface-slope, 15°; side-slope, 1½ to 1; roadbed, 24 feet.

Here the end-heights have like signs, and the lesser obviously gives a full cross-section; of course, also, the greater will, the slope being the same at each end. (Art. 34 and note.) By construction or by calculation (Art. 59) the augmented sum and the difference are found as below, and indicate the following operation by the General Rule:—

59.2 augmented sum. Tabular quantity from Table VII. under 15°	5805.6
14.2 difference. One-third of tabular quantity	111.4
Content of whole prismoid	5917.0
Redundant prism	355.6
Residual prismoid between the surface and roadbed . . .	5561.4

Example 2.—Prismoid reduced to a wedge. (Art. 37.) First end-height, +5.8; second end-height, +1.0; surface-slope, 5°; side-slope, 1 to 1; roadbed, 28 feet.

We may, for an approximate computation, disregard the partial cross-section and assume the solid to be a wedge.

33.8 augmented sum. Tabular quantity from Table IX. under 0°	1057.9
5.8 difference. One-third of tabular quantity	10.4
Content of whole prismoid	1068.3
Redundant prism	725.9
Residual prismoid or wedge	342.4

The second term is the error which would result from neglecting the difference of the end-heights and computing an approximate content by their augmented sum. This error is always in defect under plane ground. In the first example it amounts to 111 yards in 5561, or about 2 per cent. of the residual prismoid. In the second example the error is about 3 per cent. of the residual prismoid.

Consult Arts. 70 and 71 for the calculation of sums and differences in the following examples:—

Sub-Sections.

Example 1.—Truncated pyramids, Variety 11 of the General Scheme. First end-height, +2.1; second end-height, —1.0; surface-slope, 20°; roadbed, 28 feet for excavation, 24 feet for embankment.

Excavation:—

31.0 sum of bases. Tabular quantity from Table X. under 20°	254.6
8.5 difference. One-third of tabular quantity	6.4
Content of excavation	261.0

Embankment:—

21.0 sum of bases. Tabular quantity from Table VIII. under 20°	163.7
8.5 difference. One-third of tabular quantity	9.0
Content of embankment	172.7

Example 2.—Truncated pyramid of excavation and pyramid of embankment, Variety 11 of the General Scheme. First end-height, +4.37; second end-height, —3.9; surface-slope, 20°; roadbed, 28 feet for excavation, 24 feet for embankment.

Excavation:—

29.3 sum of bases. Tabular quantity from Table X. under 20°	227.5
22.7 difference. One-third of tabular quantity	45.5
Content of excavation	273.0

Embankment:—

22.7 sum of bases. Tabular quantity from Table VIII. under 20° 191.3
22.7 difference. One-third of tabular quantity . . . 63.8

Content of embankment 255.1

Example 3.—Prism of excavation: no embankment. The cross-section is neutral at both ends. Variety 9 of the General Scheme. If considered as a whole section, this piece of work belongs to Variety 1. End-heights, each +1.6; surface-slope, 10°; roadbed, 18 feet for excavation.

Excavation:—

36.0 sum of bases. Tabular quantity from Table X. under 10° 128.4
0.0 difference. One-third of tabular quantity . . . 0.0

Content of excavation 128.4

87. *The same Examples for Sub-Sections by Heights.**

Example 1.—Excavation:—

11.3 augmented sum. Tabular quantity from Table XIII. (20°) 255.8
3.1 difference. One-third of tabular quantity . . . 6.4

Content of excavation 262.2

Embankment:—

7.6 augmented sum. Tabular quantity from Table XII. (20°) 162.5
3.1 difference. One-third of tabular quantity . . . 9.1

Content of embankment 171.6

Example 2.—Excavation:—

10.7 augmented sum. Tabular quantity from Table XIII. (20°) 229.4
8.3 difference. One-third of tabular quantity . . . 46.1

Content of excavation 275.5

Embankment:—

8.3 augmented sum. Tabular quantity from Table XII. (20°) 193.6
8.3 difference. One-third of tabular quantity . . . 64.5

Content of embankment. 258.1

Example 3.—Excavation:—

6.4 augmented sum. Tabular quantity from Table XIII. (10°) 131.4
0.0 difference. One-third of tabular quantity . . . 0.0

Content of excavation 131.4

* The results found by the two methods do not quite agree, on account of small discrepancies in taking the elements.

88. Further Examples, in Whole and Sub Sections. Take the twelve consecutive sections of which the cross-sections and profiles are given upon Plates V. and VI. and the tabulation in Art. 60, and following. The elements, as found after subdividing the sections which require subdivision, and after reduction of the component solids, may be arranged as in the annexed table. The whole-section work in embankment is performed by Table VII.; in excavation, by Table IX. The sub-section work is computed by bases. For embankment, it is performed by the aid of Table VIII., and for excavation by the aid of Table X. After verifying by construction the elements recorded in the accompanying table, the student may take out the tabular quantities. After working the examples in this manner, if the student shall have become tolerably familiar with the method, it may be well to find by construction all the sums and differences of heights required for the computation of the sub-sections by heights, then to re-compute by Tables XII. and XIII. In sections No. 6 and No. 7, a plane surface is assumed, having a mean slope. If the student find difficulty in the preparation of the elements for these examples, he may consult Art. 1 of the Appendix.

Excavation.

WHOLE SECTIONS.					SUB-SECTIONS.				
Section.	Slope.	Sum.	Difference.	Length.	Slope.	Sum.	Difference.	Length.	Cubic Yards.
1	3°	34.7	5.3	88.5	....	....	....	....	354.9
2	15°	37.8	2.2	74.5	....	....	....	....	522.3
3	....	....	....	....	16°	23.5	10.8	100	110.1
4	3°	33.0	3.6	77	....	....	....	....	222.7
5	10°	34.8	1.8	43	....	....	....	....	186.0
6									
7									
8	3°	32.8	3.4	33	....	....	....	....	91.3
9	15°	35.9	0.3	61.5	....	....	....	....	344.3
10	....	....	....	....	19°	13.2	13.2	94	53.0
11	....	....	....	....	17°	41.1	4.6	100	344.8
12	....	....	....	....	19°	37.6	0.0	100	343.7

Embankment.

WHOLE SECTIONS.					SUB-SECTIONS.				
Section.	Slope.	Sum.	Difference.	Length.	Slope.	Sum.	Difference.	Length.	Cubic Yards.
1	....	....	....	....	17°	7.1	7.1	23	4.0
2	....	....	....	....	19°	9.4	9.4	51	19.8
3	....	....	....	....	16°	28.5	10.8	100	198.4
4	....	....	....	....	13°	21.5	21.5	46	46.4
5	10°	24.3	3.3	57	....	....	....	....	303.2
6	9°	33.4	5.8	100	....	....	....	....	1303.4
7	5°	35.8	3.4	100	....	....	....	....	1461.2
8	3°	24.9	7.5	67	....	....	....	....	360.1
9	....	....	....	....	20°	17.5	17.5	77	118.3
10	....	....	....	....	19°	25.7	0.0	100	217.9
11	....	....	....	....	17°	10.9	4.6	100	32.9
12	....	....	....	....	19°	7.8	7.3	56	12.5

89. Special Tables in Whole Sections for a Particular Width of Roadbed. General tables for full work, such as Tables VII., IX., and XI., require the subtraction of the redundant prism after the content of the whole ground has been computed. If the redundant prism for a particular side-slope and width of roadbed be subtracted from each quantity corresponding in the general table to a full cross-section, the diminished tabular quantities will represent the content of the ground between the roadbed and the surface. Table XIV. is an example of a special table constructed in this manner, by subtracting the redundant prism for a 24 feet roadbed from the quantities of Table VII. In a table of this sort, the number in the side column will be the sum of the end-heights without the augment, because the redundant prism has been subtracted. For the difference of the end-heights, the process is the same as before; but, for convenience, an auxiliary Second Part may be formed containing the third parts of the quantities corresponding to the differences. Hence, for Table XIV. and others similar we have the following

RULE.

90. With the sum of the end-heights enter the table, under the given slope, and take out the approximate content of the ground between the surface and the roadbed.

With the difference of the end-heights enter the Second Part of the table, under the given slope, and take out a correction, which add to the approximate content to find the true content.

Example.—End-heights, 11.6 and 5.8; surface-slope, 9°; side-slope, $1\frac{1}{2}$ to 1; roadbed, 24 feet. See section No. 6 of the previous examples.

17.4 sum.	Tabular quantity from Table XIV. . .	1286.8
5.8 difference.	Tabular quantity from Second Part .	16.6
Content	. . . .	1303.4

Unusual Cases.

91. Unequal End-Widths. Sometimes one end of a cut or embankment is wider than the other. In partial work, this is already provided for by the General Rule as applied to sub-sections. In full work, the rule still holds, except that the redundant solid between the roadbed and the side-slopes must be computed. Let A B C D (Fig. 25) and E F G H (Fig. 24) be the end cross-sections. Let the end-heights K L, M N be given, the distances K B, M E, and the end-widths A B, E F. With the given side and surface slopes and the before-mentioned data, construct the cross-sections, and prolong the side-slopes to meet in O and P. Measure the augmented end-heights O Q and P R, and the end-heights O S and P T of the redundant prismoid. Then, with the sums and the differences of the heights thus obtained, compute, as before, the whole ground and the redundant solid, and subtract the redundant solid from the whole content.

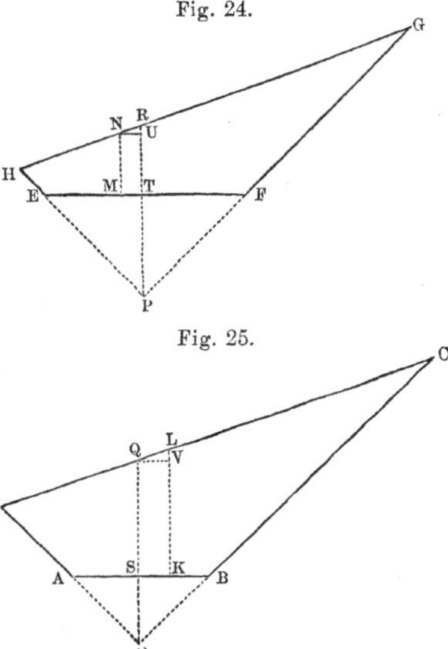

Example.—Suppose A B = 33.4; K B = 14; K L = 17.6; E F = 40; M E = 15.9; M N = 9.2; surface-slope, 10°; side-slope, 1 to 1. We find O S = 16.7; P T = 20; O Q = 33.8; P R = 29.9. Hence the computation is

36.7 sum of end-heights of the redundant prismoid under 0°, Table IX.	1247.3
3.3 difference. One-third of tabular quantity	3.4
Content of the redundant prismoid	1250.7
63.7 augmented sum of heights for whole solid, Table IX., 10° . .	3877.9
3.9 difference. One-third of tabular quantity	4.8
Content of the whole ground	3882.7
Redundant prismoid, brought down	1250.7
Residual prismoid between the surface and roadbed	2632.0

92. Inclined Surface of the Redundant Prismoid. The case above exhibited is evidently nothing more than that of a redundant prismoid with the surface inclined in the direction of the road, supposing the line of intersection of the side-slopes to remain level. The end-heights were given, not at the centre, but at a distance out from the centre. The centre-heights were obtained by construction. It is obvious that if the surface-slope A B had not been level, we must have proceeded in the same way in order to obtain the solidity of the part enclosed between E F G H and A B C D. Suppose A B and E F had had a surface-slope of 7°. Then, after drawing the cross-sections, we should have measured the heights O S and P T, and with their sum and difference we should have found the redundant prismoid in Table IX. By this method we may, if the surface through A B and E F be nearly a plane, compute approximately the quantity of excavation or embankment which has been done on an unfinished cut or fill. If there is no cause to prevent, it will be convenient to take the heights, on the field, over the centres S, T of the ends. The distances K B, M E will then become respectively equal to half the end-width, and the constructions can be made in the usual manner.

Oblique Work. If the length of the work have been measured obliquely, either horizontally or vertically, it will be necessary to obtain the direct length. (Art. 40.) This can be done, and the previous methods applied whenever the planes of the end cross-sections are parallel to each other.

93. Reduction of an Irregular Surface to a Sloping Plane Surface. Let ABCDEFGH (Fig. 27) and IKLMNOP (Fig. 26) be the end cross-sections. The points C, D, E, F, G, H, L, M, N, O, P are supposed to have been found by their heights and distances out. If a line can be drawn, as H S or T U, in such a manner as to cut off from the area of the cross-section a quantity equal to that which it adds, the area A B S H or I K U T will be the same as the original area of the cross-section. We may, therefore, measure the centre-heights R Q, V Y and the surface-

Fig. 26.

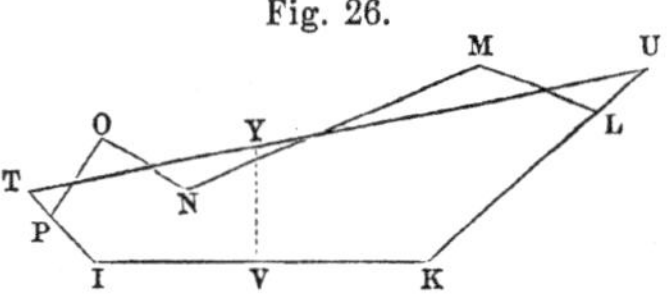

slopes of H S and T U, and proceed to compute as directed in the General Rule. We may also apply the method as in Arts. 91 and 92. When the slopes are opposite or unequal, assume a curved surface and work by Art. 104. No exact method is known for drawing the slopes so as to make the new area equal to the original. In drawing the slopes, the computer must trust to the correctness of his eye in comparing spaces of the kind in question. With careful construction, results may be obtained sufficiently accurate for some purposes of approximate calculation. As cases may, and frequently do, occur in which an expeditious computation, even though not exact, is preferred to a more correct but more laborious method, we consider this process well worthy of mention. It must be left to the judgment of the computer to decide when he will apply it.*

Fig. 27.

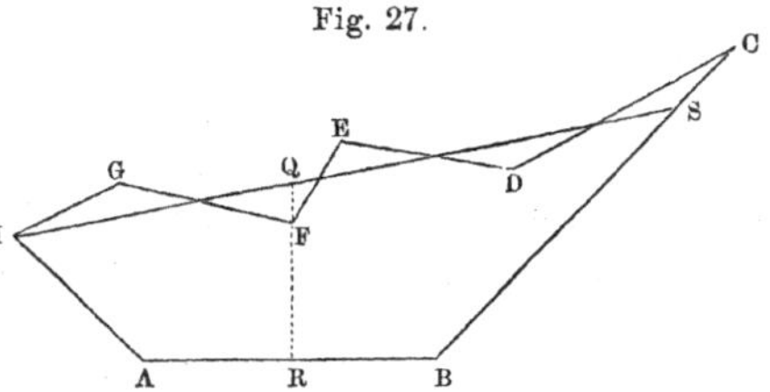

94. Applicability of the Methods by Scale and by Logarithms. The methods by general scale and by logarithms, of which we shall now treat in order, apply to all the questions of solidity which have been mentioned. It will only be necessary in the work classed under the head of "Unusual Cases" to take care to compute correctly the whole ground, and then the redundant solid within. If this solid is contained under a roadbed of equal width and horizontal transversely, it is the redundant prism of Table I. Such cases may occur when an irregular surface is reduced as in Art. 93. Special scales, such as described in Art. 97, are for particular widths of ordinary roadbed. They may also be applied when an irregular surface is reduced, if the roadbed be of the usual kind. But if the roadbed be of unequal width, or the surface of the redundant solid be inclined, those scales will not apply. Of course the logarithmic method, (Art. 102,) which supplies the place of special tables and special scales, is subject to the same restriction.

Computation by Scale.

95. Method of Use and Description of Scales. In computing by the aid of scales, the preparation of elements is made precisely as before; but, instead of entering the tables with the sums and differences, as directed by the General Rule, the sums and differences are employed to find a number upon the scale, and with the number thus found the tables are to be entered. Only one quantity is taken from the table when the scale is made use of. Scales are of two kinds, general and special. The general scale applies to both whole-section and sub-section work; special scales apply to whole-section work for particular widths of roadbed. They supply the place, in working by scale, of tables similar to Table XIV.

96. General Scale for Whole and Sub Sections. On the side marked "Sums and Depths," (Plate VIII.,) find the number denoting the augmented

* This mode of finding new end-slopes is taken from Mr. Trautwine's New Method, by his permission.

sum of the end-heights, or the sum of the bases. Extend the dividers from this point to that point on the first side of the scale which marks the difference of heights or bases, (according as heights or bases were first taken,) and set the dividers. Apply the dividers to the second side of the scale, placing one point at the mark indicating the difference of heights or bases, and read off the number to which the other point of the dividers will reach, upon the scale marked "Sums and Depths." The number last found will be a sum of heights or bases with which to enter the same table as would have been used, without the scale, in working by augmented sums of heights or sums of bases. Therefore, subtract the redundant prism, in whole sections, from the tabular quantity.

Example 1.—End-heights, 28.7 and 14.5; surface-slope, 15°; side-slope, $1\frac{1}{2}$ to 1; roadbed, 24 feet. (See Example 1, Whole Sections, Art. 86.) We place the dividers in 59.2 upon the long branch of the scale, and open them to 14.2 upon the first scale marked "Differences." Then, keeping the dividers set, place one point again in 14.2 upon the second scale marked "Differences." From this point we find them to reach to the mark, say 59.8 on the long scale. Then,

Opposite 59.8, under 15°, in Table VII. . . .	5923.9
Redundant prism	355.6
Residual prismoid between the surface and roadbed .	5568.3

Example 2.—Take the truncated pyramid of embankment in section No. 3, Art. 88. The sum of the bases is 28.5, and the difference 10.8. The slope is 16°. We find on the scale, say 29.2.

Opposite 29.2, under 16°, in Table VIII. . . . 198.6

97. SPECIAL SCALES FOR PARTICULAR WIDTHS OF ROADBED FOR WHOLE SECTIONS. On the side marked "Sums," (Plate IX.,) find the number denoting the sum of the end-heights. Extend the dividers from this point to that point on the first side of the scale which marks the difference of the heights, and set the dividers. Apply the dividers to the second side of the scale, placing one point at the mark indicating the surface-slope, and read off the number to which the other point of the dividers will reach upon the scale marked "Depths of Equivalent Prisms." The number last found will be a sum of depths of equal end-heights from the surface to the intersection of the side-slopes. The quantity found opposite to this number, under the given degree of slope, in the general table adapted to the given side-slope, will be the true content of the ground between the surface and the roadbed.

NOTE.—It is unnecessary to augment the sum of the heights before going on to the scale, because the augment is permanently supplied upon the scale, in the form of the blank space, on the side marked "Sums," between the zero-point and the branch containing the differences.

Example.—End-heights, 28.7 and 14.5; surface-slope, 15°; side-slope, $1\frac{1}{2}$ to 1; roadbed, 24 feet. (See Example 1, Art. 96.) The sum is 43.2; difference, 14.2. On the side marked "Sums," on the embankment scale, take 43.2, and extend the dividers to the difference 14.2. Keeping the dividers set, place one point at the mark of 15°,—as nearly as the place can be estimated, if not marked,—and read the number to which the dividers reach on the scale of depths, say 58 feet.

Opposite 58, under 15°, in Table VII. 5572.4

98. Computation by Equivalent Level-Heights. This method, as far as we have treated it, is best adapted to computation by the aid of scales or diagrams. It may, however, be applied by calculation. It consists in finding a new sum of such heights as A D, (Fig. 28,) each of which heights makes the area of the end cross-section A F K, as if under level ground, equal to the area of the original cross-section A B C under sloping ground. The student who desires to study this may consult the Appendix. Arts. 24, § 5, and 25, §§ 1, 2, are adapted to the wants of those who wish for practical rules without investigation of the theory. The method applies to whole-section work under a plane surface; but whole-section work of any unusual kind, if it can be reduced to an equivalent solid under a plane surface, may be computed, after reduction, by this method. It therefore applies with Arts. 91, 92, 93, and 104.

Fig. 28.

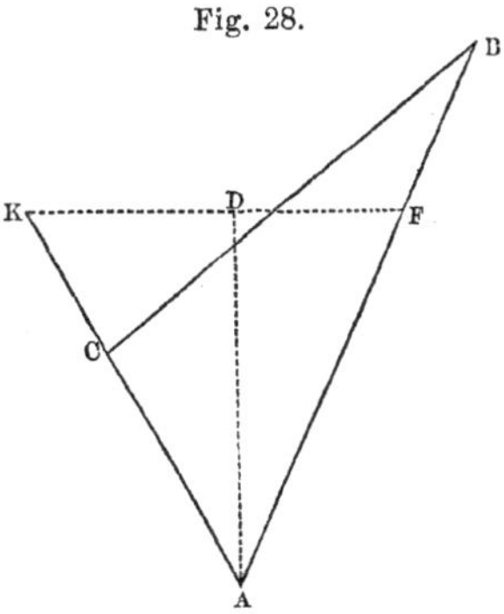

Computation by Logarithms.

99. Elements Required. These are the augmented sums and the differences of end-heights, both for whole and sub sections.* The same computations may be conveniently performed by scale, according to the method of Equivalent Square Bases. (Appendix, Arts. 13 and 25, § 5.)

RULE.

100. With the augmented sum of the heights enter the First Part of Table XV., and take out the tabular quantity.

With the difference of the heights enter the Second Part of the table, and add the quantity thus found to that previously found.

Take the common logarithm of this sum from Table XXVI. and reserve it.

Then, according as the work is in whole or sub sections, enter Table XVI. or XVII., and take out the logarithm of the multiplier for the given side-slope and surface-slope.

Add the logarithm of the multiplier to the reserved logarithm. The result is the common logarithm of the content of the whole ground for whole sections, and of the true content for sub-sections.

Example 1.—End-heights, 28.7 and 14.5; surface-slope, 15°; side-slope, 1½ to 1; roadbed, 24 feet. See Example 1, Art. 96.

---

* It is also possible to construct tables suitable for computation of sub-section work by bases.

59.2 augmented sum. Opposite 59 and under 2, Table XV. . 1622.52
14.2 difference. Opposite 14 and under 2, Second Part Table XV. 31.12

Common logarithm . . 3.2184410 of the sum 1653.64
Logarithm of multiplier . 0.5536408 opposite 15°, under $1\frac{1}{2}$ to 1, Table XVI.

Logarithm . . . 3.7720818 of whole content . . 5916.7
Redundant prism 355.6

Residual prismoid between the surface and roadbed . . . 5561.1*

Example 2.—The augmented sum of the heights is 8.2, and their difference 3.1; surface-slope, 16°; side-slope, $1\frac{1}{2}$ to 1. These are the elements, by heights, for Example 2, by General Scale, Art. 96.

8.2 augmented sum. Opposite 8 and under 2, Table XV. . . 31.12
3.1 difference. Opposite 3 and under 1, Second Part Table XV. . 1.48

Common logarithm . 1.5132176 of the sum 32.60
Logarithm of multiplier 0.7867188 opposite 16°, under $1\frac{1}{2}$ to 1, Table XVII.

Logarithm . . . 2.2999364 of content . . . . 199.5†

101. Omission of the Correction for the Difference of the End-Heights. If the computer only desire an approximate estimate, the correction for the difference of the end-heights may be omitted, especially in whole sections, where the correction is comparatively small. In working by tables of cubical content, this omission is made by taking only the tabular quantity corresponding to the augmented sum of heights, or to the sum of bases. In logarithmic computation, it is made by taking only, from the First Part of Table XV., the tabular quantity corresponding to the augmented sum of the heights, reserving the logarithm of this tabular number, and then proceeding as before, by entering Tables XVI. or XVII. Instead, however, of entering Table XV., we may more conveniently make use of a table such as XXV., which contains the logarithm to be reserved. Thus, in Example 1 of the previous article, we find

59.2 augmented sum. Opposite 59 and under 2, Table XXV. . 3.2101896
Logarithm of multiplier, as before 0.5536408

Logarithm of 5805.4, the whole content 3.7638304

This agrees sufficiently with the first term corresponding to the augmented sum of heights, found in Example 1, Whole Sections, Art. 86.

* This result would have agreed with that found in Art. 86 had the interpolation for tenths been accurately made in that case. (See § 3, Art. 11, Appendix.)

† Had the sum of the heights here corresponded precisely with the sum of the bases, the result would have agreed more nearly with that found in the table, Art. 88.

102. THE PLACE OF SPECIAL TABLES SUPPLIED BY LOGARITHMS. The place of special tables similar to Table XIV. may be supplied by logarithmic computation. For this purpose the subtraction of the redundant prism is virtually effected before the logarithm of the multiplier is employed. This subtraction consists in adding to the tabular quantity first taken from Table XV. another quantity from the same table, and then subtracting a third quantity; also from the same table. The quantity added corresponds, in Table XV., to twice the augment from Table III. for the given roadbed and surface-slope; that is, to the marginal height of the neutral cross-section. The quantity subtracted corresponds to the augment from Table II.; that is, to the sum of the end-heights of the redundant prism. An example will sufficiently explain the method. Take Example 1, Art. 100.

59.2 augmented sum.	Tabular quantity as before . . .	1622.52
14.2 difference.	Tabular quantity as before	31.12
6.4 double augment, Table III.	Tabular quantity from Table XV.	18.96
		1672.60
16 augment, Table II.	Tabular quantity from Table XV. . .	118.52
Common logarithm . .	3.1914733 of remainder . .	1554.08
Logarithm of multiplier .	0.5536408, as before.	
Logarithm . . .	3.7451141 of residual prismoid	5560.5*

Remark 1.—This method facilitates the calculation for lengths differing from one hundred feet. It is only necessary to add the logarithm of the length to the logarithms whose sum forms the logarithm of the residual prismoid, and to diminish by 2 the characteristic of the sum of all the logarithms.

Remark 2.—As the width of roadbed for the same work is generally constant for the same side-slope, the quantity from Table XV. corresponding to the augment from Table II. may be taken out and permanently recorded.

Straight Work and Curved Ground-Surface.

103. REDUCTION TO A PLANE SURFACE. The method for curved ground-surface is to find or to assume a solid with a plane surface, the content of which shall be approximately equal to the content of the given solid. After this reduction, the content of the new solid can be computed by any of the previous methods for whole sections under plane ground.

Sub-sections are not considered here, because we have already assumed their reduction to a plane surface. The same has also been done in regard to those parts of a section which, when the section is subdivided, are reduced by our method to the form of whole-section work under plane ground. Curved surfaces arise from a difference in magnitude or direction of the surface-slopes.

* By taking 6.44 for the double augment from Table III., and the tabular quantity accordingly from Table XV., the two results will agree very nearly.

RULE.

104. Find, by Art. 43, the augmented centre-height and the surface-slope of the mid cross-section. The solidity of the whole ground, from the surface to the intersection of the side-slopes, is approximately equal to a solid having a plane surface, with each of its end-heights equal to the augmented height of the mid cross-section, and with the surface-slope of that cross-section.

Hence, by the General Rule, (Art. 85,) with twice the augmented centre-height above found, for an augmented sum of heights, take out the tabular quantity as there directed. Subtract the redundant prism for the approximate content.

NOTE.—For the curved surfaces intended, (see Article 8,) the correction which is in strictness necessary cannot be made as directed in the General Rule. The student who desires to judge of the necessity of correction, and to apply it if necessary, may refer to Articles 6, 7, and 8 of the Appendix. The augmented centre-height and the surface-slope of the mid cross-section may also be found by calculation. (See Articles 75 and 79.)

Example 1.—First end-height, —28.7; surface-slope, 18° to the right; second end-height, —14.5; surface-slope, 12° to the right; side-slope, 1½ to 1; road-bed, 24.

The augmented height of the mid cross-section is found to be, say 29.84, and the slope 16°.

29.84 }
29.84 } 0.0 difference.

59.68 augmented sum. In Table VII. under 16°	6070.1
Redundant prism	355.6
Approximate residual prismoid between the surface and roadbed	5714.5

The same by Scale.—As the difference of the end-heights is here nothing, the General Scale (Art. 96) would merely reproduce the sum 59.68 which we already have.

By Special Scale.—The unaugmented sum of heights is required for this scale, (Art. 97;) but, because the difference of heights is nothing, it is the same thing to enter the second side of the scale at once with 59.68 in the dividers. Placing one point in the mark of 16°, we find, on the long scale, 57.9. Then 57.9, in Table VII. under 16°, gives for the approximate residual prismoid 5713.2.

By Equivalent Level-Heights.—We find on the diagram (Art. 25, Appendix) the equivalent level-height 66.1+, then

66.1, in Table VII. under 0°, gives	6068.5
Redundant prism	355.6
Approximate residual prismoid between the surface and roadbed . .	5712.9

The same by Table XV., Art. 25, Appendix.—Entering Table XV. with the equivalent sum of level-heights, we have—

66.1 in Table XV. gives	2022.78
Multiplier = twice the rate of side-slope	3
Content of the whole ground	6068.34
Redundant prism	355.6
Approximate residual prismoid between the surface and roadbed . .	5712.7

Example 2.—Take the previous example, except with opposite surface-slopes.

The height of the mid cross-section is found to be 34.96, and the slope 8°.

34.9+ } 0.0 difference.
34.9+ }

69.9 augmented sum.	In Table VII., under 8°	7101.8
Redundant prism	. . . .	355.6
Approximate residual prismoid between the surface and roadbed		6746.2

Curves.

105. Reduction to Straight Work. The method for curves consists in computing as if for straight work of the given end-dimensions and 100 feet in length, and then correcting for curvature. Then, if the work differ in length from 100 feet, take the corrected content proportional to the length, in the same manner as is done with the tabular content for straight work.

106. Preparation for Finding the Correction. *Whole Sections.*—Find the distances out of the mid section, (Art. 44,) and measure their difference.

By Calculation. See Examples, Articles 72 and 73.

107. To find the Correction. *Whole Sections.*—Compute the whole content from the surface to the intersection of the side-slopes as if for straight work 100 feet long. Multiply the whole content by the difference of the distances out of the mid cross-section, and divide the product by 3 and by the number of feet in the radius of the curve. The result is the correction, which is to be added to the content of the straight work when the external distance out is the greater, and subtracted when the internal distance out is the greater. This may be denoted by prefixing the sign *plus* or *minus* to the difference of distances out when found.

Note.—If the whole content found for the straight work is only approximate, the correction for curvature will only be approximate; but the error from this cause is generally small. The correction of the straight work must be first made, to insure accuracy. See note to Rule, Art. 104.

Example 1.—Suppose the piece of work given in Example 1 (Art. 86) were upon a curve of radius 700, and that the surface-slope were downward towards the centre of the curve. The external distance out will be the greater.

Whole content as if for straight work	5917.0
Multiply by the difference of distances out . . .	+42.6
Divide by	3)2520642
Divide by radius	700)84021.4
Correction	+120.0

Correction brought forward	+120.0
Whole content for straight work	5917.0
Whole content corrected	6037.0
Redundant prism	355.6
Residual curved prismoid	5681.4

Example 2.—Take Example 2, (Art. 104,) where the surface-slopes are opposite; the radius 1200, and the ground at the higher end of the work sloping upward towards the centre of the curve.

Whole content as if for straight work	7101.8
Multiply by the difference of distances out	–23.2
Divide by	3)164761.76
Divide by radius	1200)54920
Correction	–45.8
Whole content for straight work	7101.8
Whole content corrected	7056.0
Redundant prism	355.6
Residual curved prismoid	6700.4

Example 3.—Take the previous example as before, except the length, which suppose to be 55.

Residual curved prismoid as before	6700.4
Multiply by 55 and divide by 100	55
Residual curved prismoid for 55 feet	3685.2

Sub-Sections require a slight modification of the process for correction. This belongs to finding the difference of the distances out of the mid cross-section. One of these now becomes the distance out of the grade-point; the other is, as before, the distance out of the side-height, but must be augmented by half the width of the roadbed.

Let A B G (Fig. 29) be the mid cross-section of a piece of sub-section work.

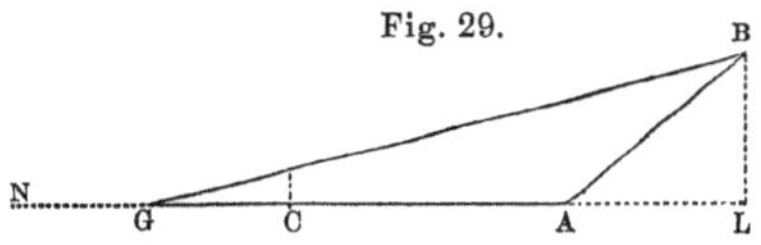

Fig. 29.

C is the centre of the roadbed. Draw the side-height B L, and make C N equal to C A. C L is the distance out, and N L the augmented distance out. C G is the distance out of the grade-point. If the grade-point G fall between C and N, subtract C G from N L; but if G fall between C and A, add C G to N L. The sum or difference thus found may be termed the *difference** required.

* When G lies between C and A, C G may be considered to have the sign *minus*, because it then diminishes the width of the base A G. The subtraction of C G is in that case equivalent to numerical addition.

To find the Correction for Sub-Sections.—Multiply the content found as for straight work by the difference of distances out, and divide the product by 3 and by the number of feet in the radius: the result is the correction.

If the side-slope A B is on the outside of the curve, the correction is to be added; but if the side-slope is on the inside of the curve, the correction is to be subtracted. This may be denoted by prefixing the sign *plus* or *minus* to the difference when found.

Example 1.—The base of the first end is 22, of the second end 16. The surface-slope is 23°, side-slope $1\frac{1}{2}$ to 1, and width of roadbed 24. The side-slope is on the inside of the curve, and the radius is 1100.

The sum of the bases is 38, and their difference 6; whence the content as if found for straight work by Table VIII. is 787.6 yards.

For the Correction.—The distance N L on the mid cross-section is found to be, say 57, and C G is 7, counting in the direction A C. The difference of the distances out is therefore 50.

Content for straight work brought down	787.6
Multiply by the difference	—50
Divide by	3)39380
Divide by radius	1100)13126
Correction	—11.9
Content for straight work	787.6
Content corrected	775.7

Example 2.—The base of the first end is 6, of the second 20. The surface-slope is 33°, side-slope 1 to 1, and width of roadbed 28. The side-slope is on the outside of the curve, and the radius is 900.

The sum of the bases is 26, and their difference 14; whence the content as if found for straight work by Table X. is 635.7 yards.

For the Correction.—The distance N L on the mid cross-section is found to be, say 52, and C G is 1, counting in the direction C A. The difference of the distances out is therefore 53.

Content for straight work brought down	635.7
Multiply by the difference	+53
Divide by	3)33692
Divide by radius	900)11231
Correction	+12.5
Content for straight work	635.7
Content corrected	648.2

Remark.—By employing the marginal radii, the method of correction may be made uniform for whole and sub sections; but the method for the first term, now uniform, will be varied. (See Art. 36.) The divisor 3 becomes 6, if the difference (or multiplier) is doubled, as in Art. 122. For a mode of computing C L when the centre-height is known, see Art. 74.

CHAPTER IV.

COMPUTATION OF EXCAVATION AND EMBANKMENT BY CENTRE AND SIDE HEIGHTS.

Straight Work.

108. DATA. When computation is to be made by centre and side heights, the subdivision of sections is made upon the field. The length of all work is supposed to be given. Besides the length, the following dimensions are given at each end of the work.

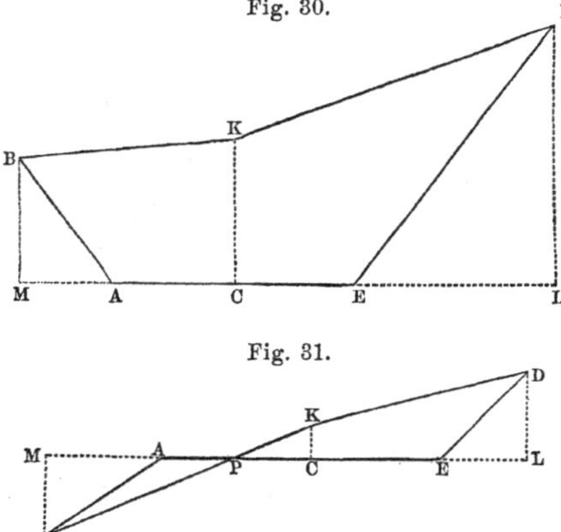

Fig. 30.

Fig. 31.

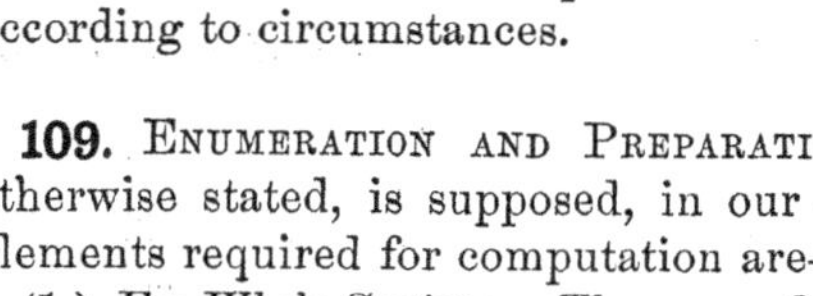

(1.) *For Whole Sections.* — The centre-height C K, (Fig. 30,) the two side-heights B M, D L, the width of roadbed A E, and the rate of side-slope.

(2.) *For Sub-Sections.* The centre-height C K, (Fig. 31,) the two side-heights B M, D L, and the distance and direction out of the grade-point P from the centre; also the width of each part C E and C A in excavation and embankment, and the rate of side-slope. Side-slope for embankment is always considered to be $1\frac{1}{2}$ to 1, which is the slope assumed by loose earth when embanked. Side-slope for excavation is generally 1 to 1, but is varied according to circumstances.

109. ENUMERATION AND PREPARATION OF ELEMENTS. The length, unless otherwise stated, is supposed, in our examples, to be 100 feet. The other elements required for computation are—

(1.) *For Whole Sections.*—The sum of the centre-heights C K (Fig. 30) at each end, augmented by the tabular augment from Table II., and the difference of the centre-heights; also the whole width M L, called the *total base*, at each end in order to find the sum and the difference of the total bases. The total base at each end is found by adding together the distances E L, A M, and the width of the roadbed A E. The distance E L or A M may be found by multiplying the given side-height D L or B M by the rate of side-slope, or by entering Table **VI.** with the side-height D L or B M. The total base M L may also be found by adding together the side-heights D L, B M, and augmenting their sum by the tabular augment from Table II.; then, with the augmented sum thus found, entering Table VI., where the tabular quantity will be the total base required. This latter method is shown in the following

EXAMPLE.

First end of the section: centre-height, 13.6; side-heights, 10 and 8. Second end of the section: centre-height, 8; side-heights, 12 and 4; width of roadbed, 18; side-slope, $1\frac{1}{2}$ to 1.

Centre-height of first end .	. 13.6	5.6 difference of centre-heights.
" " second end	. 8.0	
Whole-section augment, Table II.	12.0	
	33.6	augmented sum of centre-heights.

10.0 8.	Side-heights of first end.	Side-heights of second end	12.0 4.0
12.0	whole-section augment.	Whole-section augment .	12.0
30.0	augmented sum of side-heights.	Augmented sum of side-heights	28.0

30.0 in Table VI., under $1\frac{1}{2}$ to 1, gives total base of first end	45	3.0 difference.
28.0 " " " " " " second end	42	
Sum of total bases	87	

By this method it is not necessary to add the width of roadbed. The list of elements for whole sections is repeated (for easy reference) in Art. 111.

(2.) *For Sub-Sections.*—There are two cases, properly speaking. In one case there is a triangular cross-section P A B, (Fig. 31;) in the other, the cross-section D K P E is quadrilateral. If a grade-point occur on the median plane K C, the section should be cut at that point, so as to keep the centre-height K C always on the same side of the roadbed for any length considered as a section in computation. If this be omitted upon the field, it may be done by drawing the median profile, or by computing the length of the median abscissa. (Art. 51.) If the computer judge it to be sufficiently correct, the cross-section D K P E may sometimes be taken as a triangle. In this case, the method of computation is the same both for P A B and D K P E. It will not be necessary to divide the work at the median grade-point, when the surface-line D K P B may be considered as everywhere straight; for the sum of the end-heights C K will not then be required, because the computation may be made by bases.

For cross-sections similar to P A B, the elements are the sum and difference of the side-heights B M, and of the bases A P. (See Art. 115.)

For cross-sections similar to D K P E, the elements are the sum of the side-heights D L, and of the partial bases C E; also the sum and difference of the centre-heights C K, and of the total bases P L: this is further explained and again recited in Art. 116. Sometimes the difference of the side-heights D L, and of the partial bases C E, is required. (Art. 119.)

The method of finding the sum of the side-heights and their difference, and the same for the centre-heights when required, does not need to be explained.

The base at each end may be found by adding or subtracting the distance out of the grade-point to or from the half-width of roadbed, according to the direction of C P and the width proper for excavation or embankment. The base at each end being obtained, the sum and difference of the bases are easily found. It may also be done in the following manner:—

110. To find the Sum and Difference of Bases. Consider one direction of C P—as, for example, the direction towards the left in the figure—to be *plus*, and the other *minus;* and mark the distance out of the grade-point at each end with its proper sign. Then add together the distances out of the grade-point, giving the result its proper sign. To this result add the width of roadbed for that work which is widened by the plus sign of the distance out of the grade-point. The result is the sum of bases for that work. Then change the sign of the sum of distances out of the grade-point, and add it to the width of roadbed for that work which is narrowed by the plus sign of the distance out. The result is the sum of bases for that work.

To find the difference of the bases, take the difference of the distances out of the grade-point when they are of the same sign, but add them when of opposite sign. The result is the difference of bases, which is the same for both kinds of work.

EXAMPLE.

The width of roadbed for the work D K P E is 28, and for the work P A B, 24. The distance out C P, for the end of the work shown in the figure, is +9.3, and for the other end —6.1.

Distance out of first end	+9.3	} 15.4 difference for both kinds of work.
Distance out of second end	—6.1	

Sum of distances out .	+3.2	Sum of distances out, sign changed	—3.2
Roadbed for D K P E .	28.0	Roadbed for P A B . . .	24.0
Sum of bases for D K P E	31.2	Sum of bases for P A B . .	20.8

The distance out of the grade-point in the case of a crooked surface, such as D K P, will not change from plus to minus, or from minus to plus, if the work has been prepared upon the field: if it does, the work should be cut, as before explained, at the median grade-point, where the distance out and the centre-height are both nothing. The above method for finding the sum and difference of bases still applies. It then reduces to applying the distance out, according to its sign, to the width of roadbed belonging to the work which is widened by the plus distance, and, with sign changed, to the other width of roadbed. The difference of bases becomes simply the distance out.

We may now proceed to rules and examples in computation. As the operations can be performed by ordinary arithmetic, we shall first express the rules as if they were intended for arithmetical operations. Afterward we shall show the application of the tables. Whole sections and sub-sections will be taken in order. It will be convenient in practice to take from Tables I. and II., and to record the redundant prism and whole-section augment belonging respectively to excavation and embankment of the work in hand.

Whole Sections.

111. PREPARATION OF ELEMENTS. Find the distances out according to the width of roadbed and rate of side-slope.

Form two *total bases* by adding together the opposite distances out belonging to each of the two ends of the section.

Take the sum of the total bases and also their difference.

Take the sum and the difference of the centre-heights.

Augment the sum of the centre-heights by twice the distance from the roadbed to the intersection of the side-slopes, which quantity may be taken from Table II. of Whole-Section Augments.

Then work by the following

RULE.

112. 1st. Multiply the augmented sum of the centre-heights by the sum of the total bases and by the length of the section, and divide by 8 for a first term or approximate content of the whole solid between the surface and intersection of side-slopes.

2d. Multiply the difference of the centre-heights by the difference of the total bases and by the length of the section, and divide by 8 and by 3 for a second term.

Add the second term to the first if the greater centre-height is at the *same* end of the section with the greater total base, but if not, subtract for the true total content.

3d. From the true or the approximate total content subtract the redundant prism lying between the roadbed and intersection of side-slopes, for the true or approximate content of the section. (See Art. 21.)

NOTE.—The multiplication by the length and the division by 8, as they affect both terms, may be performed *after* the addition or subtraction of the quantities subject to these operations, as is done in the following

EXAMPLE.

What is the content of a section 100 feet long, with the side-heights at one end 10 and 8 feet and centre-height 13.6 feet, and at the other end the side-heights 12 and 4 feet and centre-height 8 feet; the width of roadbed being 18 feet, and the side-slope $1\frac{1}{2}$ to 1? (See Example, § 1, Art. 109.)

PREPARATION OF ELEMENTS.

Centre-height of first end	13.6	5.6 difference of centre-heights.
" " second end	8.0	
Whole-section augment	12.0	
	33.6	augmented sum of centre-heights.
Total base of first end	45	3 difference of total bases.
" " second end	42	
	87	sum of total bases.

OPERATION.

33.6 multiplied by 87 gives	2923.2
5.6 multiplied by 3 and divided by 3 gives 5.6 for a second term, which is additive because the greater centre-height 13.6 corresponds with the greater total base 45	5.6
Multiplying by 100, and dividing by	8)2928.8
we find the total content in cubic feet, which, reduced to yards by dividing by	27)36610
gives	1355.9
Redundant prism from Table I.	200.0
Residual prismoid in cubic yards	1155.9

THE SAME BY THE TABLE.

113. In the side column of Table XXI. find either the augmented sum of the centre-heights or the sum of the total bases, and at the top of the table find successively the figures of the other of these two factors, and take out the corresponding tabular quantities; observing, if necessary, to remove the decimal point of these quantities to correspond with the decimal value of the figure under which they are found.

Add together the several tabular quantities for the first term.

Find the second term from its proper factors, by taking out and adding the tabular quantities in the same way and dividing the result by 3.

Add or subtract the second term, and deduct the redundant prism as before.

If the length of the section differ from 100 feet, divide the result as above found by 100 and multiply by the length of the section.

OPERATION.

Opposite 33.6 and under 8 (taken ten times) . . .	1244.4
Opposite 33.6 and under 7 (taken once)	108.9
First term or approximate total content	1353.3
Opposite 5.6 and under 3, take one-third of the tabular quantity	2.6
Whole content of a hundred-feet section in cubic yards .	1355.9
Redundant prism as before	200.0
Residual prismoid in cubic yards	1155.9

114. Sub-Sections. The subdivision is supposed to have been made upon the field. There is a grade-point within the section at each end of the work. The solids will in general have the form of pyramids and truncated pyramids. If one of the grade-points fall on the edge of the roadbed, at that point there will be a neutral cross-section or the apex of a pyramid. If both grade-points fall on the same edge of the roadbed, we have for the forms of work, prisms or prismoids. All work has the same length as the section.

The total bases are the distances, at the respective ends of the work, of the grade-point from the meeting of the side-slope and roadbed; or, in other words, the lower sides of the triangular end cross-sections in excavation, and upper sides in embankment.

There are but two side-heights for each kind of work. The centre-height is only considered when the surface-line of the cross-section is so crooked as to require the centre-height being taken into account; and this will then only be for that part of the work to which the centre-height belongs.

We shall first consider the surface-line of the cross-section to be straight.

This being premised, the computation is similar to that for whole sections, taking care to employ the sum of the *side-heights* instead of the *augmented sum of the centre-heights*, as is directed in the following

RULE FOR TRIANGULAR CROSS-SECTIONS.

115. Multiply the sum of the side-heights by the sum of the total bases and by the length, and divide by 8 for the first term.

Multiply the difference of the side-heights by the difference of the total bases and by the length, and divide by 8 and by 3 for the second term.

Add the second term to the first if the greater side-height has the greater base; otherwise subtract. The result is the content required, as there is no redundant prism.

NOTE.—The multiplication by the length and the division by 8, as they affect both terms, may be performed *after* the addition or subtraction of the quantities subject to these operations, as is done in the following

EXAMPLE.

First end of the section: the side-height on the right is +10.0, (excavation;) side-height on the left, —1.8, (embankment;) centre-height, +2.5; distance out of the grade-point left, 9.3.

Second end of the section: the side-height on the right is +2.1; side-height on the left, —5.2; centre-height, —1.3; distance out of the grade-point right, 6.1; roadbed for excavation, 28 feet, and side-slope 1 to 1; roadbed for embankment, 24 feet, and side-slope 1½ to 1.

The length of the section is 50 feet. The surface-line of the cross-section is assumed to be straight; the centre-heights are not required in the computation.

PREPARATION OF ELEMENTS. (See Art. 110.)

For Excavation.				*For Embankment.*
Side-height of first end	10.0	} 7.9 diff.	Diff. 3.4 {	1.8 side-height of first end.
Side-height of second end	2.1			5.2 side-height of second "
Sum of side-heights .	12.1			7.0 sum of side-heights.
Sum of bases . .	31.2			20.8 sum of bases.
Difference of bases .	15.4			15.4 difference of bases.

OPERATION.

For Excavation.		*For Embankment.*	
12.1 multiplied by 31.2 gives	377.52	7.0 multiplied by 20.8 gives	145.60
7.9 multip'd by 15.4, div'd by 3	40.55	3.4 multip'd by 15.4, div'd by 3	17.45
Sum of the terms . . .	418.07	Sum of the terms . .	163.05
Multiply by the length . .	50	Multiply by the length .	50
Divide by	8)20903.50	Divide by . . .	8)8152.50
Content in cubic feet .	2612.9	Content in cubic feet .	1019.06
Content reduced to cubic yards	96.8	Content reduced to cubic yards	37.7

116. When the Cross-Section is Irregular, the centre-heights CK (Figs. 32 and 33) must be employed. In this case there will generally be a triangular-shaped cross-section A B P to a portion of the work. This part being small, its cross-section may be regarded as a true triangle. When this is so, the previous rule will apply to that part.

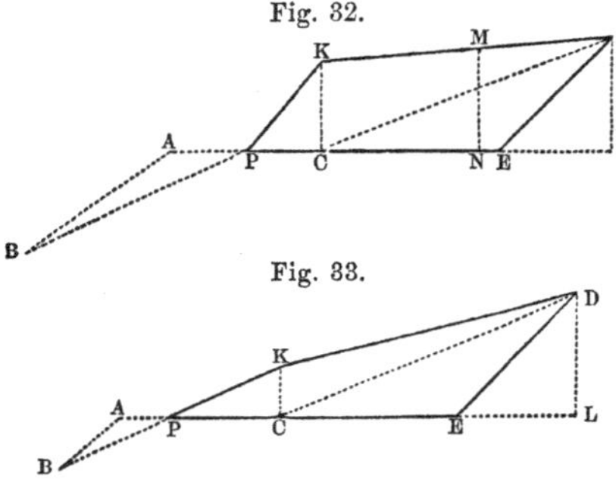

There remains to be considered the part whose cross-section is D K P E. The cross-section of this is composed of the three triangles DEC, DCK, and P C K.

The triangle D E C has its base C E equal to the half-width of the roadbed; the sum of the bases is therefore the width of the roadbed, and their difference is nothing. The solidity between the two triangles D E C can, then, be computed by the previous rule.

The triangle D C K has the base C K and the altitude C L. The triangle P C K has the same base C K, and the altitude C P. Hence the solidities for both triangles may be computed together, by adding the altitudes C P, C L and employing the common base CK. This can also be performed by the previous rule. The sum of the altitudes P L is equal to P C added to C L. The distance out of the grade-point P C will here always be *plus*.

The elements required are, then:—For the solid upon D E C, the sum of the side-heights D L, and sum of the bases C E, equal, together, to the width of roadbed; for the solid upon D K P C, the sum and difference of the centre-heights C K, and the sum and difference of the united altitudes P L. Instead of proceeding in the manner here indicated, it may sometimes answer to construct equivalent triangular cross-sections according to the method of Art. 93, and to compute as usual from the dimensions thus found. We have the following rule for computing the solidity between irregular cross-sections.

RULE FOR IRREGULAR CROSS-SECTIONS.

117. Compute the solid upon D E C as for triangular cross-sections by their side-heights and bases, (Art. 115,) observing that there is no second term for this solid.

Consider the distance out added to the distance out of the grade-point, as a *base;* make use of the centre-height instead of the side-height, and compute the solid upon D K P C as for triangular cross-sections.

Add the result of this last computation to the result of the previous computation: the sum is the required content.

EXAMPLE.

Let D L (Fig. 33) be 10.4; C K, 4.4; C P, 10.1. And let D L (Fig. 32) be 9.6; C K, 7.2; C P, 6.5. The width of roadbed is 28 feet, and the side-slope 1¼ to 1; the length, 75 feet. We shall take only the part D K P E, because the triangular part A B P is computed as in the previous example.

PREPARATION OF ELEMENTS.

10.4	side-height of first end.	*Elements for the solid upon D C E.*
9.6	side-height of second end.	
20.0	sum of side-heights.	
28.0	width of roadbed.	

Elements for the Solid upon D K P C.

13.0	given in Table VI. by the side-height 10.4.	First end.
14.0	half-width of roadbed.	
10.1	distance out of grade-point.	
37.1	base.	

	12.0	given in Table VI. by the side-height 9.6.	Second end.
	14.0	half-width of roadbed.	
	6.5	distance out of grade-point.	
Difference 4.6	32.5	base.	
	37.1	base of first end.	
	69.6	sum of bases.	
Difference 2.8	4.4	centre-height of first end.	
	7.2	centre-height of second end.	
	11.6	sum of centre-heights.	

OPERATION.

20 multiplied by 28.0 gives for the solid upon D C E .	560.00
11.6 multiplied by 69.6 gives for the solid upon DKPC	807.36
Sum of first terms	1367.36
2.8 multiplied by 4.6 and divided by 3, *subtract* . . .	4.29
Sum of all the terms	1363.07
Multiply by the length	75
Divide by	8)102230.25
Content in cubic feet	12778.78
Content reduced to cubic yards	473.3

THE SAME BY THE TABLE.

118. In the side column of Table XXI. find either the sum of heights or the sum of bases, and at the top of the table find successively the figures of the other of these two factors, and take out the corresponding tabular quantities; observing, if necessary, to remove the decimal point of these quantities to correspond with the decimal value of the figure under which they are found.

Add together the several tabular quantities for the first term.

Find the second term from its proper factors, by taking out and adding the tabular quantities in the same way and dividing the result by 3.

Add or subtract the second term as before.

If the length of the section differ from 100 feet, divide the result as above found by 100, and multiply by the length of the section.

This rule applies to triangular as well as to irregular cross-sections: it is also similar to the rule for whole sections. As the operation for irregular cross-sections is but the repetition of the process for triangular cross-sections, it will suffice to work the last example by the table.

OPERATION.

Opposite 28.0, under 2, taken 10 times	259.2
Opposite 69.6, under 1, taken 10 times	322.2
Opposite 69.6, under 1, taken once	32.2
Opposite 69.6, under 6, take one-tenth	19.3
Sum of first terms	632.9
Opposite 4.6, under 2, take one-third	1.4
Opposite 4.6, under 8, take one-third of one-tenth . . .	0.5
Second term, which subtract from the sum of the first terms, because the greater end-height has the lesser base.	1.9
	631.0
Divide by 100 and multiply by the length	75
Content of the section in cubic yards	473.25

119. HEIGHTS NOT TAKEN BOTH ON THE MEDIAN LINE. If the heights C K be not taken at the same distance from E, the foregoing method is only modified in this respect,—viz., the bases C E will then not be of the same magnitude, and their difference will give a second term in computing the solid upon D C E. It is supposed the heights differ in magnitude: if they happen to be alike, their difference, being nothing, destroys the second term.

EXAMPLE.

Let D L (Fig. 33) be 10.4; C K, 4.4; C P, 10.1; C E, 14; C L, 37.1; which makes the first end of the section the same as in the previous example. And let D L (Fig. 32) be 9.6; N M, 8.4; N P, 19.5; N E, 1.0. On this cross-section the component figures are now D N E, D M P N. The lines D N, M P must be supplied. The roadbed, side-slope, and length of the section as before. We have the following elements:—

Sum of the heights C K, N M	12.8.	Difference of the same	4.0
Sum of partial bases C E, N E	15.0.	Difference of the same	13.0
Sum of side-heights D L	20.0.	Difference of the same	0.8
Sum of total bases P L	69.6.	Difference of the same	4.6

OPERATION.

Opposite 15.0, under 2, taken ten times, Table XXI.	138.9
Opposite 13.0, under 8, take one-third of one-tenth	1.6
Sum of the terms for the solid between D C E, D N E	140.5
Opposite 69.6, under 1, taken ten times	322.2
Opposite 69.6, under 2, taken once	64.4
Opposite 69.6, under 8, take one-tenth	25.8
First term	412.4
Opposite 4.6, under 4.0, take one-third	2.8
Sum* of the terms for the solid between D K P C, D M P N	409.6
Sum of first terms brought down	140.5
Content for 100 feet in length	550.1
Divide by 100, and multiply by the length	75
Content of the section in cubic yards	412.6

If the work be not really upon the line of the road, or if neither of the heights C K fall over the centre, the same method will still apply, for it is obviously unimportant whether the distances C E represent part of a roadbed or some other ground. If these distances be equal, they may be treated as the half-width of some roadbed, and the computation made as directed in Art. 118.

* The word "sum" may be employed if we here suppose the second term to be added having a negative sign.

If the distances be unequal, the last example indicates the mode of proceeding. One thing must be observed,—viz., that neither of the heights CK or NM fall outside between E and L.

Curves.

120. Reduction to Straight Work. The method for curves consists in computing as if for straight work of the given end dimensions and 100 feet in length, and then correcting for curvature. Then, if the work differ in length from 100 feet, take the corrected content proportional to the length, in the same manner as is done with the tabular content for straight work.

The method is similar to that for transverse slopes. (See Remark, p. 55, and Articles 107, 122.)

121. Preparation for finding the Correction. *Whole Sections.*—Form two sums of distances out,—a sum of *external* distances, by adding together the pair of distances out upon the outside of the curve, and a sum of *internal* distances, by adding together the pair of distances out on the inside of the curve, and take the difference of these sums.

122. To find the Correction. *Whole Sections.*—Compute the whole content from the surface to the intersection of the side-slopes as if for straight work 100 feet long. Multiply the whole content by the difference of sums of distances out, and divide the product by 6 and by the number of feet in the radius of the curve. The result is the correction, which is to be added to the content of the straight work when the sum of external distances is greater than the sum of internal distances, and subtracted when the sum of internal distances is the greater. This may be denoted by prefixing the sign *plus* or *minus* to the difference of the sums when found.

Example 1.—First end: augmented height, 20; distance out right, 39; distance out left, 60. Second end: augmented height, 30; distance out right, 37.5; distance out left, 42. Roadbed, 24; side-slope, $1\frac{1}{2}$ to 1; radius, 800. The left-hand side of the work is towards the centre of the curve.

The computation being made as if for a straight piece, gives for the whole ground, from the surface to the intersection of the side-slopes, 4101.9 yards.

Internal distance of first end .	60	External distance of first end .	39
Internal distance of second end	42	External distance of second end	37.5
Sum of internal distances .	102	Sum of external distances .	76.5
Sum of external distances .	76.5	less than sum of internal distances, making correction subtractive.	
Difference of sums . .	—25.5		

Whole content for straight work brought down	4101.9
Multiply by difference	—25.5
Divide by	6)104598.45
Divide by radius	800)17433.07
Correction	—21.8

Correction brought forward	—21.8
Whole content for straight work	4101.9
Whole content corrected	4080.1
Redundant prism	355.6
Residual curved prismoid	3724.5

Example 2.—First end: augmented height, 34; distance out right, 63; distance out left, 38. Second end: augmented height, 23; distance out right, 33; distance out left, 40.5. Roadbed, 28; side-slope, $1\frac{1}{4}$ to 1; radius, 1200. The left-hand side of the work is towards the centre of the curve.

The work being computed as if for a straight piece, gives for the whole ground, from the surface to the intersection of the side-slopes, 4651.5 yards.

Internal distance of first end .	38	External distance of first end .	63
Internal distance of second end	40.5	External distance of second end .	33
Sum of internal distances . .	78.5	Sum of external distances . .	96
Sum of external distances . .	96.0	greater than sum of internal distances, making correction additive.	
Difference of sums . .	+17.5		

Whole content for straight work brought down	4651.5
Multiply by the difference	+17.5
Divide by	6)81401.25
Divide by radius	1200)13566.87
Correction	+11.3
Whole content for straight work	4651.5
Whole content corrected	4662.8
Redundant prism	580.7
Residual curved prismoid	4082.1

Sub-Sections require a slight modification of the process for correction. This belongs to finding the difference of the sums of distances out.

Let A B G, D H F (Fig. 34) be the end cross-sections; C K the centre-line of the roadbed. The distances out C L, K M are as for whole sections, but on the side GF the distances out are C G and K F. These are the distances out of the grade-point. As these distances may lie on either side of the centre-line, they may be *plus* or *minus*. They are plus when they count in the direction A C or D K, because they then *add* to the width of the base A G or D F. They are minus in the other direction, because they then *subtract* from the

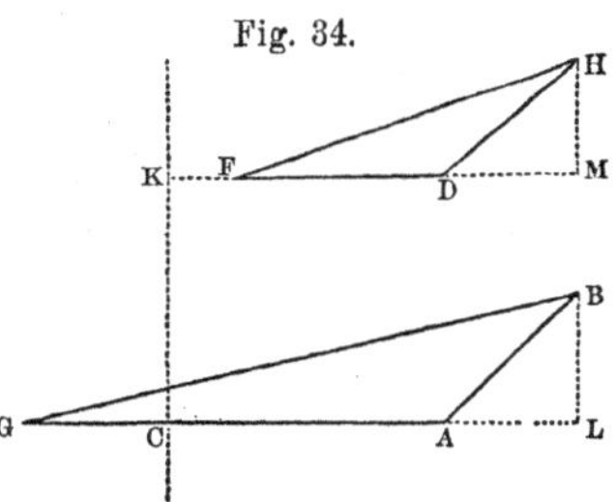

Fig. 34.

width of the base. These distances should be marked with their proper sign before beginning the computation.

To find the Difference for Sub-Sections.—Add together CL, KM and the width of the roadbed: this will form an augmented sum of internal or external distances out, according as the centre of the curve lies on the side of the slopes AB, DH, or of the grade-points G, F. The other sum is formed by adding together the distances CG, KF, giving the result its proper sign. Subtract this result from the augmented sum of CL and KM, observing that if the quantity to be subtracted has the negative sign, the subtraction is converted into addition. The result is the difference required.

To find the Correction for Sub-Sections.—Multiply the content found as if for straight work by the difference, and divide the product by 6 and by the number of feet in the radius: the result is the correction.

If the side-slopes AB, DH are on the outside of the curve, the correction is to be added; but if the side-slopes are on the inside of the curve, the correction is to be subtracted. This may be denoted by prefixing the sign *plus* or *minus* to the difference when found.

Example 1.—First end: side-height on the right, 16; distance out right, 36; distance out of the grade-point left, (*plus*,) 10. Second end: side-height on the right, 28; distance out right, 54; distance out of the grade-point left, (*plus*,) 4. Roadbed, 24; radius, 1100. The left-hand side of the work is towards the centre of the curve.

The work being computed as if for a straight piece, gives for the content 763 yards.

Distance out to side-height, 1st end	36	Distance out to grade-point, 1st end	+10
Distance out to side-height, 2d end	54	Distance out to grade-point, 2d end	+4
Width of roadbed . . .	24	Sum of distances out to grade-point,	+14
Augmented sum of distances out	114		
Sum of distances out to grade-point	+14		
Difference	+100		

Content for straight work brought down	763
Multiply by the difference	+100
Divide by	6)76300
Divide by radius	1100)12717
Correction	+11.6
Content for straight work	763.0
Content corrected	774.6

Example 2.—First end: side-height on the left, 31; distance out left, 45; distance out of the grade-point left, (*minus*,) 8. Second end: side-height on the left, 20; distance out left, 34; distance out of the grade-point right, (*plus*,) 6. Roadbed, 28; radius, 900. The left-hand side of the work is towards the centre of the curve.

The work being computed as if for a straight piece, gives for the content 590.1 yards.

Distance out to side-height, 1st end	45	Distance out to grade-point, 1st end	—8
Distance out to side-height, 2d end	34	Distance out to grade-point, 2d end	+6
Width of roadbed . . .	28	Sum of distances out to grade-point	—2
Augmented sum of distances out	107		
Sum of distances out to grade-point	—2		
Difference	—109		

Content for straight work brought down	590.1
Multiply by difference	—109
Divide by	6)64320.9
Divide by radius	900)10720.1
Correction	—11.9
Content for straight work	590.1
Content corrected	578.2

Unusual Cases, and Computation by Logarithms.

123. Unusual Cases. Under this head we shall treat of cases wherein two intermediate heights are taken on each of the end cross-sections, and of work having irregular quadrilateral cross-sections. Also of work bounded by planes having everywhere a rectangular cross-section: this may occur in the computation of borrow-pits, excavations for foundations, and other work.

If the cross-section should be everywhere a right-angled or other triangle, the computation may be made by the method of Art. 115.

The principles of Articles 91, 92, and 93 may also be applied in computations by centre and side heights.

124. Two Intermediate Level-Heights. If two intermediate level-heights are taken as at H and K (Figs. 35 and 36) and the distances out of H and K, the content may be found by computing separately, according to the rule, (Art. 112,) the solid enclosed between each pair of figures L B H E, A L E M, M C K E, then taking the sum of the solidities and deducting the redundant prism.

Fig. 35.

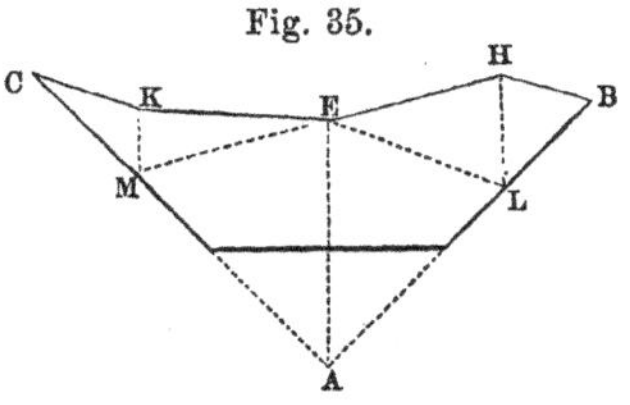

The elements may either be found by constructing the cross-sections, or by a computation which is sufficiently obvious.

If the heights at H and K be so taken as to make HL and KM respectively the same on each cross-section, the difference of the heights will vanish for the two outside solids, and there will be no second term in computing their contents.

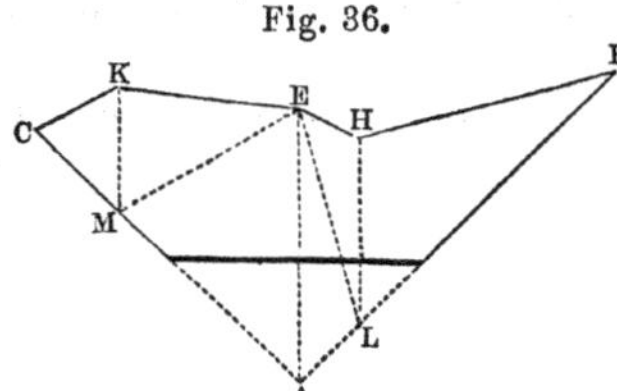

Fig. 36.

If intermediate heights have not been taken on both cross-sections upon the field, they may be supplied upon the diagram, after construction, for that cross-section which requires them.

Example.—The data are, (on Fig. 35,) height from roadbed at B, 18; height at H, 22; height at E, 16; height at K, 17; height at C, 21; distance out at H, 21; distance out at K, 22.

On Fig. 36, height from roadbed at B, 24; height at H, 15; height at E, 19; height at K, 22; height at C, 17; distance out at H, 7; distance out at K, 20. The roadbed is 28, and the side-slope 1 to 1.

From these data are derived the following elements:—

For the Figures L B H E.—Sum of the heights HL, 37; difference, 7: sum of total bases or distances out of B, 70; difference, 6.

For the Figures A L E M.—Sum of the heights E A, 63; difference, 3: sum of total bases, equal to the sum of the distances out of H and K, 70; difference, 16.

For the Figures M C K E.—Sum of the heights K M, 25; difference, 7: sum of total bases or distances out of C, 66; difference, 4.

These elements give according to the rule, (Art. 112,)

First term for the solid enclosed between the figures LBHE	1199.1
Second " " " " " " "	+6.5
Whole content " " " " " "	1205.6
First term for the solid enclosed between the figures ALEM	2041.7
Second " " " " " " "	—7.4
Whole content " " " " " "	2034.3
First term for the solid enclosed between the figures MCKE	763.9
Second " " " " " " "	—4.3
Whole content " " " " " "	759.6
Content of the whole ground equal to sum of the three totals	3999.5
Redundant prism	725.9
Residual prismoid	3273.6

NOTE. Work having cross-sections like A L E M may be computed, as above, by Art. 112 or 113, provided the end-heights, as A E, on a diagonal plane, and the distances out of the corners L and M, can be found.

125. WORK HAVING A RECTANGULAR CROSS-SECTION may be computed by Table XXI. or XXIII. The cross-section is supposed to be everywhere rectangular and the enclosing surfaces plane.

The area of a four-sided figure having two parallel sides is equal to the area of a rectangle having the same height, and with a base equal to the half-sum of those sides. Therefore in work having a cross-section with two parallel sides we may substitute a rectangle for the given cross-section, and proceed by the same

RULE.

Let A B C D, E H K L (Figs. 37 and 38) be the end cross-sections. Take one pair of the sides at each end, as A B and E H, for the bases; and another pair of sides, as B C and H K, for the heights. Then proceed according to the rule, Art. 115. Twice the quantity thus found is the content required.

Fig. 37.

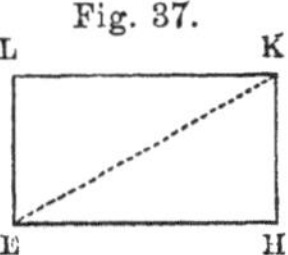

NOTE.—It is an equivalent operation to double the sum and the difference either of the heights or bases, and then proceed as in Art. 115.

Fig. 38.

D C A B

Example.—A B is 12.5, and B C 11; E H is 15.5, and H K 9.

15.5 12.5	3.0 difference of bases.	Difference of heights, 2.0	9.0 11.0
28.0 sum of bases.		Sum of heights . .	20.0

Take twice the sum of heights, 40, and twice the difference, 4.

Opposite 40.0, under 2, taken ten times, Table XXI.	. 370.4
Opposite 40.0, under 8, taken once, "	. 148.1
First term, or approximate content	. 518.5
Opposite 4.0, under 3, take one-third, which subtract,	. 1.9
Content of the work	. 516.6

The operation by Table XXIII. is only another mode of performing the same thing, and will be sufficiently understood by reference to Art. 128.

Explanation.—If each of the cross-sections be divided by a diagonal, as A C, E K, it is separated into two equal triangles. The solid between each pair of triangles would be found by the rule, Art. 115; but the solidity required is double that so derived.

126. WHEN THE RECTANGULAR CROSS-SECTION IS EVERYWHERE THE SAME, the computation may be performed as directed in Art. 125, or by the aid of Table XXII. or XXIV. It is not necessary that the end planes should be parallel, or that either of them should be at right angles to the length of the work. But the cross-section from which the solidity is computed must be at right angles to the length.

The methods of this and the following article are applicable to borrow-pits, the solidities of which are generally considered to be composed of an assemblage of vertical prisms, having cross-sections of the same size and form for all. When the cross-section is a parallelogram, the depth of the prism is the distance from the centre of one end to the centre of the other. Whether the prism be a parallelogram or a triangle, the depth is equal to the average of the corner depths.

Example.—Suppose E H (Fig. 37) to be 15.5, H K 9.7, and the length 12.5.

Opposite 15.5 and under 9, taken once, Table XXII. . .	516.7
Opposite 15.5 and under 7, take one-tenth	40.2
Content for 100 feet	556.9
Multiply by 12.5 and divide by 100	12.5
Content for 12.5 feet	69.6

The operation by Table XXIV. is only another mode of performing the same thing, and will be sufficiently understood by reference to Art. 128.

When the cross-section is a true square, the same method applies. The computation may also then be made as follows:—

127. WHEN THE CROSS-SECTION IS EVERYWHERE SQUARE. The sum of the end-heights or the sum of the bases is equal to the double height or base. The difference of the end dimensions is nothing. Enter the First Part of Table XV. with the double height or base. *Twice* the tabular quantity is the content required.

Example.—A pit has everywhere a square cross-section 9.7 feet on the side, and is 10 feet deep. What is the amount of excavation?

The double of the side of the square is here 19.4.	
Opposite 19 and under 4, in Table XV., First Part . .	174.24
Take twice the tabular quantity and divide by 10 for 10 feet .	2
Content of excavation in cubic yards	34.8

The same thing may be performed by Table XXV. This will be sufficiently understood by reference to Art. 131, recollecting that if the table be entered with the side of the square, 0.9030900, or logarithm of 8, must be added to the logarithm there found. If the table be entered with double the side of the square, 0.3010300, or logarithm of 2, must be added.

128. COMPUTATION BY LOGARITHMS. Table XXIII. contains logarithms which are proper for dispensing with the use of Table XXI. as directed in Articles 113 and 118. The computation is essentially the same, but the purpose served by Table XXI. is now fulfilled by logarithmic calculation.

RULE.

In Table XXIII., opposite to the whole feet in the side column and under the tenths upon the top, find successively the proper logarithm for the sum of the augmented heights and for the sum of the total bases. Add together these logarithms: the result is the logarithm of the first term or approximate content of the whole ground.

If the length differ from 100 feet, add the logarithm of the length to the two logarithms found from the table, and subtract 2 from the characteristic of the sum.

In the same manner the tabular number corresponding to the product of the differences may be found. But the quantity required for the second term—viz., the third part of this tabular number—may be found sufficiently near by multiplying together the differences (in feet) and again multiplying by $\frac{15}{100}$.

Example.—Take the example in Art. 112.

Opposite 33, under 6, in Table XXIII.	1.35911
Opposite 87, under 0, " "	1.77229
Logarithm of 1353.3, the first term	3.13140

The second term may be found and the operation completed as follows:—

Difference of heights	5.6
Difference of bases	3
Product of the differences	16.8
Multiply by 15 and divide by 100*.	15
Second term	2.5
First term brought down	1353.3
Whole content of a 100 feet section in yards	1355.8
Redundant prism as before	200.0
Content as before (nearly, the error is here in the second term)	1155.8

Curves.—Instead of correcting the cubic content directly, we may correct, in the same way, either the tabular length of 100 ft., or the given length: then, with the corrected length, find, as if for straight work, the corrected whole content for 100 ft., or for the given length.

Example 1.—Take Example 1, page 66, supposing the length to be 50 ft. The corrected tabular length is $100 - \frac{25.5 \times 100}{6 \times 800} = 99.469$, of which the log. is 1.99769. The logs. of the 1st and 2d terms may be found as shown above in this Article: to each of which add the log. of corrected length, and take 2 (= log. 100) from the index. We have log. 1st term 3.61384, and cubic yards 4110.0; log. 2d term 1.47614, and cubic yards 29.9. Then 4110.0 — 29.9 = 4080.1, the corrected whole content for 100 ft. And 4080.1 — 355.6, redundant prism for 100 ft., = 3724.5. Then $3724.5 \times \frac{50}{100} = 1862.2$, the residual curved prismoid for 50 ft.

Example 2.—Take Example 1, page 53, supposing the length to be 50 ft. We shall here correct the given length, 50 ft., instead of the tabular length. The corrected length is $50 + \frac{42.6 \times 50}{3 \times 700} = 51.0143$, of which the log. is 1.70769. Then 1.70769 + 3.77208 (log. of whole content for tabular length, Art. 100) — 2 = 3.47977 = log. 3018.4, corrected whole content for 50 ft. And 3018.4 — 177.8, redundant prism for 50 ft., = 2840.6, residual curved prismoid for 50 ft.

Cross-sections, like Figs. 26, 35, do not come strictly within the previous rules for curves.

* *Explanation.*—In finding the second term in cubic yards, (Art. 112,) 100 times the product of the differences is divided by 8, by 3, and by 27; that is, very nearly, multiplied by $\frac{15}{100}$.

CHAPTER V.

THE TABLES AND THEIR USE.

GENERAL DESCRIPTION—TECHNICAL TERMS—FINDING THE TABULAR QUANTITIES.

129. General Description. (1.) *Whole and Sub Section Tables.*—The tables headed "Whole Sections" apply to the computation of sections requiring no subdivision, or of those parts of sections which after subdivision take the same form as whole sections. The tables headed "Sub-Sections" apply to the computation of prisms, pyramids, and truncated pyramids, which in general form only parts of a section.

(2.) *Nature of the Tables.*—Some of the tables pertain to the cubical content of earthwork, some to the length of subdivisions, some to the dimensions of cross-sections, and others to logarithms for assisting in various computations. Tables I. to VI. inclusive are for auxiliary computations.

(3.) *Cubical Content.*—Tables of cubical content all apply directly to sections 100 feet long. Their tabular quantities are given in cubic yards. When questions arise concerning sections longer or shorter than 100 feet, the tabular quantity is to be increased or diminished in proportion to the length of the section.

(4.) *Lengths* are the subject of Table IV. The lengths found in that table correspond to a section 100 feet long. If the section be longer or shorter, the tabular lengths are to be taken in proportion.

(5.) *Dimensions of Cross-Sections* are proportional to heights or widths, as hereafter explained.

(6.) *Logarithms.*—In our examples involving the use of logarithms, the student is supposed to be familiar with that subject. Tables XVI., XVII., XIX., XX., XXIII., XXIV., XXV., and XXVI. are logarithmic tables. For each of these, under its proper title, except for Table XXVI., the method of finding the logarithm is shown.*

(7.) *Given Dimensions for Entering the Tables.*—Lengths, heights, and widths are supposed to be given in feet and tenths. Surface-slope, in whole degrees. Side-slopes will not be required in greater variety than are found in the tables.

---

* The method of finding the logarithm for Table XXVI. forms part of the rules given in works on Arithmetic, Mensuration, Surveying, or others explaining the use of logarithms. It was thought unnecessary to increase the size of this work by embodying those rules. In some of our examples a seven-figure logarithm has been used, which has been taken from a table similar to XXVI., but extended to seven figures. To such tables the computer may refer if Table XXVI. is not deemed sufficient; but in cases where it is thought sufficient, two figures may be rejected from our seven-figure logarithms of Tables XVI., XVII., and XXV.

(8.) *Decimals.*—For practical purposes, the nearest tenths will be sufficient, whether in entering the tables or in taking out tabular quantities.

130. TECHNICAL TERMS. In speaking of tables, we employ the terms *Argument*, or variable; *Tabular Quantity*, or function; *Interval*, or increment of the variable; *Difference*, or increment of the function; *Interpolation*, or finding the tabular quantity for a fractional argument.

(1.) *Argument* is a name for the number opposite to or under which we seek the quantity required. A fractional argument is one of the arguments given in a table, with a fraction annexed, as, for instance, a roadbed of 28.5 in the side column of Table I.

(2.) *Tabular Quantity* is the number sought.

(3.) *Interval* is the difference between two consecutive arguments. In these tables it is either one foot or one-tenth of a foot where feet are concerned, one degree where degrees are concerned, and $\frac{1}{4}$ to 1 in most cases where side-slopes are in question.

(4.) *Difference*, in its general sense, is the difference between two consecutive tabular quantities. In a restricted sense, a difference is some convenient fraction of the whole difference between two consecutive tabular quantities. Each of the small numbers set opposite the principal numbers in the several columns of Table VII., and others, is called a *difference*, and is the tenth part of the difference between two tabular quantities.

(5.) *Interpolation by Proportional Parts* is a process for finding a tabular quantity not given in the table, and which corresponds to an argument containing a fraction. The method consists in dividing the whole difference between two consecutive tabular quantities, in the same proportion as the interval between their arguments is divided by the fraction belonging to the given argument. The quantity thus found is to be added to or subtracted from the tabular quantity corresponding to the integral part of the given argument. Subtraction will rarely be necessary for our purposes. The nature of interpolation is further explained in the following note.

Interpolation.—We speak, at first, only of interpolation when the argument is in feet. It is founded on the assumption, not always strictly correct, that the *tabular quantity* increases in the same proportion as the *interval*. In Table VII., for example, each of the small quantities called *differences*, on the right of one of the principal numbers, is the *tenth part* of the whole difference between that principal number and the next following. Thus, in the column of 0°, opposite 59 in the side is the small number 16.53, which is one-tenth of 165.3, the whole difference between the two principal numbers 4834.7 and 5000.0. It is assumed that for every tenth of a foot in the interval between 59 and 60 in the side column, there is an increase of 16.53 in the tabular number 4834.7. If in any table the tabular numbers *decrease* as the argument *increases*, a similar assumption is made concerning the *decrease* of the tabular number.

Examination of this assumption.—If this assumption be correct, or nearly so, then any tabular number will be exactly, or nearly, equal to the half-sum of the one preceding and that following. In the case just cited, we find the half-sum of 4672.2 and 5000.0 is 4836.1, which is only 1.4 larger than 4834.7, the true quantity for the argument 59.

By this kind of comparison, we may judge of the admissibility of the assumption that the increase of the tabular quantity is proportional to the increase of the interval. The comparison may be made in going across a table as well as going down the columns; but *irregular intervals must be avoided.* Thus, in Table VI. the irregular interval between $\frac{1}{2}$ to 1 and $\frac{1}{3}$ to 1 must be left out of account. We there find that for regular intervals of $\frac{1}{4}$ to 1 in the side-slope, the tabular quantity is exactly equal to the half-sum of the two adjacent ones.

Again, in Table VII., opposite 60 and under 0° we have 5000.0; and on the same line, under 2°, 5013.8. The half-sum of these quantities is 5006.9, which differs from 5003.4, the quantity for 1°, by 3.5. Hence we infer that *for this part of Table VII.* the assumption in question holds very nearly from degree to degree. But take *another part* of the table. Opposite 60, under 27° and 29° respectively stand 12023.2 and 16198.7. Their half-sum is 14110.9, which is 370.5 greater than 13740.4 under 28°. This difference is much greater, considering the magnitude of the principal numbers in question, than was found for the first part of the table.

A similar examination of Table XI. shows that the assumption is nearly correct in all parts of that table.

131. FINDING THE TABULAR QUANTITY. This will now be explained for each table under its proper title. It will not be necessary to repeat the name of the argument, when this is sufficiently evident at the head of the side column or over the top of the table.

TABLE I.

TABULAR QUANTITY, the *Redundant Prism.*

Example.—Width of roadbed, 16.3 feet; side-slope, 2¾ to 1; length, 75 feet.

Opposite 16, under 2¾ to 1	86.2
Opposite 16, under 2¾ to 1, take three times the difference .	3.3
Content for 100 feet long	89.5
Multiply by 75 and divide by 100	75
Content for 75 feet	67.1

Other Methods.—See Example 2 under Table VII., and Example 3 under Table XXI. Also § 2, Art. 25, Appendix.

TABLE II.

TABULAR QUANTITY, the double centre-height of the *Redundant Prism*, or the *Whole-Section Augment* of the sum of the centre-heights.

Example.—Width of roadbed, 28.5; side-slope, 1½ to 1.

Opposite 28, under 1½ to 1	18.67
Opposite 5, under 1½ to 1, take the tenth part	.33
Augment	19.00

TABLE III.

TABULAR QUANTITY, the centre-height of the *Neutral Cross-Section.*

Example.—Width of roadbed, 28.5; surface-slope, 10°.

Opposite 28, under 10°	2.47
Opposite 5, under 10°, take the tenth part	.04
Centre-height of neutral cross-section	2.51

Twice this centre-height is the augment for the *sum* of the end centre-heights in computing the solidity of sub-sections. An approximate interpolation from degree to degree can be made by proportional parts.

TABLE IV.

TABULAR QUANTITY, either the *Abscissa* of the *Neutral Cross-Section*, or of the *Median Grade-Point*. The argument of the side-column is the algebraic difference of marginal heights, or of the centre-heights, according to the abscissa required. The argument for the top is the height at the origin. Each figure of this argument is taken separately. The tabular quantity remains unchanged for units of this argument, but is multiplied by ten for tens, and divided by ten for tenths.

In practice, the abscissa is rarely wanted for whole sections. The argument for the top, therefore, is generally the numerical sum of the heights.

Example 1.—Marginal heights, +6.7 and —2.8. Length of the section, 75. Height at the origin, +6.7. The numerical sum of the heights is 9.5.

Opposite 9.5, under 6 (units)	63.16
Opposite 9.5, under 7 (tenths)	7.37
Abscissa for a section 100 feet long	70.53
Multiply by 75 and divide by 100	75
Abscissa for a section 75 feet long	52.9

Example 2.—Take the preceding with the height —2.8 at the origin.

Opposite 9.5, under 2 (units)	21.05
Opposite 9.5, under 8 (tenths)	8.42
Abscissa for a section 100 feet long	29.47
Multiply by 75 and divide by 100	75
Abscissa for a section 75 feet long	22.1

TABLE V.

TABULAR QUANTITY, the *Distance Out* of the *Grade-Point.* The argument of the side column is either the centre-height of the partial cross-section, or, if the sum or difference of distances out be required, the sum or difference of centre-heights. If the argument is *minus*, the tabular quantity is also minus.

Example.—Centre-height, 5.8; surface-slope, 12°.

Opposite 5, under 12°	23.52
Opposite 8, (tenths,) under 12°	3.76
Distance out of the grade-point	27.28

TABLE VI.

Tabular Quantity, the *Distance Out.* When the side-height counts from grade, the distance out is from the edge of the roadbed. When the augmented side-height is used, the distance out counts from the centre.

Example.—Augmented side-height, 27.3; side-slope, 1½ to 1.

Opposite 27, under 1½ to 1	40.50
Opposite 3, (tenths,) under 1½ to 1	.45
Distance out from centre	40.95

TABLES VII., VIII., IX., X., XI., XII., XIII.

The Tabular Quantity in each is a *Prism of Mean Dimensions;* that is, a prism having the mean height or the mean width of the end cross-sections. The argument for the side-column is the augmented sum of the end-heights or widths, or the difference of heights or of widths. These tables are all used in the same manner. A few examples will suffice for all. Interpolation from degree to degree by proportional parts is not exact. The accuracy thus attainable may be judged of in the manner shown in the note, Art. 130. It may be necessary, in making such interpolation in Tables XII. and XIII., to observe whether the quantities increase or decrease from degree to degree, except for half-degrees. (See Examples 1 and 2, bottom of page 79.)

In Table XII. the tabular quantities decrease as the surface-slope increases, up to 19°, after which they increase. In Table XIII., the same change occurs at 28°. A greater slope than 19° will rarely be required in Table XII. The reason of this change is that while the height remains constant the area of the triangular cross-section varies, during the change of slope from 0° to the inclination of the side-slope; and this variation of the area takes place between infinite magnitudes through a series of finite values. One of the intermediate values must therefore be a minimum.

TABLE VII.

Example 1.—Sum or difference of centre-heights, 9.3 feet; surface-slope, 11°.

Opposite 9, under 11°	123.0
Opposite 9, under 11°, take three times the difference . .	8.6
Content of the prism of mean dimensions	131.6

When the argument for the side column does not exceed one-tenth of the largest number there contained, interpolation for tenths can be accurately made by taking out the tabular quantity as if for a whole number, and then dividing by 100.* Also, when the argument is greater than the number in the side column, the tabular number may be found by taking it out as if for *half* the argument, and multiplying the number thus found by four.

The Redundant Prism, when its height is known, can be taken from Tables VII., IX., or XI., under 0°.

* Because the tabular quantities are as the squares of the side numbers.

Example 2.—Sum of centre-heights of the redundant prism, 11.7; side-slope, 1½ to 1.

Opposite 117, under 0°, Table VII., divide by 100 . . 190.1

TABLE XIV.

Consists of a First and Second Part. The First Part is sufficiently designated by its position before the other. The Tabular Quantity of the First Part is the *Residual Prism of Mean Height;* that is, the prism of mean height with the redundant prism subtracted. The Tabular Quantity of the Second Part is one-third of that found in Table VII. opposite the same side number and under the same degree. The argument for the side column of the First Part is the *unaugmented* sum of the centre-heights; for the Second Part, the difference of the centre-heights.

FIRST PART.

Example.—Sum of centre-heights, 43.2; surface-slope, 15°.

Opposite 43, under 15°	5410.7
Opposite 43, under 15°, take twice the difference . . .	39.4
Content of prism of mean height	5450.1

This part of Table XIV. is used like Tables VII. to XIII. inclusive, except that the remarks following Example 1 under Table VII. do not apply.

SECOND PART.

Example.—Difference of centre-heights, 7.4; surface-slope, 15°.

Opposite 7, under 15°	27.1
Opposite 7, under 15°, take four times the difference . .	3.3
Third part of tabular number for 7.4 and 15°, in Table VII. .	30.4

PROPORTIONAL INTERPOLATION FROM DEGREE TO DEGREE.

Example 1.—What is the tabular quantity in Table VII. corresponding to 58.7 under 18½°?

Opposite 58.7, under 18°	6277.0
Opposite 58.7, under 19°	6527.2
Take the half-sum	2)12804.2
Tabular quantity for 18½°	6402.1

Example 2.—What is the tabular quantity in Table XIII. corresponding to 25.4 under 16½°?

Opposite 25.4, under 16°	1461.0
Opposite 25.4, under 17°	1407.7
Take the half-sum	2)2868.7
Tabular quantity for 16½°	1434.3

TABLE XV.

Consists of a First and Second Part. The First Part is sufficiently designated by its position before the other. The Tabular Quantity of the First Part is the one-eighth of a square prism. The argument of the side column is the whole feet in the augmented sum of centre-heights, which sum corresponds to the side of the base of the prism. The argument for the top is the tenths in the augmented sum.

The Tabular Quantity of the Second Part is one-third of that contained in the First, with an equal argument. The argument is the difference of centre-heights.

Both parts of the table are used in the same way.

Example for the First Part.—Sum of augmented centre-heights, 42.8.

Opposite 42, under 8 . . . . 848.07

Example for the Second Part.—Difference of centre-heights, 15.4.

Opposite 15, under 4 . . . . 36.6

TABLES XVI. and XVII.

Tabular Quantity, a *Logarithm* used, according to the rules of the text, for calculating cubical content. (See Articles 100 and 101.)

Example for Table XVI.—Surface-slope, 14°; side-slope, 1 to 1.

Opposite 14°, under 1 to 1. Logarithm 0.3289033

Example for Table XVII.—Surface-slope, 9°; side-slope, 1½ to 1.

Opposite 9°, under 1½ to 1. Logarithm 0.9180915

TABLE XVIII.

Tabular Quantity, the *Distance Out,* measured from the centre along the surface, either on the long side up hill or on the short side down hill. The table is for the side-slope 1 to 1. The argument for the top is the augmented centre-height.

Example.—Augmented centre-height, 42.7; surface-slope, 17°. Required the distance out up hill.

Opposite 17°, under 4 (tens)	60.2
Opposite 17°, under 2 (units)	3.0
Opposite 17°, under 7 (tenths)	1.1
Distance out up hill	64.3

TABLE XIX.

Tabular Quantity, a *Logarithm,* to be used in computing horizontal distances out. (See Articles 72 and 73.)

Example.—Surface-slope, 18°; side-slope, 1 to 1. Required the logarithm for calculating the distance out towards the lower side of the surface-slope.

Opposite 18°, under 1 to 1. Logarithm . . . . —1.57678

TABLE XX.

Tabular Quantity, a *Logarithm* for computing distances out from the centre along the surface, either on the long side up hill or the short side down hill. The distances are of the same kind as in Table XVIII. (See Art. 72.)

Example.—Surface-slope, 17°; side-slope, 1 to 1. Required the logarithm for computing the distance out up hill.

Opposite 17°, under 1 to 1. Logarithm . . . . . —1.87685

TABLE XXI.

Tabular Quantity, the *Eighth Part* of a *Rectangular Prism.* The argument for the side column is the height of the base of the prism when the argument for the top is the breadth of the base, and *vice versa.* The height or the base corresponds to the sum or the difference of augmented centre-heights or of total bases.

Example 1.—Height of the base, 33.6; breadth of the base, 87.

Opposite 33.6, under 8 (tens)	1244.44
Opposite 33.6, under 7 (units)	108.89
Eighth part of the prism	1353.33

Example 2.—Take the same with 87 in the side column and 33.6 on top.

Opposite 87, under 3 (tens)	1208.33
Opposite 87, under 3 (units)	120.83
Opposite 87, under 6 (tenths)	24.17
Eighth part of the prism	1353.33

Example 3.—*Finding the Redundant Prism.* (See Art. 112.) The sum of total bases for this prism is twice the width of roadbed. The double centre-height is found by Table II. Take the same prism, 100 feet long, given under Table I. The double width of roadbed is 32.6. The double centre-height from Table II. is 5.93. Opposite 32.6 and under 5.93 we find the content 89.5 as before.

TABLE XXII.

Tabular Quantity, the *Whole Prism* described under Table XXI. The arguments are the same, and can be changed in the same way.

Example.—Take the same given for Table XXI.

Opposite 33.6, under 8 (tens)	9955.6
Opposite 33.6, under 7 (units)	871.1
Content of the whole prism	10826.7

If in either Table XXI. or XXII. both arguments exceed 120, divide one of them by 2, and take out the tabular quantity with the half-argument in the side. Then multiply the result by 2.

TABLE XXIII.

TABULAR QUANTITY, a *Logarithm* for the calculation of the tabular quantity of Table XXI. The argument for the side column is the whole feet in the height or in the breadth of the base of the prism. The argument for the top is the tenths in the same.

Example 1.—What are the logarithms proper for the example given under Table XXI.?

Opposite 33, under 6. Logarithm 1.35911
Opposite 87, under 0. Logarithm 1.77229

It will be observed that if 5.93 in Example 3 under Table XXI. be multiplied by 10, it becomes 59.3. We may take out the logarithm for 59.3, not forgetting to subtract 1 from the index.

Example 2.—Take Example 3 under Table XXI. What are the logarithms proper for the sums of heights and bases?

Opposite 59, under 3, take 1 from the characteristic . . 0.60582
Opposite 32, under 6 . . . . 1.34599

TABLE XXIV.

TABULAR QUANTITY, a *Logarithm* for computing the tabular quantity of Table XXII. This table is employed precisely like Table XXIII.

Example.—Take the one under Table XXII.

Opposite 33, under 6. Logarithm 1.81066
Opposite 87, under 0. Logarithm 2.22384

TABLE XXV.

TABULAR QUANTITY, the *Logarithm* of the tabular quantity of Table XV. The tabular quantity is found as in that table.

Example.—The side of the square base of a prism is 9.7.

Opposite 9, under 7 . . . . 1.6390899

If 0.9030900, or logarithm of 8, be added to this logarithm, the sum will be the logarithm of the whole content of the prism.

TABLE XXVI.

TABULAR QUANTITIES, *Common Logarithms.* See Art. 129 (6) and note.

TABLE A.

TABULAR QUANTITY, the degree of *Surface-Slope* corresponding to the natural tangent to radius 1. Find the given tangent in the column headed "Tangent," and the required slope immediately opposite in the column headed "Slope."

TABLE B.

TABULAR QUANTITY, a *Multiplier* equal to twice the rate of side-slope. Under the given side-slope find the multiplier.

TABLES

FOR THE

COMPUTATION OF EARTHWORK.

Arrangement of the Tables.—In several cases the whole table is displayed at one view. Except Tables XI. and XV., all those which cannot be displayed at one view show, wherever opened, their whole extent in one direction,—either of the side column or of the top line.

Table XI., although continuous, is by its arrangement separated into two divisions. The first, ending on page 153, shows at one view the side column from 1 to 120; the second, beginning on page 154, shows at one view the side column from 121 to 240, with the same arrangement and extent of the top lines as are adopted in the first division.

Table XV. consists of two Parts. The First Part, ending on page 197, shows at one view the whole extent of the top line; the Second Part, beginning on page 198, is entirely displayed at one view. For want of space, the First Part is not designated by a separate heading. (See under Table XV., page 80.)

Advantage has been taken of the spaces left upon pages 123 and 179, by the arrangement described, to insert Tables A and B.

TABLE I. Redundant Prisms.

ROAD BEDS.	SIDE SLOPE											
	2¾ to 1.		2½ to 1.		2¼ to 1.		2 to 1.		1¾ to 1.		1½ to 1.	
1	.34	.10	.37	.11	.41	.12	.46	.14	.53	.16	.62	.19
2	1.35	.17	1.48	.19	1.65	.21	1.85	.23	2.12	.26	2.47	.31
3	3.03	.24	3.33	.26	3.70	.29	4.17	.32	4.76	.37	5.56	.43
4	5.39	.30	5.93	.33	6.58	.37	7.41	.42	8.47	.48	9.88	.56
5	8.42	.37	9.26	.41	10.29	.45	11.57	.51	13.23	.58	15.43	.68
6	12.12	.44	13.33	.48	14.81	.53	16.67	.60	19.05	.69	22.22	.80
7	16.50	.51	18.15	.56	20.16	.62	22.69	.69	25.93	.79	30.25	.93
8	21.55	.57	23.70	.63	26.34	.70	29.63	.79	33.86	.90	39.51	1.05
9	27.27	.64	30.00	.70	33.33	.78	37.50	.88	42.86	1.01	50.00	1.17
10	33.67	.71	37.04	.78	41.15	.86	46.30	.97	52.91	1.11	61.73	1.30
11	40.74	.77	44.81	.85	49.79	.95	56.02	1.06	64.02	1.22	74.69	1.42
12	48.48	.84	53.33	.93	59.26	1.03	66.67	1.16	76.19	1.32	88.89	1.54
13	56.90	.91	62.59	1.00	69.55	1.11	78.24	1.25	89.42	1.43	104.32	1.67
14	65.99	.98	72.59	1.07	80.66	1.19	90.74	1.34	103.70	1.53	120.99	1.79
15	75.76	1.04	83.33	1.15	92.59	1.28	104.17	1.44	119.05	1.64	138.89	1.91
16	86.20	1.11	94.81	1.22	105.35	1.36	118.52	1.53	135.45	1.75	158.02	2.04
17	97.31	1.18	107.04	1.30	118.93	1.44	133.80	1.62	152.91	1.85	178.40	2.16
18	109.09	1.25	120.00	1.37	133.33	1.52	150.00	1.71	171.43	1.96	200.00	2.28
19	121.55	1.31	133.70	1.44	148.56	1.60	167.13	1.81	191.01	2.06	222.84	2.41
20	134.68	1.38	148.15	1.52	164.61	1.69	185.19	1.90	211.64	2.17	246.91	2.53
21	148.48	1.45	163.33	1.59	181.48	1.77	204.17	1.99	233.33	2.28	272.22	2.65
22	162.96	1.52	179.26	1.67	199.18	1.85	224.07	2.08	256.08	2.38	298.77	2.78
23	178.11	1.58	195.93	1.74	217.70	1.93	244.91	2.18	279.89	2.49	326.54	2.90
24	193.94	1.65	213.33	1.81	237.04	2.02	266.67	2.27	304.76	2.59	355.56	3.02
25	210.44	1.72	231.48	1.89	257.20	2.10	289.35	2.36	330.69	2.70	385.80	3.15
26	227.61	1.78	250.37	1.96	278.19	2.18	312.96	2.45	357.67	2.80	417.28	3.27
27	245.45	1.85	270.00	2.04	300.00	2.26	337.50	2.55	385.71	2.91	450.00	3.40
28	263.97	1.92	290.37	2.11	322.63	2.35	362.96	2.64	414.81	3.02	483.95	3.52
29	283.16	1.99	311.48	2.19	346.09	2.43	389.35	2.73	444.97	3.12	519.14	3.64
30	303.03	2.05	333.33	2.26	370.37	2.51	416.67	2.82	476.19	3.23	555.56	3.77
31	323.57	2.12	355.93	2.33	395.47	2.59	444.91	2.92	508.47	3.33	593.21	3.89
32	344.78	2.19	379.26	2.41	421.40	2.67	474.07	3.01	541.80	3.44	632.10	4.01
33	366.67	2.25	403.33	2.48	448.15	2.76	504.17	3.10	576.19	3.54	672.22	4.14
34	389.23	2.32	428.15	2.56	475.72	2.84	535.19	3.19	611.64	3.65	713.58	4.26
35	412.46	2.39	453.70	2.63	504.12	2.92	567.13	3.29	648.15	3.76	756.17	4.38
36	436.36	2.46	480.00	2.70	533.33	3.00	600.00	3.38	685.71	3.86	800.00	4.51
ROAD BEDS.	2¾ to 1.		2½ to 1.		2¼ to 1.		2 to 1.		1¾ to 1.		1½ to 1.	

TABLE I. **Redundant Prisms.**

ROAD BEDS.	SIDE SLOPE											
	1¼ to 1.		1 to 1.		¾ to 1.		½ to 1.		⅓ to 1.		¼ to 1.	
1	.74	.22	.93	.28	1.23	.37	1.85	.56	2.78	.83	3.70	1.11
2	2.96	.37	3.70	.46	4.94	.62	7.41	.93	11.11	1.39	14.81	1.85
3	6.67	.52	8.33	.65	11.11	.86	16.67	1.30	25.00	1.94	33.33	2.59
4	11.85	.67	14.81	.83	19.75	1.11	29.63	1.67	44.44	2.50	59.26	3.33
5	18.52	.81	23.15	1.02	30.86	1.36	46.30	2.04	69.44	3.06	92.59	4.07
6	26.67	.96	33.33	1.20	44.44	1.60	66.67	2.41	100.00	3.61	133.33	4.81
7	36.30	1.11	45.37	1.39	60.49	1.85	90.74	2.78	136.11	4.17	181.48	5.56
8	47.41	1.26	59.26	1.57	79.01	2.10	118.52	3.15	177.78	4.72	237.04	6.30
9	60.00	1.41	75.00	1.76	100.00	2.35	150.00	3.52	225.00	5.28	300.00	7.04
10	74.07	1.56	92.59	1.94	123.46	2.59	185.19	3.89	277.78	5.83	370.37	7.78
11	89.63	1.70	112.04	2.13	149.38	2.84	224.07	4.26	336.11	6.39	448.15	8.52
12	106.67	1.85	133.33	2.31	177.78	3.09	266.67	4.63	400.00	6.94	533.33	9.26
13	125.19	2.00	156.48	2.50	208.64	3.33	312.96	5.00	469.44	7.50	625.93	10.00
14	145.19	2.15	181.48	2.69	241.98	3.58	362.96	5.37	544.44	8.06	725.93	10.74
15	166.67	2.30	208.33	2.87	277.78	3.83	416.67	5.74	625.00	8.61	833.33	11.48
16	189.63	2.44	237.04	3.06	316.05	4.07	474.07	6.11	711.11	9.17	948.15	12.22
17	214.07	2.59	267.59	3.24	356.79	4.32	535.19	6.48	802.78	9.72	1070.37	12.96
18	240.00	2.74	300.00	3.43	400.00	4.57	600.00	6.85	900.00	10.28	1200.00	13.70
19	267.41	2.89	334.26	3.61	445.68	4.81	668.52	7.22	1002.78	10.83	1337.04	14.44
20	296.30	3.04	370.37	3.80	493.83	5.06	740.74	7.59	1111.11	11.39	1481.48	15.19
21	326.67	3.19	408.33	3.98	544.44	5.31	816.67	7.96	1225.00	11.94	1633.33	15.93
22	358.52	3.33	448.15	4.17	597.53	5.56	896.30	8.33	1344.44	12.50	1792.59	16.67
23	391.85	3.48	489.81	4.35	653.09	5.80	979.63	8.70	1469.44	13.06	1959.26	17.41
24	426.67	3.63	533.33	4.54	711.11	6.05	1066.67	9.07	1600.00	13.61	2133.33	18.15
25	462.96	3.78	578.70	4.72	771.60	6.30	1157.41	9.44	1736.11	14.17	2314.81	18.89
26	500.74	3.93	625.93	4.91	834.57	6.54	1251.85	9.81	1877.78	14.72	2503.70	19.63
27	540.00	4.07	675.00	5.09	900.00	6.79	1350.00	10.19	2025.00	15.28	2700.00	20.37
28	580.74	4.22	725.93	5.28	967.90	7.04	1451.85	10.56	2177.78	15.83	2903.70	21.11
29	622.96	4.37	778.70	5.46	1038.27	7.28	1557.41	10.93	2336.11	16.39	3114.81	21.85
30	666.67	4.52	833.33	5.65	1111.11	7.53	1666.67	11.30	2500.00	16.94	3333.33	22.59
31	711.85	4.67	889.81	5.83	1186.42	7.78	1779.63	11.67	2669.44	17.50	3559.26	23.33
32	758.52	4.81	948.15	6.02	1264.20	8.02	1896.30	12.04	2844.44	18.06	3792.59	24.07
33	806.67	4.96	1008.33	6.20	1344.44	8.27	2016.67	12.41	3025.00	18.61	4033.33	24.81
34	856.30	5.11	1070.37	6.39	1427.16	8.52	2140.74	12.78	3211.11	19.17	4281.48	25.56
35	907.41	5.26	1134.26	6.57	1512.35	8.77	2268.52	13.15	3402.78	19.72	4537.04	26.30
36	960.00	5.41	1200.00	6.76	1600.00	9.01	2400.00	13.52	3600.00	20.28	4800.00	27.04
ROAD BEDS.	1¼ to 1.		1 to 1.		¾ to 1.		½ to 1.		⅓ to 1.		¼ to 1.	

TABLE II. **Whole-Section Augments.**

ROAD BEDS.	SIDE SLOPE					
	2¾ to 1.	2½ to 1.	2¼ to 1.	2 to 1.	1¾ to 1.	1½ to 1.
1	.36	.40	.44	.50	.57	.67
2	.73	.80	.89	1.00	1.14	1.33
3	1.09	1.20	1.33	1.50	1.71	2.00
4	1.45	1.60	1.78	2.00	2.29	2.67
5	1.82	2.00	2.22	2.50	2.86	3.33
6	2.18	2.40	2.67	3.00	3.43	4.00
7	2.55	2.80	3.11	3.50	4.00	4.67
8	2.91	3.20	3.56	4.00	4.57	5.33
9	3.27	3.60	4.00	4.50	5.14	6.00
10	3.64	4.00	4.44	5.00	5.71	6.67
11	4.00	4.40	4.89	5.50	6.29	7.33
12	4.36	4.80	5.33	6.00	6.86	8.00
13	4.73	5.20	5.78	6.50	7.43	8.67
14	5.09	5.60	6.22	7.00	8.00	9.33
15	5.45	6.00	6.67	7.50	8.57	10.00
16	5.82	6.40	7.11	8.00	9.14	10.67
17	6.18	6.80	7.56	8.50	9.71	11.33
18	6.55	7.20	8.00	9.00	10.29	12.00
19	6.91	7.60	8.44	9.50	10.86	12.67
20	7.27	8.00	8.89	10.00	11.43	13.33
21	7.64	8.40	9.33	10.50	12.00	14.00
22	8.00	8.80	9.78	11.00	12.57	14.67
23	8.36	9.20	10.22	11.50	13.14	15.33
24	8.73	9.60	10.67	12.00	13.71	16.00
25	9.09	10.00	11.11	12.50	14.29	16.67
26	9.45	10.40	11.56	13.00	14.86	17.33
27	9.82	10.80	12.00	13.50	15.43	18.00
28	10.18	11.20	12.44	14.00	16.00	18.67
29	10.55	11.60	12.89	14.50	16.57	19.33
30	10.91	12.00	13.33	15.00	17.14	20.00
31	11.27	12.40	13.78	15.50	17.71	20.67
32	11.64	12.80	14.22	16.00	18.29	21.33
33	12.00	13.20	14.67	16.50	18.86	22.00
34	12.36	13.60	15.11	17.00	19.43	22.67
35	12.73	14.00	15.56	17.50	20.00	23.33
36	13.09	14.40	16.00	18.00	20.57	24.00
ROAD BEDS.	2¾ to 1.	2½ to 1.	2¼ to 1.	2 to 1.	1¾ to 1.	1½ to 1.

TABLE II. Whole-Section Augments.

ROAD BEDS.	SIDE SLOPE					
	$1\frac{1}{4}$ to 1.	1 to 1.	$\frac{3}{4}$ to 1.	$\frac{1}{2}$ to 1.	$\frac{1}{3}$ to 1.	$\frac{1}{4}$ to 1.
1	.80	1.00	1.33	2.00	3.00	4.00
2	1.60	2.00	2.67	4.00	6.00	8.00
3	2.40	3.00	4.00	6.00	9.00	12.00
4	3.20	4.00	5.33	8.00	12.00	16.00
5	4.00	5.00	6.67	10.00	15.00	20.00
6	4.80	6.00	8.00	12.00	18.00	24.00
7	5.60	7.00	9.33	14.00	21.00	28.00
8	6.40	8.00	10.67	16.00	24.00	32.00
9	7.20	9.00	12.00	18.00	27.00	36.00
10	8.00	10.00	13.33	20.00	30.00	40.00
11	8.80	11.00	14.67	22.00	33.00	44.00
12	9.60	12.00	16.00	24.00	36.00	48.00
13	10.40	13.00	17.33	26.00	39.00	52.00
14	11.20	14.00	18.67	28.00	42.00	56.00
15	12.00	15.00	20.00	30.00	45.00	60.00
16	12.80	16.00	21.33	32.00	48.00	64.00
17	13.60	17.00	22.67	34.00	51.00	68.00
18	14.40	18.00	24.00	36.00	54.00	72.00
19	15.20	19.00	25.33	38.00	57.00	76.00
20	16.00	20.00	26.67	40.00	60.00	80.00
21	16.80	21.00	28.00	42.00	63.00	84.00
22	17.60	22.00	29.33	44.00	66.00	88.00
23	18.40	23.00	30.67	46.00	69.00	92.00
24	19.20	24.00	32.00	48.00	72.00	96.00
25	20.00	25.00	33.33	50.00	75.00	100.00
26	20.80	26.00	34.67	52.00	78.00	104.00
27	21.60	27.00	36.00	54.00	81.00	108.00
28	22.40	28.00	37.33	56.00	84.00	112.00
29	23.20	29.00	38.67	58.00	87.00	116.00
30	24.00	30.00	40.00	60.00	90.00	120.00
31	24.80	31.00	41.33	62.00	93.00	124.00
32	25.60	32.00	42.67	64.00	96.00	128.00
33	26.40	33.00	44.00	66.00	99.00	132.00
34	27.20	34.00	45.33	68.00	102.00	136.00
35	28.00	35.00	46.67	70.00	105.00	140.00
36	28.80	36.00	48.00	72.00	108.00	144.00
ROAD BEDS.	$1\frac{1}{4}$ to 1.	1 to 1.	$\frac{3}{4}$ to 1.	$\frac{1}{2}$ to 1.	$\frac{1}{3}$ to 1.	$\frac{1}{4}$ to 1.

TABLE III. Sub-Section Augments for Heights.

ROAD BEDS.	0°	1°	2°	3°	4°	5°
1	00.00	0.01	0.02	0.03	0.03	0.04
2	00.00	0.02	0.03	0.05	0.07	0.09
3	00.00	0.03	0.05	0.08	0.10	0.13
4	00.00	0.03	0.07	0.10	0.14	0.17
5	00.00	0.04	0.09	0.13	0.17	0.22
6	00.00	0.05	0.10	0.16	0.21	0.26
7	00.00	0.06	0.12	0.18	0.24	0.31
8	00.00	0.07	0.14	0.21	0.28	0.35
9	00.00	0.08	0.16	0.24	0.31	0.39
10	00.00	0.09	0.17	0.26	0.35	0.44
11	00.00	0.10	0.19	0.29	0.38	0.48
12	00.00	0.10	0.21	0.31	0.42	0.52
13	00.00	0.11	0.23	0.34	0.45	0.57
14	00.00	0.12	0.24	0.37	0.49	0.61
15	00.00	0.13	0.26	0.39	0.52	0.66
16	00.00	0.14	0.28	0.42	0.56	0.70
17	00.00	0.15	0.30	0.45	0.59	0.74
18	00.00	0.16	0.31	0.47	0.63	0.79
19	00.00	0.17	0.33	0.50	0.66	0.83
20	00.00	0.17	0.35	0.52	0.70	0.87
21	00.00	0.18	0.37	0.55	0.73	0.92
22	00.00	0.19	0.38	0.58	0.77	0.96
23	00.00	0.20	0.40	0.60	0.80	1.01
24	00.00	0.21	0.42	0.63	0.84	1.05
25	00.00	0.22	0.44	0.66	0.87	1.09
26	00.00	0.23	0.45	0.68	0.91	1.14
27	00.00	0.24	0.47	0.71	0.94	1.18
28	00.00	0.24	0.49	0.73	0.98	1.22
29	00.00	0.25	0.51	0.76	1.01	1.27
30	00.00	0.26	0.52	0.79	1.05	1.31
31	00.00	0.27	0.54	0.81	1.08	1.36
32	00.00	0.28	0.56	0.84	1.12	1.40
33	00.00	0.29	0.58	0.86	1.15	1.44
34	00.00	0.30	0.59	0.89	1.19	1.49
35	00.00	0.31	0.61	0.92	1.22	1.53
36	00.00	0.31	0.63	0.94	1.26	1.57
ROAD BEDS.	0°	1°	2°	3°	4°	5°

TABLE III. Sub-Section Augments for Heights.

ROAD BEDS.	6°	7°	8°	9°	10°	11°
1	0.05	0.06	0.07	0.08	0.09	0.10
2	0.11	0.12	0.14	0.16	0.18	0.19
3	0.16	0.18	0.21	0.24	0.26	0.29
4	0.21	0.25	0.28	0.32	0.35	0.39
5	0.26	0.31	0.35	0.40	0.44	0.49
6	0.32	0.37	0.42	0.48	0.53	0.58
7	0.37	0.43	0.49	0.55	0.62	0.68
8	0.42	0.49	0.56	0.63	0.71	0.78
9	0.47	0.55	0.63	0.71	0.79	0.87
10	0.53	0.61	0.70	0.79	0.88	0.97
11	0.58	0.68	0.77	0.87	0.97	1.07
12	0.63	0.74	0.84	0.95	1.06	1.17
13	0.68	0.80	0.91	1.03	1.15	1.26
14	0.74	0.86	0.98	1.11	1.23	1.36
15	0.79	0.92	1.05	1.19	1.32	1.46
16	0.84	0.98	1.12	1.27	1.41	1.56
17	0.89	1.04	1.19	1.35	1.50	1.65
18	0.95	1.11	1.26	1.43	1.59	1.75
19	1.00	1.17	1.34	1.50	1.68	1.85
20	1.05	1.23	1.41	1.58	1.76	1.94
21	1.10	1.29	1.48	1.66	1.85	2.04
22	1.16	1.35	1.55	1.74	1.94	2.14
23	1.21	1.41	1.62	1.82	2.03	2.24
24	1.26	1.47	1.69	1.90	2.12	2.33
25	1.31	1.53	1.76	1.98	2.20	2.43
26	1.37	1.60	1.83	2.06	2.29	2.53
27	1.42	1.66	1.90	2.14	2.38	2.62
28	1.47	1.72	1.97	2.22	2.47	2.72
29	1.52	1.78	2.04	2.30	2.56	2.82
30	1.58	1.84	2.11	2.38	2.64	2.92
31	1.63	1.90	2.18	2.45	2.73	3.01
32	1.68	1.96	2.25	2.53	2.82	3.11
33	1.73	2.03	2.32	2.61	2.91	3.21
34	1.79	2.09	2.39	2.69	3.00	3.30
35	1.84	2.15	2.46	2.77	3.09	3.40
36	1.89	2.21	2.53	2.85	3.17	3.50
ROAD BEDS.	6°	7°	8°	9°	10°	11°

TABLE III. Sub-Section Augments for Heights.

ROAD BEDS.	12°	13°	14°	15°	16°	17°
1	0.11	0.12	0.12	0.13	0.14	0.15
2	0.21	0.23	0.25	0.27	0.29	0.31
3	0.32	0.35	0.37	0.40	0.43	0.46
4	0.43	0.46	0.50	0.54	0.57	0.61
5	0.53	0.58	0.62	0.67	0.72	0.76
6	0.64	0.69	0.75	0.80	0.86	0.92
7	0.74	0.81	0.87	0.94	1.00	1.07
8	0.85	0.92	1.00	1.07	1.15	1.22
9	0.96	1.04	1.12	1.21	1.29	1.38
10	1.06	1.15	1.25	1.34	1.43	1.53
11	1.17	1.27	1.37	1.47	1.58	1.68
12	1.28	1.39	1.50	1.61	1.72	1.83
13	1.38	1.50	1.62	1.74	1.86	1.99
14	1.49	1.62	1.75	1.88	2.01	2.14
15	1.59	1.73	1.87	2.01	2.15	2.29
16	1.70	1.85	1.99	2.14	2.29	2.45
17	1.81	1.96	2.12	2.28	2.44	2.60
18	1.91	2.08	2.24	2.41	2.58	2.75
19	2.02	2.19	2.37	2.55	2.72	2.90
20	2.13	2.31	2.49	2.68	2.87	3.06
21	2.23	2.42	2.62	2.81	3.01	3.21
22	2.34	2.54	2.74	2.95	3.15	3.36
23	2.44	2.65	2.87	3.08	3.30	3.52
24	2.55	2.77	2.99	3.22	3.44	3.67
25	2.66	2.89	3.12	3.35	3.58	3.82
26	2.76	3.00	3.24	3.48	3.73	3.97
27	2.87	3.12	3.37	3.62	3.87	4.13
28	2.98	3.23	3.49	3.75	4.01	4.28
29	3.08	3.35	3.62	3.89	4.16	4.43
30	3.19	3.46	3.74	4.02	4.30	4.59
31	3.29	3.58	3.86	4.15	4.44	4.74
32	3.40	3.69	3.99	4.29	4.59	4.89
33	3.51	3.81	4.11	4.42	4.73	5.04
34	3.61	3.92	4.24	4.56	4.87	5.20
35	3.72	4.04	4.36	4.69	5.02	5.35
36	3.83	4.16	4.49	4.82	5.16	5.50
ROAD BEDS.	12°	13°	14°	15°	16°	17°

TABLE III. Sub-Section Augments for Heights.

ROAD BEDS.	18°	19°	20°	21°	22°	23°
1	0.16	0.17	0.18	0.19	0.20	0.21
2	0.32	0.34	0.36	0.38	0.40	0.42
3	0.49	0.52	0.55	0.58	0.61	0.64
4	0.65	0.69	0.73	0.77	0.81	0.85
5	0.81	0.86	0.91	0.96	1.01	1.06
6	0.97	1.03	1.09	1.15	1.21	1.27
7	1.14	1.21	1.27	1.34	1.41	1.49
8	1.30	1.38	1.46	1.54	1.62	1.70
9	1.46	1.55	1.64	1.73	1.82	1.91
10	1.62	1.72	1.82	1.92	2.02	2.12
11	1.79	1.89	2.00	2.11	2.22	2.33
12	1.95	2.07	2.18	2.30	2.42	2.55
13	2.11	2.24	2.37	2.50	2.63	2.76
14	2.27	2.41	2.55	2.69	2.83	2.97
15	2.44	2.58	2.73	2.88	3.03	3.18
16	2.60	2.75	2.91	3.07	3.23	3.40
17	2.76	2.93	3.09	3.26	3.43	3.61
18	2.92	3.10	3.28	3.45	3.64	3.82
19	3.09	3.27	3.46	3.65	3.84	4.03
20	3.25	3.44	3.64	3.84	4.04	4.24
21	3.41	3.62	3.82	4.03	4.24	4.46
22	3.57	3.79	4.00	4.22	4.44	4.67
23	3.74	3.96	4.19	4.41	4.65	4.88
24	3.90	4.13	4.37	4.61	4.85	5.09
25	4.06	4.30	4.55	4.80	5.05	5.31
26	4.22	4.48	4.73	4.99	5.25	5.52
27	4.39	4.65	4.91	5.18	5.45	5.73
28	4.55	4.82	5.10	5.37	5.66	5.94
29	4.71	4.99	5.28	5.57	5.86	6.15
30	4.87	5.16	5.46	5.76	6.06	6.37
31	5.04	5.34	5.64	5.95	6.26	6.58
32	5.20	5.51	5.82	6.14	6.46	6.79
33	5.36	5.68	6.01	6.33	6.67	7.00
34	5.52	5.85	6.19	6.53	6.87	7.22
35	5.69	6.03	6.37	6.72	7.07	7.43
36	5.85	6.20	6.55	6.91	7.27	7.64
ROAD BEDS.	18°	19°	20°	21°	22°	23°

TABLE III. Sub-Section Augments for Heights.

ROAD BEDS.	24°	25°	26°	27°	28°	29°
1	0.22	0.23	0.24	0.25	0.27	0.28
2	0.45	0.47	0.49	0.51	0.53	0.55
3	0.67	0.70	0.73	0.76	0.80	0.83
4	0.89	0.93	0.98	1.02	1.06	1.11
5	1.11	1.17	1.22	1.27	1.33	1.39
6	1.34	1.40	1.46	1.53	1.60	1.66
7	1.56	1.63	1.71	1.78	1.86	1.94
8	1.78	1.87	1.95	2.04	2.13	2.22
9	2.00	2.10	2.19	2.29	2.39	2.49
10	2.23	2.33	2.44	2.55	2.66	2.77
11	2.45	2.56	2.68	2.80	2.92	3.05
12	2.67	2.80	2.93	3.06	3.19	3.33
13	2.89	3.03	3.17	3.31	3.46	3.60
14	3.12	3.26	3.41	3.57	3.72	3.88
15	3.34	3.50	3.66	3.82	3.99	4.16
16	3.56	3.73	3.90	4.08	4.25	4.43
17	3.78	3.96	4.15	4.33	4.52	4.71
18	4.01	4.20	4.39	4.59	4.79	4.99
19	4.23	4.43	4.63	4.84	5.05	5.27
20	4.45	4.66	4.88	5.10	5.32	5.54
21	4.67	4.90	5.12	5.35	5.58	5.82
22	4.90	5.13	5.37	5.60	5.85	6.10
23	5.12	5.36	5.61	5.86	6.11	6.37
24	5.34	5.60	5.85	6.11	6.38	6.65
25	5.57	5.83	6.10	6.37	6.65	6.93
26	5.79	6.06	6.34	6.62	6.91	7.21
27	6.01	6.30	6.58	6.88	7.18	7.48
28	6.23	6.53	6.83	7.13	7.44	7.76
29	6.46	6.76	7.07	7.39	7.71	8.04
30	6.68	6.99	7.32	7.64	7.98	8.31
31	6.90	7.23	7.56	7.90	8.24	8.59
32	7.12	7.46	7.80	8.15	8.51	8.87
33	7.35	7.69	8.05	8.41	8.77	9.15
34	7.57	7.93	8.29	8.66	9.04	9.42
35	7.79	8.16	8.54	8.92	9.30	9.70
36	8.01	8.39	8.78	9.17	9.57	9.98
ROAD BEDS.	24°	25°	26°	27°	28°	29°

TABLE III. Sub-Section Augments for Heights.

ROAD BEDS.	30°	31°	32°	33°	34°	35°
1	0.29	0.30	0.31	0.32	0.34	0.35
2	0.58	0.60	0.62	0.65	0.67	0.70
3	0.87	0.90	0.94	0.97	1.01	1.05
4	1.15	1.20	1.25	1.30	1.35	1.40
5	1.44	1.50	1.56	1.62	1.69	1.75
6	1.73	1.80	1.87	1.95	2.02	2.10
7	2.02	2.10	2.19	2.27	2.36	2.45
8	2.31	2.40	2.50	2.60	2.70	2.80
9	2.60	2.70	2.81	2.92	3.04	3.15
10	2.89	3.00	3.12	3.25	3.37	3.50
11	3.18	3.30	3.44	3.57	3.71	3.85
12	3.46	3.61	3.75	3.90	4.05	4.20
13	3.75	3.91	4.06	4.22	4.38	4.55
14	4.04	4.21	4.37	4.55	4.72	4.90
15	4.33	4.51	4.69	4.87	5.06	5.25
16	4.62	4.81	5.00	5.20	5.40	5.60
17	4.91	5.11	5.31	5.52	5.73	5.95
18	5.20	5.41	5.62	5.84	6.07	6.30
19	5.48	5.71	5.94	6.17	6.41	6.65
20	5.77	6.01	6.25	6.49	6.75	7.00
21	6.06	6.31	6.56	6.82	7.08	7.35
22	6.35	6.61	6.87	7.14	7.42	7.70
23	6.64	6.91	7.19	7.47	7.76	8.05
24	6.93	7.21	7.50	7.79	8.09	8.40
25	7.22	7.51	7.81	8.12	8.43	8.75
26	7.51	7.81	8.12	8.44	8.77	9.10
27	7.79	8.11	8.44	8.77	9.11	9.45
28	8.08	8.41	8.75	9.09	9.44	9.80
29	8.37	8.71	9.06	9.42	9.78	10.15
30	8.66	9.01	9.37	9.74	10.12	10.50
31	8.95	9.31	9.69	10.07	10.45	10.85
32	9.24	9.61	10.00	10.39	10.79	11.20
33	9.53	9.91	10.31	10.72	11.13	11.55
34	9.81	10.21	10.62	11.04	11.47	11.90
35	10.10	10.52	10.94	11.36	11.80	12.25
36	10.39	10.82	11.25	11.69	12.14	12.60
ROAD BEDS.	30°	31°	32°	33°	34°	35°

TABLE IV. Lengths of Sub-Sections.

DIFF.	1	2	3	4	5	DIFF.
0.1	1000.00	2000.00	3000.00	4000.00	5000.00	**0.1**
0.2	500.00	1000.00	1500.00	2000.00	2500.00	**0.2**
0.3	333.33	666.67	1000.00	1333.33	1666.67	**0.3**
0.4	250.00	500.00	750.00	1000.00	1250.00	**0.4**
0.5	200.00	400.00	600.00	800.00	1000.00	**0.5**
0.6	166.67	333.33	500.00	666.67	833.33	**0.6**
0.7	142.86	285.71	428.57	571.43	714.29	**0.7**
0.8	125.00	250.00	375.00	500.00	625.00	**0.8**
0.9	111.11	222.22	333.33	444.44	555.56	**0.9**
1.0	100.00	200.00	300.00	400.00	500.00	**1.0**
1.1	90.91	181.82	272.73	363.64	454.55	**1.1**
1.2	83.33	166.67	250.00	333.33	416.67	**1.2**
1.3	76.92	153.85	230.77	307.69	384.62	**1.3**
1.4	71.43	142.86	214.29	285.71	357.14	**1.4**
1.5	66.67	133.33	200.00	266.67	333.33	**1.5**
1.6	62.50	125.00	187.50	250.00	312.50	**1.6**
1.7	58.82	117.65	176.47	235.29	294.12	**1.7**
1.8	55.56	111.11	166.67	222.22	277.78	**1.8**
1.9	52.63	105.26	157.89	210.53	263.16	**1.9**
2.0	50.00	100.00	150.00	200.00	250.00	**2.0**
2.1	47.62	95.24	142.86	190.48	238.10	**2.1**
2.2	45.45	90.91	136.36	181.82	227.27	**2.2**
2.3	43.48	86.96	130.43	173.91	217.39	**2.3**
2.4	41.67	83.33	125.00	166.67	208.33	**2.4**
2.5	40.00	80.00	120.00	160.00	200.00	**2.5**
2.6	38.46	76.93	115.39	153.85	192.31	**2.6**
2.7	37.04	74.07	111.11	148.15	185.19	**2.7**
2.8	35.71	71.43	107.14	142.86	178.57	**2.8**
2.9	34.48	68.97	103.45	137.93	172.41	**2.9**
3.0	33.33	66.67	100.00	133.33	166.67	**3.0**
3.1	32.26	64.52	96.77	129.03	161.29	**3.1**
3.2	31.25	62.50	93.75	125.00	156.25	**3.2**
3.3	30.30	60.61	90.91	121.21	151.52	**3.3**
3.4	29.41	58.82	88.24	117.65	147.06	**3.4**
3.5	28.57	57.14	85.71	114.29	142.86	**3.5**
3.6	27.78	55.56	83.33	111.11	138.89	**3.6**
3.7	27.03	54.05	81.08	108.11	135.14	**3.7**
3.8	26.32	52.63	78.95	105.26	131.58	**3.8**
3.9	25.64	51.28	76.92	102.56	128.21	**3.9**
4.0	25.00	50.00	75.00	100.00	125.00	**4.0**
4.1	24.39	48.78	73.17	97.56	121.95	**4.1**
4.2	23.81	47.62	71.43	95.24	119.05	**4.2**
4.3	23.26	46.51	69.77	93.02	116.28	**4.3**
4.4	22.73	45.45	68.18	90.91	113.64	**4.4**
4.5	22.22	44.44	66.67	88.89	111.11	**4.5**
4.6	21.74	43.48	65.22	86.96	108.70	**4.6**
4.7	21.28	42.55	63.83	85.11	106.38	**4.7**
4.8	20.83	41.67	62.50	83.33	104.17	**4.8**
4.9	20.41	40.82	61.22	81.63	102.04	**4.9**
5.0	20.00	40.00	60.00	80.00	100.00	**5.0**
DIFF.	1	2	3	4	5	DIFF.

TABLE IV. Lengths of Sub-Sections.

DIFF.	6	7	8	9	10	DIFF.
0.1	6000.00	7000.00	8000.00	9000.00	10000.00	**0.1**
0.2	3000.00	3500.00	4000.00	4500.00	5000.00	**0.2**
0.3	2000.00	2333.33	2666.67	3000.00	3333.33	**0.3**
0.4	1500.00	1750.00	2000.00	2250.00	2500.00	**0.4**
0.5	1200.00	1400.00	1600.00	1800.00	2000.00	**0.5**
0.6	1000.00	1166.67	1333.33	1500.00	1666.67	**0.6**
0.7	857.14	1000.00	1142.86	1285.71	1428.57	**0.7**
0.8	750.00	875.00	1000.00	1125.00	1250.00	**0.8**
0.9	666.67	777.78	888.89	1000.00	1111.11	**0.9**
1.0	600.00	700.00	800.00	900.00	1000.00	**1.0**
1.1	545.45	636.36	727.27	818.18	909.09	**1.1**
1.2	500.00	583.33	666.67	750.00	833.33	**1.2**
1.3	461.54	538.46	615.38	692.31	769.23	**1.3**
1.4	428.57	500.00	571.43	642.86	714.29	**1.4**
1.5	400.00	466.67	533.33	600.00	666.67	**1.5**
1.6	375.00	437.50	500.00	562.50	625.00	**1.6**
1.7	352.94	411.76	470.59	529.41	588.24	**1.7**
1.8	333.33	388.89	444.44	500.00	555.56	**1.8**
1.9	315.79	368.42	421.05	473.68	526.32	**1.9**
2.0	300.00	350.00	400.00	450.00	500.00	**2.0**
2.1	285.71	333.33	380.95	428.57	476.19	**2.1**
2.2	272.73	318.18	363.64	409.09	454.55	**2.2**
2.3	260.87	304.35	347.83	391.30	434.78	**2.3**
2.4	250.00	291.67	333.33	375.00	416.67	**2.4**
2.5	240.00	280.00	320.00	360.00	400.00	**2.5**
2.6	230.78	269.24	307.70	346.16	384.63	**2.6**
2.7	222.22	259.26	296.30	333.33	370.37	**2.7**
2.8	214.29	250.00	285.71	321.43	357.14	**2.8**
2.9	206.90	241.38	275.86	310.34	344.83	**2.9**
3.0	200.00	233.33	266.67	300.00	333.33	**3.0**
3.1	193.55	225.81	258.06	290.32	322.58	**3.1**
3.2	187.50	218.75	250.00	281.25	312.50	**3.2**
3.3	181.82	212.12	242.42	272.73	303.03	**3.3**
3.4	176.47	205.88	235.29	264.71	294.12	**3.4**
3.5	171.43	200.00	228.57	257.14	285.71	**3.5**
3.6	166.67	194.44	222.22	250.00	277.78	**3.6**
3.7	162.16	189.19	216.22	243.24	270.27	**3.7**
3.8	157.89	184.21	210.53	236.84	263.16	**3.8**
3.9	153.85	179.49	205.13	230.77	256.41	**3.9**
4.0	150.00	175.00	200.00	225.00	250.00	**4.0**
4.1	146.34	170.73	195.12	219.51	243.90	**4.1**
4.2	142.86	166.67	190.48	214.29	238.10	**4.2**
4.3	139.54	162.79	186.05	209.30	232.56	**4.3**
4.4	136.36	159.09	181.82	204.55	227.27	**4.4**
4.5	133.33	155.56	177.78	200.00	222.22	**4.5**
4.6	130.43	152.17	173.91	195.65	217.39	**4.6**
4.7	127.66	148.94	170.21	191.49	212.77	**4.7**
4.8	125.00	145.83	166.67	187.50	208.33	**4.8**
4.9	122.45	142.86	163.27	183.67	204.08	**4.9**
5.0	120.00	140.00	160.00	180.00	200.00	**5.0**
DIFF.	6	7	8	9	10	DIFF.

TABLE IV. **Lengths of Sub-Sections.**

DIFF.	1	2	3	4	5	DIFF.
5.1	19.61	39.22	58.82	78.43	98.04	**5.1**
5.2	19.23	38.46	57.69	76.93	96.16	**5.2**
5.3	18.87	37.74	56.60	75.47	94.34	**5.3**
5.4	18.52	37.04	55.56	74.07	92.59	**5.4**
5.5	18.18	36.36	54.55	72.73	90.91	**5.5**
5.6	17.86	35.71	53.57	71.43	89.29	**5.6**
5.7	17.54	35.09	52.63	70.18	87.72	**5.7**
5.8	17.24	34.48	51.72	68.97	86.21	**5.8**
5.9	16.95	33.90	50.85	67.80	84.75	**5.9**
6.0	16.67	33.33	50.00	66.67	83.33	**6.0**
6.1	16.39	32.79	49.18	65.57	81.97	**6.1**
6.2	16.13	32.26	48.39	64.52	80.65	**6.2**
6.3	15.87	31.75	47.62	63.49	79.37	**6.3**
6.4	15.63	31.25	46.88	62.50	78.13	**6.4**
6.5	15.38	30.77	46.15	61.54	76.92	**6.5**
6.6	15.15	30.30	45.45	60.61	75.76	**6.6**
6.7	14.93	29.85	44.78	59.70	74.63	**6.7**
6.8	14.71	29.41	44.12	58.82	73.53	**6.8**
6.9	14.49	28.99	43.48	57.97	72.46	**6.9**
7.0	14.29	28.57	42.86	57.14	71.43	**7.0**
7.1	14.08	28.17	42.25	56.34	70.42	**7.1**
7.2	13.89	27.78	41.67	55.56	69.44	**7.2**
7.3	13.70	27.40	41.10	54.79	68.49	**7.3**
7.4	13.51	27.03	40.54	54.05	67.57	**7.4**
7.5	13.33	26.67	40.00	53.33	66.67	**7.5**
7.6	13.16	26.32	39.47	52.63	65.79	**7.6**
7.7	12.99	25.97	38.96	51.95	64.94	**7.7**
7.8	12.82	25.64	38.46	51.28	64.10	**7.8**
7.9	12.66	25.32	37.97	50.63	63.29	**7.9**
8.0	12.50	25.00	37.50	50.00	62.50	**8.0**
8.1	12.35	24.69	37.04	49.38	61.73	**8.1**
8.2	12.20	24.39	36.59	48.78	60.98	**8.2**
8.3	12.05	24.10	36.14	48.19	60.24	**8.3**
8.4	11.90	23.81	35.71	47.62	59.52	**8.4**
8.5	11.76	23.53	35.29	47.06	58.82	**8.5**
8.6	11.63	23.26	34.88	46.51	58.14	**8.6**
8.7	11.49	22.99	34.48	45.98	57.47	**8.7**
8.8	11.36	22.73	34.09	45.45	56.82	**8.8**
8.9	11.24	22.47	33.71	44.94	56.18	**8.9**
9.0	11.11	22.22	33.33	44.44	55.56	**9.0**
9.1	10.99	21.98	32.97	43.96	54.95	**9.1**
9.2	10.87	21.74	32.61	43.48	54.35	**9.2**
9.3	10.75	21.51	32.26	43.01	53.76	**9.3**
9.4	10.64	21.28	31.91	42.55	53.19	**9.4**
9.5	10.53	21.05	31.58	42.11	52.63	**9.5**
9.6	10.42	20.83	31.25	41.67	52.08	**9.6**
9.7	10.31	20.62	30.93	41.24	51.55	**9.7**
9.8	10.20	20.41	30.61	40.82	51.02	**9.8**
9.9	10.10	20.20	30.30	40.40	50.51	**9.9**
10.0	10.00	20.00	30.00	40.00	50.00	**10.0**
DIFF.	1	2	3	4	5	DIFF.

TABLE IV. Lengths of Sub-Sections.

DIFF.	6	7	8	9	10	DIFF.
5.1	117.65	137.25	156.86	176.47	196.08	5.1
5.2	115.39	134.62	153.85	173.08	192.31	5.2
5.3	113.21	132.08	150.94	169.81	188.68	5.3
5.4	111.11	129.63	148.15	166.67	185.19	5.4
5.5	109.09	127.27	145.45	163.64	181.82	5.5
5.6	107.14	125.00	142.86	160.71	178.57	5.6
5.7	105.26	122.81	140.35	157.89	175.44	5.7
5.8	103.45	120.69	137.93	155.17	172.41	5.8
5.9	101.69	118.64	135.59	152.54	169.49	5.9
6.0	100.00	116.67	133.33	150.00	166.67	6.0
6.1	98.36	114.75	131.15	147.54	163.93	6.1
6.2	96.77	112.90	129.03	145.16	161.29	6.2
6.3	95.24	111.11	126.98	142.86	158.73	6.3
6.4	93.75	109.38	125.00	140.63	156.25	6.4
6.5	92.31	107.69	123.08	138.46	153.85	6.5
6.6	90.91	106.06	121.21	136.36	151.52	6.6
6.7	89.55	104.48	119.40	134.33	149.25	6.7
6.8	88.24	102.94	117.65	132.35	147.06	6.8
6.9	86.96	101.45	115.94	130.43	144.93	6.9
7.0	85.71	100.00	114.29	128.57	142.86	7.0
7.1	84.51	98.59	112.67	126.76	140.85	7.1
7.2	83.33	97.22	111.11	125.00	138.89	7.2
7.3	82.19	95.89	109.59	123.29	136.99	7.3
7.4	81.08	94.59	108.11	121.62	135.14	7.4
7.5	80.00	93.33	106.67	120.00	133.33	7.5
7.6	78.95	92.11	105.26	118.42	131.58	7.6
7.7	77.92	90.91	103.90	116.88	129.87	7.7
7.8	76.92	89.74	102.56	115.38	128.21	7.8
7.9	75.95	88.61	101.27	113.92	126.58	7.9
8.0	75.00	87.50	100.00	112.50	125.00	8.0
8.1	74.07	86.42	98.77	111.11	123.46	8.1
8.2	73.17	85.37	97.56	109.76	121.95	8.2
8.3	72.29	84.34	96.39	108.43	120.48	8.3
8.4	71.43	83.33	95.24	107.14	119.05	8.4
8.5	70.59	82.35	94.12	105.88	117.65	8.5
8.6	69.77	81.40	93.02	104.65	116.28	8.6
8.7	68.97	80.46	91.95	103.45	114.94	8.7
8.8	68.18	79.55	90.91	102.27	113.64	8.8
8.9	67.42	78.65	89.89	101.12	112.36	8.9
9.0	66.67	77.78	88.89	100.00	111.11	9.0
9.1	65.93	76.92	87.91	98.90	109.89	9.1
9.2	65.22	76.09	86.96	97.83	108.70	9.2
9.3	64.52	75.27	86.02	96.77	107.53	9.3
9.4	63.83	74.47	85.11	95.74	106.38	9.4
9.5	63.16	73.68	84.21	94.74	105.26	9.5
9.6	62.50	72.92	83.33	93.75	104.17	9.6
9.7	61.86	72.17	82.47	92.78	103.09	9.7
9.8	61.22	71.43	81.63	91.84	102.04	9.8
9.9	60.61	70.71	80.81	90.91	101.01	9.9
10.0	60.00	70.00	80.00	90.00	100.00	10.0
DIFF.	6	7	8	9	10	DIFF.

TABLE IV. **Lengths of Sub-Sections.**

DIFF.	1	2	3	4	5	DIFF.
10.1	9.90	19.80	29.70	39.60	49.50	**10.1**
10.2	9.80	19.61	29.41	39.22	49.02	**10.2**
10.3	9.71	19.42	29.13	38.83	48.54	**10.3**
10.4	9.62	19.23	28.85	38.46	48.08	**10.4**
10.5	9.52	19.05	28.57	38.10	47.62	**10.5**
10.6	9.43	18.87	28.30	37.74	47.17	**10.6**
10.7	9.35	18.69	28.04	37.38	46.73	**10.7**
10.8	9.26	18.52	27.78	37.04	46.30	**10.8**
10.9	9.17	18.35	27.52	36.70	45.87	**10.9**
11.0	9.09	18.18	27.27	36.36	45.45	**11.0**
11.1	9.01	18.02	27.03	36.04	45.05	**11.1**
11.2	8.93	17.86	26.79	35.71	44.64	**11.2**
11.3	8.85	17.70	26.55	35.40	44.25	**11.3**
11.4	8.77	17.54	26.32	35.09	43.86	**11.4**
11.5	8.70	17.39	26.09	34.78	43.48	**11.5**
11.6	8.62	17.24	25.86	34.48	43.10	**11.6**
11.7	8.55	17.09	25.64	34.19	42.74	**11.7**
11.8	8.47	16.95	25.42	33.90	42.37	**11.8**
11.9	8.40	16.81	25.21	33.61	42.02	**11.9**
12.0	8.33	16.67	25.00	33.33	41.67	**12.0**
12.1	8.26	16.53	24.79	33.06	41.32	**12.1**
12.2	8.20	16.39	24.59	32.79	40.98	**12.2**
12.3	8.13	16.26	24.39	32.52	40.65	**12.3**
12.4	8.06	16.13	24.19	32.26	40.32	**12.4**
12.5	8.00	16.00	24.00	32.00	40.00	**12.5**
12.6	7.94	15.87	23.81	31.75	39.68	**12.6**
12.7	7.87	15.75	23.62	31.50	39.37	**12.7**
12.8	7.81	15.63	23.44	31.25	39.06	**12.8**
12.9	7.75	15.50	23.26	31.01	38.76	**12.9**
13.0	7.69	15.38	23.08	30.77	38.46	**13.0**
13.1	7.63	15.27	22.90	30.53	38.17	**13.1**
13.2	7.58	15.15	22.73	30.30	37.88	**13.2**
13.3	7.52	15.04	22.56	30.08	37.59	**13.3**
13.4	7.46	14.93	22.39	29.85	37.31	**13.4**
13.5	7.41	14.81	22.22	29.63	37.04	**13.5**
13.6	7.35	14.71	22.06	29.41	36.76	**13.6**
13.7	7.30	14.60	21.90	29.20	36.50	**13.7**
13.8	7.25	14.49	21.74	28.99	36.23	**13.8**
13.9	7.19	14.39	21.58	28.78	35.97	**13.9**
14.0	7.14	14.29	21.43	28.57	35.71	**14.0**
14.1	7.09	14.18	21.28	28.37	35.46	**14.1**
14.2	7.04	14.09	21.13	28.17	35.21	**14.2**
14.3	6.99	13.99	20.98	27.97	34.97	**14.3**
14.4	6.94	13.89	20.83	27.78	34.72	**14.4**
14.5	6.90	13.79	20.69	27.59	34.48	**14.5**
14.6	6.85	13.70	20.55	27.40	34.25	**14.6**
14.7	6.80	13.61	20.41	27.21	34.01	**14.7**
14.8	6.76	13.51	20.27	27.03	33.78	**14.8**
14.9	6.71	13.42	20.13	26.85	33.56	**14.9**
15.0	6.67	13.33	20.00	26.67	33.33	**15.0**
DIFF.	1	2	3	4	5	DIFF.

TABLE IV. **Lengths of Sub-Sections.**

DIFF.	6	7	8	9	10	DIFF.
10.1	59.41	69.31	79.21	89.11	99.01	**10.1**
10.2	58.82	68.63	78.43	88.24	98.04	**10.2**
10.3	58.25	67.96	77.67	87.38	97.09	**10.3**
10.4	57.69	67.31	76.92	86.54	96.16	**10.4**
10.5	57.14	66.67	76.19	85.71	95.24	**10.5**
10.6	56.60	66.04	75.47	84.91	94.34	**10.6**
10.7	56.07	65.42	74.77	84.11	93.46	**10.7**
10.8	55.56	64.82	74.07	83.33	92.59	**10.8**
10.9	55.05	64.22	73.39	82.57	91.74	**10.9**
11.0	54.55	63.64	72.73	81.82	90.91	**11.0**
11.1	54.05	63.06	72.07	81.08	90.09	**11.1**
11.2	53.57	62.50	71.43	80.36	89.29	**11.2**
11.3	53.10	61.95	70.80	79.65	88.50	**11.3**
11.4	52.63	61.40	70.18	78.95	87.72	**11.4**
11.5	52.17	60.87	69.57	78.26	86.96	**11.5**
11.6	51.72	60.34	68.97	77.59	86.21	**11.6**
11.7	51.28	59.83	68.38	76.92	85.47	**11.7**
11.8	50.85	59.32	67.80	76.27	84.75	**11.8**
11.9	50.42	58.82	67.23	75.63	84.03	**11.9**
12.0	50.00	58.33	66.67	75.00	83.33	**12.0**
12.1	49.59	57.85	66.12	74.38	82.64	**12.1**
12.2	49.18	57.38	65.57	73.77	81.97	**12.2**
12.3	48.78	56.91	65.04	73.17	81.30	**12.3**
12.4	48.39	56.45	64.52	72.58	80.65	**12.4**
12.5	48.00	56.00	64.00	72.00	80.00	**12.5**
12.6	47.62	55.56	63.49	71.43	79.37	**12.6**
12.7	47.24	55.12	62.99	70.87	78.74	**12.7**
12.8	46.88	54.69	62.50	70.31	78.13	**12.8**
12.9	46.51	54.26	62.02	69.77	77.52	**12.9**
13.0	46.15	53.85	61.54	69.23	76.92	**13.0**
13.1	45.80	53.44	61.07	68.70	76.34	**13.1**
13.2	45.45	53.03	60.61	68.18	75.76	**13.2**
13.3	45.11	52.63	60.15	67.67	75.19	**13.3**
13.4	44.78	52.24	59.70	67.16	74.63	**13.4**
13.5	44.44	51.85	59.26	66.67	74.07	**13.5**
13.6	44.12	51.47	58.82	66.18	73.53	**13.6**
13.7	43.80	51.10	58.39	65.69	72.99	**13.7**
13.8	43.48	50.72	57.97	65.22	72.46	**13.8**
13.9	43.17	50.36	57.55	64.75	71.94	**13.9**
14.0	42.86	50.00	57.14	64.29	71.43	**14.0**
14.1	42.55	49.65	56.74	63.83	70.92	**14.1**
14.2	42.25	49.30	56.34	63.38	70.42	**14.2**
14.3	41.96	48.95	55.94	62.94	69.93	**14.3**
14.4	41.67	48.61	55.56	62.50	69.44	**14.4**
14.5	41.38	48.28	55.17	62.07	68.97	**14.5**
14.6	41.10	47.95	54.79	61.64	68.49	**14.6**
14.7	40.82	47.62	54.42	61.22	68.03	**14.7**
14.8	40.54	47.30	54.05	60.81	67.57	**14.8**
14.9	40.27	46.98	53.69	60.40	67.11	**14.9**
15.0	40.00	46.67	53.33	60.00	66.67	**15.0**
DIFF.	6	7	8	9	10	DIFF.

TABLE IV. Lengths of Sub-Sections.

DIFF.	1	2	3	4	5	DIFF.
15.1	6.62	13.25	19.87	26.49	33.11	**15.1**
15.2	6.58	13.16	19.74	26.32	32.89	**15.2**
15.3	6.54	13.07	19.61	26.14	32.68	**15.3**
15.4	6.49	12.99	19.48	25.97	32.47	**15.4**
15.5	6.45	12.90	19.35	25.81	32.26	**15.5**
15.6	6.41	12.82	19.23	25.64	32.05	**15.6**
15.7	6.37	12.74	19.11	25.48	31.85	**15.7**
15.8	6.33	12.66	18.99	25.32	31.65	**15.8**
15.9	6.29	12.58	18.87	25.16	31.45	**15.9**
16.0	6.25	12.50	18.75	25.00	31.25	**16.0**
16.1	6.21	12.42	18.63	24.84	31.06	**16.1**
16.2	6.17	12.35	18.52	24.69	30.86	**16.2**
16.3	6.13	12.27	18.40	24.54	30.67	**16.3**
16.4	6.10	12.20	18.29	24.39	30.49	**16.4**
16.5	6.06	12.12	18.18	24.24	30.30	**16.5**
16.6	6.02	12.05	18.07	24.10	30.12	**16.6**
16.7	5.99	11.98	17.96	23.95	29.94	**16.7**
16.8	5.95	11.90	17.86	23.81	29.76	**16.8**
16.9	5.92	11.83	17.75	23.67	29.59	**16.9**
17.0	5.88	11.76	17.65	23.53	29.41	**17.0**
17.1	5.85	11.70	17.54	23.39	29.24	**17.1**
17.2	5.81	11.63	17.44	23.26	29.07	**17.2**
17.3	5.78	11.56	17.34	23.12	28.90	**17.3**
17.4	5.75	11.49	17.24	22.99	28.74	**17.4**
17.5	5.71	11.43	17.14	22.86	28.57	**17.5**
17.6	5.68	11.36	17.05	22.73	28.41	**17.6**
17.7	5.65	11.30	16.95	22.60	28.25	**17.7**
17.8	5.62	11.24	16.85	22.47	28.09	**17.8**
17.9	5.59	11.17	16.76	22.35	27.93	**17.9**
18.0	5.56	11.11	16.67	22.22	27.78	**18.0**
18.1	5.52	11.05	16.57	22.10	27.62	**18.1**
18.2	5.49	10.99	16.48	21.98	27.47	**18.2**
18.3	5.46	10.93	16.39	21.86	27.32	**18.3**
18.4	5.43	10.87	16.30	21.74	27.17	**18.4**
18.5	5.41	10.81	16.22	21.62	27.03	**18.5**
18.6	5.38	10.75	16.13	21.51	26.88	**18.6**
18.7	5.35	10.70	16.04	21.39	26.74	**18.7**
18.8	5.32	10.64	15.96	21.28	26.60	**18.8**
18.9	5.29	10.58	15.87	21.16	26.46	**18.9**
19.0	5.26	10.53	15.79	21.05	26.32	**19.0**
19.1	5.24	10.47	15.71	20.94	26.18	**19.1**
19.2	5.21	10.42	15.62	20.83	26.04	**19.2**
19.3	5.18	10.36	15.54	20.73	25.91	**19.3**
19.4	5.15	10.31	15.46	20.62	25.77	**19.4**
19.5	5.13	10.26	15.38	20.51	25.64	**19.5**
19.6	5.10	10.20	15.31	20.41	25.51	**19.6**
19.7	5.08	10.15	15.23	20.30	25.38	**19.7**
19.8	5.05	10.10	15.15	20.20	25.25	**19.8**
19.9	5.03	10.05	15.08	20.10	25.13	**19.9**
20.0	5.00	10.00	15.00	20.00	25.00	**20.0**
DIFF.	1	2	3	4	5	DIFF.

TABLE IV. Lengths of Sub-Sections.

DIFF.	6	7	8	9	10	DIFF.
15.1	39.74	46.36	52.98	59.60	66.23	15.1
15.2	39.47	46.05	52.63	59.21	65.79	15.2
15.3	39.22	45.75	52.29	58.82	65.36	15.3
15.4	38.96	45.45	51.95	58.44	64.94	15.4
15.5	38.71	45.16	51.61	58.06	64.52	15.5
15.6	38.46	44.87	51.28	57.69	64.10	15.6
15.7	38.22	44.59	50.96	57.32	63.69	15.7
15.8	37.97	44.30	50.63	56.96	63.29	15.8
15.9	37.74	44.03	50.31	56.60	62.89	15.9
16.0	37.50	43.75	50.00	56.25	62.50	16.0
16.1	37.27	43.48	49.69	55.90	62.11	16.1
16.2	37.04	43.21	49.38	55.56	61.73	16.2
16.3	36.81	42.94	49.08	55.21	61.35	16.3
16.4	36.59	42.68	48.78	54.88	60.98	16.4
16.5	36.36	42.42	48.48	54.55	60.61	16.5
16.6	36.14	42.17	48.19	54.22	60.24	16.6
16.7	35.93	41.92	47.90	53.89	59.88	16.7
16.8	35.71	41.67	47.62	53.57	59.52	16.8
16.9	35.50	41.42	47.34	53.25	59.17	16.9
17.0	35.29	41.18	47.06	52.94	58.82	17.0
17.1	35.09	40.94	46.78	52.63	58.48	17.1
17.2	34.88	40.70	46.51	52.33	58.14	17.2
17.3	34.68	40.46	46.24	52.02	57.80	17.3
17.4	34.48	40.23	45.98	51.72	57.47	17.4
17.5	34.29	40.00	45.71	51.43	57.14	17.5
17.6	34.09	39.77	45.45	51.14	56.82	17.6
17.7	33.90	39.55	45.20	50.85	56.50	17.7
17.8	33.71	39.33	44.94	50.56	56.18	17.8
17.9	33.52	39.11	44.69	50.28	55.87	17.9
18.0	33.33	38.89	44.44	50.00	55.56	18.0
18.1	33.15	38.67	44.20	49.72	55.25	18.1
18.2	32.97	38.46	43.96	49.45	54.95	18.2
18.3	32.79	38.25	43.72	49.18	54.64	18.3
18.4	32.61	38.04	43.48	48.91	54.35	18.4
18.5	32.43	37.84	43.24	48.65	54.05	18.5
18.6	32.26	37.63	43.01	48.39	53.76	18.6
18.7	32.09	37.43	42.78	48.13	53.48	18.7
18.8	31.91	37.23	42.55	47.87	53.19	18.8
18.9	31.75	37.04	42.33	47.62	52.91	18.9
19.0	31.58	36.84	42.11	47.37	52.63	19.0
19.1	31.41	36.65	41.88	47.12	52.36	19.1
19.2	31.25	36.46	41.67	46.87	52.08	19.2
19.3	31.09	36.27	41.45	46.63	51.81	19.3
19.4	30.93	36.08	41.24	46.39	51.55	19.4
19.5	30.77	35.90	41.03	46.15	51.28	19.5
19.6	30.61	35.71	40.82	45.92	51.02	19.6
19.7	30.46	35.53	40.61	45.68	50.76	19.7
19.8	30.30	35.35	40.40	45.45	50.51	19.8
19.9	30.15	35.18	40.20	45.23	50.25	19.9
20.0	30.00	35.00	40.00	45.00	50.00	20.0
DIFF.	6	7	8	9	10	DIFF.

TABLE V. **Sub-Section Augments for Bases.**

S. or D.	0°	1°	2°	3°	4°	5°
1	Infinite.	57.29	28.64	19.08	14.30	11.43
2	....	114.58	57.27	38.16	28.60	22.86
3	....	171.87	85.91	57.24	42.90	34.29
4	....	229.16	114.55	76.32	57.20	45.72
5	....	286.45	143.18	95.41	71.50	57.15
6	....	343.74	171.82	114.49	85.80	68.58
7	....	401.03	200.45	133.57	100.10	80.01
8	....	458.32	229.09	152.65	114.41	91.44
9	....	515.61	257.73	171.73	128.71	102.87
10	....	572.90	286.36	190.81	143.01	114.30

S. or D.	6°	7°	8°	9°	10°	11°
1	9.51	8.14	7.12	6.31	5.67	5.14
2	19.03	16.29	14.23	12.63	11.34	10.29
3	28.54	24.43	21.35	18.94	17.01	15.43
4	38.06	32.58	28.46	25.26	22.69	20.58
5	47.57	40.72	35.58	31.57	28.36	25.72
6	57.09	48.87	42.69	37.88	34.03	30.87
7	66.60	57.01	49.81	44.20	39.70	36.01
8	76.12	65.15	56.92	50.51	45.37	41.16
9	85.63	73.30	64.04	56.82	51.04	46.30
10	95.14	81.44	71.15	63.14	56.71	51.45

S. or D.	12°	13°	14°	15°	16°	17°
1	4.70	4.33	4.01	3.73	3.49	3.27
2	9.41	8.66	8.02	7.46	6.97	6.54
3	14.11	12.99	12.03	11.20	10.46	9.81
4	18.82	17.33	16.04	14.93	13.95	13.08
5	23.52	21.66	20.05	18.66	17.44	16.35
6	28.23	25.99	24.06	22.39	20.92	19.63
7	32.93	30.32	28.08	26.12	24.41	22.90
8	37.64	34.65	32.09	29.86	27.90	26.17
9	42.34	38.98	36.10	33.59	31.39	29.44
10	47.05	43.31	40.11	37.32	34.87	32.71

TABLE V. Sub-Section Augments for Bases.

S. or D.	18°	19°	20°	21°	22°	23°
1	3.08	2.90	2.75	2.61	2.48	2.36
2	6.16	5.81	5.49	5.21	4.95	4.71
3	9.23	8.71	8.24	7.82	7.43	7.07
4	12.31	11.62	10.99	10.42	9.90	9.42
5	15.39	14.52	13.74	13.03	12.38	11.78
6	18.47	17.43	16.49	15.63	14.85	14.14
7	21.54	20.33	19.23	18.24	17.33	16.49
8	24.62	23.23	21.98	20.84	19.80	18.85
9	27.70	26.14	24.73	23.45	22.28	21.20
10	30.78	29.04	27.47	26.05	24.75	23.56

S. or D.	24°	25°	26°	27°	28°	29°
1	2.25	2.14	2.05	1.96	1.88	1.80
2	4.49	4.29	4.10	3.93	3.76	3.61
3	6.74	6.43	6.15	5.89	5.64	5.41
4	8.98	8.58	8.20	7.85	7.52	7.22
5	11.23	10.72	10.25	9.81	9.40	9.02
6	13.48	12.87	12.30	11.78	11.28	10.82
7	15.72	15.01	14.35	13.74	13.16	12.63
8	17.97	17.16	16.40	15.70	15.05	14.43
9	20.21	19.30	18.45	17.66	16.93	16.24
10	22.46	21.45	20.50	19.63	18.81	18.04

S. or D.	30°	31°	32°	33°	34°	35°
1	1.73	1.66	1.60	1.54	1.48	1.43
2	3.46	3.33	3.20	3.08	2.97	2.86
3	5.20	4.99	4.80	4.62	4.45	4.28
4	6.93	6.66	6.40	6.16	5.93	5.71
5	8.66	8.32	8.00	7.70	7.41	7.14
6	10.39	9.99	9.60	9.24	8.90	8.57
7	12.12	11.65	11.20	10.78	10.38	10.00
8	13.86	13.31	12.80	12.32	11.86	11.42
9	15.59	14.98	14.40	13.86	13.34	12.85
10	17.32	16.64	16.00	15.40	14.83	14.28

TABLE VI. **Distances out.**

Side Heights	SIDE SLOPE					
	$2\frac{3}{4}$ to 1.	**$2\frac{1}{2}$ to 1.**	**$2\frac{1}{4}$ to 1.**	**2 to 1.**	**$1\frac{3}{4}$ to 1.**	**$1\frac{1}{2}$ to 1.**
1	2.75	2.50	2.25	2.00	1.75	1.50
2	5.50	5.00	4.50	4.00	3.50	3.00
3	8.25	7.50	6.75	6.00	5.25	4.50
4	11.00	10.00	9.00	8.00	7.00	6.00
5	13.75	12.50	11.25	10.00	8.75	7.50
6	16.50	15.00	13.50	12.00	10.50	9.00
7	19.25	17.50	15.75	14.00	12.25	10.50
8	22.00	20.00	18.00	16.00	14.00	12.00
9	24.75	22.50	20.25	18.00	15.75	13.50
10	27.50	25.00	22.50	20.00	17.50	15.00
11	30.25	27.50	24.75	22.00	19.25	16.50
12	33.00	30.00	27.00	24.00	21.00	18.00
13	35.75	32.50	29.25	26.00	22.75	19.50
14	38.50	35.00	31.50	28.00	24.50	21.00
15	41.25	37.50	33.75	30.00	26.25	22.50
16	44.00	40.00	36.00	32.00	28.00	24.00
17	46.75	42.50	38.25	34.00	29.75	25.50
18	49.50	45.00	40.50	36.00	31.50	27.00
19	52.25	47.50	42.75	38.00	33.25	28.50
20	55.00	50.00	45.00	40.00	35.00	30.00
21	57.75	52.50	47.25	42.00	36.75	31.50
22	60.50	55.00	49.50	44.00	38.50	33.00
23	63.25	57.50	51.75	46.00	40.25	34.50
24	66.00	60.00	54.00	48.00	42.00	36.00
25	68.75	62.50	56.25	50.00	43.75	37.50
26	71.50	65.00	58.50	52.00	45.50	39.00
27	74.25	67.50	60.75	54.00	47.25	40.50
28	77.00	70.00	63.00	56.00	49.00	42.00
29	79.75	72.50	65.25	58.00	50.75	43.50
30	82.50	75.00	67.50	60.00	52.50	45.00
31	85.25	77.50	69.75	62.00	54.25	46.50
32	88.00	80.00	72.00	64.00	56.00	48.00
33	90.75	82.50	74.25	66.00	57.75	49.50
34	93.50	85.00	76.50	68.00	59.50	51.00
35	96.25	87.50	78.75	70.00	61.25	52.50
36	99.00	90.00	81.00	72.00	63.00	54.00
37	101.75	92.50	83.25	74.00	64.75	55.50
38	104.50	95.00	85.50	76.00	66.50	57.00
39	107.25	97.50	87.75	78.00	68.25	58.50
40	110.00	100.00	90.00	80.00	70.00	60.00
41	112.75	102.50	92.25	82.00	71.75	61.50
42	115.50	105.00	94.50	84.00	73.50	63.00
43	118.25	107.50	96.75	86.00	75.25	64.50
44	121.00	110.00	99.00	88.00	77.00	66.00
45	123.75	112.50	101.25	90.00	78.75	67.50
46	126.50	115.00	103.50	92.00	80.50	69.00
47	129.25	117.50	105.75	94.00	82.25	70.50
48	132.00	120.00	108.00	96.00	84.00	72.00
49	134.75	122.50	110.25	98.00	85.75	73.50
50	137.50	125.00	112.50	100.00	87.50	75.00
51	140.25	127.50	114.75	102.00	89.25	76.50
52	143.00	130.00	117.00	104.00	91.00	78.00
53	145.75	132.50	119.25	106.00	92.75	79.50
54	148.50	135.00	121.50	108.00	94.50	81.00
55	151.25	137.50	123.75	110.00	96.25	82.50
56	154.00	140.00	126.00	112.00	98.00	84.00
57	156.75	142.50	128.25	114.00	99.75	85.50
Side Heights	**$2\frac{3}{4}$ to 1.**	**$2\frac{1}{2}$ to 1.**	**$2\frac{1}{4}$ to 1.**	**2 to 1.**	**$1\frac{3}{4}$ to 1.**	**$1\frac{1}{2}$ to 1.**

TABLE VI. **Distances out.**

Side Heights	SIDE SLOPE					
	1¼ to 1.	1 to 1.	¾ to 1.	½ to 1.	⅓ to 1.	¼ to 1.
1	1.25	1.00	0.75	0.50	0.33	0.25
2	2.50	2.00	1.50	1.00	0.67	0.50
3	3.75	3.00	2.25	1.50	1.00	0.75
4	5.00	4.00	3.00	2.00	1.33	1.00
5	6.25	5.00	3.75	2.50	1.67	1.25
6	7.50	6.00	4.50	3.00	2.00	1.50
7	8.75	7.00	5.25	3.50	2.33	1.75
8	10.00	8.00	6.00	4.00	2.67	2.00
9	11.25	9.00	6.75	4.50	3.00	2.25
10	12.50	10.00	7.50	5.00	3.33	2.50
11	13.75	11.00	8.25	5.50	3.67	2.75
12	15.00	12.00	9.00	6.00	4.00	3.00
13	16.25	13.00	9.75	6.50	4.33	3.25
14	17.50	14.00	10.50	7.00	4.67	3.50
15	18.75	15.00	11.25	7.50	5.00	3.75
16	20.00	16.00	12.00	8.00	5.33	4.00
17	21.25	17.00	12.75	8.50	5.67	4.25
18	22.50	18.00	13.50	9.00	6.00	4.50
19	23.75	19.00	14.25	9.50	6.33	4.75
20	25.00	20.00	15.00	10.00	6.67	5.00
21	26.25	21.00	15.75	10.50	7.00	5.25
22	27.50	22.00	16.50	11.00	7.33	5.50
23	28.75	23.00	17.25	11.50	7.67	5.75
24	30.00	24.00	18.00	12.00	8.00	6.00
25	31.25	25.00	18.75	12.50	8.33	6.25
26	32.50	26.00	19.50	13.00	8.67	6.50
27	33.75	27.00	20.25	13.50	9.00	6.75
28	35.00	28.00	21.00	14.00	9.33	7.00
29	36.25	29.00	21.75	14.50	9.67	7.25
30	37.50	30.00	22.50	15.00	10.00	7.50
31	38.75	31.00	23.25	15.50	10.33	7.75
32	40.00	32.00	24.00	16.00	10.67	8.00
33	41.25	33.00	24.75	16.50	11.00	8.25
34	42.50	34.00	25.50	17.00	11.33	8.50
35	43.75	35.00	26.25	17.50	11.67	8.75
36	45.00	36.00	27.00	18.00	12.00	9.00
37	46.25	37.00	27.75	18.50	12.33	9.25
38	47.50	38.00	28.50	19.00	12.67	9.50
39	48.75	39.00	29.25	19.50	13.00	9.75
40	50.00	40.00	30.00	20.00	13.33	10.00
41	51.25	41.00	30.75	20.50	13.67	10.25
42	52.50	42.00	31.50	21.00	14.00	10.50
43	53.75	43.00	32.25	21.50	14.33	10.75
44	55.00	44.00	33.00	22.00	14.67	11.00
45	56.25	45.00	33.75	22.50	15.00	11.25
46	57.50	46.00	34.50	23.00	15.33	11.50
47	58.75	47.00	35.25	23.50	15.67	11.75
48	60.00	48.00	36.00	24.00	16.00	12.00
49	61.25	49.00	36.75	24.50	16.33	12.25
50	62.50	50.00	37.50	25.00	16.67	12.50
51	63.75	51.00	38.25	25.50	17.00	12.75
52	65.00	52.00	39.00	26.00	17.33	13.00
53	66.25	53.00	39.75	26.50	17.67	13.25
54	67.50	54.00	40.50	27.00	18.00	13.50
55	68.75	55.00	41.25	27.50	18.33	13.75
56	70.00	56.00	42.00	28.00	18.67	14.00
57	71.25	57.00	42.75	28.50	19.00	14.25
Side Heights	1¼ to 1.	1 to 1.	¾ to 1.	½ to 1.	⅓ to 1.	¼ to 1.

TABLE VI. Distances out.

Side Heights	SIDE SLOPE					
	2¾ to 1.	2½ to 1.	2¼ to 1.	2 to 1.	1¾ to 1.	1½ to 1.
58	159.50	145.00	130.50	116.00	101.50	87.00
59	162.25	147.50	132.75	118.00	103.25	88.50
60	165.00	150.00	135.00	120.00	105.00	90.00
61	167.75	152.50	137.25	122.00	106.75	91.50
62	170.50	155.00	139.50	124.00	108.50	93.00
63	173.25	157.50	141.75	126.00	110.25	94.50
64	176.00	160.00	144.00	128.00	112.00	96.00
65	178.75	162.50	146.25	130.00	113.75	97.50
66	181.50	165.00	148.50	132.00	115.50	99.00
67	184.25	167.50	150.75	134.00	117.25	100.50
68	187.00	170.00	153.00	136.00	119.00	102.00
69	189.75	172.50	155.25	138.00	120.75	103.50
70	192.50	175.00	157.50	140.00	122.50	105 00
71	195.25	177.50	159.75	142.00	124.25	106.50
72	198.00	180.00	162.00	144.00	126.00	108.00
73	200.75	182.50	164.25	146.00	127.75	109.50
74	203.50	185.00	166.50	148.00	129.50	111.00
75	206.25	187.50	168.75	150.00	131.25	112.50
76	209.00	190.00	171.00	152.00	133.00	114.00
77	211.75	192.50	173.25	154.00	134.75	115.50
78	214.50	195.00	175.50	156.00	136.50	117.00
79	217.25	197.50	177.75	158.00	138.25	118.50
80	220.00	200.00	180.00	160.00	140.00	120.00
81	222.75	202.50	182.25	162.00	141.75	121.50
82	225.50	205.00	184.50	164.00	143.50	123.00
83	228.25	207.50	186.75	166.00	145.25	124.50
84	231.00	210.00	189.00	168.00	147.00	126.00
85	233.75	212.50	191.25	170.00	148.75	127.50
86	236.50	215.00	193.50	172.00	150.50	129.00
87	239.25	217.50	195.75	174.00	152.25	130.50
88	242.00	220.00	198.00	176.00	154.00	132.00
89	244.75	222.50	200.25	178.00	155.75	133.50
90	247.50	225.00	202.50	180.00	157.50	135.00
91	250.25	227.50	204.75	182.00	159.25	136.50
92	253.00	230.00	207.00	184.00	161.00	138.00
93	255.75	232.50	209.25	186.00	162.75	139.50
94	258.50	235.00	211.50	188.00	164.50	141.00
95	261.25	237.50	213.75	190.00	166.25	142.50
96	264.00	240.00	216.00	192.00	168.00	144.00
97	266.75	242.50	218.25	194.00	169.75	145.50
98	269.50	245.00	220.50	196.00	171.50	147.00
99	272.25	247.50	222.75	198.00	173.25	148.50
100	275.00	250.00	225.00	200.00	175.00	150.00
101	277.75	252.50	227.25	202.00	176.75	151.50
102	280.50	255.00	229.50	204.00	178.50	153.00
103	283.25	257.50	231.75	206.00	180.25	154.50
104	286.00	260.00	234.00	208.00	182.00	156.00
105	288.75	262.50	236.25	210.00	183.75	157.50
106	291.50	265.00	238.50	212.00	185.50	159.00
107	294.25	267.50	240.75	214.00	187.25	160.50
108	297.00	270.00	243.00	216.00	189.00	162.00
109	299.75	272.50	245.25	218.00	190.75	163.50
110	302.50	275.00	247.50	220.00	192.50	165.00
111	305.25	277.50	249.75	222.00	194.25	166.50
112	308.00	280.00	252.00	224.00	196.00	168.00
113	310.75	282.50	254.25	226.00	197.75	169.50
114	313.50	285.00	256.50	228.00	199.50	171.00
Side Heights	2¾ to 1.	2½ to 1.	2¼ to 1.	2 to 1.	1¾ to 1.	1½ to 1.

TABLE VI. **Distances out.**

Side Heights	SIDE SLOPE					
	$1\frac{1}{4}$ to 1.	1 to 1.	$\frac{3}{4}$ to 1.	$\frac{1}{2}$ to 1.	$\frac{1}{3}$ to 1.	$\frac{1}{4}$ to 1.
58	72.50	58.00	43.50	29.00	19.33	14.50
59	73.75	59.00	44.25	29.50	19.67	14.75
60	75.00	60.00	45.00	30.00	20.00	15.00
61	76.25	61.00	45.75	30.50	20.33	15.25
62	77.50	62.00	46.50	31.00	20.67	15.50
63	78.75	63.00	47.25	31.50	21.00	15.75
64	80.00	64.00	48.00	32.00	21.33	16.00
65	81.25	65.00	48.75	32.50	21.67	16.25
66	82.50	66.00	49.50	33.00	22.00	16.50
67	83.75	67.00	50.25	33.50	22.33	16.75
68	85.00	68.00	51.00	34.00	22.67	17.00
69	86.25	69.00	51.75	34.50	23.00	17.25
70	87.50	70.00	52.50	35.00	23.33	17.50
71	88.75	71.00	53.25	35.50	23.67	17.75
72	90.00	72.00	54.00	36.00	24.00	18.00
73	91.25	73.00	54.75	36.50	24.33	18.25
74	92.50	74.00	55.50	37.00	24.67	18.50
75	93.75	75.00	56.25	37.50	25.00	18.75
76	95.00	76.00	57.00	38.00	25.33	19.00
77	96.25	77.00	57.75	38.50	25.67	19.25
78	97.50	78.00	58.50	39.00	26.00	19.50
79	98.75	79.00	59.25	39.50	26.33	19.75
80	100.00	80.00	60.00	40.00	26.67	20.00
81	101.25	81.00	60.75	40.50	27.00	20.25
82	102.50	82.00	61.50	41.00	27.33	20.50
83	103.75	83.00	62.25	41.50	27.67	20.75
84	105.00	84.00	63.00	42.00	28.00	21.00
85	106.25	85.00	63.75	42.50	28.33	21.25
86	107.50	86.00	64.50	43.00	28.67	21.50
87	108.75	87.00	65.25	43.50	29.00	21.75
88	110.00	88.00	66.00	44.00	29.33	22.00
89	111.25	89.00	66.75	44.50	29.67	22.25
90	112.50	90.00	67.50	45.00	30.00	22.50
91	113.75	91.00	68.25	45.50	30.33	22.75
92	115.00	92.00	69.00	46.00	30.67	23.00
93	116.25	93.00	69.75	46.50	31.00	23.25
94	117.50	94.00	70.50	47.00	31.33	23.50
95	118.75	95.00	71.25	47.50	31.67	23.75
96	120.00	96.00	72.00	48.00	32.00	24.00
97	121.25	97.00	72.75	48.50	32.33	24.25
98	122.50	98.00	73.50	49.00	32.67	24.50
99	123.75	99.00	74.25	49.50	33.00	24.75
100	125.00	100.00	75.00	50.00	33.33	25.00
101	126.25	101.00	75.75	50.50	33.67	25.25
102	127.50	102.00	76.50	51.00	34.00	25.50
103	128.75	103.00	77.25	51.50	34.33	25.75
104	130.00	104.00	78.00	52.00	34.67	26.00
105	131.25	105.00	78.75	52.50	35.00	26.25
106	132.50	106.00	79.50	53.00	35.33	26.50
107	133.75	107.00	80.25	53.50	35.67	26.75
108	135.00	108.00	81.00	54.00	36.00	27.00
109	136.25	109.00	81.75	54.50	36.33	27.25
110	137.50	110.00	82.50	55.00	36.67	27.50
111	138.75	111.00	83.25	55.50	37.00	27.75
112	140.00	112.00	84.00	56.00	37.33	28.00
113	141.25	113.00	84.75	56.50	37.67	28.25
114	142.50	114.00	85.50	57.00	38.00	28.50
Side Heights	$1\frac{1}{4}$ to 1.	1 to 1.	$\frac{3}{4}$ to 1.	$\frac{1}{2}$ to 1.	$\frac{1}{3}$ to 1.	$\frac{1}{4}$ to 1.

TABLE VII. Whole Sections. Side Slope $1\frac{1}{2}$ to 1.

SUMS.	0°		1°		2°		3°		4°		5°	
1	1.4	0.42	1.4	0.42	1.4	0.42	1.4	0.42	1.4	0.42	1.4	0.42
2	5.6	0.69	5.6	0.69	5.6	0.70	5.6	0.70	5.6	0.70	5.7	0.71
3	12.5	0.97	12.5	0.97	12.5	0.97	12.6	0.98	12.6	0.98	12.7	0.99
4	22.2	1.25	22.2	1.25	22.3	1.25	22.4	1.26	22.5	1.26	22.6	1.27
5	34.7	1.53	34.7	1.53	34.8	1.53	34.9	1.54	35.1	1.54	35.3	1.55
6	50.0	1.81	50.0	1.81	50.1	1.81	50.3	1.82	50.6	1.83	50.9	1.84
7	68.1	2.08	68.1	2.08	68.2	2.09	68.5	2.10	68.8	2.11	69.2	2.12
8	88.9	2.36	88.9	2.36	89.1	2.37	89.4	2.38	89.9	2.39	90.4	2.40
9	112.5	2.64	112.6	2.64	112.8	2.65	113.2	2.66	113.8	2.67	114.5	2.69
10	138.9	2.92	139.0	2.92	139.3	2.92	139.8	2.93	140.4	2.95	141.3	2.97
11	168.1	3.19	168.2	3.20	168.5	3.20	169.1	3.21	169.9	3.23	171.0	3.25
12	200.0	3.47	200.1	3.47	200.6	3.48	201.2	3.49	202.2	3.51	203.5	3.53
13	234.7	3.75	234.9	3.75	235.4	3.76	236.2	3.77	237.3	3.79	238.8	3.82
14	272.2	4.03	272.4	4.03	273.0	4.04	273.9	4.05	275.3	4.07	277.0	4.10
15	312.5	4.31	312.7	4.31	313.4	4.32	314.4	4.33	316.0	4.35	318.0	4.38
16	355.6	4.58	355.8	4.59	356.5	4.60	357.8	4.61	359.5	4.63	361.8	4.66
17	401.4	4.86	401.7	4.86	402.5	4.87	403.9	4.89	405.9	4.92	408.4	4.95
18	450.0	5.14	450.3	5.14	451.2	5.15	452.8	5.17	455.0	5.20	457.9	5.23
19	501.4	5.42	501.7	5.42	502.8	5.43	504.5	5.45	507.0	5.48	510.2	5.51
20	555.6	5.69	555.9	5.70	557.1	5.71	559.0	5.73	561.7	5.76	565.3	5.79
21	612.5	5.97	612.9	5.98	614.2	5.99	616.3	6.01	619.3	6.04	623.2	6.08
22	672.2	6.25	672.7	6.25	674.1	6.27	676.4	6.29	679.7	6.32	684.0	6.36
23	734.7	6.53	735.2	6.53	736.7	6.55	739.3	6.57	742.9	6.60	747.6	6.64
24	800.0	6.81	800.5	6.81	802.2	6.82	805.0	6.85	808.9	6.88	814.0	6.92
25	868.1	7.08	868.7	7.09	870.4	7.10	873.5	7.13	877.7	7.16	883.3	7.21
26	938.9	7.36	939.5	7.37	941.5	7.38	944.7	7.41	949.3	7.44	955.3	7.49
27	1012.5	7.64	1013.2	7.64	1015.3	7.66	1018.8	7.69	1023.8	7.72	1030.2	7.77
28	1088.9	7.92	1089.6	7.92	1091.9	7.94	1095.7	7.97	1101.0	8.00	1108.0	8.06
29	1168.1	8.19	1168.9	8.20	1171.3	8.22	1175.3	8.25	1181.0	8.29	1188.5	8.34
30	1250.0	8.47	1250.9	8.48	1253.4	8.50	1257.8	8.52	1263.9	8.57	1271.9	8.62
31	1334.7	8.75	1335.6	8.76	1338.4	8.77	1343.0	8.80	1349.6	8.85	1358.1	8.90
32	1422.2	9.03	1423.2	9.03	1426.1	9.05	1431.1	9.08	1438.0	9.13	1447.1	9.19
33	1512.5	9.31	1513.5	9.31	1516.7	9.33	1521.9	9.36	1529.3	9.41	1539.0	9.47
34	1605.6	9.58	1606.7	9.59	1610.0	9.61	1615.5	9.64	1623.4	9.69	1633.7	9.75
35	1701.4	9.86	1702.6	9.87	1706.1	9.89	1712.0	9.92	1720.3	9.97	1731.2	10.03
36	1800.0	10.14	1801.2	10.15	1805.0	10.17	1811.2	10.20	1820.0	10.25	1831.5	10.32
37	1901.4	10.42	1902.7	10.42	1906.6	10.45	1913.2	10.48	1922.5	10.53	1934.7	10.60
38	2005.6	10.69	2006.9	10.70	2011.1	10.72	2018.0	10.76	2027.9	10.81	2040.7	10.88
39	2112.5	10.97	2113.9	10.98	2118.3	11.00	2125.6	11.04	2136.0	11.09	2149.5	11.16
40	2222.2	11.25	2223.7	11.26	2228.3	11.28	2236.0	11.32	2246.9	11.38	2261.2	11.45
41	2334.7	11.53	2336.3	11.54	2341.1	11.56	2349.2	11.60	2360.7	11.66	2375.6	11.73
42	2450.0	11.81	2451.7	11.81	2456.7	11.84	2465.2	11.88	2477.3	11.94	2492.9	12.01
43	2568.1	12.08	2569.8	12.09	2575.1	12.12	2584.0	12.16	2596.6	12.22	2613.1	12.30
44	2688.9	12.36	2690.7	12.37	2696.3	12.40	2705.6	12.44	2718.8	12.50	2736.0	12.58
45	2812.5	12.64	2814.4	12.65	2820.2	12.67	2830.0	12.72	2843.8	12.78	2861.8	12.86
46	2938.9	12.92	2940.9	12.93	2947.0	12.95	2957.2	13.00	2971.6	13.06	2990.4	13.14
47	3068.1	13.19	3070.2	13.20	3076.5	13.23	3087.1	13.28	3102.2	13.34	3121.8	13.43
48	3200.0	13.47	3202.2	13.48	3208.8	13.51	3219.9	13.56	3235.6	13.62	3256.1	13.71
49	3334.7	13.75	3337.0	13.76	3343.9	13.79	3355.5	13.84	3371.8	13.90	3393.2	13.99
50	3472.2	14.03	3474.6	14.04	3481.8	14.07	3493.8	14.12	3510.9	14.18	3533.1	14.27
51	3612.5	14.31	3615.0	14.32	3622.4	14.34	3635.0	14.39	3652.7	14.46	3675.8	14.56
52	3755.6	14.58	3758.1	14.59	3765.9	14.62	3778.9	14.67	3797.3	14.75	3821.4	14.84
53	3901.4	14.86	3904.1	14.87	3912.1	14.90	3925.7	14.95	3944.8	15.03	3969.8	15.12
54	4050.0	15.14	4052.8	15.15	4061.1	15.18	4075.2	15.23	4095.1	15.31	4121.0	15.40
55	4201.4	15.42	4204.3	15.43	4213.0	15.46	4227.5	15.51	4248.1	15.59	4275.0	15.69
56	4355.6	15.69	4358.5	15.71	4367.5	15.74	4382.6	15.79	4404.0	15.87	4431.9	15.97
57	4512.5	15.97	4515.6	15.98	4524.9	16.02	4540.6	16.07	4562.7	16.15	4591.6	16.25
58	4672.2	16.25	4675.4	16.26	4685.1	16.29	4701.3	16.35	4724.2	16.43	4754.1	16.53
59	4834.7	16.53	4838.0	16.54	4848.0	16.57	4864.8	16.63	4888.5	16.71	4919.4	16.82
60	5000.0	16.81	5003.4	16.82	5013.8	16.85	5031.1	16.91	5055.6	16.99	5087.6	17.10
SUMS.	0°		1°		2°		3°		4°		5°	

TABLE VII. Whole Sections. Side Slope $1\frac{1}{2}$ to 1.

SUMS.	0°		1°		2°		3°		4°		5°	
61	5168.1	17.08	5171.6	17.10	5182.3	17.13	5200.2	17.19	5225.5	17.27	5258.6	17.38
62	5338.9	17.36	5342.6	17.37	5353.6	17.41	5372.1	17.47	5398.3	17.55	5432.4	17.67
63	5512.5	17.64	5516.3	17.65	5527.7	17.69	5546.8	17.75	5573.8	17.84	5609.1	17.95
64	5688.9	17.92	5692.8	17.93	5704.5	17.97	5724.3	18.03	5752.2	18.12	5788.6	18.23
65	5868.1	18.19	5872.1	18.21	5884.2	18.24	5904.5	18.31	5933.3	18.40	5970.9	18.51
66	6050.0	18.47	6054.2	18.48	6066.6	18.52	6087.6	18.59	6117.3	18.68	6156.0	18.80
67	6234.7	18.75	6239.0	18.76	6251.9	18.80	6273.5	18.87	6304.1	18.96	6344.0	19.08
68	6422.2	19.03	6426.6	19.04	6439.9	19.08	6462.2	19.15	6493.7	19.24	6534.8	19.36
69	6612.5	19.31	6617.0	19.32	6630.7	19.36	6653.6	19.43	6686.1	19.52	6728.4	19.64
70	6805.6	19.58	6810.2	19.60	6824.3	19.64	6847.9	19.71	6881.3	19.80	6924.8	19.93
71	7001.4	19.86	7006.2	19.87	7020.7	19.92	7044.9	19.98	7079.3	20.08	7124.1	20.21
72	7200.0	20.14	7204.9	20.15	7219.8	20.19	7244.8	20.26	7280.1	20.36	7326.2	20.49
73	7401.4	20.42	7406.5	20.43	7421.8	20.47	7447.4	20.54	7483.7	20.64	7531.1	20.77
74	7605.6	20.69	7610.8	20.71	7626.5	20.75	7652.9	20.82	7690.2	20.92	7738.8	21.06
75	7812.5	20.97	7817.9	20.99	7834.0	21.03	7861.1	21.10	7899.4	21.21	7949.4	21.34
76	8022.2	21.25	8027.7	21.26	8044.3	21.31	8072.1	21.38	8111.5	21.49	8162.8	21.62
77	8234.7	21.53	8240.4	21.54	8257.4	21.59	8285.9	21.66	8326.3	21.77	8379.0	21.91
78	8450.0	21.81	8455.8	21.82	8473.3	21.87	8502.5	21.94	8544.0	22.05	8598.1	22.19
79	8668.1	22.08	8674.0	22.10	8691.9	22.14	8722.0	22.22	8764.5	22.33	8820.0	22.47
80	8888.9	22.36	8895.0	22.38	8913.4	22.42	8944.2	22.50	8987.8	22.61	9044.7	22.75
81	9112.5	22.64	9118.8	22.65	9137.6	22.70	9169.2	22.78	9213.9	22.89	9272.2	23.04
82	9338.9	22.92	9345.3	22.93	9364.6	22.98	9397.0	23.06	9442.8	23.17	9502.5	23.32
83	9568.1	23.19	9574.6	23.21	9594.4	23.26	9627.6	23.34	9674.5	23.45	9735.7	23.60
84	9800.0	23.47	9806.7	23.49	9827.0	23.54	9860.9	23.62	9909.0	23.73	9971.7	23.88
85	10034.7	23.75	10041.6	23.77	10062.3	23.82	10097.1	23.90	10146.4	24.01	10210.6	24.17
86	10272.2	24.03	10279.3	24.04	10300.5	24.09	10336.1	24.18	10386.5	24.30	10452.2	24.45
87	10512.5	24.31	10519.7	24.32	10541.4	24.37	10577.9	24.46	10629.4	24.58	10696.7	24.73
88	10755.6	24.58	10762.9	24.60	10785.2	24.65	10822.4	24.74	10875.2	24.86	10944.0	25.01
89	11001.4	24.86	11008.9	24.88	11031.7	24.93	11069.8	25.02	11123.8	25.14	11194.2	25.30
90	11250.0	25.14	11257.7	25.16	11281.0	25.21	11320.0	25.30	11375.2	25.42	11447.1	25.58
91	11501.4	25.42	11509.3	25.43	11533.0	25.49	11572.9	25.57	11629.3	25.70	11702.9	25.86
92	11755.6	25.69	11763.6	25.71	11787.9	25.77	11828.7	25.85	11886.3	25.98	11961.6	26.14
93	12012.5	25.97	12020.7	25.99	12045.6	26.04	12087.2	26.13	12146.1	26.26	12223.0	26.43
94	12272.2	26.25	12280.6	26.27	12306.0	26.32	12348.5	26.41	12408.7	26.54	12487.3	26.71
95	12534.7	26.53	12543.3	26.55	12569.2	26.60	12612.7	26.69	12674.2	26.82	12754.4	26.99
96	12800.0	26.81	12808.8	26.82	12835.2	26.88	12879.6	26.97	12942.4	27.10	13024.3	27.28
97	13068.1	27.08	13077.0	27.10	13104.0	27.16	13149.3	27.25	13213.4	27.38	13297.1	27.56
98	13338.9	27.36	13348.0	27.38	13375.6	27.44	13421.8	27.53	13487.3	27.67	13572.6	27.84
99	13612.5	27.64	13621.8	27.66	13650.0	27.71	13697.2	27.81	13763.9	27.95	13851.0	28.12
100	13888.9	27.92	13898.4	27.94	13927.1	27.99	13975.3	28.09	14043.4	28.23	14132.3	28.41
101	14168.1	28.19	14177.8	28.21	14207.0	28.27	14256.2	28.37	14325.7	28.51	14416.3	28.69
102	14450.0	28.47	14459.9	28.49	14489.8	28.55	14539.9	28.65	14610.8	28.79	14703.2	28.97
103	14734.7	28.75	14744.8	28.77	14775.3	28.83	14826.4	28.93	14898.6	29.07	14992.9	29.25
104	15022.2	29.03	15032.5	29.05	15063.6	29.11	15115.6	29.21	15189.3	29.35	15285.5	29.54
105	15312.5	29.31	15323.0	29.33	15354.6	29.39	15407.7	29.49	15482.8	29.63	15580.8	29.82
106	15605.6	29.58	15616.3	29.60	15648.5	29.66	15702.6	29.77	15779.2	29.91	15879.0	30.10
107	15901.4	29.86	15912.3	29.88	15945.1	29.94	16000.3	30.05	16078.3	30.19	16180.0	30.38
108	16200.0	30.14	16211.1	30.16	16244.6	30.22	16300.7	30.33	16380.2	30.47	16483.9	30.67
109	16501.4	30.42	16512.7	30.44	16546.8	30.50	16604.0	30.61	16685.0	30.76	16790.6	30.95
110	16805.6	30.69	16817.1	30.72	16851.8	30.78	16910.1	30.89	16992.5	31.04	17100.1	31.23
111	17112.5	30.97	17124.2	30.99	17159.6	31.06	17218.9	31.16	17302.9	31.32	17412.4	31.52
112	17422.2	31.25	17434.2	31.27	17470.2	31.34	17530.6	31.44	17616.0	31.60	17727.5	31.80
113	17734.7	31.53	17746.9	31.55	17783.5	31.61	17845.0	31.72	17932.0	31.88	18045.5	32.08
114	18050.0	31.81	18062.4	31.83	18099.7	31.89	18162.2	32.00	18250.8	32.16	18366.3	32.36
115	18368.1	32.08	18380.7	32.11	18418.6	32.17	18482.3	32.28	18572.4	32.44	18689.9	32.65
116	18688.9	32.36	18701.7	32.38	18740.3	32.45	18805.1	32.56	18896.8	32.72	19016.4	32.93
117	19012.5	32.64	19025.5	32.66	19064.8	32.73	19130.7	32.84	19224.0	33.00	19345.7	33.21
118	19338.9	32.92	19352.2	32.94	19392.1	33.01	19459.2	33.12	19554.0	33.28	19677.8	33.49
119	19668.1	33.19	19681.6	33.22	19722.2	33.29	19790.4	33.40	19886.9	33.56	20012.7	33.78
120	20000.0	33.47	20013.7	33.50	20055.0	33.56	20124.4	33.68	20222.5	33.84	20350.5	34.06
SUMS.	0°		1°		2°		3°		4°		5°	

TABLE VII. Whole Sections. Side Slope $1\frac{1}{2}$ to 1.

SUMS.	6°		7°		8°		9°		10°		11°	
1	1.4	0.43	1.4	0.43	1.5	0.44	1.5	0.44	1.5	0.45	1.5	0.46
2	5.7	0.71	5.8	0.72	5.8	0.73	5.9	0.74	6.0	0.75	6.1	0.76
3	12.8	1.00	12.9	1.01	13.1	1.02	13.2	1.03	13.4	1.05	13.7	1.06
4	22.8	1.28	23.0	1.29	23.3	1.31	23.6	1.32	23.9	1.34	24.3	1.37
5	35.6	1.57	35.9	1.58	36.3	1.60	36.8	1.62	37.3	1.64	37.9	1.67
6	51.3	1.85	51.8	1.87	52.3	1.89	53.0	1.91	53.8	1.94	54.6	1.97
7	69.8	2.14	70.4	2.16	71.2	2.18	72.1	2.21	73.2	2.24	74.4	2.28
8	91.2	2.42	92.0	2.44	93.0	2.47	94.2	2.50	95.6	2.54	97.1	2.58
9	115.4	2.71	116.5	2.73	117.7	2.76	119.2	2.80	121.0	2.84	123.0	2.88
10	142.4	2.99	143.8	3.02	145.3	3.05	147.2	3.09	149.3	3.14	151.8	3.19
11	172.3	3.28	174.0	3.31	175.9	3.34	178.1	3.39	180.7	3.43	183.7	3.49
12	205.1	3.56	207.0	3.59	209.3	3.63	212.0	3.68	215.0	3.73	218.6	3.79
13	240.7	3.85	243.0	3.88	245.6	3.92	248.8	3.97	252.4	4.03	256.5	4.10
14	279.2	4.13	281.8	4.17	284.9	4.22	288.5	4.27	292.7	4.33	297.5	4.40
15	320.5	4.42	323.5	4.46	327.0	4.51	331.2	4.56	336.0	4.63	341.5	4.71
16	364.6	4.70	368.0	4.74	372.1	4.80	376.8	4.86	382.3	4.93	388.6	5.01
17	411.6	4.99	415.5	5.03	420.1	5.09	425.4	5.15	431.6	5.23	438.7	5.31
18	461.5	5.27	465.8	5.32	470.9	5.38	476.9	5.45	483.8	5.53	491.8	5.62
19	514.2	5.55	519.0	5.61	524.7	5.67	531.4	5.74	539.1	5.82	548.0	5.92
20	569.7	5.84	575.1	5.89	581.4	5.96	588.8	6.04	597.3	6.12	607.2	6.22
21	628.1	6.12	634.0	6.18	641.0	6.25	649.1	6.33	658.6	6.42	669.4	6.53
22	689.4	6.41	695.8	6.47	703.5	6.54	712.4	6.62	722.8	6.72	734.7	6.83
23	753.4	6.69	760.5	6.76	768.9	6.83	778.7	6.92	790.0	7.02	803.0	7.13
24	820.4	6.98	828.1	7.04	837.2	7.12	847.9	7.21	860.2	7.32	874.3	7.44
25	890.2	7.26	898.5	7.33	908.4	7.41	920.0	7.51	933.3	7.62	948.7	7.74
26	962.8	7.55	971.9	7.62	982.6	7.70	995.1	7.80	1009.5	7.91	1026.1	8.05
27	1038.8	7.83	1048.1	7.91	1059.6	7.99	1073.1	8.10	1088.7	8.21	1106.6	8.35
28	1116.6	8.12	1127.1	8.19	1139.5	8.28	1154.0	8.39	1170.8	8.51	1190.1	8.65
29	1197.8	8.40	1209.1	8.48	1222.4	8.58	1237.9	8.68	1255.9	8.81	1276.6	8.96
30	1281.9	8.69	1293.9	8.77	1308.1	8.87	1324.8	8.98	1344.0	9.11	1366.1	9.26
31	1368.7	8.97	1381.6	9.06	1396.8	9.16	1414.6	9.27	1435.1	9.41	1458.7	9.56
32	1458.5	9.26	1472.2	9.34	1488.4	9.45	1507.3	9.57	1529.2	9.71	1554.4	9.87
33	1551.1	9.54	1565.6	9.63	1582.8	9.74	1603.0	9.86	1626.3	10.01	1653.0	10.17
34	1646.5	9.83	1661.9	9.92	1680.2	10.03	1701.6	10.16	1726.3	10.30	1754.7	10.47
35	1744.8	10.11	1761.1	10.21	1780.5	10.32	1803.2	10.45	1829.4	10.60	1859.5	10.78
36	1845.9	10.40	1863.2	10.49	1883.7	10.61	1907.7	10.75	1935.4	10.90	1967.2	11.08
37	1949.9	10.68	1968.2	10.78	1989.8	10.90	2015.1	11.04	2044.4	11.20	2078.1	11.38
38	2056.7	10.97	2076.0	11.07	2098.8	11.19	2125.5	11.33	2156.4	11.50	2191.9	11.69
39	2166.3	11.25	2186.7	11.36	2210.8	11.48	2238.9	11.63	2271.4	11.80	2308.8	11.99
40	2278.9	11.54	2300.3	11.65	2325.6	11.77	2355.2	11.92	2389.4	12.10	2428.7	12.30
41	2394.2	11.82	2416.7	11.93	2443.3	12.06	2474.4	12.22	2510.3	12.39	2551.6	12.60
42	2512.4	12.11	2536.0	12.22	2563.9	12.35	2596.6	12.51	2634.3	12.69	2677.6	12.90
43	2633.5	12.39	2658.2	12.51	2687.5	12.65	2721.7	12.81	2761.2	12.99	2806.7	13.21
44	2757.4	12.68	2783.3	12.80	2813.9	12.94	2849.7	13.10	2891.1	13.29	2938.7	13.51
45	2884.2	12.96	2911.3	13.08	2943.3	13.23	2980.7	13.39	3024.1	13.59	3073.8	13.81
46	3013.8	13.25	3042.1	13.37	3075.6	13.52	3114.7	13.69	3159.9	13.89	3211.9	14.12
47	3146.3	13.53	3175.8	13.66	3210.7	13.81	3251.6	13.98	3298.8	14.19	3353.1	14.42
48	3281.6	13.82	3312.4	13.95	3348.8	14.10	3391.4	14.28	3440.7	14.49	3497.3	14.72
49	3419.7	14.10	3451.8	14.23	3489.8	14.39	3534.2	14.57	3585.6	14.78	3644.6	15.03
50	3560.7	14.39	3594.1	14.52	3633.7	14.68	3679.9	14.87	3733.4	15.08	3794.8	15.33
51	3704.6	14.67	3739.3	14.81	3780.5	14.97	3828.6	15.16	3884.2	15.38	3948.1	15.63
52	3851.3	14.96	3887.4	15.10	3930.2	15.26	3980.2	15.46	4038.0	15.68	4104.5	15.94
53	4000.8	15.24	4038.4	15.38	4082.8	15.55	4134.8	15.75	4194.8	15.98	4263.9	16.24
54	4153.2	15.52	4192.2	15.67	4238.4	15.84	4292.3	16.04	4354.6	16.28	4426.3	16.55
55	4308.5	15.81	4348.9	15.96	4396.8	16.13	4452.7	16.34	4517.4	16.58	4591.8	16.85
56	4466.6	16.09	4508.5	16.25	4558.1	16.42	4616.1	16.63	4683.2	16.87	4760.2	17.15
57	4627.5	16.38	4670.9	16.53	4722.4	16.72	4782.4	16.93	4851.9	17.17	4931.8	17.46
58	4791.3	16.66	4836.3	16.82	4889.5	17.01	4951.7	17.22	5023.7	17.47	5106.3	17.76
59	4958.0	16.95	5004.5	17.11	5059.6	17.30	5123.9	17.52	5198.4	17.77	5283.9	18.06
60	5127.4	17.23	5175.6	17.40	5232.5	17.59	5299.1	17.81	5376.1	18.07	5464.6	18.37
SUMS.	6°		7°		8°		9°		10°		11°	

SUMS.	6°		7°		8°		9°		10°		11°	
61	5299.8	17.52	5349.5	17.68	5408.4	17.88	5477.2	18.11	5556.8	18.37	5648.2	18.67
62	5475.0	17.80	5526.4	17.97	5587.2	18.17	5658.3	18.40	5740.5	18.67	5834.9	18.97
63	5653.0	18.09	5706.1	18.26	5768.9	18.46	5842.3	18.69	5927.1	18.97	6024.7	19.28
64	5833.9	18.37	5888.6	18.55	5953.5	18.75	6029.2	18.99	6116.8	19.26	6217.5	19.58
65	6017.6	18.66	6074.1	18.83	6141.0	19.04	6219.1	19.28	6309.4	19.56	6413.3	19.88
66	6204.2	18.94	6262.4	19.12	6331.4	19.33	6411.9	19.58	6505.1	19.86	6612.1	20.19
67	6393.6	19.23	6453.6	19.41	6524.7	19.62	6607.7	19.87	6703.7	20.16	6814.0	20.49
68	6585.9	19.51	6647.7	19.70	6720.9	19.91	6806.4	20.17	6905.3	20.46	7018.9	20.80
69	6781.0	19.80	6844.7	19.98	6920.0	20.20	7008.1	20.46	7109.9	20.76	7226.9	21.10
70	6979.0	20.08	7044.5	20.27	7122.1	20.49	7212.7	20.75	7317.5	21.06	7437.9	21.40
71	7179.9	20.37	7247.2	20.56	7327.0	20.78	7420.2	21.05	7528.0	21.36	7651.9	21.71
72	7383.5	20.65	7452.8	20.85	7534.9	21.08	7630.7	21.34	7741.6	21.65	7869.0	22.01
73	7590.0	20.94	7661.3	21.13	7745.6	21.37	7844.1	21.64	7958.1	21.95	8089.1	22.31
74	7799.4	21.22	7872.6	21.42	7959.3	21.66	8060.5	21.93	8177.6	22.25	8312.2	22.62
75	8011.6	21.51	8086.8	21.71	8175.9	21.95	8279.8	22.23	8400.1	22.55	8538.4	22.92
76	8226.7	21.79	8303.9	22.00	8395.3	22.24	8502.1	22.52	8625.6	22.85	8767.6	23.22
77	8444.6	22.08	8523.9	22.28	8617.7	22.53	8727.3	22.82	8854.1	23.15	8999.8	23.53
78	8665.4	22.36	8746.7	22.57	8843.0	22.82	8955.5	23.11	9085.6	23.45	9235.1	23.83
79	8889.0	22.65	8972.4	22.86	9071.2	23.11	9186.6	23.40	9320.1	23.74	9473.4	24.14
80	9115.5	22.93	9201.0	23.15	9302.3	23.40	9420.6	23.70	9557.5	24.04	9714.8	24.44
81	9344.8	23.22	9432.5	23.43	9536.3	23.69	9657.6	23.99	9797.9	24.34	9959.2	24.74
82	9576.9	23.50	9666.8	23.72	9773.2	23.98	9897.5	24.29	10041.3	24.64	10206.6	25.05
83	9811.9	23.79	9904.0	24.01	10013.1	24.27	10140.4	24.58	10287.8	24.94	10457.0	25.35
84	10049.8	24.07	10144.1	24.30	10255.8	24.56	10386.2	24.88	10537.1	25.24	10710.5	25.65
85	10290.5	24.36	10387.1	24.58	10501.4	24.85	10635.0	25.17	10789.5	25.54	10967.1	25.96
86	10534.1	24.64	10632.9	24.87	10750.0	25.15	10886.7	25.47	11044.9	25.84	11226.6	26.26
87	10780.5	24.93	10881.6	25.16	11001.4	25.44	11141.4	25.76	11303.2	26.13	11489.2	26.56
88	11029.7	25.21	11133.2	25.45	11255.8	25.73	11399.0	26.05	11564.6	26.43	11754.9	26.87
89	11281.8	25.49	11387.7	25.73	11513.1	26.02	11659.5	26.35	11828.9	26.73	12023.6	27.17
90	11536.8	25.78	11645.0	26.02	11773.2	26.31	11923.0	26.64	12096.2	27.03	12295.3	27.47
91	11794.6	26.06	11905.2	26.31	12036.3	26.60	12189.4	26.94	12366.5	27.33	12570.0	27.78
92	12055.2	26.35	12168.3	26.60	12302.3	26.89	12458.8	27.23	12639.8	27.63	12847.8	28.08
93	12318.7	26.63	12434.3	26.88	12571.2	27.18	12731.1	27.53	12916.1	27.93	13128.6	28.39
94	12585.0	26.92	12703.1	27.17	12843.0	27.47	13006.3	27.82	13195.3	28.22	13412.5	28.69
95	12854.2	27.20	12974.9	27.46	13117.7	27.76	13284.5	28.11	13477.6	28.52	13699.4	28.99
96	13126.3	27.49	13249.4	27.75	13395.3	28.05	13565.7	28.41	13762.8	28.82	13989.3	29.30
97	13401.2	27.77	13526.9	28.03	13675.8	28.34	13849.8	28.70	14051.0	29.12	14282.2	29.60
98	13678.9	28.06	13807.3	28.32	13959.3	28.63	14136.8	29.00	14342.2	29.42	14578.2	29.90
99	13959.5	28.34	14090.5	28.61	14245.6	28.92	14426.8	29.29	14636.4	29.72	14877.3	30.21
100	14242.9	28.63	14376.6	28.90	14534.9	29.22	14719.7	29.59	14933.6	30.02	15179.8	30.51
101	14529.2	28.91	14665.5	29.18	14827.0	29.51	15015.6	29.88	15233.8	30.32	15484.4	30.81
102	14818.3	29.20	14957.4	29.47	15122.1	29.80	15314.4	30.18	15536.9	30.61	15792.6	31.12
103	15110.3	29.48	15252.1	29.76	15420.0	30.09	15616.2	30.47	15843.0	30.91	16103.8	31.42
104	15405.1	29.77	15549.7	30.05	15720.9	30.38	15920.8	30.76	16152.2	31.21	16418.0	31.72
105	15702.8	30.05	15850.2	30.33	16024.7	30.67	16228.5	31.06	16464.3	31.51	16735.2	32.03
106	16003.3	30.34	16153.5	30.62	16331.4	30.96	16539.1	31.35	16779.4	31.81	17055.5	32.33
107	16306.7	30.62	16459.7	30.91	16640.9	31.25	16852.6	31.65	17097.5	32.11	17378.8	32.64
108	16612.9	30.91	16768.8	31.20	16953.4	31.54	17169.1	31.94	17418.5	32.41	17705.2	32.94
109	16922.0	31.19	17080.8	31.48	17268.9	31.83	17488.5	32.24	17742.6	32.70	18034.6	33.24
110	17233.9	31.48	17395.6	31.77	17587.2	32.12	17810.9	32.53	18069.6	33.00	18367.0	33.55
111	17548.7	31.76	17713.4	32.06	17908.4	32.41	18136.2	32.82	18399.7	33.30	18702.5	33.85
112	17866.3	32.05	18034.0	32.35	18232.5	32.70	18464.4	33.12	18732.7	33.60	19041.0	34.15
113	18186.8	32.33	18357.4	32.63	18559.5	32.99	18795.6	33.41	19068.7	33.90	19382.5	34.46
114	18510.1	32.62	18683.8	32.92	18889.5	33.28	19129.7	33.71	19407.7	34.20	19727.1	34.76
115	18836.2	32.90	19013.0	33.21	19222.3	33.58	19466.8	34.00	19749.7	34.50	20074.7	35.06
116	19165.3	33.19	19345.1	33.50	19558.1	33.87	19806.9	34.30	20094.6	34.80	20425.3	35.37
117	19497.1	33.47	19680.1	33.78	19896.8	34.16	20149.8	34.59	20442.6	35.09	20779.0	35.67
118	19831.8	33.76	20017.9	34.07	20238.3	34.45	20495.7	34.89	20793.5	35.39	21135.7	35.98
119	20169.4	34.04	20358.7	34.36	20582.8	34.74	20844.6	35.18	21147.5	35.69	21495.5	36.28
120	20509.8	34.33	20702.3	34.65	20930.2	35.03	21196.4	35.47	21504.4	35.99	21858.2	36.58
SUMS.	6°		7°		8°		9°		10°		11°	

SUMS.	12°		13°		14°		15°		16°		17°	
1	1.5	0.46	1.6	0.47	1.6	0.48	1.7	0.50	1.7	0.51	1.8	0.53
2	6.2	0.77	6.3	0.79	6.5	0.81	6.6	0.83	6.8	0.85	7.0	0.88
3	13.9	1.08	14.2	1.10	14.5	1.13	14.9	1.16	15.3	1.19	15.8	1.23
4	24.7	1.39	25.3	1.42	25.8	1.45	26.5	1.49	27.3	1.53	28.1	1.58
5	38.7	1.70	39.5	1.74	40.4	1.78	41.4	1.82	42.6	1.87	44.0	1.93
6	55.7	2.01	56.8	2.05	58.1	2.10	59.6	2.15	61.3	2.22	63.3	2.29
7	75.8	2.32	77.3	2.37	79.1	2.42	81.2	2.48	83.5	2.56	86.2	2.64
8	98.9	2.63	101.0	2.68	103.3	2.75	106.0	2.82	109.1	2.90	112.6	2.99
9	125.2	2.94	127.8	3.00	130.8	3.07	134.2	3.15	138.0	3.24	142.5	3.34
10	154.6	3.25	157.8	3.31	161.5	3.39	165.6	3.48	170.4	3.58	175.9	3.69
11	187.1	3.56	191.0	3.63	195.4	3.71	200.4	3.81	206.2	3.92	212.8	4.05
12	222.6	3.87	227.3	3.95	232.5	4.04	238.5	4.14	245.4	4.26	253.3	4.40
13	261.3	4.17	266.7	4.26	272.9	4.36	279.9	4.47	288.0	4.60	297.2	4.75
14	303.0	4.48	309.3	4.58	316.5	4.68	324.7	4.80	334.0	4.94	344.7	5.10
15	347.9	4.79	355.1	4.89	363.3	5.01	372.7	5.14	383.4	5.28	395.7	5.45
16	395.8	5.10	404.0	5.21	413.4	5.33	424.1	5.47	436.3	5.62	450.2	5.80
17	446.8	5.41	456.1	5.52	466.7	5.65	478.7	5.80	492.5	5.96	508.3	6.16
18	500.9	5.72	511.3	5.84	523.2	5.97	536.7	6.13	552.1	6.31	569.8	6.51
19	558.1	6.03	569.7	6.15	582.9	6.30	598.0	6.46	615.2	6.65	634.9	6.86
20	618.4	6.34	631.3	6.47	645.9	6.62	662.6	6.79	681.7	6.99	703.5	7.21
21	681.8	6.65	696.0	6.79	712.1	6.94	730.5	7.12	751.5	7.33	775.6	7.56
22	748.3	6.96	763.8	7.10	781.5	7.27	801.7	7.45	824.8	7.67	851.2	7.91
23	817.9	7.27	834.8	7.42	854.2	7.59	876.3	7.79	901.5	8.01	930.4	8.27
24	890.5	7.58	909.0	7.73	930.1	7.91	954.1	8.12	981.6	8.35	1013.1	8.62
25	966.3	7.88	986.3	8.05	1009.2	8.24	1035.3	8.45	1065.1	8.69	1099.2	8.97
26	1045.1	8.19	1066.8	8.36	1091.6	8.56	1119.8	8.78	1152.0	9.03	1188.9	9.32
27	1127.1	8.50	1150.5	8.68	1177.1	8.88	1207.6	9.11	1242.3	9.37	1282.1	9.67
28	1212.1	8.81	1237.3	9.00	1266.0	9.20	1298.7	9.44	1336.1	9.71	1378.9	10.03
29	1300.2	9.12	1327.2	9.31	1358.0	9.53	1393.1	9.77	1433.2	10.05	1479.1	10.38
30	1391.4	9.43	1420.3	9.63	1453.3	9.85	1490.8	10.10	1533.7	10.40	1582.9	10.73
31	1485.8	9.74	1516.6	9.94	1551.8	10.17	1591.9	10.44	1637.7	10.74	1690.2	11.08
32	1583.2	10.05	1616.0	10.26	1653.5	10.50	1696.2	10.77	1745.1	11.08	1801.0	11.43
33	1683.7	10.36	1718.6	10.57	1758.5	10.82	1803.9	11.10	1855.8	11.42	1915.3	11.78
34	1787.2	10.67	1824.3	10.89	1866.6	11.14	1914.9	11.43	1970.0	11.76	2033.1	12.14
35	1893.9	10.98	1933.2	11.20	1978.1	11.46	2029.2	11.76	2087.6	12.10	2154.5	12.49
36	2003.7	11.29	2045.3	11.52	2092.7	11.79	2146.8	12.09	2208.6	12.44	2279.4	12.84
37	2116.5	11.60	2160.5	11.84	2210.6	12.11	2267.7	12.42	2333.0	12.78	2407.8	13.19
38	2232.5	11.90	2278.8	12.15	2331.7	12.43	2392.0	12.75	2460.8	13.12	2539.7	13.54
39	2351.5	12.21	2400.4	12.47	2456.0	12.76	2519.5	13.09	2592.0	13.46	2675.1	13.89
40	2473.7	12.52	2525.0	12.78	2583.6	13.08	2650.4	13.42	2726.7	13.80	2814.0	14.25
41	2598.9	12.83	2652.9	13.10	2714.4	13.40	2784.5	13.75	2864.7	14.14	2956.5	14.60
42	2727.2	13.14	2783.9	13.41	2848.4	13.73	2922.0	14.08	3006.1	14.49	3102.5	14.95
43	2858.7	13.45	2918.0	13.73	2985.7	14.05	3062.8	14.41	3151.0	14.83	3252.0	15.30
44	2993.2	13.76	3055.3	14.05	3126.1	14.37	3207.0	14.74	3299.3	15.17	3405.0	15.65
45	3130.8	14.07	3195.8	14.36	3269.9	14.69	3354.4	15.07	3450.9	15.51	3561.5	16.00
46	3271.5	14.38	3339.4	14.68	3416.8	15.02	3505.1	15.41	3606.0	15.85	3721.6	16.36
47	3415.2	14.69	3486.1	14.99	3567.0	15.34	3659.2	15.74	3764.5	16.19	3885.1	16.71
48	3562.1	15.00	3636.1	15.31	3720.4	15.66	3816.5	16.07	3926.4	16.53	4052.2	17.06
49	3712.1	15.31	3789.1	15.62	3877.0	15.99	3977.2	16.40	4091.7	16.87	4222.8	17.41
50	3865.1	15.62	3945.4	15.94	4036.9	16.31	4141.2	16.73	4260.4	17.21	4396.9	17.76
51	4021.3	15.92	4104.8	16.25	4199.9	16.63	4308.5	17.06	4432.5	17.55	4574.6	18.12
52	4180.5	16.23	4267.3	16.57	4366.3	16.95	4479.1	17.39	4608.1	17.89	4755.7	18.47
53	4342.9	16.54	4433.0	16.89	4535.8	17.28	4653.1	17.72	4787.0	18.23	4940.4	18.82
54	4508.3	16.85	4601.9	17.20	4708.6	17.60	4830.3	18.06	4969.3	18.58	5128.6	19.17
55	4676.8	17.16	4773.9	17.52	4884.6	17.92	5010.9	18.39	5155.1	18.92	5320.3	19.52
56	4848.4	17.47	4949.1	17.83	5063.8	18.25	5194.7	18.72	5344.3	19.26	5515.5	19.87
57	5023.1	17.78	5127.4	18.15	5246.3	18.57	5381.9	19.05	5536.8	19.60	5714.3	20.23
58	5200.9	18.09	5308.9	18.46	5432.0	18.89	5572.4	19.38	5732.8	19.94	5916.5	20.58
59	5381.8	18.40	5493.5	18.78	5620.9	19.22	5766.2	19.71	5932.2	20.28	6122.3	20.93
60	5565.8	18.71	5681.3	19.10	5813.1	19.54	5963.3	20.04	6135.0	20.62	6331.6	21.28
SUMS.	12°		13°		14°		15°		16°		17°	

SUMS.	12°		13°		14°		15°		16°		17°	
61	5752.9	19.02	5872.3	19.41	6008.5	19.86	6163.8	20.37	6341.2	20.96	6544.4	21.63
62	5943.0	19.33	6066.4	19.73	6207.1	20.18	6367.5	20.71	6550.8	21.30	6760.7	21.98
63	6136.3	19.63	6263.7	20.04	6408.9	20.51	6574.6	21.04	6763.8	21.64	6980.6	22.34
64	6332.6	19.94	6464.1	20.36	6614.0	20.83	6785.0	21.37	6980.3	21.98	7204.0	22.69
65	6532.1	20.25	6667.7	20.67	6822.3	21.15	6998.6	21.70	7200.1	22.32	7430.8	23.04
66	6734.6	20.56	6874.4	20.99	7033.8	21.48	7215.6	22.03	7423.3	22.67	7661.2	23.39
67	6940.2	20.87	7084.3	21.31	7248.6	21.80	7436.0	22.36	7650.0	23.01	7895.2	23.74
68	7149.0	21.18	7297.4	21.62	7466.6	22.12	7659.6	22.69	7880.0	23.35	8132.6	24.10
69	7360.8	21.49	7513.6	21.94	7687.8	22.44	7886.5	23.03	8113.5	23.69	8373.5	24.45
70	7575.7	21.80	7732.9	22.25	7912.2	22.77	8116.8	23.36	8350.4	24.03	8618.0	24.80
71	7793.7	22.11	7955.5	22.57	8139.9	23.09	8350.3	23.69	8590.7	24.37	8866.0	25.15
72	8014.7	22.42	8181.1	22.88	8370.8	23.41	8587.2	24.02	8834.4	24.71	9117.5	25.50
73	8238.9	22.73	8410.0	23.20	8605.0	23.74	8827.4	24.35	9081.5	25.05	9372.5	25.85
74	8466.2	23.04	8641.9	23.51	8842.3	24.06	9070.9	24.68	9332.0	25.39	9631.1	26.21
75	8696.6	23.35	8877.1	23.83	9082.9	24.38	9317.7	25.01	9585.9	25.73	9893.1	26.56
76	8930.0	23.65	9115.4	24.15	9326.8	24.71	9567.8	25.34	9843.2	26.07	10158.7	26.91
77	9166.6	23.96	9356.9	24.46	9573.8	25.03	9821.3	25.68	10104.0	26.41	10427.8	27.26
78	9406.2	24.27	9601.5	24.78	9824.1	25.35	10078.0	26.01	10368.1	26.76	10700.4	27.61
79	9648.9	24.58	9849.2	25.09	10077.6	25.67	10338.1	26.34	10635.7	27.10	10976.5	27.96
80	9894.8	24.89	10100.2	25.41	10334.4	26.00	10601.5	26.67	10906.6	27.44	11256.2	28.32
81	10143.7	25.20	10354.2	25.72	10594.3	26.32	10868.2	27.00	11181.0	27.78	11539.3	28.67
82	10395.7	25.51	10611.5	26.04	10857.5	26.64	11138.2	27.33	11458.8	28.12	11826.0	29.02
83	10650.8	25.82	10871.9	26.36	11124.0	26.97	11411.5	27.66	11740.0	28.46	12116.2	29.37
84	10909.0	26.13	11135.4	26.67	11393.6	27.29	11688.1	27.99	12024.6	28.80	12409.9	29.72
85	11170.2	26.44	11402.1	26.99	11666.5	27.61	11968.1	28.33	12312.6	29.14	12707.2	30.07
86	11434.6	26.75	11672.0	27.30	11942.6	27.94	12251.3	28.66	12604.0	29.48	13007.9	30.43
87	11702.1	27.06	11945.0	27.62	12222.0	28.26	12537.9	28.99	12898.8	29.82	13312.2	30.78
88	11972.6	27.37	12221.2	27.93	12504.6	28.58	12827.8	29.32	13197.0	30.16	13620.0	31.13
89	12246.3	27.67	12500.5	28.25	12790.4	28.90	13121.0	29.65	13498.7	30.50	13931.3	31.48
90	12523.0	27.98	12783.0	28.56	13079.4	29.23	13417.5	29.98	13803.7	30.85	14246.1	31.83
91	12802.9	28.29	13068.7	28.88	13371.7	29.55	13717.3	30.31	14112.2	31.19	14564.4	32.19
92	13085.8	28.60	13357.5	29.20	13667.2	29.87	14020.5	30.64	14424.0	31.53	14886.3	32.54
93	13371.8	28.91	13649.4	29.51	13965.9	30.20	14326.9	30.98	14739.3	31.87	15211.7	32.89
94	13660.9	29.22	13944.5	29.83	14267.9	30.52	14636.7	31.31	15058.0	32.21	15540.6	33.24
95	13953.1	29.53	14242.8	30.14	14573.1	30.84	14949.8	31.64	15380.1	32.55	15873.0	33.59
96	14248.4	29.84	14544.2	30.46	14881.5	31.16	15266.1	31.97	15705.6	32.89	16208.9	33.94
97	14546.8	30.15	14848.8	30.77	15193.1	31.49	15585.8	32.30	16034.5	33.23	16548.4	34.30
98	14848.3	30.46	15156.6	31.09	15508.0	31.81	15908.9	32.63	16366.8	33.57	16891.3	34.65
99	15152.9	30.77	15467.4	31.41	15826.1	32.13	16235.2	32.96	16702.5	33.91	17237.8	35.00
100	15460.6	31.08	15781.5	31.72	16147.4	32.46	16564.8	33.30	17041.6	34.25	17587.8	35.35
101	15771.3	31.38	16098.7	32.04	16472.0	32.78	16897.8	33.63	17384.2	34.59	17941.3	35.70
102	16085.2	31.69	16419.1	32.35	16799.8	33.10	17234.0	33.96	17730.1	34.94	18298.3	36.05
103	16402.1	32.00	16742.6	32.67	17130.8	33.43	17573.6	34.29	18079.5	35.28	18658.9	36.41
104	16722.1	32.31	17069.3	32.98	17465.1	33.75	17916.5	34.62	18432.2	35.62	19023.0	36.76
105	17045.3	32.62	17399.1	33.30	17802.6	34.07	18262.7	34.95	18788.4	35.96	19390.5	37.11
106	17371.5	32.93	17732.1	33.61	18143.3	34.39	18612.2	35.28	19148.0	36.30	19761.6	37.46
107	17700.8	33.24	18068.2	33.93	18487.2	34.72	18965.1	35.61	19511.0	36.64	20136.3	37.81
108	18033.2	33.55	18407.5	34.25	18834.4	35.04	19321.2	35.95	19877.4	36.98	20514.4	38.17
109	18368.7	33.86	18750.0	34.56	19184.8	35.36	19680.7	36.28	20247.2	37.32	20896.1	38.52
110	18707.3	34.17	19095.6	34.88	19538.4	35.69	20043.4	36.61	20620.4	37.66	21281.2	38.87
111	19048.9	34.48	19444.4	35.19	19895.3	36.01	20409.5	36.94	20997.0	38.00	21669.9	39.22
112	19393.7	34.79	19796.3	35.51	20255.3	36.33	20778.9	37.27	21377.0	38.34	22062.1	39.57
113	19741.6	35.10	20151.4	35.82	20618.7	36.65	21151.6	37.60	21760.5	38.68	22457.8	39.92
114	20092.5	35.40	20509.6	36.14	20985.2	36.98	21527.7	37.93	22147.3	39.03	22857.1	40.28
115	20446.6	35.71	20871.0	36.46	21355.0	37.30	21907.0	38.26	22537.6	39.37	23259.9	40.63
116	20803.7	36.02	21235.6	36.77	21728.0	37.62	22289.6	38.60	22931.2	39.71	23666.1	40.98
117	21163.9	36.33	21603.3	37.09	22104.2	37.95	22675.6	38.93	23328.3	40.05	24075.9	41.33
118	21527.3	36.64	21974.2	37.40	22483.7	38.27	23064.9	39.26	23728.8	40.39	24489.2	41.68
119	21893.7	36.95	22348.2	37.72	22866.4	38.59	23457.5	39.59	24132.7	40.73	24906.1	42.03
120	22263.2	37.26	22725.4	38.03	23252.3	38.92	23853.4	39.92	24539.9	41.07	25326.4	42.39
SUMS.	12°		13°		14°		15°		16°		17°	

TABLE VII. Whole Sections. Side Slope 1½ to 1.

SUMS.	18°		19°		20°		21°		22°		23°	
1	1.8	0.55	1.9	0.57	2.0	0.59	2.1	0.62	2.2	0.66	2.3	0.70
2	7.3	0.91	7.6	0.95	7.9	0.99	8.3	1.04	8.8	1.10	9.3	1.17
3	16.4	1.28	17.0	1.33	17.8	1.39	18.7	1.45	19.8	1.54	21.0	1.64
4	29.1	1.64	30.3	1.70	31.7	1.78	33.2	1.87	35.1	1.98	37.4	2.10
5	45.5	2.00	47.4	2.08	49.5	2.18	51.9	2.29	54.9	2.41	58.4	2.57
6	65.6	2.37	68.2	2.46	71.2	2.57	74.8	2.70	79.0	2.85	84.1	3.04
7	89.3	2.73	92.8	2.84	97.0	2.97	101.8	3.12	107.6	3.29	114.5	3.50
8	116.6	3.10	121.2	3.22	126.6	3.36	133.0	3.53	140.5	3.73	149.5	3.97
9	147.5	3.46	153.4	3.60	160.3	3.76	168.3	3.95	177.8	4.17	189.2	4.44
10	182.2	3.83	189.4	3.98	197.9	4.16	207.8	4.36	219.5	4.61	233.6	4.91
11	220.4	4.19	229.2	4.36	239.4	4.55	251.4	4.78	265.6	5.05	282.6	5.37
12	262.3	4.55	272.8	4.74	284.9	4.95	299.2	5.19	316.1	5.49	336.4	5.84
13	307.8	4.92	320.1	5.11	334.4	5.34	351.1	5.61	371.0	5.93	394.8	6.31
14	357.0	5.28	371.3	5.49	387.8	5.74	407.2	6.03	430.2	6.37	457.8	6.77
15	409.9	5.65	426.2	5.87	445.2	6.13	467.5	6.44	493.9	6.80	525.6	7.24
16	466.3	6.01	484.9	6.25	506.5	6.53	531.9	6.86	562.0	7.24	598.0	7.71
17	526.4	6.38	547.4	6.63	571.8	6.93	600.5	7.27	634.4	7.68	675.1	8.18
18	590.2	6.74	613.7	7.01	641.1	7.32	673.2	7.69	711.2	8.12	756.8	8.64
19	657.6	7.10	683.8	7.39	714.3	7.72	750.1	8.10	792.4	8.56	843.2	9.11
20	728.6	7.47	757.7	7.77	791.5	8.11	831.1	8.52	878.0	9.00	934.3	9.58
21	803.3	7.83	835.3	8.15	872.6	8.51	916.3	8.93	968.0	9.44	1030.1	10.04
22	881.6	8.20	916.8	8.52	957.7	8.90	1005.6	9.35	1062.4	9.88	1130.6	10.51
23	963.6	8.56	1002.0	8.90	1046.7	9.30	1099.1	9.77	1161.2	10.32	1235.7	10.98
24	1049.2	8.93	1091.1	9.28	1139.7	9.70	1196.8	10.18	1264.4	10.76	1345.4	11.45
25	1138.5	9.29	1183.9	9.66	1236.7	10.09	1298.6	10.60	1372.0	11.20	1459.9	11.91
26	1231.4	9.65	1280.5	10.04	1337.6	10.49	1404.6	11.01	1483.9	11.63	1579.0	12.38
27	1327.9	10.02	1380.9	10.42	1442.4	10.88	1514.7	11.43	1600.2	12.07	1702.8	12.85
28	1428.1	10.38	1485.0	10.80	1551.3	11.28	1629.0	11.84	1721.0	12.51	1831.3	13.31
29	1532.0	10.75	1593.0	11.18	1664.1	11.67	1747.4	12.26	1846.1	12.95	1964.4	13.78
30	1639.4	11.11	1704.8	11.55	1780.8	12.07	1870.0	12.67	1975.6	13.39	2102.3	14.25
31	1750.5	11.48	1820.3	11.93	1901.5	12.47	1996.7	13.09	2109.5	13.83	2244.8	14.72
32	1865.3	11.84	1939.7	12.31	2026.2	12.86	2127.6	13.51	2247.8	14.27	2391.9	15.18
33	1983.7	12.20	2062.8	12.69	2154.8	13.26	2262.7	13.92	2390.5	14.71	2543.7	15.65
34	2105.8	12.57	2189.7	13.07	2287.3	13.65	2401.9	14.34	2537.6	15.15	2700.2	16.12
35	2231.4	12.93	2320.4	13.45	2423.9	14.05	2545.2	14.75	2689.0	15.59	2861.4	16.58
36	2360.8	13.30	2454.9	13.83	2564.3	14.44	2692.8	15.17	2844.9	16.02	3027.3	17.05
37	2493.8	13.66	2593.1	14.21	2708.8	14.84	2844.4	15.58	3005.1	16.46	3197.8	17.52
38	2630.4	14.03	2735.2	14.59	2857.2	15.24	3000.3	16.00	3169.8	16.90	3373.0	17.99
39	2770.6	14.39	2881.1	14.96	3009.5	15.63	3160.3	16.41	3338.8	17.34	3552.8	18.45
40	2914.5	14.75	3030.7	15.34	3165.9	16.03	3324.4	16.83	3512.2	17.78	3737.4	18.92
41	3062.1	15.12	3184.1	15.72	3326.1	16.42	3492.7	17.25	3690.0	18.22	3926.6	19.39
42	3213.3	15.48	3341.4	16.10	3490.4	16.82	3665.2	17.66	3872.2	18.66	4120.4	19.85
43	3368.1	15.85	3502.4	16.48	3658.6	17.21	3841.8	18.08	4058.8	19.10	4319.0	20.32
44	3526.6	16.21	3667.2	16.86	3830.7	17.61	4022.5	18.49	4249.8	19.54	4522.2	20.79
45	3688.7	16.58	3835.7	17.24	4006.8	18.01	4207.5	18.91	4445.1	19.98	4730.1	21.26
46	3854.5	16.94	4008.1	17.62	4186.9	18.40	4396.5	19.32	4644.9	20.41	4942.7	21.72
47	4023.9	17.31	4184.3	17.99	4370.9	18.80	4589.8	19.74	4849.0	20.85	5159.9	22.19
48	4196.9	17.67	4364.2	18.37	4558.8	19.19	4787.1	20.15	5057.6	21.29	5381.8	22.66
49	4373.6	18.03	4548.0	18.75	4750.8	19.59	4988.7	20.57	5270.5	21.73	5608.4	23.12
50	4554.0	18.40	4735.5	19.13	4946.7	19.98	5194.4	20.99	5487.8	22.17	5839.6	23.59
51	4738.0	18.76	4926.8	19.51	5146.5	20.38	5404.2	21.40	5709.5	22.61	6075.5	24.06
52	4925.6	19.13	5121.9	19.89	5350.3	20.78	5618.2	21.82	5935.6	23.05	6316.1	24.53
53	5116.8	19.49	5320.8	20.27	5558.1	21.17	5836.4	22.23	6166.1	23.49	6561.4	24.99
54	5311.8	19.86	5523.5	20.65	5769.8	21.57	6058.7	22.65	6401.0	23.93	6811.3	25.46
55	5510.3	20.22	5729.9	21.03	5985.5	21.96	6285.2	23.06	6640.3	24.37	7065.9	25.93
56	5712.5	20.58	5940.2	21.40	6205.1	22.36	6515.8	23.48	6883.9	24.80	7325.2	26.40
57	5918.3	20.95	6154.2	21.78	6428.7	22.75	6750.6	23.89	7132.0	25.24	7589.2	26.86
58	6127.8	21.31	6372.1	22.16	6656.2	23.15	6989.6	24.31	7384.4	25.68	7857.8	27.33
59	6340.9	21.68	6593.7	22.54	6887.7	23.55	7232.7	24.73	7641.2	26.12	8131.1	27.80
60	6557.7	22.04	6819.1	22.92	7123.2	23.94	7479.9	25.14	7902.4	26.56	8409.1	28.26
SUMS.	18°		19°		20°		21°		22°		23°	

SUMS.	18°		19°		20°		21°		22°		23°	
61	6778.1	22.41	7048.3	23.30	7362.6	24.34	7731.3	25.56	8168.1	27.00	8691.7	28.73
62	7002.2	22.77	7281.3	23.68	7606.0	24.73	7986.9	25.97	8438.1	27.44	8979.0	29.20
63	7229.9	23.13	7518.0	24.06	7853.3	25.13	8246.6	26.39	8712.4	27.88	9271.0	29.67
64	7461.2	23.50	7758.6	24.44	8104.6	25.52	8510.5	26.80	8991.2	28.32	9567.6	30.13
65	7696.2	23.86	8003.0	24.81	8359.9	25.92	8778.5	27.22	9274.4	28.76	9869.0	30.60
66	7934.8	24.23	8251.1	25.19	8619.1	26.32	9050.7	27.63	9562.0	29.20	10175.0	31.07
67	8177.1	24.59	8503.0	25.57	8882.2	26.71	9327.0	28.05	9853.9	29.63	10485.6	31.53
68	8423.0	24.96	8758.7	25.95	9149.3	27.11	9607.5	28.47	10150.3	30.07	10801.0	32.00
69	8672.6	25.32	9018.2	26.33	9420.4	27.50	9892.2	28.88	10451.0	30.51	11121.0	32.47
70	8925.8	25.68	9281.5	26.71	9695.5	27.90	10181.0	29.30	10756.1	30.95	11445.7	32.94
71	9182.6	26.05	9548.6	27.09	9974.5	28.29	10474.0	29.71	11065.6	31.39	11775.0	33.40
72	9443.1	26.41	9819.5	27.47	10257.4	28.69	10771.1	30.13	11379.5	31.83	12109.0	33.87
73	9707.2	26.78	10094.1	27.84	10544.3	29.09	11072.4	30.54	11697.8	32.27	12447.7	34.34
74	9975.0	27.14	10372.6	28.22	10835.2	29.48	11377.8	30.96	12020.5	32.71	12791.1	34.80
75	10246.4	27.51	10654.8	28.60	11130.0	29.88	11687.4	31.37	12347.6	33.15	13139.2	35.27
76	10521.5	27.87	10940.9	28.98	11428.8	30.27	12001.1	31.79	12679.0	33.59	13491.9	35.74
77	10800.2	28.23	11230.7	29.36	11731.5	30.67	12319.0	32.21	13014.9	34.02	13849.3	36.21
78	11082.5	28.60	11524.3	29.74	12038.2	31.07	12641.1	32.62	13355.1	34.46	14211.3	36.67
79	11368.5	28.96	11821.7	30.12	12348.8	31.46	12967.3	33.04	13699.8	34.90	14578.0	37.14
80	11658.2	29.33	12122.8	30.50	12663.5	31.86	13297.6	33.45	14048.8	35.34	14949.4	37.61
81	11951.4	29.69	12427.8	30.88	12982.0	32.25	13632.1	33.87	14402.2	35.78	15325.5	38.07
82	12248.4	30.06	12736.5	31.25	13304.5	32.65	13970.8	34.28	14760.0	36.22	15706.3	38.54
83	12548.9	30.42	13049.1	31.63	13631.0	33.04	14313.6	34.70	15122.2	36.66	16091.7	39.01
84	12853.1	30.78	13365.4	32.01	13961.5	33.44	14660.6	35.11	15488.8	37.10	16481.8	39.48
85	13161.0	31.15	13685.5	32.39	14295.9	33.84	15011.8	35.53	15859.8	37.54	16876.5	39.94
86	13472.5	31.51	14009.4	32.77	14634.2	34.23	15367.1	35.94	16235.1	37.98	17275.9	40.41
87	13787.6	31.88	14337.1	33.15	14976.5	34.63	15726.5	36.36	16614.9	38.41	17680.0	40.88
88	14106.4	32.24	14668.6	33.53	15322.8	35.02	16090.1	36.78	16999.0	38.85	18088.8	41.34
89	14428.8	32.61	15003.9	33.91	15673.0	35.42	16457.9	37.19	17387.6	39.29	18502.3	41.81
90	14754.9	32.97	15343.0	34.28	16027.2	35.81	16829.8	37.61	17780.5	39.73	18920.4	42.28
91	15084.6	33.34	15685.8	34.66	16385.3	36.21	17205.9	38.02	18177.8	40.17	19343.2	42.75
92	15417.9	33.70	16032.4	35.04	16747.4	36.61	17586.1	38.44	18579.5	40.61	19770.6	43.21
93	15754.9	34.06	16382.9	35.42	17113.5	37.00	17970.5	38.85	18985.6	41.05	20202.8	43.68
94	16095.6	34.43	16737.1	35.80	17483.5	37.40	18359.0	39.27	19396.1	41.49	20639.6	44.15
95	16439.8	34.79	17095.1	36.18	17857.5	37.79	18751.7	39.69	19811.0	41.93	21081.0	44.61
96	16787.8	35.16	17456.9	36.56	18235.4	38.19	19148.6	40.10	20230.3	42.37	21527.2	45.08
97	17139.3	35.52	17822.5	36.94	18617.3	38.58	19549.6	40.52	20653.9	42.80	21978.0	45.55
98	17494.5	35.89	18191.8	37.32	19003.1	38.98	19954.7	40.93	21082.0	43.24	22433.5	46.02
99	17853.4	36.25	18565.0	37.69	19392.9	39.38	20364.1	41.35	21514.4	43.68	22893.7	46.48
100	18215.9	36.61	18941.9	38.07	19786.7	39.77	20777.5	41.76	21951.2	44.12	23358.5	46.95
101	18582.0	36.98	19322.7	38.45	20184.4	40.17	21195.2	42.18	22392.5	44.56	23828.0	47.42
102	18951.8	37.34	19707.2	38.83	20586.0	40.56	21617.0	42.59	22838.1	45.00	24302.2	47.88
103	19325.2	37.71	20095.5	39.21	20991.7	40.96	22042.9	43.01	23288.1	45.44	24781.0	48.35
104	19702.3	38.07	20487.6	39.59	21401.2	41.35	22473.0	43.43	23742.5	45.88	25264.6	48.82
105	20083.0	38.44	20883.5	39.97	21814.8	41.75	22907.2	43.84	24201.2	46.32	25752.7	49.29
106	20467.4	38.80	21283.1	40.35	22232.3	42.15	23345.6	44.26	24664.4	46.76	26245.6	49.75
107	20855.4	39.16	21686.6	40.73	22653.7	42.54	23788.2	44.67	25132.0	47.20	26743.1	50.22
108	21247.0	39.53	22093.9	41.10	23079.1	42.94	24234.9	45.09	25603.9	47.63	27245.4	50.69
109	21642.3	39.89	22504.9	41.48	23508.5	43.33	24685.8	45.50	26080.3	48.07	27752.2	51.16
110	22041.2	40.26	22919.7	41.86	23941.8	43.73	25140.8	45.92	26561.0	48.51	28263.8	51.62
111	22443.8	40.62	23338.3	42.24	24379.1	44.12	25600.0	46.33	27046.1	48.95	28780.0	52.09
112	22850.0	40.99	23760.7	42.62	24820.4	44.52	26063.3	46.75	27535.6	49.39	29300.9	52.56
113	23259.9	41.35	24186.9	43.00	25265.6	44.92	26530.8	47.17	28029.5	49.83	29826.5	53.02
114	23673.4	41.71	24616.9	43.38	25714.7	45.31	27002.5	47.58	28527.8	50.27	30356.7	53.49
115	24090.5	42.08	25050.7	43.76	26167.8	45.71	27478.3	48.00	29030.5	50.71	30891.6	53.96
116	24511.3	42.44	25488.2	44.13	26624.9	46.10	27958.3	48.41	29537.6	51.15	31431.2	54.43
117	24935.7	42.81	25929.6	44.51	27085.9	46.50	28442.4	48.83	30049.1	51.59	31975.5	54.89
118	25363.8	43.17	26374.7	44.89	27550.9	46.89	28930.6	49.24	30564.9	52.02	32524.4	55.36
119	25795.5	43.54	26823.7	45.27	28019.9	47.29	29423.1	49.66	31085.2	52.46	33078.0	55.83
120	26230.9	43.90	27276.4	45.65	28492.8	47.69	29919.7	50.07	31609.8	52.90	33636.2	56.29
SUMS.	18°		19°		20°		21°		22°		23°	

TABLE VII. Whole Sections. Side Slope 1½ to 1.

SUMS.	24°		25°		26°		27°		28°		29°	
1	2.5	0.75	2.7	0.82	3.0	0.90	3.3	1.00	3.8	1.15	4.5	1.35
2	10.0	1.25	10.9	1.36	12.0	1.49	13.4	1.67	15.3	1.91	18.0	2.25
3	22.6	1.75	24.5	1.90	26.9	2.09	30.1	2.34	34.4	2.67	40.5	3.15
4	40.1	2.26	43.5	2.45	47.8	2.69	53.4	3.01	61.1	3.44	72.0	4.05
5	62.7	2.76	68.0	2.99	74.7	3.29	83.5	3.67	95.4	4.20	112.5	4.95
6	90.3	3.26	97.9	3.54	107.6	3.88	120.2	4.34	137.4	4.96	162.0	5.85
7	122.8	3.76	133.2	4.08	146.4	4.48	163.6	5.01	187.0	5.73	220.5	6.75
8	160.5	4.26	174.0	4.62	191.3	5.08	213.7	5.68	244.3	6.49	288.0	7.65
9	203.1	4.76	220.3	5.17	242.1	5.68	270.5	6.35	309.2	7.25	364.5	8.55
10	250.7	5.26	271.9	5.71	298.8	6.28	334.0	7.01	381.7	8.02	450.0	9.45
11	303.4	5.77	329.0	6.25	361.6	6.87	404.1	7.68	461.8	8.78	544.5	10.35
12	361.0	6.27	391.6	6.80	430.3	7.47	480.9	8.35	549.6	9.54	647.9	11.25
13	423.7	6.77	459.6	7.34	505.0	8.07	564.4	9.02	645.0	10.31	760.4	12.15
14	491.4	7.27	533.0	7.89	585.7	8.67	654.6	9.69	748.1	11.07	881.9	13.05
15	564.1	7.77	611.8	8.43	672.4	9.26	751.5	10.35	858.8	11.83	1012.4	13.95
16	641.8	8.27	696.1	8.97	765.0	9.86	855.0	11.02	977.1	12.60	1151.9	14.85
17	724.5	8.77	785.9	9.52	863.6	10.46	965.2	11.69	1103.0	13.36	1300.4	15.75
18	812.3	9.28	881.1	10.06	968.2	11.06	1082.1	12.36	1236.6	14.12	1457.9	16.65
19	905.1	9.78	981.7	10.61	1078.8	11.65	1205.7	13.03	1377.9	14.89	1624.4	17.55
20	1002.8	10.28	1087.7	11.15	1195.4	12.25	1335.9	13.69	1526.7	15.65	1799.9	18.45
21	1105.6	10.78	1199.2	11.69	1317.9	12.85	1472.8	14.36	1683.2	16.41	1984.3	19.35
22	1213.4	11.28	1316.1	12.24	1446.4	13.45	1616.5	15.03	1847.3	17.18	2177.8	20.25
23	1326.3	11.78	1438.5	12.78	1580.9	14.05	1766.7	15.70	2019.1	17.94	2380.3	21.15
24	1444.1	12.28	1566.3	13.32	1721.3	14.64	1923.7	16.36	2198.5	18.70	2591.8	22.05
25	1566.9	12.79	1699.6	13.87	1867.7	15.24	2087.4	17.03	2385.5	19.47	2812.3	22.95
26	1694.8	13.29	1838.2	14.41	2020.1	15.84	2257.7	17.70	2580.1	20.23	3041.7	23.85
27	1827.7	13.79	1982.4	14.96	2178.5	16.44	2434.7	18.37	2782.4	20.99	3280.2	24.75
28	1965.6	14.29	2131.9	15.50	2342.9	17.03	2618.4	19.04	2992.4	21.76	3527.7	25.65
29	2108.5	14.79	2286.9	16.04	2513.2	17.63	2808.8	19.70	3209.9	22.52	3784.2	26.55
30	2256.4	15.29	2447.4	16.59	2689.5	18.23	3005.8	20.37	3435.1	23.28	4049.7	27.45
31	2409.3	15.79	2613.2	17.13	2871.8	18.83	3209.5	21.04	3667.9	24.05	4324.1	28.35
32	2567.3	16.30	2784.6	17.68	3060.1	19.42	3419.9	21.71	3908.4	24.81	4607.6	29.25
33	2730.2	16.80	2961.3	18.22	3254.3	20.02	3637.0	22.38	4156.5	25.57	4900.1	30.15
34	2898.2	17.30	3143.5	18.76	3454.6	20.62	3860.8	23.04	4412.2	26.34	5201.6	31.05
35	3071.2	17.80	3331.1	19.31	3660.8	21.22	4091.2	23.71	4675.6	27.10	5512.0	31.95
36	3249.2	18.30	3524.2	19.85	3872.9	21.82	4328.4	24.38	4946.5	27.86	5831.5	32.85
37	3432.2	18.80	3722.7	20.39	4091.1	22.41	4572.2	25.05	5225.2	28.63	6160.0	33.75
38	3620.2	19.30	3926.7	20.94	4315.2	23.01	4822.6	25.72	5511.4	29.39	6497.5	34.65
39	3813.3	19.81	4136.1	21.48	4545.3	23.61	5079.8	26.38	5805.3	30.15	6843.9	35.55
40	4011.3	20.31	4350.9	22.03	4781.4	24.21	5343.6	27.05	6106.8	30.92	7199.4	36.45
41	4214.4	20.81	4571.1	22.57	5023.5	24.80	5614.2	27.72	6416.0	31.68	7563.9	37.35
42	4422.5	21.31	4796.8	23.11	5271.5	25.40	5891.4	28.39	6732.8	32.44	7937.3	38.25
43	4635.6	21.81	5028.0	23.66	5525.5	26.00	6175.2	29.06	7057.2	33.21	8319.8	39.15
44	4853.7	22.31	5264.6	24.20	5785.5	26.60	6465.8	29.72	7389.3	33.97	8711.3	40.05
45	5076.9	22.81	5506.6	24.75	6051.5	27.19	6763.1	30.39	7729.0	34.73	9111.7	40.95
46	5305.0	23.32	5754.0	25.29	6323.4	27.79	7067.0	31.06	8076.3	35.50	9521.2	41.85
47	5538.2	23.82	6006.9	25.83	6601.3	28.39	7377.6	31.73	8431.3	36.26	9939.7	42.75
48	5776.3	24.32	6265.3	26.38	6885.2	28.99	7694.8	32.40	8793.9	37.02	10367.1	43.65
49	6019.5	24.82	6529.0	26.92	7175.1	29.58	8018.8	33.06	9164.1	37.79	10803.6	44.55
50	6267.7	25.32	6798.2	27.46	7470.9	30.18	8349.4	33.73	9541.9	38.55	11249.1	45.45
51	6520.9	25.82	7072.9	28.01	7772.8	30.78	8686.8	34.40	9927.4	39.31	11703.5	46.35
52	6779.2	26.32	7353.0	28.55	8080.6	31.38	9030.8	35.07	10320.6	40.08	12167.0	47.25
53	7042.4	26.83	7638.5	29.10	8394.4	31.98	9381.4	35.74	10721.3	40.84	12639.5	48.15
54	7310.7	27.33	7929.5	29.64	8714.1	32.57	9738.8	36.40	11129.7	41.60	13120.9	49.05
55	7583.9	27.83	8225.9	30.18	9039.8	33.17	10102.8	37.07	11545.7	42.37	13611.4	49.95
56	7862.2	28.33	8527.7	30.73	9371.6	33.77	10473.5	37.74	11969.4	43.13	14110.8	50.85
57	8145.5	28.83	8835.0	31.27	9709.2	34.37	10850.9	38.41	12400.7	43.89	14619.3	51.75
58	8433.8	29.33	9147.7	31.82	10052.9	34.96	11235.0	39.08	12839.6	44.66	15136.8	52.65
59	8727.2	29.83	9465.9	32.36	10402.5	35.56	11625.8	39.74	13286.2	45.42	15663.2	53.55
60	9025.5	30.34	9789.5	32.90	10758.2	36.16	12023.2	40.41	13740.4	46.18	16198.7	54.45
SUMS.	24°		25°		26°		27°		28°		29°	

SUMS.	24°		25°		26°		27°		28°		29°	
61	9328.9	30.84	10118.5	33.45	11119.8	36.76	12427.3	41.08	14202.2	46.95	16743.1	55.35
62	9637.3	31.34	10453.0	33.99	11487.3	37.35	12838.1	41.75	14671.7	47.71	17296.6	56.25
63	9950.6	31.84	10792.9	34.54	11860.9	37.95	13255.6	42.42	15148.8	48.47	17859.0	57.15
64	10269.0	32.34	11138.2	35.08	12240.4	38.55	13679.7	43.08	15633.5	49.24	18430.5	58.05
65	10592.5	32.84	11489.0	35.62	12625.9	39.15	14110.6	43.75	16125.9	50.00	19010.9	58.95
66	10920.9	33.34	11845.3	36.17	13017.4	39.75	14548.1	44.42	16625.9	50.76	19600.4	59.85
67	11254.3	33.85	12206.9	36.71	13414.8	40.34	14992.3	45.09	17133.5	51.53	20198.8	60.74
68	11592.8	34.35	12574.0	37.25	13818.3	40.94	15443.1	45.75	17648.8	52.29	20806.3	61.64
69	11936.3	34.85	12946.6	37.80	14227.7	41.54	15900.7	46.42	18171.7	53.05	21422.7	62.54
70	12284.7	35.35	13324.6	38.34	14643.1	42.14	16364.9	47.09	18702.2	53.82	22048.2	63.44
71	12638.2	35.85	13708.0	38.89	15064.4	42.73	16835.8	47.76	19240.4	54.58	22682.6	64.34
72	12996.7	36.35	14096.8	39.43	15491.8	43.33	17313.4	48.43	19786.2	55.34	23326.1	65.24
73	13360.3	36.85	14491.1	39.98	15925.1	43.93	17797.7	49.09	20339.6	56.11	23978.5	66.14
74	13728.8	37.36	14890.9	40.52	16364.4	44.53	18288.6	49.76	20900.7	56.87	24640.0	67.04
75	14102.4	37.86	15296.1	41.06	16809.6	45.12	18786.3	50.43	21469.4	57.63	25310.4	67.94
76	14480.9	38.36	15706.7	41.60	17260.9	45.72	19290.6	51.10	22045.7	58.40	25989.9	68.84
77	14864.5	38.86	16122.7	42.15	17718.1	46.32	19801.5	51.77	22629.7	59.16	26678.3	69.74
78	15253.1	39.36	16544.2	42.69	18181.3	46.92	20319.2	52.43	23221.3	59.92	27375.7	70.64
79	15646.7	39.86	16971.1	43.24	18650.5	47.52	20843.6	53.10	23820.5	60.69	28082.2	71.54
80	16045.4	40.36	17403.5	43.78	19125.6	48.11	21374.6	53.77	24427.4	61.45	28797.6	72.44
81	16449.0	40.87	17841.3	44.32	19606.8	48.71	21912.3	54.44	25041.9	62.21	29522.1	73.34
82	16857.7	41.37	18284.6	44.87	20093.9	49.31	22456.7	55.11	25664.0	62.98	30255.5	74.24
83	17271.3	41.87	18733.2	45.41	20586.9	49.91	23007.7	55.77	26293.8	63.74	30997.9	75.14
84	17690.0	42.37	19187.4	45.96	21086.0	50.50	23565.5	56.44	26931.2	64.50	31749.4	76.04
85	18113.7	42.87	19646.9	46.50	21591.0	51.10	24129.9	57.11	27576.2	65.27	32509.8	76.94
86	18542.4	43.37	20111.9	47.04	22102.1	51.70	24701.0	57.78	28228.9	66.03	33279.3	77.84
87	18976.2	43.87	20582.4	47.59	22619.0	52.30	25278.8	58.45	28889.2	66.79	34057.7	78.74
88	19414.9	44.38	21058.2	48.13	23142.0	52.89	25863.2	59.11	29557.1	67.56	34845.1	79.64
89	19858.7	44.88	21539.6	48.68	23670.9	53.49	26454.4	59.78	30232.7	68.32	35641.6	80.54
90	20307.4	45.38	22026.3	49.22	24205.9	54.09	27052.2	60.45	30915.9	69.08	36447.0	81.44
91	20761.2	45.88	22518.5	49.76	24746.8	54.69	27656.7	61.12	31606.7	69.85	37261.4	82.34
92	21220.0	46.38	23016.1	50.31	25293.6	55.29	28267.9	61.79	32305.2	70.61	38084.9	83.24
93	21683.8	46.88	23519.2	50.85	25846.5	55.88	28885.7	62.45	33011.3	71.37	38917.3	84.14
94	22152.6	47.38	24027.7	51.39	26405.3	56.48	29510.3	63.12	33725.0	72.14	39758.7	85.04
95	26626.5	47.89	24541.7	51.94	26970.1	57.08	30141.5	63.79	34446.4	72.90	40609.2	85.94
96	23105.3	48.39	25061.0	52.48	27540.9	57.68	30779.4	64.46	35175.4	73.66	41468.6	86.84
97	23589.2	48.89	25585.9	53.03	28117.7	58.27	31424.0	65.13	35912.0	74.43	42337.0	87.74
98	24078.1	49.39	26116.1	53.57	28700.4	58.87	32075.2	65.79	36656.3	75.19	43214.4	88.64
99	24572.0	49.89	26651.8	54.11	29289.1	59.47	32733.2	66.46	37408.2	75.95	44100.9	89.54
100	25070.9	50.39	27193.0	54.66	29883.8	60.07	33397.8	67.13	38167.8	76.72	44996.3	90.44
101	25574.8	50.89	27739.6	55.20	30484.5	60.66	34069.1	67.80	38934.9	77.48	45900.7	91.34
102	26083.8	51.40	28291.6	55.75	31091.1	61.26	34747.1	68.47	39709.7	78.24	46814.1	92.24
103	26597.7	51.90	28849.0	56.29	31703.7	61.86	35431.7	69.13	40492.2	79.01	47736.6	93.14
104	27116.7	52.40	29411.9	56.83	32322.3	62.46	36123.0	69.80	41282.2	79.77	48668.0	94.04
105	27640.7	52.90	29980.3	57.38	32946.9	63.05	36821.1	70.47	42080.0	80.53	49608.4	94.94
106	28169.7	53.40	30554.0	57.92	33577.4	63.65	37525.7	71.14	42885.3	81.30	50557.8	95.84
107	28703.7	53.90	31133.2	58.46	34214.0	64.25	38237.1	71.81	43698.3	82.06	51516.2	96.74
108	29242.7	54.40	31717.9	59.01	34856.5	64.85	38955.2	72.47	44518.9	82.82	52483.7	97.64
109	29786.7	54.91	32308.0	59.55	35504.9	65.45	39679.9	73.14	45347.1	83.59	53460.1	98.54
110	30335.8	55.41	32903.5	60.10	36159.4	66.04	40411.3	73.81	46183.0	84.35	54445.5	99.44
111	30889.8	55.91	33504.5	60.64	36819.8	66.64	41149.4	74.48	47026.5	85.11	55439.9	100.34
112	31448.9	56.41	34110.9	61.18	37486.2	67.24	41894.2	75.15	47877.6	85.88	56443.3	101.24
113	32013.0	56.91	34722.7	61.73	38158.6	67.84	42645.6	75.81	48736.4	86.64	57455.8	102.14
114	32582.1	57.41	35340.0	62.27	38837.0	68.43	43403.8	76.48	49602.8	87.40	58477.2	103.04
115	33156.3	57.91	35962.7	62.82	39521.3	69.03	44168.6	77.15	50476.9	88.17	59507.6	103.94
116	33735.4	58.42	36590.9	63.36	40211.6	69.63	44940.1	77.82	51358.5	88.93	60547.0	104.84
117	34319.5	58.92	37224.5	63.90	40907.9	70.23	45718.2	78.48	52247.8	89.69	61595.4	105.74
118	34908.7	59.42	37863.5	64.45	41610.2	70.82	46503.1	79.15	53144.8	90.46	62652.8	106.64
119	35502.9	59.92	38508.0	64.99	42318.4	71.42	47294.6	79.82	54049.4	91.22	63719.2	107.54
120	36102.1	60.42	39157.9	65.54	43032.7	72.02	48092.8	80.49	54961.6	91.98	64794.7	108.44
SUMS.	24°		25°		26°		27°		28°		29°	

TABLE VIII. **Sub-Sections.** **Side Slope 1½ to 1.**

SUMS.	0°	1°		2°		3°		4°		5°	
1	Nothing.	.0	.00	.0	.01	.0	.01	.0	.01	.0	.01
2	....	.0	.00	.1	.01	.1	.01	.1	.02	.2	.02
3	....	.1	.01	.2	.01	.2	.02	.3	.03	.4	.03
4	....	.1	.01	.3	.02	.4	.02	.6	.03	.7	.04
5	....	.2	.01	.4	.02	.7	.03	.9	.04	1.2	.05
6	....	.3	.01	.6	.02	.9	.03	1.3	.05	1.7	.06
7	....	.4	.01	.8	.03	1.3	.04	1.8	.05	2.3	.07
8	....	.5	.01	1.1	.03	1.7	.04	2.3	.06	3.0	.08
9	....	.7	.02	1.4	.03	2.1	.05	2.9	.07	3.8	.09
10	....	.8	.02	1.7	.04	2.6	.06	3.6	.08	4.7	.10
11	....	1.0	.02	2.1	.04	3.2	.06	4.4	.08	5.6	.11
12	....	1.2	.02	2.5	.04	3.8	.07	5.2	.09	6.7	.12
13	....	1.4	.02	2.9	.05	4.4	.07	6.1	.10	7.9	.13
14	....	1.6	.02	3.3	.05	5.2	.08	7.1	.10	9.1	.14
15	....	1.9	.03	3.8	.05	5.9	.08	8.1	.11	10.5	.14
16	....	2.1	.03	4.4	.06	6.7	.09	9.3	.12	11.9	.15
17	....	2.4	.03	4.9	.06	7.6	.09	10.5	.13	13.5	.16
18	....	2.7	.03	5.5	.06	8.5	.10	11.7	.13	15.1	.17
19	....	3.0	.03	6.2	.07	9.5	.10	13.1	.14	16.8	.18
20	....	3.3	.03	6.8	.07	10.5	.11	14.5	.15	18.6	.19
21	....	3.7	.04	7.5	.07	11.6	.11	16.0	.16	20.6	.20
22	....	4.0	.04	8.3	.08	12.7	.12	17.5	.16	22.6	.21
23	....	4.4	.04	9.0	.08	13.9	.12	19.1	.17	24.7	.22
24	....	4.8	.04	9.8	.08	15.2	.13	20.8	.18	26.9	.23
25	....	5.2	.04	10.7	.09	16.5	.13	22.6	.18	29.1	.24
26	....	5.6	.04	11.5	.09	17.8	.14	24.5	.19	31.5	.25
27	....	6.1	.05	12.4	.09	19.2	.14	26.4	.20	34.0	.26
28	....	6.5	.05	13.4	.10	20.6	.15	28.4	.21	36.6	.27
29	....	7.0	.05	14.3	.10	22.1	.16	30.4	.21	39.2	.28
30	....	7.5	.05	15.4	.10	23.7	.16	32.6	.22	42.0	.28
31	....	8.0	.05	16.4	.11	25.3	.17	34.8	.23	44.8	.29
32	....	8.5	.05	17.5	.11	27.0	.17	37.0	.24	47.7	.30
33	....	9.0	.06	18.6	.11	28.7	.18	39.4	.24	50.8	.31
34	....	9.6	.06	19.7	.12	30.4	.18	41.8	.25	53.9	.32
35	....	10.2	.06	20.9	.12	32.3	.19	44.3	.26	57.1	.33
36	....	10.8	.06	22.1	.12	34.1	.19	46.9	.26	60.4	.34
37	....	11.4	.06	23.4	.13	36.0	.20	49.5	.27	63.8	.35
38	....	12.0	.06	24.6	.13	38.0	.20	52.2	.28	67.3	.36
39	....	12.6	.07	25.9	.13	40.0	.21	55.0	.29	70.9	.37
40	....	13.3	.07	27.3	.14	42.1	.21	57.9	.29	74.6	.38
41	....	14.0	.07	28.7	.14	44.3	.22	60.8	.30	78.4	.39
42	....	14.6	.07	30.1	.15	46.4	.22	63.8	.31	82.2	.40
43	....	15.3	.07	31.5	.15	48.7	.23	66.9	.31	86.2	.41
44	....	16.1	.07	33.0	.15	51.0	.23	70.0	.32	90.3	.41
45	....	16.8	.08	34.5	.16	53.3	.24	73.2	.33	94.4	.42
46	....	17.6	.08	36.1	.16	55.7	.24	76.5	.34	98.6	.43
47	....	18.3	.08	37.7	.16	58.2	.25	79.9	.34	103.0	.44
48	....	19.1	.08	39.3	.17	60.7	.26	83.3	.35	107.4	.45
49	....	19.9	.08	41.0	.17	63.2	.26	86.8	.36	111.9	.46
50	....	20.8	.08	42.7	.17	65.8	.27	90.4	.37	116.6	.47
51	....	21.6	.09	44.4	.18	68.5	.27	94.1	.37	121.3	.48
52	....	22.4	.09	46.1	.18	71.2	.28	97.8	.38	126.1	.49
53	....	23.3	.09	47.9	.18	74.0	.28	101.6	.39	131.0	.50
54	....	24.2	.09	49.7	.19	76.8	.29	105.5	.39	135.9	.51
55	....	25.1	.09	51.6	.19	79.6	.29	109.4	.40	141.0	.52
56	....	26.0	.09	53.5	.19	82.6	.30	113.4	.41	146.2	.53
57	....	27.0	.10	55.4	.20	85.5	.30	117.5	.42	151.5	.54
58	....	27.9	.10	57.4	.20	88.6	.31	121.7	.42	156.8	.55
59	....	28.9	.10	59.4	.20	91.7	.31	125.9	.43	162.3	.55
60	....	29.9	.10	61.4	.21	94.8	.32	130.2	.44	167.8	.56
SUMS.	0°	1°		2°		3°		4°		5°	

TABLE VIII. Sub-Sections. Side Slope $1\frac{1}{2}$ to 1.

SUMS.	6°		7°		8°		9°		10°		11°	
1	.1	.02	.1	.02	.1	.02	.1	.03	.1	.03	.1	.04
2	.2	.03	.3	.03	.3	.04	.4	.05	.4	.06	.5	.06
3	.5	.04	.6	.05	.7	.06	.9	.07	1.0	.08	1.1	.09
4	.9	.05	1.1	.06	1.3	.07	1.5	.09	1.8	.10	2.0	.11
5	1.4	.06	1.7	.08	2.1	.09	2.4	.11	2.8	.12	3.2	.14
6	2.1	.08	2.5	.09	3.0	.11	3.5	.13	4.0	.14	4.6	.17
7	2.8	.09	3.4	.10	4.0	.12	4.7	.14	5.4	.17	6.2	.19
8	3.7	.10	4.5	.12	5.3	.14	6.2	.16	7.1	.19	8.1	.22
9	4.7	.11	5.6	.13	6.7	.16	7.8	.18	9.0	.21	10.3	.24
10	5.8	.12	7.0	.15	8.2	.17	9.6	.20	11.1	.23	12.7	.27
11	7.0	.13	8.4	.16	10.0	.19	11.6	.22	13.4	.26	15.4	.29
12	8.3	.14	10.0	.17	11.9	.21	13.8	.24	16.0	.28	18.3	.32
13	9.8	.16	11.8	.19	13.9	.22	16.3	.26	18.8	.30	21.5	.34
14	11.3	.17	13.7	.20	16.2	.24	18.9	.28	21.8	.32	24.9	.37
15	13.0	.18	15.7	.22	18.6	.26	21.6	.30	25.0	.34	28.6	.39
16	14.8	.19	17.8	.23	21.1	.27	24.6	.32	28.4	.37	32.5	.42
17	16.7	.20	20.1	.24	23.8	.29	27.8	.34	32.1	.39	36.7	.44
18	18.7	.21	22.6	.26	26.7	.31	31.2	.36	36.0	.41	41.2	.47
19	20.9	.23	25.2	.27	29.8	.32	34.7	.38	40.1	.43	45.9	.50
20	23.1	.24	27.9	.29	33.0	.34	38.5	.39	44.4	.46	50.8	.52
21	25.5	.25	30.7	.30	36.4	.35	42.4	.41	48.9	.48	56.0	.55
22	28.0	.26	33.7	.31	39.9	.37	46.6	.43	53.7	.50	61.5	.57
23	30.6	.27	36.9	.33	43.6	.39	50.9	.45	58.7	.52	67.2	.60
24	33.3	.28	40.1	.34	47.5	.40	55.4	.47	63.9	.54	73.2	.62
25	36.1	.29	43.6	.36	51.5	.42	60.1	.49	69.4	.57	79.4	.65
26	39.1	.31	47.1	.37	55.7	.44	65.0	.51	75.0	.59	85.9	.67
27	42.1	.32	50.8	.38	60.1	.45	70.1	.53	80.9	.61	92.6	.70
28	45.3	.33	54.6	.40	64.6	.47	75.4	.55	87.0	.63	99.6	.72
29	48.6	.34	58.6	.41	69.3	.49	80.9	.57	93.3	.65	106.8	.75
30	52.0	.35	62.7	.43	74.2	.50	86.6	.59	99.9	.68	114.3	.77
31	55.5	.36	67.0	.44	79.2	.52	92.4	.61	106.7	.70	122.1	.80
32	59.2	.38	71.4	.45	84.4	.54	98.5	.63	113.7	.72	130.1	.83
33	62.9	.39	75.9	.47	89.8	.55	104.7	.64	120.9	.74	138.3	.85
34	66.8	.40	80.6	.48	95.3	.57	111.2	.66	128.3	.77	146.8	.88
35	70.8	.41	85.4	.49	101.0	.59	117.8	.68	136.0	.79	155.6	.90
36	74.9	.42	90.3	.51	106.9	.60	124.6	.70	143.8	.81	164.6	.93
37	79.1	.43	95.4	.52	112.9	.62	131.7	.72	151.9	.83	173.9	.95
38	83.4	.44	100.6	.54	119.1	.63	138.9	.74	160.3	.85	183.4	.98
39	87.9	.46	106.0	.55	125.4	.65	146.3	.76	168.8	.88	193.2	1.00
40	92.4	.47	111.5	.56	131.9	.67	153.9	.78	177.6	.90	203.2	1.03
41	97.1	.48	117.1	.58	138.6	.68	161.7	.80	186.6	.92	213.5	1.05
42	101.9	.49	122.9	.59	145.4	.70	169.7	.82	195.8	.94	224.1	1.08
43	106.8	.50	128.8	.61	152.5	.72	177.8	.84	205.2	.97	234.9	1.11
44	111.8	.51	134.9	.62	159.6	.73	186.2	.86	214.9	.99	245.9	1.13
45	117.0	.53	141.1	.63	167.0	.75	194.8	.88	224.8	1.01	257.2	1.16
46	122.2	.54	147.4	.65	174.5	.77	203.5	.89	234.9	1.03	268.8	1.18
47	127.6	.55	153.9	.66	182.1	.78	212.5	.91	245.2	1.05	280.6	1.21
48	133.1	.56	160.5	.68	190.0	.80	221.6	.93	255.7	1.08	292.7	1.23
49	138.7	.57	167.3	.69	198.0	.82	230.9	.95	266.5	1.10	305.0	1.26
50	144.4	.58	174.2	.70	206.1	.83	240.5	.97	277.5	1.12	317.6	1.28
51	150.3	.60	181.2	.72	214.5	.85	250.2	.99	288.7	1.14	330.4	1.31
52	156.2	.61	188.4	.73	222.9	.87	260.1	1.01	300.1	1.17	343.5	1.33
53	162.3	.62	195.7	.75	231.6	.88	270.2	1.03	311.8	1.19	356.8	1.36
54	168.5	.63	203.2	.76	240.4	.90	280.5	1.05	323.6	1.21	370.4	1.38
55	174.8	.64	210.8	.77	249.4	.92	290.9	1.07	335.7	1.23	384.3	1.41
56	181.2	.65	218.5	.79	258.6	.93	301.6	1.09	348.1	1.25	398.4	1.44
57	187.7	.66	226.4	.80	267.9	.95	312.5	1.11	360.6	1.28	412.7	1.46
58	194.3	.68	234.4	.82	277.4	.96	323.5	1.13	373.4	1.30	427.8	1.49
59	201.1	.69	242.6	.83	287.0	.98	334.8	1.14	386.4	1.32	442.2	1.51
60	208.0	.70	250.8	.84	296.8	1.00	346.2	1.16	399.6	1.34	457.3	1.54
SUMS.	6°		7°		8°		9°		10°		11°	

TABLE VIII. **Sub-Sections.** **Side Slope $1\frac{1}{2}$ to 1.**

SUMS.	12°		13°		14°		15°		16°		17°	
1	.1	.04	.2	.05	.2	.06	.2	.06	.2	.07	3	.08
2	.6	.07	.7	.08	.7	.09	.8	.10	.9	.12	1.0	.13
3	1.3	.10	1.5	.11	1.7	.13	1.9	.15	2.1	.16	2.4	.18
4	2.3	.13	2.6	.15	3.0	.17	3.3	.19	3.7	.21	4.2	.24
5	3.6	.16	4.1	.18	4.6	.20	5.2	.23	5.8	.26	6.5	.29
6	5.2	.19	5.9	.21	6.6	.24	7.5	.27	8.4	.30	9.4	.34
7	7.1	.22	8.0	.25	9.0	.28	10.2	.31	11.4	.35	12.8	.39
8	9.2	.25	10.5	.28	11.8	.31	13.3	.35	14.9	.40	16.7	.44
9	11.7	.27	13.2	.31	14.9	.35	16.8	.39	18.9	.44	21.2	.50
10	14.4	.30	16.4	.34	18.4	.39	20.7	.44	23.3	.49	26.1	.55
11	17.5	.33	19.8	.38	22.3	.42	25.1	.48	28.2	.54	31.6	.60
12	20.8	.36	23.5	.41	26.6	.46	29.9	.52	33.5	.58	37.6	.65
13	24.4	.39	27.6	.44	31.2	.50	35.1	.56	39.4	.63	44.2	.71
14	28.3	.42	32.0	.47	36.1	.53	40.7	.60	45.7	.68	51.2	.76
15	32.5	.45	36.8	.51	41.5	.57	46.7	.64	52.4	.72	58.8	.81
16	37.0	.48	41.9	.54	47.2	.61	53.1	.68	59.6	.77	66.9	.86
17	41.8	.51	47.3	.57	53.3	.65	59.9	.73	67.3	.82	75.6	.92
18	46.8	.53	53.0	.60	59.7	.68	67.2	.77	75.5	.86	84.7	.97
19	52.2	.56	59.0	.64	66.6	.72	74.9	.81	84.1	.91	94.4	1.02
20	57.8	.59	65.4	.67	73.8	.76	83.0	.85	93.2	.96	104.6	1.07
21	63.7	.62	72.1	.70	81.3	.79	91.5	.89	102.7	1.00	115.3	1.12
22	69.9	.65	79.1	.74	89.2	.83	100.4	.93	112.7	1.05	126.5	1.18
23	76.4	.68	86.5	.77	97.5	.87	109.7	.97	123.2	1.09	138.3	1.23
24	83.2	.71	94.2	.80	106.2	.90	119 5	1.02	134.2	1.14	150.6	1.28
25	90.3	.74	102.2	.83	115.2	.94	129.6	1.06	145.6	1.19	163.4	1.33
26	97.7	.77	110.5	.87	124.6	.98	140.2	1.10	157.5	1.23	176.7	1.39
27	105.3	.79	119.2	.90	134.4	1.01	151.2	1.14	169.8	1.28	190.6	1.44
28	113.3	.82	128.2	.93	144.6	1.05	162.6	1.18	182.6	1.33	205.0	1.49
29	121.5	.85	137.5	.96	155.1	1.09	174.4	1.22	195.9	1.37	219.9	1.54
30	130.0	.88	147.2	1.00	166.0	1.12	186.7	1.27	209.7	1.42	235.3	1.59
31	138.8	.91	157.1	1.03	177.2	1.16	199.3	1.31	223.9	1.47	251.2	1.65
32	147.9	.94	167.4	1.06	188.8	1.20	212.4	1.35	238.5	1.51	267.7	1.70
33	157.3	.97	178.1	1.10	200.8	1.24	225.9	1.39	253.7	1.56	284.7	1.75
34	167.0	1.00	189.0	1.13	213.2	1.27	239.3	1.43	269.3	1.61	302.2	1.80
35	177.0	1.03	200.3	1.16	225.9	1.31	254.1	1.47	285.4	1.65	320.3	1.86
36	187.2	1.05	211.9	1.19	239.0	1.35	268.8	1.51	301.9	1.70	338.8	1.91
37	197.8	1.08	223.8	1.23	252.4	1.38	284.0	1.56	318.9	1.75	357.9	1.96
38	208.6	1.11	236.1	1.26	266.3	1.42	299.5	1.60	336.4	1.79	377.5	2.01
39	219.7	1.14	248.7	1.29	280.5	1.46	315.5	1.64	354.3	1.84	397.7	2.07
40	231.2	1.17	261 6	1.32	295.0	1.49	331.9	1.68	372.7	1.89	418.3	2.12
41	242.9	1.20	274.9	1.36	310.0	1.53	348.7	1.72	391.6	1.93	439.5	2.17
42	254.8	1.23	288.4	1.39	325.3	1.57	365.9	1.76	410.9	1.98	461.2	2.22
43	267.1	1.26	302.3	1.42	340.9	1.60	383.5	1.80	430.7	2.03	483.4	2.27
44	279.7	1.29	316.6	1.46	357.0	1.64	401.6	1.85	451.0	2.07	506.1	2.33
45	292.6	1.31	331.1	1.49	373.4	1.68	420.0	1.89	471.7	2.12	529.4	2.38
46	305.7	1.34	346.0	1.52	390.2	1.71	438.9	1.93	492.9	2.17	553.2	2.43
47	319.1	1.37	361.2	1.55	407.3	1.75	458.2	1.97	514.6	2.21	577.5	2.48
48	332.9	1.40	376.7	1.59	424.8	1.79	477.9	2.01	536.7	2.26	602.4	2.54
49	346.9	1.43	392.6	1.62	442.7	1.83	498.0	2.05	559.3	2.31	627.7	2.59
50	361.2	1.46	408.8	1.65	461.0	1.86	518.6	2.09	582.4	2.35	653.6	2.64
51	375.8	1.49	425.3	1.68	479.6	1.90	539.5	2.14	605.9	2.40	680.0	2.69
52	390.6	1.52	442.1	1.72	498.6	1.94	560.9	2.18	629.9	2.45	706.9	2.75
53	405.8	1.55	459.3	1.75	518.0	1.97	582.6	2.22	654.4	2.49	734.4	2.80
54	421.3	1.57	476.8	1.78	537.7	2.01	604.8	2.26	679.3	2.54	762.4	2.85
55	437.0	1.60	494.6	1.81	557.8	2.05	627.4	2.30	704.7	2.59	790.9	2.90
56	453.1	1.63	512.8	1.85	578.2	2.08	650.5	2.34	730.5	2.63	819.9	2.95
57	469.4	1.66	531.2	1.88	599.1	2.12	673.9	2.39	756.9	2.68	849.4	3.01
58	486.0	1.69	550.0	1.91	620.3	2.16	697.8	2.43	783.6	2.73	879.5	3.06
59	502.9	1.72	569.2	1.95	641.9	2.19	722.0	2.47	810.9	2.77	910.1	3.11
60	520.1	1.75	588.6	1.98	663.8	2.23	746.7	2.51	838.6	2.82	941.2	3.16
SUMS.	12°		13°		14°		15°		16°		17°	

TABLE VIII. Sub-Sections. Side Slope 1½ to 1.

SUMS.	18°		19°		20°		21°		22°		23°	
1	.3	.09	.3	.10	.4	.11	.4	.13	.5	.14	.5	.16
2	1.2	.15	1.3	.16	1.5	.19	1.7	.21	1.9	.24	2.2	.27
3	2.6	.21	3.0	.23	3.3	.26	3.8	.29	4.3	.33	4.9	.38
4	4.7	.26	5.3	.30	5.9	.33	6.7	.38	7.6	.43	8.7	.49
5	7.3	.32	8.2	.36	9.3	.41	10.5	.46	11.9	.52	13.5	.60
6	10.6	.38	11.9	.43	13.4	.48	15.1	.54	17.1	.62	19.5	.70
7	14.4	.44	16.2	.49	18.2	.56	20.5	.63	23.3	.71	26.5	.81
8	18.8	.50	21.1	.56	23.8	.63	26.8	.71	30.4	.81	34.6	.92
9	23.8	.56	26.7	.63	30.1	.71	33.9	.80	38.5	.90	43.8	1.03
10	29.3	.62	33.0	.69	37.1	.78	41.9	.88	47.5	1.00	54.1	1.14
11	35.5	.67	39.9	.76	44.9	.85	50.7	.96	57.4	1.09	65.5	1.24
12	42.3	.73	47.5	.82	53.4	.93	60.3	1.05	68.4	1.19	77.9	1.35
13	49.6	.79	55.7	.89	62.7	1.00	70.8	1.13	80.2	1.28	91.4	1.46
14	57.5	.85	64.6	.96	72.7	1.08	82.1	1.21	93.1	1.38	106.0	1.57
15	66.0	.91	74.2	1.02	83.5	1.15	94.3	1.30	106.8	1.47	121.7	1.68
16	75.1	.97	84.4	1.09	95.0	1.22	107.2	1.38	121.5	1.57	138.5	1.79
17	84.8	1.03	95.3	1.15	107.3	1.30	121.1	1.47	137.2	1.66	156.3	1.89
18	95.1	1.09	106.8	1.22	120.2	1.37	135.7	1.55	153.8	1.76	175.3	2.00
19	105.9	1.14	119.0	1.29	134.0	1.45	151.2	1.63	171.4	1.85	195.3	2.11
20	117.4	1.20	131.9	1.35	148.4	1.52	167.6	1.72	189.9	1.95	216.4	2.22
21	129.4	1.26	145.4	1.42	163.7	1.60	184.8	1.80	209.4	2.04	238.6	2.33
22	142.0	1.32	159.6	1.48	179.6	1.67	202.8	1.89	229.8	2.14	261.8	2.43
23	155.2	1.38	174.4	1.55	196.3	1.74	221.6	1.97	251.2	2.23	286.2	2.54
24	169.0	1.44	189.9	1.62	213.8	1.82	241.3	2.05	273.5	2.33	311.6	2.65
25	183.4	1.50	206.1	1.68	232.0	1.89	261.8	2.14	296.7	2.42	338.1	2.76
26	198.4	1.56	222.9	1.75	250.9	1.97	283.2	2.22	321.0	2.52	365.7	2.87
27	213.9	1.61	240.4	1.81	270.5	2.04	305.4	2.30	346.1	2.61	394.3	2.98
28	230.1	1.67	258.5	1.88	291.0	2.12	328.4	2.39	372.2	2.71	424.1	3.08
29	246.8	1.73	277.3	1.95	312.1	2.19	352.3	2.47	399.3	2.80	454.9	3.19
30	264.1	1.79	296.7	2.01	334.0	2.26	377.0	2.56	427.3	2.90	486.8	3.30
31	282.0	1.85	316.8	2.08	356.6	2.34	402.6	2.64	456.3	2.99	519.8	3.41
32	300.5	1.91	337.6	2.14	380.0	2.41	429.0	2.72	486.2	3.09	553.9	3.52
33	319.6	1.97	359.0	2.21	404.1	2.49	456.2	2.81	517.0	3.18	589.1	3.62
34	339.2	2.02	381.1	2.27	429.0	2.56	484.3	2.89	548.9	3.28	625.3	3.73
35	359.5	2.08	403.9	2.34	454.6	2.63	513.2	2.97	581.6	3.37	662.7	3.84
36	380.3	2.14	427.3	2.41	481.0	2.71	542.9	3.06	615.3	3.47	701.1	3.95
37	401.7	2.20	451.4	2.47	508.1	2.78	573.5	3.14	650.0	3.56	740.5	4.06
38	423.7	2.26	476.1	2.54	535.9	2.86	604.9	3.23	685.6	3.66	781.1	4.17
39	446.3	2.32	501.5	2.60	564.5	2.93	637.2	3.31	722.2	3.75	822.8	4.27
40	469.5	2.38	527.5	2.67	593.8	3.01	670.3	3.39	759.7	3.85	865.5	4.38
41	493.3	2.44	554.2	2.74	623.9	3.08	704.2	3.48	798.1	3.94	909.3	4.49
42	517.6	2.49	581.6	2.80	654.7	3.15	739.0	3.56	837.5	4.04	954.2	4.60
43	542.6	2.55	609.6	2.87	686.2	3.23	774.6	3.64	877.9	4.13	1000.2	4.71
44	568.1	2.61	638.3	2.93	718.5	3.30	811.1	3.73	919.2	4.23	1047.3	4.81
45	594.2	2.67	667.6	3.00	751.5	3.38	848.4	3.81	961.4	4.32	1095.4	4.92
46	620.9	2.73	697.6	3.07	785.3	3.45	886.5	3.90	1004.7	4.42	1144.6	5.03
47	648.2	2.79	728.3	3.13	819.8	3.53	925.4	3.98	1048.8	4.51	1194.9	5.14
48	676.1	2.85	759.6	3.20	855.1	3.60	965.2	4.06	1093.9	4.61	1246.3	5.25
49	704.5	2.91	791.6	3.26	891.1	3.67	1005.9	4.15	1140.0	4.70	1298.8	5.36
50	733.6	2.96	824.3	3.33	927.8	3.75	1047.4	4.23	1187.0	4.80	1352.4	5.46
51	763.2	3.02	857.5	3.40	965.3	3.82	1089.7	4.32	1234.9	4.89	1407.0	5.57
52	793.5	3.08	891.5	3.46	1003.5	3.90	1132.8	4.40	1283.8	4.99	1462.7	5.68
53	824.3	3.14	926.1	3.53	1042.5	3.97	1176.8	4.48	1333.7	5.08	1519.5	5.79
54	855.7	3.20	961.4	3.59	1082.2	4.05	1221.6	4.57	1384.5	5.18	1577.4	5.90
55	887.7	3.26	997.3	3.66	1122.6	4.12	1267.3	4.65	1436.2	5.27	1636.3	6.00
56	920.2	3.32	1033.9	3.73	1163.8	4.19	1313.8	4.73	1488.9	5.37	1696.4	6.11
57	953.4	3.37	1071.2	3.79	1205.8	4.27	1361.1	4.82	1542.6	5.46	1757.5	6.22
58	987.1	3.43	1109.1	3.86	1248.4	4.34	1409.3	4.90	1597.2	5.56	1819.7	6.33
59	1021.5	3.49	1147.7	3.92	1291.9	4.42	1458.3	4.99	1652.7	5.65	1883.0	6.44
60	1056.4	3.55	1186.9	3.99	1336.0	4.49	1508.2	5.07	1709.2	5.74	1947.4	6.55
SUMS.	18°		19°		20°		21°		22°		23°	

SUMS.	24°		25°		26°		27°		28°		29°	
1	.6	.19	.7	.22	.8	.25	1.0	.30	1.2	.36	1.5	.46
2	2.5	.31	2.9	.36	3.4	.42	4.0	.50	4.9	.61	6.1	.76
3	5.6	.43	6.5	.50	7.6	.59	9.0	.70	10.9	.85	13.7	1.07
4	9.9	.56	11.5	.65	13.5	.76	16.0	.90	19.5	1.09	24.4	1.37
5	15.5	.68	18.0	.79	21.0	.93	25.0	1.10	30.4	1.34	38.1	1.67
6	22.3	.81	25.9	.93	30.3	1.09	36.0	1.30	43.8	1.58	54.8	1.98
7	30.4	.93	35.2	1.08	41.2	1.26	49.0	1.50	59.6	1.82	74.6	2.28
8	39.7	1.05	46.0	1.22	53.8	1.43	64.0	1.70	77.8	2.07	97.5	2.59
9	50.3	1.18	58.2	1.36	68.1	1.60	81.1	1.90	98.5	2.31	123.3	2.89
10	62.1	1.30	71.8	1.51	84.1	1.77	100.1	2.10	121.6	2.55	152.3	3.20
11	75.1	1.43	86.9	1.65	101.8	1.93	121.1	2.30	147.1	2.80	184.2	3.50
12	89.4	1.55	103.4	1.80	121.1	2.10	144.1	2.50	175.1	3.04	219.3	3.81
13	104.9	1.68	121.4	1.94	142.2	2.27	169.1	2.70	205.5	3.28	257.3	4.11
14	121.6	1.80	140.8	2.08	164.9	2.44	196.1	2.90	238.3	3.53	298.4	4.42
15	139.6	1.92	161.6	2.23	189.3	2.61	225.2	3.10	273.6	3.77	342.6	4.72
16	158.9	2.05	183.9	2.37	215.4	2.78	256.2	3.30	311.3	4.01	389.8	5.02
17	179.3	2.17	207.6	2.51	243.1	2.94	289.2	3.50	351.4	4.26	440.1	5.33
18	201.1	2.30	232.7	2.66	272.6	3.11	324.2	3.70	394.0	4.50	493.3	5.63
19	224.0	2.42	259.3	2.80	303.7	3.28	361.3	3.90	439.0	4.74	549.7	5.94
20	248.2	2.54	287.3	2.95	336.5	3.45	400.3	4.10	486.4	4.99	609.1	6.24
21	273.7	2.67	316.8	3.09	371.0	3.62	441.3	4.30	536.3	5.23	671.5	6.55
22	300.4	2.79	347.7	3.23	407.2	3.79	484.4	4.50	588.5	5.47	737.0	6.85
23	328.3	2.92	380.0	3.38	445.0	3.95	529.4	4.70	643.3	5.72	805.5	7.16
24	357.4	3.04	413.8	3.52	484.6	4.12	576.4	4.90	700.4	5.96	877.1	7.46
25	387.9	3.16	449.0	3.66	525.8	4.29	625.5	5.10	760.0	6.20	951.7	7.77
26	419.5	3.29	485.6	3.81	568.7	4.46	676.5	5.30	822.0	6.44	1029.3	8.07
27	452.4	3.41	523.7	3.95	613.3	4.63	729.6	5.50	886.5	6.69	1110.0	8.37
28	486.5	3.54	563.2	4.09	659.6	4.80	784.6	5.70	953.4	6.93	1193.8	8.68
29	521.9	3.66	604.1	4.24	707.5	4.96	841.6	5.90	1022.7	7.17	1280.6	8.98
30	558.5	3.79	646.5	4.38	757.2	5.13	900.7	6.10	1094.4	7.42	1370.4	9.29
31	596.4	3.91	690.3	4.53	808.5	5.30	961.7	6.30	1168.6	7.66	1463.3	9.59
32	635.5	4.03	735.6	4.67	861.5	5.47	1024.8	6.50	1245.2	7.90	1559.2	9.90
33	675.8	4.16	782.3	4.81	916.2	5.64	1089.8	6.71	1324.2	8.15	1658.2	10.20
34	717.4	4.28	830.4	4.96	972.5	5.80	1156.9	6.91	1405.7	8.39	1760.2	10.51
35	760.2	4.41	879.9	5.10	1030.6	5.97	1225.9	7.11	1489.6	8.63	1865.3	10.81
36	804.2	4.53	930.9	5.24	1090.3	6.14	1297.0	7.31	1575.9	8.88	1973.4	11.12
37	849.5	4.65	983.4	5.39	1151.7	6.31	1370.0	7.51	1664.7	9.12	2084.5	11.42
38	896.1	4.78	1037.3	5.53	1214.8	6.48	1445.1	7.71	1755.9	9.36	2198.7	11.72
39	943.9	4.90	1092.6	5.67	1279.6	6.65	1522.2	7.91	1849.6	9.61	2316.0	12.03
40	992.9	5.03	1149.3	5.82	1346.1	6.81	1601.2	8.11	1945.6	9.85	2436.3	12.33
41	1043.2	5.15	1207.5	5.96	1414.2	6.98	1682.3	8.31	2044.1	10.09	2559.6	12.64
42	1094.7	5.27	1267.1	6.11	1484.0	7.15	1765.3	8.51	2145.0	10.34	2686.0	12.94
43	1147.4	5.40	1328.2	6.25	1555.5	7.32	1850.4	8.71	2248.4	10.58	2815.4	13.25
44	1201.4	5.52	1390.7	6.39	1628.7	7.49	1937.5	8.91	2354.2	10.82	2947.9	13.55
45	1256.6	5.65	1454.6	6.54	1703.6	7.66	2026.5	9.11	2462.4	11.07	3083.4	13.86
46	1313.1	5.77	1520.0	6.68	1780.2	7.82	2117.6	9.31	2573.1	11.31	3222.0	14.16
47	1370.8	5.90	1586.8	6.82	1858.4	7.99	2210.7	9.51	2686.2	11.55	3363.6	14.47
48	1429.8	6.02	1655.0	6.97	1938.3	8.16	2305.8	9.71	2801.7	11.80	3508.2	14.77
49	1490.0	6.14	1724.7	7.11	2019.9	8.33	2402.8	9.91	2919.6	12.04	3655.9	15.07
50	1551.4	6.27	1795.8	7.26	2103.2	8.50	2501.9	10.11	3040.0	12.28	3806.7	15.38
51	1614.1	6.39	1868.4	7.40	2188.2	8.67	2603.0	10.31	3162.8	12.52	3960.5	15.68
52	1678.0	6.52	1942.3	7.54	2274.8	8.83	2706.1	10.51	3288.1	12.77	4117.3	15.99
53	1743.2	6.64	2017.8	7.69	2363.2	9.00	2811.1	10.71	3415.8	13.01	4277.2	16.29
54	1809.6	6.76	2094.6	7.83	2453.2	9.17	2918.2	10.91	3545.9	13.25	4440.1	16.60
55	1877.2	6.89	2172.9	7.97	2544.9	9.34	3027.3	11.11	3678.4	13.50	4606.1	16.90
56	1946.1	7.01	2252.7	8.12	2638.3	9.51	3138.4	11.31	3813.4	13.74	4775.1	17.21
57	2016.2	7.14	2333.8	8.26	2733.4	9.67	3251.5	11.51	3950.8	13.98	4947.2	17.51
58	2087.6	7.26	2416.4	8.40	2830.1	9.84	3366.6	11.71	4090.7	14.23	5122.3	17.82
59	2160.2	7.38	2500.5	8.55	2928.5	10.01	3483.6	11.91	4232.9	14.47	5300.4	18.12
60	2234.0	7.51	2586.0	8.69	3028.6	10.18	3602.7	12.11	4377.6	14.71	5481.6	18.42
SUMS.	24°		25°		26°		27°		28°		29°	

TABLE A. **Surface-Slopes.**

Tangent.	Slope.	Tangent.	Slope.	Tangent.	Slope.	Tangent.	Slope.	Tangent.	Slope.
.0044	¼°	.2726	15¼°	.5832	30¼°	1.0088	45¼°	1.7496	60¼°
.0087	½	.2773	15½	.5890	30½	1.0176	45½	1.7675	60½
.0131	¾	.2820	15¾	.5949	30¾	1.0265	45¾	1.7856	60¾
.0175	**1°**	.2867	**16°**	.6009	**31°**	1.0355	**46°**	1.8040	**61°**
.0218	1¼	.2915	16¼	.6068	31¼	1.0446	46¼	1.8228	61¼
.0262	1½	.2962	16½	.6128	31½	1.0538	46½	1.8418	61½
.0306	1¾	.3010	16¾	.6188	31¾	1.0630	46¾	1.8611	61¾
.0349	**2°**	.3057	**17°**	.6249	**32°**	1.0724	**47°**	1.8807	**62°**
.0393	2¼	.3105	17¼	.6310	32¼	1.0818	47¼	1.9007	62¼
.0437	2½	.3153	17½	.6371	32½	1.0913	47½	1.9210	62½
.0480	2¾	.3201	17¾	.6432	32¾	1.1009	47¾	1.9416	62¾
.0524	**3°**	.3249	**18°**	.6494	**33°**	1.1106	**48°**	1.9626	**63°**
.0568	3¼	.3298	18¼	.6556	33¼	1.1204	48¼	1.9840	63¼
.0612	3½	.3346	18½	.6619	33½	1.1303	48½	2.0057	63½
.0655	3¾	.3395	18¾	.6682	33¾	1.1403	48¾	2.0278	63¾
.0699	**4°**	.3443	**19°**	.6745	**34°**	1.1504	**49°**	2.0503	**64°**
.0743	4¼	.3492	19¼	.6809	34¼	1.1606	49¼	2.0732	64¼
.0787	4½	.3541	19½	.6873	34½	1.1708	49½	2.0965	64½
.0831	4¾	.3590	19¾	.6937	34¾	1.1812	49¾	2.1203	64¾
.0875	**5°**	.3640	**20°**	.7002	**35°**	1.1918	**50°**	2.1445	**65°**
.0919	5¼	.3689	20¼	.7067	35¼	1.2024	50¼	2.1692	65¼
.0963	5½	.3739	20½	.7133	35½	1.2131	50½	2.1943	65½
.1007	5¾	.3789	20¾	.7199	35¾	1.2239	50¾	2.2199	65¾
.1051	**6°**	.3839	**21°**	.7265	**36°**	1.2349	**51°**	2.2460	**66°**
.1095	6¼	.3889	21¼	.7332	36¼	1.2460	51¼	2.2727	66¼
.1139	6½	.3939	21½	.7400	36½	1.2572	51½	2.2998	66½
.1184	6¾	.3990	21¾	.7467	36¾	1.2685	51¾	2.3276	66¾
.1228	**7°**	.4040	**22°**	.7536	**37°**	1.2799	**52°**	2.3559	**67°**
.1272	7¼	.4091	22¼	.7604	37¼	1.2915	52¼	2.3847	67¼
.1317	7½	.4142	22½	.7673	37½	1.3032	52½	2.4142	67½
.1361	7¾	.4193	22¾	.7743	37¾	1.3151	52¾	2.4443	67¾
.1405	**8°**	.4245	**23°**	.7813	**38°**	1.3270	**53°**	2.4751	**68°**
.1450	8¼	.4296	23¼	.7883	38¼	1.3392	53¼	2.5065	68¼
.1495	8½	.4348	23½	.7954	38½	1.3514	53½	2.5386	68½
.1539	8¾	.4400	23¾	.8026	38¾	1.3638	53¾	2.5715	68¾
.1584	**9°**	.4452	**24°**	.8098	**39°**	1.3764	**54°**	2.6051	**69°**
.1629	9¼	.4505	24¼	.8170	39¼	1.3891	54¼	2.6395	69¼
.1673	9½	.4557	24½	.8243	39½	1.4019	54½	2.6746	69½
.1718	9¾	.4610	24¾	.8317	39¾	1.4150	54¾	2.7106	69¾
.1763	**10°**	.4663	**25°**	.8391	**40°**	1.4281	**55°**	2.7475	**70°**
.1808	10¼	.4716	25¼	.8466	40¼	1.4415	55¼	2.7852	70¼
.1853	10½	.4770	25½	.8541	40½	1.4550	55½	2.8239	70½
.1899	10¾	.4823	25¾	.8617	40¾	1.4687	55¾	2.8636	70¾
.1944	**11°**	.4877	**26°**	.8693	**41°**	1.4826	**56°**	2.9042	**71°**
.1989	11¼	.4931	26¼	.8770	41¼	1.4966	56¼	2.9459	71¼
.2035	11½	.4986	26½	.8847	41½	1.5108	56½	2.9887	71½
.2080	11¾	.5040	26¾	.8925	41¾	1.5253	56¾	3.0326	71¾
.2126	**12°**	.5095	**27°**	.9004	**42°**	1.5399	**57°**	3.0777	**72°**
.2171	12¼	.5150	27¼	.9083	42¼	1.5547	57¼	3.1240	72¼
.2217	12½	.5206	27½	.9163	42½	1.5697	57½	3.1716	72½
.2263	12¾	.5261	27¾	.9244	42¾	1.5849	57¾	3.2205	72¾
.2309	**13°**	.5317	**28°**	.9325	**43°**	1.6003	**58°**	3.2709	**73°**
.2355	13¼	.5373	28¼	.9407	43¼	1.6160	58¼	3.3226	73¼
.2401	13½	.5430	28½	.9490	43½	1.6319	58½	3.3759	73½
.2447	13¾	.5486	28¾	.9573	43¾	1.6479	58¾	3.4308	73¾
.2493	**14°**	.5543	**29°**	.9657	**44°**	1.6643	**59°**	3.4874	**74°**
.2540	14¼	.5600	29¼	.9742	44¼	1.6808	59¼	3.5457	74¼
.2586	14½	.5658	29½	.9827	44½	1.6977	59½	3.6059	74½
.2633	14¾	.5715	29¾	.9913	44¾	1.7147	59¾	3.6680	74¾
.2679	**15°**	.5774	**30°**	1.0000	**45°**	1.7321	**60°**	3.7321	**75°**

TABLE IX. Whole Sections. Side Slope 1 to 1.

SUMS.	0°		1°		2°		3°		4°		5°	
1	0.9	0.28	0.9	0.28	0.9	0.28	0.9	0.28	0.9	0.28	0.9	0.28
2	3.7	0.46	3.7	0.46	3.7	0.46	3.7	0.46	3.7	0.47	3.7	0.47
3	8.3	0.65	8.3	0.65	8.3	0.65	8.4	0.65	8.4	0.65	8.4	0.65
4	14.8	0.83	14.8	0.83	14.8	0.83	14.9	0.84	14.9	0.84	14.9	0.84
5	23.1	1.02	23.2	1.02	23.2	1.02	23.2	1.02	23.3	1.02	23.3	1.03
6	33.3	1.20	33.3	1.20	33.4	1.21	33.4	1.21	33.5	1.21	33.6	1.21
7	45.4	1.39	45.4	1.39	45.4	1.39	45.5	1.39	45.6	1.40	45.7	1.40
8	59.3	1.57	59.3	1.57	59.3	1.58	59.4	1.58	59.6	1.58	59.7	1.59
9	75.0	1.76	75.0	1.76	75.1	1.76	75.2	1.76	75.4	1.77	75.6	1.77
10	92.6	1.94	92.6	1.95	92.7	1.95	92.8	1.95	93.0	1.95	93.3	1.96
11	112.0	2.13	112.1	2.13	112.2	2.13	112.3	2.14	112.6	2.14	112.9	2.15
12	133.3	2.31	133.4	2.32	133.5	2.32	133.7	2.32	134.0	2.33	134.4	2.33
13	156.5	2.50	156.5	2.50	156.7	2.50	156.9	2.51	157.3	2.51	157.7	2.52
14	181.5	2.69	181.5	2.69	181.7	2.69	182.0	2.69	182.4	2.70	182.9	2.71
15	208.3	2.87	208.4	2.87	208.6	2.87	208.9	2.88	209.4	2.88	209.9	2.89
16	237.0	3.06	237.1	3.06	237.3	3.06	237.7	3.06	238.2	3.07	238.9	3.08
17	267.6	3.24	267.7	3.24	267.9	3.24	268.3	3.25	268.9	3.26	269.7	3.27
18	300.0	3.43	300.1	3.43	300.4	3.43	300.8	3.44	301.5	3.44	302.3	3.45
19	334.3	3.61	334.4	3.61	334.7	3.62	335.2	3.62	335.9	3.63	336.8	3.64
20	370.4	3.80	370.5	3.80	370.8	3.80	371.4	3.81	372.2	3.81	373.2	3.83
21	408.3	3.98	408.5	3.98	408.8	3.99	409.5	3.99	410.3	4.00	411.5	4.01
22	448.1	4.17	448.3	4.17	448.7	4.17	449.4	4.18	450.4	4.19	451.6	4.20
23	489.8	4.35	490.0	4.35	490.4	4.36	491.2	4.36	492.2	4.37	493.6	4.39
24	533.3	4.54	533.5	4.54	534.0	4.54	534.8	4.55	536.0	4.56	537.4	4.57
25	578.7	4.72	578.9	4.72	579.4	4.73	580.3	4.74	581.5	4.75	583.2	4.76
26	625.9	4.91	626.1	4.91	626.7	4.91	627.6	4.92	629.0	4.93	630.8	4.95
27	675.0	5.09	675.2	5.09	675.8	5.10	676.9	5.11	678.3	5.12	680.2	5.13
28	725.9	5.28	726.1	5.28	726.8	5.28	727.9	5.29	729.5	5.30	731.5	5.32
29	778.7	5.46	778.9	5.46	779.7	5.47	780.8	5.48	782.5	5.49	784.7	5.51
30	833.3	5.65	833.6	5.65	834.4	5.66	835.6	5.66	837.4	5.68	839.8	5.69
31	889.8	5.83	890.1	5.84	890.9	5.84	892.3	5.85	894.2	5.86	896.7	5.88
32	948.1	6.02	948.4	6.02	949.3	6.03	950.8	6.04	952.8	6.05	955.5	6.06
33	1008.3	6.20	1008.6	6.21	1009.6	6.21	1011.1	6.22	1013.3	6.23	1016.1	6.25
34	1070.4	6.39	1070.7	6.39	1071.7	6.40	1073.3	6.41	1075.6	6.42	1078.6	6.44
35	1134.3	6.57	1134.6	6.58	1135.6	6.58	1137.4	6.59	1139.8	6.61	1143.0	6.62
36	1200.0	6.76	1200.4	6.76	1201.5	6.77	1203.3	6.78	1205.9	6.79	1209.3	6.81
37	1267.6	6.94	1268.0	6.95	1269.1	6.95	1271.1	6.96	1273.8	6.98	1277.4	7.00
38	1337.0	7.13	1337.4	7.13	1338.7	7.14	1340.7	7.15	1343.6	7.16	1347.4	7.18
39	1408.3	7.31	1408.8	7.32	1410.1	7.32	1412.2	7.33	1415.3	7.35	1419.2	7.37
40	1481.5	7.50	1481.9	7.50	1483.3	7.51	1485.6	7.52	1488.8	7.54	1492.9	7.56
41	1556.5	7.69	1557.0	7.69	1558.4	7.69	1560.8	7.71	1564.1	7.72	1568.5	7.74
42	1633.3	7.87	1633.8	7.87	1635.3	7.88	1637.8	7.89	1641.4	7.91	1645.9	7.93
43	1712.0	8.06	1712.6	8.06	1714.1	8.07	1716.8	8.08	1720.5	8.10	1725.2	8.12
44	1792.6	8.24	1793.1	8.24	1794.8	8.25	1797.5	8.26	1801.4	8.28	1806.4	8.30
45	1875.0	8.43	1875.6	8.43	1877.3	8.44	1880.2	8.45	1884.2	8.47	1889.5	8.49
46	1959.3	8.61	1959.9	8.61	1961.7	8.62	1964.7	8.63	1968.9	8.65	1974.4	8.68
47	2045.4	8.80	2046.0	8.80	2047.9	8.81	2051.0	8.82	2055.4	8.84	2061.1	8.86
48	2133.3	8.98	2134.0	8.98	2135.9	8.99	2139.2	9.01	2143.8	9.03	2149.8	9.05
49	2223.1	9.17	2223.8	9.17	2225.9	9.18	2229.3	9.19	2234.1	9.21	2240.3	9.24
50	2314.8	9.35	2315.5	9.35	2317.6	9.36	2321.2	9.38	2326.2	9.40	2332.7	9.42
51	2408.3	9.54	2409.1	9.54	2411.3	9.55	2415.0	9.56	2420.2	9.58	2426.9	9.61
52	2503.7	9.72	2504.5	9.73	2506.8	9.73	2510.6	9.75	2516.0	9.77	2523.0	9.80
53	2600.9	9.91	2601.7	9.91	2604.1	9.92	2608.1	9.93	2613.7	9.96	2621.0	9.98
54	2700.0	10.09	2700.8	10.10	2703.3	10.10	2707.4	10.12	2713.3	10.14	2720.8	10.17
55	2800.9	10.28	2801.8	10.28	2804.3	10.29	2808.6	10.31	2814.7	10.33	2822.5	10.36
56	2903.7	10.46	2904.6	10.47	2907.2	10.48	2911.7	10.49	2918.0	10.51	2926.1	10.54
57	3008.3	10.65	3009.2	10.65	3012.0	10.66	3016.6	10.68	3023.1	10.70	3031.5	10.73
58	3114.8	10.83	3115.8	10.84	3118.6	10.85	3123.4	10.86	3130.1	10.89	3138.8	10.92
59	3223.1	11.02	3224.1	11.02	3227.1	11.03	3232.0	11.05	3239.0	11.07	3248.0	11.10
60	3333.3	11.20	3334.3	11.21	3337.4	11.22	3342.5	11.23	3349.7	11.26	3359.0	11.29
SUMS.	0°		1°		2°		3°		4°		5°	

TABLE IX. **Whole Sections.** **Side Slope 1 to 1.**

SUMS.	0°		1°		2°		3°		4°		5°	
61	3445.4	11.39	3446.4	11.39	3449.6	11.40	3454.9	11.42	3462.3	11.44	3471.9	11.48
62	3559.3	11.57	3560.3	11.58	3563.6	11.59	3569.1	11.61	3576.7	11.63	3586.7	11.66
63	3675.0	11.76	3676.1	11.76	3679.5	11.77	3685.1	11.79	3693.1	11.82	3703.3	11.85
64	3792.6	11.94	3793.7	11.95	3797.2	11.96	3803.0	11.98	3811.2	12.00	3821.8	12.04
65	3912.0	12.13	3913.2	12.13	3916.8	12.14	3922.8	12.16	3931.3	12.19	3942.2	12.22
66	4033.3	12.31	4034.6	12.32	4038.3	12.33	4044.4	12.35	4053.2	12.38	4064.4	12.41
67	4156.5	12.50	4157.7	12.50	4161.6	12.52	4167.9	12.53	4176.9	12.56	4188.5	12.60
68	4281.5	12.69	4282.8	12.69	4286.7	12.70	4293.3	12.72	4302.5	12.75	4314.5	12.78
69	4408.3	12.87	4409.7	12.87	4413.7	12.89	4420.5	12.91	4430.0	12.93	4442.3	12.97
70	4537.0	13.06	4538.4	13.06	4542.6	13.07	4549.5	13.09	4559.8	13.12	4572.0	13.16
71	4667.6	13.24	4669.0	13.24	4673.3	13.26	4680.4	13.28	4690.5	13.31	4703.6	13.34
72	4800.0	13.43	4801.5	13.43	4805.9	13.44	4813.2	13.46	4823.6	13.49	4837.0	13.53
73	4934.3	13.61	4935.8	13.62	4940.3	13.63	4947.8	13.65	4958.5	13.68	4972.3	13.72
74	5070.4	13.80	5071.9	13.80	5076.6	13.81	5084.3	13.83	5095.3	13.86	5109.5	13.90
75	5208.3	13.98	5209.9	13.99	5214.7	14.00	5222.7	14.02	5233.9	14.05	5248.5	14.09
76	5348.1	14.17	5349.8	14.17	5354.7	14.18	5362.9	14.21	5374.4	14.24	5389.4	14.28
77	5489.8	14.35	5491.5	14.36	5496.5	14.37	5504.9	14.39	5516.8	14.42	5532.2	14.46
78	5633.3	14.54	5635.0	14.54	5640.2	14.55	5648.8	14.58	5661.0	14.61	5676.8	14.65
79	5778.7	14.72	5780.5	14.73	5785.8	14.74	5794.6	14.76	5807.1	14.79	5823.3	14.84
80	5925.9	14.91	5927.7	14.91	5933.2	14.93	5942.2	14.95	5955.0	14.98	5971.6	15.02
81	6075.0	15.09	6076.8	15.10	6082.4	15.11	6091.7	15.13	6104.9	15.17	6121.9	15.21
82	6225.9	15.28	6227.8	15.28	6233.5	15.30	6243.1	15.32	6256.5	15.35	6273.9	15.40
83	6378.7	15.46	6380.6	15.47	6386.5	15.48	6396.3	15.51	6410.0	15.54	6427.9	15.58
84	6533.3	15.65	6535.3	15.65	6541.3	15.67	6551.3	15.69	6565.4	15.73	6583.7	15.77
85	6689.8	15.83	6691.8	15.84	6698.0	15.85	6708.2	15.88	6722.7	15.91	6741.4	15.96
86	6848.1	16.02	6850.2	16.02	6856.5	16.04	6867.0	16.06	6881.8	16.10	6901.0	16.14
87	7008.3	16.20	7010.5	16.21	7016.9	16.22	7027.6	16.25	7042.8	16.28	7062.4	16.33
88	7170 4	16.39	7172.6	16.39	7179.1	16.41	7190.1	16.43	7205.6	16.47	7225.7	16.53
89	7334 3	16.57	7336.5	16.58	7343.2	16.59	7354.5	16.62	7370.3	16.66	7390.9	16.71
90	7500.0	16.76	7502.3	16.76	7509.2	16.78	7520.7	16.81	7536.9	16.84	7557.9	16.89
91	7667.6	16.94	7669.9	16.95	7677.0	16.97	7688.7	16.99	7705.3	17.03	7726.7	17.08
92	7837.0	17.13	7839.4	17.13	7846.6	17.15	7858.6	17.18	7875.5	17.21	7897.5	17.26
93	8008.3	17.31	8010.8	17.32	8018.1	17.34	8030.4	17.36	8047.7	17.40	8070.1	17.45
94	8181.5	17.50	8184.0	17.51	8191.5	17.52	8204.0	17.55	8221.7	17.59	8244.6	17.63
95	8356.5	17.69	8359.0	17.69	8366.7	17.71	8379.5	17.73	8397.5	17.77	8420.9	17.82
96	8533.3	17.87	8535.9	17.88	8543.7	17.89	8556.8	17.92	8575.3	17.96	8599.2	18.01
97	8712.0	18.06	8714.7	18.06	8722.7	18.08	8736.0	18.11	8754.8	18.14	8779.2	18.19
98	8892.6	18.24	8895.3	18.25	8903.4	18.26	8917.1	18.29	8936.3	18.33	8961.2	18.38
99	9075.0	18.43	9077.8	18.43	9086.1	18.45	9100.0	18.48	9119.6	18.52	9145.0	18.57
100	9259.3	18.61	9262.1	18.62	9270.6	18.63	9284.8	18.66	9304.8	18.70	9330.7	18.75
101	9445.4	18.80	9448.2	18.80	9456.9	18.82	9471.4	18.85	9491.8	18.89	9518.2	18.94
102	9633.3	18.98	9636.3	18.99	9645.1	19.00	9659.9	19.03	9680.7	19.07	9707.6	19.13
103	9823.1	19.17	9826.1	19.17	9835.1	19.19	9850.2	19.22	9871.4	19.26	9898.9	19.31
104	10014.8	19.35	10017.9	19.36	10027.0	19.38	10042.4	19.41	10064.0	19.45	10092.1	19.50
105	10208.3	19.54	10211.4	19.54	10220.8	19.56	10236.4	19.59	10258.5	19.63	10287.1	19.69
106	10403.7	19.72	10406.9	19.73	10416.4	19.75	10432.4	19.78	10454.8	19.82	10484.0	19.87
107	10600.9	19.91	10604.2	19.91	10613.9	19.93	10630.1	19.96	10653.0	20.01	10682.7	20.06
108	10800.0	20.09	10803.3	20.10	10813.2	20.12	10829.7	20.15	10853.1	20.19	10883.3	20.25
109	11000.9	20.28	11004.3	20.28	11014.4	20.30	11031.2	20.33	11055.0	20.38	11085.8	20.43
110	11203.7	20.46	11207.1	20.47	11217.4	20.49	11234.6	20.52	11258.8	20.56	11290.1	20.62
111	11408.3	20.65	11411.8	20.65	11422.3	20.67	11439.8	20.71	11464.4	20.75	11496.3	20.81
112	11614.8	20.83	11618.3	20.84	11629.0	20.86	11646.8	20.89	11671.9	20.94	11704.4	20.99
113	11823.1	21.02	11826.7	21.02	11837.6	21.04	11855.7	21.08	11881.2	21.12	11914.3	21.18
114	12033.3	21.20	12037.0	21.21	12048.0	21.23	12066.5	21.26	12092.5	21.31	12126.2	21.37
115	12245.4	21.39	12249.1	21.40	12260.3	21.41	12279.1	21.45	12305.5	21.49	12339.8	21.55
116	12459.3	21.57	12463.0	21.58	12474.5	21.60	12493.6	21.63	12520.5	21.68	12555.4	21.74
117	12675.0	21.76	12678.9	21.77	12690.5	21.79	12709.9	21.82	12737.3	21.87	12772.8	21.93
118	12892.6	21.94	12896.5	21.95	12908.3	21.97	12928.1	22.00	12955.9	22.05	12992.0	22.11
119	13112.0	22.13	13116.0	22.14	13128.0	22.16	13148.1	22.19	13176.5	22.24	13213.2	22.30
120	13333.3	22.31	13337.4	22.32	13349.6	22.34	13370.1	22.38	13398.9	22.42	13436.2	22.49
SUMS.	0°		1°		2°		3°		4°		5°	

TABLE IX. Whole Sections. Side Slope 1 to 1.

SUMS.	6°		7°		8°		9°		10°		11°	
1	0.9	0.28	0.9	0.28	0.9	0.28	0.9	0.28	1.0	0.29	1.0	0.29
2	3.7	0.47	3.8	0.47	3.8	0.47	3.8	0.47	3.8	0.48	3.8	0.48
3	8.4	0.66	8.5	0.66	8.5	0.66	8.5	0.66	8.6	0.67	8.7	0.67
4	15.0	0.84	15.0	0.85	15.1	0.85	15.2	0.85	15.3	0.86	15.4	0.87
5	23.4	1.03	23.5	1.03	23.6	1.04	23.7	1.04	23.9	1.05	24.1	1.06
6	33.7	1.22	33.8	1.22	34.0	1.23	34.2	1.23	34.4	1.24	34.6	1.25
7	45.9	1.40	46.1	1.41	46.3	1.42	46.5	1.42	46.8	1.43	47.2	1.44
8	59.9	1.59	60.2	1.60	60.5	1.61	60.8	1.61	61.2	1.62	61.6	1.64
9	75.8	1.78	76.1	1.79	76.5	1.79	76.9	1.80	77.4	1.82	77.9	1.83
10	93.6	1.97	94.0	1.97	94.5	1.98	95.0	1.99	95.6	2.01	96.2	2.02
11	113.3	2.15	113.8	2.16	114.3	2.17	114.9	2.18	115.6	2.20	116.4	2.21
12	134.8	2.34	135.4	2.35	136.0	2.36	136.8	2.37	137.6	2.39	138.6	2.41
13	158.2	2.53	158.9	2.54	159.6	2.55	160.5	2.56	161.5	2.58	162.6	2.60
14	183.5	2.72	184.3	2.73	185.1	2.74	186.2	2.75	187.3	2.77	188.6	2.79
15	210.7	2.90	211.5	2.91	212.5	2.93	213.7	2.94	215.0	2.96	216.5	2.98
16	239.7	3.09	240.7	3.10	241.8	3.12	243.1	3.13	244.6	3.15	246.3	3.18
17	270.6	3.28	271.7	3.29	273.0	3.31	274.5	3.32	276.2	3.34	278.1	3.37
18	303.4	3.46	304.6	3.48	306.0	3.49	307.7	3.51	309.6	3.54	311.8	3.56
19	338.0	3.65	339.4	3.67	341.0	3.68	342.9	3.70	345.0	3.73	347.4	3.75
20	374.5	3.84	376.0	3.85	377.8	3.87	379.9	3.89	382.3	3.92	384.9	3.95
21	412.9	4.03	414.6	4.04	416.6	4.06	418.8	4.08	421.4	4.11	424.4	4.14
22	453.2	4.21	455.0	4.23	457.2	4.25	459.7	4.27	462.5	4.30	465.7	4.33
23	495.3	4.40	497.3	4.42	499.7	4.44	502.4	4.46	505.5	4.49	509.0	4.52
24	539.3	4.59	541.5	4.61	544.1	4.63	547.1	4.65	550.4	4.68	554.3	4.72
25	585.2	4.77	587.6	4.79	590.4	4.82	593.6	4.84	597.3	4.87	601.4	4.91
26	632.9	4.96	635.5	4.98	638.5	5.01	642.0	5.03	646.0	5.06	650.5	5.10
27	682.5	5.15	685.3	5.17	688.6	5.20	692.4	5.22	696.7	5.26	701.5	5.29
28	734.0	5.34	737.0	5.36	740.6	5.38	744.6	5.41	749.2	5.45	754.4	5.49
29	787.4	5.52	790.6	5.55	794.4	5.57	798.7	5.60	803.7	5.64	809.3	5.68
30	842.6	5.71	846.1	5.73	850.1	5.76	854.8	5.79	860.1	5.83	866.1	5.87
31	899.8	5.90	903.4	5.92	907.7	5.95	912.7	5.98	918.4	6.02	924.8	6.06
32	958.7	6.09	962.7	6.11	967.3	6.14	972.5	6.17	978.6	6.21	985.4	6.25
33	1019.6	6.27	1023.8	6.30	1028.7	6.33	1034.3	6.36	1040.7	6.40	1047.9	6.45
34	1082.3	6.46	1086.8	6.49	1091.9	6.52	1097.9	6.55	1104.7	6.59	1112.4	6.64
35	1146.9	6.65	1151.6	6.67	1157.1	6.71	1163.4	6.74	1170.7	6.79	1178.8	6.83
36	1213.4	6.83	1218.4	6.86	1224.2	6.90	1230.9	6.93	1238.5	6.98	1247.1	7.02
37	1281.8	7.02	1287.0	7.05	1293.1	7.08	1300.2	7.12	1308.3	7.17	1317.4	7.22
38	1352.0	7.21	1357.5	7.24	1364.0	7.27	1371.4	7.31	1379.9	7.36	1389.5	7.41
39	1424.1	7.40	1429.9	7.43	1436.7	7.46	1444.6	7.50	1453.5	7.55	1463.6	7.60
40	1498.0	7.58	1504.2	7.61	1511.3	7.65	1519.6	7.69	1529.0	7.74	1539.7	7.79
41	1573.9	7.77	1580.3	7.80	1587.8	7.84	1596.5	7.88	1606.4	7.93	1617.6	7.99
42	1651.6	7.96	1658.3	7.99	1666.2	8.03	1675.4	8.07	1685.7	8.12	1697.5	8.18
43	1731.2	8.15	1738.2	8.18	1746.5	8.22	1756.1	8.26	1767.0	8.31	1779.3	8.37
44	1812.6	8.33	1820.0	8.37	1828.7	8.41	1838.7	8.45	1850.1	8.51	1863.0	8.56
45	1895.9	8.52	1903.7	8.55	1912.8	8.60	1923.2	8.64	1935.2	8.70	1948.6	8.76
46	1981.1	8.71	1989.2	8.74	1998.7	8.78	2009.7	8.83	2022.1	8.89	2036.2	8.95
47	2068.2	8.89	2076.7	8.93	2086.6	8.97	2098.0	9.02	2111.0	9.08	2125.7	9.14
48	2157.2	9.08	2166.0	9.12	2176.3	9.16	2188.2	9.21	2201.8	9.27	2217.1	9.33
49	2248.0	9.27	2257.2	9.31	2267.9	9.35	2280.4	9.40	2294.5	9.46	2310.4	9.53
50	2340.7	9.46	2350.2	9.49	2361.5	9.54	2374.4	9.59	2389.1	9.65	2405.7	9.72
51	2435.2	9.64	2445.2	9.68	2456.9	9.73	2470.3	9.78	2485.6	9.84	2502.9	9.91
52	2531.7	9.83	2542.0	9.87	2554.2	9.92	2568.1	9.97	2584.0	10.03	2602.0	10.10
53	2630.0	10.02	2640.7	10.06	2653.3	10.11	2667.9	10.16	2684.4	10.23	2703.1	10.30
54	2730.2	10.21	2741.3	10.25	2754.4	10.30	2769.5	10.35	2786.6	10.42	2806.0	10.49
55	2832.2	10.39	2843.8	10.44	2857.4	10.48	2873.0	10.54	2890.8	10.61	2910.9	10.68
56	2936.1	10.58	2948.2	10.62	2962.2	10.67	2978.4	10.73	2996.9	10.80	3017.7	10.87
57	3041.9	10.77	3054.4	10.81	3069.0	10.86	3085.7	10.92	3104.9	10.99	3126.5	11.07
58	3149.6	10.95	3162.5	11.00	3177.6	11.05	3195.0	11.11	3214.8	11.18	3237.1	11.26
59	3259.1	11.14	3272.5	11.19	3288.1	11.24	3306.1	11.30	3326.6	11.37	3349.7	11.45
60	3370.6	11.33	3384.4	11.38	3400.5	11.43	3419.1	11.49	3440.3	11.56	3464.2	11.64
SUMS.	6°		7°		8°		9°		10°		11°	

TABLE IX. Whole Sections. Side Slope 1 to 1.

SUMS.	6°	7°	8°	9°	10°	11°
61	3483.9 11.52	3498.1 11.56	3514.8 11.62	3534.0 11.68	3555.9 11.75	3580.7 11.84
62	3599.0 11.70	3613.7 11.75	3631.0 11.81	3650.8 11.87	3673.5 11.95	3699.0 12.03
63	3716.0 11.89	3731.3 11.94	3749.0 12.00	3769.6 12.06	3792.9 12.14	3819.3 12.22
64	3835.0 12.08	3850.6 12.13	3869.0 12.19	3890.2 12.25	3914.3 12.33	3941.5 12.41
65	3955.7 12.27	3971.9 12.32	3990.9 12.37	4012.7 12.44	4037.6 12.52	4065.6 12.61
66	4078.4 12.45	4095.1 12.50	4114.6 12.56	4137.1 12.63	4162.8 12.71	4191.7 12.80
67	4202.9 12.64	4220.1 12.69	4240.2 12.75	4263.4 12.82	4289.9 12.90	4319.7 13.00
68	4329.3 12.83	4347.0 12.88	4367.8 12.94	4391.6 13.01	4418.9 13.09	4449.6 13.18
69	4457.6 13.01	4475.8 13.07	4497.2 13.13	4521.8 13.20	4549.8 13.28	4581.4 13.38
70	4587.7 13.20	4606.5 13.26	4628.5 13.32	4653.8 13.39	4682.6 13.47	4715.2 13.57
71	4719.7 13.39	4739.0 13.44	4761.6 13.51	4787.7 13.58	4817.4 13.67	4850.9 13.76
72	4853.6 13.58	4873.5 13.63	4896.7 13.70	4923.5 13.77	4954.0 13.86	4988.5 13.95
73	4989.4 13.76	5009.8 13.82	5033.7 13.89	5061.2 13.96	5092.6 14.05	5128.0 14.15
74	5127.0 13.95	5148.0 14.01	5172.5 14.07	5200.8 14.15	5233.1 14.24	5269.5 14.34
75	5266.5 14.14	5288.1 14.20	5313.3 14.26	5342.3 14.34	5375.5 14.43	5412.8 14.53
76	5407.9 14.32	5430.0 14.38	5455.9 14.45	5485.8 14.53	5519.8 14.62	5558.2 14.72
77	5551.1 14.51	5573.8 14.57	5600.4 14.64	5631.1 14.72	5666.0 14.81	5705.4 14.92
78	5696.3 14.70	5719.6 14.76	5746.8 14.83	5778.3 14.91	5814.1 15.00	5854.5 15.11
79	5843.2 14.89	5867.2 14.95	5895.1 15.02	5927.4 15.10	5964.1 15.19	6005.6 15.30
80	5992.1 15.07	6016.6 15.14	6045.3 15.21	6078.4 15.29	6116.1 15.39	6158.6 15.49
81	6142.9 15.26	6168.0 15.32	6197.4 15.40	6231.3 15.48	6269.9 15.58	6313.5 15.69
82	6295.5 15.45	6321.2 15.51	6351.4 15.59	6386.1 15.67	6425.7 15.77	6470.4 15.88
83	6450.0 15.64	6476.3 15.70	6507.2 15.77	6542.8 15.86	6583.4 15.96	6629.2 16.07
84	6606.3 15.82	6633.3 15.89	6665.0 15.96	6701.4 16.05	6743.0 16.15	6789.9 16.26
85	6764.5 16.01	6792.2 16.08	6824.6 16.15	6862.0 16.24	6904.5 16.34	6952.5 16.46
86	6924.6 16.20	6953.0 16.26	6986.1 16.34	7024.4 16.43	7067.9 16.53	7117.1 16.65
87	7086.6 16.38	7115.6 16.45	7149.5 16.53	7188.7 16.62	7233.2 16.72	7283.5 16.84
88	7250.5 16.57	7280.1 16.64	7314.9 16.72	7354.9 16.81	7400.5 16.91	7451.9 17.03
89	7416.2 16.76	7446.5 16.83	7482.0 16.91	7523.0 17.00	7569.6 17.11	7622.3 17.22
90	7583.8 16.95	7614.8 17.02	7651.1 17.10	7693.0 17.19	7740.7 17.30	7794.5 17.42
91	7753.2 17.13	7785.0 17.20	7822.1 17.29	7864.9 17.38	7913.6 17.49	7968.7 17.61
92	7924.6 17.32	7957.0 17.39	7995.0 17.47	8038.7 17.57	8088.5 17.68	8144.8 17.80
93	8097.8 17.51	8130.9 17.58	8169.7 17.66	8214.4 17.76	8265.3 17.87	8322.8 17.99
94	8272.9 17.70	8306.7 17.77	8346.3 17.85	8392.0 17.95	8444.0 18.06	8502.7 18.19
95	8449.8 17.88	8484.4 17.96	8524.9 18.04	8571.5 18.14	8624.6 18.25	8684.6 18.38
96	8628.6 18.07	8664.0 18.14	8705.3 18.23	8752.9 18.33	8807.2 18.44	8868.4 18.57
97	8809.3 18.26	8845.4 18.33	8887.6 18.42	8936.2 18.52	8991.6 18.63	9054.1 18.76
98	8991.9 18.44	9028.7 18.52	9071.8 18.61	9121.4 18.71	9177.9 18.83	9241.8 13.96
99	9176.4 18.63	9213.9 18.71	9257.9 18.80	9308.5 18.90	9366.2 19.02	9431.3 19.15
100	9362.7 18.82	9401.0 18.90	9445.8 18.99	9497.5 19.09	9556.4 19.21	9622.8 19.34
101	9550.9 19.01	9589.9 19.08	9635.7 19.18	9688.4 19.28	9748.5 19.40	9816.3 19.53
102	9740.9 19.19	9780.8 19.27	9827.4 19.36	9881.2 19.47	9942.5 19.59	10011.6 19.73
103	9932.9 19.38	9973.5 19.46	10021.1 19.55	10075.9 19.66	10138.4 19.78	10208.9 19.92
104	10126.7 19.57	10168.1 19.65	10216.6 19.74	10272.5 19.85	10336.2 19.97	10408.1 20.11
105	10322.4 19.76	10364.6 19.84	10414.0 19.93	10471.0 20.04	10535.9 20.16	10609.2 20.30
106	10519.9 19.94	10563.0 20.02	10613.3 20.12	10671.4 20.23	10737.5 20.36	10812.2 20.50
107	10719.3 20.13	10763.2 20.21	10814.5 20.31	10873.7 20.42	10941.1 20.55	11017.2 20.69
108	10920.6 20.32	10965.3 20.40	11017.6 20.50	11077.9 20.61	11146.6 20.74	11224.1 20.88
109	11123.8 20.50	11169.3 20.59	11222.6 20.69	11284.0 20.80	11353.9 20.93	11432.9 21.07
110	11328.8 20.69	11375.2 20.78	11429.5 20.88	11492.0 20.99	11563.2 21.12	11643.6 21.27
111	11535.8 20.88	11583.0 20.96	11638.2 21.06	11701.9 21.18	11774.4 21.31	11856.3 21.46
112	11744.5 21.07	11792.6 21.15	11848.8 21.25	11913.7 21.37	11987.5 21.50	12070.9 21.65
113	11955.2 21.25	12004.1 21.34	12061.4 21.44	12127.4 21.56	12202.5 21.69	12287.4 21.84
114	12167.7 21.44	12217.5 21.53	12275.8 21.63	12343.0 21.75	12419.5 21.88	12505.8 22.04
115	12382.1 21.63	12432.8 21.72	12492.1 21.82	12560.5 21.94	12638.3 22.08	12726.2 22.23
116	12598.4 21.82	12650.0 21.90	12710.3 22.01	12779.8 22.13	12859.1 22.27	12948.5 22.42
117	12816.6 22.00	12869.0 22.09	12930.4 22.20	13001.1 22.32	13081.7 22.46	13172.7 22.61
118	13036.6 22.19	13089.9 22.28	13152.4 22.39	13224.3 22.51	13306.3 22.65	13398.8 22.81
119	13258.5 22.38	13312.7 22.47	13376.2 22.58	13449.4 22.70	13532.8 22.84	13626.9 23.00
120	13482.3 22.56	13537.4 22.66	13602.0 22.76	13676.4 22.89	13761.2 23.03	13856.9 23.19
SUMS.	6°	7°	8°	9°	10°	11°

TABLE IX. Whole Sections. Side Slope 1 to 1.

SUMS.	12°		13°		14°		15°		16°		17°	
1	1.0	0.29	1.0	0.29	1.0	0.30	1.0	0.30	1.0	0.30	1.0	0.31
2	3.9	0.48	3.9	0.49	3.9	0.49	4.0	0.49	4.0	0.50	4.1	0.51
3	8.7	0.68	8.8	0.68	8.9	0.69	9.0	0.70	9.1	0.71	9.2	0.71
4	15.5	0.87	15.6	0.88	15.8	0.89	16.0	0.90	16.1	0.91	16.3	0.92
5	24.2	1.07	24.5	1.08	24.7	1.09	24.9	1.10	25.2	1.11	25.5	1.12
6	34.9	1.26	35.2	1.27	35.5	1.28	35.9	1.30	36.3	1.31	36.8	1.33
7	47.5	1.45	47.9	1.47	48.4	1.48	48.9	1.50	49.4	1.51	50.0	1.53
8	62.1	1.65	62.6	1.66	63.2	1.68	63.8	1.70	64.6	1.72	65.4	1.74
9	78.5	1.84	79.2	1.86	80.0	1.88	80.8	1.90	81.7	1.92	82.7	1.94
10	97.0	2.04	97.8	2.05	98.7	2.07	99.8	2.09	100.9	2.12	102.1	2.14
11	117.3	2.23	118.3	2.25	119.5	2.27	120.7	2.29	122.1	2.32	123.6	2.35
12	139.6	2.42	140.8	2.45	142.2	2.47	143.6	2.49	145.3	2.52	147.1	2.55
13	163.9	2.62	165.3	2.64	166.9	2.67	168.6	2.69	170.5	2.72	172.6	2.76
14	190.1	2.81	191.7	2.84	193.5	2.86	195.5	2.89	197.7	2.93	200.2	2.96
15	218.2	3.01	220.1	3.03	222.1	3.06	224.4	3.09	227.0	3.13	229.8	3.17
16	248.3	3.20	250.4	3.23	252.7	3.26	255.4	3.29	258.3	3.33	261.5	3.37
17	280.3	3.39	282.7	3.42	285.3	3.46	288.3	3.49	291.6	3.53	295.2	3.57
18	314.2	3.59	316.9	3.62	319.9	3.65	323.2	3.69	326.9	3.73	330.9	3.78
19	350.1	3.79	353.1	3.81	356.4	3.85	360.1	3.89	364.2	3.93	368.7	3.98
20	387.9	3.98	391.2	4.01	394.9	4.05	399.0	4.09	403.6	4.14	408.6	4.19
21	427.7	4.17	431.3	4.21	435.4	4.25	439.9	4.29	444.9	4.34	450.4	4.39
22	469.4	4.36	473.4	4.40	477.9	4.44	482.8	4.49	488.3	4.54	494.4	4.60
23	513.0	4.56	517.4	4.60	522.3	4.64	527.7	4.69	533.7	4.74	540.3	4.80
24	558.6	4.75	563.4	4.79	568.7	4.84	574.6	4.89	581.1	4.94	588.3	5.00
25	606.1	4.95	611.3	4.99	617.1	5.04	623.5	5.09	630.5	5.15	638.4	5.21
26	655.5	5.14	661.2	5.18	667.4	5.23	674.3	5.29	682.0	5.35	690.5	5.41
27	706.9	5.33	713.0	5.38	719.7	5.43	727.2	5.49	735.5	5.55	744.6	5.62
28	760.3	5.53	766.8	5.57	774.0	5.63	782.1	5.69	791.0	5.75	800.8	5.82
29	815.6	5.72	822.5	5.77	830.3	5.83	838.9	5.89	848.5	5.95	859.0	6.03
30	872.8	5.92	880.3	5.97	888.6	6.02	897.8	6.09	908.0	6.15	919.3	6.23
31	931.9	6.11	939.9	6.16	948.8	6.22	958.6	6.28	969.5	6.36	981.6	6.43
32	993.0	6.30	1001.5	6.36	1011.0	6.42	1021.5	6.48	1033.1	6.56	1045.9	6.64
33	1056.0	6.50	1065.1	6.55	1075.2	6.61	1086.3	6.68	1098.7	6.76	1112.3	6.84
34	1121.0	6.69	1130.6	6.75	1141.3	6.81	1153.2	6.88	1166.3	6.96	1180.7	7.05
35	1187.9	6.89	1198.1	6.94	1209.4	7.01	1222.0	7.08	1235.9	7.16	1251.2	7.25
36	1256.8	7.08	1267.6	7.14	1279.5	7.21	1292.8	7.28	1307.5	7.36	1323.7	7.46
37	1327.6	7.27	1339.0	7.34	1351.6	7.40	1365.6	7.48	1381.2	7.57	1398.3	7.66
38	1400.3	7.47	1412.3	7.53	1425.7	7.60	1440.5	7.68	1456.8	7.77	1474.9	7.86
39	1475.0	7.66	1487.6	7.73	1501.7	7.80	1517.3	7.88	1534.5	7.97	1553.5	8.07
40	1551.6	7.85	1564.9	7.92	1579.7	8.00	1596.1	8.08	1614.2	8.17	1634.2	8.27
41	1630.1	8.05	1644.1	8.12	1659.7	8.19	1676.9	8.28	1695.9	8.37	1717.0	8.48
42	1710.6	8.24	1725.3	8.31	1741.6	8.39	1759.7	8.48	1779.7	8.58	1801.7	8.68
43	1793.0	8.44	1808.4	8.51	1825.5	8.59	1844.5	8.68	1865.4	8.78	1888.6	8.89
44	1877.4	8.63	1893.5	8.70	1911.4	8.79	1931.3	8.88	1953.2	8.98	1977.4	9.09
45	1963.7	8.82	1980.6	8.90	1999.3	8.98	2020.0	9.08	2043.0	9.18	2068.3	9.29
46	2052.0	9.02	2069.6	9.10	2089.1	9.18	2110.8	9.28	2134.8	9.38	2161.3	9.50
47	2142.2	9.21	2160.5	9.29	2180.9	9.38	2203.6	9.48	2228.6	9.58	2256.3	9.70
48	2234.3	9.41	2253.4	9.49	2274.7	9.58	2298.3	9.68	2324.5	9.79	2353.3	9.91
49	2328.3	9.60	2348.3	9.68	2370.5	9.77	2395.1	9.88	2422.3	9.99	2452.4	10.11
50	2424.3	9.79	2445.1	9.88	2468.3	9.97	2493.9	10.08	2522.2	10.19	2553.5	10.32
51	2522.3	9.99	2543.9	10.07	2568.0	10.17	2594.6	10.28	2624.1	10.39	2656.7	10.52
52	2622.2	10.18	2644.7	10.26	2669.7	10.37	2697.4	10.47	2728.0	10.59	2761.9	10.72
53	2724.0	10.38	2747.4	10.47	2773.3	10.56	2802.1	10.67	2833.9	10.80	2869.1	10.93
54	2827.8	10.57	2852.0	10.66	2879.0	10.76	2908.8	10.87	2941.9	11.00	2978.4	11.13
55	2933.5	10.76	2958.6	10.86	2986.6	10.96	3017.6	11.07	3051.9	11.20	3089.7	11.34
56	3041.1	10.96	3067.2	11.05	3096.2	11.16	3128.3	11.27	3163.8	11.40	3203.1	11.54
57	3150.7	11.15	3177.7	11.25	3207.7	11.35	3241.0	11.47	3277.8	11.60	3318.5	11.75
58	3262.2	11.35	3290.2	11.44	3321.3	11.55	3355.7	11.67	3393.9	11.80	3436.0	11.95
59	3375.7	11.54	3404.6	11.64	3436.8	11.75	3472.5	11.87	3511.9	12.01	3555.5	12.15
60	3491.1	11.73	3521.0	11.83	3554.3	11.95	3591.2	12.07	3632.0	12.21	3677.0	12.36
SUMS.	12°		13°		14°		15°		16°		17°	

TABLE IX. Whole Sections. Side Slope 1 to 1.

SUMS.	12°	13°	14°	15°	16°	17°
61	3608.4 11.93	3639.3 12.03	3673.7 12.14	3711.9 12.27	3754.0 12.41	3800.6 12.56
62	3727.7 12.12	3759.6 12.23	3795.2 12.34	3834.6 12.47	3878.1 12.61	3926.3 12.77
63	3848.9 12.32	3881.9 12.42	3918.6 12.54	3959.3 12.67	4004.2 12.81	4053.9 12.97
64	3972.1 12.51	4006.1 12.62	4044.0 12.74	4086.0 12.87	4132.4 13.01	4183.6 13.18
65	4097.1 12.70	4132.3 12.81	4171.3 12.93	4214.6 13.07	4262.5 13.22	4315.4 13.38
66	4224.2 12.90	4260.4 13.01	4300.7 13.13	4345.3 13.27	4394.7 13.42	4449.2 13.58
67	4353.2 13.09	4390.5 13.20	4432.0 13.33	4478.0 13.47	4528.9 13.62	4585.1 13.79
68	4484.1 13.29	4522.5 13.40	4565.3 13.53	4612.7 13.67	4665.1 13.82	4722.9 13.99
69	4616.9 13.48	4656.5 13.59	4700.5 13.72	4749.3 13.87	4803.3 14.02	4862.9 14.20
70	4751.7 13.67	4792.5 13.79	4837.8 13.92	4888.0 14.07	4943.5 14.23	5004.8 14.40
71	4888.5 13.87	4930.4 13.99	4977.0 14.12	5028.6 14.26	5085.8 14.43	5148.9 14.61
72	5027.1 14.06	5070.2 14.18	5118.2 14.32	5171.3 14.46	5230.0 14.63	5294.9 14.81
73	5167.7 14.26	5212.1 14.38	5261.3 14.51	5315.9 14.66	5376.3 14.83	5443.0 15.01
74	5310.3 14.45	5355.8 14.57	5406.5 14.71	5462.6 14.86	5524.6 15.03	5593.2 15.22
75	5454.8 14.64	5501.6 14.77	5553.6 14.91	5611.2 15.06	5674.9 15.23	5745.4 15.42
76	5601.2 14.84	5649.3 14.96	5702.7 15.11	5761.8 15.26	5827.3 15.44	5899.6 15.63
77	5749.6 15.03	5798.9 15.16	5853.7 15.30	5914.5 15.46	5981.6 15.64	6055.9 15.83
78	5899.9 15.22	5950.5 15.36	6006.7 15.50	6069.1 15.66	6138.0 15.84	6214.2 16.04
79	6052.1 15.42	6104.0 15.55	6161.7 15.70	6225.7 15.86	6296.4 16.04	6374.5 16.24
80	6206.3 15.61	6259.6 15.75	6318.7 15.90	6384.3 16.06	6456.8 16.24	6536.9 16.44
81	6362.5 15.81	6417.0 15.94	6477.7 16.09	6544.9 16.26	6619.3 16.44	6701.4 16.65
82	6520.5 16.00	6576.4 16.14	6638.6 16.29	6707.5 16.46	6783.7 16.65	6867.9 16.85
83	6680.5 16.19	6737.8 16.33	6801.5 16.49	6872.1 16.66	6950.2 16.85	7036.4 17.06
84	6842.5 16.39	6901.2 16.53	6966.4 16.69	7038.7 16.86	7118.7 17.05	7207.0 17.26
85	7006.4 16.58	7066.5 16.72	7133.2 16.88	7207.3 17.06	7289.2 17.25	7379.6 17.47
86	7172.2 16.78	7233.7 16.92	7302.1 17.08	7377.9 17.26	7461.7 17.45	7554.3 17.67
87	7340.0 16.97	7402.9 17.12	7472.9 17.28	7550.4 17.46	7636.2 17.66	7731.0 17.87
88	7509.7 17.16	7574.1 17.31	7645.7 17.48	7725.0 17.66	7812.8 17.86	7909.7 18.08
89	7681.3 17.36	7747.2 17.51	7820.4 17.67	7901.6 17.86	7991.3 18.06	8090.5 18.28
90	7854.9 17.55	7922.3 17.70	7997.1 17.87	8080.1 18.06	8171.9 18.26	8273.3 18.49
91	8030.4 17.75	8099.3 17.90	8175.8 18.07	8260.7 18.26	8354.5 18.46	8458.2 18.69
92	8207.9 17.94	8278.3 18.09	8356.5 18.27	8443.2 18.45	8539.2 18.66	8645.1 18.90
93	8387.3 18.13	8459.2 18.29	8539.2 18.46	8627.8 18.65	8725.8 18.87	8834.1 19.10
94	8568.6 18.33	8642.1 18.49	8723.8 18.66	8814.3 18.85	8914.5 19.07	9025.1 19.30
95	8751.9 18.52	8827.0 18.68	8910.4 18.86	9002.9 19.05	9105.1 19.27	9218.1 19.51
96	8937.1 18.72	9013.8 18.88	9099.0 19.05	9193.4 19.25	9297.8 19.47	9413.2 19.71
97	9124.3 18.91	9202.5 19.07	9289.5 19.25	9385.9 19.45	9492.5 19.67	9610.3 19.92
98	9313.4 19.10	9393.2 19.27	9482.0 19.45	9580.4 19.65	9689.3 19.87	9809.5 20.12
99	9504.4 19.30	9585.9 19.46	9676.5 19.65	9777.0 19.85	9888.0 20.08	10010.7 20.33
100	9697.4 19.49	9780.6 19.66	9873.0 19.84	9975.5 20.05	10088.8 20.28	10214.0 20.53
101	9892.3 19.69	9977.1 19.85	10071.5 20.04	10176.0 20.25	10291.6 20.48	10419.3 20.73
102	10089.2 19.88	10175.7 20.05	10271.9 20.24	10378.5 20.45	10496.4 20.68	10626.6 20.94
103	10288.0 20.07	10376.2 20.25	10474.3 20.44	10583.0 20.65	10703.2 20.88	10836.0 21.14
104	10488.7 20.27	10578.7 20.44	10678.6 20.63	10789.5 20.85	10912.0 21.09	11047.4 21.35
105	10691.4 20.46	10783.1 20.64	10885.0 20.83	10998.0 21.05	11122.9 21.29	11260.9 21.55
106	10896.0 20.66	10989.4 20.83	11093.3 21.03	11208.4 21.25	11335.8 21.49	11476.4 21.76
107	11102.5 20.85	11197.8 21.03	11303.6 21.23	11420.9 21.45	11550.7 21.69	11694.0 21.96
108	11311.0 21.04	11408.0 21.22	11515.9 21.42	11635.4 21.65	11767.6 21.89	11913.6 22.16
109	11521.5 21.24	11620.3 21.42	11730.1 21.62	11851.9 21.85	11986.5 22.09	12135.2 22.37
110	11733.8 21.43	11834.5 21.62	11946.3 21.82	12070.3 22.05	12207.4 22.30	12358.9 22.57
111	11948.2 21.63	12050.6 21.81	12164.5 22.02	12290.8 22.25	12430.4 22.50	12584.6 22.78
112	12164.4 21.82	12268.7 22.01	12384.7 22.21	12513.2 22.44	12655.4 22.70	12812.4 22.98
113	12382.6 22.01	12488.8 22.20	12606.8 22.41	12737.7 22.64	12882.4 22.90	13042.2 23.19
114	12602.7 22.21	12710.8 22.40	12831.0 22.61	12964.1 22.84	13111.4 23.10	13274.1 23.39
115	12824.8 22.40	12934.8 22.59	13057.1 22.81	13192.6 23.04	13342.4 23.31	13508.0 23.59
116	13048.8 22.59	13160.7 22.79	13285.1 23.00	13423.0 23.24	13575.5 23.51	13743.9 23.80
117	13274.8 22.79	13388.6 22.98	13515.2 23.20	13655.4 23.44	13810.5 23.71	13981.9 24.00
118	13502.6 22.98	13618.5 23.18	13747.2 23.40	13889.8 23.64	14047.6 23.91	14221.9 24.21
119	13732.5 23.18	13850.3 23.38	13981.2 23.60	14126.3 23.84	14286.7 24.11	14464.0 24.41
120	13964.2 23.37	14084.0 23.57	14217.1 23.79	14364.7 24.04	14527.9 24.31	14708.1 24.62
SUMS.	12°	13°	14°	15°	16°	17°

TABLE IX. **Whole Sections.** **Side Slope 1 to 1.**

SUMS.	18°		19°		20°		21°		22°		23°	
1	1.0	0.31	1.1	0.32	1.1	0.32	1.1	0.33	1.1	0.33	1.1	0.34
2	4.1	0.52	4.2	0.53	4.3	0.53	4.3	0.54	4.4	0.55	4.5	0.56
3	9.3	0.72	9.5	0.74	9.6	0.75	9.8	0.76	10.0	0.77	10.2	0.79
4	16.6	0.93	16.8	0.95	17.1	0.96	17.4	0.98	17.7	1.00	18.1	1.02
5	25.9	1.14	26.3	1.16	26.7	1.17	27.1	1.19	27.7	1.22	28.2	1.24
6	37.3	1.35	37.8	1.37	38.4	1.39	39.1	1.41	39.8	1.44	40.7	1.47
7	50.7	1.55	51.5	1.58	52.3	1.60	53.2	1.63	54.2	1.66	55.3	1.69
8	66.3	1.76	67.2	1.79	68.3	1.81	69.5	1.85	70.8	1.88	72.3	1.92
9	83.9	1.97	85.1	2.00	86.5	2.03	88.0	2.06	89.6	2.10	91.5	2.15
10	103.5	2.17	105.0	2.21	106.7	2.24	108.6	2.28	110.7	2.32	112.9	2.37
11	125.3	2.38	127.1	2.42	129.1	2.45	131.4	2.50	133.9	2.55	136.7	2.60
12	149.1	2.59	151.3	2.63	153.7	2.67	156.4	2.71	159.3	2.77	162.6	2.82
13	175.0	2.80	177.5	2.84	180.4	2.89	183.5	2.93	187.0	2.99	190.9	3.05
14	202.9	3.00	205.9	3.05	209.2	3.10	212.8	3.15	216.9	3.21	221.4	3.28
15	232.9	3.21	236.4	3.26	240.1	3.31	244.3	3.37	249.0	3.43	254.1	3.50
16	265.0	3.42	268.9	3.47	273.2	3.52	278.0	3.58	283.3	3.65	289.1	3.73
17	299.2	3.62	303.6	3.68	308.5	3.74	313.8	3.80	319.8	3.87	326.4	3.95
18	335.4	3.83	340.4	3.89	345.8	3.95	351.8	4.02	358.5	4.09	365.9	4.18
19	373.7	4.04	379.2	4.10	385.3	4.16	392.0	4.24	399.5	4.32	407.7	4.40
20	414.1	4.24	420.2	4.31	426.9	4.38	434.4	4.45	442.6	4.54	451.8	4.63
21	456.5	4.45	463.3	4.52	470.7	4.59	478.9	4.67	488.0	4.76	498.1	4.86
22	501.0	4.66	508.4	4.73	516.6	4.80	525.6	4.89	535.6	4.98	546.6	5.08
23	547.6	4.87	555.7	4.94	564.6	5.02	574.5	5.10	585.4	5.20	597.5	5.31
24	596.3	5.07	605.1	5.15	614.8	5.23	625.5	5.32	637.4	5.42	650.5	5.53
25	647.0	5.28	656.5	5.36	667.1	5.44	678.7	5.54	691.6	5.64	705.9	5.76
26	699.8	5.49	710.1	5.57	721.5	5.66	734.1	5.76	748.0	5.86	763.5	5.99
27	754.7	5.69	765.8	5.78	778.1	5.87	791.7	5.97	806.7	6.09	823.4	6.21
28	811.6	5.90	823.6	5.99	836.8	6.08	851.4	6.19	867.5	6.31	885.5	6.44
29	870.6	6.11	883.4	6.20	897.6	6.30	913.3	6.41	930.6	6.53	949.8	6.66
30	931.7	6.31	945.4	6.41	960.6	6.51	977.3	6.62	995.9	6.75	1016.5	6.89
31	994.8	6.52	1009.5	6.62	1025.7	6.72	1043.6	6.84	1063.4	6.97	1085.4	7.11
32	1060.1	6.73	1075.7	6.83	1092.9	6.94	1112.0	7.06	1133.1	7.19	1156.5	7.34
33	1127.4	6.94	1144.0	7.04	1162.3	7.15	1182.6	7.28	1205.0	7.41	1229.9	7.57
34	1196.7	7.14	1214.3	7.25	1233.8	7.36	1255.3	7.49	1279.2	7.64	1305.6	7.79
35	1268.1	7.35	1286.8	7.46	1307.5	7.58	1330.3	7.71	1355.5	7.86	1383.5	8.02
36	1341.6	7.56	1361.4	7.67	1383.2	7.79	1407.4	7.93	1434.1	8.08	1463.7	8.24
37	1417.2	7.76	1438.1	7.88	1461.2	8.00	1486.7	8.14	1514.9	8.30	1546.2	8.47
38	1494.9	7.97	1516.9	8.09	1541.2	8.22	1568.1	8.36	1597.9	8.52	1630.9	8.70
39	1574.6	8.18	1597.8	8.30	1623.4	8.43	1651.7	8.58	1683.1	8.74	1717.9	8.92
40	1656.3	8.39	1680.8	8.51	1707.7	8.65	1737.5	8.80	1770.5	8.96	1807.1	9.15
41	1740.2	8.59	1765.8	8.72	1794.2	8.86	1825.5	9.01	1860.1	9.18	1898.6	9.37
42	1826.1	8.80	1853.0	8.93	1882.7	9.07	1915.6	9.23	1952.0	9.41	1992.3	9.60
43	1914.1	9.01	1942.3	9.14	1973.5	9.29	2007.9	9.45	2046.0	9.63	2088.3	9.83
44	2004.2	9.21	2033.7	9.35	2066.3	9.50	2102.4	9.66	2142.3	9.85	2186.6	10.05
45	2096.3	9.42	2127.2	9.56	2161.3	9.71	2199.0	9.88	2240.8	10.07	2287.1	10.28
46	2190.5	9.63	2222.8	9.77	2258.4	9.93	2297.9	10.10	2341.5	10.29	2389.9	10.50
47	2286.8	9.83	2320.5	9.98	2357.7	10.14	2398.8	10.32	2444.4	10.51	2494.9	10.73
48	2385.1	10.04	2420.3	10.19	2459.1	10.35	2502.0	10.53	2549.5	10.73	2602.2	10.96
49	2485.6	10.25	2522.2	10.40	2562.6	10.57	2607.3	10.75	2656.8	10.95	2711.7	11.18
50	2588.0	10.46	2626.2	10.61	2668.3	10.78	2714.9	10.97	2766.4	11.18	2823.6	11.41
51	2692.6	10.66	2732.3	10.82	2776.1	10.99	2824.5	11.19	2878.2	11.40	2937.6	11.63
52	2799.2	10.87	2840.5	11.03	2886.0	11.21	2936.4	11.40	2992.1	11.62	3054.0	11.86
53	2907.9	11.08	2950.8	11.24	2998.1	11.42	3050.4	11.62	3108.3	11.84	3172.6	12.08
54	3018.7	11.28	3063.2	11.45	3112.3	11.63	3166.6	11.84	3226.7	12.06	3293.4	12.31
55	3131.5	11.49	3177.7	11.66	3228.6	11.85	3285.0	12.05	3347.3	12.28	3416.5	12.54
56	3246.4	11.70	3294.3	11.87	3347.1	12.06	3405.5	12.27	3470.2	12.50	3541.9	12.76
57	3363.4	11.90	3413.0	12.08	3467.7	12.27	3528.2	12.49	3595.2	12.73	3669.5	12.99
58	3482.5	12.11	3533.8	12.29	3590.5	12.49	3653.1	12.71	3722.5	12.95	3799.4	13.21
59	3603.6	12.32	3656.7	12.50	3715.3	12.70	3780.2	12.92	3851.9	13.17	3931.5	13.44
60	3726.8	12.53	3781.7	12.71	3842.3	12.91	3909.4	13.14	3983.6	13.39	4065.9	13.67
SUMS.	18°		19°		20°		21°		22°		23°	

SUMS.	18°		19°		20°		21°		22°		23°	
61	3852.0	12.73	3908.8	12.92	3971.5	13.13	4040.8	13.36	4117.5	13.61	4202.6	13.89
62	3979.4	12.94	4038.0	13.13	4102.8	13.34	4174.4	13.57	4253.6	13.83	4341.5	14.12
63	4108.8	13.15	4169.3	13.34	4236.2	13.55	4310.1	13.79	4391.9	14.05	4482.7	14.34
64	4240.2	13.35	4302.7	13.55	4371.7	13.77	4448.0	14.01	4532.5	14.27	4626.1	14.57
65	4373.8	13.56	4438.2	13.76	4509.4	13.98	4588.1	14.23	4675.2	14.50	4771.8	14.80
66	4509.4	13.77	4575.9	13.97	4649.2	14.20	4730.4	14.44	4820.2	14.72	4919.8	15.02
67	4647.1	13.98	4715.6	14.18	4791.2	14.41	4874.8	14.66	4967.3	14.94	5070.0	15.25
68	4786.8	14.18	4857.4	14.39	4935.3	14.62	5021.4	14.88	5116.7	15.16	5222.5	15.47
69	4928.7	14.39	5001.3	14.60	5081.5	14.84	5170.2	15.09	5268.3	15.38	5377.2	15.70
70	5072.6	14.60	5147.3	14.81	5229.9	15.05	5321.1	15.31	5422.1	15.60	5534.2	15.92
71	5218.5	14.80	5295.4	15.02	5380.4	15.26	5474.2	15.53	5578.2	15.82	5693.4	16.15
72	5366.6	15.01	5445.6	15.23	5533.0	15.48	5629.5	15.75	5736.4	16.05	5854.9	16.38
73	5516.7	15.22	5598.0	15.44	5687.7	15.69	5787.0	15.96	5896.8	16.27	6018.7	16.60
74	5668.8	15.42	5752.4	15.65	5844.6	15.90	5946.6	16.18	6059.5	16.49	6184.7	16.83
75	5823.1	15.63	5908.9	15.86	6003.7	16.12	6108.4	16.40	6224.4	16.71	6353.0	17.05
76	5979.4	15.84	6067.5	16.07	6164.8	16.33	6272.4	16.61	6391.5	16.93	6523.6	17.28
77	6137.8	16.05	6228.2	16.28	6328.1	16.54	6438.5	16.83	6560.8	17.15	6696.4	17.51
78	6298.3	16.25	6391.1	16.49	6493.6	16.76	6606.9	17.05	6732.3	17.37	6871.4	17.73
79	6460.8	16.46	6556.0	16.70	6661.1	16.97	6777.4	17.27	6906.0	17.59	7048.7	17.96
80	6625.4	16.67	6723.0	16.91	6830.8	17.18	6950.0	17.48	7082.0	17.82	7228.3	18.18
81	6792.1	16.87	6892.1	17.12	7002.7	17.40	7124.9	17.70	7260.1	18.04	7410.2	18.41
82	6960.8	17.08	7063.4	17.33	7176.6	17.61	7301.9	17.92	7440.5	18.26	7594.2	18.64
83	7131.6	17.29	7236.7	17.54	7352.8	17.82	7481.0	18.14	7623.1	18.48	7780.6	18.86
84	7304.5	17.50	7412.1	17.75	7531.0	18.04	7662.4	18.35	7807.9	18.70	7969.2	19.09
85	7479.4	17.70	7589.7	17.96	7711.4	18.25	7845.9	18.57	7994.9	18.92	8160.1	19.31
86	7656.5	17.91	7769.3	18.17	7893.9	18.46	8031.6	18.79	8184.1	19.14	8353.2	19.54
87	7835.5	18.12	7951.0	18.38	8078.5	18.68	8219.5	19.00	8375.5	19.36	8548.6	19.76
88	8016.7	18.32	8134.8	18.59	8265.3	18.89	8409.5	19.22	8569.2	19.59	8746.3	19.99
89	8199.9	18.53	8320.8	18.80	8454.2	19.10	8601.7	19.44	8765.0	19.81	8946.2	20.22
90	8385.2	18.74	8508.8	19.01	8645.3	19.32	8796.1	19.66	8963.1	20.03	9148.3	20.44
91	8572.6	18.94	8699.0	19.22	8838.5	19.53	8992.7	19.87	9163.4	20.25	9352.8	20.67
92	8762.1	19.15	8891.2	19.43	9033.8	19.75	9191.4	20.09	9365.9	20.47	9559.4	20.89
93	8953.6	19.36	9085.5	19.64	9231.2	19.96	9392.3	20.31	9570.6	20.69	9768.4	21.12
94	9147.2	19.57	9282.0	19.85	9430.8	20.17	9595.4	20.52	9777.5	20.91	9979.6	21.35
95	9342.8	19.77	9480.5	20.06	9632.5	20.39	9800.6	20.74	9986.7	21.14	10193.1	21.57
96	9540.6	19.98	9681.1	20.27	9836.4	20.60	10008.0	20.96	10198.0	21.36	10408.8	21.80
97	9740.3	20.19	9883.9	20.48	10042.4	20.81	10217.6	21.18	10411.6	21.58	10626.8	22.02
98	9942.2	20.39	10088.7	20.69	10250.5	21.03	10429.4	21.39	10627.4	21.80	10847.0	22.25
99	10146.2	20.60	10295.7	20.90	10460.8	21.24	10643.3	21.61	10845.4	22.02	11069.5	22.48
100	10352.2	20.81	10504.7	21.11	10673.2	21.45	10859.4	21.83	11065.6	22.24	11294.2	22.70
101	10560.2	21.01	10715.9	21.32	10887.7	21.67	11077.7	22.04	11288.0	22.46	11521.3	22.93
102	10770.4	21.22	10929.1	21.53	11104.4	21.88	11298.1	22.26	11512.6	22.68	11750.5	23.15
103	10982.6	21.43	11144.4	21.74	11323.2	22.09	11520.7	22.48	11739.5	22.91	11982.1	23.38
104	11196.9	21.64	11361.9	21.95	11544.1	22.31	11745.5	22.70	11968.5	23.13	12215.8	23.60
105	11413.3	21.84	11581.4	22.16	11767.2	22.52	11972.5	22.91	12199.8	23.35	12451.9	23.83
106	11631.7	22.05	11803.1	22.38	11992.4	22.73	12201.6	23.13	12433.3	23.57	12690.2	24.06
107	11852.2	22.26	12026.8	22.59	12219.7	22.95	12432.9	23.35	12669.0	23.79	12930.8	24.28
108	12074.8	22.46	12252.7	22.80	12449.2	23.16	12666.4	23.56	12906.9	24.01	13173.6	24.51
109	12299.4	22.67	12480.6	23.01	12680.8	23.37	12902.1	23.78	13147.0	24.23	13418.7	24.73
110	12526.1	22.88	12710.7	23.22	12914.5	23.59	13139.9	24.00	13389.4	24.45	13666.0	24.96
111	12754.9	23.09	12942.9	23.43	13150.4	23.80	13379.9	24.22	13633.9	24.68	13915.6	25.19
112	12985.7	23.29	13177.1	23.64	13388.4	24.01	13622.0	24.43	13880.7	24.90	14167.5	25.41
113	13218.7	23.50	13413.5	23.85	13628.6	24.23	13866.4	24.65	14129.6	25.12	14421.6	25.64
114	13453.7	23.71	13651.9	24.06	13870.9	24.44	14112.9	24.87	14380.8	25.34	14678.0	25.86
115	13690.7	23.91	13892.5	24.27	14115.3	24.66	14361.6	25.09	14634.2	25.56	14936.6	26.09
116	13929.9	24.12	14135.1	24.48	14361.8	24.87	14612.4	25.30	14889.8	25.78	15197.5	26.32
117	14171.1	24.33	14379.9	24.69	14610.5	25.08	14865.4	25.52	15147.7	26.00	15460.7	26.54
118	14415.3	24.53	14626.8	24.90	14861.3	25.30	15120.6	25.74	15407.7	26.23	15726.1	26.77
119	14659.7	24.74	14875.7	25.11	15114.3	25.51	15378.0	25.95	15670.0	26.45	15993.8	26.99
120	14907.1	24.95	15126.8	25.32	15369.4	25.72	15637.6	26.17	15934.4	26.67	16263.7	27.22
SUMS.	18°		19°		20°		21°		22°		23°	

SUMS.	24°		25°		26°		27°		28°		29°	
1	1.2	0.35	1.2	0.35	1.2	0.36	1.3	0.38	1.3	0.39	1.3	0.40
2	4.6	0.58	4.7	0.59	4.9	0.61	5.0	0.63	5.2	0.65	5.3	0.67
3	10.4	0.81	10.6	0.83	10.9	0.85	11.3	0.88	11.6	0.90	12.0	0.94
4	18.5	1.04	18.9	1.06	19.4	1.09	20.0	1.13	20.7	1.16	21.4	1.20
5	28.9	1.27	29.6	1.30	30.4	1.34	31.3	1.38	32.3	1.42	33.4	1.47
6	41.6	1.50	42.6	1.54	43.7	1.58	45.0	1.63	46.5	1.68	48.1	1.74
7	56.6	1.73	58.0	1.77	59.5	1.82	61.3	1.88	63.3	1.94	65.5	2.00
8	73.9	1.96	75.7	2.01	77.8	2.07	80.0	2.13	82.6	2.19	85.5	2.27
9	93.5	2.19	95.8	2.25	98.4	2.31	101.3	2.38	104.6	2.45	108.3	2.54
10	115.5	2.43	118.3	2.48	121.5	2.55	125.1	2.63	129.1	2.71	133.7	2.81
11	139.7	2.66	143.2	2.72	147.0	2.79	151.3	2.88	156.2	2.97	161.7	3.07
12	166.3	2.89	170.4	2.96	175.0	3.04	180.1	3.13	185.9	3.23	192.5	3.34
13	195.2	3.12	200.0	3.19	205.3	3.28	211.4	3.38	218.2	3.49	225.9	3.61
14	226.4	3.35	231.9	3.43	238.1	3.52	245.1	3.63	253.0	3.74	262.0	3.88
15	259.8	3.58	266.2	3.67	273.4	3.77	281.4	3.88	290.4	4.00	300.7	4.14
16	295.6	3.81	302.9	3.90	311.0	4.01	320.2	4.13	330.5	4.26	342.2	4.41
17	333.8	4.04	341.9	4.14	351.1	4.25	361.4	4.38	373.1	4.52	386.3	4.68
18	374.2	4.27	383.4	4.38	393.6	4.50	405.2	4.63	418.2	4.78	433.1	4.95
19	416.9	4.50	427.1	4.61	438.6	4.74	451.5	4.88	466.0	5.03	482.5	5.21
20	461.9	4.74	473.3	4.85	486.0	4.98	500.2	5.13	516.3	5.29	534.6	5.48
21	509.3	4.97	521.8	5.09	535.8	5.22	551.5	5.38	569.3	5.55	589.4	5.75
22	558.9	5.20	572.7	5.32	588.0	5.47	605.3	5.63	624.8	5.81	646.9	6.01
23	610.9	5.43	625.9	5.56	642.7	5.71	661.6	5.88	682.9	6.07	707.1	6.28
24	665.2	5.66	681.5	5.80	699.8	5.95	720.3	6.13	743.5	6.33	769.9	6.55
25	721.8	5.89	739.5	6.03	759.3	6.20	781.6	6.38	806.8	6.58	835.4	6.82
26	780.7	6.12	799.8	6.27	821.3	6.44	845.4	6.63	872.6	6.84	903.5	7.08
27	841.9	6.35	862.6	6.51	885.7	6.68	911.7	6.88	941.0	7.10	974.4	7.35
28	905.4	6.58	927.6	6.74	952.5	6.93	980.5	7.13	1012.0	7.36	1047.9	7.62
29	971.2	6.81	995.1	6.98	1021.8	7.17	1051.8	7.38	1085.6	7.62	1124.1	7.89
30	1039.4	7.04	1064.9	7.22	1093.4	7.41	1125.5	7.63	1161.8	7.87	1202.9	8.15
31	1109.8	7.28	1137.1	7.45	1167.6	7.65	1201.8	7.88	1240.5	8.13	1284.5	8.42
32	1182.6	7.51	1211.6	7.69	1244.1	7.90	1280.6	8.13	1321.9	8.39	1368.7	8.69
33	1257.6	7.74	1288.5	7.93	1323.1	8.14	1361.9	8.38	1405.8	8.65	1455.6	8.96
34	1335.0	7.97	1367.8	8.16	1404.5	8.38	1445.7	8.63	1492.3	8.91	1545.1	9.22
35	1414.7	8.20	1449.4	8.40	1488.3	8.63	1532.0	8.88	1581.3	9.17	1637.3	9.49
36	1496.7	8.43	1533.4	8.64	1574.6	8.87	1620.8	9.13	1673.0	9.42	1732.2	9.76
37	1581.0	8.66	1619.8	8.87	1663.3	9.11	1712.1	9.38	1767.2	9.68	1829.8	10.02
38	1667.6	8.89	1708.5	9.11	1754.4	9.36	1805.9	9.63	1864.0	9.94	1930.1	10.29
39	1756.5	9.12	1799.7	9.35	1847.9	9.60	1902.2	9.88	1963.4	10.20	2033.0	10.56
40	1847.8	9.35	1893.1	9.58	1943.9	9.84	2001.0	10.13	2065.4	10.46	2138.6	10.83
41	1941.3	9.59	1989.0	9.82	2042.3	10.08	2102.3	10.38	2170.0	10.71	2246.8	11.09
42	2037.2	9.82	2087.2	10.06	2143.2	10.33	2206.1	10.63	2277.1	10.97	2357.8	11.36
43	2135.3	10.05	2187.7	10.29	2246.4	10.57	2312.4	10.88	2386.8	11.23	2471.4	11.63
44	2235.8	10.28	2290.7	10.53	2352.1	10.81	2421.2	11.13	2499.1	11.49	2587.7	11.90
45	2338.6	10.51	2396.0	10.77	2460.3	11.06	2532.5	11.38	2614.0	11.75	2706.6	12.16
46	2443.7	10.74	2503.7	11.00	2570.8	11.30	2646.3	11.63	2731.5	12.01	2828.3	12.43
47	2551.1	10.97	2613.7	11.24	2683.8	11.54	2762.6	11.88	2851.5	12.26	2952.6	12.70
48	2660.8	11.20	2726.1	11.48	2799.2	11.78	2881.4	12.13	2974.2	12.52	3079.6	12.97
49	2772.8	11.43	2840.9	11.71	2917.1	12.03	3002.7	12.38	3099.4	12.78	3209.2	13.23
50	2887.1	11.66	2958.0	11.95	3037.3	12.27	3126.5	12.63	3227.2	13.04	3341.5	13.50
51	3003.8	11.89	3077.5	12.19	3160.1	12.51	3252.8	12.88	3357.6	13.30	3476.5	13.77
52	3122.7	12.13	3199.4	12.42	3285.2	12.76	3381.6	13.13	3490.5	13.55	3614.2	14.03
53	3244.0	12.36	3323.6	12.66	3412.8	13.00	3512.9	13.38	3626.1	13.81	3754.5	14.30
54	3367.5	12.59	3450.2	12.90	3542.8	13.24	3646.8	13.63	3764.2	14.07	3897.6	14.57
55	3493.4	12.82	3579.2	13.13	3675.2	13.49	3783.1	13.88	3904.9	14.33	4043.2	14.84
56	3621.6	13.05	3710.5	13.37	3810.0	13.73	3921.9	14.13	4048.2	14.59	4191.6	15.10
57	3752.1	13.28	3844.2	13.61	3947.3	13.97	4063.2	14.38	4194.1	14.85	4342.6	15.37
58	3884.9	13.51	3980.3	13.84	4087.1	14.21	4207.0	14.63	4342.5	15.10	4496.4	15.64
59	4020.0	13.74	4118.7	14.08	4229.2	14.46	4353.3	14.88	4493.5	15.36	4652.7	15.91
60	4157.5	13.97	4259.5	14.32	4373.8	14.70	4502.2	15.13	4647.2	15.62	4811.8	16.17
SUMS.	24°		25°		26°		27°		28°		29°	

TABLE IX. Whole Sections. Side Slope 1 to 1.

SUMS.	24°		25°		26°		27°		28°		29°	
61	4297.2	14.20	4402.7	14.55	4520.8	14.94	4653.5	15.38	4803.3	15.88	4973.5	16.44
62	4439.2	14.44	4548.2	14.79	4670.2	15.19	4807.3	15.63	4962.1	16.14	5137.9	16.71
63	4583.6	14.67	4696.1	15.03	4822.1	15.43	4963.6	15.88	5123.5	16.39	5305.0	16.97
64	4730.3	14.90	4846.4	15.26	4976.4	15.67	5122.5	16.13	5287.4	16.65	5474.8	17.24
65	4879.2	15.13	4999.0	15.50	5133.1	15.92	5283.8	16.38	5453.9	16.91	5647.2	17.51
66	5030.5	15.36	5154.0	15.74	5292.3	16.16	5447.6	16.63	5623.1	17.17	5822.3	17.78
67	5184.1	15.59	5311.4	15.97	5453.9	16.40	5614.0	16.88	5794.7	17.43	6000.0	18.04
68	5340.0	15.82	5471.1	16.21	5617.9	16.64	5782.8	17.13	5969.0	17.68	6180.5	18.31
69	5498.2	16.05	5633.2	16.45	5784.3	16.89	5954.1	17.38	6145.9	17.94	6363.6	18.58
70	5658.8	16.28	5797.7	16.68	5953.2	17.13	6128.0	17.63	6325.3	18.20	6549.4	18.85
71	5821.6	16.51	5964.5	16.92	6124.5	17.37	6304.3	17.88	6507.3	18.46	6737.9	19.11
72	5986.7	16.75	6133.7	17.16	6298.2	17.62	6483.1	18.13	6691.9	18.72	6929.0	19.38
73	6154.2	16.98	6305.3	17.39	6474.4	17.86	6664.5	18.38	6879.1	18.98	7122.8	19.65
74	6324.0	17.21	6479.2	17.63	6653.0	18.10	6848.3	18.63	7068.8	19.23	7319.3	19.92
75	6496.0	17.44	6655.5	17.87	6834.0	18.35	7034.6	18.88	7261.2	19.49	7518.4	20.18
76	6670.4	17.67	6834.2	18.10	7017.5	18.59	7223.5	19.13	7456.1	19.75	7720.3	20.45
77	6847.1	17.90	7015.2	18.34	7203.4	18.83	7414.8	19.38	7653.6	20.01	7924.8	20.72
78	7026.1	18.13	7198.6	18.58	7391.7	19.07	7608.7	19.63	7853.7	20.27	8131.9	20.98
79	7207.4	18.36	7384.4	18.81	7582.4	19.32	7805.0	19.88	8056.4	20.52	8341.8	21.25
80	7391.0	18.59	7572.5	19.05	7775.6	19.56	8003.9	20.13	8261.6	20.78	8554.3	21.52
81	7577.0	18.82	7763.0	19.29	7971.2	19.80	8205.2	20.38	8469.4	21.04	8769.5	21.79
82	7765.2	19.06	7955.9	19.52	8169.2	20.05	8409.1	20.63	8679.8	21.30	8987.4	22.05
83	7955.8	19.29	8151.1	19.76	8369.7	20.29	8615.4	20.89	8892.8	21.56	9207.9	22.32
84	8148.6	19.52	8348.7	20.00	8572.6	20.53	8824.3	21.14	9108.4	21.82	9431.1	22.59
85	8343.8	19.75	8548.7	20.23	8777.9	20.78	9035.6	21.39	9326.6	22.07	9657.0	22.86
86	8541.3	19.98	8751.0	20.47	8985.7	21.02	9249.5	21.64	9547.3	22.33	9885.6	23.12
87	8741.1	20.21	8955.7	20.71	9195.9	21.26	9465.8	21.89	9770.6	22.59	10116.8	23.39
88	8943.2	20.44	9162.7	20.94	9408.5	21.50	9684.7	22.14	9996.5	22.85	10350.7	23.66
89	9147.6	20.67	9372.2	21.18	9623.5	21.75	9906.0	22.39	10225.0	23.11	10587.3	23.93
90	9354.3	20.90	9584.0	21.42	9841.0	21.99	10129.9	22.64	10456.1	23.36	10826.5	24.19
91	9563.3	21.13	9798.1	21.65	10060.9	22.23	10356.2	22.89	10689.7	23.62	11068.5	24.46
92	9774.7	21.36	10014.6	21.89	10283.2	22.48	10585.1	23.14	10926.0	23.88	11313.1	24.73
93	9988.3	21.60	10233.5	22.13	10508.0	22.72	10816.5	23.39	11164.8	24.14	11560.3	24.99
94	10204.3	21.83	10454.8	22.36	10735.2	22.96	11050.3	23.64	11406.2	24.40	11810.3	25.26
95	10422.5	22.06	10678.4	22.60	10964.8	23.21	11286.7	23.89	11650.1	24.66	12062.9	25.53
96	10643.1	22.29	10904.4	22.84	11196.9	23.45	11525.6	24.14	11896.7	24.91	12318.2	25.80
97	10866.0	22.52	11132.8	23.07	11431.4	23.69	11766.9	24.39	12145.8	25.17	12576.2	26.06
98	11091.2	22.75	11363.5	23.31	11668.3	23.93	12010.8	24.64	12397.6	25.43	12836.8	26.33
99	11318.7	22.98	11596.6	23.55	11907.6	24.18	12257.2	24.89	12651.9	25.69	13100.1	26.60
100	11548.5	23.21	11832.1	23.78	12149.4	24.42	12506.0	25.14	12908.8	25.95	13366.1	26.87
101	11780.6	23.44	12069.9	24.02	12393.6	24.66	12757.4	25.39	13168.2	26.20	13634.8	27.13
102	12015.1	23.67	12310.1	24.26	12640.2	24.91	13011.3	25.64	13430.3	26.46	13906.1	27.40
103	12251.8	23.91	12552.6	24.49	12889.3	25.15	13267.6	25.89	13694.9	26.72	14180.1	27.67
104	12490.9	24.14	12797.5	24.73	13140.8	25.39	13526.5	26.14	13962.1	26.98	14456.8	27.94
105	12732.2	24.37	13044.8	24.97	13394.7	25.64	13787.9	26.39	14231.9	27.24	14736.1	28.20
106	12975.9	24.60	13294.5	25.20	13651.1	25.88	14051.8	26.64	14504.3	27.50	15018.2	28.47
107	13221.9	24.83	13546.5	25.44	13909.8	26.12	14318.2	26.89	14779.2	27.75	15302.9	28.74
108	13470.2	25.06	13800.9	25.68	14171.0	26.36	14587.0	27.14	15056.8	28.01	15590.2	29.00
109	13720.8	25.29	14057.7	25.91	14434.7	26.61	14858.4	27.39	15336.9	28.27	15880.3	29.27
110	13973.7	25.52	14316.8	26.15	14700.8	26.85	15132.3	27.64	15619.6	28.53	16173.0	29.54
111	14228.9	25.75	14578.3	26.39	14969.3	27.09	15408.7	27.89	15904.9	28.79	16468.4	29.81
112	14486.4	25.98	14842.1	26.62	15240.2	27.34	15687.6	28.14	16192.7	29.04	16766.4	30.07
113	14746.3	26.22	15108.3	26.86	15513.6	27.58	15968.9	28.39	16483.2	29.30	17067.2	30.34
114	15008.4	26.45	15376.9	27.10	15789.3	27.82	16252.8	28.64	16776.2	29.56	17370.6	30.61
115	15272.9	26.68	15647.9	27.33	16067.6	28.07	16539.2	28.89	17071.8	29.82	17676.7	30.88
116	15539.7	26.91	15921.2	27.57	16348.2	28.31	16828.1	29.14	17370.0	30.08	17985.4	31.14
117	15808.7	27.14	16196.9	27.81	16631.3	28.55	17119.5	29.39	17670.8	30.34	18296.9	31.41
118	16080.1	27.37	16474.9	28.04	16916.8	28.79	17413.4	29.64	17974.1	30.59	18611.0	31.68
119	16353.8	27.60	16755.4	28.28	17204.8	29.04	17709.8	29.89	18280.1	30.85	18927.7	31.95
120	16629.8	27.83	17038.2	28.52	17495.1	29.28	18008.7	30.14	18588.6	31.11	19247.2	32.21
SUMS.	24°		25°		26°		27°		28°		29°	

TABLE IX. Whole Sections. Side Slope 1 to 1.

SUMS.	30°		31°		32°		33°		34°		35°	
1	1.4	0.42	1.4	0.43	1.5	0.46	1.6	0.48	1.7	0.51	1.8	0.54
2	5.6	0.69	5.8	0.72	6.1	0.76	6.4	0.80	6.8	0.85	7.3	0.91
3	12.5	0.97	13.0	1.01	13.7	1.06	14.4	1.12	15.3	1.19	16.3	1.27
4	22.2	1.25	23.2	1.30	24.3	1.37	25.6	1.44	27.2	1.53	29.1	1.63
5	34.7	1.53	36.2	1.59	38.0	1.67	40.0	1.76	42.5	1.87	45.4	2.00
6	50.0	1.81	52.2	1.88	54.7	1.97	57.6	2.08	61.2	2.21	65.4	2.36
7	68.1	2.08	71.0	2.17	74.4	2.28	78.5	2.40	83.2	2.55	89.0	2.72
8	88.9	2.36	92.7	2.46	97.2	2.58	102.5	2.72	108.7	2.89	116.3	3.09
9	112.5	2.64	117.4	2.75	123.0	2.89	129.7	3.04	137.6	3.23	147.1	3.45
10	138.9	2.92	144.9	3.04	151.9	3.19	160.1	3.36	169.9	3.57	181.7	3.81
11	168.1	3.19	175.3	3.33	183.8	3.49	193.7	3.68	205.6	3.91	219.8	4.18
12	200.0	3.47	208.7	3.62	218.7	3.80	230.6	4.00	244.6	4.25	261.6	4.54
13	234.7	3.75	244.9	3.91	256.7	4.10	270.6	4.32	287.1	4.59	307.0	4.90
14	272.2	4.03	284.0	4.20	297.7	4.41	313.8	4.64	333.0	4.93	356.0	5.27
15	312.5	4.31	326.0	4.49	341.8	4.71	360.3	4.96	382.2	5.27	408.7	5.63
16	355.6	4.58	371.0	4.78	388.9	5.01	409.9	5.28	434.9	5.61	465.0	5.99
17	401.4	4.86	418.8	5.07	439.0	5.32	462.7	5.60	491.0	5.95	525.0	6.36
18	450.0	5.14	469.5	5.36	492.2	5.62	518.8	5.92	550.4	6.29	588.6	6.72
19	501.4	5.42	523.1	5.65	548.4	5.92	578.0	6.24	613.3	6.63	655.8	7.08
20	555.6	5.69	579.6	5.94	607.6	6.23	640.5	6.56	679.5	6.97	726.6	7.45
21	612.5	5.97	639.1	6.23	669.9	6.53	706.1	6.89	749.2	7.30	801.1	7.81
22	672.2	6.25	701.4	6.52	735.2	6.84	775.0	7.21	822.2	7.64	879.2	8.17
23	734.7	6.53	766.6	6.81	803.6	7.14	847.0	7.53	898.7	7.98	961.0	8.54
24	800.0	6.81	834.7	7.10	875.0	7.44	922.3	7.85	978.5	8.32	1046.3	8.90
25	868.1	7.08	905.7	7.39	949.4	7.75	1000.8	8.17	1061.8	8.66	1135.4	9.26
26	938.9	7.36	979.6	7.68	1026.9	8.05	1082.4	8.49	1148.4	9.00	1228.0	9.63
27	1012.5	7.64	1056.4	7.97	1107.4	8.35	1167.3	8.81	1238.4	9.34	1324.3	9.99
28	1088.9	7.92	1136.1	8.26	1190.9	8.66	1255.3	9.13	1331.9	9.68	1424.2	10.35
29	1168.1	8.19	1218.7	8.55	1277.5	8.96	1346.6	9.45	1428.7	10.02	1527.7	10.72
30	1250.0	8.47	1304.2	8.84	1367.2	9.27	1441.1	9.77	1528.9	10.36	1634.9	11.08
31	1334.7	8.75	1392.6	9.13	1459.8	9.57	1538.8	10.09	1632.6	10.70	1745.7	11.44
32	1422.2	9.03	1483.9	9.42	1555.5	9.87	1639.6	10.41	1739.6	11.04	1860.2	11.81
33	1512.5	9.31	1578.1	9.71	1654.3	10.18	1743.7	10.73	1850.0	11.38	1978.3	12.17
34	1605.6	9.58	1675.2	10.00	1756.0	10.48	1851.0	11.05	1963.8	11.72	2100.0	12.53
35	1701.4	9.86	1775.1	10.29	1860.8	10.79	1961.5	11.37	2081.1	12.06	2225.3	12.90
36	1800.0	10.14	1878.0	10.58	1968.7	11.09	2075.2	11.69	2201.7	12.40	2354.3	13.26
37	1901.4	10.42	1983.8	10.87	2079.6	11.39	2192.0	12.01	2325.7	12.74	2486.9	13.62
38	2005.6	10.69	2092.5	11.16	2193.5	11.70	2312.1	12.33	2453.1	13.08	2623.1	13.99
39	2112.5	10.97	2204.1	11.45	2310.5	12.00	2435.4	12.65	2583.9	13.42	2763.0	14.35
40	2222.2	11.25	2318.6	11.74	2430.5	12.30	2561.9	12.97	2718.1	13.76	2906.5	14.71
41	2334.7	11.53	2435.9	12.03	2553.5	12.61	2691.6	13.29	2855.7	14.10	3053.7	15.08
42	2450.0	11.81	2556.2	12.32	2679.6	12.91	2824.5	13.61	2996.7	14.44	3204.4	15.44
43	2568.1	12.08	2679.4	12.61	2808.7	13.22	2960.6	13.93	3141.1	14.78	3358.8	15.80
44	2688.9	12.36	2805.5	12.90	2940.9	13.52	3099.9	14.25	3288.9	15.12	3516.9	16.17
45	2812.5	12.64	2934.4	13.19	3076.1	13.82	3242.4	14.57	3440.1	15.46	3678.6	16.53
46	2938.9	12.92	3066.3	13.48	3214.3	14.13	3388.1	14.89	3594.7	15.80	3843.9	16.89
47	3068.1	13.19	3201.1	13.77	3355.6	14.43	3537.1	15.21	3752.7	16.14	4012.8	17.26
48	3200.0	13.47	3338.7	14.06	3499.9	14.73	3689.2	15.53	3914.1	16.48	4185.4	17.62
49	3334.7	13.75	3479.3	14.35	3647.3	15.04	3844.5	15.85	4078.9	16.82	4361.6	17.98
50	3472.2	14.03	3622.7	14.64	3797.7	15.34	4003.0	16.17	4247.1	17.16	4541.4	18.35
51	3612.5	14.31	3769.1	14.93	3951.1	15.65	4164.7	16.49	4418.6	17.50	4724.9	18.71
52	3755.6	14.58	3918.4	15.22	4107.5	15.95	4329.6	16.81	4593.6	17.84	4912.0	19.07
53	3901.4	14.86	4070.5	15.51	4267.0	16.25	4497.8	17.13	4772.0	18.18	5102.8	19.44
54	4050.0	15.14	4225.6	15.80	4429.6	16.56	4669.1	17.45	4953.8	18.52	5297.1	19.80
55	4201.4	15.42	4383.5	16.08	4595.2	16.86	4843.6	17.77	5139.0	18.86	5495.1	20.16
56	4355.6	15.69	4544.4	16.37	4763.8	17.17	5021.4	18.09	5327.5	19.20	5696.8	20.53
57	4512.5	15.97	4708.1	16.66	4935.4	17.47	5202.3	18.41	5519.5	19.54	5902.1	20.89
58	4672.2	16.25	4874.8	16.95	5110.1	17.77	5386.4	18.73	5714.9	19.88	6111.0	21.25
59	4834.7	16.53	5044.3	17.24	5287.9	18.08	5573.8	19.05	5913.6	20.22	6328.5	21.62
60	5000.0	16.81	5216.8	17.53	5468.6	18.38	5764.3	19.37	6115.8	20.56	6539.7	21.98
SUMS.	30°		31°		32°		33°		34°		35°	

TABLE IX. Whole Sections. Side Slope 1 to 1.

SUMS.	30°		31°		32°		33°		34°		35°	
61	5168.1	17.08	5392.1	17.82	5652.4	18.68	5958.1	19.69	6321.3	20.90	6759.5	22.34
62	5338.9	17.36	5570.3	18.11	5839.3	18.99	6155.0	20.02	6530.3	21.24	6982.9	22.71
63	5512.5	17.64	5751.5	18.40	6029.2	19.29	6355.2	20.34	6742.6	21.58	7210.0	23.07
64	5688.9	17.92	5935.5	18.69	6222.1	19.60	6558.5	20.66	6958.4	21.91	7440.7	23.43
65	5868.1	18.19	6122.4	18.98	6418.0	19.90	6765.1	20.98	7177.5	22.25	7675.0	23.80
66	6050.0	18.47	6312.3	19.27	6617.0	20.20	6974.8	21.30	7400.1	22.59	7913.0	24.16
67	6234.7	18.75	6505.0	19.56	6819.1	20.51	7187.8	21.62	7626.0	22.93	8154.6	24.52
68	6422.2	19.03	6700.6	19.85	7024.1	20.81	7403.9	21.94	7855.4	23.27	8399.8	24.89
69	6612.5	19.31	6899.2	20.14	7232.2	21.11	7623.3	22.26	8088.1	23.61	8648.7	25.25
70	6805.6	19.58	7100.6	20.43	7443.4	21.42	7845.9	22.58	8324.3	23.95	8901.2	25.61
71	7001.4	19.86	7304.9	20.72	7657.6	21.72	8071.6	22.90	8563.8	24.29	9157.4	25.98
72	7200.0	20.14	7512.1	21.01	7874.8	22.03	8300.6	23.22	8806.7	24.63	9417.1	26.34
73	7401.4	20.42	7722.2	21.30	8095.1	22.33	8532.8	23.54	9053.0	24.97	9680.5	26.70
74	7605.6	20.69	7935.3	21.59	8318.4	22.63	8768.2	23.86	9302.8	25.31	9947.6	27.07
75	7812.5	20.97	8151.2	21.88	8544.7	22.94	9006.8	24.18	9555.9	25.65	10218.2	27.43
76	8022.2	21.25	8370.0	22.17	8774.1	23.24	9248.5	24.50	9812.4	25.99	10492.5	27.79
77	8234.7	21.53	8591.7	22.46	9006.5	23.55	9493.5	24.82	10072.3	26.33	10770.5	28.16
78	8450.0	21.81	8816.3	22.75	9242.0	23.85	9741.7	25.14	10335.7	26.67	11052.0	28.52
79	8668.1	22.08	9043.8	23.04	9480.5	24.15	9993.1	25.46	10602.4	27.01	11337.3	28.88
80	8888.9	22.36	9274.2	23.33	9722.0	24.46	10247.7	25.78	10872.5	27.35	11626.1	29.25
81	9112.5	22.64	9507.5	23.62	9966.6	24.76	10505.5	26.10	11146.0	27.69	11918.6	29.61
82	9338.9	22.92	9743.7	23.91	10214.2	25.06	10766.5	26.42	11422.9	28.03	12214.7	29.97
83	9568.1	23.19	9982.8	24.20	10464.8	25.37	11030.7	26.74	11703.2	28.37	12514.4	30.34
84	9800.0	23.47	10224.8	24.49	10718.5	25.67	11298.1	27.06	11986.9	28.71	12817.8	30.70
85	10034.7	23.75	10469.7	24.78	10975.2	25.98	11568.7	27.38	12274.0	29.05	13124.8	31.06
86	10272.2	24.03	10717.5	25.07	11235.0	26.28	11842.5	27.70	12564.5	29.39	13435.4	31.43
87	10512.5	24.31	10968.2	25.36	11497.8	26.58	12119.5	28.02	12858.4	29.73	13749.7	31.79
88	10755.6	24.58	11221.8	25.65	11763.6	26.89	12399.7	28.34	13155.7	30.07	14067.6	32.15
89	11001.4	24.86	11478.3	25.94	12032.5	27.19	12683.1	28.66	13456.4	30.41	14389.1	32.52
90	11250.0	25.14	11737.7	26.23	12304.4	27.50	12969.7	28.98	13760.5	30.75	14714.3	32.88
91	11501.4	25.42	12000.0	26.52	12579.3	27.80	13259.5	29.30	14068.0	31.09	15043.1	33.24
92	11755.6	25.69	12265.2	26.81	12857.3	28.10	13552.6	29.62	14378.9	31.43	15375.5	33.61
93	12012.5	25.97	12533.3	27.10	13138.4	28.41	13848.8	29.94	14693.2	31.77	15711.6	33.97
94	12272.2	26.25	12804.2	27.39	13422.4	28.71	14148.2	30.26	15010.8	32.11	16051.3	34.33
95	12534.7	26.53	13078.1	27.68	13709.5	29.01	14450.8	30.58	15331.9	32.45	16394.6	34.70
96	12800.0	26.81	13354.9	27.97	13999.7	29.32	14756.7	30.90	15656.4	32.79	16741.6	35.06
97	13068.1	27.08	13634.6	28.26	14292.8	29.62	15065.7	31.22	15984.3	33.13	17092.2	35.42
98	13338.9	27.36	13917.1	28.55	14589.1	29.93	15377.9	31.54	16315.5	33.47	17446.4	35.79
99	13612.5	27.64	14202.6	28.84	14888.3	30.23	15693.4	31.86	16650.2	33.81	17804.3	36.15
100	13888.9	27.92	14491.0	29.13	15190.6	30.53	16012.0	32.18	16988.3	34.15	18165.8	36.51
101	14168.1	28.19	14782.3	29.42	15495.9	30.84	16333.8	32.50	17329.7	34.49	18530.9	36.88
102	14450.0	28.47	15076.4	29.71	15804.3	31.14	16658.9	32.82	17674.6	34.83	18899.7	37.24
103	14734.7	28.75	15373.5	30.00	16115.7	31.44	16987.1	33.14	18022.0	35.17	19272.1	37.60
104	15022.2	29.03	15673.5	30.29	16430.2	31.75	17318.6	33.47	18374.5	35.51	19648.1	37.97
105	15312.5	29.31	15976.3	30.58	16747.6	32.05	17653.2	33.79	18729.6	35.85	20027.8	38.33
106	15605.6	29.58	16282.1	30.87	17068.2	32.36	17991.1	34.11	19088.0	36.19	20411.0	38.69
107	15901.4	29.86	16590.7	31.16	17391.7	32.66	18332.1	34.43	19449.9	36.52	20798.0	39.06
108	16200.0	30.14	16902.3	31.45	17718.3	32.96	18676.4	34.75	19815.1	36.86	21188.5	39.42
109	16501.4	30.42	17216.7	31.74	18048.0	33.27	19023.9	35.07	20183.8	37.20	21582.7	39.78
110	16805.6	30.69	17534.1	32.03	18380.6	33.57	19374.5	35.39	20555.8	37.54	21980.6	40.15
111	17112.5	30.97	17854.3	32.31	18716.4	33.88	19728.4	35.71	20931.2	37.88	22382.0	40.51
112	17422.2	31.25	18177.5	32.60	19055.1	34.18	20085.5	36.03	21310.1	38.22	22787.1	40.87
113	17734.7	31.53	18503.5	32.89	19396.9	34.48	20445.7	36.35	21692.3	38.56	23195.9	41.24
114	18050.0	31.81	18832.5	33.18	19741.7	34.79	20809.2	36.67	22078.0	38.90	23608.2	41.60
115	18368.1	32.08	19164.3	33.47	20089.6	35.09	21175.9	36.99	22467.0	39.24	24024.2	41.96
116	18688.9	32.36	19499.1	33.76	20440.5	35.39	21545.7	37.31	22859.4	39.58	24443.8	42.33
117	19012.5	32.64	19836.7	34.05	20794.4	35.70	21918.8	37.63	23255.2	39.92	24867.1	42.69
118	19338.9	32.92	20177.3	34.34	21151.4	36.00	22295.1	37.95	23654.5	40.26	25294.0	43.05
119	19668.1	33.19	20520.7	34.63	21511.4	36.31	22674.6	38.27	24057.1	40.60	25724.5	43.42
120	20000.0	33.47	20867.0	34.92	21874.5	36.61	23057.3	38.59	24463.1	40.94	26158.7	43.78
SUMS.	30°		31°		32°		33°		34°		35°	

TABLE X. Sub-Sections. Side Slope 1 to 1.

SUMS.	0°	1°		2°		3°		4°		5°	
1	Nothing.	.0	.00	.0	.01	.0	.01	.0	.01	.0	.01
2	....	.0	.00	.1	.01	.1	.01	.1	.02	.2	.02
3	....	.1	.01	.2	.01	.2	.02	.3	.02	.4	.03
4	....	.1	.01	.3	.02	.4	.02	.6	.03	.7	.04
5	....	.2	.01	.4	.02	.6	.03	.9	.04	1.1	.05
6	....	.3	.01	.6	.02	.9	.03	1.3	.05	1.6	.06
7	....	.4	.01	.8	.03	1.3	.04	1.7	.05	2.2	.07
8	....	.5	.01	1.1	.03	1.6	.04	2.2	.06	2.8	.08
9	....	.7	.02	1.4	.03	2.1	.05	2.8	.07	3.6	.08
10	....	.8	.02	1.7	.04	2.6	.05	3.5	.07	4.4	.09
11	....	1.0	.02	2.0	.04	3.1	.06	4.2	.08	5.4	.10
12	....	1.2	.02	2.4	.04	3.7	.06	5.0	.09	6.4	.11
13	....	1.4	.02	2.8	.05	4.3	.07	5.9	.09	7.5	.12
14	....	1.6	.02	3.3	.05	5.0	.07	6.8	.10	8.7	.13
15	....	1.8	.03	3.8	.05	5.8	.08	7.8	.11	10.0	.14
16	....	2.1	.03	4.3	.06	6.6	.08	8.9	.11	11.4	.15
17	....	2.4	.03	4.8	.06	7.4	.09	10.1	.12	12.8	.16
18	....	2.7	.03	5.4	.06	8.3	.09	11.3	.13	14.4	.16
19	....	3.0	.03	6.0	.07	9.2	.10	12.6	.14	16.0	.17
20	....	3.3	.03	6.7	.07	10.2	.10	13.9	.14	17.8	.18
21	....	3.6	.04	7.4	.07	11.3	.11	15.4	.15	19.6	.19
22	....	4.0	.04	8.1	.08	12.4	.12	16.8	.16	21.5	.20
23	....	4.3	.04	8.9	.08	13.5	.12	18.4	.16	23.5	.21
24	....	4.7	.04	9.6	.08	14.7	.13	20.1	.17	25.6	.22
25	....	5.1	.04	10.5	.09	16.0	.13	21.8	.18	27.7	.23
26	....	5.6	.04	11.3	.09	17.3	.14	23.5	.18	30.0	.24
27	....	6.0	.05	12.2	.09	18.7	.14	25.4	.19	32.4	.24
28	....	6.4	.05	13.1	.10	20.1	.15	27.3	.20	34.8	.25
29	....	6.9	.05	14.1	.10	21.5	.15	29.3	.21	37.3	.26
30	....	7.4	.05	15.1	.10	23.0	.16	31.3	.21	40.0	.27
31	....	7.9	.05	16.1	.11	24.5	.16	33.5	.22	42.7	.28
32	....	8.4	.05	17.2	.11	26.2	.17	35.6	.23	45.5	.29
33	....	9.0	.06	18.2	.11	27.9	.17	37.9	.23	48.3	.30
34	....	9.5	.06	19.4	.12	29.6	.18	40.2	.24	51.3	.31
35	....	10.1	.06	20.5	.12	31.4	.18	42.6	.25	54.4	.32
36	....	10.7	.06	21.7	.12	33.2	.19	45.1	.25	57.5	.32
37	....	11.3	.06	22.9	.13	35.0	.19	47.7	.26	60.8	.33
38	....	11.9	.06	24.2	.13	37.0	.20	50.3	.27	64.1	.34
39	....	12.5	.06	25.5	.13	38.9	.20	52.9	.27	67.5	.35
40	....	13.2	.07	26.8	.14	41.0	.21	55.7	.28	71.0	.36
41	....	13.8	.07	28.2	.14	43.0	.21	58.5	.29	74.6	.37
42	....	14.5	.07	29.5	.14	45.2	.22	61.4	.30	78.3	.38
43	....	15.2	.07	31.0	.15	47.3	.22	64.4	.30	82.1	.39
44	....	15.9	.07	32.4	.15	49.6	.23	67.4	.31	85.9	.40
45	....	16.6	.07	33.9	.15	51.8	.23	70.5	.32	89.9	.40
46	....	17.4	.08	35.4	.16	54.2	.24	73.7	.32	93.9	.41
47	....	18.2	.08	37.0	.16	56.6	.24	76.9	.33	98.1	.42
48	....	18.9	.08	38.6	.16	59.0	.25	80.2	.34	102.3	.43
49	....	19.7	.08	40.2	.17	61.5	.25	83.6	.34	106.6	.44
50	....	20.6	.08	41.9	.17	64.0	.26	87.0	.35	111.0	.45
51	....	21.4	.08	43.6	.17	66.6	.26	90.5	.36	115.5	.46
52	....	22.2	.09	45.3	.18	69.2	.27	94.1	.37	120.0	.47
53	....	23.1	.09	47.1	.18	71.9	.27	97.8	.37	124.7	.47
54	....	24.0	.09	48.8	.18	74.6	.28	101.5	.38	129.4	.48
55	....	24.9	.09	50.7	.19	77.4	.28	105.3	.39	134.3	.49
56	....	25.8	.09	52.5	.19	80.3	.29	109.2	.39	139.2	.50
57	....	26.7	.09	54.4	.19	83.2	.29	113.1	.40	144.2	.51
58	....	27.7	.10	56.3	.20	86.1	.30	117.1	.41	149.3	.52
59	....	28.6	.10	58.3	.20	89.1	.30	121.2	.41	154.5	.53
60	....	29.6	.10	60.3	.20	92.2	.31	125.3	.42	159.8	.54
SUMS.	0°	1°		2°		3°		4°		5°	

TABLE X. Sub-Sections. Side Slope 1 to 1.

SUMS.	6°		7°		8°		9°		10°		11°	
1	.1	.02	.1	.02	.1	.02	.1	.03	.1	.03	.1	.03
2	.2	.03	.3	.03	.3	.04	.3	.04	.4	.05	.4	.06
3	.5	.04	.6	.05	.7	.05	.8	.06	.9	.07	1.0	.08
4	.9	.05	1.0	.06	1.2	.07	1.4	.08	1.6	.09	1.8	.10
5	1.4	.06	1.6	.07	1.9	.08	2.2	.10	2.5	.11	2.8	.12
6	2.0	.07	2.3	.08	2.7	.10	3.1	.11	3.6	.13	4.0	.15
7	2.7	.08	3.2	.10	3.7	.11	4.3	.13	4.9	.15	5.5	.17
8	3.5	.09	4.1	.11	4.8	.13	5.6	.15	6.3	.17	7.1	.19
9	4.4	.10	5.2	.12	6.1	.14	7.1	.17	8.0	.19	9.0	.21
10	5.4	.11	6.5	.14	7.6	.16	8.7	.18	9.9	.21	11.2	.23
11	6.6	.13	7.8	.15	9.2	.17	10.5	.20	12.0	.23	13.5	.26
12	7.8	.14	9.3	.16	10.9	.19	12.5	.22	14.3	.25	16.1	.28
13	9.2	.15	11.0	.17	12.8	.20	14.7	.24	16.7	.27	18.9	.30
14	10.7	.16	12.7	.19	14.8	.22	17.1	.25	19.4	.29	21.9	.32
15	12.2	.17	14.6	.20	17.0	.23	19.6	.27	22.3	.31	25.1	.35
16	13.9	.18	16.6	.21	19.4	.25	22.3	.29	25.4	.33	28.6	.37
17	15.7	.19	18.7	.23	21.9	.26	25.2	.30	28.6	.35	32.3	.39
18	17.6	.20	21.0	.24	24.5	.28	28.2	.32	32.1	.37	36.2	.41
19	19.6	.21	23.4	.25	27.3	.30	31.5	.34	35.8	.39	40.3	.44
20	21.7	.22	25.9	.27	30.3	.31	34.9	.36	39.6	.41	44.7	.46
21	24.0	.23	28.6	.28	33.4	.33	38.4	.37	43.7	.43	49.3	.48
22	26.3	.24	31.4	.29	36.6	.34	42.2	.39	48.0	.45	54.1	.50
23	28.8	.26	34.3	.30	40.0	.36	46.1	.41	52.4	.47	59.1	.52
24	31.3	.27	37.3	.32	43.6	.37	50.2	.43	57.1	.49	64.3	.55
25	34.0	.28	40.5	.33	47.3	.39	54.5	.44	61.9	.51	69.8	.57
26	36.8	.29	43.8	.34	51.2	.40	58.9	.46	67.0	.53	75.5	.59
27	39.6	.30	47.2	.36	55.2	.42	63.5	.48	72.3	.55	81.4	.61
28	42.6	.31	50.8	.37	59.3	.43	68.3	.50	77.7	.56	87.6	.64
29	45.7	.32	54.5	.38	63.7	.45	73.3	.51	83.4	.58	93.9	.66
30	48.9	.33	58.3	.40	68.1	.46	78.4	.53	89.2	.60	100.5	.68
31	52.2	.34	62.3	.41	72.7	.48	83.7	.55	95.2	.62	107.3	.70
32	55.7	.35	66.4	.42	77.5	.49	89.2	.57	101.5	.64	114.4	.73
33	59.2	.36	70.6	.43	82.4	.51	94.9	.58	107.9	.66	121.6	.75
34	62.9	.38	74.9	.45	87.5	.52	100.7	.60	114.6	.68	129.1	.77
35	66.6	.39	79.4	.46	92.7	.54	106.7	.62	121.4	.70	136.8	.79
36	70.5	.40	84.0	.47	98.1	.55	112.9	.64	128.4	.72	144.8	.82
37	74.4	.41	88.7	.49	103.6	.57	119.3	.65	135.7	.74	152.9	.84
38	78.5	.42	93.6	.50	109.3	.58	125.8	.67	143.1	.76	161.3	.86
39	82.7	.43	98.6	.51	115.1	.60	132.5	.69	150.7	.78	169.9	.88
40	87.0	.44	103.7	.52	121.1	.61	139.4	.71	158.6	.80	178.7	.90
41	91.4	.45	108.9	.54	127.3	.63	146.5	.72	166.6	.82	187.8	.93
42	95.9	.46	114.3	.55	133.5	.64	153.7	.74	174.8	.84	197.0	.95
43	100.5	.47	119.8	.56	140.0	.66	161.1	.76	183.3	.86	206.5	.97
44	105.3	.48	125.5	.58	146.6	.67	168.7	.78	191.9	.88	216.3	.99
45	110.1	.49	131.2	.59	153.3	.69	176.4	.79	200.7	.90	226.2	1.02
46	115.0	.51	137.1	60	160.2	.70	184.4	.81	209.7	.92	236.4	1.04
47	120.1	.52	143.1	.62	167.2	.72	192.5	.83	218.9	.94	246.7	1.06
48	125.3	.53	149.3	.63	174.4	.73	200.7	.85	228.3	.96	257.4	1.08
49	130.5	.54	155.6	.64	181.8	.75	209.2	.86	238.0	.98	268.2	1.11
50	135.9	.55	162.0	.65	189.3	.76	217.8	.88	247.8	1.00	279.3	1.13
51	141.4	.56	168.5	.67	196.9	.78	226.6	.90	257.8	1.02	290.5	1.15
52	147.0	.57	175.2	.68	204.7	.79	235.6	.91	268.0	1.04	302.0	1.17
53	152.7	.58	182.0	.69	212.6	.81	244.7	.93	278.4	1.06	313.8	1.20
54	158.5	.59	189.0	.71	220.7	.83	254.1	.95	289.0	1.08	325.7	1.22
55	164.5	.60	196.0	.72	229.0	.84	263.6	.97	299.8	1.10	337.9	1.24
56	170.5	.61	203.2	.73	237.4	.86	273.2	.98	310.8	1.12	350.3	1.26
57	176.6	.63	210.5	.75	245.9	.87	283.1	1.00	322.0	1.14	362.9	1.28
58	182.9	.64	218.0	.76	254.7	.89	293.1	1.02	333.4	1.16	375.8	1.31
59	189.3	.65	225.6	.77	263.5	.90	303.3	1.04	345.0	1.18	388.8	1.33
60	195.7	.67	233.3	.78	272.5	.92	313.7	1.05	356.8	1.20	402.1	1.35
SUMS.	6°		7°		8°		9°		10°		11°	

TABLE X. Sub-Sections. Side Slope 1 to 1.

SUMS.	12°		13°		14°		15°		16°		17°	
1	.1	.04	.1	.04	.2	.05	.2	.05	.2	.06	.2	.06
2	.5	.06	.6	.07	.6	.08	.7	.08	.7	.09	.8	.10
3	1.1	.09	1.3	.10	1.4	.11	1.5	.12	1.7	.13	1.8	.14
4	2.0	.11	2.2	.13	2.5	.14	2.7	.15	3.0	.17	3.3	.18
5	3.1	.14	3.5	.15	3.8	.17	4.2	.19	4.7	.20	5.1	.22
6	4.5	.16	5.0	.18	5.5	.20	6.1	.22	6.7	.24	7.3	.27
7	6.1	.19	6.8	.21	7.5	.23	8.3	.25	9.1	.28	10.0	.31
8	8.0	.21	8.9	.24	9.8	.26	10.8	.29	11.9	.32	13.0	.35
9	10.1	.24	11.3	.26	12.5	.29	13.7	.32	15.1	.35	16.5	.39
10	12.5	.26	13.9	.29	15.4	.32	16.9	.36	18.6	.39	20.4	.43
11	15.1	.29	16.8	.32	18.6	.35	20.5	.39	22.5	.43	24.7	.47
12	18.0	.31	20.0	.35	22.1	.38	24.4	.42	26.8	.47	29.4	.51
13	21.1	.34	23.5	.38	26.0	.42	28.6	.46	31.5	.50	34.5	.55
14	24.5	.36	27.2	.40	30.1	.45	33.2	.49	36.5	.54	40.0	.59
15	28.1	.39	31.3	.43	34.6	.48	38.1	.53	41.9	.58	45.9	.63
16	32.0	.41	35.6	.46	39.4	.51	43.4	.56	47.6	.61	52.2	.67
17	36.1	.44	40.2	.49	44.4	.54	49.0	.59	53.8	.65	58.9	.71
18	40.5	.46	45.0	.51	49.8	.57	54.9	.63	60.3	.69	66.1	.75
19	45.1	.49	50.2	.54	55.5	.60	61.2	.66	67.2	.73	73.6	.80
20	50.0	.51	55 6	.57	61.5	.63	67.8	.69	74.4	.76	81.5	.84
21	55.1	.54	61.3	.60	67.8	.66	74.7	.73	82.1	.80	89.9	.88
22	60.5	.56	67.3	.63	74.4	.69	82.0	.76	90.1	.84	98.7	.92
23	66.1	.59	73.5	.65	81.3	.72	89.6	.80	98.5	.87	107.8	.96
24	72.0	.61	80.0	.68	88.6	.75	97.6	.83	107.2	.91	117.4	1.00
25	78.1	.64	86.9	.71	96.1	.78	105.9	.86	116.3	.95	127.4	1.04
26	84.5	.66	93.9	.74	103.9	.81	114.6	.90	125.8	.99	137.8	1.08
27	91.1	.69	101.3	.76	112.1	.85	123.5	.93	135.7	1.02	148.6	1.12
28	98.0	.71	108.9	.79	120.6	.88	132.9	.97	145.9	1.06	159.8	1.16
29	105.1	.74	116.9	.82	129.3	.91	142.5	1.00	156.5	1.10	171.5	1.20
30	112.5	.76	125.1	.85	138.4	.94	152.5	1.03	167.5	1.14	183.5	1.24
31	120.1	.79	133.5	.88	147.8	.97	162.9	1.07	178.9	1.17	195.9	1.28
32	128.0	.81	142.3	.90	157.5	1.00	173.5	1.10	190.6	1.21	208.8	1.33
33	136.1	.84	151.3	.93	167.5	1.03	184.5	1.14	202.7	1.25	222.0	1.37
34	144.5	.86	160.6	.96	177.8	1.06	195.9	1.17	215.2	1.28	235.7	1.41
35	153.1	.89	170.2	.99	188.4	1.09	207.6	1.20	228.0	1.32	249.7	1.45
36	162.0	.91	180.1	1.01	199.3	1.12	219.6	1.24	241.2	1.36	264.2	1.49
37	171.1	.94	190.2	1.04	210.5	1.15	232.0	1.27	254.8	1.40	279.1	1.53
38	180.5	.96	200.7	1.07	222.0	1.18	244.7	1.30	268.8	1.43	294.4	1.57
39	190.1	.99	211.4	1.10	233.9	1.21	257.7	1.34	283.1	1.47	310.1	1.61
40	200.0	1.01	222.3	1.13	246.0	1.25	271.1	1.37	297.8	1.51	326.2	1.65
41	210.1	1.04	233.6	1.15	258.5	1.28	284.9	1.41	312.9	1.54	342.7	1.69
42	220.4	1.06	245.1	1.18	271.3	1.31	298.9	1.44	328.3	1.58	359.6	1.73
43	231.1	1.09	256.9	1.21	284.3	1.34	313.3	1.47	344.1	1.62	377.0	1.77
44	241.9	1.11	269.0	1.24	297.7	1.37	328.1	1.51	360.3	1.66	394.7	1.81
45	253.1	1.14	281.4	1.26	311.4	1.40	343.2	1.54	376.9	1.69	412.8	1.86
46	264.4	1.16	294.0	1.29	325.4	1.43	358.6	1.58	393.8	1.73	431.4	1.90
47	276.1	1.19	307.0	1.32	339.7	1.46	374.3	1.61	411.1	1.77	450.3	1.94
48	287.9	1.21	320.2	1.35	354.3	1.49	390.4	1.64	428.8	1.81	469.7	1.98
49	300.1	1.24	333.6	1.38	369.2	1.52	406.9	1.68	446.9	1.84	489.5	2.02
50	312.4	1.26	347.4	1.40	384.4	1.55	423.7	1.71	465.3	1.88	509.7	2.06
51	325.0	1.29	361.4	1.43	400.0	1.58	440.8	1.75	484.1	1.92	530.3	2.10
52	337.9	1.31	375.7	1.46	415.8	1.61	458.2	1.78	503.3	1.95	551.3	2.14
53	351.0	1.34	390.3	1.49	431.9	1.65	476.0	1.81	522.8	1.99	572.7	2.18
54	364.4	1.36	405.2	1.51	448.4	1.68	494.1	1.85	542.7	2.03	594.5	2.22
55	378.0	1.39	420.4	1.54	465.2	1.71	512.6	1.88	563.0	2.07	616.7	2.26
56	391.9	1.41	435.8	1.57	482.2	1.74	531.4	1.91	583.7	2.10	639.3	2.30
57	406.0	1.44	451.5	1.60	499.6	1.77	550.6	1.95	604.7	2.14	662.4	2.34
58	420.4	1.46	467.5	1.63	517.3	1.80	570.1	1.98	626.1	2.18	685.8	2.39
59	435.0	1.49	483.7	1.65	535.3	1.83	589.9	2.02	647.9	2.21	709.7	2.43
60	449.9	1.51	500.3	1.68	553.6	1.86	610.1	2.05	670.0	2.25	733.9	2.47
SUMS.	12°		13°		14°		15°		16°		17°	

SUMS.	18°		19°		20°		21°		22°		23°	
1	.2	.07	.2	.07	.3	.08	.3	.09	.3	.09	.3	.10
2	.9	.11	1.0	.12	1.1	.13	1.2	.14	1.3	.16	1.4	.17
3	2.0	.16	2.2	.17	2.4	.19	2.6	.20	2.8	.22	3.1	.24
4	3.6	.20	3.9	.22	4.2	.24	4.6	.26	5.0	.28	5.5	.31
5	5.6	.25	6.1	.27	6.6	.29	7.2	.32	7.8	.35	8.5	.38
6	8.0	.29	8.8	.32	9.5	.34	10.4	.37	11.3	.41	12.3	.44
7	10.9	.33	11.9	.36	13.0	.40	14.1	.43	15.4	.47	16.7	.51
8	14.3	.38	15.6	.41	17.0	.45	18.5	.49	20.1	.53	21.9	.58
9	18.0	.42	19.7	.46	21.5	.50	23.4	.55	25.4	.60	27.7	.65
10	22.3	.47	24.3	.51	26.5	.56	28.8	.61	31.4	.66	34.1	.72
11	27.0	.51	29.4	.56	32.1	.61	34.9	.66	38.0	.72	41.3	.79
12	32.1	.56	35.0	.61	38.1	.66	41.5	.72	45.2	.78	49.2	.85
13	37.7	.60	41.1	.66	44.8	.72	48.7	.78	53.0	.85	57.7	.92
14	43.7	.65	47.7	.71	51.9	.77	56.5	.84	61.5	.91	66.9	.99
15	50.1	.69	54.7	.75	59.6	.82	64.9	.89	70.6	.97	76.8	1.06
16	57.0	.74	62.2	.80	67.8	.87	73.8	.95	80.3	1.04	87.4	1.13
17	64.4	.78	70.3	.85	76.6	.93	83.4	1.01	90.7	1.10	98.7	1.20
18	72.2	.82	78.8	.90	85.8	.98	93.5	1.07	101.7	1.16	110.6	1.26
19	80.4	.87	87.8	.95	95.6	1.03	104.1	1.12	113.3	1.22	123.3	1.33
20	89.1	.91	97.3	1.00	106.0	1.09	115.4	1.18	125.5	1.29	136.6	1.40
21	98.3	.96	107.2	1.05	116.8	1.14	127.2	1.24	138.4	1.35	150.6	1.47
22	107.8	1.00	117.7	1.09	128.2	1.19	139.6	1.30	151.9	1.41	165.3	1.54
23	117.9	1.05	128.6	1.14	140.1	1.25	152.6	1.36	166.0	1.48	180.6	1.60
24	128.4	1.09	140.0	1.19	152.6	1.30	166.1	1.41	180.8	1.54	196.7	1.67
25	139.3	1.14	152.0	1.24	165.6	1.35	180.3	1.47	196.2	1.60	213.4	1.74
26	150.6	1.18	164.4	1.29	179.1	1.40	195.0	1.53	212.2	1.66	230.8	1.81
27	162.4	1.23	177.2	1.34	193.1	1.46	210.3	1.59	228.8	1.73	248.9	1.88
28	174.7	1.27	190.6	1.39	207.7	1.51	226.1	1.64	246.1	1.79	267.7	1.95
29	187.4	1.31	204.5	1.43	222.8	1.56	242.6	1.70	263.9	1.85	287.2	2.01
30	200.5	1.36	218.8	1.48	238.4	1.62	259.6	1.76	282.5	1.91	307.3	2.08
31	214.1	1.40	233.6	1.53	254.6	1.67	277.2	1.82	301.6	1.98	328.1	2.15
32	228.2	1.45	249.0	1.58	271.3	1.72	295.4	1.87	321.4	2.04	349.7	2.22
33	242.7	1.49	264.8	1.63	288.5	1.78	314.1	1.93	341.8	2.10	371.8	2.29
34	257.6	1.54	281.1	1.68	306.3	1.83	333.4	1.99	362.8	2.17	394.7	2.36
35	273.0	1.58	297.8	1.73	324.5	1.88	353.3	2.05	384.5	2.23	418.3	2.42
36	288.8	1.63	315.1	1.77	343.3	1.93	373.8	2.11	406.7	2.29	442.5	2.49
37	305.1	1.67	332.8	1.82	362.7	1.99	394.9	2.16	429.7	2.35	467.5	2.56
38	321.8	1.72	351.1	1.87	382.6	2.04	416.5	2.22	453.2	2.42	493.1	2.63
39	338.9	1.76	369.8	1.92	403.0	2.09	438.7	2.28	477.4	2.48	519.4	2.70
40	356.5	1.80	389.0	1.97	423.9	2.15	461.5	2.34	502.2	2.54	546.3	2.77
41	374.6	1.85	408.7	2.02	445.3	2.20	484.9	2.39	527.6	2.60	574.0	2.83
42	393.1	1.89	428.9	2.07	467.3	2.25	508.8	2.45	553.6	2.67	602.3	2.90
43	412.0	1.94	449.5	2.12	489.9	2.30	533.3	2.51	580.3	2.73	631.4	2.97
44	431.4	1.98	470.7	2.16	512.9	2.36	558.4	2.57	607.6	2.79	661.1	3.04
45	451.2	2.03	492.3	2.21	536.5	2.41	584.1	2.62	635.5	2.86	691.5	3.11
46	471.5	2.07	514.5	2.26	560.6	2.46	610.3	2.68	664.1	2.92	722.5	3.18
47	492.2	2.12	537.1	2.31	585.2	2.52	637.1	2.74	693.3	2.98	754.3	3.24
48	513.4	2.16	560.2	2.36	610.4	2.57	664.5	2.80	723.1	3.04	786.7	3.31
49	535.0	2.21	583.8	2.41	636.1	2.62	692.5	2.86	753.6	3.11	819.8	3.38
50	557.1	2.25	607.8	2.46	662.3	2.68	721.1	2.91	784.6	3.17	853.7	3.45
51	579.6	2.30	632.4	2.50	689.1	2.73	750.2	2.97	816.3	3.23	888.1	3.52
52	602.5	2.34	657.4	2.55	716.4	2.78	779.9	3.03	848.7	3.30	923.3	3.59
53	625.9	2.38	683.0	2.60	744.2	2.83	810.2	3.09	881.6	3.36	959.2	3.65
54	649.8	2.43	709.0	2.65	772.5	2.89	841.1	3.14	915.2	3.42	995.7	3.72
55	674.1	2.47	735.5	2.70	801.4	2.94	872.5	3.20	949.4	3.48	1032.9	3.79
56	698.8	2.52	762.5	2.75	830.8	2.99	904.5	3.26	984.2	3.55	1070.8	3.86
57	724.0	2.56	789.9	2.80	860.8	3.05	937.1	3.32	1019.7	3.61	1109.4	3.93
58	749.6	2.61	817.9	2.84	891.2	3.10	970.3	3.37	1055.8	3.67	1148.7	4.00
59	775.7	2.65	846.3	2.89	922.2	3.15	1004.0	3.43	1092.5	3.73	1188.6	4.06
60	802.2	2.70	875.3	2.94	953.7	3.21	1038.3	3.49	1129.9	3.80	1229.3	4.13
SUMS.	18°		19°		20°		21°		22°		23°	

SUMS.	24°		25°		26°		27°		28°		29°	
1	.4	.11	.4	.12	.4	.13	.5	.14	.5	.16	.6	.17
2	1.5	.19	1.6	.20	1.8	.22	1.9	.24	2.1	.26	2.3	.29
3	3.3	.26	3.6	.28	4.0	.31	4.3	.34	4.7	.37	5.2	.40
4	5.9	.33	6.5	.36	7.1	.40	7.7	.43	8.4	.47	9.2	.52
5	9.3	.41	10.1	.44	11.0	.48	12.0	.53	13.1	.58	14.4	.63
6	13.4	.48	14.6	.53	15.9	.57	17.3	.63	18.9	.68	20.7	.75
7	18.2	.56	19.8	.61	21.6	.66	23.6	.72	25.8	.79	28.2	.86
8	23.8	.63	25.9	.69	28.2	.75	30.8	.82	33.6	.89	36.9	.98
9	30.1	.71	32.8	.77	35.7	.84	39.0	.91	42.6	1.00	46.6	1.09
10	37.2	.78	40.5	.85	44.1	.93	48.1	1.01	52.6	1.10	57.6	1.21
11	45.0	.85	48.9	.93	53.3	1.01	58.2	1.11	63.6	1.21	69.7	1.32
12	53.5	.93	58.2	1.01	63.5	1.10	69.3	1.20	75.7	1.31	82.9	1.44
13	62.8	1.00	68.4	1.09	74.5	1.19	81.3	1.30	88.8	1.42	97.3	1.55
14	72.8	1.08	79.3	1.17	86.4	1.28	94.3	1.39	103.0	1.52	112.9	1.67
15	83.6	1.15	91.0	1.25	99.2	1.37	108.2	1.49	118.3	1.63	129.6	1.78
16	95.1	1.23	103.6	1.33	112.8	1.45	123.1	1.59	134.6	1.73	147.4	1.90
17	107.4	1.30	116.9	1.42	127.4	1.54	139.0	1.68	151.9	1.84	166.4	2.02
18	120.4	1.37	131.1	1.50	142.8	1.63	155.8	1.78	170.3	1.94	186.6	2.13
19	134.1	1.45	146.0	1.58	159.1	1.72	173.6	1.88	189.8	2.05	207.9	2.25
20	148.6	1.52	161.8	1.66	176.3	1.81	192.4	1.97	210.3	2.16	230.3	2.36
21	163.9	1.60	178.4	1.74	194.4	1.90	212.1	2.07	231.8	2.26	253.9	2.48
22	179.8	1.67	195.8	1.82	213.3	1.98	232.8	2.16	254.4	2.37	278.7	2.59
23	196.5	1.75	214.0	1.90	233.2	2.07	254.4	2.26	278.1	2.47	304.6	2.71
24	214.0	1.82	233.0	1.98	253.9	2.16	277.0	2.36	302.8	2.58	331.7	2.82
25	232.2	1.89	252.8	2.06	275.5	2.25	300.6	2.45	328.5	2.68	359.9	2.94
26	251.2	1.97	273.4	2.14	298.0	2.34	325.1	2.55	355.3	2.79	389.2	3.05
27	270.9	2.04	294.9	2.22	321.3	2.42	350.6	2.65	383.2	2.89	419.8	3.17
28	291.3	2.12	317.1	2.31	345.6	2.51	377.1	2.74	412.1	3.00	451.4	3.28
29	312.5	2.19	340.2	2.39	370.7	2.60	404.5	2.84	442.1	3.10	484.2	3.40
30	334.4	2.27	364.1	2.47	396.7	2.69	432.9	2.93	473.1	3.21	518.2	3.51
31	357.1	2.34	388.7	2.55	423.6	2.78	462.2	3.03	505.2	3.31	553.3	3.63
32	380.5	2.42	414.2	2.63	451.4	2.87	492.5	3.13	538.3	3.42	589.6	3.74
33	404.6	2.49	440.5	2.71	480.0	2.95	523.8	3.22	572.4	3.52	627.0	3.86
34	429.5	2.56	467.6	2.79	509.6	3.04	556.0	3.32	607.7	3.63	665.6	3.97
35	455.1	2.64	495.5	2.87	540.0	3.13	589.2	3.41	643.9	3.73	705.3	4.09
36	481.5	2.71	524.2	2.95	571.3	3.22	623.3	3.51	681.3	3.84	746.2	4.20
37	508.7	2.79	553.8	3.03	603.4	3.31	658.4	3.61	719.6	3.94	788.3	4.32
38	536.5	2.86	584.1	3.11	636.5	3.39	694.5	3.70	759.1	4.05	831.4	4.43
39	565.1	2.94	615.3	3.20	670.4	3.48	731.5	3.80	799.5	4.15	875.8	4.55
40	594.5	3.01	647.2	3.28	705.3	3.57	769.5	3.90	841.1	4.26	921.3	4.66
41	624.6	3.08	680.0	3.36	741.0	3.66	808.5	3.99	883.6	4.36	967.9	4.78
42	655.4	3.16	713.6	3.44	777.6	3.75	848.4	4.09	927.3	4.47	1015.7	4.89
43	687.0	3.23	747.9	3.52	815.0	3.83	889.3	4.18	971.9	4.57	1064.6	5.01
44	719.3	3.31	783.1	3.60	853.4	3.92	931.1	4.28	1017.7	4.68	1114.7	5.12
45	752.4	3.38	819.1	3.68	892.6	4.01	973.9	4.38	1064.5	4.78	1166.0	5.24
46	786.2	3.46	855.9	3.76	932.7	4.10	1017.7	4.47	1112.3	4.89	1218.4	5.35
47	820.8	3.53	893.6	3.84	973.7	4.19	1062.4	4.57	1161.2	4.99	1271.9	5.47
48	856.1	3.60	932.0	3.92	1015.6	4.28	1108.1	4.67	1211.1	5.10	1326.6	5.59
49	892.1	3.68	971.2	4.00	1058.3	4.36	1154.8	4.76	1262.1	5.20	1382.5	5.70
50	928.9	3.75	1011.3	4.09	1102.0	4.45	1202.4	4.86	1314.2	5.31	1439.5	5.82
51	966.4	3.83	1052.1	4.17	1146.5	4.54	1251.0	4.95	1367.2	5.41	1497.6	5.93
52	1004.7	3.90	1093.8	4.25	1191.9	4.63	1300.5	5.05	1421.4	5.52	1556.9	6.05
53	1043.7	3.98	1136.3	4.33	1238.2	4.72	1351.0	5.15	1476.6	5.62	1617.4	6.16
54	1083.4	4.05	1179.6	4.41	1285.3	4.80	1402.5	5.24	1532.8	5.73	1679.0	6.28
55	1123.9	4.12	1223.6	4.49	1333.4	4.89	1454.9	5.34	1590.1	5.83	1741.8	6.39
56	1165.2	4.20	1268.5	4.57	1382.3	4.98	1508.3	5.43	1648.5	5.94	1805.7	6.51
57	1207.2	4.27	1314.3	4.65	1432.1	5.07	1562.6	5.53	1707.9	6.05	1870.7	6.62
58	1249.9	4.35	1360.8	4.73	1482.8	5.16	1617.9	5.63	1768.3	6.15	1937.0	6.74
59	1293.4	4.42	1408.1	4.81	1534.4	5.25	1674.2	5.72	1829.8	6.26	2004.3	6.85
60	1337.6	4.50	1456.2	4.89	1586.8	5.33	1731.4	5.82	1892.4	6.36	2072.3	6.97
SUMS.	24°		25°		26°		27°		28°		29°	

TABLE X. Sub-Sections. Side Slope 1 to 1.

SUMS.	30°		31°		32°		33°		34°		35°	
1	.6	.19	.7	.21	.8	.23	.9	.26	1.0	.29	1.1	.32
2	2.5	.32	2.8	.35	3.1	.39	3.4	.43	3.8	.48	4.3	.54
3	5.7	.44	6.3	.49	6.9	.54	7.7	.60	8.6	.67	9.7	.76
4	10.1	.57	11.2	.63	12.3	.69	13.7	.77	15.4	.86	17.3	.97
5	15.8	.70	17.4	.77	19.3	.85	21.4	.94	24.0	1.06	27.0	1.19
6	22.8	.82	25.1	.91	27.8	1.00	30.9	1.11	34.5	1.25	38.9	1.41
7	31.0	.95	34.2	1.05	37.8	1.16	42.0	1.29	47.0	1.44	53.0	1.62
8	40.5	1.08	44.6	1.18	49.4	1.31	54.9	1.46	61.4	1.63	69.2	1.84
9	51.2	1.20	56.5	1.32	62.5	1.47	69.5	1.63	77.7	1.82	87.6	2.05
10	63.2	1.33	69.7	1.46	77.1	1.62	85.8	1.80	95.9	2.01	108.1	2.27
11	76.5	1.45	84.3	1.60	93.3	1.77	103.8	1.97	116.1	2.21	130.8	2.49
12	91.1	1.58	100.4	1.74	111.0	1.93	123.5	2.14	138.2	2.40	155.7	2.70
13	106.9	1.71	117.8	1.88	130.3	2.08	144.9	2.32	162.1	2.59	182.7	2.92
14	124.0	1.83	136.6	2.02	151.2	2.24	168.1	2.49	188.0	2.78	211.9	3.14
15	142.3	1.96	156.8	2.16	173.5	2.39	193.0	2.66	215.9	2.97	243.3	3.35
16	161.9	2.09	178.4	2.30	197.4	2.54	219.5	2.83	245.6	3.17	276.8	3.57
17	182.8	2.21	201.4	2.44	222.9	2.70	247.8	3.00	277.3	3.36	312.5	3.78
18	204.9	2.34	225.8	2.58	249.9	2.85	277.8	3.17	310.8	3.55	350.3	4.00
19	228.3	2.47	251.6	2.72	278.4	3.01	309.6	3.34	346.3	3.74	390.4	4.22
20	253.0	2.59	278.8	2.86	308.5	3.16	343.0	3.52	383.8	3.93	432.5	4.43
21	278.9	2.72	307.4	3.00	340.1	3.32	378.2	3.69	423.1	4.13	476.9	4.65
22	306.1	2.85	337.3	3.14	373.3	3.47	415.1	3.86	464.3	4.32	523.4	4.87
23	334.6	2.97	368.7	3.28	408.0	3.62	453.6	4.03	507.5	4.51	572.0	5.08
24	364.3	3.10	401.4	3.42	444.2	3.78	494.0	4.20	552.6	4.70	622.8	5.30
25	395.3	3.23	435.6	3.55	482.0	3.93	536.0	4.37	599.6	4.89	675.8	5.51
26	427.5	3.35	471.1	3.69	521.3	4.09	579.7	4.55	648.5	5.08	731.0	5.73
27	461.0	3.48	508.1	3.83	562.2	4.24	625.2	4.72	699.4	5.28	788.3	5.95
28	495.8	3.60	546.4	3.97	604.6	4.40	672.3	4.89	752.2	5.47	847.8	6.16
29	531.9	3.73	586.1	4.11	648.6	4.55	721.2	5.06	806.8	5.66	909.4	6.38
30	569.2	3.86	627.2	4.25	694.1	4.70	771.8	5.23	863.5	5.85	973.2	6.60
31	607.8	3.98	669.8	4.39	741.1	4.86	824.1	5.40	922.0	6.04	1039.1	6.81
32	647.6	4.11	713.7	4.53	789.7	5.01	878.1	5.57	982.4	6.24	1107.3	7.03
33	688.7	4.24	759.0	4.67	839.8	5.17	933.9	5.75	1044.8	6.43	1177.6	7.24
34	731.1	4.36	805.7	4.81	891.5	5.32	991.3	5.92	1109.1	6.62	1250.0	7.46
35	774.7	4.49	853.8	4.95	944.7	5.48	1050.5	6.09	1175.3	6.81	1324.6	7.68
36	819.6	4.62	903.2	5.09	999.4	5.63	1111.4	6.26	1243.4	7.00	1401.4	7.89
37	865.8	4.74	954.1	5.23	1055.7	5.78	1174.0	6.43	1313.4	7.20	1480.3	8.11
38	913.2	4.87	1006.4	5.37	1113.6	5.94	1238.3	6.60	1385.4	7.39	1561.4	8.33
39	961.9	5.00	1060.0	5.51	1173.0	6.09	1304.3	6.77	1459.2	7.58	1644.7	8.54
40	1011.9	5.12	1115.1	5.65	1233.9	6.25	1372.1	6.95	1535.0	7.77	1730.1	8.76
41	1063.1	5.25	1171.6	5.78	1296.4	6.40	1441.6	7.12	1612.7	7.96	1817.7	8.97
42	1115.6	5.38	1229.4	5.92	1360.4	6.56	1512.7	7.29	1692.4	8.15	1907.4	9.19
43	1169.3	5.50	1288.6	6.06	1425.9	6.71	1585.6	7.46	1773.9	8.35	1999.4	9.41
44	1224.4	5.63	1349.3	6.20	1493.0	6.86	1660.2	7.63	1857.4	8.54	2093.4	9.62
45	1280.7	5.76	1411.3	6.34	1561.6	7.02	1736.6	7.80	1942.8	8.73	2189.7	9.84
46	1338.2	5.88	1474.7	6.48	1631.8	7.17	1814.6	7.98	2030.1	8.92	2288.1	10.06
47	1397.0	6.01	1539.5	6.62	1703.5	7.33	1894.4	8.15	2119.3	9.11	2388.6	10.27
48	1457.1	6.13	1605.7	6.76	1776.8	7.48	1975.8	8.32	2210.4	9.31	2491.4	10.49
49	1518.4	6.26	1673.4	6.90	1851.6	7.63	2059.0	8.49	2303.5	9.50	2596.2	10.71
50	1581.1	6.39	1742.4	7.04	1928.0	7.79	2143.9	8.66	2398.5	9.69	2703.3	10.92
51	1644.9	6.51	1812.7	7.18	2005.8	7.94	2230.5	8.83	2495.4	9.88	2812.5	11.14
52	1710.1	6.64	1884.5	7.32	2085.3	8.10	2318.8	9.00	2594.2	10.07	2923.9	11.35
53	1776.5	6.77	1957.7	7.46	2166.2	8.25	2408.9	9.18	2694.9	10.27	3037.4	11.57
54	1844.1	6.89	2032.3	7.60	2248.8	8.41	2500.6	9.35	2797.6	10.46	3153.1	11.79
55	1913.1	7.02	2108.2	7.74	2332.8	8.56	2594.1	9.52	2902.2	10.65	3271.0	12.00
56	1983.3	7.15	2185.6	7.88	2418.4	8.71	2689.3	9.69	3008.6	10.84	3391.0	12.22
57	2054.7	7.27	2264.4	8.01	2505.6	8.87	2786.2	9.86	3117.1	11.03	3513.2	12.44
58	2127.5	7.40	2344.5	8.15	2594.2	9.02	2884.8	10.03	3227.4	11.22	3637.6	12.65
59	2201.5	7.53	2426.0	8.29	2684.5	9.18	2985.2	10.20	3339.6	11.42	3764.1	12.87
60	2276.7	7.65	2509.0	8.43	2776.2	9.33	3087.2	10.38	3453.8	11.61	3892.8	13.08
SUMS.	30°		31°		32°		33°		34°		35°	

TABLE XI. **Whole Sections.** **Side Slope ¼ to 1.**

SUMS.	0°		1°		2°		3°		4°		5°	
1	0.2	0.07	0.2	0.07	0.2	0.07	0.2	0.07	0.2	0.07	0.2	0.07
2	0.9	0.12	0.9	0.12	0.9	0.12	0.9	0.12	0.9	0.12	0.9	0.12
3	2.1	0.16	2.1	0.16	2.1	0.16	2.1	0.16	2.1	0.16	2.1	0.16
4	3.7	0.21	3.7	0.21	3.7	0.21	3.7	0.21	3.7	0.21	3.7	0.21
5	5.8	0.25	5.8	0.25	5.8	0.25	5.8	0.25	5.8	0.25	5.8	0.25
6	8.3	0.30	8.3	0.30	8.3	0.30	8.3	0.30	8.3	0.30	8.3	0.30
7	11.3	0.35	11.3	0.35	11.3	0.35	11.3	0.35	11.3	0.35	11.3	0.35
8	14.8	0.39	14.8	0.39	14.8	0.39	14.8	0.39	14.8	0.39	14.8	0.39
9	18.7	0.44	18.8	0.44	18.8	0.44	18.8	0.44	18.8	0.44	18.8	0.44
10	23.1	0.49	23.1	0.49	23.1	0.49	23.2	0.49	23.2	0.49	23.2	0.49
11	28.0	0.53	28.0	0.53	28.0	0.53	28.0	0.53	28.0	0.53	28.0	0.53
12	33.3	0.58	33.3	0.58	33.3	0.58	33.3	0.58	33.3	0.58	33.3	0.58
13	39.1	0.62	39.1	0.63	39.1	0.63	39.1	0.63	39.1	0.63	39.1	0.63
14	45.4	0.67	45.4	0.67	45.4	0.67	45.4	0.67	45.4	0.67	45.4	0.67
15	52.1	0.72	52.1	0.72	52.1	0.72	52.1	0.72	52.1	0.72	52.1	0.72
16	59.3	0.76	59.3	0.76	59.3	0.76	59.3	0.76	59.3	0.76	59.3	0.76
17	66.9	0.81	66.9	0.81	66.9	0.81	66.9	0.81	66.9	0.81	66.9	0.81
18	75.0	0.86	75.0	0.86	75.0	0.86	75.0	0.86	75.0	0.86	75.0	0.86
19	83.6	0.90	83.6	0.90	83.6	0.90	83.6	0.90	83.6	0.90	83.6	0.90
20	92.6	0.95	92.6	0.95	92.6	0.95	92.6	0.95	92.6	0.95	92.6	0.95
21	102.1	1.00	102.1	1.00	102.1	1.00	102.1	1.00	102.1	1.00	102.1	1.00
22	112.0	1.04	112.0	1.04	112.0	1.04	112.1	1.04	112.1	1.04	112.1	1.04
23	122.5	1.09	122.5	1.09	122.5	1.09	122.5	1.09	122.5	1.09	122.5	1.09
24	133.3	1.13	133.3	1.13	133.3	1.13	133.4	1.13	133.4	1.13	133.4	1.13
25	144.7	1.18	144.7	1.18	144.7	1.18	144.7	1.18	144.7	1.18	144.7	1.18
26	156.5	1.23	156.5	1.23	156.5	1.23	156.5	1.23	156.5	1.23	156.6	1.23
27	168.7	1.27	168.8	1.27	168.8	1.27	168.8	1.27	168.8	1.27	168.8	1.27
28	181.5	1.32	181.5	1.32	181.5	1.32	181.5	1.32	181.5	1.32	181.6	1.32
29	194.7	1.37	194.7	1.37	194.7	1.37	194.7	1.37	194.7	1.37	194.8	1.37
30	208.3	1.41	208.3	1.41	208.3	1.41	208.4	1.41	208.4	1.41	208.4	1.41
31	222.5	1.46	222.5	1.46	222.5	1.46	222.5	1.46	222.5	1.46	222.6	1.46
32	237.0	1.50	237.0	1.50	237.1	1.50	237.1	1.50	237.1	1.51	237.2	1.51
33	252.1	1.55	252.1	1.55	252.1	1.55	252.1	1.55	252.2	1.55	252.2	1.55
34	267.6	1.60	267.6	1.60	267.6	1.60	267.6	1.60	267.7	1.60	267.7	1.60
35	283.6	1.64	283.6	1.64	283.6	1.64	283.6	1.64	283.7	1.64	283.7	1.64
36	300.0	1.69	300.0	1.69	300.0	1.69	300.1	1.69	300.1	1.69	300.1	1.69
37	316.9	1.74	316.9	1.74	316.9	1.74	317.0	1.74	317.0	1.74	317.0	1.74
38	334.3	1.78	334.3	1.78	334.3	1.78	334.3	1.78	334.4	1.78	334.4	1.78
39	352.1	1.83	352.1	1.83	352.1	1.83	352.1	1.83	352.2	1.83	352.3	1.83
40	370.4	1.87	370.4	1.88	370.4	1.88	370.4	1.88	370.5	1.88	370.5	1.88
41	389.1	1.92	389.1	1.92	389.2	1.92	389.2	1.92	389.2	1.92	389.3	1.92
42	408.3	1.97	408.3	1.97	408.4	1.97	408.4	1.97	408.5	1.97	408.5	1.97
43	428.0	2.01	428.0	2.01	428.0	2.01	428.1	2.01	428.1	2.01	428.2	2.01
44	448.1	2.06	448.2	2.06	448.2	2.06	448.2	2.06	448.3	2.06	448.4	2.06
45	468.7	2.11	468.8	2.11	468.8	2.11	468.8	2.11	468.9	2.11	469.0	2.11
46	489.8	2.15	489.8	2.15	489.9	2.15	489.9	2.15	490.0	2.15	490.0	2.15
47	511.3	2.20	511.4	2 20	511.4	2.20	511.4	2.20	511.5	2.20	511.6	2.20
48	533.3	2.25	533.3	2.25	533.4	2.25	533.4	2.25	533.5	2.25	533.6	2.25
49	555.8	2.29	555.8	2.29	555.8	2.29	555.9	2.29	556.0	2.29	556.1	2.29
50	578.7	2.34	578.7	2.34	578.7	2.34	578.8	2.34	578.9	2.34	579.0	2.34
51	602.1	2.38	602.1	2.38	602.1	2.38	602.2	2.38	602.3	2.38	602.4	2.39
52	625.9	2.43	625.9	2.43	626.0	2.43	626.0	2.43	626.1	2.43	626.2	2.43
53	650.2	2.48	650.2	2.48	650.3	2.48	650.3	2.48	650.4	2.48	650.5	2.48
54	675.0	2.52	675.0	2.52	675.1	2.52	675.1	2.52	675.2	2.52	675.3	2.52
55	700.2	2.57	700.2	2.57	700.3	2.57	700.4	2.57	700.4	2.57	700.6	2.57
56	725.9	2.62	725.9	2.62	726.0	2.62	726.1	2.62	726.1	2.62	726.3	2.62
57	752.1	2.66	752.1	2.66	752.1	2.66	752.2	2.66	752.3	2.66	752.4	2.66
58	778.7	2.71	778.7	2.71	778.8	2.71	778.8	2.71	778.9	2.71	779.1	2.71
59	805.8	2.75	805.8	2.75	805.8	2.75	805.9	2.76	806.0	2.76	806.2	2.76
60	833.3	2.80	833.3	2.80	833.4	2.80	833.5	2.80	833.6	2.80	833.7	2.80
SUMS.	0°		1°		2°		3°		4°		5°	

SUMS.	0°		1°		2°		3°		4°		5°	
61	861.3	2.85	861.4	2.85	861.4	2.85	861.5	2.85	861.6	2.85	861.8	2.85
62	889.8	2.89	889.8	2.89	889.9	2.89	890.0	2.89	890.1	2.89	890.2	2.89
63	918.7	2.94	918.8	2.94	918.8	2.94	918.9	2.94	919.0	2.94	919.2	2.94
64	948.1	2.99	948.2	2.99	948.2	2.99	948.3	2.99	948.4	2.99	948.6	2.99
65	978.0	3.03	978.0	3.03	978.1	3.03	978.2	3.03	978.3	3.03	978.5	3.03
66	1008.3	3.08	1008.4	3.08	1008.4	3.08	1008.5	3.08	1008.6	3.08	1008.8	3.08
67	1039.1	3.12	1039.1	3.13	1039.2	3.13	1039.3	3.13	1039.4	3.13	1039.6	3.13
68	1070.4	3.17	1070.4	3.17	1070.5	3.17	1070.6	3.17	1070.7	3.17	1070.9	3.17
69	1102.1	3.22	1102.1	3.22	1102.2	3.22	1102.3	3.22	1102.4	3.22	1102.6	3.22
70	1134.3	3.26	1134.3	3.26	1134.3	3.26	1134.5	3.26	1134.6	3.26	1134.8	3.27
71	1166.9	3.31	1166.9	3.31	1167.0	3.31	1167.1	3.31	1167.3	3.31	1167.5	3.31
72	1200.0	3.36	1200.0	3.36	1200.1	3.36	1200.2	3.36	1200.4	3.36	1200.6	3.36
73	1233.6	3.40	1233.6	3.40	1233.7	3.40	1233.8	3.40	1233.9	3.40	1234.2	3.40
74	1267.6	3.45	1267.6	3.45	1267.7	3.45	1267.8	3.45	1268.0	3.45	1268.2	3.45
75	1302.1	3.50	1302.1	3.50	1302.2	3.50	1302.3	3.50	1302.5	3.50	1302.7	3.50
76	1337.0	3.54	1337.1	3.54	1337.1	3.54	1337.3	3.54	1337.4	3.54	1337.7	3.54
77	1372.5	3.59	1372.5	3.59	1372.6	3.59	1372.7	3.59	1372.9	3.59	1373.1	3.59
78	1408.3	3.63	1408.4	3.63	1408.4	3.63	1408.6	3.63	1408.8	3.64	1409.0	3.64
79	1444.7	3.68	1444.7	3.68	1444.8	3.68	1444.9	3.68	1445.1	3.68	1445.4	3.68
80	1481.5	3.73	1481.5	3.73	1481.6	3.73	1481.7	3.73	1481.9	3.73	1482.2	3.73
81	1518.7	3.77	1518.8	3.77	1518.9	3.77	1519.0	3.77	1519.2	3.77	1519.5	3.77
82	1556.5	3.82	1556.5	3.82	1556.6	3.82	1556.7	3.82	1557.0	3.82	1557.2	3.82
83	1594.7	3.87	1594.7	3.87	1594.8	3.87	1595.0	3.87	1595.2	3.87	1595.4	3.87
84	1633.3	3.91	1633.4	3.91	1633.5	3.91	1633.6	3.91	1633.8	3.91	1634.1	3.91
85	1672.5	3.96	1672.5	3.96	1672.6	3.96	1672.7	3.96	1673.0	3.96	1673.3	3.96
86	1712.0	4.00	1712.1	4.00	1712.2	4.00	1712.3	4.01	1712.6	4.01	1712.9	4.01
87	1752.1	4.05	1752.1	4.05	1752.2	4.05	1752.4	4.05	1752.6	4.05	1752.9	4.05
88	1792.6	4.10	1792.6	4.10	1792.7	4.10	1792.9	4.10	1793.1	4.10	1793.5	4.10
89	1833.6	4.14	1833.6	4.14	1833.7	4.14	1833.9	4.14	1834.1	4.14	1834.4	4.15
90	1875.0	4.19	1875.0	4.19	1875.1	4.19	1875.3	4.19	1875.6	4.19	1875.9	4.19
91	1916.9	4.24	1916.9	4.24	1917.0	4.24	1917.2	4.24	1917.5	4.24	1917.8	4.24
92	1959.3	4.28	1959.3	4.28	1959.4	4.28	1959.6	4.28	1959.9	4.28	1960.2	4.28
93	2002.1	4.33	2002.1	4.33	2002.2	4.33	2002.4	4.33	2002.7	4.33	2003.0	4.33
94	2045.4	4.37	2045.4	4.38	2045.5	4.38	2045.7	4.38	2046.0	4.38	2046.3	4.38
95	2089.1	4.42	2089.2	4.42	2089.3	4.42	2089.5	4.42	2089.8	4.42	2090.1	4.42
96	2133.3	4.47	2133.4	4.47	2133.5	4.47	2133.7	4.47	2134.0	4.47	2134.4	4.47
97	2178.0	4.51	2178.1	4.51	2178.2	4.51	2178.4	4.51	2178.7	4.52	2179.1	4.52
98	2223.1	4.56	2223.2	4.56	2223.3	4.56	2223.5	4.56	2223.8	4.56	2224.2	4.56
99	2268.7	4.61	2268.8	4.61	2268.9	4.61	2269.1	4.61	2269.4	4.61	2269.8	4.61
100	2314.8	4.65	2314.9	4.65	2315.0	4.65	2315.2	4.65	2315.5	4.65	2315.9	4.66
101	2361.3	4.70	2361.4	4.70	2361.5	4.70	2361.7	4.70	2362.1	4.70	2362.5	4.70
102	2408.3	4.75	2408.4	4.75	2408.5	4.75	2408.7	4.75	2409.1	4.75	2409.5	4.75
103	2455.8	4.79	2455.8	4.79	2456.0	4.79	2456.2	4.79	2456.5	4.79	2457.0	4.79
104	2503.7	4.84	2503.8	4.84	2503.9	4.84	2504.1	4.84	2504.5	4.84	2504.9	4.84
105	2552.1	4.88	2552.1	4.88	2552.3	4.88	2552.5	4.89	2552.9	4.89	2553.3	4.89
106	2600.9	4.93	2601.0	4.93	2601.1	4.93	2601.4	4.93	2601.7	4.93	2602.2	4.93
107	2650.2	4.98	2650.3	4.98	2650.4	4.98	2650.7	4.98	2651.0	4.98	2651.5	4.98
108	2700.0	5.02	2700.1	5.02	2700.2	5.02	2700.5	5.02	2700.8	5.02	2701.3	5.03
109	2750.2	5.07	2750.3	5.07	2750.4	5.07	2750.7	5.07	2751.1	5.07	2751.5	5.07
110	2800.9	5.12	2801.0	5.12	2801.1	5.12	2801.4	5.12	2801.8	5.12	2802.3	5.12
111	2852.1	5.16	2852.1	5.16	2852.3	5.16	2852.6	5.16	2853.0	5.16	2853.4	5.16
112	2903.7	5.21	2903.8	5.21	2903.9	5.21	2904.2	5.21	2904.6	5.21	2905.1	5.21
113	2955.8	5.25	2955.8	5.25	2956.0	5.26	2956.3	5.26	2956.7	5.26	2957.2	5.26
114	3008.3	5.30	3008.4	5.30	3008.6	5.30	3008.9	5.30	3009.3	5.30	3009.8	5.30
115	3061.3	5.35	3061.4	5.35	3061.6	5.35	3061.9	5.35	3062.3	5.35	3062.8	5.35
116	3114.8	5.39	3114.9	5.39	3115.1	5.39	3115.4	5.39	3115.8	5.40	3116.3	5.40
117	3168.7	5.44	3168.8	5.44	3169.0	5.44	3169.3	5.44	3169.7	5.44	3170.3	5.44
118	3223.1	5.49	3223.2	5.49	3223.4	5.49	3223.7	5.49	3224.1	5.49	3224.7	5.49
119	3278.0	5.53	3278.1	5.53	3278.3	5.53	3278.6	5.53	3279.0	5.53	3279.6	5.54
120	3333.3	5.58	3333.4	5.58	3333.6	5.58	3333.9	5.58	3334.4	5.58	3334.9	5.58
SUMS.	0°		1°		2°		3°		4°		5°	

TABLE XI. **Whole Sections.** **Side Slope ¼ to 1.**

SUMS.	6°		7°		8°		9°		10°		11°	
1	0.2	0.07	0.2	0.07	0.2	0.07	0.2	0.07	0.2	0.07	0.2	0.07
2	0.9	0.12	0.9	0.12	0.9	0.12	0.9	0.12	0.9	0.12	0.9	0.12
3	2.1	0.16	2.1	0.16	2.1	0.16	2.1	0.16	2.1	0.16	2.1	0.16
4	3.7	0.21	3.7	0.21	3.7	0.21	3.7	0.21	3.7	0.21	3.7	0.21
5	5.8	0.25	5.8	0.25	5.8	0.25	5.8	0.26	5.8	0.26	5.8	0.26
6	8.3	0.30	8.3	0.30	8.3	0.30	8.3	0.30	8.3	0.30	8.4	0.30
7	11.4	0.35	11.4	0.35	11.4	0.35	11.4	0.35	11.4	0.35	11.4	0.35
8	14.8	0.39	14.8	0.39	14.8	0.39	14.8	0.39	14.8	0.39	14.8	0.39
9	18.8	0.44	18.8	0.44	18.8	0.44	18.8	0.44	18.8	0.44	18.8	0.44
10	23.2	0.49	23.2	0.49	23.2	0.49	23.2	0.49	23.2	0.49	23.2	0.49
11	28.0	0.53	28.0	0.53	28.0	0.53	28.1	0.53	28.1	0.53	28.1	0.53
12	33.4	0.58	33.4	0.58	33.4	0.58	33.4	0.58	33.4	0.58	33.4	0.58
13	39.1	0.63	39.2	0.63	39.2	0.63	39.2	0.63	39.2	0.63	39.2	0.63
14	45.4	0.67	45.4	0.67	45.4	0.67	45.4	0.67	45.5	0.67	45.5	0.67
15	52.1	0.72	52.1	0.72	52.1	0.72	52.2	0.72	52.2	0.72	52.2	0.72
16	59.3	0.76	59.3	0.76	59.3	0.76	59.4	0.77	59.4	0.77	59.4	0.77
17	66.9	0.81	67.0	0.81	67.0	0.81	67.0	0.81	67.0	0.81	67.1	0.81
18	75.1	0.86	75.1	0.86	75.1	0.86	75.1	0.86	75.1	0.86	75.2	0.86
19	83.6	0.90	83.6	0.90	83.7	0.90	83.7	0.90	83.7	0.90	83.8	0.90
20	92.7	0.95	92.7	0.95	92.7	0.95	92.7	0.95	92.8	0.95	92.8	0.95
21	102.2	1.00	102.2	1.00	102.2	1.00	102.2	1.00	102.3	1.00	102.3	1.00
22	112.1	1.04	112.1	1.04	112.2	1.04	112.2	1.04	112.3	1.04	112.3	1.04
23	122.5	1.09	122.6	1.09	122.6	1.09	122.6	1.09	122.7	1.09	122.7	1.09
24	133.4	1.14	133.5	1.14	133.5	1.14	133.5	1.14	133.6	1.14	133.6	1.14
25	144.8	1.18	144.8	1.18	144.9	1.18	144.9	1.18	145.0	1.18	145.0	1.18
26	156.6	1.23	156.6	1.23	156.7	1.23	156.7	1.23	156.8	1.23	156.9	1.23
27	168.9	1.27	168.9	1.27	169.0	1.27	169.0	1.28	169.1	1.28	169.1	1.28
28	181.6	1.32	181.7	1.32	181.7	1.32	181.8	1.32	181.8	1.32	181.9	1.32
29	194.8	1.37	194.9	1.37	194.9	1.37	195.0	1.37	195.1	1.37	195.1	1.37
30	208.5	1.41	208.5	1.41	208.6	1.41	208.7	1.41	208.7	1.41	208.8	1.42
31	222.6	1.46	222.7	1.46	222.7	1.46	222.8	1.46	222.9	1.46	223.0	1.46
32	237.2	1.51	237.3	1.51	237.3	1.51	237.4	1.51	237.5	1.51	237.6	1.51
33	252.3	1.55	252.3	1.55	252.4	1.55	252.5	1.55	252.6	1.55	252.7	1.55
34	267.8	1.60	267.8	1.60	267.9	1.60	268.0	1.60	268.1	1.60	268.2	1.60
35	283.8	1.64	283.8	1.65	283.9	1.65	284.0	1.65	284.1	1.65	284.2	1.65
36	300.2	1.69	300.3	1.69	300.4	1.69	300.5	1.69	300.6	1.69	300.7	1.69
37	317.1	1.74	317.2	1.74	317.3	1.74	317.4	1.74	317.5	1.74	317.6	1.74
38	334.5	1.78	334.6	1.78	334.7	1.78	334.8	1.79	334.9	1.79	335.1	1.79
39	352.3	1.83	352.4	1.83	352.5	1.83	352.6	1.83	352.8	1.83	352.9	1.83
40	370.6	1.88	370.7	1.88	370.8	1.88	371.0	1.88	371.1	1.88	371.2	1.88
41	389.4	1.92	389.5	1.92	389.6	1.92	389.7	1.92	389.9	1.93	390.0	1.93
42	408.6	1.97	408.7	1.97	408.8	1.97	409.0	1.97	409.1	1.97	409.3	1.97
43	428.3	2.02	428.4	2.02	428.5	2.02	428.7	2.02	428.8	2.02	429.0	2.02
44	448.5	2.06	448.6	2.06	448.7	2.06	448.9	2.06	449.0	2.06	449.2	2.07
45	469.1	2.11	469.2	2.11	469.3	2.11	469.5	2.11	469.7	2.11	469.9	2.11
46	490.2	2.15	490.3	2.15	490.4	2.16	490.6	2.16	490.8	2.16	491.0	2.16
47	511.7	2.20	511.8	2 20	512.0	2.20	512.1	2.20	512.3	2.20	512.6	2.20
48	533.7	2.25	533.8	2.25	534.0	2.25	534.2	2.25	534.4	2.25	534.6	2.25
49	556.2	2.29	556.3	2.29	556.5	2.29	556.7	2.30	556.9	2.30	557.1	2.30
50	579.1	2.34	579.2	2.34	579.4	2.34	579.6	2.34	579.8	2.34	580.1	2.34
51	602.5	2.39	602.7	2.39	602.8	2.39	603.0	2.39	603.3	2.39	603.5	2.39
52	626.4	2.43	626.5	2.43	626.7	2.43	626.9	2.43	627.1	2.44	627.4	2.44
53	650.7	2.48	650.8	2.48	651.0	2.48	651.3	2.48	651.5	2.48	651.8	2.48
54	675.5	2.52	675.6	2.53	675.8	2.53	676.1	2.53	676.3	2.53	676.6	2.53
55	700.7	2.57	700.9	2.57	701.1	2.57	701.3	2.57	701.6	2.57	701.9	2.58
56	726.4	2.62	726.6	2.62	726.8	2.62	727.1	2.62	727.3	2.62	727.6	2.62
57	752.6	2.66	752.8	2.66	753.0	2.67	753.3	2.67	753.5	2.67	753.9	2.67
58	779.2	2.71	779.4	2.71	779.7	2.71	779.9	2.71	780.2	2.71	780.5	2.71
59	806.3	2.76	806.5	2.76	806.8	2.76	807.1	2.76	807.4	2.76	807.7	2.76
60	833.9	2.80	834.1	2.80	834.4	2.80	834.6	2.81	835.0	2.81	835.3	2.81
SUMS.	6°		7°		8°		9°		10°		11°	

SUMS.	6°		7°		8°		9°		10°		11°	
61	861.9	2.85	862.2	2.85	862.4	2.85	862.7	2.85	863.0	2.85	863.4	2.85
62	890.4	2.90	890.7	2.90	890.9	2.90	891.2	2.90	891.5	2.90	891.9	2.90
63	919.4	2.94	919.6	2.94	919.9	2.94	920.2	2.94	920.5	2.95	920.9	2.95
64	948.8	2.99	949.0	2.99	949.3	2.99	949.6	2.99	950.0	2.99	950.4	2.99
65	978.7	3.03	978.9	3.04	979.2	3.04	979.5	3.04	979.9	3.04	980.3	3.04
66	1009.0	3.08	1009.3	3.08	1009.6	3.08	1009.9	3.08	1010.3	3.08	1010.7	3.09
67	1039.8	3.13	1040.1	3.13	1040.4	3.13	1040.8	3.13	1041.1	3.13	1041.6	3.13
68	1071.1	3.17	1071.4	3.17	1071.7	3.18	1072.1	3.18	1072.5	3.18	1072.9	3.18
69	1102.9	3.22	1103.1	3.22	1103.4	3.22	1103.8	3.22	1104.2	3.22	1104.7	3.23
70	1135.1	3.27	1135.3	3.27	1135.7	3.27	1136.0	3.27	1136.5	3.27	1136.9	3.27
71	1167.7	3.31	1168.0	3.31	1168.3	3.31	1168.7	3.32	1169.2	3.32	1169.7	3.32
72	1200.8	3.36	1201.1	3.36	1201.5	3.36	1201.9	3.36	1202.3	3.36	1202.8	3.36
73	1234.4	3.41	1234.7	3.41	1235.1	3.41	1235.5	3.41	1236.0	3.41	1236.5	3.41
74	1268.5	3.45	1268.8	3.45	1269.2	3.45	1269.6	3.45	1270.1	3.46	1270.6	3.46
75	1303.0	3.50	1303.3	3.50	1303.7	3.50	1304.1	3.50	1304.6	3.50	1305.2	3.50
76	1338.0	3.54	1338.3	3.55	1338.7	3.55	1339.1	3.55	1339.6	3.55	1340.2	3.55
77	1373.4	3.59	1373.7	3.59	1374.2	3.59	1374.6	3.59	1375.1	3.59	1375.7	3.60
78	1409.3	3.64	1409.7	3.64	1410.1	3.64	1410.5	3.64	1411.1	3.64	1411.7	3.64
79	1445.7	3.68	1446.0	3.68	1446.5	3.69	1446.9	3.69	1447.5	3.69	1448.1	3.69
80	1482.5	3.73	1482.9	3.73	1483.3	3.73	1483.8	3.73	1484.4	3.73	1485.0	3.74
81	1519.8	3.78	1520.2	3.78	1520.6	3.78	1521.1	3.78	1521.7	3.78	1522.3	3.78
82	1557.6	3.82	1557.9	3.82	1558.4	3.82	1558.9	3.83	1559.5	3.83	1560.2	3.83
83	1595.8	3.87	1596.2	3.87	1596.6	3.87	1597.2	3.87	1597.8	3.87	1598.5	3.87
84	1634.5	3.91	1634.9	3.92	1635.4	3.92	1635.9	3.92	1636.5	3.92	1637.2	3.92
85	1673.6	3.96	1674.0	3.96	1674.5	3.96	1675.1	3.96	1675.7	3.97	1676.4	3.97
86	1713.2	4.01	1713.7	4.01	1714.2	4.01	1714.7	4.01	1715.4	4.01	1716.1	4.01
87	1753.3	4.05	1753.7	4.05	1754.2	4.06	1754.8	4.06	1755.5	4.06	1756.2	4.06
88	1793.8	4.10	1794.3	4.10	1794.8	4.10	1795.4	4.10	1796.1	4.11	1796.8	4.11
89	1834.8	4.15	1835.3	4.15	1835.8	4.15	1836.4	4.15	1837.1	4.15	1837.9	4.15
90	1876.3	4.19	1876.8	4.19	1877.3	4.19	1877.9	4.20	1878.7	4.20	1879.4	4.20
91	1918.2	4.24	1918.7	4.24	1919.3	4.24	1919.9	4.24	1920.6	4.24	1921.4	4.25
92	1960.6	4.29	1961.1	4.29	1961.7	4.29	1962.3	4.29	1963.1	4.29	1963.9	4.29
93	2003.5	4.33	2004.0	4.33	2004.6	4.33	2005.2	4.34	2006.0	4.34	2006.8	4.34
94	2046.8	4.38	2047.3	4.38	2047.9	4.38	2048.6	4.38	2049.4	4.38	2050.2	4.39
95	2090.6	4.42	2091.1	4.43	2091.7	4.43	2092.4	4.43	2093.2	4.43	2094.1	4.43
96	2134.8	4.47	2135.3	4.47	2136.0	4.47	2136.7	4.47	2137.5	4.48	2138.4	4.48
97	2179.5	4.52	2180.1	4.52	2180.7	4.52	2181.4	4.52	2182.3	4.52	2183.2	4.52
98	2224.7	4.56	2225.2	4.56	2225.9	4.57	2226.6	4.57	2227.5	4.57	2228.4	4.57
99	2270.3	4.61	2270.9	4.61	2271.6	4.61	2272.3	4.61	2273.2	4.62	2274.1	4.62
100	2316.4	4.66	2317.0	4.66	2317.7	4.66	2318.4	4.66	2319.3	4.66	2320.3	4.66
101	2363.0	4.70	2363.6	4.70	2364.3	4.70	2365.0	4.71	2365.9	4.71	2366.9	4.71
102	2410.0	4.75	2410.6	4.75	2411.3	4.75	2412.1	4.75	2413.0	4.75	2414.0	4.76
103	2457.5	4.80	2458.1	4.80	2458.8	4.80	2459.6	4.80	2460.6	4.80	2461.6	4.80
104	2505.5	4.84	2506.1	4.84	2506.8	4.84	2507.6	4.85	2508.6	4.85	2509.6	4.85
105	2553.9	4.89	2554.5	4.89	2555.2	4.89	2556.1	4.89	2557.1	4.89	2558.1	4.90
106	2602.7	4.93	2603.4	4.94	2604.1	4.94	2605.0	4.94	2606.0	4.94	2607.1	4.94
107	2652.1	4.98	2652.7	4.98	2653.5	4.98	2654.4	4.98	2655.4	4.99	2656.5	4.99
108	2701.9	5.03	2702.5	5.03	2703.3	5.03	2704.2	5.03	2705.3	5.03	2706.4	5.04
109	2752.2	5.07	2752.8	5.07	2753.6	5.08	2754.5	5.08	2755.6	5.08	2756.7	5.08
110	2802.9	5.12	2803.6	5.12	2804.4	5.12	2805.3	5.12	2806.4	5.13	2807.6	5.13
111	2854.1	5.17	2854.8	5.17	2855.6	5.17	2856.6	5.17	2857.6	5.17	2858.8	5.17
112	2905.7	5.21	2906.4	5.21	2907.3	5.21	2908.3	5.22	2909.4	5.22	2910.6	5.22
113	2957.8	5.26	2958.6	5.26	2959.4	5.26	2960.4	5.26	2961.5	5.26	2962.8	5.27
114	3010.4	5.30	3011.2	5.31	3012.1	5.31	3013.1	5.31	3014.2	5.31	3015.5	5.31
115	3063.5	5.35	3064.2	5.35	3065.1	5.35	3066.1	5.36	3067.3	5.36	3068.6	5.36
116	3117.0	5.40	3117.7	5.40	3118.7	5.40	3119.7	5.40	3120.9	5.40	3122.2	5.41
117	3171.0	5.44	3171.7	5.44	3172.7	5.45	3173.7	5.45	3174.9	5.45	3176.3	5.45
118	3225.4	5.49	3226.2	5.49	3227.1	5.49	3228.2	5.49	3229.4	5.50	3230.8	5.50
119	3280.3	5.54	3281.1	5.54	3282.1	5.54	3283.2	5.54	3284.4	5.54	3285.8	5.55
120	3335.7	5.58	3336.5	5.58	3337.5	5.59	3338.6	5.59	3339.8	5.59	3341.2	5.59
SUMS.	6°		7°		8°		9°		10°		11°	

TABLE XI. Whole Sections. Side Slope ¼ to 1.

SUMS.	12°		13°		14°		15°		16°		17°	
1	0.2	0.07	0.2	0.07	0.2	0.07	0.2	0.07	0.2	0.07	0.2	0.07
2	0.9	0.12	0.9	0.12	0.9	0.12	0.9	0.12	0.9	0.12	0.9	0.12
3	2.1	0.16	2.1	0.16	2.1	0.16	2.1	0.16	2.1	0.16	2.1	0.16
4	3.7	0.21	3.7	0.21	3.7	0.21	3.7	0.21	3.7	0.21	3.7	0.21
5	5.8	0.26	5.8	0.26	5.8	0.26	5.8	0.26	5.8	0.26	5.8	0.26
6	8.4	0.30	8.4	0.30	8.4	0.30	8.4	0.30	8.4	0.30	8.4	0.30
7	11.4	0.35	11.4	0.35	11.4	0.35	11.4	0.35	11.4	0.35	11.4	0.35
8	14.9	0.39	14.9	0.39	14.9	0.40	14.9	0.40	14.9	0.40	14.9	0.40
9	18.8	0.44	18.8	0.44	18.8	0.44	18.8	0.44	18.8	0.44	18.9	0.44
10	23.2	0.49	23.2	0.49	23.2	0.49	23.3	0.49	23.3	0.49	23.3	0.49
11	28.1	0.53	28.1	0.53	28.1	0.53	28.1	0.53	28.2	0.54	28.2	0.54
12	33.4	0.58	33.4	0.58	33.5	0.58	33.5	0.58	33.5	0.58	33.5	0.58
13	39.2	0.63	39.3	0.63	39.3	0.63	39.3	0.63	39.3	0.63	39.4	0.63
14	45.5	0.67	45.5	0.67	45.5	0.67	45.6	0.67	45.6	0.67	45.6	0.68
15	52.2	0.72	52.3	0.72	52.3	0.72	52.3	0.72	52.4	0.72	52.4	0.72
16	59.4	0.77	59.5	0.77	59.5	0.77	59.5	0.77	59.6	0.77	59.6	0.77
17	67.1	0.81	67.1	0.81	67.2	0.81	67.2	0.81	67.2	0.81	67.3	0.81
18	75.2	0.86	75.3	0.86	75.3	0.86	75.3	0.86	75.4	0.86	75.4	0.86
19	83.8	0.91	83.8	0.91	83.9	0.91	83.9	0.91	84.0	0.91	84.1	0.91
20	92.9	0.95	92.9	0.95	93.0	0.95	93.0	0.95	93.1	0.95	93.1	0.95
21	102.4	1.00	102.4	1.00	102.5	1.00	102.5	1.00	102.6	1.00	102.7	1.00
22	112.4	1.04	112.4	1.05	112.5	1.05	112.5	1.05	112.6	1.05	112.7	1.05
23	122.8	1.09	122.9	1.09	122.9	1.09	123.0	1.09	123.1	1.09	123.2	1.09
24	133.7	1.14	133.8	1.14	133.9	1.14	133.9	1.14	134.0	1.14	134.1	1.14
25	145.1	1.18	145.2	1.18	145.2	1.19	145.3	1.19	145.4	1.19	145.5	1.19
26	156.9	1.23	157.0	1.23	157.1	1.23	157.2	1.23	157.3	1.23	157.4	1.23
27	169.2	1.28	169.3	1.28	169.4	1.28	169.5	1.28	169.6	1.28	169.7	1.28
28	182.0	1.32	182.1	1.32	182.2	1.32	182.3	1.33	182.4	1.33	182.5	1.33
29	195.2	1.37	195.3	1.37	195.4	1.37	195.6	1.37	195.7	1.37	195.8	1.37
30	208.9	1.42	209.0	1.42	209.1	1.42	209.3	1.42	209.4	1.42	209.6	1.42
31	223.1	1.46	223.2	1.46	223.3	1.46	223.5	1.46	223.6	1.47	223.8	1.47
32	237.7	1.51	237.8	1.51	238.0	1.51	238.1	1.51	238.3	1.51	238.4	1.51
33	252.8	1.56	252.9	1.56	253.1	1.56	253.2	1.56	253.4	1.56	253.6	1.56
34	268.4	1.60	268.5	1.60	268.6	1.60	268.8	1.60	269.0	1.61	269.2	1.61
35	284.4	1.65	284.5	1.65	284.7	1.65	284.8	1.65	285.0	1.65	285.2	1.65
36	300.8	1.69	301.0	1.70	301.2	1.70	301.4	1.70	301.5	1.70	301.8	1.70
37	317.8	1.74	318.0	1.74	318.1	1.74	318.3	1.74	318.5	1.75	318.8	1.75
38	335.2	1.79	335.4	1.79	335.6	1.79	335.8	1.79	336.0	1.79	336.2	1.79
39	353.1	1.83	353.3	1.83	353.5	1.84	353.7	1.84	353.9	1.84	354.2	1.84
40	371.4	1.88	371.6	1.88	371.8	1.88	372.0	1.88	372.3	1.88	372.5	1.89
41	390.2	1.93	390.4	1.93	390.6	1.93	390.9	1.93	391.1	1.93	391.4	1.93
42	409.5	1.97	409.7	1.97	409.9	1.98	410.2	1.98	410.4	1.98	410.7	1.98
43	429.2	2.02	429.4	2.02	429.7	2.02	429.9	2.02	430.2	2.02	430.5	2.03
44	449.4	2.07	449.6	2.07	449.9	2.07	450.2	2.07	450.5	2.07	450.8	2.07
45	470.1	2.11	470.3	2.11	470.6	2.11	470.9	2.12	471.2	2.12	471.5	2.12
46	491.2	2.16	491.5	2.16	491.7	2.16	492.0	2.16	492.3	2.16	492.7	2.17
47	512.8	2.21	513.1	2.21	513.3	2.21	513.6	2.21	514.0	2.21	514.3	2.21
48	534.8	2.25	535.1	2.25	535.4	2.25	535.7	2.26	536.1	2.26	536.5	2.26
49	557.4	2.30	557.6	2.30	558.0	2.30	558.3	2.30	558.7	2.30	559.1	2.31
50	580.3	2.34	580.6	2.35	581.0	2.35	581.3	2.35	581.7	2.35	582.1	2.35
51	603.8	2.39	604.1	2.39	604.4	2.39	604.8	2.40	605.2	2.40	605.6	2.40
52	627.7	2.44	628.0	2.44	628.4	2.44	628.7	2.44	629.2	2.44	629.6	2.44
53	652.1	2.48	652.4	2.49	652.8	2.49	653.2	2.49	653.6	2.49	654.1	2.49
54	676.9	2.53	677.3	2.53	677.6	2.53	678.0	2.53	678.5	2.54	679.0	2.54
55	702.2	2.58	702.6	2.58	703.0	2.58	703.4	2.58	703.8	2.58	704.3	2.58
56	728.0	2.62	728.4	2.62	728.8	2.63	729.2	2.63	729.7	2.63	730.2	2.63
57	754.2	2.67	754.6	2.67	755.0	2.67	755.5	2.67	756.0	2.68	756.5	2.68
58	780.9	2.72	781.3	2.72	781.7	2.72	782.2	2.72	782.7	2.72	783.3	2.72
59	808.1	2.76	808.5	2.76	808.9	2.77	809.4	2.77	809.9	2.77	810.5	2.77
60	835.7	2.81	836.1	2.81	836.6	2.81	837.1	2.81	837.6	2.82	838.2	2.82
SUMS.	12°		13°		14°		15°		16°		17°	

TABLE XI. **Whole Sections.** **Side Slope ½ to 1.**

SUMS.	12°		13°		14°		15°		16°		17°	
61	863.8	2.86	864.2	2.86	864.7	2.86	865.2	2.86	865.8	2.86	866.4	2.86
62	892.3	2.90	892.8	2.90	893.3	2.90	893.8	2.91	894.4	2.91	895.0	2.91
63	921.4	2.95	921.8	2.95	922.3	2.95	922.9	2.95	923.5	2.96	924.1	2.96
64	950.8	2.99	951.3	3.00	951.8	3.00	952.4	3.00	953.0	3.00	953.7	3.00
65	980.8	3.04	981.3	3.04	981.8	3.04	982.4	3.05	983.1	3.05	983.8	3.05
66	1011.2	3.09	1011.7	3.09	1012.3	3.09	1012.9	3.09	1013.5	3.09	1014.3	3.10
67	1042.1	3.13	1042.6	3.14	1043.2	3.14	1043.8	3.14	1044.5	3.14	1045.2	3.14
68	1073.4	3.18	1073.9	3.18	1074.5	3.18	1075.2	3.19	1075.9	3.19	1076.7	3.19
69	1105.2	3.23	1105.8	3.23	1106.4	3.23	1107.1	3.23	1107.8	3.23	1108.6	3.24
70	1137.5	3.27	1138.1	3.27	1138.7	3.28	1139.4	3.28	1140.1	3.28	1140.9	3.28
71	1170.2	3.32	1170.8	3.32	1171.4	3.32	1172.2	3.33	1172.9	3.33	1173.8	3.33
72	1203.4	3.37	1204.0	3.37	1204.7	3.37	1205.4	3.37	1206.2	3.37	1207.1	3.38
73	1237.1	3.41	1237.7	3.41	1238.4	3.42	1239.1	3.42	1239.9	3.42	1240.8	3.42
74	1271.2	3.46	1271.8	3.46	1272.5	3.46	1273.3	3.46	1274.1	3.47	1275.0	3.47
75	1305.8	3.51	1306.4	3.51	1307.2	3.51	1308.0	3.51	1308.8	3.51	1309.7	3.52
76	1340.8	3.55	1341.5	3.55	1342.3	3.56	1343.1	3.56	1343.9	3.56	1344.9	3.56
77	1376.3	3.60	1377.0	3.60	1377.8	3.60	1378.6	3.60	1379.5	3.61	1380.5	3.61
78	1412.3	3.64	1413.0	3.65	1413.8	3.65	1414.7	3.65	1415.6	3.65	1416.6	3.66
79	1448.8	3.69	1449.5	3.69	1450.3	3.69	1451.2	3.70	1452.1	3.70	1453.2	3.70
80	1485.7	3.74	1486.4	3.74	1487.3	3.74	1488.2	3.74	1489.1	3.75	1490.2	3.75
81	1523.1	3.78	1523.8	3.79	1524.7	3.79	1525.6	3.79	1526.6	3.79	1527.7	3.80
82	1560.9	3.83	1561.7	3.83	1562.6	3.83	1563.5	3.84	1564.5	3.84	1565.6	3.84
83	1599.2	3.88	1600.0	3.88	1600.9	3.88	1601.9	3.88	1602.9	3.89	1604.0	3.89
84	1638.0	3.92	1638.8	3.93	1639.7	3.93	1640.7	3.93	1641.8	3.93	1642.9	3.94
85	1677.2	3.97	1678.0	3.97	1679.0	3.97	1680.0	3.98	1681.1	3.98	1682.3	3.98
86	1716.9	4.02	1717.8	4.02	1718.7	4.02	1719.8	4.02	1720.9	4.03	1722.1	4.03
87	1757.0	4.06	1757.9	4.06	1758.9	4.07	1760.0	4.07	1761.1	4.07	1762.4	4.07
88	1797.7	4.11	1798.6	4.11	1799.6	4.11	1800.7	4.12	1801.9	4.12	1803.1	4.12
89	1838.8	4.16	1839.7	4.16	1840.7	4.16	1841.8	4.16	1843.0	4.16	1844.3	4.17
90	1880.3	4.20	1881.3	4.20	1882.3	4.21	1883.5	4.21	1884.7	4.21	1886.0	4.21
91	1922.3	4.25	1923.3	4.25	1924.4	4.25	1925.5	4.26	1926.8	4.26	1928.2	4.26
92	1964.8	4.29	1965.8	4.30	1966.9	4.30	1968.1	4.30	1969.4	4.30	1970.8	4.31
93	2007.8	4.34	2008.8	4.34	2009.9	4.35	2011.1	4.35	2012.4	4.35	2013.8	4.35
94	2051.2	4.39	2052.2	4.39	2053.3	4.39	2054.6	4.39	2055.9	4.40	2057.4	4.40
95	2095.0	4.43	2096.1	4.44	2097.3	4.44	2098.5	4.44	2099.9	4.44	2101.4	4.45
96	2139.4	4.48	2140.5	4.48	2141.7	4.49	2143.0	4.49	2144.4	4.49	2145.9	4.49
97	2184.2	4.53	2185.3	4.53	2186.5	4.53	2187.8	4.53	2189.3	4.54	2190.8	4.54
98	2229.4	4.57	2230.6	4.58	2231.8	4.58	2233.2	4.58	2234.6	4.58	2236.2	4.59
99	2275.2	4.62	2276.3	4.62	2277.6	4.62	2279.0	4.63	2280.5	4.63	2282.1	4.63
100	2321.4	4.67	2322.6	4.67	2323.8	4.67	2325.3	4.67	2326.8	4.68	2328.4	4.68
101	2368.0	4.71	2369.2	4.71	2370.6	4.72	2372.0	4.72	2373.5	4.72	2375.2	4.73
102	2415.2	4.76	2416.4	4.76	2417.7	4.76	2419.2	4.77	2420.8	4.77	2422.5	4.77
103	2462.7	4.81	2464.0	4.81	2465.4	4.81	2466.9	4.81	2468.5	4.82	2470.2	4.82
104	2510.8	4.85	2512.1	4.85	2513.5	4.86	2515.0	4.86	2516.6	4.86	2518.4	4.87
105	2559.3	4.90	2560.6	4.90	2562.0	4.90	2563.6	4.91	2565.3	4.91	2567.1	4.91
106	2608.3	4.94	2609.6	4.95	2611.1	4.95	2612.7	4.95	2614.4	4.96	2616.2	4.96
107	2657.7	4.99	2659.1	4.99	2660.6	5.00	2662.2	5.00	2663.9	5.00	2665.8	5.01
108	2707.6	5.04	2709.0	5.04	2710.5	5.04	2712.2	5.05	2713.9	5.05	2715.9	5.05
109	2758.0	5.08	2759.4	5.09	2761.0	5.09	2762.6	5.09	2764.4	5.10	2766.4	5.10
110	2808.9	5.13	2810.3	5.13	2811.9	5.14	2813.6	5.14	2815.4	5.14	2817.4	5.15
111	2860.2	5.18	2861.6	5.18	2863.2	5.18	2864.9	5.19	2866.8	5.19	2868.8	5.19
112	2911.9	5.22	2913.4	5.23	2915.0	5.23	2916.8	5.23	2918.7	5.24	2920.8	5.24
113	2964.2	5.27	2965.7	5.27	2967.3	5.28	2969.1	5.28	2971.1	5.28	2973.2	5.29
114	3016.9	5.32	3018.4	5.32	3020.1	5.32	3021.9	5.32	3023.9	5.33	3026.0	5.33
115	3070.0	5.36	3071.6	5.37	3073.3	5.37	3075.1	5.37	3077.2	5.37	3079.3	5.38
116	3123.6	5.41	3125.2	5.41	3127.0	5.41	3128.9	5.42	3130.9	5.42	3133.1	5.43
117	3177.7	5.46	3179.3	5.46	3181.1	5.46	3183.0	5.46	3185.1	5.47	3187.4	5.47
118	3232.3	5.50	3233.9	5.50	3235.7	5.51	3237.7	5.51	3239.8	5.51	3242.1	5.52
119	3287.3	5.55	3289.0	5.55	3290.8	5.55	3292.8	5.56	3294.9	5.56	3297.3	5.56
120	3342.8	5.59	3344.5	5.60	3346.3	5.60	3348.4	5.60	3350.6	5.61	3352.9	5.61
SUMS.	12°		13°		14°		15°		16°		17°	

SUMS.	18°		19°		20°		21°		22°		23°	
1	0.2	0.07	0.2	0.07	0.2	0.07	0.2	0.07	0.2	0.07	0.2	0.07
2	0.9	0.12	0.9	0.12	0.9	0.12	0.9	0.12	0.9	0.12	0.9	0.12
3	2.1	0.16	2.1	0.16	2.1	0.16	2.1	0.16	2.1	0.16	2.1	0.16
4	3.7	0.21	3.7	0.21	3.7	0.21	3.7	0.21	3.7	0.21	3.7	0.21
5	5.8	0.26	5.8	0.26	5.8	0.26	5.8	0.26	5.8	0.26	5.9	0.26
6	8.4	0.30	8.4	0.30	8.4	0.30	8.4	0.30	8.4	0.30	8.4	0.30
7	11.4	0.35	11.4	0.35	11.4	0.35	11.4	0.35	11.5	0.35	11.5	0.35
8	14.9	0.40	14.9	0.40	14.9	0.40	15.0	0.40	15.0	0.40	15.0	0.40
9	18.9	0.44	18.9	0.44	18.9	0.44	18.9	0.44	18.9	0.44	19.0	0.44
10	23.3	0.49	23.3	0.49	23.3	0.49	23.4	0.49	23.4	0.49	23.4	0.49
11	28.2	0.54	28.2	0.54	28.2	0.54	28.3	0.54	28.3	0.54	28.3	0.54
12	33.6	0.58	33.6	0.58	33.6	0.58	33.6	0.58	33.7	0.58	33.7	0.59
13	39.4	0.63	39.4	0.63	39.4	0.63	39.5	0.63	39.5	0.63	39.6	0.63
14	45.7	0.68	45.7	0.68	45.7	0.68	45.8	0.68	45.8	0.68	45.9	0.68
15	52.4	0.72	52.5	0.72	52.5	0.72	52.6	0.72	52.6	0.72	52.7	0.73
16	59.7	0.77	59.7	0.77	59.8	0.77	59.8	0.77	59.9	0.77	59.9	0.77
17	67.3	0.82	67.4	0.82	67.5	0.82	67.5	0.82	67.6	0.82	67.7	0.82
18	75.5	0.86	75.6	0.86	75.6	0.86	75.7	0.86	75.8	0.87	75.9	0.87
19	84.1	0.91	84.2	0.91	84.3	0.91	84.3	0.91	84.4	0.91	84.5	0.91
20	93.2	0.96	93.3	0.96	93.4	0.96	93.5	0.96	93.5	0.96	93.6	0.96
21	102.8	1.00	102.8	1.00	102.9	1.00	103.0	1.00	103.1	1.01	103.2	1.01
22	112.8	1.05	112.9	1.05	113.0	1.05	113.1	1.05	113.2	1.05	113.3	1.05
23	123.3	1.10	123.4	1.10	123.5	1.10	123.6	1.10	123.7	1.10	123.8	1.10
24	134.2	1.14	134.3	1.14	134.4	1.14	134.6	1.14	134.7	1.15	134.9	1.15
25	145.6	1.19	145.8	1.19	145.9	1.19	146.0	1.19	146.2	1.19	146.3	1.19
26	157.5	1.24	157.6	1.24	157.8	1.24	157.9	1.24	158.1	1.24	158.3	1.24
27	169.9	1.28	170.0	1.28	170.2	1.28	170.3	1.28	170.5	1.29	170.7	1.29
28	182.7	1.33	182.8	1.33	183.0	1.33	183.2	1.33	183.4	1.33	183.5	1.33
29	196.0	1.37	196.1	1.38	196.3	1.38	196.5	1.38	196.7	1.38	196.9	1.38
30	209.7	1.42	209.9	1.42	210.1	1.42	210.3	1.43	210.5	1.43	210.7	1.43
31	223.9	1.47	224.1	1.47	224.3	1.47	224.5	1.47	224.7	1.47	225.0	1.47
32	238.6	1.51	238.8	1.52	239.0	1.52	239.2	1.52	239.5	1.52	239.7	1.52
33	253.8	1.56	254.0	1.56	254.2	1.56	254.4	1.57	254.7	1.57	255.0	1.57
34	269.4	1.61	269.6	1.61	269.8	1.61	270.1	1.61	270.4	1.61	270.6	1.62
35	285.4	1.65	285.7	1.66	285.9	1.66	286.2	1.66	286.5	1.66	286.8	1.66
36	302.0	1.70	302.2	1.70	302.5	1.70	302.8	1.71	303.1	1.71	303.4	1.71
37	319.0	1.75	319.3	1.75	319.5	1.75	319.8	1.75	320.2	1.75	320.5	1.76
38	336.5	1.79	336.8	1.80	337.1	1.80	337.4	1.80	337.7	1.80	338.1	1.80
39	354.4	1.84	354.7	1.84	355.0	1.84	355.4	1.85	355.7	1.85	356.1	1.85
40	372.8	1.89	373.1	1.89	373.5	1.89	373.8	1.89	374.2	1.89	374.6	1.90
41	391.7	1.93	392.0	1.94	392.4	1.94	392.7	1.94	393.1	1.94	393.5	1.94
42	411.0	1.98	411.4	1.98	411.7	1.98	412.1	1.99	412.5	1.99	413.0	1.99
43	430.9	2.03	431.2	2.03	431.6	2.03	432.0	2.03	432.4	2.03	432.9	2.04
44	451.1	2.07	451.5	2.08	451.9	2.08	452.3	2.08	452.8	2.08	453.2	2.08
45	471.9	2.12	472.2	2.12	472.7	2.12	473.1	2.13	473.6	2.13	474.1	2.13
46	493.1	2.17	493.5	2.17	493.9	2.17	494.4	2.17	494.9	2.17	495.4	2.18
47	514.7	2.21	515.2	2.22	515.6	2.22	516.1	2.22	516.6	2.22	517.2	2.22
48	536.9	2.26	537.3	2.26	537.8	2.26	538.3	2.27	538.8	2.27	539.4	2.27
49	559.5	2.31	559.9	2.31	560.4	2.31	561.0	2.31	561.5	2.32	562.1	2.32
50	582.5	2.35	583.0	2.36	583.5	2.36	584.1	2.36	584.7	2.36	585.3	2.36
51	606.1	2.40	606.6	2.40	607.1	2.40	607.7	2.41	608.3	2.41	608.9	2.41
52	630.1	2.45	630.6	2.45	631.2	2.45	631.7	2.45	632.4	2.46	633.0	2.46
53	654.6	2.49	655.1	2.50	655.7	2.50	656.3	2.50	656.9	2.50	657.6	2.51
54	679.5	2.54	680.0	2.54	680.6	2.54	681.3	2.55	682.0	2.55	682.7	2.55
55	704.9	2.59	705.5	2.59	706.1	2.59	706.7	2.59	707.4	2.60	708.2	2.60
56	730.7	2.63	731.3	2.64	732.0	2.64	732.7	2.64	733.4	2.64	734.2	2.65
57	757.1	2.68	757.7	2.68	758.4	2.68	759.1	2.69	759.8	2.69	760.6	2.69
58	783.9	2.73	784.5	2.73	785.2	2.73	785.9	2.73	786.7	2.74	787.6	2.74
59	811.1	2.77	811.8	2.78	812.5	2.78	813.3	2.78	814.1	2.78	815.0	2.79
60	838.9	2.82	839.6	2.82	840.3	2.82	841.1	2.83	841.9	2.83	842.8	2.83
SUMS.	18°		19°		20°		21°		22°		23°	

TABLE XI. Whole Sections. Side Slope ¼ to 1.

SUMS.	18°		19°		20°		21°		22°		23°	
61	867.1	2.87	867.8	2.87	868.5	2.87	869.3	2.87	870.2	2.88	871.1	2.88
62	895.7	2.91	896.5	2.92	897.2	2.92	898.1	2.92	899.0	2.92	899.9	2.93
63	924.9	2.96	925.6	2.96	926.4	2.96	927.3	2.97	928.2	2.97	929.2	2.97
64	954.4	3.01	955.2	3.01	956.1	3.01	957.0	3.01	957.9	3.02	958.9	3.02
65	984.5	3.05	985.3	3.06	986.2	3.06	987.1	3.06	988.1	3.06	989.1	3.07
66	1015.0	3.10	1015.9	3.10	1016.8	3.10	1017.7	3.11	1018.7	3.11	1019.8	3.11
67	1046.0	3.15	1046.9	3.15	1047.8	3.15	1048.8	3.15	1049.8	3.16	1050.9	3.16
68	1077.5	3.19	1078.4	3.19	1079.3	3.20	1080.3	3.20	1081.4	3.20	1082.6	3.21
69	1109.4	3.24	1110.3	3.24	1111.3	3.24	1112.3	3.25	1113.4	3.25	1114.6	3.25
70	1141.8	3.29	1142.7	3.29	1143.7	3.29	1144.8	3.29	1146.0	3.30	1147.2	3.30
71	1174.7	3.33	1175.6	3.33	1176.6	3.34	1177.7	3.34	1178.9	3.34	1180.2	3.35
72	1208.0	3.38	1209.0	3.38	1210.0	3.38	1211.2	3.39	1212.4	3.39	1213.7	3.39
73	1241.8	3.43	1242.8	3.43	1243.9	3.43	1245.0	3.43	1246.3	3.44	1247.6	3.44
74	1276.0	3.47	1277.1	3.47	1278.2	3.48	1279.4	3.48	1280.7	3.48	1282.0	3.49
75	1310.7	3.52	1311.8	3.52	1313.0	3.52	1314.2	3.53	1315.5	3.53	1316.9	3.54
76	1345.9	3.57	1347.0	3.57	1348.2	3.57	1349.5	3.57	1350.8	3.58	1352.3	3.58
77	1381.6	3.61	1382.7	3.61	1383.9	3.62	1385.2	3.62	1386.6	3.62	1388.1	3.63
78	1417.7	3.66	1418.8	3.66	1420.1	3.66	1421.4	3.67	1422.9	3.67	1424.4	3.68
79	1454.3	3.71	1455.5	3.71	1456.7	3.71	1458.1	3.71	1459 6	3.72	1461.1	3.72
80	1491.3	3.75	1492.5	3.75	1493.9	3.76	1495.3	3.76	1496.8	3.77	1498.3	3.77
81	1528.8	3.80	1530.1	3.80	1531.4	3.80	1532.9	3.81	1534.4	3.81	1536.0	3.82
82	1566.8	3.84	1568.1	3.85	1569.5	3.85	1570.9	3.85	1572.5	3.86	1574.2	3.86
83	1605.3	3.89	1606.6	3.89	1608.0	3.90	1609.5	3.90	1611.1	3.91	1612.8	3.91
84	1644.2	3.94	1645.5	3.94	1647.0	3.94	1648.5	3.95	1650.2	3.95	1651.9	3.96
85	1683.6	3.98	1684.9	3.99	1686.4	3.99	1688.0	4.00	1689.7	4.00	1691.5	4.00
86	1723.4	4.03	1724.8	4.03	1726.3	4.04	1728.0	4.04	1729.7	4.05	1731.5	4.05
87	1763.7	4.08	1765.2	4.08	1766.7	4.08	1768.4	4.09	1770.1	4.09	1772.0	4.10
88	1804.5	4.12	1806.0	4.13	1807.6	4.13	1809.3	4.14	1811.1	4.14	1813.0	4.14
89	1845.7	4.17	1847.3	4.17	1848.9	4.18	1850.6	4.18	1852.5	4.19	1854.4	4.19
90	1887.5	4.22	1889.0	4.22	1890.7	4.22	1892.4	4.23	1894.3	4.23	1896.3	4.24
91	1929.6	4.26	1931.2	4.27	1932.9	4.27	1934.7	4.28	1936.7	4.28	1938.7	4.28
92	1972.3	4.31	1973.9	4.31	1975.6	4.32	1977.5	4.32	1979.5	4.33	1981.6	4.33
93	2015.4	4.36	2017.0	4.36	2018.8	4.36	2020.7	4.37	2022.7	4.37	2024.9	4.38
94	2059.0	4.40	2060.6	4.41	2062.4	4.41	2064.4	4.42	2066.5	4.42	2068.6	4.42
95	2103.0	4.45	2104.7	4.45	2106.6	4.46	2108.5	4.46	2110.7	4.47	2112.9	4.47
96	2147.5	4.50	2149.3	4.50	2151.1	4.50	2153.2	4.51	2155.3	4.51	2157.6	4.52
97	2192.5	4.54	2194.3	4.55	2196.2	4.55	2198.3	4.56	2200.5	4.56	2202.8	4.57
98	2237.9	4.59	2239.7	4.59	2241.7	4.60	2243.8	4.60	2246.1	4.61	2248.4	4.61
99	2283.8	4.64	2285.7	4.64	2287.7	4.64	2289.8	4.65	2292.1	4.65	2294.6	4.66
100	2330.2	4.68	2332.1	4.69	2334.1	4.69	2336.3	4.70	2338.7	4.70	2341.2	4.71
101	2377.0	4.73	2379.0	4.73	2381.1	4.74	2383.3	4.74	2385.7	4.75	2388.2	4.75
102	2424.3	4.78	2426.3	4.78	2428.4	4.78	2430.7	4.79	2433.2	4.79	2435.7	4.80
103	2472.1	4.82	2474.1	4.83	2476.3	4.83	2478.6	4.84	2481.1	4.84	2483.7	4.85
104	2520.3	4.87	2522.4	4.87	2524.6	4.88	2527.0	4.88	2529.5	4.89	2532.2	4.89
105	2569.0	4.92	2571.1	4.92	2573.4	4.93	2575.8	4.93	2578.4	4.93	2581.1	4.94
106	2618.2	4.96	2620.3	4.97	2622.6	4.97	2625.1	4.98	2627.7	4.98	2630.5	4.99
107	2667.8	5.01	2670.0	5.01	2672.4	5.02	2674.9	5.02	2677.6	5.03	2680.4	5.03
108	2717.9	5.06	2720.2	5.06	2722.5	5.07	2725.1	5.07	2727.8	5.07	2730.7	5.08
109	2768.5	5.10	2770.8	5.11	2773.2	5.11	2775.8	5.12	2778.6	5.12	2781.5	5.13
110	2819.5	5.15	2821.8	5.15	2824.3	5.16	2827.0	5.16	2829.8	5.17	2832.8	5.17
111	2871.0	5.20	2873.4	5.20	2875.9	5.21	2878.6	5.21	2881.5	5.22	2884.5	5.22
112	2923.0	5.24	2925.4	5.25	2927.9	5.25	2930.7	5.26	2933.6	5.26	2936.7	5.27
113	2975.4	5.29	2977.9	5.29	2980.5	5.30	2983.3	5.30	2986.3	5.31	2989.4	5.31
114	3028.3	5.34	3030.8	5.34	3033.5	5.35	3036.3	5.35	3039.3	5.36	3042.6	5.36
115	3081.7	5.38	3084.2	5.39	3086.9	5.39	3089.8	5.40	3092.9	5.40	3096.2	5.41
116	3135.5	5.43	3138.1	5.43	3140.8	5.44	3143.8	5.44	3146.9	5.45	3150.3	5.45
117	3189.8	5.48	3192.4	5.48	3195.2	5.49	3198.2	5.49	3201.4	5.50	3204.8	5.50
118	3244.6	5.52	3247.2	5.53	3250.1	5.53	3253.1	5.54	3256.4	5.54	3259.8	5.55
119	3299.8	5.57	3302.5	5.57	3305.4	5.58	3308.5	5.58	3311.8	5.59	3315.3	5.60
120	3355.5	5.62	3358.2	5.62	3361.2	5.63	3364.3	5.63	3367.7	5.64	3371.3	5.64
SUMS.	18°		19°		20°		21°		22°		23°	

TABLE XI. Whole Sections. Side Slope $\frac{1}{4}$ to 1.

SUMS.	24°		25°		26°		27°		28°		29°	
1	0.2	0.07	0.2	0.07	0.2	0.07	0.2	0.07	0.2	0.07	0.2	0.07
2	0.9	0.12	0.9	0.12	0.9	0.12	0.9	0.12	0.9	0.12	0.9	0.12
3	2.1	0.16	2.1	0.16	2.1	0.16	2.1	0.16	2.1	0.16	2.1	0.17
4	3.8	0.21	3.8	0.21	3.8	0.21	3.8	0.21	3.8	0.21	3.8	0.21
5	5.9	0.26	5.9	0.26	5.9	0.26	5.9	0.26	5.9	0.26	5.9	0.26
6	8.4	0.30	8.4	0.31	8.5	0.31	8.5	0.31	8.5	0.31	8.5	0.31
7	11.5	0.35	11.5	0.35	11.5	0.35	11.5	0.35	11.5	0.35	11.6	0.35
8	15.0	0.40	15.0	0.40	15.0	0.40	15.1	0.40	15.1	0.40	15.1	0.40
9	19.0	0.45	19.0	0.45	19.0	0.45	19.1	0.45	19.1	0.45	19.1	0.45
10	23.4	0.49	23.5	0.49	23.5	0.49	23.5	0.49	23.6	0.49	23.6	0.50
11	28.4	0.54	28.4	0.54	28.4	0.54	28.5	0.54	28.5	0.54	28.6	0.54
12	33.8	0.59	33.8	0.59	33.8	0.59	33.9	0.59	33.9	0.59	34.0	0.59
13	39.6	0.63	39.7	0.63	39.7	0.63	39.8	0.64	39.8	0.64	39.9	0.64
14	45.9	0.68	46.0	0.68	46.1	0.68	46.1	0.68	46.2	0.68	46.3	0.68
15	52.7	0.73	52.8	0.73	52.9	0.73	52.9	0.73	53.0	0.73	53.1	0.73
16	60.0	0.77	60.1	0.77	60.2	0.78	60.2	0.78	60.3	0.78	60.4	0.78
17	67.7	0.82	67.8	0.82	67.9	0.82	68.0	0.82	68.1	0.82	68.2	0.83
18	75.9	0.87	76.0	0.87	76.1	0.87	76.2	0.87	76.3	0.87	76.5	0.87
19	84.6	0.91	84.7	0.92	84.8	0.92	84.9	0.92	85.1	0.92	85.2	0.92
20	93.8	0.96	93.9	0.96	94.0	0.96	94.1	0.96	94.3	0.97	94.4	0.97
21	103.4	1.01	103.5	1.01	103.6	1.01	103.8	1.01	103.9	1.01	104.1	1.01
22	113.4	1.05	113.6	1.06	113.7	1.06	113.9	1.06	114.1	1.06	114.2	1.06
23	124.0	1.10	124.1	1.10	124.3	1.10	124.5	1.11	124.7	1.11	124.9	1.11
24	135.0	1.15	135.2	1.15	135.3	1.15	135.5	1.15	135.7	1.15	135.9	1.16
25	146.5	1.20	146.7	1.20	146.9	1.20	147.1	1.20	147.3	1.20	147.5	1.20
26	158.4	1.24	158.6	1.24	158.8	1.25	159.1	1.25	159.3	1.25	159.5	1.25
27	170.9	1.29	171.1	1.29	171.3	1.29	171.5	1.29	171.8	1.30	172.1	1.30
28	183.8	1.34	184.0	1.34	184.2	1.34	184.5	1.34	184.7	1.34	185.0	1.35
29	197.1	1.38	197.4	1.38	197.6	1.39	197.9	1.39	198.2	1.39	198.5	1.39
30	210.9	1.43	211.2	1.43	211.5	1.43	211.8	1.44	212.1	1.44	212.4	1.44
31	225.2	1.48	225.5	1.48	225.8	1.48	226.1	1.48	226.5	1.48	226.8	1.49
32	240.0	1.52	240.3	1.53	240.6	1.53	240.9	1.53	241.3	1.53	241.7	1.53
33	255.2	1.57	255.6	1.57	255.9	1.57	256.2	1.58	256.6	1.58	257.0	1.58
34	270.9	1.62	271.3	1.62	271.6	1.62	272.0	1.62	272.4	1.63	272.8	1.63
35	287.1	1.66	287.5	1.67	287.8	1.67	288.2	1.67	288.7	1.67	289.1	1.68
36	303.8	1.71	304.1	1.71	304.5	1.72	304.9	1.72	305.4	1.72	305.9	1.72
37	320.9	1.76	321.3	1.76	321.7	1.76	322.1	1.76	322.6	1.77	323.1	1.77
38	338.5	1.80	338.9	1.81	339.3	1.81	339.8	1.81	340.3	1.81	340.8	1.82
39	356.5	1.85	356.9	1.85	357.4	1.86	357.9	1.86	358.4	1.86	359.0	1.86
40	375.0	1.90	375.5	1.90	376.0	1.90	376.5	1.91	377.0	1.91	377.6	1.91
41	394.0	1.95	394.5	1.95	395.0	1.95	395.5	1.95	396.1	1.96	396.7	1.96
42	413.5	1.99	414.0	1.99	414.5	2.00	415.1	2.00	415.7	2.00	416.3	2.01
43	433.4	2.04	433.9	2.04	434.5	2.04	435.1	2.05	435.7	2.05	436.4	2.05
44	453.8	2.09	454.3	2.09	454.9	2.09	455.5	2.09	456.2	2.10	456.9	2.10
45	474.6	2.13	475.2	2.14	475.8	2.14	476.5	2.14	477.2	2.14	477.9	2.15
46	496.0	2.18	496.6	2.18	497.2	2.19	497.9	2.19	498.6	2.19	499.4	2.19
47	517.8	2.23	518.4	2.23	519.1	2.23	519.8	2.24	520.5	2.24	521.4	2.24
48	540.0	2.27	540.7	2.28	541.4	2.28	542.1	2.28	542.9	2.29	543.8	2.29
49	562.8	2.32	563.4	2.32	564.2	2.33	565.0	2.33	565.8	2.33	566.7	2.34
50	586.0	2.37	586.7	2.37	587.4	2.37	588.2	2.38	589.1	2.38	590.0	2.38
51	609.6	2.41	610.4	2.42	611.2	2.42	612.0	2.42	612.9	2.43	613.9	2.43
52	633.8	2.46	634.5	2.46	635.4	2.47	636.2	2.47	637.2	2.47	638.2	2.48
53	658.4	2.51	659.2	2.51	660.0	2.51	661.0	2.52	661.9	2.52	663.0	2.53
54	683.5	2.55	684.3	2.56	685.2	2.56	686.1	2.56	687.1	2.57	688.2	2.57
55	709.0	2.60	709.9	2.60	710.8	2.61	711.8	2.61	712.8	2.62	713.9	2.62
56	735.0	2.65	735.9	2.65	736.9	2.66	737.9	2.66	739.0	2.66	740.1	2.67
57	761.5	2.70	762.4	2.70	763.4	2.70	764.5	2.71	765.6	2.71	766.8	2.71
58	788.5	2.74	789.4	2.75	790.5	2.75	791.5	2.75	792.7	2.76	794.0	2.76
59	815.9	2.79	816.9	2.79	817.9	2.80	819.1	2.80	820.3	2.80	821.6	2.81
60	843.8	2.84	844.8	2.84	845.9	2.84	847.1	2.85	848.3	2.85	849.7	2.86
SUMS.	24°		25°		26°		27°		28°		29°	

TABLE XI. **Whole Sections.** **Side Slope $\frac{1}{4}$ to 1.**

SUMS.	24°		25°		26°		27°		28°		29°	
61	872.1	2.88	873.2	2.89	874.3	2.89	875.5	2.89	876.8	2.90	878.2	2.90
62	901.0	2.93	902.1	2.93	903.2	2.94	904.5	2.94	905.8	2.95	907.2	2.95
63	930.3	2.98	931.4	2.98	932.6	2.98	933.9	2.99	935.3	2.99	936.7	3.00
64	960.0	3.02	961.2	3.03	962.5	3.03	963.8	3.04	965.2	3.04	966.7	3.04
65	990.3	3.07	991.5	3.07	992.8	3.08	994.1	3.08	995.6	3.09	997.2	3.09
66	1021.0	3.12	1022.2	3.12	1023.6	3.13	1025.0	3.13	1026.5	3.13	1028.1	3.14
67	1052.2	3.16	1053.4	3.17	1054.8	3.17	1056.3	3.18	1057.8	3.18	1059.5	3.19
68	1083.8	3.21	1085.1	3.21	1086.5	3.22	1088.0	3.22	1089.6	3.23	1091.3	3.23
69	1115.9	3.26	1117.3	3.26	1118.7	3.27	1120.3	3.27	1121.9	3.28	1123.7	3.28
70	1148.5	3.30	1149.9	3.31	1151.4	3.31	1153.0	3.32	1154.7	3.32	1156.5	3.33
71	1181.5	3.35	1183.0	3.36	1184.5	3.36	1186.1	3.36	1187.9	3.37	1189.7	3.37
72	1215.1	3.40	1216.5	3.40	1218.1	3.41	1219.8	3.41	1221.6	3.42	1223.5	3.42
73	1249.0	3.45	1250.6	3.45	1252.2	3.45	1253.9	3.46	1255.8	3.46	1257.7	3.47
74	1283.5	3.49	1285.1	3.50	1286.7	3.50	1288.5	3.51	1290.4	3.51	1292.4	3.52
75	1318.4	3.54	1320.0	3.54	1321.7	3.55	1323.6	3.55	1325.5	3.56	1327.6	3.56
76	1353.8	3.59	1355.5	3.59	1357.2	3.60	1359.1	3.60	1361.1	3.61	1363.2	3.61
77	1389.7	3.63	1391.4	3.64	1393.2	3.64	1395.1	3.65	1397.1	3.65	1399.3	3.66
78	1426.0	3.68	1427.7	3.68	1429.6	3.69	1431.6	3.69	1433.7	3.70	1435.9	3.71
79	1462.8	3.73	1464.6	3.73	1466.5	3.74	1468.5	3.74	1470.7	3.75	1473.0	3.75
80	1500.1	3.77	1501.9	3.78	1503.8	3.78	1505.9	3.79	1508.1	3.79	1510.5	3.80
81	1537.8	3.82	1539.7	3.83	1541.7	3.83	1543.8	3.84	1546.1	3.84	1548.5	3.85
82	1576.0	3.87	1577.9	3.87	1580.0	3.88	1582.2	3.88	1584.5	3.89	1587.0	3.89
83	1614.7	3.91	1616.6	3.92	1618.7	3.92	1621.0	3.93	1623.4	3.94	1625.9	3.94
84	1653.8	3.96	1655.8	3.97	1658.0	3.97	1660.3	3.98	1662.7	3.98	1665.3	3.99
85	1693.4	4.01	1695.5	4.01	1697.7	4.02	1700.0	4.02	1702.5	4.03	1705.2	4.04
86	1733.5	4.05	1735.6	4.06	1737.9	4.07	1740.3	4.07	1742.8	4.08	1745.6	4.08
87	1774.1	4.10	1776.2	4.11	1778.5	4.11	1781.0	4.12	1783.6	4.12	1786.4	4.13
88	1815.1	4.15	1817.3	4.15	1819.6	4.16	1822.2	4.16	1824.8	4.17	1827.7	4.18
89	1856.6	4.20	1858.8	4.20	1861.2	4.21	1863.8	4.21	1866.5	4.22	1869.5	4.22
90	1898.5	4.24	1900.8	4.25	1903.3	4.25	1905.9	4.26	1908.7	4.27	1911.7	4.27
91	1940.9	4.29	1943.3	4.29	1945.8	4.30	1948.5	4.31	1951.4	4.31	1954.4	4.32
92	1983.8	4.34	1986.3	4.34	1988.8	4.35	1991.6	4.35	1994.5	4.36	1997.6	4.37
93	2027.2	4.38	2029.7	4.39	2032.3	4.39	2035.1	4.40	2038.1	4.41	2041.3	4.41
94	2071.0	4.43	2073.6	4.44	2076.2	4.44	2079.1	4.45	2082.2	4.45	2085.4	4.46
95	2115.3	4.48	2117.9	4.48	2120.7	4.49	2123.6	4.49	2126.7	4.50	2130.0	4.51
96	2160.1	4.52	2162.7	4.53	2165.5	4.54	2168.5	4.54	2171.7	4.55	2175.1	4.56
97	2205.3	4.57	2208.0	4.58	2210.9	4.58	2213.9	4.59	2217.2	4.60	2220.7	4.60
98	2251.0	4.62	2253.8	4.62	2256.7	4.63	2259.8	4.64	2263.1	4.64	2266.7	4.65
99	2297.2	4.66	2300.0	4.67	2303.0	4.68	2306.2	4.68	2309.6	4.69	2313.2	4.70
100	2343.9	4.71	2346.7	4.72	2349.8	4.72	2353.0	4.73	2356.5	4.74	2360.1	4.74
101	2391.0	4.76	2393.9	4.76	2397.0	4.77	2400.3	4.78	2403.8	4.78	2407.6	4.79
102	2438.5	4.80	2441.5	4.81	2444.7	4.82	2448.1	4.82	2451.7	4.83	2455.5	4.84
103	2486.6	4.85	2489.6	4.86	2492.9	4.86	2496.3	4.87	2500.0	4.88	2503.9	4.89
104	2535.1	4.90	2538.2	4.90	2541.5	4.91	2545.0	4.92	2548.7	4.92	2552.7	4.93
105	2584.1	4.95	2587.2	4.95	2590.6	4.96	2594.2	4.96	2598.0	4.97	2602.1	4.98
106	2633.6	4.99	2636.8	5.00	2640.2	5.00	2643.8	5.01	2647.7	5.02	2651.9	5.03
107	2683.5	5.04	2686.7	5.05	2690.2	5.05	2693.9	5.06	2697.9	5.07	2702.1	5.07
108	2733.9	5.09	2737.2	5.09	2740.7	5.10	2744.5	5.11	2748.6	5.11	2752.9	5.12
109	2784.7	5.13	2788.1	5.14	2791.7	5.15	2795.6	5.15	2799.7	5.16	2804.1	5.17
110	2836.1	5.18	2839.5	5.19	2843.2	5.19	2847.1	5.20	2851.3	5.21	2855.8	5.22
111	2887.9	5.23	2891.4	5.23	2895.1	5.24	2899.1	5.25	2903.4	5.25	2907.9	5.26
112	2940.1	5.27	2943.7	5.28	2947.5	5.29	2951.6	5.29	2955.9	5.30	2960.6	5.31
113	2992.9	5.32	2996.5	5.33	3000.4	5.33	3004.5	5.34	3009.0	5.35	3013.7	5.36
114	3046.1	5.37	3049.8	5.37	3053.7	5.38	3058.0	5.39	3062.4	5.40	3067.2	5.40
115	3099.7	5.41	3103.5	5.42	3107.5	5.43	3111.8	5.44	3116.4	5.44	3121.3	5.45
116	3153.9	5.46	3157.7	5.47	3161.8	5.47	3166.2	5.48	3170.8	5.49	3175.8	5.50
117	3208.5	5.51	3212.4	5.51	3216.6	5.52	3221.0	5.53	3225.7	5.54	3230.8	5.55
118	3263.6	5.55	3267.6	5.56	3271.8	5.57	3276.3	5.58	3281.1	5.58	3286.3	5.59
119	3319.1	5.60	3323.2	5.61	3327.5	5.62	3332.1	5.62	3337.0	5.63	3342.2	5.64
120	3375.1	5.65	3379.3	5.66	3383.6	5.66	3388.3	5.67	3393.3	5.68	3398.6	5.69
SUMS.	24°		25°		26°		27°		28°		29°	

TABLE XI. Whole Sections. Side Slope ¼ to 1.

SUMS.	30°		31°		32°		33°		34°		35°	
1	0.2	0.07	0.2	0.07	0.2	0.07	0.2	0.07	0.2	0.07	0.2	0.07
2	0.9	0.12	0.9	0.12	0.9	0.12	1.0	0.12	1.0	0.12	1.0	0.12
3	2.1	0.17	2.1	0.17	2.1	0.17	2.1	0.17	2.1	0.17	2.1	0.17
4	3.8	0.21	3.8	0.21	3.8	0.21	3.8	0.21	3.8	0.21	3.8	0.21
5	5.9	0.26	5.9	0.26	5.9	0.26	5.9	0.26	6.0	0.26	6.0	0.26
6	8.5	0.31	8.5	0.31	8.5	0.31	8.6	0.31	8.6	0.31	8.6	0.31
7	11.6	0.35	11.6	0.36	11.6	0.36	11.6	0.36	11.7	0.36	11.7	0.36
8	15.1	0.40	15.2	0.40	15.2	0.40	15.2	0.40	15.2	0.41	15.3	0.41
9	19.1	0.45	19.2	0.45	19.2	0.45	19.3	0.45	19.3	0.45	19.3	0.45
10	23.6	0.50	23.7	0.50	23.7	0.50	23.8	0.50	23.8	0.50	23.9	0.50
11	28.6	0.54	28.7	0.54	28.7	0.55	28.8	0.55	28.8	0.55	28.9	0.55
12	34.0	0.59	34.1	0.59	34.2	0.59	34.2	0.59	34.3	0.60	34.4	0.60
13	40.0	0.64	40.0	0.64	40.1	0.64	40.2	0.64	40.3	0.64	40.4	0.64
14	46.3	0.69	46.4	0.69	46.5	0.69	46.6	0.69	46.7	0.69	46.8	0.69
15	53.2	0.73	53.3	0.73	53.4	0.74	53.5	0.74	53.6	0.74	53.7	0.74
16	60.5	0.78	60.6	0.78	60.7	0.78	60.9	0.78	61.0	0.79	61.1	0.79
17	68.3	0.83	68.4	0.83	68.6	0.83	68.7	0.83	68.9	0.83	69.0	0.84
18	76.6	0.87	76.7	0.88	76.9	0.88	77.0	0.88	77.2	0.88	77.4	0.88
19	85.3	0.92	85.5	0.92	85.7	0.93	85.8	0.93	86.0	0.93	86.2	0.93
20	94.6	0.97	94.7	0.97	94.9	0.97	95.1	0.97	95.3	0.98	95.5	0.98
21	104.3	1.02	104.4	1.02	104.6	1.02	104.8	1.02	105.1	1.02	105.3	1.03
22	114.4	1.06	114.6	1.07	114.8	1.07	115.1	1.07	115.3	1.07	115.6	1.07
23	125.1	1.11	125.3	1.11	125.5	1.12	125.8	1.12	126.0	1.12	126.3	1.12
24	136.2	1.16	136.4	1.16	136.7	1.16	136.9	1.16	137.2	1.17	137.5	1.17
25	147.8	1.21	148.0	1.21	148.3	1.21	148.6	1.21	148.9	1.22	149.2	1.22
26	159.8	1.25	160.1	1.26	160.4	1.26	160.7	1.26	161.1	1.26	161.4	1.27
27	172.3	1.30	172.6	1.30	173.0	1.30	173.3	1.31	173.7	1.31	174.1	1.31
28	185.3	1.35	185.7	1.35	186.0	1.35	183.4	1.36	186.8	1.36	187.2	1.36
29	198.8	1.39	199.2	1.40	199.5	1.40	199.9	1.40	200.4	1.41	200.8	1.41
30	212.8	1.44	213.1	1.44	213.5	1.45	214.0	1.45	214.4	1.45	214.9	1.46
31	227.2	1.49	227.6	1.49	228.0	1.49	223.5	1.50	229.0	1.50	229.5	1.50
32	242.1	1.54	242.5	1.54	243.0	1.54	243.5	1.55	244.0	1.55	244.5	1.55
33	257.4	1.58	257.9	1.59	258.4	1.59	253.9	1.59	259.5	1.60	260.1	1.60
34	273.3	1.63	273.8	1.63	274.3	1.64	274.8	1.64	275.4	1.64	276.1	1.65
35	289.6	1.68	290.1	1.68	290.7	1.68	291.2	1.69	291.9	1.69	292.5	1.70
36	306.4	1.73	306.9	1.73	307.5	1.73	308.1	1.74	308.8	1.74	309.5	1.74
37	323.6	1.77	324.2	1.78	324.8	1.78	325.5	1.78	326.2	1.79	326.9	1.79
38	341.4	1.82	342.0	1.82	342.6	1.83	343.3	1.83	344.0	1.83	344.8	1.84
39	359.6	1.87	360.2	1.87	360.9	1.87	361.6	1.88	362.4	1.88	363.2	1.89
40	378.3	1.91	378.9	1.92	379.6	1.92	380.4	1.93	381.2	1.93	382.1	1.93
41	397.4	1.96	398.1	1.97	398.9	1.97	399.7	1.97	400.5	1.98	401.4	1.98
42	417.0	2.01	417.8	2.01	418.5	2.02	419.4	2.02	420.3	2.03	421.2	2.03
43	437.1	2.06	437.9	2.06	438.7	2.06	439.6	2.07	440.5	2.07	441.5	2.08
44	457.7	2.10	458.5	2.11	459.4	2.11	460.3	2.12	461.3	2.12	462.3	2.13
45	478.7	2.15	479.6	2.16	480.5	2.16	481.4	2.16	482.5	2.17	483.6	2.17
46	500.2	2.20	501.1	2.20	502.1	2.21	503.1	2.21	504.2	2.22	505.3	2.22
47	522.2	2.25	523.1	2.25	524.1	2.25	525.2	2.26	526.3	2.26	527.5	2.27
48	544.7	2.29	545.6	2.30	546.7	2.30	547.8	2.31	548.9	2.31	550.2	2.32
49	567.6	2.34	568.6	2.34	569.7	2.35	570.8	2.35	572.1	2.36	573.4	2.36
50	591.0	2.39	592.1	2.39	593.2	2.40	594.4	2.40	595.6	2.41	597.0	2.41
51	614.9	2.43	616.0	2.44	617.1	2.44	618.4	2.45	619.7	2.45	621.1	2.46
52	639.2	2.48	640.4	2.49	641.6	2.49	642.9	2.50	644.2	2.50	645.7	2.51
53	664.1	2.53	665.2	2.53	666.5	2.54	667.8	2.54	669.3	2.55	670.8	2.56
54	689.4	2.58	690.6	2.58	691.9	2.59	693.3	2.59	694.8	2.60	696.3	2.60
55	715.1	2.62	716.4	2.63	717.7	2.63	719.2	2.64	720.7	2.64	722.4	2.65
56	741.4	2.67	742.7	2.68	744.1	2.68	745.6	2.69	747.2	2.69	748.9	2.70
57	768.1	2.72	769.4	2.72	770.9	2.73	772.4	2.73	774.1	2.74	775.9	2.75
58	795.3	2.77	796.7	2.77	798.2	2.78	799.8	2.78	801.5	2.79	803.3	2.79
59	822.9	2.81	824.4	2.82	825.9	2.82	827.6	2.83	829.4	2.84	831.3	2.84
60	851.1	2.86	852.6	2.87	854.2	2.87	855.9	2.88	857.7	2.88	859.7	2.89
SUMS.	30°		31°		32°		33°		34°		35°	

SUMS.	30°		31°		32°		33°		34°		35°	
61	879.7	2.91	881.2	2.91	882.9	2.92	884.7	2.92	886.6	2.93	888.6	2.94
62	908.7	2.96	910.4	2.96	912.1	2.97	913.9	2.97	915.9	2.98	917.9	2.98
63	938.3	3.00	940.0	3.01	941.7	3.01	943.6	3.02	945.6	3.03	947.8	3.03
64	968.3	3.05	970.0	3.06	971.9	3.06	973.8	3.07	975.9	3.07	978.1	3.08
65	998.8	3.10	1000.6	3.10	1002.5	3.11	1004.5	3.11	1006.6	3.12	1008.9	3.13
66	1029.8	3.14	1031.6	3.15	1033.6	3.16	1035.6	3.16	1037.8	3.17	1040.2	3.18
67	1061.2	3.19	1063.1	3.20	1065.1	3.20	1067.3	3.21	1069.5	3.22	1072.0	3.22
68	1093.1	3.24	1095.1	3.24	1097.1	3.25	1099.3	3.26	1101.7	3.26	1104.2	3.27
69	1125.5	3.29	1127.5	3.29	1129.7	3.30	1131.9	3.30	1134.3	3.31	1136.9	3.32
70	1158.4	3.33	1160.4	3.34	1162.6	3.35	1165.0	3.35	1167.5	3.36	1170.1	3.37
71	1191.7	3.38	1193.8	3.39	1196.1	3.39	1198.5	3.40	1201.1	3.41	1203.8	3.41
72	1225.5	3.43	1227.7	3.43	1230.0	3.44	1232.5	3.45	1235.1	3.45	1237.9	3.46
73	1259.8	3.48	1262.0	3.48	1264.4	3.49	1267.0	3.49	1269.7	3.50	1272.6	3.51
74	1294.6	3.52	1296.9	3.53	1299.3	3.54	1301.9	3.54	1304.7	3.55	1307.7	3.56
75	1329.8	3.57	1332.1	3.58	1334.7	3.58	1337.3	3.59	1340.2	3.60	1343.2	3.61
76	1365.5	3.62	1367.9	3.62	1370.5	3.63	1373.2	3.64	1376.2	3.65	1379.3	3.65
77	1401.7	3.66	1404.1	3.67	1406.8	3.68	1409.6	3.69	1412.6	3.69	1415.8	3.70
78	1438.3	3.71	1440.8	3.72	1443.6	3.73	1446.5	3.73	1449.6	3.74	1452.9	3.75
79	1475.4	3.76	1478.0	3.77	1480.8	3.77	1483.8	3.78	1487.0	3.79	1490.3	3.80
80	1513.0	3.81	1515.7	3.81	1518.5	3.82	1521.6	3.83	1524.8	3.84	1528.3	3.84
81	1551.1	3.85	1553.8	3.86	1556.7	3.87	1559.9	3.88	1563.2	3.88	1566.8	3.89
82	1589.6	3.90	1592.4	3.91	1595.4	3.91	1598.6	3.92	1602.0	3.93	1605.7	3.94
83	1628.6	3.95	1631.5	3.95	1634.6	3.96	1637.8	3.97	1641.3	3.98	1645.1	3.99
84	1668.1	4.00	1671.0	4.00	1674.2	4.01	1677.6	4.02	1681.1	4.03	1685.0	4.04
85	1708.0	4.04	1711.1	4.05	1714.3	4.06	1717.7	4.07	1721.4	4.07	1725.3	4.08
86	1748.5	4.09	1751.6	4.10	1754.9	4.10	1758.4	4.11	1762.1	4.12	1766.2	4.13
87	1789.4	4.14	1792.5	4.14	1795.9	4.15	1799.5	4.16	1803.4	4.17	1807.5	4.18
88	1830.7	4.18	1834.0	4.19	1837.4	4.20	1841.1	4.21	1845.1	4.22	1849.3	4.23
89	1872.6	4.23	1875.9	4.24	1879.4	4.25	1883.2	4.26	1887.2	4.26	1891.5	4.27
90	1914.9	4.28	1918.3	4.29	1921.9	4.29	1925.8	4.30	1929.9	4.31	1934.3	4.32
91	1957.7	4.33	1961.2	4.33	1964.8	4.34	1968.8	4.35	1973.0	4.36	1977.5	4.37
92	2000.9	4.37	2004.5	4.38	2008.3	4.39	2012.3	4.40	2016.6	4.41	2021.2	4.42
93	2044.7	4.42	2048.3	4.43	2052.2	4.44	2056.3	4.45	2060.7	4.46	2065.4	4.47
94	2088.9	4.47	2092.6	4.48	2096.5	4.48	2100.7	4.49	2105.2	4.50	2110.0	4.51
95	2133.6	4.52	2137.3	4.52	2141.4	4.53	2145.7	4.54	2150.3	4.55	2155.2	4.56
96	2178.7	4.56	2182.6	4.57	2186.7	4.58	2191.1	4.59	2195.8	4.60	2200.8	4.61
97	2224.4	4.61	2228.3	4.62	2232.5	4.63	2237.0	4.64	2241.8	4.65	2246.9	4.66
98	2270.4	4.66	2274.5	4.67	2278.8	4.67	2283.3	4.68	2288.2	4.69	2293.4	4.70
99	2317.0	4.70	2321.1	4.71	2325.5	4.72	2330.2	4.73	2335.2	4.74	2340.5	4.75
100	2364.1	4.75	2368.3	4.76	2372.7	4.77	2377.5	4.78	2382.6	4.79	2388.0	4.80
101	2411.6	4.80	2415.9	4.81	2420.4	4.82	2425.3	4.83	2430.5	4.84	2436.0	4.85
102	2459.6	4.85	2463.9	4.85	2468.6	4.86	2473.5	4.87	2478.8	4.88	2484.5	4.90
103	2508.0	4.89	2512.5	4.90	2517.2	4.91	2522.3	4.92	2527.7	4.93	2533.4	4.94
104	2557.0	4.94	2561.5	4.95	2566.3	4.96	2571.5	4.97	2577.0	4.98	2582.9	4.99
105	2606.4	4.99	2611.0	5.00	2615.9	5.01	2621.2	5.02	2626.8	5.03	2632.8	5.04
106	2656.3	5.04	2661.0	5.04	2666.0	5.05	2671.3	5.06	2677.0	5.07	2683.1	5.09
107	2706.6	5.08	2711.4	5.09	2716.5	5.10	2722.0	5.11	2727.8	5.12	2734.0	5.13
108	2757.4	5.13	2762.3	5.14	2767.5	5.15	2773.1	5.16	2779.0	5.17	2785.4	5.18
109	2808.7	5.18	2813.7	5.19	2819.0	5.20	2824.7	5.21	2830.7	5.22	2837.2	5.23
110	2860.5	5.22	2865.6	5.23	2871.0	5.24	2876.8	5.25	2882.9	5.27	2889.5	5.28
111	2912.8	5.27	2917.9	5.28	2923.4	5.29	2929.3	5.30	2935.6	5.31	2942.2	5.33
112	2965.5	5.32	2970.7	5.33	2976.3	5.34	2982.3	5.35	2988.7	5.36	2995.5	5.37
113	3018.7	5.37	3024.0	5.38	3029.7	5.39	3035.8	5.40	3042.3	5.41	3049.2	5.42
114	3072.3	5.41	3077.8	5.42	3083.6	5.43	3089.8	5.44	3096.4	5.46	3103.4	5.47
115	3126.5	5.46	3132.0	5.47	3137.9	5.48	3144.2	5.49	3150.9	5.50	3158.1	5.52
116	3181.1	5.51	3186.7	5.52	3192.7	5.53	3199.1	5.54	3206.0	5.55	3213.3	5.56
117	3236.2	5.56	3241.9	5.57	3248.0	5.58	3254.5	5.59	3261.5	5.60	3268.9	5.61
118	3291.7	5.60	3297.6	5.61	3303.8	5.62	3310.4	5.63	3317.5	5.65	3325.0	5.66
119	3347.8	5.65	3353.7	5.66	3360.0	5.67	3366.8	5.68	3373.9	5.69	3381.6	5.71
120	3404.3	5.70	3410.3	5.71	3416.7	5.72	3423.6	5.73	3430.9	5.74	3438.7	5.76
SUMS.	30°		31°		32°		33°		34°		35°	

SUMS.	0°		1°		2°		3°		4°		5°	
121	3389.1	5.62	3389.2	5.63	3389.4	5.63	3389.7	5.63	3390.2	5.63	3390.7	5.63
122	3445.4	5.67	3445.4	5.67	3445.6	5.67	3446.0	5.67	3446.4	5.67	3447.0	5.67
123	3502.1	5.72	3502.2	5.72	3502.4	5.72	3502.7	5.72	3503.2	5.72	3503.8	5.72
124	3559.3	5.76	3559.3	5.76	3559.5	5.76	3559.9	5.76	3560.3	5.77	3561.0	5.77
125	3616.9	5.81	3617.0	5.81	3617.2	5.81	3617.5	5.81	3618.0	5.81	3618.6	5.81
126	3675.0	5.86	3675.1	5.86	3675.3	5.86	3675.6	5.86	3676.1	5.86	3676.8	5.86
127	3733.6	5.90	3733.6	5.90	3733.9	5.90	3734.2	5.90	3734.7	5.90	3735.4	5.91
128	3792.6	5.95	3792.7	5.95	3792.9	5.95	3793.2	5.95	3793.8	5.95	3794.4	5.95
129	3852.1	6.00	3852.2	6.00	3852.4	6.00	3852.7	6.00	3853.3	6.00	3853.9	6.00
130	3912.0	6.04	3912.1	6.04	3912.3	6.04	3912.7	6.04	3913.2	6.04	3913.9	6.04
131	3972.5	6.09	3972.5	6.09	3972.8	6.09	3973.1	6.09	3973.7	6.09	3974.4	6.09
132	4033.3	6.13	4033.4	6.13	4033.6	6.13	4034.0	6.14	4034.6	6.14	4035.3	6.14
133	4094.7	6.18	4094.8	6.18	4095.0	6.18	4095.4	6.18	4095.9	6.18	4096.6	6.18
134	4156.5	6.23	4156.6	6.23	4156.8	6.23	4157.2	6.23	4157.8	6.23	4158.5	6.23
135	4218.7	6.27	4218.8	6.27	4219.1	6.27	4219.5	6.27	4220.0	6.28	4220.8	6.28
136	4281.5	6.32	4281.6	6.32	4281.8	6.32	4282.2	6.32	4282.8	6.32	4283.5	6.32
137	4344.7	6.37	4344.8	6.37	4345.0	6.37	4345.4	6.37	4346.0	6.37	4346.8	6.37
138	4408.3	6.41	4408.4	6.41	4408.7	6.41	4409.1	6.41	4409.7	6.41	4410.4	6.42
139	4472.5	6.46	4472.5	6.46	4472.8	6.46	4473.2	6.46	4473.8	6.46	4474.6	6.46
140	4537.0	6.50	4537.1	6.50	4537.4	6.51	4537.8	6.51	4538.4	6.51	4539.2	6.51
141	4602.1	6.55	4602.2	6.55	4602.4	6.55	4602.9	6.55	4603.5	6.55	4604.3	6.55
142	4667.6	6.60	4667.7	6.60	4668.0	6.60	4668.4	6.60	4669.0	6.60	4669.8	6.60
143	4733.6	6.64	4733.7	6.64	4733.9	6.64	4734.4	6.64	4735.0	6.65	4735.8	6.65
144	4800.0	6.69	4800.1	6.69	4800.4	6.69	4800.8	6.69	4801.5	6.69	4802.3	6.69
145	4866.9	6.74	4867.0	6.74	4867.3	6.74	4867.7	6.74	4868.4	6.74	4869.2	6.74
146	4934.3	6.78	4934.4	6.78	4934.6	6.78	4935.1	6.78	4935.8	6.78	4936.6	6.79
147	5002.1	6.83	5002.2	6.83	5002.5	6.83	5002.9	6.83	5003.6	6.83	5004.5	6.83
148	5070.4	6.87	5070.5	6.88	5070.8	6.88	5071.2	6.88	5071.9	6.88	5072.8	6.88
149	5139.1	6.92	5139.2	6.92	5139.5	6.92	5140.0	6.92	5140.7	6.92	5141.6	6.92
150	5208.3	6.97	5208.4	6.97	5208.7	6.97	5209.2	6.97	5209.9	6.97	5210.8	6.97
151	5278.0	7.01	5278.1	7.01	5278.4	7.01	5278.9	7.02	5279.6	7.02	5280.5	7.02
152	5348.1	7.06	5348.3	7.06	5348.6	7.06	5349.1	7.06	5349.8	7.06	5350.7	7.06
153	5418.7	7.11	5418.9	7.11	5419.2	7.11	5419.7	7.11	5420.4	7.11	5421.3	7.11
154	5489.8	7.15	5489.9	7.15	5490.2	7.15	5490.8	7.15	5491.5	7.15	5492.4	7.16
155	5561.3	7.20	5561.4	7.20	5561.8	7.20	5562.3	7.20	5563.0	7.20	5564.0	7.20
156	5633.3	7.25	5633.4	7.25	5633.8	7.25	5634.3	7.25	5635.1	7.25	5636.0	7.25
157	5705.8	7.29	5705.9	7.29	5706.2	7.29	5706.8	7.29	5707.5	7.29	5708.5	7.30
158	5778.7	7.34	5778.8	7.34	5779.1	7.34	5779.7	7.34	5780.5	7.34	5781.5	7.34
159	5852.1	7.38	5852.2	7.38	5852.5	7.38	5853.1	7.39	5853.9	7.39	5854.9	7.39
160	5925.9	7.43	5926.0	7.43	5926.4	7.43	5926.9	7.43	5927.7	7.43	5928.8	7.43
161	6000.2	7.48	6000.3	7.48	6000.7	7.48	6001.3	7.48	6002.1	7.48	6003.1	7.48
162	6075.0	7.52	6075.1	7.52	6075.5	7.52	6076.0	7.52	6076.9	7.53	6077.9	7.53
163	6150.2	7.57	6150.3	7.57	6150.7	7.57	6151.3	7.57	6152.1	7.57	6153.2	7.57
164	6225.9	7.62	6226.0	7.62	6226.4	7.62	6227.0	7.62	6227.8	7.62	6228.9	7.62
165	6302.1	7.66	6302.2	7.66	6302.6	7.66	6303.2	7.66	6304.0	7.66	6305.1	7.67
166	6378.7	7.71	6378.8	7.71	6379.2	7.71	6379.8	7.71	6380.7	7.71	6381.8	7.71
167	6455.8	7.75	6455.9	7.75	6456.3	7.76	6456.9	7.76	6457.8	7.76	6458.9	7.76
168	6533.3	7.80	6533.5	7.80	6533.8	7.80	6534.5	7.80	6535.3	7.80	6536.5	7.80
169	6611.3	7.85	6611.5	7.85	6611.9	7.85	6612.5	7.85	6613.4	7.85	6614.5	7.85
170	6689.8	7.89	6689.9	7.89	6690.3	7.89	6691.0	7.89	6691.9	7.90	6693.0	7.90
171	6768.7	7.94	6768.9	7.94	6769.3	7.94	6769.9	7.94	6770.8	7.94	6772.0	7.94
172	6848.1	7.99	6848.3	7.99	6848.7	7.99	6849.3	7.99	6850.2	7.99	6851.4	7.99
173	6928.0	8.03	6928.1	8.03	6928.5	8.03	6929.2	8.03	6930.1	8.03	6931.3	8.04
174	7008.3	8.08	7008.5	8.08	7008.9	8.08	7009.5	8.08	7010.5	8.08	7011.7	8.08
175	7089.1	8.12	7089.3	8.13	7089.7	8.13	7090.3	8.13	7091.3	8.13	7092.5	8.13
176	7170.4	8.17	7170.5	8.17	7170.9	8.17	7171.6	8.17	7172.6	8.17	7173.8	8.18
177	7252.1	8.22	7252.2	8.22	7252.6	8.22	7253.3	8.22	7254.3	8.22	7255.6	8.22
178	7334.3	8.26	7334.4	8.26	7334.8	8.26	7335.5	8.27	7336.5	8.27	7337.8	8.27
179	7416.9	8.31	7417.0	8.31	7417.5	8.31	7418.2	8.31	7419.2	8.31	7420.4	8.31
180	7500.0	8.36	7500.1	8.36	7500.6	8.36	7501.3	8.36	7502.3	8.36	7503.6	8.36
SUMS.	0°		1°		2°		3°		4°		5°	

TABLE XI. Whole Sections. Side Slope ¼ to 1.

SUMS.	0°		1°		2°		3°		4°		5°	
181	7583.6	8.40	7583.7	8.40	7584.1	8.40	7584.9	8.40	7585.9	8.41	7587.2	8.41
182	7667.6	8.45	7667.7	8.45	7668.2	8.45	7668.9	8.45	7669.9	8.45	7671.3	8.45
183	7752.1	8.50	7752.2	8.50	7752.7	8.50	7753.4	8.50	7754.5	8.50	7755.8	8.50
184	7837.0	8.54	7837.2	8.54	7837.6	8.54	7838.4	8.54	7839.4	8.54	7840.8	8.55
185	7922.5	8.59	7922.6	8.59	7923.1	8.59	7923.8	8.59	7924.9	8.59	7926.2	8.59
186	8008.3	8.63	8008.5	8.63	8008.9	8.63	8009.7	8.64	8010.8	8.64	8012.2	8.64
187	8094.7	8.68	8094.8	8.68	8095.3	8.68	8096.1	8.68	8097.2	8.68	8098.6	8.68
188	8181.5	8.73	8181.6	8.73	8182.1	8.73	8182.9	8.73	8184.0	8.73	8185.4	8.73
189	8268.7	8.77	8268.9	8.77	8269.4	8.77	8270.2	8.77	8271.3	8.78	8272.7	8.78
190	8356.5	8.82	8356.6	8.82	8357.1	8.82	8357.9	8.82	8359.0	8.82	8360.5	8.82
191	8444.7	8.87	8444.8	8.87	8445.3	8.87	8446.1	8.87	8447.3	8.87	8448.7	8.87
192	8533.3	8.91	8533.5	8.91	8534.0	8.91	8534.8	8.91	8535.9	8.91	8537.4	8.92
193	8622.5	8.96	8622.6	8.96	8623.1	8.96	8623.9	8.96	8625.1	8.96	8626.6	8.96
194	8712.0	9.00	8712.2	9.00	8712.7	9.01	8713.5	9.01	8714.7	9.01	8716.2	9.01
195	8802.1	9.05	8802.3	9.05	8802.8	9.05	8803.6	9.05	8804.8	9.05	8806.3	9.06
196	8892.6	9.10	8892.8	9.10	8893.3	9.10	8894.1	9.10	8895.3	9.10	8896.8	9.10
197	8983.6	9.14	8983.7	9.14	8984.3	9.14	8985.1	9.15	8986.3	9.15	8987.9	9.15
198	9075.0	9.19	9075.2	9.19	9075.7	9.19	9076.6	9.19	9077.8	9.19	9079.3	9.19
199	9166.9	9.24	9167.1	9.24	9167.6	9.24	9168.5	9.24	9169.7	9.24	9171.3	9.24
200	9259.3	9.28	9259.4	9.28	9260.0	9.28	9260.9	9.28	9262.1	9.29	9263.7	9.29
201	9352.1	9.33	9352.3	9.33	9352.8	9.33	9353.7	9.33	9354.9	9.33	9356.6	9.33
202	9445.4	9.37	9445.6	9.38	9446.1	9.38	9447.0	9.38	9448.3	9.38	9449.9	9.38
203	9539.1	9.42	9539.3	9.42	9539.9	9.42	9540.8	9.42	9542.0	9.42	9543.7	9.43
204	9633.3	9.47	9633.5	9.47	9634.1	9.47	9635.0	9.47	9636.3	9.47	9637.9	9.47
205	9728.0	9.51	9728.2	9.51	9728.8	9.51	9729.7	9.52	9731.0	9.52	9732.7	9.52
206	9823.1	9.56	9823.3	9.56	9823.9	9.56	9824.8	9.56	9826.2	9.56	9827.9	9.56
207	9918.7	9.61	9918.9	9.61	9919.5	9.61	9920.5	9.61	9921.8	9.61	9923.5	9.61
208	10014.8	9.65	10015.0	9.65	10015.6	9.65	10016.5	9.65	10017.9	9.66	10019.6	9.66
209	10111.3	9.70	10111.5	9.70	10112.1	9.70	10113.1	9.70	10114.4	9.70	10116.2	9.70
210	10208.3	9.75	10208.5	9.75	10209.1	9.75	10210.1	9.75	10211.5	9.75	10213.2	9.75
211	10305.8	9.79	10306.0	9.79	10306.6	9.79	10307.6	9.79	10308.9	9.79	10310.7	9.80
212	10403.7	9.84	10403.9	9.84	10404.5	9.84	10405.5	9.84	10406.9	9.84	10408.7	9.84
213	10502.1	9.88	10502.3	9.88	10502.9	9.89	10503.9	9.89	10505.3	9.89	10507.1	9.89
214	10600.9	9.93	10601.1	9.93	10601.7	9.93	10602.7	9.93	10604.2	9.93	10606.0	9.94
215	10700.2	9.98	10700.4	9.98	10701.1	9.98	10702.1	9.98	10703.5	9.98	10705.4	9.98
216	10800.0	10.02	10800.2	10.02	10800.8	10.02	10801.9	10.02	10803.3	10.03	10805.2	10.03
217	10900.2	10.07	10900.4	10.07	10901.1	10.07	10902.1	10.07	10903.6	10.07	10905.4	10.07
218	11000.9	10.12	11001.1	10.12	11001.8	10.12	11002.8	10.12	11004.3	10.12	11006.2	10.12
219	11102.1	10.16	11102.3	10.16	11102.9	10.16	11104.0	10.16	11105.5	10.17	11107.4	10.17
220	11203.7	10.21	11203.9	10.21	11204.6	10.21	11205.6	10.21	11207.1	10.21	11209.1	10.21
221	11305.8	10.25	11306.0	10.25	11306.7	10.26	11307.7	10.26	11309.2	10.26	11311.2	10.26
222	11408.3	10.30	11408.6	10.30	11409.2	10.30	11410.3	10.30	11411.8	10.30	11413.8	10.31
223	11511.3	10.35	11511.6	10.35	11512.2	10.35	11513.3	10.35	11514.9	10.35	11516.9	10.35
224	11614.8	10.39	11615.0	10.39	11615.7	10.39	11616.8	10.40	11618.4	10.40	11620.4	10.40
225	11718.7	10.44	11719.0	10.44	11719.7	10.44	11720.8	10.44	11722.3	10.44	11724.4	10.44
226	11823.1	10.49	11823.4	10.49	11824.1	10.49	11825.2	10.49	11826.8	10.49	11828.8	10.49
227	11928.0	10.53	11928.2	10.53	11928.9	10.53	11930.1	10.53	11931.7	10.54	11933.7	10.54
228	12033.3	10.58	12033.6	10.58	12034.3	10.58	12035.4	10.58	12037.0	10.58	12039.1	10.58
229	12139.1	10.62	12139.4	10.63	12140.1	10.63	12141.2	10.63	12142.8	10.63	12144.9	10.63
230	12245.4	10.67	12245.6	10.67	12246.3	10.67	12247.5	10.67	12249.1	10.67	12251.2	10.68
231	12352.1	10.72	12352.3	10.72	12353.0	10.72	12354.2	10.72	12355.9	10.72	12358.0	10.72
232	12459.3	10.76	12459.5	10.76	12460.2	10.76	12461.4	10.77	12463.1	10.77	12465.2	10.77
233	12566.9	10.81	12567.1	10.81	12567.9	10.81	12569.1	10.81	12570.7	10.81	12572.9	10.82
234	12675.0	10.86	12675.2	10.86	12676.0	10.86	12677.2	10.86	12678.9	10.86	12681.1	10.86
235	12783.6	10.90	12783.8	10.90	12784.5	10.90	12785.8	10.90	12787.5	10.91	12789.7	10.91
236	12892.6	10.95	12892.8	10.95	12893.6	10.95	12894.8	10.95	12896.5	10.95	12898.8	10.95
237	13002.1	11.00	13002.3	11.00	13003.1	11.00	13004.3	11.00	13006.1	11.00	13008.3	11.00
238	13112.0	11.04	13112.3	11.04	13113.0	11.04	13114.3	11.04	13116.0	11.05	13118.3	11.05
239	13222.4	11.09	13222.7	11.09	13223.5	11.09	13224.7	11.09	13226.5	11.09	13228.8	11.09
240	13333.3	11.13	13333.6	11.13	13334.4	11.14	13335.6	11.14	13337.4	11.14	13339.7	11.14
SUMS.	0°		1°		2°		3°		4°		5°	

TABLE XI. Whole Sections. Side Slope ¼ to 1.

SUMS.	6°		7°		8°		9°		10°		11°	
121	3391.5	5.63	3392.3	5.63	3393.3	5.63	3394.4	5.63	3395.7	5.64	3397.1	5.64
122	3447.8	5.68	3448.6	5.68	3449.6	5.68	3450.8	5.68	3452.1	5.68	3453.5	5.68
123	3504.5	5.72	3505.4	5.72	3506.4	5.72	3507.6	5.73	3508.9	5.73	3510.4	5.73
124	3561.7	5.77	3562.6	5.77	3563.7	5.77	3564.8	5.77	3566.2	5.78	3567.7	5.78
125	3619.4	5.81	3620.3	5.82	3621.4	5.82	3622.6	5.82	3623.9	5.82	3625.5	5.82
126	3677.6	5.86	3678.5	5.86	3679.5	5.86	3680.8	5.87	3682.2	5.87	3683.7	5.87
127	3736.2	5.91	3737.1	5.91	3738.2	5.91	3739.4	5.91	3740.8	5.91	3742.4	5.92
128	3795.2	5.95	3796.2	5.95	3797.3	5.96	3798.5	5.96	3800.0	5.96	3801.6	5.96
129	3854.8	6.00	3855.7	6.00	3856.8	6.00	3858.1	6.00	3859.6	6.01	3861.2	6.01
130	3914.8	6.05	3915.7	6.05	3916.9	6.05	3918.2	6.05	3919.7	6.05	3921.3	6.06
131	3975.2	6.09	3976.2	6.09	3977.4	6.10	3978.7	6.10	3980.2	6.10	3981.9	6.10
132	4036.1	6.14	4037.1	6.14	4038.3	6.14	4039.7	6.14	4041.2	6.15	4042.9	6.15
133	4097.5	6.18	4098.5	6.19	4099.7	6.19	4101.1	6.19	4102.6	6.19	4104.4	6.20
134	4159.4	6.23	4160.4	6.23	4161.6	6.23	4163.0	6.24	4164.6	6.24	4166.3	6.24
135	4221.7	6.28	4222.7	6.28	4224.0	6.28	4225.4	6.28	4227.0	6.29	4228.7	6.29
136	4284.5	6.32	4285.5	6.33	4286.8	6.33	4288.2	6.33	4289.8	6.33	4291.6	6.33
137	4347.7	6.37	4348.8	6.37	4350.0	6.37	4351.5	6.38	4353.1	6.38	4355.0	6.38
138	4411.4	6.42	4412.5	6.42	4413.8	6.42	4415.3	6.42	4416.9	6.42	4418.8	6.43
139	4475.6	6.46	4476.7	6.46	4478.0	6.47	4479.5	6.47	4481.2	6.47	4483.0	6.47
140	4540.2	6.51	4541.3	6.51	4542.6	6.51	4544.2	6.51	4545.9	6.52	4547.8	6.52
141	4605.3	6.56	4606.4	6.56	4607.8	6.56	4609.3	6.56	4611.0	6.56	4613.0	6.57
142	4670.8	6.60	4672.0	6.60	4673.4	6.61	4674.9	6.61	4676.7	6.61	4678.6	6.61
143	4736.9	6.65	4738.0	6.65	4739.4	6.65	4741.0	6.65	4742.8	6.66	4744.8	6.66
144	4803.3	6.69	4804.5	6.70	4805.9	6.70	4807.5	6.70	4809.3	6.70	4811.4	6.71
145	4870.3	6.74	4871.5	6.74	4872.9	6.74	4874.5	6.75	4876.4	6.75	4878.4	6.75
146	4937.7	6.79	4938.9	6.79	4940.4	6.79	4942.0	6.79	4943.9	6.80	4945.9	6.80
147	5005.6	6.83	5006.8	6.84	5008.3	6.84	5009.9	6.84	5011.8	6.84	5013.9	6.84
148	5073.9	6.88	5075.1	6.88	5076.6	6.88	5078.3	6.89	5080.2	6.89	5082.4	6.89
149	5142.7	6.93	5144.0	6.93	5145.5	6.93	5147.2	6.93	5149.1	6.93	5151.3	6.94
150	5212.0	6.97	5213.2	6.97	5214.8	6.98	5216.5	6.98	5218.5	6.98	5220.7	6.98
151	5281.7	7.02	5283.0	7.02	5284.5	7.02	5286.3	7.02	5288.3	7.03	5290.5	7.03
152	5351.9	7.07	5353.2	7.07	5354.8	7.07	5356.5	7.07	5358.6	7.07	5360.8	7.08
153	5422.5	7.11	5423.9	7.11	5425.5	7.12	5427.3	7.12	5429.3	7.12	5431.6	7.12
154	5493.6	7.16	5495.0	7.16	5496.6	7.16	5498.4	7.16	5500.5	7.17	5502.8	7.17
155	5565.2	7.20	5566.6	7.21	5568.2	7.21	5570.1	7.21	5572.2	7.21	5574.5	7.22
156	5637.3	7.25	5638.6	7.25	5640.3	7.25	5642.2	7.26	5644.3	7.26	5646.7	7.26
157	5709.8	7.30	5711.2	7.30	5712.8	7.30	5714.7	7.30	5716.9	7.31	5719.3	7.31
158	5782.7	7.34	5784.1	7.34	5785.8	7.35	5787.8	7.35	5790.0	7.35	5792.4	7.36
159	5856.2	7.39	5857.6	7.39	5859.3	7.39	5861.3	7.40	5863.5	7.40	5865.9	7.40
160	5930.1	7.44	5931.5	7.44	5933.3	7.44	5935.2	7.44	5937.5	7.45	5940.0	7.45
161	6004.4	7.48	6005.9	7.48	6007.7	7.49	6009.7	7.49	6011.9	7.49	6014.4	7.49
162	6079.2	7.53	6080.7	7.53	6082.5	7.53	6084.5	7.53	6086.8	7.54	6089.4	7.54
163	6154.5	7.57	6156.0	7.58	6157.8	7.58	6159.9	7.58	6162.2	7.58	6164.8	7.59
164	6230.3	7.62	6231.8	7.62	6233.6	7.63	6235.7	7.63	6238.0	7.63	6240.7	7.63
165	6306.5	7.67	6308.0	7.67	6309.9	7.67	6312.0	7.67	6314.4	7.68	6317.0	7.68
166	6383.2	7.71	6384.7	7.72	6386.6	7.72	6388.7	7.72	6391.1	7.72	6393.8	7.73
167	6460.3	7.76	6461.9	7.76	6463.8	7.76	6465.9	7.77	6468.4	7.77	6471.1	7.77
168	6537.9	7.81	6539.5	7.81	6541.4	7.81	6543.6	7.81	6546.1	7.82	6548.8	7.82
169	6616.0	7.85	6617.6	7.85	6619.5	7.86	6621.7	7.86	6624.2	7.86	6627.0	7.87
170	6694.5	7.90	6696.1	7.90	6698.1	7.90	6700.3	7.91	6702.8	7.91	6705.7	7.91
171	6773.5	7.95	6775.1	7.95	6777.1	7.95	6779.4	7.95	6781.9	7.96	6784.8	7.96
172	6852.9	7.99	6854.6	7.99	6856.6	8.00	6858.9	8.00	6861.5	8.00	6864.4	8.01
173	6932.8	8.04	6934.5	8.04	6936.6	8.04	6938.9	8.05	6941.5	8.05	6944.4	8.05
174	7013.2	8.08	7014.9	8.09	7017.0	8.09	7019.3	8.09	7022.0	8.09	7024.9	8.10
175	7094.1	8.13	7095.8	8.13	7097.9	8.14	7100.3	8.14	7102.9	8.14	7105.9	8.14
176	7175.4	8.18	7177.1	8.18	7179.2	8.18	7181.6	8.18	7184.3	8.19	7187.3	8.19
177	7257.1	8.22	7258.9	8.23	7261.1	8.23	7263.5	8.23	7266.2	8.23	7269.3	8.24
178	7339.4	8.27	7341.2	8.27	7343.3	8.27	7345.8	8.28	7348.5	8.28	7351.6	8.28
179	7422.1	8.32	7423.9	8.32	7426.1	8.32	7428.5	8.32	7431.3	8.33	7434.5	8.33
180	7505.2	8.36	7507.1	8.36	7509.3	8.37	7511.8	8.37	7514.6	8.37	7517.8	8.38
SUMS.	6°		7°		8°		9°		10°		11°	

TABLE XI. Whole Sections. Side Slope ¼ to 1.

SUMS.	6°		7°		8°		9°		10°		11°	
181	7588.9	8.41	7590.7	8.41	7592.9	8.41	7595.5	8.42	7598.3	8.42	7601.5	8.42
182	7672.9	8.45	7674.8	8.46	7677.1	8.46	7679.6	8.46	7682.5	8.47	7685.7	8.47
183	7757.5	8.50	7759.4	8.50	7761.7	8.51	7764.3	8.51	7767.2	8.51	7770.4	8.52
184	7842.5	8.55	7844.4	8.55	7846.7	8.55	7849.3	8.56	7852.3	8.56	7855.6	8.56
185	7928.0	8.59	7929.9	8.60	7932.2	8.60	7934.9	8.60	7937.9	8.60	7941.2	8.61
186	8013.9	8.64	8015.9	8.64	8018.2	8.64	8020.9	8.65	8023.9	8.65	8027.3	8.65
187	8100.3	8.69	8102.3	8.69	8104.7	8.69	8107.4	8.69	8110.4	8.70	8113.8	8.70
188	8187.2	8.73	8189.2	8.74	8191.6	8.74	8194.3	8.74	8197.4	8.74	8200.9	8.75
189	8274.5	8.78	8276.5	8.78	8279.0	8.78	8281.7	8.79	8284.9	8.79	8288.3	8.79
190	8362.3	8.83	8364.4	8.83	8366.8	8.83	8369.6	8.83	8372.8	8.84	8376.3	8.84
191	8450.6	8.87	8452.6	8.87	8455.1	8.88	8457.9	8.88	8461.1	8.88	8464.7	8.89
192	8539.3	8.92	8541.4	8.92	8543.9	8.92	8546.7	8.93	8549.9	8.93	8553.5	8.93
193	8628.5	8.96	8630.6	8.97	8633.1	8.97	8636.0	8.97	8639.2	8.98	8642.9	8.98
194	8718.1	9.01	8720.2	9.01	8722.8	9.02	8725.7	9.02	8729.0	9.02	8732.7	9.03
195	8808.2	9.06	8810.4	9.06	8813.0	9.06	8815.9	9.07	8819.2	9.07	8822.9	9.07
196	8898.8	9.10	8901.0	9.11	8903.6	9.11	8906.6	9.11	8909.9	9.11	8913.6	9.12
197	8989.8	9.15	8992.0	9.15	8994.7	9.15	8997.7	9.16	9001.1	9.16	9004.8	9.17
198	9081.3	9.20	9083.6	9.20	9086.2	9.20	9089.2	9.20	9092.7	9.21	9096.5	9.21
199	9173.3	9.24	9175.5	9.24	9178.2	9.25	9181.3	9.25	9184.7	9.25	9188.6	9.26
200	9265.7	9.29	9268.0	9.29	9270.7	9.29	9273.8	9.30	9277.3	9.30	9281.2	9.30
201	9358.6	9.34	9360.9	9.34	9363.6	9.34	9366.8	9.34	9370.3	9.35	9374.2	9.35
202	9452.0	9.38	9454.3	9.38	9457.0	9.39	9460.2	9.39	9463.8	9.39	9467.7	9.40
203	9545.8	9.43	9548.1	9.43	9550.9	9.43	9554.1	9.44	9557.7	9.44	9561.7	9.44
204	9640.1	9.47	9642.4	9.48	9645.2	9.48	9648.5	9.48	9652.1	9.49	9656.1	9.49
205	9734.8	9.52	9737.2	9.52	9740.0	9.53	9743.3	9.53	9747.0	9.53	9751.0	9.54
206	9830.0	9.57	9832.4	9.57	9835.3	9.57	9838.6	9.58	9842.3	9.58	9846.4	9.58
207	9925.7	9.61	9928.1	9.62	9931.0	9.62	9934.3	9.62	9938.1	9.63	9942.2	9.63
208	10021.8	9.66	10024.3	9.66	10027.2	9.66	10030.5	9.67	10034.3	9.67	10038.5	9.68
209	10118.4	9.71	10120.9	9.71	10123.8	9.71	10127.2	9.71	10131.0	9.72	10135.3	9.72
210	10215.5	9.75	10218.0	9.75	10221.0	9.76	10224.4	9.76	10228.2	9.76	10232.5	9.77
211	10313.0	9.80	10315.5	9.80	10318.5	9.80	10322.0	9.81	10325.9	9.81	10330.2	9.81
212	10411.0	9.84	10413.5	9.85	10416.6	9.85	10420.0	9.85	10424.0	9.86	10428.3	9.86
213	10509.4	9.89	10512.0	9.89	10515.1	9.90	10518.6	9.90	10522.5	9.90	10527.0	9.91
214	10608.3	9.94	10610.9	9.94	10614.0	9.94	10617.6	9.95	10621.6	9.95	10626.0	9.95
215	10707.7	9.98	10710.3	9.99	10713.5	9.99	10717.0	9.99	10721.1	10.00	10725.6	10.00
216	10807.5	10.03	10810.2	10.03	10813.4	10.04	10817.0	10.04	10821.0	10.04	10825.6	10.05
217	10907.8	10.08	10910.5	10.08	10913.7	10.08	10917.3	10.09	10921.5	10.09	10926.0	10.09
218	11008.6	10.12	11011.3	10.13	11014.5	10.13	11018.2	10.13	11022.3	10.14	11027.0	10.14
219	11109.8	10.17	11112.5	10.17	11115.8	10.17	11119.5	10.18	11123.7	10.18	11128.4	10.19
220	11211.5	10.22	11214.3	10.22	11217.6	10.22	11221.3	10.22	11225.5	10.23	11230.2	10.23
221	11313.7	10.26	11316.4	10.26	11319.8	10.27	11323.5	10.27	11327.8	10.27	11332.6	10.28
222	11416.3	10.31	11419.1	10.31	11422.4	10.31	11426.2	10.32	11430.5	10.32	11435.3	10.33
223	11519.4	10.35	11522.2	10.36	11525.6	10.36	11529.4	10.36	11533.8	10.37	11538.6	10.37
224	11622.9	10.40	11625.8	10.40	11629.2	10.41	11633.0	10.41	11637.4	10.41	11642.3	10.42
225	11726.9	10.45	11729.8	10.45	11733.2	10.45	11737.1	10.46	11741.6	10.46	11746.5	10.46
226	11831.4	10.49	11834.3	10.50	11837.8	10.50	11841.7	10.50	11846.2	10.51	11851.1	10.51
227	11936.3	10.54	11939.2	10.54	11942.8	10.55	11946.7	10.55	11951.2	10.55	11956.3	10.56
228	12041.7	10.59	12044.7	10.59	12048.2	10.59	12052.2	10.60	12056.8	10.60	12061.8	10.60
229	12147.6	10.63	12150.6	10.64	12154.1	10.64	12158.2	10.64	12162.8	10.65	12167.9	10.65
230	12253.9	10.68	12256.9	10.68	12260.5	10.68	12264.6	10.69	12269.2	10.69	12274.4	10.70
231	12360.7	10.73	12363.7	10.73	12367.4	10.73	12371.5	10.73	12376.1	10.74	12381.3	10.74
232	12468.0	10.77	12471.0	10.77	12474.7	10.78	12478.8	10.78	12483.5	10.78	12488.8	10.79
233	12575.7	10.82	12578.7	10.82	12582.4	10.82	12586.6	10.83	12591.4	10.83	12596.7	10.84
234	12683.8	10.86	12686.9	10.87	12690.7	10.87	12694.9	10.87	12699.7	10.88	12705.0	10.88
235	12792.5	10.91	12795.6	10.91	12799.4	10.92	12803.6	10.92	12808.5	10.92	12813.8	10.93
236	12901.6	10.96	12904.7	10.96	12908.5	10.96	12912.8	10.97	12917.7	10.97	12923.1	10.98
237	13011.2	11.00	13014.3	11.01	13018.2	11.01	13022.5	11.01	13027.4	11.02	13032.9	11.02
238	13121.2	11.05	13124.4	11.05	13128.2	11.06	13132.6	11.06	13137.6	11.06	13143.1	11.07
239	13231.7	11.10	13234.9	11.10	13238.8	11.10	13243.2	11.11	13248.2	11.11	13253.8	11.11
240	13342.6	11.14	13345.9	11.14	13349.8	11.15	13354.3	11.15	13359.3	11.16	13364.9	11.16
SUMS.	6°		7°		8°		9°		10°		11°	

TABLE XI. Whole Sections. Side Slope $\frac{1}{4}$ to 1.

SUMS.	12°		13°		14°		15°		16°		17°	
121	3398.7	5.64	3400.4	5.64	3402.3	5.65	3404.4	5.65	3406.6	5.65	3409.0	5.66
122	3455.1	5.69	3456.9	5.69	3458.8	5.69	3460.9	5.70	3463.2	5.70	3465.6	5.70
123	3512.0	5.73	3513.8	5.74	3515.7	5.74	3517.9	5.74	3520.2	5.75	3522.7	5.75
124	3569.3	5.78	3571.2	5.78	3573.1	5.79	3575.3	5.79	3577.6	5.79	3580.2	5.80
125	3627.1	5.83	3629.0	5.83	3631.0	5.83	3633.2	5.84	3635.6	5.84	3638.2	5.84
126	3685.4	5.87	3687.3	5.88	3689.3	5.88	3691.6	5.88	3694.0	5.89	3696.6	5.89
127	3744.1	5.92	3746.0	5.92	3748.1	5.93	3750.4	5.93	3752.9	5.93	3755.5	5.94
128	3803.3	5.97	3805.3	5.97	3807.4	5.97	3809.7	5.98	3812.2	5.98	3814.9	5.98
129	3863.0	6.01	3865.0	6.02	3867.1	6.02	3869.4	6.02	3872.0	6.03	3874.7	6.03
130	3923.1	6.06	3925.1	6.06	3927.3	6.07	3929.7	6.07	3932.2	6.07	3935.0	6.08
131	3983.7	6.11	3985.7	6.11	3987.9	6.11	3990.4	6.12	3993.0	6.12	3995.8	6.12
132	4044.8	6.15	4046.8	6.15	4049.1	6.16	4051.5	6.16	4054.2	6.17	4057.0	6.17
133	4106.3	6.20	4108.4	6.20	4110.6	6.20	4113.1	6.21	4115.8	6.21	4118.7	6.22
134	4168.3	6.24	4170.4	6.25	4172.7	6.25	4175.2	6.25	4178.0	6.26	4180.9	6.26
135	4230.7	6.29	4232.9	6.29	4235.2	6.30	4237.8	6.30	4240.5	6.31	4243.5	6.31
136	4293.6	6.34	4295.8	6.34	4298.2	6.34	4300.8	6.35	4303.6	6.35	4306.6	6.36
137	4357.0	6.38	4359.2	6.39	4361.6	6.39	4364.3	6.39	4367.1	6.40	4370.2	6.40
138	4420.8	6.43	4423.1	6.43	4425.5	6.44	4428.2	6.44	4431.1	6.45	4434.2	6.45
139	4485.1	6.48	4487.4	6.48	4489.9	6.48	4492.6	6.49	4495.6	6.49	4498.7	6.50
140	4549.9	6.52	4552.2	6.53	4554.7	6.53	4557.5	6.53	4560.5	6.54	4563.7	6.54
141	4615.1	6.57	4617.5	6.57	4620.0	6.58	4622.8	6.58	4625.9	6.58	4629.1	6.59
142	4680.8	6.62	4683.2	6.62	4685.8	6.62	4688.6	6.63	4691.7	6.63	4695.0	6.64
143	4747.0	6.66	4749.4	6.67	4752.0	6.67	4754.9	6.67	4758.0	6.68	4761.4	6.68
144	4813.6	6.71	4816.0	6.71	4818.7	6.72	4821.6	6.72	4824.8	6.72	4828.2	6.73
145	4880.7	6.76	4883.2	6.76	4885.9	6.76	4888.8	6.77	4892.0	6.77	4895.5	6.78
146	4948.2	6.80	4950.8	6.81	4953.5	6.81	4956.5	6.81	4959.7	6.82	4963.3	6.82
147	5016.2	6.85	5018.8	6.85	5021.6	6.86	5024.6	6.86	5027.9	6.86	5031.5	6.87
148	5084.7	6.89	5087.3	6.90	5090.1	6.90	5093.2	6.91	5096.6	6.91	5100.2	6.92
149	5153.7	6.94	5156.3	6.94	5159.2	6.95	5162.3	6.95	5165.7	6.96	5169.3	6.96
150	5223.1	6.99	5225.7	6.99	5228.6	6.99	5231.8	7.00	5235.2	7.00	5238.9	7.01
151	5293.0	7.03	5295.7	7.04	5298.6	7.04	5301.8	7.05	5305.3	7.05	5309.0	7.06
152	5363.3	7.08	5366.0	7.08	5369.0	7.09	5372.3	7.09	5375.8	7.10	5379.6	7.10
153	5434.1	7.13	5436.9	7.13	5439.9	7.13	5443.2	7.14	5446.7	7.14	5450.6	7.15
154	5505.4	7.17	5508.2	7.18	5511.2	7.18	5514.6	7.19	5518.2	7.19	5522.1	7.19
155	5577.1	7.22	5579.9	7.22	5583.0	7.23	5586.4	7.23	5590.1	7.24	5594.0	7.24
156	5649.3	7.27	5652.2	7.27	5655.3	7.27	5658.7	7.28	5662.4	7.28	5666.4	7.29
157	5721.9	7.31	5724.9	7.32	5728.0	7.32	5731.5	7.32	5735.3	7.33	5739.3	7.33
158	5795.1	7.36	5798.0	7.36	5801.2	7.37	5804.8	7.37	5808.6	7.38	5812.7	7.38
159	5868.7	7.41	5871.6	7.41	5874.9	7.41	5878.5	7.42	5882.3	7.42	5886.5	7.43
160	5942.7	7.45	5945.7	7.46	5949.0	7.46	5952.6	7.46	5956.5	7.47	5960.8	7.47
161	6017.2	7.50	6020.3	7.50	6023.6	7.51	6027.3	7.51	6031.2	7.52	6035.5	7.52
162	6092.2	7.54	6095.3	7.55	6098.7	7.55	6102.4	7.56	6106.4	7.56	6110.7	7.57
163	6167.6	7.59	6170.8	7.59	6174.2	7.60	6178.0	7.60	6182.0	7.61	6186.4	7.61
164	6243.6	7.64	6246.7	7.64	6250.2	7.65	6254.0	7.65	6258.1	7.66	6262.5	7.66
165	6319.9	7.68	6323.1	7.69	6326.7	7.69	6330.5	7.70	6334.6	7.70	6339.1	7.71
166	6396.8	7.73	6400.0	7.73	6403.6	7.74	6407.5	7.74	6411.7	7.75	6416.2	7.75
167	6474.1	7.78	6477.4	7.78	6481.0	7.78	6484.9	7.79	6489.1	7.79	6493.7	7.80
168	6551.8	7.82	6555.2	7.83	6558.8	7.83	6562.8	7.84	6567.1	7.84	6571.7	7.85
169	6630.1	7.87	6633.4	7.87	6637.1	7.88	6641.1	7.88	6645.5	7.89	6650.2	7.89
170	6708.8	7.92	6712.2	7.92	6715.9	7.92	6720.0	7.93	6724.4	7.93	6729.1	7.94
171	6787.9	7.96	6791.4	7.97	6795.1	7.97	6799.3	7.98	6803.7	7.98	6808.5	7.99
172	6867.5	8.01	6871.0	8.01	6874.9	8.02	6879.0	8.02	6883.5	8.03	6888.4	8.03
173	6947.6	8.06	6951.2	8.06	6955.0	8.06	6959.2	8.07	6963.8	8.07	6968.7	8.08
174	7028.2	8.10	7031.8	8.11	7035.7	8.11	7039.9	8.12	7044.5	8.12	7049.5	8.13
175	7109.2	8.15	7112.8	8.15	7116.8	8.16	7121.1	8.16	7125.7	8.17	7130.8	8.17
176	7190.7	8.19	7194.3	8.20	7198.3	8.20	7202.7	8.21	7207.4	8.21	7212.5	8.22
177	7272.6	8.24	7276.3	8.25	7280.4	8.25	7284.8	8.25	7289.5	8.26	7294.7	8.27
178	7355.0	8.29	7358.8	8.29	7362.9	8.30	7367.3	8.30	7372.1	8.31	7377.4	8.31
179	7437.9	8.33	7441.7	8.34	7445.8	8.34	7450.3	8.35	7455.2	8.35	7460.5	8.36
180	7521.2	8.38	7525.1	8.38	7529.3	8.39	7533.8	8.39	7538.7	8.40	7544.1	8.41
SUMS.	12°		13°		14°		15°		16°		17°	

TABLE XI. **Whole Sections.** **Side Slope ¼ to 1.**

SUMS.	12°		13°		14°		15°		16°		17°	
181	7605.0	8.43	7608.9	8.43	7613.1	8.44	7617.8	8.44	7622.7	8.45	7628.1	8.45
182	7689.3	8.47	7693.2	8.48	7697.5	8.48	7702.2	8.49	7707.2	8.49	7712.7	8.50
183	7774.0	8.52	7778.0	8.52	7782.3	8.53	7787.0	8.53	7792.1	8.54	7797.6	8.55
184	7859.2	8.57	7863.2	8.57	7867.6	8.57	7872.4	8.58	7877.5	8.59	7883.1	8.59
185	7944.9	8.61	7948.9	8.62	7953.4	8.62	7958.2	8.63	7963.4	8.63	7969.0	8.64
186	8031.0	8.66	8035.1	8.66	8039.6	8.67	8044.4	8.67	8049.7	8.68	8055.4	8.68
187	8117.6	8.71	8121.7	8.71	8126.2	8.71	8131.2	8.72	8136.5	8.73	8142.2	8.73
188	8204.7	8.75	8208.8	8.76	8213.4	8.76	8218.4	8.77	8223.7	8.77	8229.6	8.78
189	8292.2	8.80	8296.4	8.80	8301.0	8.81	8306.0	8.81	8311.5	8.82	8317.3	8.82
190	8380.1	8.84	8384.4	8.85	8389.1	8.85	8394.2	8.86	8399.6	8.87	8405.6	8.87
191	8468.6	8.89	8472.9	8.90	8477.6	8.90	8482.7	8.91	8488.3	8.91	8494.3	8.92
192	8557.5	8.94	8561.9	8.94	8566.6	8.95	8571.8	8.95	8577.4	8.96	8583.5	8.96
193	8646.9	8.98	8651.3	8.99	8656.1	8.99	8661.3	9.00	8667.0	9.00	8673.1	9.01
194	8736.7	9.03	8741.2	9.03	8746.0	9.04	8751.3	9.05	8757.0	9.05	8763.2	9.06
195	8827.0	9.08	8831.5	9.08	8836.4	9.09	8841.8	9.09	8847.6	9.10	8853.8	9.10
196	8917.8	9.12	8922.3	9.13	8927.3	9.13	8932.7	9.14	8938.5	9.14	8944.9	9.15
197	9009.0	9.17	9013.6	9.17	9018.6	9.18	9024.1	9.18	9030.0	9.19	9036.4	9.20
198	9100.7	9.22	9105.3	9.22	9110.4	9.23	9115.9	9.23	9121.9	9.24	9128.3	9.24
199	9192.9	9.26	9197.5	9.27	9202.7	9.27	9208.2	9.28	9214.2	9.28	9220.8	9.29
200	9285.5	9.31	9290.2	9.31	9295.4	9.32	9301.0	9.32	9307.1	9.33	9313.7	9.34
201	9378.6	9.36	9383.3	9.36	9388.6	9.37	9394.2	9.37	9400.4	9.38	9407.0	9.38
202	9472.1	9.40	9476.9	9.41	9482.2	9.41	9488.0	9.42	9494.2	9.42	9500.9	9.43
203	9566.1	9.45	9571.0	9.45	9576.3	9.46	9582.1	9.46	9588.4	9.47	9595.2	9.48
204	9660.6	9.49	9665.5	9.50	9670.9	9.50	9676.8	9.51	9683.1	9.52	9689.9	9.52
205	9755.6	9.54	9760.5	9.55	9766.0	9.55	9771.9	9.56	9778.3	9.56	9785.2	9.57
206	9851.0	9.59	9856.0	9.59	9861.5	9.60	9867.4	9.60	9873.9	9.61	9880.9	9.62
207	9946.8	9.63	9951.9	9.64	9957.4	9.64	9963.5	9.65	9970.0	9.66	9977.0	9.66
208	10043.2	9.68	10048.3	9.69	10053.9	9.69	10060.0	9.70	10066.5	9.70	10073.7	9.71
209	10140.0	9.73	10145.1	9.73	10150.8	9.74	10156.9	9.74	10163.6	9.75	10170.8	9.76
210	10237.2	9.77	10242.5	9.78	10248.1	9.78	10254.4	9.79	10261.1	9.80	10268.3	9.80
211	10335.0	9.82	10340.2	9.82	10346.0	9.83	10352.2	9.84	10359.0	9.84	10366.3	9.85
212	10433.2	9.87	10438.5	9.87	10444.3	9.88	10450.6	9.88	10457.4	9.89	10464.8	9.90
213	10531.8	9.91	10537.2	9.92	10543.0	9.92	10549.4	9.93	10556.3	9.94	10563.8	9.94
214	10630.9	9.96	10636.4	9.96	10642.3	9.97	10648.7	9.98	10655.7	9.98	10663.2	9.99
215	10730.5	10.01	10736.0	10.01	10742.0	10.02	10748.5	10.02	10755.5	10.03	10763.1	10.04
216	10830.6	10.05	10836.1	10.06	10842.1	10.06	10848.7	10.07	10855.8	10.07	10863.5	10.08
217	10931.1	10.10	10936.7	10.10	10942.7	10.11	10949.4	10.11	10956.5	10.12	10964.3	10.13
218	11032.1	10.14	11037.7	10.15	11043.8	10.16	11050.5	10.16	11057.8	10.17	11065.6	10.18
219	11133.5	10.19	11139.2	10.20	11145.4	10.20	11152.1	10.21	11159.4	10.21	11167.3	10.22
220	11235.4	10.24	11241.2	10.24	11247.4	10.25	11254.2	10.25	11261.6	10.26	11269.5	10.27
221	11337.8	10.28	11343.6	10.29	11349.9	10.29	11356.8	10.30	11364.2	10.31	11372.2	10.31
222	11440.6	10.33	11446.5	10.34	11452.8	10.34	11459.8	10.35	11467.3	10.35	11475.4	10.36
223	11543.9	10.38	11549.8	10.38	11556.2	10.39	11563.2	10.39	11570.8	10.40	11579.0	10.41
224	11647.7	10.42	11653.6	10.43	11660.1	10.43	11667.2	10.44	11674.8	10.45	11683.1	10.45
225	11751.9	10.47	11757.9	10.47	11764.5	10.48	11771.6	10.49	11779.3	10.49	11787.6	10.50
226	11856.6	10.52	11862.7	10.52	11869.3	10.53	11876.4	10.53	11884.2	10.54	11892.6	10.55
227	11961.8	10.56	11967.9	10.57	11974.5	10.57	11981.8	10.58	11989.6	10.59	11998.1	10.59
228	12067.4	10.61	12073.6	10.61	12080.3	10.62	12087.6	10.63	12095.5	10.63	12104.0	10.64
229	12173.5	10.66	12179.7	10.66	12186.5	10.67	12193.8	10.67	12201.8	10.68	12210.5	10.69
230	12280.0	10.70	12286.3	10.71	12293.1	10.71	12300.6	10.72	12308.6	10.73	12317.3	10.73
231	12387.1	10.75	12393.4	10.75	12400.3	10.76	12407.8	10.77	12415.9	10.77	12424.7	10.78
232	12494.5	10.79	12500.9	10.80	12507.9	10.81	12515.4	10.81	12523.6	10.82	12532.5	10.83
233	12602.5	10.84	12608.9	10.85	12615.9	10.85	12623.5	10.86	12631.8	10.87	12640.7	10.87
234	12710.9	10.89	12717.4	10.89	12724.4	10.90	12732.1	10.91	12740.5	10.91	12749.5	10.92
235	12819.8	10.93	12826.3	10.94	12833.4	10.95	12841.2	10.95	12849.6	10.96	12858.7	10.97
236	12929.1	10.98	12935.7	10.99	12942.9	10.99	12950.7	11.00	12959.2	11.01	12968.4	11.01
237	13038.9	11.03	13045.5	11.03	13052.8	11.04	13060.7	11.04	13069.2	11.05	13078.5	11.06
238	13149.2	11.07	13155.9	11.08	13163.2	11.08	13171.1	11.09	13179.8	11.10	13189.1	11.11
239	13259.9	11.12	13266.6	11.13	13274.0	11.13	13282.1	11.14	13290.8	11.15	13300.2	11.15
240	13371.1	11.17	13377.9	11.17	13385.3	11.18	13393.4	11.18	13402.2	11.19	13411.7	11.20
SUMS.	12°		13°		14°		15°		16°		17°	

SUMS.	18°		19°		20°		21°		22°		23°	
121	3411.6	5.66	3414.4	5.67	3417.4	5.67	3420.6	5.68	3424.1	5.68	3427.7	5.69
122	3468.3	5.71	3471.1	5.71	3474.1	5.72	3477.4	5.72	3480.9	5.73	3484.6	5.74
123	3525.3	5.76	3528.2	5.76	3531.3	5.77	3534.6	5.77	3538.2	5.78	3541.9	5.78
124	3582.9	5.80	3585.8	5.81	3589.0	5.81	3592.3	5.82	3595.9	5.82	3599.8	5.83
125	3640.9	5.85	3643.9	5.85	3647.1	5.86	3650.5	5.86	3654.2	5.87	3658.1	5.88
126	3699.4	5.90	3702.4	5.90	3705.7	5.91	3709.2	5.91	3712.9	5.92	3716.8	5.92
127	3758.4	5.94	3761.4	5.95	3764.7	5.95	3768.3	5.96	3772.1	5.96	3776.1	5.97
128	3817.8	5.99	3820.9	5.99	3824.3	6.00	3827.8	6.00	3831.7	6.01	3835.8	6.02
129	3877.7	6.04	3880.8	6.04	3884.2	6.05	3887.9	6.05	3891.8	6.06	3895.9	6.06
130	3938.0	6.08	3941.2	6.09	3944.7	6.09	3948.4	6.10	3952.4	6.10	3956.6	6.11
131	3998.8	6.13	4002.1	6.13	4005.6	6.14	4009.4	6.14	4013.4	6.15	4017.7	6.16
132	4060.1	6.18	4063.4	6.18	4067.0	6.19	4070.8	6.19	4074.9	6.20	4079.2	6.20
133	4121.9	6.22	4125.2	6.23	4128.9	6.23	4132.7	6.24	4136.9	6.24	4141.3	6.25
134	4184.1	6.27	4187.5	6.27	4191.2	6.28	4195.1	6.28	4199.3	6.29	4203.8	6.30
135	4246.8	6.31	4250.2	6.32	4254.0	6.33	4258.0	6.33	4262.2	6.34	4266.8	6.34
136	4309.9	6.36	4313.4	6.37	4317.2	6.37	4321.3	6.38	4325.6	6.38	4330.2	6.39
137	4373.5	6.41	4377.1	6.41	4381.0	6.42	4385.1	6.42	4389.5	6.43	4394.1	6.44
138	4437.6	6.45	4441.2	6.46	4445.1	6.47	4449.3	6.47	4453.8	6.48	4458.5	6.49
139	4502.2	6.50	4505.8	6.51	4509.8	6.51	4514.0	6.52	4518.6	6.52	4523.4	6.53
140	4567.2	6.55	4570.9	6.55	4574.9	6.56	4579.2	6.57	4583.8	6.57	4588.7	6.58
141	4632.7	6.59	4636.4	6.60	4640.5	6.61	4644.9	6.61	4649.5	6.62	4654.5	6.63
142	4698.6	6.64	4702.4	6.65	4706.6	6.65	4711.0	6.66	4715.7	6.67	4720.7	6.67
143	4765.0	6.69	4768.9	6.69	4773.1	6.70	4777.6	6.71	4782.4	6.71	4787.4	6.72
144	4831.9	6.73	4835.8	6.74	4840.1	6.75	4844.6	6.75	4849.5	6.76	4854.6	6.77
145	4899.2	6.78	4903.2	6.79	4907.5	6.79	4912.1	6.80	4917.1	6.81	4922.3	6.81
146	4967.0	6.83	4971.1	6.83	4975.5	6.84	4980.1	6.85	4985.1	6.85	4990.4	6.86
147	5035.3	6.87	5039.4	6.88	5043.8	6.89	5048.6	6.89	5053.6	6.90	5059.0	6.91
148	5104.1	6.92	5108.2	6.93	5112.7	6.93	5117.5	6.94	5122.6	6.95	5128.1	6.95
149	5173.3	6.97	5177.5	6.97	5182.0	6.98	5186.9	6.99	5192.1	6.99	5197.6	7.00
150	5242.9	7.01	5247.2	7.02	5251.8	7.03	5256.7	7.03	5262.0	7.04	5267.6	7.05
151	5313.1	7.06	5317.4	7.07	5322.1	7.07	5327.1	7.08	5332.4	7.09	5338.1	7.09
152	5383.7	7.11	5388.1	7.11	5392.8	7.12	5397.9	7.13	5403.3	7.13	5409.0	7.14
153	5454.7	7.15	5459.2	7.16	5464.0	7.17	5469.1	7.17	5474.6	7.18	5480.4	7.19
154	5526.3	7.20	5530.8	7.21	5535.7	7.21	5540.8	7.22	5546.4	7.23	5552.3	7.23
155	5598.3	7.25	5602.9	7.25	5607.8	7.26	5613.0	7.27	5618.7	7.27	5624.6	7.28
156	5670.8	7.29	5675.4	7.30	5680.4	7.31	5685.7	7.31	5691.4	7.32	5697.4	7.33
157	5743.7	7.34	5748.4	7.35	5753.4	7.35	5758.8	7.36	5764.6	7.37	5770.7	7.37
158	5817.1	7.39	5821.8	7.39	5827.0	7.40	5832.4	7.41	5838.3	7.41	5844.5	7.42
159	5891.0	7.43	5895.8	7.44	5900.9	7.45	5906.5	7.45	5912.4	7.46	5918.7	7.47
160	5965.3	7.48	5970.2	7.49	5975.4	7.49	5981.0	7.50	5987.0	7.51	5993.4	7.52
161	6040.1	7.53	6045.0	7.53	6050.3	7.54	6056.0	7.55	6062.1	7.55	6068.5	7.56
162	6115.4	7.57	6120.4	7.58	6125.7	7.59	6131.5	7.59	6137.6	7.60	6144.1	7.61
163	6191.1	7.62	6196.1	7.63	6201.6	7.63	6207.4	7.64	6213.6	7.65	6220.2	7.66
164	6267.3	7.67	6272.4	7.67	6277.9	7.68	6283.8	7.69	6290.1	7.69	6296.8	7.70
165	6344.0	7.71	6349.1	7.72	6354.7	7.73	6360.7	7.73	6367.0	7.74	6373.8	7.75
166	6421.1	7.76	6426.3	7.77	6432.0	7.77	6438.0	7.78	6444.5	7.79	6451.3	7.80
167	6498.7	7.81	6504.0	7.81	6509.7	7.82	6515.8	7.83	6522.3	7.83	6529.3	7.84
168	6576.7	7.85	6582.1	7.86	6587.9	7.87	6594.1	7.87	6600.7	7.88	6607.7	7.89
169	6655.3	7.90	6660.7	7.91	6666.5	7.91	6672.8	7.92	6679.5	7.93	6686.6	7.94
170	6734.3	7.95	6739.8	7.95	6745.7	7.96	6752.0	7.97	6758.8	7.97	6765.9	7.98
171	6813.7	7.99	6819.3	8.00	6825.3	8.01	6831.7	8.01	6838.5	8.02	6845.8	8.03
172	6893.6	8.04	6899.3	8.05	6905.3	8.05	6911.3	8.06	6918.7	8.07	6926.1	8.08
173	6974.0	8.09	6979.7	8.09	6985.9	8.10	6992.4	8.11	6999.4	8.12	7006.9	8.12
174	7054.9	8.13	7060.7	8.14	7066.8	8.15	7073.5	8.15	7080.6	8.16	7088.1	8.17
175	7136.2	8.18	7142.0	8.19	7148.3	8.19	7155.0	8.20	7162.2	8.21	7169.8	8.22
176	7218.0	8.23	7223.9	8.23	7230.2	8.24	7237.0	8.25	7244.3	8.26	7252.0	8.26
177	7300.3	8.27	7306.2	8.28	7312.6	8.29	7319.5	8.29	7326.8	8.30	7334.6	8.31
178	7383.0	8.32	7389.0	8.33	7395.5	8.33	7402.4	8.34	7409.9	8.35	7417.7	8.36
179	7466.2	8.37	7472.3	8.37	7478.8	8.38	7485.8	8.39	7493.4	8.40	7501.3	8.40
180	7549.8	8.41	7556.0	8.42	7562.6	8.43	7569.7	8.43	7577.3	8.44	7585.4	8.45
SUMS.	18°		19°		20°		21°		22°		23°	

SUMS.	18°		19°		20°		21°		22°		23°	
181	7633.9	8.46	7640.2	8.47	7646.9	8.47	7654.1	8.48	7661.7	8.49	7669.9	8.50
182	7718.5	8.51	7724.8	8.51	7731.6	8.52	7738.9	8.53	7746.6	8.54	7754.9	8.55
183	7803.6	8.55	7810.0	8.56	7816.8	8.57	7824.1	8.57	7832.0	8.58	7840.3	8.59
184	7889.1	8.60	7895.5	8.61	7902.5	8.61	7909.9	8.62	7917.8	8.63	7926.2	8.64
185	7975.1	8.65	7981.6	8.65	7988.6	8.66	7996.1	8.67	8004.1	8.68	8012.6	8.69
186	8061.5	8.69	8068.1	8.70	8075.2	8.71	8082.8	8.71	8090.9	8.72	8099.5	8.73
187	8148.5	8.74	8155.1	8.75	8162.3	8.75	8169.9	8.76	8178.1	8.77	8186.8	8.78
188	8235.8	8.78	8242.6	8.79	8249.8	8.80	8257.5	8.81	8265.8	8.82	8274.6	8.83
189	8323.7	8.83	8330.5	8.84	8337.8	8.85	8345.6	8.85	8354.0	8.86	8362.9	8.87
190	8412.0	8.88	8418.9	8.89	8426.3	8.89	8434.2	8.90	8442.6	8.91	8451.6	8.92
191	8500.8	8.92	8507.7	8.93	8515.2	8.94	8523.2	8.95	8531.7	8.96	8540.8	8.97
192	8590.0	8.97	8597.0	8.98	8604.6	8.99	8612.7	8.99	8621.3	9.00	8630.4	9.01
193	8679.7	9.02	8686.8	9.03	8694.4	9.03	8702.6	9.04	8711.3	9.05	8720.6	9.06
194	8769.9	9.06	8777.1	9.07	8784.8	9.08	8793.0	9.09	8801.8	9.10	8811.2	9.11
195	8860.6	9.11	8867.8	9.12	8875.6	9.13	8883.9	9.14	8892.8	9.14	8902.3	9.15
196	8951.7	9.16	8959.0	9.17	8966.8	9.17	8975.3	9.18	8984.3	9.19	8993.8	9.20
197	9043.2	9.20	9050.6	9.21	9058.6	9.22	9067.1	9.23	9076.2	9.24	9085.8	9.25
198	9135.3	9.25	9142.8	9.26	9150.8	9.27	9159.4	9.28	9168.5	9.28	9178.3	9.29
199	9227.8	9.30	9235.3	9.31	9243.4	9.31	9252.1	9.32	9261.4	9.33	9271.2	9.34
200	9320.8	9.34	9328.4	9.35	9336.6	9.36	9345.3	9.37	9354.7	9.38	9364.6	9.39
201	9414.2	9.39	9421.9	9.40	9430.2	9.41	9439.0	9.42	9448.5	9.42	9458.5	9.43
202	9508.1	9.44	9515.9	9.44	9524.2	9.45	9533.2	9.46	9542.7	9.47	9552.9	9.48
203	9602.5	9.48	9610.3	9.49	9618.8	9.50	9627.8	9.51	9637.4	9.52	9647.7	9.53
204	9697.3	9.53	9705.3	9.54	9713.8	9.55	9722.9	9.56	9732.6	9.57	9743.0	9.58
205	9792.6	9.58	9800.6	9.58	9809.2	9.59	9818.4	9.60	9828.3	9.61	9838.7	9.62
206	9888.4	9.62	9896.5	9.63	9905.2	9.64	9914.5	9.65	9924.4	9.66	9934.9	9.67
207	9984.6	9.67	9992.8	9.68	10001.6	9.69	10010.9	9.70	10021.0	9.71	10031.6	9.72
208	10081.3	9.72	10089.6	9.72	10098.4	9.73	10107.9	9.74	10118.0	9.75	10128.8	9.76
209	10178.5	9.76	10186.8	9.77	10195.8	9.78	10205.3	9.79	10215.6	9.80	10226.4	9.81
210	10276.2	9.81	10284.5	9.82	10293.6	9.83	10303.2	9.84	10313.6	9.85	10324.5	9.86
211	10374.3	9.86	10382.7	9.86	10391.8	9.87	10401.6	9.88	10412.0	9.89	10423.1	9.90
212	10472.8	9.90	10481.4	9.91	10490.6	9.92	10500.4	9.93	10510.9	9.94	10522.1	9.95
213	10571.9	9.95	10580.5	9.96	10589.8	9.97	10599.7	9.98	10610.3	9.99	10621.6	10.00
214	10671.4	10.00	10680.1	10.00	10689.4	10.01	10699.5	10.02	10710.2	10.03	10721.6	10.04
215	10771.3	10.04	10780.1	10.05	10789.6	10.06	10799.7	10.07	10810.5	10.08	10822.0	10.09
216	10871.7	10.09	10880.6	10.10	10890.2	10.11	10900.4	10.12	10911.3	10.13	10922.9	10.14
217	10972.6	10.14	10981.6	10.14	10991.2	10.15	11001.6	10.16	11012.6	10.17	11024.3	10.18
218	11074.0	10.18	11083.1	10.19	11092.8	10.20	11103.2	10.21	11114.3	10.22	11126.1	10.23
219	11175 8	10.23	11185.0	10.24	11194.8	10.25	11205.3	10.26	11216.5	10.27	11228.4	10.28
220	11278.1	10.28	11287.3	10.28	11297.2	10.29	11307.8	10.30	11319.2	10.31	11331.2	10.32
221	11380.9	10.32	11390.2	10.33	11400.2	10.34	11410.9	10.35	11422.3	10.36	11434.4	10.37
222	11484.1	10.37	11493.5	10.38	11503.6	10.39	11514.4	10.40	11525.9	10.41	11538.2	10.42
223	11587.8	10.42	11597.3	10.42	11607.5	10.43	11618.3	10.44	11630.0	10.45	11642.3	10.46
224	11692.0	10.46	11701.5	10.47	11711.8	10.48	11722.8	10.49	11734.5	10.50	11747.0	10.51
225	11796.6	10.51	11806.2	10.52	11816.6	10.53	11827.7	10.54	11839.5	10.55	11852.1	10.56
226	11901.7	10.56	11911.4	10.56	11921.9	10.57	11933.0	10.58	11945.0	10.59	11957.7	10.61
227	12007.3	10.60	12017.1	10.61	12027.6	10.62	12038.9	10.63	12051.0	10.64	12063.8	10.65
228	12113.3	10.65	12123.2	10.66	12133.8	10.67	12145.2	10.68	12157.4	10.69	12170.3	10.70
229	12219.8	10.70	12229.7	10.70	12240.5	10.71	12252.0	10.72	12264.3	10.73	12277.3	10.75
230	12326.7	10.74	12336.8	10.75	12347.6	10.76	12359.2	10.77	12371.6	10.78	12384.7	10.79
231	12434.1	10.79	12444.3	10.80	12455.2	10.81	12466.9	10.82	12479.4	10.83	12492.7	10.84
232	12542.0	10.84	12552.3	10.84	12563.3	10.85	12575.1	10.86	12587.7	10.87	12601.0	10.89
233	12650.4	10.88	12660.7	10.89	12671.8	10.90	12683.7	10.91	12696.4	10.92	12709.9	10.93
234	12759.2	10.93	12769.6	10.94	12780.8	10.95	12792.8	10.96	12805.7	10.97	12819.2	10.98
235	12868.5	10.98	12879.0	10.98	12890.3	10.99	12902.4	11.00	12915.3	11.02	12929.0	11.03
236	12978.2	11.02	12988.8	11.03	13000.2	11.04	13012.4	11.05	13025.5	11.06	13039.3	11.07
237	13088.5	11.07	13099.2	11.08	13110.6	11.09	13122.9	11.10	13136.1	11.11	13150.1	11.12
238	13199.1	11.12	13209.9	11.12	13221.5	11.13	13233.9	11.14	13247.2	11.16	13261.3	11.17
239	13310.3	11.16	13321.2	11.17	13332.9	11.18	13345.4	11.19	13358.8	11.20	13372.9	11.21
240	13421.9	11.21	13432.9	11.22	13444.7	11.23	13457.3	11.24	13470.8	11.25	13485.1	11.26
SUMS.	18°		19°		20°		21°		22°		23°	

TABLE XI. Whole Sections. Side Slope ¼ to 1.

SUMS.	24°		25°		26°		27°		28°		29°	
121	3431.6	5.70	3435.8	5.70	3440.3	5.71	3445.0	5.72	3450.1	5.73	3455.5	5.74
122	3488.6	5.74	3492.8	5.75	3497.4	5.76	3502.2	5.76	3507.3	5.77	3512.8	5.78
123	3546.0	5.79	3550.3	5.80	3554.9	5.80	3559.8	5.81	3565.1	5.82	3570.7	5.83
124	3603.9	5.84	3608.3	5.84	3613.0	5.85	3618.0	5.86	3623.3	5.87	3628.9	5.88
125	3662.3	5.88	3666.7	5.89	3671.5	5.90	3676.6	5.91	3682.0	5.91	3687.7	5.92
126	3721.1	5.93	3725.6	5.94	3730.5	5.94	3735.6	5.95	3741.1	5.96	3747.0	5.97
127	3780.4	5.98	3785.0	5.98	3789.9	5.99	3795.1	6.00	3800.7	6.01	3806.7	6.02
128	3840.2	6.02	3844.8	6.03	3849.8	6.04	3855.1	6.05	3860.8	6.06	3866.9	6.07
129	3900.4	6.07	3905.2	6.08	3910.2	6.09	3915.6	6.09	3921.4	6.10	3927.5	6.11
130	3961.1	6.12	3965.9	6.12	3971.1	6.13	3976.6	6.14	3982.4	6.15	3988.6	6.16
131	4022.3	6.16	4027.2	6.17	4032.4	6.18	4038.0	6.19	4043.9	6.20	4050.2	6.21
132	4083.9	6.21	4088.9	6.22	4094.2	6.23	4099.9	6.24	4105.9	6.24	4112.3	6.25
133	4146.0	6.26	4151.1	6.27	4156.5	6.27	4162.2	6.28	4168.3	6.29	4174.8	6.30
134	4208.6	6.30	4213.7	6.31	4219.2	6.32	4225.0	6.33	4231.2	6.34	4237.9	6.35
135	4271.7	6.35	4276.9	6.36	4282.4	6.37	4288.3	6.38	4294.6	6.39	4301.4	6.40
136	4335.2	6.40	4340.5	6.41	4346.1	6.41	4352.1	6.42	4358.5	6.43	4365.3	6.44
137	4399.2	6.45	4404.5	6.45	4410.2	6.46	4416.3	6.47	4422.8	6.48	4429.7	6.49
138	4463.6	6.49	4469.1	6.50	4474.9	6.51	4481.0	6.52	4487.6	6.53	4494.6	6.54
139	4528.6	6.54	4534.1	6.55	4540.0	6.56	4546.2	6.56	4552.9	6.57	4560.0	6.58
140	4594.0	6.59	4599.5	6.59	4605.5	6.60	4611.9	6.61	4618.6	6.62	4625.9	6.63
141	4659.8	6.63	4665.5	6.64	4671.5	6.65	4678.0	6.66	4684.9	6.67	4692.2	6.68
142	4726.1	6.68	4731.9	6.69	4738.0	6.70	4744.6	6.71	4751.6	6.72	4759.0	6.73
143	4792.9	6.73	4798.8	6.74	4805.0	6.74	4811.6	6.75	4818.7	6.76	4826.2	6.77
144	4860.2	6.77	4866.1	6.78	4872.4	6.79	4879.2	6.80	4886.3	6.81	4894.0	6.82
145	4928.0	6.82	4934.0	6.83	4940.4	6.84	4947.2	6.85	4954.4	6.86	4962.2	6.87
146	4996.2	6.87	5002.2	6.88	5008.7	6.88	5015.6	6.89	5023.0	6.90	5030.9	6.92
147	5064.8	6.91	5071.0	6.92	5077.6	6.93	5084.6	6.94	5092.1	6.95	5100.0	6.96
148	5134.0	6.96	5140.2	6.97	5146.9	6.98	5154.0	6.99	5161.6	7.00	5169.6	7.01
149	5203.6	7.01	5209.9	7.02	5216.7	7.03	5223.9	7.04	5231.6	7.05	5239.7	7.06
150	5273.7	7.06	5280.1	7.06	5286.9	7.07	5294.2	7.08	5302.0	7.09	5310.3	7.10
151	5344.2	7.10	5350.7	7.11	5357.7	7.12	5365.1	7.13	5372.9	7.14	5381.4	7.15
152	5415.2	7.15	5421.8	7.16	5428.9	7.17	5436.4	7.18	5444.3	7.19	5452.9	7.20
153	5486.7	7.20	5493.4	7.20	5500.5	7.21	5508.1	7.22	5516.2	7.23	5524.8	7.25
154	5558.7	7.24	5565.5	7.25	5572.7	7.26	5580.4	7.27	5588.6	7.28	5597.3	7.29
155	5631.1	7.29	5638.0	7.30	5645.3	7.31	5653.1	7.32	5661.4	7.33	5670.2	7.34
156	5704.0	7.34	5710.9	7.35	5718.4	7.35	5726.2	7.36	5734.7	7.38	5743.6	7.39
157	5777.4	7.38	5784.4	7.39	5791.0	7.40	5799.9	7.41	5808.4	7.42	5817.5	7.43
158	5851.2	7.43	5858.3	7.44	5865.9	7.45	5874.0	7.46	5882.6	7.47	5891.9	7.48
159	5925.5	7.48	5932.7	7.49	5940.4	7.50	5948.6	7.51	5957.3	7.52	5966.7	7.53
160	6000.3	7.52	6007.6	7.53	6015.4	7.54	6023.7	7.55	6032.5	7.56	6042.0	7.58
161	6075.5	7.57	6082.9	7.58	6090.8	7.59	6099.2	7.60	6108.2	7.61	6117.7	7.62
162	6151.2	7.62	6158.7	7.63	6166.7	7.64	6175.2	7.65	6184.3	7.66	6193.9	7.67
163	6227.4	7.66	6235.0	7.67	6243.1	7.68	6251.7	7.69	6260.9	7.71	6270.7	7.72
164	6304.0	7.71	6311.7	7.72	6319.9	7.73	6328.6	7.74	6337.9	7.75	6347.8	7.76
165	6381.1	7.76	6388.9	7.77	6397.2	7.78	6406.0	7.79	6415.4	7.80	6425.5	7.81
166	6458.7	7.81	6466.6	7.81	6475.0	7.82	6483.9	7.84	6493.4	7.85	6503.6	7.86
167	6536.8	7.85	6544.7	7.86	6553.2	7.87	6562.3	7.88	6571.9	7.89	6582.2	7.91
168	6615.3	7.90	6623.3	7.91	6631.9	7.92	6641.1	7.93	6650.9	7.94	6661.3	7.95
169	6694.3	7.95	6702.4	7.96	6711.1	7.97	6720.4	7.98	6730.3	7.99	6740.8	8.00
170	6773.7	7.99	6782.0	8.00	6790.8	8.01	6800.2	8.02	6810.1	8.04	6820.8	8.05
171	6853.7	8.04	6862.0	8.05	6870.9	8.06	6880.4	8.07	6890.5	8.08	6901.3	8.10
172	6934.1	8.09	6942.5	8.10	6951.5	8.11	6961.1	8.12	6971.3	8.13	6982.2	8.14
173	7014.9	8.13	7023.5	8.14	7032.6	8.15	7042.3	8.16	7052.6	8.18	7063.7	8.19
174	7096.3	8.18	7104.9	8.19	7114.1	8.20	7123.9	8.21	7134.4	8.22	7145.6	8.24
175	7178.1	8.23	7186.8	8.24	7196.1	8.25	7206.0	8.26	7216.6	8.27	7227.9	8.28
176	7260.3	8.27	7269.2	8.28	7278.6	8.29	7288.6	8.31	7299.3	8.32	7310.8	8.33
177	7343.1	8.32	7352.0	8.33	7361.5	8.34	7371.7	8.35	7382.5	8.37	7394.1	8.38
178	7426.3	8.37	7435.3	8.38	7445.0	8.39	7455.2	8.40	7466.2	8.41	7477.9	8.43
179	7509.9	8.41	7519.1	8.42	7528.8	8.44	7539.2	8.45	7550.3	8.46	7562.1	8.47
180	7594.1	8.46	7603.3	8.47	7613.2	8.48	7623.7	8.49	7634.9	8.51	7646.9	8.52
SUMS.	24°		25°		26°		27°		28°		29°	

SUMS.	24°		25°		26°		27°		28°		29°	
181	7678.7	8.51	7688.0	8.52	7698.0	8.53	7708.6	8.54	7720.0	8.55	7732.1	8.57
182	7763.8	8.56	7773.2	8.57	7783.3	8.58	7794.1	8.59	7805.5	8.60	7817.7	8.61
183	7849.3	8.60	7858.9	8.61	7869.1	8.62	7879.9	8.64	7891.5	8.65	7903.9	8.66
184	7935.4	8.65	7945.0	8.66	7955.3	8.67	7966.3	8.68	7978.0	8.70	7990.5	8.71
185	8021.8	8.70	8031.6	8.71	8042.0	8.72	8053.1	8.73	8065.0	8.74	8077.6	8.76
186	8108.8	8.74	8118.7	8.75	8129.2	8.76	8140.4	8.78	8152.4	8.79	8165.1	8.80
187	8196.2	8.79	8206.2	8.80	8216.8	8.81	8228.2	8.82	8240.3	8.84	8253.2	8.85
188	8284.1	8.84	8294.2	8.85	8305.0	8.86	8316.4	8.87	8328.6	8.88	8341.7	8.90
189	8372.5	8.88	8382.7	8.89	8393.5	8.91	8405.1	8.92	8417.5	8.93	8430.7	8.94
190	8461.3	8.93	8471.6	8.94	8482.6	8.95	8494.3	8.96	8506.8	8.98	8520.1	8.99
191	8550.6	8.98	8561.0	8.99	8572.1	9.00	8584.0	9.01	8596.6	9.03	8610.0	9.04
192	8640.4	9.02	8650.9	9.03	8662.1	9.05	8674.1	9.06	8686.8	9.07	8700.4	9.09
193	8730.6	9.07	8741.3	9.08	8752.6	9.09	8764.7	9.11	8777.6	9.12	8791.3	9.13
194	8821.3	9.12	8832.1	9.13	8843.5	9.14	8855.7	9.15	8868.7	9.17	8882.6	9.18
195	8912.5	9.16	8923.4	9.18	8934.9	9.19	8947.3	9.20	8960.4	9.21	8974.4	9.23
196	9004.1	9.21	9015.1	9.22	9026.8	9.23	9039.3	9.25	9052.5	9.26	9066.7	9.28
197	9096.3	9.26	9107.3	9.27	9119.1	9.28	9131.7	9.29	9145.2	9.31	9159.5	9.32
198	9188.8	9.31	9200.0	9.32	9212.0	9.33	9224.7	9.34	9238.2	9.36	9252.7	9.37
199	9281.9	9.35	9293.2	9.36	9305.2	9.38	9318.1	9.39	9331.8	9.40	9346.4	9.42
200	9375.4	9.40	9386.8	9.41	9399.0	9.42	9412.0	9.44	9425.8	9.45	9440.6	9.46
201	9469.4	9.45	9480.9	9.46	9493.2	9.47	9506.3	9.48	9520.3	9.50	9535.2	9.51
202	9563.9	9.49	9575.5	9.50	9587.9	9.52	9601.2	9.53	9615.3	9.54	9630.3	9.56
203	9658.8	9.54	9670.5	9.55	9683.1	9.56	9696.5	9.58	9710.7	9.59	9725.9	9.61
204	9754.2	9.59	9766.1	9.60	9778.7	9.61	9792.2	9.62	9806.6	9.64	9822.0	9.65
205	9850.0	9.63	9862.0	9.64	9874.8	9.66	9888.5	9.67	9903.0	9.69	9918.5	9.70
206	9946.4	9.68	9958.5	9.69	9971.4	9.70	9985.2	9.72	9999.8	9.73	10015.5	9.75
207	10043.2	9.73	10055.4	9.74	10068.4	9.75	10082.3	9.76	10097.2	9.78	10113.0	9.79
208	10140.4	9.77	10152.8	9.79	10166.0	9.80	10180.0	9.81	10195.0	9.83	10210.9	9.84
209	10238.2	9.82	10250.7	9.83	10263.9	9.85	10278.1	9.86	10293.2	9.87	10309.3	9.89
210	10336.4	9.87	10349.0	9.88	10362.4	9.89	10376.7	9.91	10392.0	9.92	10408.2	9.94
211	10435.1	9.91	10447.8	9.93	10461.3	9.94	10475.8	9.95	10491.2	9.97	10507.6	9.98
212	10534.2	9.96	10547.0	9.97	10560.7	9.99	10575.3	10.00	10590.8	10.01	10607.4	10.03
213	10633.8	10.01	10646.8	10.02	10660.6	10.03	10675.3	10.05	10691.0	10.06	10707.7	10.08
214	10733.9	10.06	10747.0	10.07	10760.9	10.08	10775.8	10.09	10791.6	10.11	10808.5	10.12
215	10834.5	10.10	10847.7	10.11	10861.7	10.13	10876.7	10.14	10892.7	10.16	10909.7	10.17
216	10935.5	10.15	10948.8	10.16	10963.0	10.17	10978.1	10.19	10994.3	10.20	11011.5	10.22
217	11037.0	10.20	11050.4	10.21	11064.7	10.22	11080.0	10.24	11096.3	10.25	11113.7	10.27
218	11138.9	10.24	11152.5	10.26	11167.0	10.27	11182.4	10.28	11198.8	10.30	11216.3	10.31
219	11241.4	10.29	11255.0	10.30	11269.6	10.32	11285.2	10.33	11301.8	10.34	11319.5	10.36
220	11344.3	10.34	11358.1	10.35	11372.8	10.36	11388.5	10.38	11405.2	10.39	11423.1	10.41
221	11447.6	10.38	11461.6	10.40	11476.4	10.41	11492.3	10.42	11509.2	10.44	11527.2	10.46
222	11551.5	10.43	11565.5	10.44	11580.5	10.46	11596.5	10.47	11613.5	10.49	11631.7	10.50
223	11655.8	10.48	11669.9	10.49	11685.1	10.50	11701.2	10.52	11718.4	10.53	11736.7	10.55
224	11760.5	10.52	11774.8	10.54	11790.1	10.55	11806.4	10.56	11823.7	10.58	11842.2	10.60
225	11865.8	10.57	11880.2	10.58	11895.6	10.60	11912.0	10.61	11929.5	10.63	11948.2	10.64
226	11971.5	10.62	11986.0	10.63	12001.6	10.64	12018.2	10.66	12035.8	10.67	12054.6	10.69
227	12077.6	10.66	12092.4	10.68	12108.0	10.69	12124.7	10.71	12142.6	10.72	12161.6	10.74
228	12184.3	10.71	12199.1	10.72	12214.9	10.74	12231.8	10.75	12249.8	10.77	12268.9	10.79
229	12291.4	10.76	12306.4	10.77	12322.3	10.79	12339.3	10.80	12357.5	10.82	12376.8	10.83
230	12399.0	10.81	12414.1	10.82	12430.2	10.83	12447.3	10.85	12465.6	10.86	12485.1	10.88
231	12507.0	10.85	12522.3	10.87	12538.5	10.88	12555.8	10.89	12574.3	10.91	12593.9	10.93
232	12615.6	10.90	12630.9	10.91	12647.3	10.93	12664.8	10.94	12683.4	10.96	12703.2	10.97
233	12724.5	10.95	12740.0	10.96	12756.6	10.97	12774.2	10.99	12792.9	11.00	12813.0	11.02
234	12834.0	10.99	12849.6	11.01	12866.3	11.02	12884.1	11.04	12903.0	11.05	12923.2	11.07
235	12943.9	11.04	12959.7	11.05	12976.5	11.07	12994.4	11.08	13013.5	11.10	13033.9	11.12
236	13054.3	11.09	13070,2	11.10	13087.2	11.11	13105.2	11.13	13124.5	11.15	13145.0	11.16
237	13165.2	11.13	13181.2	11.15	13198.3	11.16	13216.5	11.18	13236.0	11.19	13256.7	11.21
238	13276.5	11.18	13292.7	11.19	13309.9	11.21	13328.3	11.22	13347.9	11.24	13368.8	11.26
239	13388.3	11.23	13404.6	11.24	13422.0	11.26	13440.5	11.27	13460.3	11.29	13481.3	11.31
240	13500.6	11.27	13517.0	11.29	13534.6	11.30	13553.3	11.32	13573.2	11.33	13594.4	11.35
SUMS.	24°		25°		26°		27°		28°		29°	

SUMS.	30°		31°		32°		33°		34°		35°	
121	3461.2	5.74	3467.4	5.75	3473.9	5.77	3480.9	5.78	3488.3	5.79	3496.3	5.80
122	3518.7	5.79	3524.9	5.80	3531.6	5.81	3538.6	5.82	3546.2	5.84	3554.8	5.85
123	3576.6	5.84	3582.9	5.85	3589.7	5.86	3596.9	5.87	3604.6	5.88	3612.8	5.90
124	3635.0	5.89	3641.4	5.90	3648.3	5.91	3655.6	5.92	3663.4	5.93	3671.8	5.95
125	3693.9	5.93	3700.4	5.94	3707.4	5.96	3714.8	5.97	3722.8	5.98	3731.2	5.99
126	3753.2	5.98	3759.8	5.99	3766.9	6.00	3774.5	6.02	3782.6	6.03	3791.2	6.04
127	3813.0	6.03	3819.8	6.04	3827.0	6.05	3834.6	6.06	3842.8	6.08	3851.6	6.09
128	3873.3	6.08	3880.1	6.09	3887.5	6.10	3895.3	6.11	3903.6	6.12	3912.5	6.14
129	3934.0	6.12	3941.0	6.13	3948.4	6.15	3956.4	6.16	3964.8	6.17	3973.9	6.18
130	3995.3	6.17	4002.3	6.18	4009.9	6.19	4017.9	6.21	4026.5	6.22	4035.7	6.23
131	4057.0	6.22	4064.2	6.23	4071.8	6.24	4080.0	6.25	4088.7	6.27	4098.0	6.28
132	4119.2	6.26	4126.4	6.28	4134.2	6.29	4142.5	6.30	4151.4	6.31	4160.8	6.33
133	4181.8	6.31	4189.2	6.32	4197.1	6.34	4205.5	6.35	4214.5	6.36	4224.1	6.38
134	4244.9	6.36	4252.4	6.37	4260.5	6.38	4269.0	6.40	4278.1	6.41	4287.9	6.42
135	4308.5	6.41	4316.1	6.42	4324.3	6.43	4333.0	6.44	4342.2	6.46	4352.1	6.47
136	4372.6	6.45	4380.3	6.47	4388.6	6.48	4397.4	6.49	4406.8	6.50	4416.8	6.52
137	4437.1	6.50	4445.0	6.51	4453.4	6.52	4462.3	6.54	4471.8	6.55	4482.0	6.57
138	4502.1	6.55	4510.1	6.56	4518.6	6.57	4527.7	6.59	4537.4	6.60	4547.7	6.61
139	4567.6	6.60	4575.7	6.61	4584.3	6.62	4593.5	6.63	4603.4	6.65	4613.8	6.66
140	4633.6	6.64	4641.8	6.65	4650.5	6.67	4659.9	6.68	4669.8	6.70	4680.5	6.71
141	4700.0	6.69	4708.3	6.70	4717.2	6.71	4726.7	6.73	4736.8	6.74	4747.6	6.76
142	4766.9	6.74	4775.3	6.75	4784.4	6.76	4794.0	6.78	4804.2	6.79	4815.1	6.81
143	4834.3	6.78	4842.8	6.80	4852.0	6.81	4861.7	6.82	4872.1	6.84	4883.2	6.85
144	4902.1	6.83	4910.8	6.84	4920.1	6.86	4929.9	6.87	4940.5	6.89	4951.7	6.90
145	4970.5	6.88	4979.3	6.89	4988.6	6.90	4998.7	6.92	5009.3	6.93	5020.8	6.95
146	5039.2	6.93	5048.2	6.94	5057.7	6.95	5067.8	6.97	5078.7	6.98	5090.2	7.00
147	5108.5	6.97	5117.6	6.99	5127.2	7.00	5137.5	7.01	5148.5	7.03	5160.2	7.04
148	5178.3	7.02	5187.4	7.03	5197.2	7.05	5207.6	7.06	5218.8	7.08	5230.7	7.09
149	5248.5	7.07	5257.8	7.08	5267.7	7.09	5278.2	7.11	5289.5	7.12	5301.6	7.14
150	5319.2	7.12	5328.6	7.13	5338.6	7.14	5349.3	7.16	5360.8	7.17	5373.0	7.19
151	5390.3	7.16	5399.9	7.18	5410.0	7.19	5420.9	7.20	5432.5	7.22	5444.9	7.24
152	5461.9	7.21	5471.6	7.22	5481.9	7.24	5492.9	7.25	5504.7	7.27	5517.2	7.28
153	5534.0	7.26	5543.8	7.27	5554.3	7.28	5565.4	7.30	5577.3	7.31	5590.0	7.33
154	5606.6	7.30	5616.6	7.32	5627.1	7.33	5638.4	7.35	5650.5	7.36	5663.4	7.38
155	5679.7	7.35	5689.7	7.37	5700.5	7.38	5711.9	7.39	5724.1	7.41	5737.1	7.43
156	5753.2	7.40	5763.4	7.41	5774.2	7.43	5785.8	7.44	5798.2	7.46	5811.4	7.47
157	5827.2	7.45	5837.5	7.46	5848.5	7.47	5860.3	7.49	5872.8	7.51	5886.2	7.52
158	5901.7	7.49	5912.1	7.51	5923.3	7.52	5935.1	7.54	5947.8	7.55	5961.4	7.57
159	5976.6	7.54	5987.2	7.55	5998.5	7.57	6010.5	7.58	6023.4	7.60	6037.1	7.62
160	6052.0	7.59	6062.7	7.60	6074.2	7.62	6086.4	7.63	6099.4	7.65	6113.3	7.67
161	6127.9	7.64	6138.8	7.65	6150.3	7.66	6162.7	7.68	6175.8	7.70	6189.9	7.71
162	6204.3	7.68	6215.2	7.70	6227.0	7.71	6239.5	7.73	6252.8	7.74	6267.0	7.76
163	6281.1	7.73	6292.2	7.74	6304.1	7.76	6316.7	7.77	6330.2	7.79	6344.7	7.81
164	6358.4	7.78	6369.7	7.79	6381.7	7.81	6394.5	7.82	6408.1	7.84	6422.7	7.86
165	6436.2	7.83	6447.6	7.84	6459.7	7.85	6472.7	7.87	6486.5	7.89	6501.3	7.90
166	6514.4	7.87	6526.0	7.89	6538.3	7.90	6551.4	7.92	6565.4	7.93	6580.3	7.95
167	6593.1	7.92	6604.8	7.93	6617.3	7.95	6630.6	7.96	6644.7	7.98	6659.9	8.00
168	6672.3	7.97	6684.2	7.98	6696.8	8.00	6710.2	8.01	6724.5	8.03	6739.9	8.05
169	6752.0	8.01	6764.0	8.03	6776.7	8.04	6790.3	8.06	6804.8	8.08	6820.3	8.10
170	6832.2	8.06	6844.3	8.08	6857.2	8.09	6870.9	8.11	6885.6	8.12	6901.3	8.14
171	6912.8	8.11	6925.0	8.12	6938.1	8.14	6952.0	8.15	6966.9	8.17	6982.7	8.19
172	6993.9	8.16	7006.2	8.17	7019.5	8.19	7033.5	8.20	7048.6	8.22	7064.6	8.24
173	7075.4	8.20	7087.9	8.22	7101.3	8.23	7115.6	8.25	7130.8	8.27	7147.0	8.29
174	7157.4	8.25	7170.1	8.27	7183.6	8.28	7198.1	8.30	7213.5	8.32	7229.9	8.33
175	7240.0	8.30	7252.8	8.31	7266.5	8.33	7281.0	8.34	7296.6	8.36	7313.2	8.38
176	7322.9	8.35	7335.9	8.36	7349.7	8.38	7364.5	8.39	7380.2	8.41	7397.0	8.43
177	7406.4	8.39	7419.5	8.41	7433.5	8.42	7448.4	8.44	7464.3	8.46	7481.3	8.48
178	7490.3	8.44	7503.6	8.45	7517.7	8.47	7532.8	8.49	7548.9	8.51	7566.1	8.53
179	7574.7	8.49	7588.1	8.50	7602.4	8.52	7617.7	8.54	7634.0	8.55	7651.4	8.57
180	7659.6	8.53	7673.1	8.55	7687.6	8.57	7703.0	8.58	7719.5	8.60	7737.1	8.62
SUMS.	30°		31°		32°		33°		34°		35°	

SUMS	30°		31°		32°		33°		34°		35°	
181	7744.9	8.58	7758.6	8.60	7773.3	8.61	7788.9	8.63	7805.5	8.65	7823.3	8.67
182	7830.7	8.63	7844.6	8.64	7859.4	8.66	7875.2	8.68	7892.0	8.70	7910.0	8.72
183	7917.0	8.68	7931.0	8.69	7946.0	8.71	7961.9	8.73	7979.0	8.74	7997.1	8.76
184	8003.8	8.72	8018.0	8.74	8033.1	8.76	8049.2	8.77	8066.4	8.79	8084.8	8.81
185	8091.0	8.77	8105.3	8.79	8120.6	8.80	8136.9	8.82	8154.3	8.84	8172.9	8.86
186	8178.7	8.82	8193.2	8.83	8208.7	8.85	8225.1	8.87	8242.7	8.89	8261.5	8.91
187	8266.9	8.87	8281.5	8.88	8297.2	8.90	8313.8	8.92	8331.6	8.93	8350.6	8.95
188	8355.6	8.91	8370.4	8.93	8386.1	8.95	8403.0	8.96	8420.9	8.98	8440.1	9.00
189	8444.7	8.96	8459.6	8.98	8475.6	8.99	8492.6	9.01	8510.8	9.03	8530.1	9.05
190	8534.3	9.01	8549.4	9.02	8565.5	9.04	8582.7	9.06	8601.1	9.08	8620.6	9.10
191	8624.4	9.05	8639.6	9.07	8655.9	9.09	8673.3	9.11	8691.8	9.13	8711.6	9.15
192	8714.9	9.10	8730.3	9.12	8746.8	9.13	8764.3	9.15	8783.1	9.17	8803.1	9.19
193	8805.9	9.15	8821.5	9.17	8838.1	9.18	8855.9	9.20	8874.8	9.22	8895.0	9.24
194	8897.4	9.20	8913.2	9.21	8930.0	9.23	8947.9	9.25	8967.0	9.27	8987.4	9.29
195	8989.4	9.24	9005.3	9.26	9022.3	9.28	9040.4	9.30	9059.7	9.32	9080.3	9.34
196	9081.8	9.29	9097.9	9.31	9115.0	9.32	9133.3	9.34	9152.9	9.36	9173.7	9.38
197	9174.7	9.34	9191.0	9.35	9208.3	9.37	9226.8	9.39	9246.5	9.41	9267.6	9.43
198	9268.1	9.39	9284.5	9.40	9302.0	9.42	9320.7	9.44	9340.6	9.46	9361.9	9.48
199	9361.9	9.43	9378.5	9.45	9396.2	9.47	9415.1	9.49	9435.2	9.51	9456.7	9.53
200	9456.3	9.48	9473.0	9.50	9490.9	9.51	9509.9	9.53	9530.3	9.55	9552.0	9.58
201	9551.1	9.53	9568.0	9.54	9586.0	9.56	9605.3	9.58	9625.8	9.60	9647.7	9.62
202	9646.3	9.57	9663.4	9.59	9681.6	9.61	9701.1	9.63	9721.8	9.65	9744.0	9.67
203	9742.1	9.62	9759.3	9.64	9777.7	9.66	9797.4	9.68	9818.3	9.70	9840.7	9.72
204	9838.3	9.67	9855.7	9.69	9874.3	9.70	9894.1	9.72	9915.3	9.74	9937.9	9.77
205	9935.0	9.72	9952.6	9.73	9971.4	9.75	9991.4	9.77	10012.7	9.79	10035.5	9.81
206	10032.2	9.76	10049.9	9.78	10068.9	9.80	10089.1	9.82	10110.6	9.84	10133.7	9.86
207	10129.8	9.81	10147.7	9.83	10166.9	9.85	10187.3	9.87	10209.0	9.89	10232.3	9.91
208	10227.9	9.86	10246.0	9.88	10265.3	9.89	10285.9	9.91	10307.9	9.94	10331.4	9.96
209	10326.5	9.91	10344.8	9.92	10364.3	9.94	10385.1	9.96	10407.3	9.98	10431.0	10.01
210	10425.5	9.95	10444.0	9.97	10463.7	9.99	10484.7	10.01	10507.1	10.03	10531.0	10.05
211	10525.1	10.00	10543.7	10.02	10563.6	10.04	10584.8	10.06	10607.4	10.08	10631.6	10.10
212	10625.1	10.05	10643.9	10.07	10663.9	10.08	10685.4	10.10	10708.2	10.13	10732.6	10.15
213	10725.5	10.09	10744.5	10.11	10764.8	10.13	10786.4	10.15	10809.5	10.17	10834.1	10.20
214	10826.5	10.14	10845.7	10.16	10866.1	10.18	10887.9	10.20	10911.2	10.22	10936.0	10.24
215	10927.9	10.19	10947.3	10.21	10967.9	10.23	10989.9	10.25	11013.4	10.27	11038.5	10.29
216	11029.8	10.24	11049.3	10.25	11070.2	10.27	11092.4	10.29	11116.1	10.32	11141.4	10.34
217	11132.2	10.28	11151.9	10.30	11172.9	10.32	11195.3	10.34	11219.3	10.36	11244.8	10.39
218	11235.0	10.33	11254.9	10.35	11276.1	10.37	11298.7	10.39	11322.9	10.41	11348.7	10.44
219	11338.3	10.38	11358.4	10.40	11379.8	10.42	11402.6	10.44	11427.0	10.46	11453.0	10.48
220	11442.1	10.43	11462.3	10.44	11484.0	10.46	11507.0	10.48	11531.6	10.51	11557.9	10.53
221	11546.3	10.47	11566.8	10.49	11588.6	10.51	11611.9	10.53	11636.7	10.55	11663.2	10.58
222	11651.1	10.52	11671.7	10.54	11693.7	10.56	11717.2	10.58	11742.2	10.60	11769.0	10.63
223	11756.3	10.57	11777.1	10.59	11799.3	10.61	11823.0	10.63	11848.3	10.65	11875.2	10.67
224	11861.9	10.61	11883.0	10.63	11905.4	10.65	11929.2	10.67	11954.8	10.70	11982.0	10.72
225	11968.1	10.66	11989.3	10.68	12011.9	10.70	12036.0	10.72	12061.7	10.75	12089.2	10.77
226	12074.7	10.71	12096.1	10.73	12118.9	10.75	12143.2	10.77	12169.2	10.79	12196.9	10.82
227	12181.8	10.76	12203.4	10.78	12226.4	10.80	12250.9	10.82	12277.1	10.84	12305.1	10.87
228	12289.4	10.80	12311.1	10.82	12334.3	10.84	12359.1	10.87	12385.5	10.89	12413.7	10.91
229	12397.4	10.85	12419.4	10.87	12442.8	10.89	12467.7	10.91	12494.4	10.94	12522.9	10.96
230	12505.9	10.90	12528.1	10.92	12551.7	10.94	12576.9	10.96	12603.8	10.98	12632.5	11.01
231	12614.9	10.95	12637.2	10.97	12661.1	10.99	12686.5	11.01	12713.6	11.03	12742.6	11.06
232	12724.4	10.99	12746.9	11.01	12770.9	11.03	12796.6	11.06	12823.9	11.08	12853.1	11.10
233	12834.3	11.04	12857.0	11.06	12881.3	11.08	12907.1	11.10	12934.7	11.13	12964.2	11.15
234	12944.7	11.09	12967.6	11.11	12992.1	11.13	13018.1	11.15	13046.0	11.17	13075.7	11.20
235	13055.6	11.13	13078.7	11.15	13103.3	11.18	13129.6	11.20	13157.7	11.22	13187.7	11.25
236	13166.9	11.18	13190.2	11.20	13215.1	11.22	13241.6	11.25	13269.9	11.27	13300.2	11.30
237	13278.7	11.23	13302.2	11.25	13327.3	11.27	13354.1	11.29	13382.6	11.32	13413.1	11.34
238	13391.0	11.28	13414.7	11.30	13440.0	11.32	13467.0	11.34	13495.8	11.36	13526.5	11.39
239	13503.8	11.32	13527.7	11.34	13553.2	11.37	13580.4	11.39	13609.4	11.41	13640.4	11.44
240	13617.0	11.37	13641.1	11.39	13666.9	11.41	13694.3	11.44	13723.6	11.46	13754.8	11.49
SUMS.	30°		31°		32°		33°		34°		35°	

FOR COMPUTATION BY END HEIGHTS.

SUMS.	1°		2°		3°		4°		5°		SUMS.
1	27.2	8.17	14.0	4.20	9.6	2.88	7.4	2.22	6.1	1.83	1
2	108.9	13.62	56.0	7.00	38.4	4.79	29.6	3.70	24.4	3.05	2
3	245.1	19.07	125.9	9.79	86.3	6.71	66.6	5.18	54.8	4.26	3
4	435.8	24.51	223.8	12.59	153.4	8.63	118.3	6.66	97.5	5.48	4
5	680.9	29.96	349.8	15.39	239.7	10.55	184.9	8.14	152.3	6.70	5
6	980.5	35.41	503.7	18.19	345.2	12.46	266.3	9.62	219.3	7.92	6
7	1334.6	40.85	685.5	20.99	469.8	14.38	362.4	11.09	298.5	9.14	7
8	1743.1	46.30	895.4	23.78	613.6	16.30	473.4	12.57	389.8	10.35	8
9	2206.1	51.75	1133.2	26.58	776.6	18.22	599.1	14.05	493.4	11.57	9
10	2723.6	57.20	1399.0	29.38	958.8	20.13	739.6	15.53	609.1	12.79	10
11	3295.6	62.64	1692.8	32.18	1160.1	22.05	895.0	17.01	737.0	14.01	11
12	3922.0	68.09	2014.6	34.98	1380.6	23.97	1065.1	18.49	877.1	15.23	12
13	4602.9	73.54	2364.4	37.77	1620.3	25.89	1250.0	19.97	1029.4	16.45	13
14	5338.3	78.99	2742.1	40.57	1879.2	27.80	1449.7	21.45	1193.8	17.66	14
15	6128.2	84.43	3147.8	43.37	2157.2	29.72	1664.2	22.93	1370.5	18.88	15
16	6972.5	89.88	3581.5	46.17	2454.4	31.64	1893.5	24.41	1559.3	20.10	16
17	7871.3	95.33	4043.2	48.97	2770.8	33.56	2137.6	25.89	1760.3	21.32	17
18	8824.5	100.77	4532.9	51.76	3106.4	35.47	2396.5	27.37	1973.5	22.54	18
19	9832.3	106.22	5050.5	54.56	3461.1	37.39	2670.1	28.85	2198.9	23.76	19
20	10894.5	111.67	5596.1	57.36	3835.0	39.31	2958.6	30.33	2436.4	24.97	20
21	12011.2	117.12	6169.7	60.16	4228.1	41.23	3261.9	31.80	2686.1	26.19	21
22	13182.3	122.56	6771.3	62.96	4640.4	43.14	3579.9	33.28	2948.1	27.41	22
23	14408.0	128.01	7400.9	65.75	5071.8	45.06	3912.7	34.76	3222.2	28.63	23
24	15688.1	133.46	8058.4	68.55	5522.4	46.98	4260.4	36.24	3508.4	29.85	24
25	17022.7	138.90	8744.0	71.35	5992.2	48.90	4622.8	37.72	3806.9	31.06	25
26	18411.7	144.35	9457.5	74.15	6481.2	50.81	5000.0	39.20	4117.5	32.28	26
27	19855.2	149.80	10199.0	76.95	6989.3	52.73	5392.0	40.68	4440.4	33.50	27
28	21353.2	155.25	10968.4	79.75	7516.6	54.65	5798.9	42.16	4775.4	34.72	28
29	22905.7	160.69	11765.9	82.54	8063.1	56.57	6220.5	43.64	5122.6	35.94	29
30	24512.6	166.14	12591.3	85.34	8628.8	58.48	6656.8	45.12	5481.9	36.16	30
SUMS.	1°		2°		3°		4°		5°		SUMS.

FOR COMPUTATION BY END HEIGHTS.

SUMS.	6°		7°		8°		9°		10°		SUMS.
1	5.2	1.57	4.6	1.39	4.2	1.25	3.8	1.15	3.6	1.07	1
2	20.9	2.61	18.5	2.31	16.7	2.09	15.3	1.92	14.3	1.78	2
3	47.1	3.66	41.6	3.24	37.6	2.92	34.5	2.68	32.1	2.50	3
4	83.7	4.71	73.9	4.16	66.8	3.76	61.3	3.45	57.1	3.21	4
5	130.7	5.75	115.5	5.08	104.4	4.59	95.8	4.22	89.2	3.93	5
6	188.3	6.80	166.4	6.01	150.3	5.43	138.0	4.98	128.5	4.64	6
7	256.2	7.84	226.5	6.93	204.5	6.26	187.9	5.75	174.9	5.35	7
8	334.7	8.89	295.8	7.86	267.1	7.10	245.4	6.52	228.5	6.07	8
9	423.6	9.94	374.4	8.78	338.1	7.93	310.5	7.28	289.2	6.78	9
10	522.9	10.98	462.2	9.71	417.4	8.77	383.4	8.05	357.0	7.50	10
11	632.7	12.03	559.2	10.63	505.1	9.60	463.9	8.82	431.9	8.21	11
12	753.0	13.07	665.5	11.55	601.1	10.44	552.1	9.58	514.0	8.92	12
13	883.7	14.12	781.1	12.48	705.4	11.27	647.9	10.35	603.3	9.64	13
14	1024.9	15.16	905.9	13.40	818.1	12.10	751.4	11.12	699.7	10.35	14
15	1176.6	16.21	1039.9	14.33	939.2	12.94	862.6	11.89	803.2	11.07	15
16	1338.7	17.26	1183.2	15.25	1068.6	13.77	981.5	12.65	913.9	11.78	16
17	1511.2	18.30	1335.7	16.18	1206.8	14.61	1108.0	13.42	1031.7	12.49	17
18	1694.3	19.35	1497.4	17.10	1352.4	15.44	1242.2	14.19	1156.6	13.21	18
19	1887.7	20.39	1668.5	18.02	1506.9	16.28	1384.0	14.95	1288.7	13.92	19
20	2091.7	21.44	1848.7	18.95	1669.6	17.11	1533.6	15.72	1427.9	14.64	20
21	2306.1	22.49	2038.2	19.87	1840.8	17.95	1690.7	16.49	1574.3	15.35	21
22	2530.9	23.53	2236.9	20.80	2020.3	18.78	1855.6	17.25	1727.8	16.06	22
23	2766.3	24.58	2444.9	21.72	2208.1	19.62	2028.1	18.02	1888.4	16.78	23
24	3012.0	25.62	2662.1	22.65	2404.3	20.45	2208.3	18.79	2056.2	17.49	24
25	3268.3	26.67	2888.6	23.57	2608.8	21.29	2396.2	19.55	2231.1	18.21	25
26	3535.0	27.71	3124.8	24.50	2821.7	22.12	2591.7	20.32	2413.2	18.92	26
27	3812.1	28.76	3369.3	25.42	3042.9	22.96	2794.9	21.09	2602.4	19.63	27
28	4099.7	29.81	3623.5	26.34	3272.5	23.79	3005.8	21.85	2798.7	20.35	28
29	4397.8	30.85	3886.9	27.27	3510.4	24.63	3224.3	22.62	3002.2	21.06	29
30	4706.3	31.90	4159.6	28.19	3756.7	25.46	3450.5	22.39	3212.8	21.78	30
SUMS.	6°		7°		8°		9°		10°		SUMS.

FOR COMPUTATION BY END HEIGHTS.

SUMS.	11°		12°		13°		14°		15°		SUMS.
1	3.4	1.01	3.2	0.95	3.1	0.92	3.0	0.89	2.9	0.87	1
2	13.4	1.68	12.8	1.60	12.3	1.53	11.9	1.48	11.6	1.44	2
3	30.3	2.35	28.8	2.24	27.6	2.15	26.7	2.08	26.0	2.02	3
4	53.8	3.03	51.2	2.88	49.1	2.76	47.5	2.67	46.2	2.60	4
5	84.0	3.70	79.9	3.52	76.7	3.37	74.2	3.26	72.2	3.18	5
6	121.0	4.37	115.1	4.16	110.4	3.99	106.8	3.86	104.0	3.76	6
7	164.7	5.04	156.7	4.80	150.3	4.60	145.3	4.45	141.6	4.33	7
8	215.2	5.72	204.6	5.44	196.3	5.21	189.8	5.04	184.9	4.91	8
9	272.3	6.39	259.0	6.08	248.5	5.83	240.3	5.64	234.0	5.49	9
10	336.2	7.06	319.8	6.71	306.8	6.44	296.6	6.23	288.9	6.07	10
11	406.8	7.73	386.9	7.35	371.2	7.06	358.9	6.82	349.6	6.64	11
12	484.1	8.40	460.4	7.99	441.7	7.67	427.1	7.42	416.0	7.22	12
13	568.2	9.08	540.4	8.63	518.4	8.28	501.3	8.01	488.2	7.80	13
14	659.0	9.75	626.7	9.27	601.3	8.90	581.4	8.60	566.2	8.38	14
15	756.4	10.42	719.5	9.91	690.2	9.51	667.4	9.20	650.0	8.96	15
16	860.7	11.09	818.6	10.55	785.3	10.12	759.3	9.79	739.6	9.53	16
17	971.6	11.77	924.1	11.19	886.5	10.74	857.2	10.38	834.9	10.11	17
18	1089.3	12.44	1036.0	11.83	993.9	11.35	961.0	10.97	936.0	10.69	18
19	1213.7	13.11	1154.3	12.47	1107.4	11.96	1070.8	11.57	1042.9	11.27	19
20	1344.8	13.78	1279.0	13.11	1227.1	12.58	1186.5	12.16	1155.6	11.84	20
21	1482.6	14.46	1410.1	13.75	1352.8	13.19	1308.1	12.75	1274.0	12.42	21
22	1627.2	15.13	1547.6	14.39	1484.7	13.80	1435.6	13.35	1398.2	13.00	22
23	1778.5	15.80	1691.5	15.03	1622.8	14.42	1569.1	13.94	1528.2	13.58	23
24	1936.5	16.47	1841.8	15.67	1767.0	15.03	1708.5	14.53	1664.0	14.16	24
25	2101.2	17.15	1998.5	16.31	1917.3	15.64	1853.9	15.13	1805.6	14.73	25
26	2272.7	17.82	2161.6	16.95	2073.7	16.26	2005.1	15.72	1952.9	15.31	26
27	2450.9	18.49	2331.0	17.59	2236.3	16.87	2162.3	16.31	2106.0	15.89	27
28	2635.8	19.16	2506.9	18.23	2405.0	17.49	2325.5	16.91	2264.9	16.47	28
29	2827.4	19.84	2689.2	18.37	2579.9	18.10	2494.5	17.50	2429.6	17.04	29
30	3025.8	20.51	2877.8	19.51	2760.9	18.71	2669.5	18.09	2600.0	17.62	30
SUMS.	11°		12°		13°		14°		15°		SUMS.

FOR COMPUTATION BY END HEIGHTS.

SUMS.	16°		17°		18°		19°		20°		SUMS.
1	2.8	0.85	2.8	0.84	2.8	0.83	2.8	0.83	2.8	0.84	1
2	11.3	1.42	11.2	1.40	11.1	1.39	11.1	1.39	11.2	1.40	2
3	25.5	1.98	25.2	1.96	25.0	1.95	25.0	1.95	25.2	1.96	3
4	45.3	2.55	44.8	2.52	44.5	2.50	44.5	2.50	44.8	2.52	4
5	70.8	3.12	69.9	3.08	69.5	3.06	69.5	3.06	70.0	3.08	5
6	102.0	3.68	100.7	3.64	100.1	3.61	100.1	3.62	100.9	3.64	6
7	138.8	4.25	137.1	4.20	136.2	4.17	136.3	4.17	137.3	4.20	7
8	181.3	4.82	179.0	4.75	177.9	4.73	178.0	4.73	179.3	4.76	8
9	229.5	5.38	226.6	5.31	225.1	5.28	225.2	5.28	226.9	5.32	9
10	283.3	5.95	279.7	5.87	278.0	5.84	278.1	5.84	280.1	5.88	10
11	342.8	6.52	338.4	6.43	336.3	6.39	336.5	6.40	339.0	6.44	11
12	408.0	7.08	402.8	6.99	400.3	6.95	400.4	6.95	403.4	7.00	12
13	478.8	7.65	472.7	7.55	469.7	7.50	470.0	7.51	473.4	7.56	13
14	555.3	8.22	548.2	8.11	544.8	8.06	545.0	8.06	549.1	8.12	14
15	687.5	8.78	629.3	8.67	625.4	8.62	625.7	8.62	630.3	8.68	15
16	725.3	9.35	716.0	9.23	711.6	9.17	711.9	9.18	717.2	9.24	16
17	818.8	9.92	808.3	9.79	803.3	9.73	803.7	9.73	809.6	9.81	17
18	917.9	10.48	906.2	10.35	900.6	10.28	901.0	10.29	907.7	10.37	18
19	1022.8	11.05	1009.7	10.91	1003.4	10.84	1003.9	10.85	1011.3	10.93	19
20	1133.2	11.62	1118.8	11.47	1111.8	11.40	1112.3	11.40	1120.6	11.49	20
21	1249.4	12.18	1233.5	12.03	1225.8	11.95	1226.3	11.96	1235.4	12.05	21
22	1371.2	12.75	1353.7	12.59	1345.3	12.51	1345.9	12.51	1355.9	12.61	22
23	1498.7	13.32	1479.6	13.15	1470.4	13.06	1471.0	13.07	1482.0	13.17	23
24	1631.9	13.88	1611.0	13.71	1601.0	13.62	1601.7	13.63	1613.6	13.73	24
25	1770.7	14.45	1748.1	14.26	1737.2	14.18	1738.0	14.18	1750.9	14.29	25
26	1915.2	15.02	1890.7	14.82	1879.0	14.73	1879.8	14.74	1893.8	14.85	26
27	2065.3	15.58	2039.0	15.38	2026.3	15.29	2027.2	15.29	2042.3	15.41	27
28	2221.2	16.15	2192.8	15.94	2179.2	15.84	2180.2	15.85	2196.3	15.97	28
29	2882.7	16.72	2352.2	16.50	2337.6	16.40	2338.7	16.41	2356.0	16.53	29
30	2549.8	17.28	2517.3	17.06	2501.6	16.96	2502.7	16.96	2521.3	17.09	30
SUMS.	16°		17°		18°		19°		20°		SUMS.

FOR COMPUTATION BY END HEIGHTS.

SUMS.	21°		22°		23°		24°		25°		SUMS.
1	2.8	0.85	2.9	0.87	3.0	0.90	3.1	0.94	3.3	0.99	1
2	11.4	1.42	11.6	1.45	12.0	1.50	12.5	1.57	13.2	1.65	2
3	25.6	1.99	26.2	2.04	27.0	2.10	28.2	2.19	29.7	2.31	3
4	45.5	2.56	46.5	2.52	48.0	2.70	50.1	2.82	52.9	2.97	4
5	71.1	3.13	72.7	3.20	75.1	3.30	78.3	3.44	82.6	3.63	5
6	102.4	3.70	104.7	3.78	108.1	3.90	112.7	4.07	118.9	4.29	6
7	139.3	4.26	142.5	4.36	147.1	4.50	153.4	4.70	161.9	4.96	7
8	182.0	4.83	186.2	4.94	192.1	5.10	200.4	5.32	211.4	5.62	8
9	230.3	5.40	235.6	5.53	243.2	5.70	253.6	5.95	267.6	6.28	9
10	284.3	5.97	290.9	6.11	300.2	6.30	313.1	6.57	330.3	6.94	10
11	344.0	6.54	351.9	6.69	363.3	6.91	378.8	7.20	399.7	7.60	11
12	409.4	7.11	418.8	7.27	432.3	7.51	450.8	7.83	475.7	8.26	12
13	480.5	7.68	491.6	7.85	507.4	8.11	529.1	8.45	558.3	8.92	13
14	557.3	8.25	570.1	8.43	588.4	8.71	613.6	9.08	647.5	9.58	14
15	639.7	8.81	654.4	9.02	675.5	9.31	704.4	9.70	743.3	10.24	15
16	727.8	9.38	744.6	9.60	768.6	9.91	801.4	10.33	845.7	10.90	16
17	821.7	9.95	840.6	10.18	867.6	10.51	904.7	10.96	954.7	11.56	17
18	921.2	10.52	942.4	10.76	972.7	11.11	1014.3	11.58	1070.3	12.22	18
19	1026.4	11.09	1050.0	11.34	1083.8	11.71	1130.1	12.21	1192.6	12.88	19
20	1137.2	11.66	1163.4	11.93	1200.9	12.31	1252.2	12.84	1321.4	13.54	20
21	1253.8	12.23	1282.7	12.51	1324.0	12.91	1380.6	13.46	1456.8	14.21	21
22	1376.1	12.79	1407.8	13.09	1453.1	13.51	1515.2	14.09	1598.9	14.87	22
23	1504.0	13.36	1538.6	13.67	1588.2	14.11	1656.1	14.71	1747.6	15.53	23
24	1637.6	13.93	1675.4	14.25	1729.3	14.71	1803.2	15.34	1902.8	16.19	24
25	1776.9	14.50	1817.9	14.83	1876.4	15.31	1956.6	15.97	2064.7	16.85	25
26	1921.9	15.07	1966.2	15.42	2029.5	15.91	2116.2	16.59	2233.2	17.51	26
27	2072.6	15.64	2120.4	16.00	2188.6	16.51	2282.2	17.22	2408.3	18.17	27
28	2229.0	16.21	2280.3	16.58	2353.7	17.11	2454.3	17.84	2589.9	18.83	28
29	2391.1	16.77	2446.1	17.16	2524.9	17.71	2632.8	18.47	2778.2	19.49	29
30	2558.8	17.34	2617.7	17.74	2702.0	18.31	2817.5	19.10	2973.1	20.15	30
SUMS.	21°		22°		23°		24°		25°		SUMS.

FOR COMPUTATION BY END HEIGHTS.

SUMS.	26°		27°		28°		29°		30°		SUMS.
1	3.5	1.06	3.9	1.16	4.3	1.29	5.0	1.49	6.0	1.80	1
2	14.1	1.77	15.4	1.93	17.2	2.15	19.8	2.48	23.9	2.99	2
3	31.8	2.48	34.7	2.70	38.7	3.01	44.6	3.47	53.9	4.19	3
4	56.6	3.18	61.7	3.47	68.8	3.87	79.3	4.46	95.8	5.39	4
5	88.4	3.89	96.4	4.24	107.5	4.73	123.9	5.45	149.6	6.58	5
6	127.3	4.60	138.8	5.01	154.8	5.59	178.4	6.44	215.5	7.78	6
7	173.3	5.30	188.9	5.78	210.8	6.45	242.8	7.43	293.3	8.98	7
8	226.3	6.01	246.7	6.55	275.3	7.31	317.2	8.42	383.1	10.18	8
9	286.5	6.72	312.2	7.32	348.4	8.17	401.4	9.42	484.8	11.37	9
10	353.7	7.43	385.5	8.10	430.1	9.03	495.6	10.41	598.5	12.57	10
11	427.9	8.13	466.4	8.87	520.4	9.89	599.6	11.40	724.2	13.77	11
12	509.3	8.84	555.1	9.64	619.4	10.75	713.6	12.39	861.9	14.96	12
13	597.7	9.55	651.5	10.41	726.9	11.61	837.5	13.38	1011.5	16.16	13
14	693.2	10.26	755.5	11.18	843.0	12.47	971.3	14.37	1173.1	17.36	14
15	795.7	10.96	867.3	11.95	967.8	13.33	1115.0	15.36	1346.7	18.55	15
16	905.4	11.67	986.8	12.72	1101.1	14.19	1268.6	16.35	1532.2	19.75	16
17	1022.1	12.38	1114.0	13.49	1243.0	15.05	1432.2	17.34	1729.8	20.95	17
18	1145.8	13.09	1248.9	14.26	1393.6	15.91	1605.6	18.34	1939.2	22.15	18
19	1276.7	13.79	1391.6	15.03	1552.7	16.77	1789.0	19.33	2160.7	23.34	19
20	1414.6	14.50	1541.9	15.80	1720.5	17.63	1982.3	20.32	2394.1	24.54	20
21	1559.6	15.21	1700.0	16.58	1896.8	18.49	2185.4	21.31	2639.5	25.74	21
22	1711.7	15.91	1865.7	17.35	2081.8	19.36	2398.5	22.30	2896.9	26.93	22
23	1870.8	16.62	2039.2	18.12	2275.3	20.22	2621.5	23.29	3166.2	28.13	23
24	2037.1	17.33	2220.4	18.89	2477.5	21.08	2854.5	24.28	3447.5	29.33	24
25	2210.3	18.04	2409.2	19.66	2688.2	21.94	3097.3	25.27	3740.8	30.53	25
26	2390.7	18.74	2605.8	20.43	2907.6	22.80	3350.0	26.27	4046.1	31.72	26
27	2578.2	19.45	2810.1	21.20	3135.5	23.66	3612.7	27.26	4363.3	32.92	27
28	2772.7	20.16	3022.1	21.97	3372.1	24.52	3885.2	28.25	4692.5	34.12	28
29	2974.2	20.87	3241.9	22.74	3617.3	25.38	4167.7	29.24	5033.6	35.31	29
30	3182.9	21.77	3469.3	23.51	3871.0	26.24	4460.1	30.23	5386.8	36.51	30
SUMS.	26°		27°		28°		29°		30°		SUMS.

FOR COMPUTATION BY END HEIGHTS.

SUMS.	1°		2°		3°		4°		5°		SUMS.
1	27.0	8.10	13.7	4.12	9.8	2.80	7.1	2.14	5.8	1.74	1
2	108.0	13.50	54.9	6.87	37.3	4.66	28.5	3.56	23.2	2.90	2
3	242.9	18.90	123.6	9.62	83.9	6.53	64.1	4.98	52.2	4.06	3
4	431.9	24.29	219.8	12.36	149.2	8.39	113.9	6.41	92.8	5.22	4
5	674.9	29.69	343.4	15.11	233.1	10.25	178.0	7.83	145.0	6.38	5
6	971.8	35.09	494.5	17.86	335.6	12.12	256.3	9.25	208.8	7.54	6
7	1322.7	40.49	673.1	20.61	456.8	13.98	348.8	10.68	284.2	8.70	7
8	1727.6	45.89	879.2	23.35	596.6	15.85	455.6	12.10	371.1	9.86	8
9	2186.5	51.29	1112.7	26.10	755.1	17.71	576.6	13.53	469.7	11.02	9
10	2699.4	56.69	1373.7	28.85	932.2	19.58	711.8	14.95	579.9	12.18	10
11	3266.3	62.09	1662.2	31.60	1128.0	21.44	861.3	16.37	701.7	13.34	11
12	3887.2	67.49	1978.2	34.34	1342.4	23.31	1025.1	17.80	835.1	14.50	12
13	4562.0	72.88	2321.6	37.09	1575.5	25.17	1203.0	19.22	980.0	15.66	13
14	5290.9	78.28	2692.5	39.84	1827.2	27.04	1395.2	20.64	1136.6	16.82	14
15	6073.7	83.68	3090.9	42.59	2097.5	28.90	1601.7	22.07	1304.8	17.98	15
16	6910.5	89.08	3516.7	45.35	2386.5	30.76	1822.3	23.49	1484.6	19.14	16
17	7801.4	94.48	3970.1	48.08	2694.2	32.63	2057.2	24.91	1675.9	20.30	17
18	8746.2	99.88	4450.9	50.83	3020.5	34.49	2306.4	26.34	1878.9	21.46	18
19	9744.9	105.28	4959.1	53.58	3365.4	36.36	2569.8	27.76	2093.5	22.62	19
20	10797.7	110.68	5494.9	56.32	3729.0	38.22	2847.4	29.19	2319.6	23.78	20
21	11904.5	116.08	6058.1	59.07	4111.2	40.09	3139.2	30.61	2557.4	24.94	21
22	13065.2	121.47	6648.8	61.82	4512.1	41.95	3445.3	32.03	2806.7	26.10	22
23	14280.0	126.87	7267.0	64.57	4931.6	43.82	3765.7	33.46	3067.7	27.26	23
24	15548.7	132.27	7912.7	67.31	5369.7	45.68	4100.2	34.88	3340.2	28.42	24
25	16871.4	137.67	8585.8	70.05	5826.5	47.54	4449.0	36.30	3624.4	29.58	25
26	18248.2	143.07	9286.4	72.81	6302.0	49.41	4812.1	37.73	3920.2	30.73	26
27	19678.9	148.47	10014.4	75.55	6796.0	51.27	5189.3	39.15	4227.5	31.89	27
28	21163.5	153.87	10770.0	78.30	7308.8	53.14	5580.9	40.58	4546.4	33.05	28
29	22702.2	159.27	11553.0	81.05	7840.2	55.00	5986.6	42.00	4877.0	34.21	29
30	24294.9	164.67	12363.5	83.80	8390.2	56.87	6406.6	43.42	5219.1	35.37	30
SUMS.	1°		2°		3°		4°		5°		SUMS.

FOR COMPUTATION BY END HEIGHTS.

SUMS.	6°		7°		8°		9°		10°		SUMS.
1	4.9	1.48	4.3	1.29	3.8	1.15	3.5	1.04	3.2	0.96	1
2	19.7	2.46	17.2	2.15	15.3	1.92	13.9	1.74	12.8	1.59	2
3	44.3	3.45	38.7	3.01	34.5	2.68	31.3	2.43	28.7	2.23	3
4	78.8	4.43	68.8	3.87	61.3	3.45	55.6	3.13	51.0	2.87	4
5	123.1	5.41	107.5	4.73	95.8	4.22	86.8	3.82	79.7	3.51	5
6	177.2	6.40	154.7	5.59	138.0	4.98	125.0	4.52	114.8	4.14	6
7	241.2	7.38	210.6	6.45	187.8	5.75	170.2	5.21	156.2	4.78	7
8	315.0	8.37	275.1	7.31	245.3	6.52	222.3	5.90	204.0	5.42	8
9	398.7	9.35	348.2	8.17	310.5	7.28	281.3	6.60	258.2	6.06	9
10	492.2	10.34	429.8	9.03	383.3	8.05	347.3	7.29	318.8	6.69	10
11	595.6	11.32	520.1	9.89	463.8	8.82	420.2	7.99	385.7	7.33	11
12	708.8	12.31	619.0	10.75	551.9	9.58	500.1	8.68	459.0	7.97	12
13	831.8	13.29	726.4	11.61	647.7	10.35	587.0	9.38	538.7	8.61	13
14	964.7	14.27	842.5	12.47	751.2	11.12	680.7	10.07	624.8	9.24	14
15	1107.5	15.26	967.1	13.32	862.4	11.88	781.5	10.77	717.2	9.88	15
16	1260.1	16.24	1100.4	14.18	981.2	12.65	889.1	11.46	816.0	10.52	16
17	1422.5	17.23	1242.2	15.04	1107.7	13.41	1003.7	12.16	921.2	11.16	17
18	1594.8	18.21	1392.6	15.90	1241.8	14.18	1125.3	12.85	1032.8	11.79	18
19	1776.9	19.20	1551.7	16.76	1383.6	14.95	1253.8	13.55	1150.7	12.43	19
20	1968.9	20.18	1719.3	17.62	1533.1	15.71	1389.2	14.24	1275.1	13.07	20
21	2170.7	21.17	1895.5	18.48	1690.3	16.48	1531.6	14.93	1405.8	13.71	21
22	2382.3	22.15	2080.4	19.34	1855.1	17.25	1681.0	15.63	1542.8	14.34	22
23	2603.8	23.13	2273.8	20.20	2027.6	18.01	1837.3	16.32	1686.3	14.98	23
24	2835.1	24.12	2475.8	21.06	2207.7	18.78	2000.5	17.02	1836.1	15.62	24
25	3076.3	25.10	2686.4	21.92	2395.5	19.55	2170.7	17.71	1992.3	16.26	25
26	3327.4	26.09	2905.6	22.78	2591.0	20.31	2347.8	18.41	2154.9	16.89	26
27	3588.2	27.07	3133.5	23.64	2794.1	21.08	2531.9	19.10	2323.8	17.53	27
28	3859.0	28.06	3369.9	24.50	3004.9	21.85	2722.9	19.80	2499.1	18.17	28
29	4139.5	29.04	3614.9	25.36	3222.4	22.61	2920.9	20.49	2680.8	18.81	29
30	4429.9	30.03	3868.5	26.22	3449.5	23.38	3125.8	21.19	2868.9	19.44	30
SUMS.	6°		7°		8°		9°		10°		SUMS.

FOR COMPUTATION BY END HEIGHTS.

SUMS.	11°		12°		13°		14°		15°		SUMS.
1	3.0	0.89	2.8	0.83	2.6	0.78	2.5	0.74	2.4	0.71	1
2	11.8	1.48	11.1	1.38	10.4	1.30	9.9	1.24	9.4	1.18	2
3	26.6	2.07	24.9	1.94	23.5	1.83	22.3	1.73	21.2	1.65	3
4	47.3	2.66	44.3	2.49	41.7	2.35	39.6	2.23	37.8	2.12	4
5	73.9	3.25	69.2	3.04	65.2	2.87	61.8	2.72	59.0	2.60	5
6	106.4	3.84	99.6	3.60	93.9	3.39	89.0	3.22	85.0	3.07	6
7	144.9	4.43	135.5	4.15	127.8	3.91	121.2	3.71	115.7	3.54	7
8	189.2	5.03	177.0	4.70	166.9	4.43	158.3	4.21	151.1	4.01	8
9	239.5	5.62	224.0	5.26	211.2	4.95	200.4	4.70	191.2	4.48	9
10	295.6	6.21	276.6	5.81	260.7	5.48	247.4	5.19	236.0	4.96	10
11	357.7	6.80	334.7	6.36	315.5	6.00	299.3	5.69	285.6	5.43	11
12	425.7	7.39	398.3	6.92	375.4	6.52	356.2	6.18	339.9	5.90	12
13	499.6	7.98	467.5	7.47	440.6	7.04	418.0	6.68	398.9	6.37	13
14	579.5	8.57	542.1	8.02	511.0	7.56	484.8	7.17	462.6	6.84	14
15	665.2	9.16	622.4	8.57	586.6	8.08	556.6	7.67	531.0	7.32	15
16	756.8	9.76	708.1	9.13	667.5	8.60	633.2	8.16	604.2	7.79	16
17	854.4	10.35	799.4	9.68	753.5	9.13	714.9	8.66	682.1	8.26	17
18	957.9	10.94	896.2	10.23	844.7	9.65	801.4	9.15	764.7	8.73	18
19	1067.3	11.53	998.5	10.79	941.2	10.17	893.0	9.65	852.0	9.20	19
20	1182.6	12.12	1106.4	11.34	1042.9	10.69	989.4	10.14	944.1	9.68	20
21	1303.8	12.71	1219.8	11.89	1149.8	11.21	1090.8	10.64	1040.9	10.15	21
22	1430.9	13.30	1338.7	12.45	1261.9	11.73	1197.2	11.13	1142.3	10.62	22
23	1563.9	13.90	1463.2	13.00	1379.2	12.25	1308.5	11.63	1248.6	11.09	23
24	1702.9	14.49	1593.2	13.55	1501.8	12.78	1424.8	12.12	1359.5	11.57	24
25	1847.8	15.08	1728.8	14.11	1629.5	13.30	1546.0	12.62	1475.1	12.04	25
26	1998.5	15.67	1869.8	14.66	1762.5	13.82	1672.1	13.11	1595.5	12.51	26
27	2155.2	16.26	2016.4	15.21	1900.7	14.34	1803.2	13.60	1720.6	12.98	27
28	2317.8	16.85	2168.5	15.77	2044.1	14.86	1939.3	14.10	1850.4	13.45	28
29	2486.3	17.44	2326.2	16.32	2192.7	15.38	2080.3	14.59	1984.9	13.93	29
30	2660.8	18.03	2489.4	16.87	2346.5	15.90	2226.2	15.09	2124.2	14.40	30
SUMS.	11°		12°		13°		14°		15°		SUMS

FOR COMPUTATION BY END HEIGHTS.

SUMS.	16°		17°		18°		19°		20°		SUMS.
1	2.3	0.68	2.2	0.65	2.1	0.63	2.1	0.62	2.0	0.60	1
2	9.1	1.13	8.7	1.09	8.4	1.06	8.2	1.03	8.0	1.00	2
3	20.4	1.58	19.6	1.53	19.0	1.48	18.5	1.44	18.0	1.40	3
4	36.2	2.04	34.9	1.96	33.8	1.90	32.8	1.85	32.0	1.80	4
5	56.6	2.49	54.5	2.40	52.8	2.32	51.3	2.26	50.0	2.20	5
6	81.5	2.94	78.5	2.84	76.0	2.74	73.8	2.67	72.0	2.60	6
7	110.9	3.40	106.9	3.27	103.4	3.17	100.5	3.08	98.0	3.00	7
8	144.9	3.85	139.6	3.71	135.1	3.59	131.2	3.49	128.0	3.40	8
9	183.4	4.30	176.7	4.14	171.0	4.01	166.1	3.90	162.0	3.80	9
10	226.4	4.75	218.1	4.58	211.1	4.43	205.1	4.31	200.0	4.20	10
11	273.9	5.21	263.9	5.02	255.4	4.85	248.1	4.72	242.0	4.60	11
12	326.0	5.66	314.1	5.45	303.9	5.28	295.3	5.13	288.0	5.00	12
13	382.6	6.11	368.6	5.89	356.7	5.70	346.6	5.54	338.0	5.40	13
14	443.7	6.56	427.5	6.33	413.7	6.12	401.9	5.95	392.0	5.80	14
15	509.3	7.02	490.8	6.76	474.9	6.54	461.4	6.36	450.0	6.20	15
16	579.5	7.47	558.4	7.20	540.3	6.97	525.0	6.77	512.0	6.60	16
17	654.2	7.92	630.3	7.63	610.0	7.39	592.6	7.18	578.0	7.00	17
18	733.4	8.38	706.7	8.07	683.8	7.81	664.4	7.59	648.0	7.40	18
19	817.2	8.83	787.4	8.51	761.9	8.23	740.3	8.00	722.0	7.80	19
20	905.5	9.28	872.4	8.94	844.3	8.65	820.3	8.41	799.9	8.20	20
21	998.3	9.73	961.9	9.38	930.8	9.08	904.3	8.82	881.9	8.60	21
22	1095.6	10.19	1055.7	9.82	1021.6	9.50	992.5	9.23	967.9	9.00	22
23	1197.5	10.64	1153.8	10.25	1116.5	9.92	1084.8	9.64	1057.9	9.40	23
24	1303.8	11.09	1256.3	10.69	1215.7	10.34	1181.2	10.05	1151.9	9.80	24
25	1414.8	11.54	1363.2	11.12	1319.2	10.76	1281.6	10.46	1249.9	10.20	25
26	1530.2	12.00	1474.4	11.56	1426.8	11.19	1386.2	10.87	1351.9	10.60	26
27	1650.2	12.45	1590.0	12.00	1538.7	11.61	1494.9	11.28	1457.9	11.00	27
28	1774.7	12.90	1710.0	12.43	1654.7	12.03	1607.7	11.69	1567.9	11.40	28
29	1903.7	13.36	1834.3	12.87	1775.0	12.45	1724.6	12.10	1681.9	11.80	29
30	2037.3	13.81	1963.0	13.30	1899.6	12.87	1845.6	12.51	1799.9	12.20	30
SUMS.	16°		17°		18°		19°		20°		SUMS.

FOR COMPUTATION BY END HEIGHTS.

SUMS.	21°		22°		23°		24°		25°		SUMS.
1	2.0	0.59	1.9	0.58	1.9	0.57	1.9	0.56	1.9	0.56	**1**
2	7.8	0.98	7.7	0.96	7.6	0.95	7.5	0.94	7.4	0.93	**2**
3	17.6	1.37	17.3	1.35	17.1	1.33	16.9	1.31	16.7	1.30	**3**
4	31.3	1.76	30.8	1.73	30.3	1.71	30.0	1.69	29.8	1.67	**4**
5	48.9	2.15	48.1	2.11	47.4	2.08	46.9	2.06	46.5	2.05	**5**
6	70.5	2.54	69.2	2.50	68.2	2.46	67.5	2.44	67.0	2.42	**6**
7	95.9	2.94	94.2	2.88	92.9	2.84	91.8	2.81	91.2	2.79	**7**
8	125.3	3.33	123.1	3.27	121.3	3.22	120.0	3.19	119.1	3.16	**8**
9	158.6	3.72	155.7	3.65	153.5	3.60	151.8	3.56	150.7	3.53	**9**
10	195.7	4.11	192.3	4.04	189.5	3.98	187.4	3.94	186.0	3.91	**10**
11	236.9	4.50	232.6	4.42	229.3	4.36	226.8	4.31	225.1	4.28	**11**
12	281.9	4.89	276.9	4.81	272.9	4.74	269.9	4.69	267.9	4.65	**12**
13	330.8	5.29	324.9	5.19	320.3	5.12	316.8	5.06	314.4	5.02	**13**
14	383.7	5.68	376.8	5.58	371.4	5.50	367.4	5.44	364.6	5.39	**14**
15	440.4	6.07	432.6	5.96	426.4	5.87	421.7	5.81	418.6	5.77	**15**
16	501.1	6.46	492.2	6.34	485.1	6.25	479.8	6.19	476.2	6.14	**16**
17	565.7	6.85	555.7	6.73	547.7	6.63	541.7	6.56	537.6	6.51	**17**
18	634.2	7.24	623.0	7.11	614.0	7.01	607.3	6.94	602.7	6.88	**18**
19	706.6	7.63	694.1	7.50	684.1	7.39	676.6	7.31	671.6	7.26	**19**
20	783.0	8.03	769.1	7.88	758.0	7.77	749.7	7.68	744.1	7.63	**20**
21	863.2	8.42	847.9	8.27	835.7	8.15	826.6	8.06	820.4	8.00	**21**
22	947.4	8.81	930.6	8.65	917.2	8.53	907.2	8.43	900.4	8.37	**22**
23	1035.5	9.20	1017.1	9.04	1002.5	8.91	991.5	8.81	984.1	8.74	**23**
24	1127.5	9.59	1107.5	9.42	1091.6	9.29	1079.6	9.18	1071.5	9.12	**24**
25	1223.4	9.98	1201.7	9.81	1184.4	9.66	1171.5	9.56	1162.7	9.49	**25**
26	1323.2	10.37	1299.7	10.19	1281.1	10.04	1267.1	9.93	1257.6	9.86	**26**
27	1427.0	10.77	1401.6	10.57	1381.5	10.42	1366.4	10.31	1356.2	10.23	**27**
28	1534.6	11.16	1507.4	10.96	1485.7	10.80	1469.5	10.68	1458.5	10.60	**28**
29	1646.2	11.55	1617.0	11.34	1593.7	11.18	1576.3	11.06	1564.5	10.98	**29**
30	1761.7	11.94	1730.4	11.73	1705.6	11.56	1686.9	11.43	1674.3	11.35	**30**
SUMS.	21°		22°		23°		24°		25°		SUMS.

FOR COMPUTATION BY END HEIGHTS.

SUMS.	26°		27°		28°		29°		30°		SUMS.
1	1.9	0.56	1.9	0.56	1.9	0.56	1.9	0.56	1.9	0.57	1
2	7.4	0.93	7.4	0.93	7.4	0.93	7.5	0.94	7.6	0.95	2
3	16.7	1.30	16.7	1.30	16.7	1.30	16.9	1.31	17.1	1.33	3
4	29.6	1.67	29.6	1.67	29.7	1.67	30.0	1.69	30.4	1.71	4
5	46.3	2.04	46.3	2.04	46.5	2.05	46.8	2.06	47.4	2.09	5
6	66.7	2.41	66.7	2.41	66.9	2.42	67.5	2.44	68.3	2.47	6
7	90.8	2.78	90.8	2.78	91.1	2.79	91.8	2.81	93.0	2.85	7
8	118.6	3.15	118.6	3.15	119.0	3.16	119.9	3.19	121.4	3.23	8
9	150.1	3.52	150.1	3.52	150.6	3.53	151.8	3.56	153.7	3.60	9
10	185.3	3.89	185.3	3.89	185.9	3.90	187.4	3.94	189.7	3.98	10
11	224.2	4.26	224.2	4.26	225.0	4.28	226.7	4.31	229.6	4.36	11
12	266.8	4.63	266.8	4.63	267.7	4.65	269.9	4.68	273.2	4.74	12
13	313.2	5.00	313.1	5.00	314.2	5.02	316.7	5.06	320.6	5.12	13
14	363.2	5.37	363.1	5.37	364.4	5.39	367.3	5.43	371.9	5.50	14
15	416.9	5.74	416.8	5.74	418.3	5.76	421.6	5.81	426.9	5.88	15
16	474.4	6.11	474.2	6.11	476.0	6.14	479.7	6.18	485.7	6.26	16
17	535.5	6.49	535.4	6.48	537.3	6.51	541.6	6.56	548.3	6.64	17
18	600.4	6.86	600.2	6.85	602.4	6.88	607.2	6.93	614.7	7.02	18
19	668.9	7.23	668.8	7.22	671.2	7.25	676.5	7.31	684.9	7.40	19
20	741.2	7.60	741.0	7.60	743.7	7.62	749.6	7.68	758.9	7.78	20
21	817.2	7.97	817.0	7.97	820.0	8.00	826.4	8.06	836.7	8.16	21
22	896.8	8.34	896.6	8.34	899.9	8.37	907.0	8.43	918.3	8.54	22
23	980.2	8.71	980.0	8.71	983.6	8.74	991.3	8.81	1003.6	8.92	23
24	1067.3	9.08	1067.1	9.08	1071.0	9.11	1079.4	9.18	1092.8	9.30	24
25	1158.1	9.45	1157.8	9.45	1162.1	9.48	1171.2	9.56	1185.8	9.68	25
26	1252.6	9.82	1252.3	9.82	1256.9	9.85	1266.8	9.93	1282.5	10.06	26
27	1350.8	10.19	1350.5	10.19	1355.5	10.23	1366.1	10.31	1383.1	10.43	27
28	1452.7	10.56	1452.4	10.56	1457.7	10.60	1469.2	10.68	1487.4	10.81	28
29	1558.3	10.93	1558.0	10.93	1563.7	10.97	1576.0	11.06	1595.6	11.19	29
30	1667.7	11.30	1667.3	11.30	1673.4	11.34	1686.6	11.43	1707.5	11.57	30
SUMS.	26°		27°		28°		29°		30°		SUMS.

FOR COMPUTATION BY END HEIGHTS.

SUMS.	31°		32°		33°		34°		35°		SUMS.
1	1.9	0.58	2.0	0.59	2.0	0.61	2.1	0.63	2.2	0.66	1
2	7.7	0.97	7.9	0.99	8.1	1.02	8.4	1.05	8.8	1.10	2
3	17.4	1.35	17.8	1.38	18.3	1.42	19.0	1.48	19.8	1.54	3
4	30.9	1.74	31.6	1.78	32.5	1.83	33.7	1.90	35.3	1.98	4
5	48.3	2.12	49.4	2.17	50.8	2.24	52.7	2.32	55.1	2.43	5
6	69.5	2.51	71.1	2.57	73.2	2.64	75.9	2.74	79.4	2.87	6
7	94.6	2.90	96.8	2.96	99.6	3.05	103.3	3.16	108.1	3.31	7
8	123.5	3.28	126.4	3.36	130.1	3.46	135.0	3.58	141.1	3.75	8
9	156.4	3.67	160.0	3.75	164.7	3.86	170.8	4.01	178.6	4.19	9
10	193.0	4.05	197.5	4.15	203.3	4.27	210.9	4.43	220.5	4.63	10
11	233.6	4.44	239.0	4.54	246.0	4.68	255.2	4.85	266.9	5.07	11
12	278.0	4.83	284.4	4.94	292.8	5.08	303.7	5.27	317.6	5.51	12
13	326.2	5.21	333.8	5.33	343.6	5.49	356.4	5.69	372.7	5.95	13
14	378.4	5.60	387.1	5.73	398.5	5.90	413.3	6.12	432.3	6.40	14
15	434.3	5.98	444.4	6.12	457.5	6.30	474.5	6.54	496.2	6.84	15
16	494.2	6.37	505.6	6.52	520.6	6.71	539.8	6.96	564.6	7.28	16
17	557.9	6.76	570.8	6.91	587.7	7.12	609.4	7.38	637.4	7.72	17
18	625.5	7.14	639.9	7.31	658.8	7.52	683.2	7.80	714.6	8.16	18
19	696.9	7.53	713.0	7.70	734.1	7.93	761.2	8.22	796.2	8.60	19
20	772.2	7.91	790.0	8.10	813.4	8.34	843.5	8.65	882.2	9.04	20
21	851.3	8.30	871.0	8.49	896.7	8.74	929.9	9.07	972.6	9.48	21
22	934.3	8.69	955.9	8.89	984.2	9.15	1020.6	9.49	1067.4	9.92	22
23	1021.2	9.07	1044.8	9.28	1075.7	9.56	1115.5	9.91	1166.7	10.37	23
24	1111.9	9.46	1137.6	9.68	1171.2	9.96	1214.6	10.33	1270.3	10.81	24
25	1206.5	9.85	1234.4	10.07	1270.9	10.37	1318.0	10.75	1378.4	11.25	25
26	1305.0	10.23	1335.1	10.47	1374.6	10.78	1425.5	11.18	1490.9	11.69	26
27	1407.3	10.62	1439.8	10.86	1482.4	11.18	1537.3	11.60	1607.8	12.13	27
28	1513.4	11.00	1548.4	11.26	1594.2	11.59	1653.2	12.02	1729.1	12.57	28
29	1623.5	11.39	1661.0	11.65	1710.1	12.00	1773.4	12.44	1854.8	13.01	29
30	1737.4	11.78	1777.5	12.05	1830.1	12.40	1897.8	12.86	1984.9	13.45	30
SUMS.	31°		32°		33°		34°		35°		SUMS.

TABLE B. **Multipliers.**

Side-Slope	2¾ to 1	2½ to 1	2¼ to 1	2 to 1	1¾ to 1	1½ to 1	1¼ to 1	1 to 1	¾ to 1	½ to 1	⅓ to 1	¼ to 1
Multiplier	5½	5	4½	4	3½	3	2½	2	1½	1	⅔	½

TABLE XIV. Whole Sections.—Roadbed 24 ft. Side Slope 1½ to 1.

SUMS.	0°		1°		2°		3°		4°		5°	
1	45.8	4.86	46.1	4.86	46.9	4.87	......	......	......	......	......	......
2	94.4	5.14	94.8	5.14	95.7	5.15	97.2	5.17	99.5	5.20	102.3	5.23
3	145.8	5.42	146.2	5.42	147.2	5.43	148.9	5.45	151.4	5.48	154.6	5.51
4	200.0	5.69	200.4	5.70	201.5	5.71	203.5	5.73	206.2	5.76	209.7	5.79
5	256.9	5.97	257.4	5.98	258.6	5.99	260.7	6.01	263.8	6.04	267.7	6.08
6	316.7	6.25	317.1	6.26	318.5	6.27	320.8	6.29	324.1	6.32	328.4	6.36
7	379.2	6.53	379.7	6.53	381.2	6.55	383.7	6.57	387.3	6.60	392.0	6.64
8	444.4	6.81	445.0	6.81	446.6	6.82	449.4	6.85	453.3	6.88	458.5	6.92
9	512.5	7.08	513.1	7.09	514.9	7.10	517.9	7.13	522.2	7.16	527.7	7.21
10	583.3	7.36	584.0	7.37	585.9	7.38	589.2	7.41	593.8	7.44	599.8	7.49
11	656.9	7.64	657.6	7.64	659.7	7.66	663.2	7.69	668.2	7.72	674.7	7.77
12	733.3	7.92	734.1	7.92	736.3	7.94	740.1	7.97	745.4	8.00	752.4	8.06
13	812.5	8.19	813.3	8.20	815.7	8.22	819.8	8.25	825.5	8.29	833.0	8.34
14	894.4	8.47	895.3	8.48	897.9	8.50	902.2	8.52	908.4	8.57	916.3	8.62
15	979.2	8.75	980.1	8.76	982.8	8.77	987.5	8.80	994.0	8.85	1002.6	8.90
16	1066.7	9.03	1067.6	9.03	1070.6	9.05	1075.5	9.08	1082.5	9.13	1091.6	9.19
17	1156.9	9.31	1158.0	9.31	1161.1	9.33	1166.4	9.36	1173.8	9.41	1183.4	9.47
18	1250.0	9.58	1251.1	9.59	1254.4	9.61	1260.0	9.64	1267.9	9.69	1278.1	9.75
19	1345.8	9.86	1347.0	9.87	1350.5	9.89	1356.4	9.92	1364.8	9.97	1375.6	10.03
20	1444.4	10.14	1445.7	10.15	1449.4	10.17	1455.6	10.20	1464.5	10.25	1476.0	10.32
21	1545.8	10.42	1547.1	10.42	1551.1	10.45	1557.7	10.48	1567.0	10.53	1579.2	10.60
22	1650.0	10.69	1651.4	10.70	1655.5	10.72	1662.5	10.76	1672.3	10.81	1685.1	10.88
23	1756.9	10.97	1758.4	10.98	1762.8	11.00	1770.1	11.04	1780.4	11.09	1794.0	11.16
24	1866.7	11.25	1868.2	11.26	1872.8	11.28	1880.5	11.32	1891.4	11.38	1905.6	11.45
25	1979.2	11.53	1980.8	11.54	1985.6	11.56	1993.7	11.60	2005.1	11.66	2020.1	11.73
26	2094.4	11.81	2096.1	11.81	2101.2	11.84	2109.7	11.88	2121.7	11.94	2137.4	12.01
27	2212.5	12.08	2214.3	12.09	2219.6	12.12	2228.5	12.16	2241.1	12.22	2257.5	12.30
28	2333.3	12.36	2335.2	12.37	2340.7	12.40	2350.1	12.44	2363.2	12.50	2380.5	12.58
29	2456.9	12.64	2458.9	12.65	2464.7	12.67	2474.4	12.72	2488.2	12.78	2506.2	12.86
30	2583.3	12.92	2585.4	12.93	2591.4	12.95	2601.6	13.00	2616.0	13.06	2634.8	13.15
31	2712.5	13.19	2714.6	13.20	2720.9	13.23	2731.6	13.28	2746.6	13.34	2766.3	13.43
32	2844.4	13.47	2846.6	13.48	2853.2	13.51	2864.3	13.56	2880.0	13.62	2900.5	13.71
33	2979.2	13.75	2981.5	13.76	2988.3	13.79	2999.9	13.84	3016.3	13.90	3037.6	13.99
34	3116.7	14.03	3119.0	14.04	3126.2	14.07	3138.3	14.12	3155.3	14.18	3177.5	14.27
35	3256.9	14.31	3259.4	14.32	3266.9	14.34	3279.4	14.39	3297.1	14.46	3320.3	14.56
36	3400.0	14.58	3402.6	14.59	3410.3	14.62	3423.4	14.67	3441.8	14.75	3465.8	14.84
37	3545.8	14.86	3548.5	14.87	3556.6	14.90	3570.1	14.95	3589.2	15.03	3614.2	15.12
38	3694.4	15.14	3697.2	15.15	3705.6	15.18	3719.6	15.23	3739.5	15.31	3765.4	15.40
39	3845.8	15.42	3848.7	15.43	3857.4	15.46	3872.0	15.51	3892.6	15.59	3919.5	15.69
40	4000.0	15.69	4003.0	15.71	4012.0	15.74	4027.1	15.79	4048.5	15.87	4076.3	15.97
41	4156.9	15.97	4160.0	15.98	4169.4	16.02	4185.0	16.07	4207.1	16.15	4236.0	16.25
42	4316.7	16.25	4319.9	16.26	4329.5	16.29	4345.7	16.35	4368.6	16.43	4398.5	16.53
43	4479.2	16.53	4482.5	16.54	4492.5	16.57	4509.2	16.63	4533.0	16.71	4563.9	16.82
44	4644.4	16.81	4647.9	16.82	4658.2	16.85	4675.5	16.91	4700.1	16.99	4732.1	17.10
45	4812.5	17.08	4816.0	17.10	4826.7	17.13	4844.6	17.19	4870.0	17.27	4903.1	17.38
46	4983.3	17.36	4987.0	17.37	4998.0	17.41	5016.5	17.47	5042.7	17.55	5076.9	17.67
47	5156.9	17.64	5160.7	17.65	5172.1	17.69	5191.2	17.75	5218.3	17.84	5253.5	17.95
48	5333.3	17.92	5337.2	17.93	5349.0	17.97	5368.7	18.03	5396.6	18.12	5433.0	18.23
49	5512.5	18.19	5516.5	18.21	5528.6	18.24	5549.0	18.31	5577.8	18.40	5615.3	18.51
50	5694.4	18.47	5698.6	18.48	5711.1	18.52	5732.1	18.59	5761.7	18.68	5800.5	18.80
51	5879.2	18.75	5883.4	18.76	5896.3	18.80	5917.9	18.87	5948.5	18.96	5988.4	19.08
52	6066.7	19.03	6071.1	19.04	6084.3	19.08	6106.6	19.15	6138.1	19.24	6179.2	19.36
53	6256.9	19.31	6261.5	19.32	6275.1	19.36	6298.1	19.43	6330.5	19.52	6372.8	19.64
54	6450.0	19.58	6454.7	19.60	6468.7	19.64	6492.3	19.71	6525.7	19.80	6569.3	19.93
55	6645.8	19.86	6650.6	19.87	6665.1	19.92	6689.4	19.98	6723.7	20.08	6768.5	20.21
56	6844.4	20.14	6849.4	20.15	6864.3	20.19	6889.2	20.26	6924.5	20.36	6970.6	20.49
57	7045.8	20.42	7050.9	20.43	7066.2	20.47	7091.9	20.54	7128.2	20.64	7175.5	20.77
58	7250.0	20.69	7255.2	20.71	7270.9	20.75	7297.3	20.82	7334.6	20.92	7383.3	21.06
59	7456.9	20.97	7462.3	20.99	7478.4	21.03	7505.5	21.10	7543.9	21.21	7593.9	21.34
60	7666.7	21.25	7672.2	21.26	7688.7	21.31	7716.6	21.38	7755.9	21.49	7807.2	21.62
SUMS.	0°		1°		2°		3°		4°		5°	

TABLE XIV. Whole Sections.—Roadbed 24 ft. Side Slope 1½ to 1.

SUMS.	0°		1°		2°		3°		4°		5°	
61	7879.2	21.53	7884.8	21.54	7901.8	21.59	7930.4	21.66	7970.8	21.77	8023.5	21.91
62	8094.4	21.81	8100.2	21.82	8117.7	21.87	8147.0	21.94	8188.4	22.05	8242.5	22.19
63	8312.5	22.08	8318.4	22.10	8336.4	22.14	8366.4	22.22	8408.9	22.33	8464.4	22.47
64	8533.3	22.36	8539.4	22.38	8557.8	22.42	8588.6	22.50	8632.2	22.61	8689.1	22.75
65	8756.9	22.64	8763.2	22.65	8782.0	22.70	8813.6	22.78	8858.3	22.89	8916.6	23.04
66	8983.3	22.92	8989.7	22.93	9009.0	22.98	9041.4	23.06	9087.2	23.17	9147.0	23.32
67	9212.5	23.19	9219.1	23.21	9238.8	23.26	9272.0	23.34	9318.9	23.45	9380.2	23.60
68	9444.4	23.47	9451.2	23.49	9471.4	23.54	9505.4	23.62	9553.5	23.73	9616.2	23.88
69	9679.2	23.75	9686.1	23.77	9706.8	23.82	9741.6	23.90	9790.8	24.01	9855.0	24.17
70	9916.7	24.03	9923.7	24.04	9944.9	24.09	9980.5	24.18	10030.9	24.30	10096.7	24.45
71	10156.9	24.31	10164.2	24.32	10185.9	24.37	10222.3	24.46	10273.9	24.58	10341.2	24.73
72	10400.0	24.58	10407.4	24.60	10429.6	24.65	10466.9	24.74	10519.7	24.86	10588.5	25.01
73	10645.8	24.86	10653.4	24.88	10676.1	24.93	10714.2	25.02	10768.2	25.14	10838.6	25.30
74	10894.4	25.14	10902.2	25.16	10925.4	25.21	10964.4	25.30	11019.6	25.42	11091.6	25.58
75	11145.8	25.42	11153.7	25.43	11177.5	25.49	11217.4	25.57	11273.8	25.70	11347.4	25.86
76	11400.0	25.69	11408.1	25.71	11432.4	25.77	11473.1	25.85	11530.8	25.98	11606.0	26.14
77	11656.9	25.97	11665.2	25.99	11690.0	26.04	11731.6	26.13	11790.6	26.26	11867.5	26.43
78	11916.7	26.25	11925.1	26.27	11950.4	26.32	11993.0	26.41	12053.2	26.54	12131.7	26.71
79	12179.2	26.53	12187.8	26.55	12213.7	26.60	12257.1	26.69	12318.6	26.82	12398.8	26.99
80	12444.4	26.81	12453.2	26.82	12479.7	26.88	12524.0	26.97	12586.8	27.10	12668.8	27.28
81	12712.5	27.08	12721.5	27.10	12748.5	27.16	12793.8	27.25	12857.9	27.38	12941.5	27.56
82	12983.3	27.36	12992.5	27.38	13020.0	27.44	13066.3	27.53	13131.7	27.67	13217.1	27.84
83	13256.9	27.64	13266.3	27.66	13294.4	27.71	13341.6	27.81	13408.4	27.95	13495.5	28.12
84	13533.3	27.92	13542.9	27.94	13571.6	27.99	13619.7	28.09	13687.8	28.23	13776.7	28.41
85	13812.5	28.19	13822.2	28.21	13851.5	28.27	13900.6	28.37	13970.1	28.51	14060.8	28.69
86	14094.4	28.47	14104.4	28.49	14134.2	28.55	14184.3	28.65	14255.2	28.79	14347.7	28.97
87	14379.2	28.75	14389.3	28.77	14419.7	28.83	14470.8	28.93	14543.1	29.07	14637.4	29.25
88	14666.7	29.03	14677.0	29.05	14708.0	29.11	14760.1	29.21	14833.8	29.35	14929.9	29.54
89	14956.9	29.31	14967.5	29.33	14999.1	29.39	15052.2	29.49	15127.3	29.63	15225.3	29.82
90	15250.0	29.58	15260.7	29.60	15292.9	29.66	15347.0	29.77	15423.6	29.91	15523.5	30.10
91	15545.8	29.86	15556.7	29.88	15589.6	29.94	15644.7	30.05	15722.7	30.19	15824.5	30.38
92	15844.4	30.14	15855.6	30.16	15889.0	30.22	15945.2	30.33	16024.7	30.47	16128.3	30.67
93	16145.8	30.42	16157.2	30.44	16191.2	30.50	16248.5	30.61	16329.4	30.76	16435.0	30.95
94	16450.0	30.69	16461.5	30.72	16496.2	30.78	16554.5	30.89	16637.0	31.04	16744.5	31.23
95	16756.9	30.97	16768.7	30.99	16804.0	31.06	16863.4	31.16	16947.3	31.32	17056.8	31.52
96	17066.7	31.25	17078.6	31.27	17114.6	31.34	17175.0	31.44	17260.5	31.60	17372.0	31.80
97	17379.2	31.53	17391.3	31.55	17428.0	31.61	17489.5	31.72	17576.5	31.88	17690.0	32.08
98	17694.4	31.81	17706.8	31.83	17744.1	31.89	17806.7	32.00	17895.2	32.16	18010.8	32.36
99	18012.5	32.08	18025.1	32.11	18063.0	32.17	18126.7	32.28	18216.8	32.44	18334.4	32.65
100	18333.3	32.36	18346.2	32.38	18384.8	32.45	18449.6	32.56	18541.2	32.72	18660.8	32.93
SUMS.	0°		1°		2°		3°		4°		5°	

SECOND PART.

DIFF.	0°		1°		2°		3°		4°		5°	
1	.5	0.14	.5	0.14	.5	0.14	.5	0.14	.5	0.14	.5	0.14
2	1.9	0.23	1.9	0.23	1.9	0.23	1.9	0.23	1.9	0.23	1.9	0.24
3	4.2	0.32	4.2	0.32	4.2	0.32	4.2	0.33	4.2	0.33	4.2	0.33
4	7.4	0.42	7.4	0.42	7.4	0.42	7.5	0.42	7.5	0.42	7.5	0.42
5	11.6	0.51	11.6	0.51	11.6	0.51	11.6	0.51	11.7	0.51	11.8	0.52
6	16.7	0.60	16.7	0.60	16.7	0.60	16.8	0.61	16.9	0.61	17.0	0.61
7	22.7	0.69	22.7	0.69	22.7	0.70	22.8	0.70	22.9	0.70	23.1	0.71
8	29.6	0.79	29.6	0.79	29.7	0.79	29.8	0.79	30.0	0.80	30.1	0.80
9	37.5	0.88	37.5	0.88	37.6	0.88	37.7	0.89	37.9	0.89	38.2	0.90
10	46.3	0.97	46.3	0.97	46.4	0.97	46.6	0.98	46.8	0.98	47.1	0.99
DIFF.	0°		1°		2°		3°		4°		5°	

TABLE XIV. Whole Sections.—Roadbed 24 ft. Side Slope 1½ to 1.

SUMS.	6°		7°		8°		9°		10°		11°	
1	....		....		....		....		....		....	
2	....		....		....		....		....		....	
3	158.6	5.55	163.4	5.61	....		....		....		....	
4	214.2	5.84	219.5	5.89	225.8	5.96	233.2	6.04	....		....	
5	272.6	6.12	278.5	6.18	285.4	6.25	293.6	6.33	303.0	6.42	313.9	6.53
6	333.8	6.41	340.3	6.47	347.9	6.54	356.9	6.62	367.2	6.72	379.1	6.83
7	397.9	6.69	405.0	6.76	413.3	6.83	423.1	6.92	434.4	7.02	447.4	7.13
8	464.8	6.98	472.5	7.04	481.7	7.12	492.3	7.21	504.6	7.32	518.8	7.44
9	534.6	7.26	543.0	7.33	552.9	7.41	564.4	7.51	577.8	7.62	593.2	7.74
10	607.3	7.55	616.3	7.62	627.0	7.70	639.5	7.80	654.0	7.91	670.6	8.05
11	682.8	7.83	692.5	7.91	704.0	7.99	717.5	8.10	733.1	8.21	751.0	8.35
12	761.1	8.12	771.6	8.19	784.0	8.28	798.5	8.39	815.2	8.51	834.5	8.65
13	842.3	8.40	853.5	8.48	866.8	8.58	882.4	8.68	900.4	8.81	921.0	8.96
14	926.3	8.69	938.3	8.77	952.6	8.87	969.2	8.98	988.5	9.11	1010.6	9.26
15	1013.2	8.97	1026.0	9.06	1041.2	9.16	1059.0	9.27	1079.6	9.41	1103.2	9.56
16	1102.9	9.26	1116.6	9.34	1132.8	9.45	1151.7	9.57	1173.6	9.71	1198.8	9.87
17	1195.5	9.54	1210.1	9.63	1227.3	9.74	1247.4	9.86	1270.7	10.01	1297.5	10.17
18	1290.9	9.83	1306.4	9.92	1324.7	10.03	1346.0	10.16	1370.8	10.30	1399.2	10.47
19	1389.2	10.11	1405.6	10.21	1425.0	10.32	1447.6	10.45	1473.8	10.60	1503.9	10.78
20	1490.3	10.40	1507.6	10.49	1528.2	10.61	1552.1	10.75	1579.8	10.90	1611.7	11.08
21	1594.3	10.68	1612.6	10.78	1634.3	10.90	1659.6	11.04	1688.9	11.20	1722.5	11.38
22	1701.1	10.97	1720.4	11.07	1743.3	11.19	1770.0	11.33	1800.9	11.50	1836.3	11.69
23	1810.8	11.25	1831.1	11.36	1855.2	11.48	1883.3	11.63	1915.8	11.80	1953.2	11.99
24	1923.3	11.54	1944.7	11.65	1970.0	11.77	1999.6	11.92	2033.8	12.10	2073.1	12.30
25	2038.7	11.82	2061.1	11.93	2087.8	12.06	2118.8	12.22	2154.8	12.39	2196.1	12.60
26	2156.9	12.11	2180.5	12.22	2208.4	12.35	2241.0	12.51	2278.7	12.69	2322.1	12.90
27	2278.0	12.39	2302.7	12.51	2331.9	12.65	2366.1	12.81	2405.7	12.99	2451.1	13.21
28	2401.9	12.68	2427.7	12.80	2458.4	12.94	2494.2	13.10	2535.6	13.29	2583.2	13.51
29	2528.6	12.96	2555.7	13.08	2587.8	13.23	2625.2	13.39	2668.5	13.59	2718.3	13.81
30	2658.2	13.25	2686.5	13.37	2720.0	13.52	2759.1	13.69	2804.4	13.89	2856.4	14.12
31	2790.7	13.53	2820.2	13.66	2855.2	13.81	2896.0	13.98	2943.3	14.19	2997.6	14.42
32	2926.0	13.82	2956.8	13.95	2993.3	14.10	3035.9	14.28	3085.1	14.49	3141.8	14.72
33	3064.2	14.10	3096.3	14.23	3134.3	14.39	3178.6	14.57	3230.0	14.78	3289.0	15.03
34	3205.2	14.39	3238.6	14.52	3278.2	14.68	3324.4	14.87	3377.8	15.08	3439.3	15.33
35	3349.0	14.67	3383.8	14.81	3425.0	14.97	3473.0	15.16	3528.7	15.38	3592.6	15.63
36	3495.7	14.96	3531.9	15.10	3574.7	15.26	3624.7	15.46	3682.5	15.68	3748.9	15.94
37	3645.3	15.24	3682.8	15.38	3727.3	15.55	3779.2	15.75	3839.3	15.98	3908.3	16.24
38	3797.7	15.52	3836.7	15.67	3882.8	15.84	3936.7	16.04	3999.1	16.28	4070.7	16.55
39	3952.9	15.81	3993.4	15.96	4041.2	16.13	4097.2	16.33	4161.9	16.58	4236.2	16.85
40	4111.0	16.09	4152.9	16.25	4202.6	16.42	4260.5	16.63	4327.6	16.87	4404.7	17.15
41	4272.0	16.38	4315.4	16.53	4366.8	16.72	4426.9	16.93	4496.4	17.17	4576.2	17.46
42	4435.8	16.66	4480.7	16.82	4534.0	17.01	4596.1	17.22	4668.1	17.47	4750.8	17.76
43	4602.4	16.95	4648.9	17.11	4704.0	17.30	4768.4	17.52	4842.8	17.77	4928.4	18.06
44	4771.9	17.23	4820.0	17.40	4877.0	17.59	4943.5	17.81	5020.5	18.07	5109.0	18.37
45	4944.2	17.52	4994.0	17.68	5052.9	17.88	5121.6	18.11	5201.2	18.37	5292.7	18.67
46	5119.4	17.80	5170.8	17.97	5231.6	18.17	5302.7	18.40	5384.9	18.67	5479.4	18.97
47	5297.5	18.09	5350.5	18.26	5413.3	18.46	5486.7	18.69	5571.6	18.97	5669.1	19.28
48	5478.3	18.37	5533.1	18.55	5597.9	18.75	5673.6	18.99	5761.2	19.26	5861.9	19.58
49	5662.1	18.66	5718.5	18.83	5785.4	19.04	5863.5	19.28	5953.9	19.56	6057.7	19.88
50	5848.7	18.94	5906.9	19.12	5975.8	19.33	6056.4	19.58	6149.5	19.86	6256.6	20.19
51	6038.1	19.23	6098.1	19.41	6169.1	19.62	6252.1	19.87	6348.1	20.16	6458.5	20.49
52	6230.4	19.51	6292.2	19.70	6365.4	19.91	6450.8	20.17	6549.7	20.46	6663.4	20.80
53	6425.5	19.80	6489.1	19.98	6564.5	20.20	6652.5	20.46	6754.3	20.76	6871.3	21.10
54	6623.5	20.08	6689.0	20.27	6766.5	20.49	6857.1	20.75	6961.9	21.06	7082.3	21.40
55	6824.3	20.37	6891.7	20.56	6971.5	20.78	7064.7	21.05	7172.5	21.36	7296.3	21.71
56	7028.0	20.65	7097.3	20.85	7179.3	21.08	7275.1	21.34	7386.0	21.65	7513.4	22.01
57	7234.5	20.94	7305.7	21.13	7390.1	21.37	7488.6	21.64	7602.6	21.95	7733.5	22.31
58	7443.9	21.22	7517.1	21.42	7603.7	21.66	7705.0	21.93	7822.1	22.25	7956.7	22.62
59	7656.1	21.51	7731.3	21.71	7820.3	21.95	7924.3	22.23	8044.6	22.55	8182.8	22.92
60	7871.1	21.79	7948.4	22.00	8039.8	22.24	8146.5	22.52	8270.1	22.85	8412.0	23.22
SUMS.	6°		7°		8°		9°		10°		11°	

TABLE XIV. Whole Sections.—Roadbed 24 ft. Side Slope 1½ to 1.

SUMS.	6°	7°	8°	9°	10°	11°
61	8089.1 22.07	8168.3 22.28	8262.2 22.53	8371.8 22.82	8498.6 23.15	8644.3 23.53
62	8309.8 22.36	8391.1 22.57	8487.4 22.82	8599.9 23.11	8730.0 23.45	8879.6 23.83
63	8533.5 22.65	8616.9 22.86	8715.6 23.11	8831.0 23.40	8964.5 23.74	9117.9 24.14
64	8759.9 22.93	8845.4 23.15	8946.7 23.40	9065.1 23.70	9201.9 24.04	9359.2 24.44
65	8989.2 23.22	9076.9 23.43	9180.8 23.69	9302.1 23.99	9442.4 24.34	9603.6 24.74
66	9221.4 23.50	9311.3 23.72	9417.7 23.98	9542.0 24.29	9685.8 24.64	9851.0 25.05
67	9456.4 23.79	9548.5 24.01	9657.5 24.27	9784.9 24.58	9932.2 24.94	10101.5 25.35
68	9694.2 24.07	9788.6 24.30	9900.2 24.56	10030.7 24.88	10181.6 25.24	10355.0 25.65
69	9934.9 24.36	10031.5 24.58	10145.9 24.85	10279.4 25.17	10434.0 25.54	10611.5 25.96
70	10178.5 24.64	10277.4 24.87	10394.4 25.15	10531.1 25.47	10689.3 25.84	10871.1 26.26
71	10424.9 24.93	10526.1 25.16	10645.9 25.44	10785.8 25.76	10947.7 26.13	11133.7 26.56
72	10674.2 25.21	10777.7 25.45	10900.2 25.73	11043.4 26.05	11209.0 26.43	11399.3 26.87
73	10926.3 25.49	11032.1 25.73	11157.5 26.02	11304.0 26.35	11473.3 26.73	11668.0 27.17
74	11181.2 25.78	11289.5 26.02	11417.7 26.31	11567.4 26.64	11740.7 27.03	11939.7 27.47
75	11439.0 26.06	11549.7 26.31	11680.8 26.60	11833.9 26.94	12011.0 27.33	12214.5 27.78
76	11699.6 26.35	11812.8 26.60	11946.7 26.89	12103.2 27.23	12284.2 27.63	12492.2 28.08
77	11963.1 26.63	12078.7 26.88	12215.6 27.18	12375.6 27.53	12560.5 27.93	12773.1 28.39
78	12229.5 26.92	12347.6 27.17	12487.4 27.47	12650.8 27.82	12839.8 28.22	13056.9 28.69
79	12498.7 27.20	12619.3 27.46	12762.1 27.76	12929.0 28.11	13122.0 28.52	13343.8 28.99
80	12770.7 27.49	12893.9 27.75	13039.8 28.05	13210.2 28.41	13407.2 28.82	13633.7 29.30
81	13045.6 27.77	13171.4 28.03	13320.3 28.34	13494.3 28.70	13695.5 29.12	13926.7 29.60
82	13323.3 28.06	13451.7 28.32	13603.7 28.63	13781.3 29.00	13986.7 29.42	14222.7 29.90
83	13603.9 28.34	13734.9 28.61	13890.1 28.92	14071.2 29.29	14280.9 29.72	14521.7 30.21
84	13887.4 28.63	14021.0 28.90	14179.3 29.22	14364.1 29.59	14578.0 30.02	14823.8 30.51
85	14173.6 28.91	14310.0 29.18	14471.4 29.51	14660.0 29.88	14878.2 30.32	15128.9 30.81
86	14462.8 29.20	14601.8 29.47	14766.5 29.80	14958.8 30.18	15181.4 30.61	15437.0 31.12
87	14754.7 29.48	14896.5 29.76	15064.5 30.09	15260.6 30.47	15487.5 30.91	15748.2 31.42
88	15049.6 29.77	15194.1 30.05	15365.3 30.38	15565.3 30.76	15796.6 31.21	16062.4 31.72
89	15347.3 30.05	15494.6 30.33	15669.1 30.67	15872.9 31.06	16108.7 31.51	16379.7 32.03
90	15647.8 30.34	15798.0 30.62	15975.8 30.96	16183.5 31.35	16423.8 31.81	16700.0 32.33
91	15951.2 30.62	16104.2 30.91	16285.4 31.25	16497.0 31.65	16741.9 32.11	17023.3 32.64
92	16257.4 30.91	16413.3 31.20	16597.9 31.54	16813.5 31.94	17063.0 32.41	17349.6 32.94
93	16566.4 31.19	16725.2 31.48	16913.3 31.83	17132.9 32.24	17387.0 32.70	17679.0 33.24
94	16878.4 31.48	17040.1 31.77	17231.6 32.12	17455.3 32.53	17714.1 33.00	18011.4 33.55
95	17193.1 31.76	17357.8 32.06	17552.8 32.41	17780.6 32.82	18044.1 33.30	18346.9 33.85
96	17510.8 32.05	17678.4 32.35	17877.0 32.70	18108.9 33.12	18377.1 33.60	18685.4 34.15
97	17831.2 32.33	18001.9 32.63	18204.0 32.99	18440.0 33.41	18713.1 33.90	19027.0 34.46
98	18154.5 32.62	18328.2 32.92	18533.9 33.28	18774.2 33.71	19052.1 34.20	19371.5 34.76
99	18480.7 32.90	18657.5 33.21	18866.8 33.58	19111.3 34.00	19394.1 34.50	19719.1 35.06
100	18809.7 33.19	18989.6 33.50	19202.5 33.87	19451.2 34.30	19739.1 34.80	20069.8 35.37
SUMS.	6°	7°	8°	9°	10°	11°

SECOND PART.

DIFF.	6°	7°	8°	9°	10°	11°
1	.5 0.14	.5 0.14	.5 0.15	.5 0.15	.5 0.15	.5 0.15
2	1.9 0.24	1.9 0.24	1.9 0.24	2.0 0.25	2.0 0.25	2.0 0.25
3	4.3 0.33	4.3 0.34	4.4 0.34	4.4 0.34	4.5 0.35	4.6 0.35
4	7.6 0.43	7.7 0.43	7.8 0.44	7.9 0.44	8.0 0.45	8.1 0.46
5	11.9 0.52	12.0 0.53	12.1 0.53	12.3 0.54	12.4 0.55	12.6 0.56
6	17.1 0.62	17.3 0.62	17.4 0.63	17.7 0.64	17.9 0.65	18.2 0.66
7	23.3 0.71	23.5 0.72	23.7 0.73	24.0 0.74	24.4 0.75	24.8 0.76
8	30.4 0.81	30.7 0.81	31.0 0.82	31.4 0.83	31.9 0.85	32.4 0.86
9	38.5 0.90	38.8 0.91	39.2 0.92	39.7 0.93	40.3 0.95	41.0 0.96
10	47.5 1.00	47.9 1.01	48.4 1.02	49.1 1.03	49.8 1.05	50.6 1.06
DIFF.	6°	7°	8°	9°	10°	11°

TABLE XIV. Whole Sections.—Roadbed 24 ft. Side Slope 1½ to 1.

SUMS.	12°		13°		14°		15°		16°		17°	
1	....		....		....		....		....		....	
2	....		....		....		....		....		....	
3	....		....		....		....		....		....	
4	....		....		....		....		....		....	
5	326.8	6.65	....		....		....		....		....	
6	392.7	6.96	408.3	7.10	426.0	7.27	....		....		....	
7	462.3	7.27	479.3	7.42	498.6	7.59	520.7	7.79	545.9	8.01	....	
8	535.0	7.58	553.5	7.73	574.5	7.91	598.6	8.12	626.0	8.35	657.5	8.62
9	610.7	7.88	630.8	8.05	653.7	8.24	679.7	8.45	709.5	8.69	743.7	8.97
10	689.6	8.19	711.3	8.36	736.0	8.56	764.2	8.78	796.5	9.03	833.4	9.32
11	771.5	8.50	794.9	8.68	821.6	8.88	852.0	9.11	886.8	9.37	926.6	9.67
12	856.6	8.81	881.7	9.00	910.4	9.20	943.1	9.44	980.5	9.71	1023.3	10.03
13	944.7	9.12	971.7	9.31	1002.4	9.53	1037.5	9.77	1077.6	10.05	1123.6	10.38
14	1035.9	9.43	1064.8	9.63	1097.7	9.85	1135.3	10.10	1178.2	10.40	1227.3	10.73
15	1130.2	9.74	1161.0	9.94	1196.2	10.17	1236.3	10.44	1282.1	10.74	1334.6	11.08
16	1227.6	10.05	1260.5	10.26	1297.9	10.50	1340.7	10.77	1389.5	11.08	1445.4	11.43
17	1328.1	10.36	1363.0	10.57	1402.9	10.82	1448.4	11.10	1500.3	11.42	1559.8	11.78
18	1431.7	10.67	1468.8	10.89	1511.1	11.14	1559.3	11.43	1614.5	11.76	1677.6	12.14
19	1538.4	10.98	1577.7	11.20	1622.5	11.46	1673.6	11.76	1732.0	12.10	1798.9	12.49
20	1648.1	11.29	1689.7	11.52	1737.2	11.79	1791.2	12.09	1853.0	12.44	1923.8	12.84
21	1761.0	11.60	1804.9	11.84	1855.0	12.11	1912.2	12.42	1977.4	12.78	2052.2	13.19
22	1876.9	11.90	1923.3	12.15	1976.1	12.43	2036.4	12.75	2105.3	13.12	2184.1	13.54
23	1996.0	12.21	2044.8	12.47	2100.5	12.76	2164.0	13.09	2236.5	13.46	2319.5	13.89
24	2118.1	12.52	2169.5	12.78	2228.0	13.08	2294.8	13.42	2371.1	13.80	2458.5	14.25
25	2243.4	12.83	2297.3	13.10	2358.8	13.40	2429.0	13.75	2509.1	14.14	2601.0	14.60
26	2371.7	13.14	2428.3	13.41	2492.9	13.73	2566.5	14.08	2650.6	14.49	2746.9	14.95
27	2503.1	13.45	2562.4	13.73	2630.1	14.05	2707.3	14.41	2795.4	14.83	2896.4	15.30
28	2637.6	13.76	2699.7	14.05	2770.6	14.37	2851.4	14.74	2943.7	15.17	3049.4	15.65
29	2775.2	14.07	2840.2	14.36	2914.3	14.69	2998.8	15.07	3095.4	15.51	3206.0	16.00
30	2915.9	14.38	2983.8	14.68	3061.2	15.02	3149.6	15.41	3250.4	15.85	3366.0	16.36
31	3059.7	14.69	3130.6	14.99	3211.4	15.34	3303.6	15.74	3408.9	16.19	3529.6	16.71
32	3206.6	15.00	3280.5	15.31	3364.8	15.66	3461.0	16.07	3570.8	16.53	3696.7	17.06
33	3356.5	15.31	3433.6	15.62	3521.4	15.99	3621.7	16.40	3736.1	16.87	3867.3	17.41
34	3509.6	15.62	3589.8	15.94	3681.3	16.31	3785.7	16.73	3904.8	17.21	4041.4	17.76
35	3665.7	15.92	3749.2	16.25	3844.4	16.63	3953.0	17.06	4077.0	17.55	4219.0	18.12
36	3825.0	16.23	3911.8	16.57	4010.7	16.95	4123.6	17.39	4252.5	17.89	4400.2	18.47
37	3987.3	16.54	4077.5	16.89	4180.3	17.28	4297.5	17.72	4431.4	18.23	4584.9	18.82
38	4152.7	16.85	4246.3	17.20	4353.0	17.60	4474.7	18.06	4613.8	18.58	4773.0	19.17
39	4321.3	17.16	4418.3	17.52	4529.0	17.92	4655.3	18.39	4799.5	18.92	4964.8	19.52
40	4492.9	17.47	4593.5	17.83	4708.3	18.25	4839.2	18.72	4988.7	19.26	5160.0	19.87
41	4667.6	17.78	4771.9	18.15	4890.7	18.57	5026.4	19.05	5181.3	19.60	5358.7	20.23
42	4845.4	18.09	4953.3	18.46	5076.4	18.89	5216.9	19.38	5377.2	19.94	5561.0	20.58
43	5026.3	18.40	5138.0	18.78	5265.4	19.22	5410.7	19.71	5576.6	20.28	5766.8	20.93
44	5210.2	18.71	5325.8	19.10	5457.5	19.54	5607.8	20.04	5779.4	20.62	5976.0	21.28
45	5397.3	19.02	5516.7	19.41	5652.9	19.86	5808.2	20.37	5985.6	20.96	6188.9	21.63
46	5587.5	19.33	5710.9	19.73	5851.5	20.18	6012.0	20.71	6195.2	21.30	6405.2	21.98
47	5780.7	19.63	5908.1	20.04	6053.4	20.51	6219.0	21.04	6408.3	21.64	6625.0	22.34
48	5977.1	19.94	6108.5	20.36	6258.4	20.83	6429.4	21.37	6624.7	21.98	6848.4	22.69
49	6176.5	20.25	6312.1	20.67	6466.7	21.15	6643.1	21.70	6844.5	22.32	7075.3	23.04
50	6379.1	20.56	6518.9	20.99	6678.3	21.48	6860.1	22.03	7067.8	22.67	7305.7	23.39
51	6584.7	20.87	6728.8	21.30	6893.0	21.80	7080.4	22.36	7294.4	23.01	7539.6	23.74
52	6793.4	21.18	6941.8	21.62	7111.0	22.12	7304.0	22.69	7524.5	23.35	7777.0	24.10
53	7005.2	21.49	7158.0	21.94	7332.2	22.44	7531.0	23.03	7758.0	23.69	8018.0	24.45
54	7220.1	21.80	7377.4	22.25	7556.7	22.77	7761.2	23.36	7994.8	24.03	8262.5	24.80
55	7438.1	22.11	7599.9	22.57	7784.4	23.09	7994.8	23.69	8235.1	24.37	8510.4	25.15
56	7659.2	22.42	7825.6	22.88	8015.3	23.41	8231.7	24.02	8478.8	24.71	8762.0	25.50
57	7883.4	22.73	8054.4	23.20	8249.4	23.74	8471.8	24.35	8725.9	25.05	9017.0	25.85
58	8110.6	23.04	8286.4	23.51	8486.8	24.06	8715.3	24.68	8976.4	25.39	9275.5	26.21
59	8341.0	23.35	8521.5	23.83	8727.4	24.38	8962.2	25.01	9230.4	25.73	9537.6	26.56
60	8574.5	23.65	8759.8	24.15	8971.2	24.71	9212.3	25.34	9487.7	26.07	9803.2	26.91
SUMS.	12°		13°		14°		15°		16°		17°	

TABLE XIV. Whole Sections.—Roadbed 24 ft. Side Slope 1½ to 1.

SUMS.	12°	13°	14°	15°	16°	17°
61	8811.0 23.96	9001.3 24.46	9218.3 25.03	9465.7 25.68	9748.4 26.41	10072.3 27.26
62	9050.6 24.27	9245.9 24.78	9468.5 25.35	9722.5 26.01	10012.6 26.76	10344.9 27.61
63	9293.4 24.58	9493.7 25.09	9722.1 25.67	9982.6 26.34	10280.1 27.10	10621.0 27.96
64	9539.2 24.89	9744.6 25.41	9978.8 26.00	10245.9 26.67	10551.1 27.44	10900.6 28.32
65	9788.1 25.20	9998.7 25.72	10238.8 26.32	10512.6 27.00	10825.5 27.78	11183.8 28.67
66	10040.1 25.51	10255.9 26.04	10502.0 26.64	10782.6 27.33	11103.2 28.12	11470.5 29.02
67	10295.2 25.82	10516.3 26.36	10768.4 26.97	11056.0 27.66	11384.4 28.46	11760.7 29.37
68	10553.4 26.13	10779.9 26.67	11038.1 27.29	11332.6 27.99	11669.0 28.80	12054.4 29.72
69	10814.7 26.44	11046.6 26.99	11311.0 27.61	11612.5 28.33	11957.0 29.14	12351.6 30.08
70	11079.1 26.75	11316.4 27.30	11587.1 27.94	11895.8 28.66	12248.4 29.48	12652.4 30.43
71	11346.5 27.06	11589.5 27.62	11866.4 28.26	12182.4 28.99	12543.2 29.82	12956.6 30.78
72	11617.1 27.37	11865.6 27.93	12149.0 28.58	12472.2 29.32	12841.5 30.16	13264.4 31.13
73	11890.7 27.67	12145.0 28.25	12434.8 28.90	12765.4 29.65	13143.1 30.50	13575.7 31.48
74	12167.5 27.98	12427.5 28.56	12723.9 29.23	13062.0 29.98	13448.2 30.85	13890.6 31.83
75	12447.3 28.29	12713.1 28.88	13016.1 29.55	13361.8 30.31	13756.6 31.19	14208.9 32.19
76	12730.3 28.60	13001.9 29.20	13311.6 29.87	13664.9 30.64	14068.5 31.53	14530.7 32.54
77	13016.3 28.91	13293.9 29.51	13610.4 30.20	13971.4 30.98	14383.7 31.87	14856.1 32.89
78	13305.4 29.22	13589.0 29.83	13912.3 30.52	14281.1 31.31	14702.4 32.21	15185.0 33.24
79	13597.6 29.53	13887.2 30.14	14217.5 30.84	14594.2 31.64	15024.5 32.55	15517.4 33.59
80	13892.9 29.84	14188.7 30.46	14525.9 31.16	14910.6 31.97	15350.0 32.89	15853.4 33.94
81	14191.3 30.15	14493.3 30.77	14837.6 31.49	15230.3 32.30	15678.9 33.23	16192.8 34.30
82	14492.8 30.46	14801.0 31.09	15152.4 31.81	15553.3 32.63	16011.2 33.57	16535.8 34.65
83	14797.3 30.77	15111.9 31.41	15470.5 32.13	15879.6 32.96	16346.9 33.91	16882.2 35.00
84	15105.0 31.08	15425.9 31.72	15791.9 32.46	16209.3 33.30	16686.1 34.25	17232.2 35.35
85	15415.8 31.38	15743.2 32.04	16116.4 32.78	16542.2 33.63	17028.6 34.59	17585.7 35.70
86	15729.6 31.69	16063.5 32.35	16444.2 33.10	16878.5 33.96	17374.6 34.94	17942.8 36.05
87	16046.5 32.00	16387.0 32.67	16775.3 33.43	17218.1 34.29	17723.9 35.28	18303.3 36.41
88	16366.6 32.31	16713.7 32.98	17109.5 33.75	17561.0 34.62	18076.7 35.62	18667.4 36.76
89	16689.7 32.62	17043.5 33.30	17447.0 34.07	17907.2 34.95	18432.8 35.96	19035.0 37.11
90	17015.9 32.93	17376.5 33.61	17787.7 34.39	18256.7 35.28	18792.4 36.30	19406.1 37.46
91	17345.2 33.24	17712.7 33.93	18131.6 34.72	18609.5 35.61	19155.4 36.64	19780.7 37.81
92	17677.6 33.55	18052.0 34.25	18478.8 35.04	18965.7 35.95	19521.8 36.98	20158.8 38.17
93	18013.1 33.86	18394.4 34.56	18829.2 35.36	19325.1 36.28	19891.6 37.32	20540.5 38.52
94	18351.7 34.17	18740.1 34.88	19182.8 35.69	19687.9 36.61	20264.8 37.66	20925.7 38.87
95	18693.4 34.48	19088.8 35.19	19539.7 36.01	20054.0 36.94	20641.4 38.00	21314.4 39.22
96	19038.2 34.79	19440.8 35.51	19899.8 36.33	20423.4 37.27	21021.5 38.34	21706.6 39.57
97	19386.0 35.10	19795.8 35.82	20263.1 36.65	20796.1 37.60	21404.9 38.68	22102.3 39.92
98	19737.0 35.40	20154.1 36.14	20629.7 36.98	21172.1 37.93	21791.7 39.02	22501.5 40.28
99	20091.0 35.71	20515.5 36.46	20999.4 37.30	21551.4 38.26	22182.0 39.37	22904.3 40.63
100	20448.2 36.02	20880.0 36.77	21372.4 37.62	21934.1 38.60	22575.7 39.71	23310.6 40.98
SUMS.	12°	13°	14°	15°	16°	17°

SECOND PART.

DIFF.	12°	13°	14°	15°	16°	17°
1	.5 0.15	.5 0.16	.5 0.16	.6 0.17	.6 0.17	.6 0.18
2	2.1 0.26	2.1 0.26	2.2 0.27	2.2 0.28	2.3 0.28	2.3 0.29
3	4.6 0.36	4.7 0.37	4.8 0.38	5.0 0.39	5.1 0.40	5.3 0.41
4	8.2 0.46	8.4 0.47	8.6 0.48	8.8 0.50	9.1 0.51	9.4 0.53
5	12.9 0.57	13.2 0.58	13.5 0.59	13.8 0.61	14.2 0.62	14.7 0.64
6	18.6 0.67	18.9 0.68	19.4 0.70	19.9 0.72	20.4 0.74	21.1 0.76
7	25.3 0.77	25.8 0.79	26.4 0.81	27.1 0.83	27.8 0.85	28.7 0.88
8	33.0 0.88	33.7 0.89	34.4 0.92	35.3 0.94	36.4 0.97	37.5 1.00
9	41.7 0.98	42.6 1.00	43.6 1.02	44.7 1.05	46.0 1.08	47.5 1.11
10	51.5 1.08	52.6 1.10	53.8 1.13	55.2 1.16	56.8 1.19	58.6 1.23
DIFF.	12°	13°	14°	15°	16°	17°

TABLE XIV. Whole Sections.—Roadbed 24 ft. Side Slope 1½ to 1.

SUMS.	18°	19°	20°	21°	22°	23°
1	....	....	....	....	....	....
2	....	....	....	....	....	....
3	....	....	....	....	....	....
4	....	....	....	....	....	....
5	....	....	....	....	....	....
6	....	....	....	....	....	....
7	....	....	....	....	....	....
8	698.7 8.93	....	....	....	....	....
9	782.9 9.29	828.3 9.66	881.1 10.09	....	....	....
10	875.8 9.65	924.9 10.04	982.0 10.49	1049.0 11.01	1128.2 11.63	....
11	972.4 10.02	1026.3 10.42	1086.9 10.88	1159.1 11.43	1244.7 12.07	1347.3 12.85
12	1072.6 10.38	1129.5 10.80	1195.7 11.28	1273.4 11.84	1365.4 12.51	1475.8 13.31
13	1176.4 10.75	1237.5 11.18	1308.5 11.67	1391.8 12.26	1490.5 12.95	1608.9 13.78
14	1283.9 11.11	1349.2 11.55	1425.2 12.07	1514.4 12.67	1620.1 13.39	1746.7 14.25
15	1395.0 11.48	1464.8 11.93	1545.9 12.47	1641.2 13.09	1754.0 13.83	1889.2 14.72
16	1509.8 11.84	1584.1 12.31	1670.6 12.86	1772.1 13.51	1892.3 14.27	2036.4 15.18
17	1628.2 12.20	1707.2 12.69	1799.2 13.26	1907.1 13.92	2034.9 14.71	2188.2 15.65
18	1750.2 12.57	1834.1 13.07	1931.8 13.65	2046.3 14.34	2182.0 15.15	2344.7 16.12
19	1875.9 12.93	1964.8 13.45	2068.3 14.05	2189.7 14.75	2333.5 15.59	2505.9 16.59
20	2005.2 13.30	2099.3 13.83	2208.8 14.44	2337.2 15.17	2489.3 16.02	2671.7 17.05
21	2138.2 13.66	2237.6 14.21	2353.2 14.84	2488.9 15.58	2649.6 16.46	2842.2 17.52
22	2274.8 14.03	2379.7 14.58	2501.6 15.24	2644.7 16.00	2814.2 16.90	3017.4 17.99
23	2415.1 14.39	2525.5 14.97	2654.0 15.63	2804.7 16.41	2983.2 17.34	3197.3 18.45
24	2559.0 14.75	2675.2 15.34	2810.3 16.03	2968.9 16.83	3156.6 17.78	3381.8 18.92
25	2706.5 15.12	2828.6 15.72	2970.6 16.42	3137.1 17.25	3334.4 18.22	3571.0 19.39
26	2857.7 15.48	2985.8 16.10	3134.8 16.82	3309.3 17.66	3516.6 18.66	3764.9 19.85
27	3012.6 15.85	3146.8 16.48	3303.0 17.21	3483.2 18.08	3703.2 19.10	3963.4 20.32
28	3171.0 16.21	3311.6 16.86	3475.1 17.61	3667.0 18.49	3894.2 19.54	4166.7 20.79
29	3333.2 16.58	3480.2 17.24	3651.2 18.01	3851.9 18.91	4089.6 19.98	4374.5 21.26
30	3498.9 16.94	3652.6 17.62	3831.3 18.40	4041.0 19.32	4289.3 20.41	4587.1 21.72
31	3668.3 17.31	3828.7 17.99	4015.3 18.80	4234.2 19.74	4493.5 20.85	4804.3 22.19
32	3841.4 17.67	4008.7 18.37	4203.3 19.19	4431.6 20.15	4702.0 21.29	5026.2 22.66
33	4018.1 18.03	4192.4 18.75	4395.2 19.59	4633.1 20.57	4914.9 21.73	5252.8 23.12
34	4198.4 18.40	4379.9 19.13	4591.1 19.98	4838.8 20.99	5132.3 22.17	5484.1 23.59
35	4382.4 18.76	4571.2 19.51	4791.0 20.38	5048.7 21.40	5354.0 22.61	5720.0 24.06
36	4570.0 19.13	4766.3 19.89	4994.8 20.78	5262.7 21.82	5580.1 23.05	5960.6 24.53
37	4761.3 19.49	4965.2 20.27	5202.5 21.17	5480.9 22.23	5810.5 23.49	6205.8 24.99
38	4956.2 19.86	5167.9 20.65	5414.2 21.57	5703.2 22.65	6045.4 23.93	6455.8 25.46
39	5154.7 20.22	5374.4 21.03	5629.9 21.96	5929.7 23.06	6284.7 24.37	6710.4 25.93
40	5356.9 20.58	5584.6 21.40	5849.5 22.36	6160.3 23.48	6528.4 24.80	6969.7 26.40
41	5562.8 20.95	5798.7 21.78	6073.1 22.75	6395.1 23.89	6776.4 25.24	7233.6 26.86
42	5772.3 21.31	6016.5 22.16	6300.7 23.15	6634.0 24.31	7028.8 25.68	7502.2 27.33
43	5985.4 21.68	6238.1 22.54	6532.2 23.55	6877.1 24.73	7285.7 26.12	7775.5 27.80
44	6202.2 22.04	6463.5 22.92	6767.6 23.94	7124.4 25.14	7546.9 26.56	8053.5 28.26
45	6422.6 22.41	6692.7 23.30	7007.1 24.34	7375.8 25.56	7812.5 27.00	8336.1 28.73
46	6646.6 22.77	6925.7 23.68	7250.4 24.73	7631.3 25.97	8082.5 27.44	8623.4 29.20
47	6874.3 23.13	7162.5 24.06	7497.8 25.13	7891.1 26.39	8356.9 27.88	8915.4 29.67
48	7105.7 23.50	7403.1 24.44	7749.1 25.52	8154.9 26.80	8635.7 28.32	9212.1 30.13
49	7340.7 23.86	7647.4 24.81	8004.3 25.92	8423.0 27.22	8918.8 28.76	9513.4 30.60
50	7579.3 24.23	7895.5 25.19	8263.5 26.32	8695.1 27.63	9206.4 29.20	9819.4 31.07
51	7821.6 24.59	8147.5 25.57	8526.7 26.71	8971.5 28.05	9498.4 29.63	10130.1 31.53
52	8067.5 24.96	8403.2 25.95	8793.8 27.11	9252.0 28.47	9794.7 30.07	10445.4 32.00
53	8317.0 25.32	8662.7 26.33	9064.9 27.50	9536.6 28.88	10095.4 30.51	10765.4 32.47
54	8570.2 25.68	8926.0 26.71	9339.9 27.90	9825.4 29.30	10400.6 30.95	11090.1 32.94
55	8827.1 26.05	9193.1 27.09	9618.9 28.29	10118.4 29.71	10710.1 31.39	11419.5 33.40
56	9087.6 26.41	9463.9 27.47	9901.8 28.69	10415.5 30.13	11024.0 31.83	11753.5 33.87
57	9351.7 26.78	9738.6 27.84	10188.8 29.09	10716.8 30.54	11342.3 32.27	12092.2 34.34
58	9619.5 27.14	10017.0 28.22	10479.6 29.48	11022.2 30.96	11664.9 32.71	12435.6 34.80
59	9890.9 27.51	10299.3 28.60	10774.4 29.88	11331.8 31.37	11992.0 33.15	12783.6 35.27
60	10165.9 27.87	10585.3 28.98	11073.2 30.27	11645.6 31.79	12323.5 33.59	13136.3 35.74
SUMS.	18°	19°	20°	21°	22°	23°

TABLE XIV. Whole Sections.—Roadbed 24 ft. Side Slope 1½ to 1.

SUMS.	18°		19°		20°		21°		22°		23°	
61	10444.6	28.23	10875.1	29.36	11375.9	30.67	11963.4	32.21	12659.3	34.02	13493.7	36.21
62	10727.0	28.60	11168.7	29.74	11682.6	31.07	12285.5	32.62	12999.6	34.46	13855.8	36.67
63	11013.0	28.96	11466.1	30.12	11993.3	31.46	12611.7	33.04	13344.2	34.90	14222.5	37.14
64	11302.6	29.33	11767.3	30.50	12307.9	31.86	12942.1	33.45	13693.2	35.34	14593.9	37.61
65	11595.9	29.69	12072.2	30.88	12626.5	32.25	13276.6	33.87	14046.7	35.78	14970.0	38.07
66	11892.8	30.06	12381.0	31.25	12949.0	32.65	13615.3	34.28	14404.5	36.22	15350.7	38.54
67	12193.4	30.42	12693.5	31.63	13275.5	33.04	13958.1	34.70	14766.7	36.66	15736.1	39.01
68	12497.6	30.78	13009.9	32.01	13605.9	33.44	14305.1	35.11	15133.2	37.10	16126.2	39.48
69	12805.4	31.15	13330.0	32.39	13940.3	33.84	14656.2	35.53	15504.2	37.54	16521.0	39.94
70	13116.9	31.51	13653.9	32.77	14278.7	34.23	15011.5	35.95	15879.6	37.98	16920.4	40.41
71	13432.0	31.88	13981.6	33.15	14621.0	34.63	15371.0	36.36	16259.3	38.41	17324.5	40.88
72	13750.8	32.24	14313.1	33.53	14967.2	35.02	15734.6	36.78	16643.5	38.85	17733.3	41.34
73	14073.2	32.61	14648.3	33.91	15317.4	35.42	16102.3	37.19	17032.0	39.29	18146.7	41.81
74	14399.3	32.97	14987.4	34.28	15671.6	35.81	16474.3	37.61	17424.9	39.73	18564.8	42.28
75	14729.0	33.34	15330.2	34.66	16029.8	36.21	16850.3	38.02	17822.3	40.17	18987.6	42.75
76	15062.4	33.70	15676.9	35.04	16391.9	36.61	17230.6	38.44	18224.0	40.61	19415.1	43.21
77	15399.4	34.06	16027.3	35.42	16757.9	37.00	17614.9	38.85	18630.1	41.05	19847.2	43.68
78	15740.0	34.43	16381.5	35.80	17127.9	37.40	18003.5	39.27	19040.6	41.49	20284.0	44.15
79	16084.3	34.79	16739.5	36.18	17501.9	37.79	18396.2	39.69	19455.4	41.93	20725.5	44.61
80	16432.2	35.16	17101.3	36.56	17879.8	38.19	18793.0	40.10	19874.7	42.37	21171.6	45.08
81	16783.8	35.52	17466.9	36.94	18261.7	38.58	19194.0	40.52	20298.4	42.80	21622.5	45.55
82	17139.0	35.89	17836.3	37.32	18647.5	38.98	19599.2	40.93	20726.4	43.24	22077.9	46.02
83	17497.8	36.25	18209.4	37.69	19037.3	39.38	20008.5	41.35	21158.9	43.68	22538.1	46.48
84	17860.3	36.61	18586.4	38.07	19431.1	39.77	20422.0	41.76	21595.7	44.12	23002.9	46.95
85	18226.5	36.98	18967.1	38.45	19828.8	40.17	20839.6	42.18	22036.9	44.56	23472.5	47.42
86	18596.2	37.34	19351.6	38.83	20230.5	40.56	21261.4	42.59	22482.5	45.00	23946.6	47.89
87	18969.7	37.71	19739.9	39.21	20636.1	40.96	21687.3	43.01	22932.5	45.44	24425.5	48.35
88	19346.7	38.07	20132.0	39.59	21045.7	41.35	22117.4	43.43	23386.9	45.88	24909.0	48.82
89	19727.5	38.44	20527.9	39.97	21459.2	41.75	22551.7	43.84	23845.7	46.32	25397.2	49.29
90	20111.8	38.80	20927.6	40.35	21876.7	42.15	22990.1	44.26	24308.9	46.76	25890.1	49.75
91	20499.8	39.16	21331.0	40.73	22298.2	42.54	23432.6	44.67	24776.4	47.20	26387.6	50.22
92	20891.4	39.53	21738.3	41.10	22723.6	42.94	23879.4	45.09	25248.4	47.63	26889.8	50.69
93	21286.7	39.89	22149.3	41.48	23153.0	43.33	24330.2	45.50	25724.7	48.07	27396.7	51.16
94	21685.7	40.26	22564.2	41.86	23586.3	43.73	24785.3	45.92	26205.4	48.51	27908.2	51.62
95	22088.2	40.62	22982.8	42.24	24023.6	44.12	25244.5	46.33	26690.6	48.95	28424.5	52.09
96	22494.4	40.99	23405.2	42.62	24464.8	44.52	25707.8	46.75	27180.1	49.39	28945.3	52.56
97	22904.3	41.35	23831.4	43.00	24910.0	44.92	26175.3	47.17	27674.0	49.83	29470.9	53.02
98	23317.8	41.71	24261.4	43.38	25359.2	45.31	26646.9	47.58	28172.3	50.27	30001.2	53.49
99	23734.9	42.08	24695.1	43.76	25812.3	45.71	27122.7	48.00	28675.0	50.71	30536.1	53.96
100	24155.7	42.44	25132.7	44.13	26269.4	46.10	27602.7	48.41	29182.0	51.15	31075.6	54.43
SUMS.	18°		19°		20°		21°		22°		23°	

SECOND PART.

DIFF.	18°		19°		20°		21°		22°		23°	
1	.6	0.18	.6	0.19	.7	0.20	.7	0.21	.7	0.22	.8	0.23
2	2.4	0.30	2.5	0.32	2.6	0.33	2.8	0.35	2.9	0.37	3.1	0.39
3	5.5	0.43	5.7	0.44	5.9	0.46	6.2	0.48	6.6	0.51	7.0	0.55
4	9.7	0.55	10.1	0.57	10.6	0.59	11.1	0.62	11.7	0.66	12.5	0.70
5	15.2	0.67	15.8	0.69	16.5	0.73	17.3	0.76	18.3	0.80	19.5	0.86
6	21.9	0.79	22.7	0.82	23.7	0.86	24.9	0.90	26.3	0.95	28.0	1.01
7	29.8	0.91	30.9	0.95	32.3	0.99	33.9	1.04	35.9	1.10	38.2	1.17
8	38.9	1.03	40.4	1.07	42.2	1.12	44.3	1.18	46.8	1.24	49.8	1.32
9	49.2	1.15	51.1	1.20	53.4	1.25	56.1	1.32	59.3	1.39	63.1	1.48
10	60.7	1.28	63.1	1.33	66.0	1.39	69.3	1.45	73.2	1.54	77.9	1.64
DIFF.	18°		19°		20°		21°		22°		23°	

TABLE XIV. Whole Sections.—Roadbed 24 ft. Side Slope 1½ to 1.

SUMS.	24°	25°	26°	27°	28°	29°
1	....	....	....	....	....	....
2	....	....	....	....	....	....
3	....	....	....	....	....	....
4	....	....	....	....	....	....
5	....	....	....	....	....	....
6	....	....	....	....	....	....
7	....	....	....	....	....	....
8	....	....	....	....	....	....
9	....	....	....	....	....	....
10	....	....	....	....	....	....
11	1472.1 13.79	....	....	....	....	....
12	1610.0 14.29	1776.4 15.50	1987.3 17.03	....	....	....
13	1752.9 14.79	1931.4 16.04	2157.7 17.63	2453.2 19.70	2854.4 22.52	....
14	1900.8 15.29	2091.8 16.59	2334.0 18.23	2650.2 20.37	3079.5 23.28	3694.1 27.45
15	2053.8 15.79	2257.7 17.13	2516.3 18.83	2854.0 21.04	3312.4 24.05	3968.6 28.35
16	2211.7 16.30	2429.0 17.68	2704.5 19.42	3064.4 21.71	3552.8 24.81	4252.1 29.25
17	2374.7 16.80	2605.8 18.22	2898.8 20.02	3281.5 22.38	3800.9 25.57	4544.5 30.15
18	2542.6 17.30	2788.0 18.76	3099.0 20.62	3505.2 23.04	4056.6 26.34	4846.0 31.05
19	2715.6 17.80	2975.6 19.31	3305.2 21.22	3735.7 23.71	4320.0 27.10	5156.5 31.95
20	2893.6 18.30	3168.7 19.85	3517.4 21.82	3972.8 24.38	4591.0 27.86	5476.0 32.85
21	3076.6 18.80	3367.2 20.39	3735.5 22.41	4216.6 25.05	4869.6 28.63	5804.4 33.75
22	3264.7 19.30	3571.1 20.94	3959.7 23.01	4467.1 25.72	5155.9 29.39	6141.9 34.65
23	3457.7 19.81	3780.5 21.48	4189.8 23.61	4724.2 26.38	5449.8 30.15	6488.4 35.55
24	3655.8 20.31	3995.3 22.03	4425.9 24.21	4988.1 27.05	5751.3 30.92	6843.9 36.45
25	3858.9 20.81	4215.6 22.57	4667.9 24.80	5258.6 27.72	6060.4 31.68	7208.3 37.35
26	4066.9 21.31	4441.3 23.11	4915.9 25.40	5535.8 28.39	6377.2 32.44	7581.8 38.25
27	4280.1 21.81	4672.4 23.66	5170.0 26.00	5819.7 29.06	6701.7 33.21	7964.3 39.15
28	4498.2 22.31	4909.0 24.20	5429.9 26.60	6110.3 29.72	7033.7 33.97	8355.7 40.05
29	4721.3 22.81	5151.0 24.75	5695.9 27.19	6407.5 30.39	7373.4 34.73	8756.2 40.95
30	4949.4 23.32	5398.5 25.29	5967.9 27.79	6711.4 31.06	7720.7 35.50	9165.7 41.85
31	5182.6 23.82	5651.4 25.83	6245.8 28.39	7022.0 31.73	8075.7 36.26	9584.1 42.75
32	5420.8 24.32	5909.7 26.38	6529.7 28.99	7339.3 32.40	8438.3 37.02	10011.6 43.65
33	5664.0 24.82	6173.5 26.92	6819.5 29.58	7663.3 33.06	8808.5 37.79	10448.1 44.55
34	5912.2 25.32	6442.7 27.46	7115.4 30.18	7993.9 33.73	9186.4 38.55	10893.5 45.45
35	6165.4 25.82	6717.3 28.01	7417.2 30.78	8331.2 34.40	9571.9 39.31	11348.0 46.35
36	6423.6 26.32	6997.4 28.55	7725.0 31.38	8675.2 35.07	9965.0 40.08	11811.4 47.25
37	6686.9 26.83	7283.0 29.10	8038.8 31.98	9025.9 35.74	10365.8 40.84	12283.9 48.15
38	6955.1 27.33	7573.9 29.64	8358.6 32.57	9383.2 36.40	10774.2 41.60	12765.4 49.05
39	7228.4 27.83	7870.3 30.18	8684.3 33.17	9747.3 37.07	11190.2 42.37	13255.8 49.95
40	7506.7 28.33	8172.2 30.73	9016.0 33.77	10118.0 37.74	11613.9 43.13	13755.3 50.85
41	7790.0 28.83	8479.4 31.27	9353.7 34.37	10495.4 38.41	12045.1 43.89	14263.7 51.75
42	8078.3 29.33	8792.2 31.82	9697.4 34.96	10879.5 39.08	12484.1 44.66	14781.2 52.65
43	8371.6 29.83	9110.3 32.36	10047.0 35.56	11270.2 39.74	12930.6 45.42	15307.7 53.55
44	8670.0 30.34	9433.9 32.90	10402.6 36.16	11667.6 40.41	13384.8 46.18	15843.1 54.45
45	8973.3 30.84	9763.0 33.45	10764.2 36.76	12071.8 41.08	13846.7 46.95	16387.6 55.35
46	9281.7 31.34	10097.4 33.99	11131.8 37.35	12482.6 41.75	14316.1 47.71	16941.0 56.25
47	9595.1 31.84	10437.3 34.54	11505.3 37.95	12900.0 42.42	14793.2 48.47	17503.5 57.15
48	9913.5 32.34	10782.7 35.08	11884.8 38.55	13324.2 43.08	15278.0 49.24	18074.9 58.05
49	10236.9 32.84	11133.5 35.62	12270.3 39.15	13755.0 43.75	15770.3 50.00	18655.4 58.95
50	10565.3 33.34	11489.7 36.17	12661.8 39.75	14192.5 44.42	16270.3 50.76	19244.8 59.85
51	10898.8 33.85	11851.4 36.71	13059.3 40.34	14636.7 45.09	16778.0 51.53	19843.3 60.74
52	11237.2 34.35	12218.5 37.25	13462.7 40.94	15087.6 45.75	17293.2 52.29	20450.7 61.64
53	11580.7 34.85	12591.0 37.80	13872.1 41.54	15545.1 46.42	17816.1 53.05	21067.2 62.54
54	11929.2 35.35	12969.0 38.34	14287.5 42.14	16009.4 47.09	18346.6 53.82	21692.6 63.44
55	12282.7 35.85	13352.4 38.89	14708.9 42.73	16480.3 47.76	18884.8 54.58	22327.1 64.34
56	12641.2 36.35	13741.3 39.43	15136.2 43.33	16957.9 48.43	19430.6 55.34	22970.5 65.24
57	13004.7 36.85	14135.6 39.97	15569.5 43.93	17442.1 49.09	19984.0 56.11	23623.0 66.14
58	13373.3 37.36	14535.3 40.52	16008.8 44.53	17933.1 49.76	20545.1 56.87	24284.4 67.04
59	13746.8 37.86	14940.5 41.06	16454.1 45.12	18430.7 50.43	21113.8 57.63	24954.9 67.94
60	14125.4 38.36	15351.1 41.61	16905.3 45.72	18935.0 51.10	21690.1 58.40	25634.3 68.84
SUMS.	24°	25°	26°	27°	28°	29°

TABLE XIV. Whole Sections.—Roadbed 24 ft. Side Slope $1\frac{1}{2}$ to 1.

SUMS.	24°		25°		26°		27°		28°		29°	
61	14509.0	38.86	15767.2	42.15	17362.6	46.32	19446.0	51.77	22274.1	59.16	26322.7	69.74
62	14897.6	39.36	16188.7	42.69	17825.7	46.92	19963.7	52.43	22865.7	59.92	27020.2	70.64
63	15291.2	39.86	16615.6	43.24	18294.9	47.52	20488.0	53.10	23464.9	60.69	27726.6	71.54
64	15689.8	40.36	17048.0	43.78	18770.1	48.11	21019.0	53.77	24071.8	61.45	28442.1	72.44
65	16093.5	40.87	17485.8	44.32	19251.2	48.71	21556.7	54.44	24686.3	62.21	29166.5	73.34
66	16502.1	41.37	17929.0	44.87	19738.3	49.31	22101.1	55.11	25308.4	62.98	29899.9	74.24
67	16915.8	41.87	18377.7	45.41	20231.4	49.91	22652.2	55.77	25938.2	63.74	30642.4	75.14
68	17334.5	42.37	18831.8	45.96	20730.4	50.50	23209.9	56.44	26575.6	64.50	31393.8	76.04
69	17758.2	42.87	19291.4	46.50	21235.5	51.10	23774.3	57.11	27220.7	65.27	32154.3	76.94
70	18186.9	43.37	19756.4	47.04	21746.5	51.70	24345.4	57.78	27873.3	66.03	32923.7	77.84
71	18620.6	43.87	20226.8	47.59	22263.5	52.30	24923.2	58.45	28533.6	66.79	33702.1	78.74
72	19059.3	44.38	20702.7	48.13	22786.5	52.89	25507.7	59.11	29201.6	67.56	34489.6	79.64
73	19503.1	44.88	21184.0	48.68	23315.4	53.49	26098.8	59.78	29877.1	68.32	35286.0	80.54
74	19951.9	45.38	21670.8	49.22	23850.3	54.09	26696.6	60.45	30560.3	69.08	36091.4	81.44
75	20405.6	45.88	22162.9	49.76	24391.2	54.69	27301.1	61.12	31251.2	69.85	36905.9	82.34
76	20864.4	46.38	22660.6	50.31	24938.1	55.29	27912.3	61.79	31949.6	70.61	37729.3	83.24
77	21328.3	46.88	23163.7	50.85	25490.9	55.88	28530.2	62.45	32655.7	71.37	38561.7	84.14
78	21797.1	47.38	23672.2	51.39	26049.8	56.48	29154.7	63.12	33369.5	72.14	39403.2	85.04
79	22270.9	47.89	24186.1	51.94	26614.6	57.08	29785.9	63.79	34090.8	72.90	40253.6	85.94
80	22749.8	48.39	24705.5	52.48	27185.3	57.68	30423.8	64.46	34819.9	73.66	41113.0	86.84
81	23233.6	48.89	25230.3	53.03	27762.1	58.27	31068.4	65.13	35556.5	74.43	41981.5	87.74
82	23722.5	49.39	25760.6	53.57	28344.8	58.87	31719.7	65.79	36300.8	75.19	42858.9	88.64
83	24216.4	49.89	26296.3	54.11	28933.5	59.47	32377.6	66.46	37052.7	75.95	43745.3	89.54
84	24715.3	50.39	26837.4	54.66	29528.2	60.07	33042.2	67.13	37812.2	76.72	44640.7	90.44
85	25219.3	50.89	27384.0	55.20	30128.9	60.66	33713.5	67.80	38579.4	77.48	45545.2	91.34
86	25728.2	51.40	27936.0	55.75	30735.5	61.26	34391.5	68.47	39354.2	78.24	46458.6	92.24
87	26242.2	51.90	28493.5	56.29	31348.2	61.86	35076.1	69.13	40136.6	79.01	47381.0	93.14
88	26761.1	52.40	29056.4	56.83	31966.8	62.46	35767.5	69.80	40926.7	79.77	48312.4	94.04
89	27285.1	52.90	29624.7	57.38	32591.3	63.05	36465.5	70.47	41724.4	80.53	49252.9	94.94
90	27814.1	53.40	30198.5	57.92	33221.9	63.65	37170.2	71.14	42529.7	81.30	50202.3	95.84
91	28348.1	53.90	30777.7	58.46	33858.4	64.25	37881.6	71.81	43342.7	82.06	51160.7	96.74
92	28887.1	54.40	31362.3	59.01	34500.9	64.85	38599.6	72.47	44163.3	82.82	52128.1	97.64
93	29431.2	54.91	31952.4	59.55	35149.4	65.45	39324.3	73.14	44991.6	83.59	53104.5	98.54
94	29980.2	55.41	32548.0	60.10	35803.8	66.04	40055.8	73.81	45827.4	84.35	54090.0	99.44
95	30534.3	55.91	33148.9	60.64	36464.3	66.64	40793.8	74.48	46670.9	85.11	55084.4	100.34
96	31093.4	56.41	33755.3	61.18	37130.7	67.24	41538.6	75.15	47522.1	85.88	56087.8	101.24
97	31657.5	56.91	34367.2	61.73	37803.1	67.84	42290.1	75.81	48380.9	86.64	57100.2	102.14
98	32226.6	57.41	34984.4	62.27	38481.4	68.43	43048.2	76.48	49247.3	87.40	58121.6	103.04
99	32800.7	57.91	35607.2	62.82	39165.8	69.03	43813.0	77.15	50121.3	88.17	59152.0	103.94
100	33379.8	58.42	36235.3	63.36	39856.1	69.63	44584.5	77.82	51003.0	88.93	60191.5	104.84
SUMS.	24°		25°		26°		27°		28°		29°	

SECOND PART.

DIFF.	24°		25°		26°		27°		28°		29°	
1	.8	0.25	.9	0.27	1.0	0.30	1.1	0.33	1.3	0.38	1.5	0.45
2	3.3	0.42	3.6	0.45	4.0	0.50	4.5	0.56	5.1	0.64	6.0	0.75
3	7.5	0.58	8.2	0.63	9.0	0.70	10.0	0.78	11.5	0.89	13.5	1.05
4	13.4	0.75	14.5	0.82	15.9	0.90	17.8	1.00	20.4	1.15	24.0	1.35
5	20.9	0.92	22.7	1.00	24.9	1.10	27.8	1.22	31.8	1.40	37.5	1.65
6	30.1	1.09	32.6	1.18	35.9	1.29	40.1	1.45	45.8	1.65	54.0	1.95
7	40.9	1.25	44.4	1.36	48.8	1.49	54.5	1.67	62.3	1.91	73.5	2.25
8	53.5	1.42	58.0	1.54	63.8	1.69	71.2	1.89	81.4	2.16	96.0	2.55
9	67.7	1.59	73.4	1.72	80.7	1.89	90.2	2.12	103.1	2.42	121.5	2.85
10	83.6	1.75	90.6	1.90	99.6	2.09	111.3	2.34	127.2	2.67	150.0	3.15
DIFF.	24°		25°		26°		27°		28°		29°	

TABLE XV. Whole or Sub Sections.

SUMS.	0	1	2	3	4	SUMS.
1	.46	.56	.67	.78	.91	1
2	1.85	2.04	2.24	2.45	2.67	2
3	4.17	4.45	4.74	5.04	5.35	3
4	7.41	7.78	8.17	8.56	8.96	4
5	11.57	12.04	12.52	13.00	13.50	5
6	16.67	17.23	17.80	18.38	18.96	6
7	22.69	23.34	24.00	24.67	25.35	7
8	29.63	30.37	31.13	31.89	32.67	8
9	37.50	38.34	39.19	40.04	40.91	9
10	46.30	47.23	48.17	49.12	50.07	10
11	56.02	57.04	58.07	59.12	60.17	11
12	66.67	67.78	68.91	70.04	71.19	12
13	78.24	79.45	80.67	81.89	83.13	13
14	90.74	92.04	93.35	94.67	96.00	14
15	104.17	105.56	106.96	108.37	109.80	15
16	118.52	120.00	121.50	123.00	124.52	16
17	133.80	135.38	136.96	138.56	140.17	17
18	150.00	151.67	153.35	155.04	156.74	18
19	167.13	168.89	170.67	172.45	174.24	19
20	185.19	187.04	188.91	190.78	192.67	20
21	204.17	206.12	208.07	210.04	212.02	21
22	224.07	226.12	228.17	230.23	232.30	22
23	244.91	247.04	249.19	251.34	253.50	23
24	266.67	268.89	271.13	273.37	275.63	24
25	289.35	291.67	294.00	296.34	298.69	25
26	312.96	315.38	317.80	320.23	322.67	26
27	337.50	340.00	342.52	345.04	347.57	27
28	362.96	365.56	368.17	370.78	373.41	28
29	389.35	392.04	394.74	397.45	400.17	29
30	416.67	419.45	422.24	425.04	427.85	30
31	444.91	447.78	450.67	453.56	456.46	31
32	474.07	477.04	480.02	483.00	486.00	32
33	504.17	507.23	510.30	513.37	516.46	33
34	535.19	538.34	541.50	544.67	547.85	34
35	567.13	570.37	573.63	576.89	580.17	35
36	600.00	603.34	606.69	610.04	613.41	36
37	633.80	637.23	640.67	644.12	647.57	37
38	668.52	672.04	675.57	679.12	682.67	38
39	704.17	707.78	711.41	715.04	718.69	39
40	740.74	744.45	748.17	751.89	755.63	40
41	778.24	782.04	785.85	789.67	793.50	41
42	816.67	820.56	824.46	828.38	832.30	42
43	856.02	860.00	864.00	868.00	872.02	43
44	896.30	900.37	904.46	908.56	912.67	44
45	937.50	941.67	945.85	950.04	954.24	45
46	979.63	983.89	988.17	992.45	996.74	46
47	1022.69	1027.04	1031.41	1035.78	1040.17	47
48	1066.67	1071.12	1075.57	1080.04	1084.52	48
49	1111.57	1116.12	1120.67	1125.23	1129.80	49
50	1157.41	1162.04	1166.69	1171.34	1176.00	50
51	1204.17	1208.89	1213.63	1218.37	1223.13	51
52	1251.85	1256.67	1261.50	1266.34	1271.19	52
53	1300.46	1305.37	1310.30	1315.23	1320.17	53
54	1350.00	1355.00	1360.02	1365.04	1370.07	54
55	1400.46	1405.56	1410.67	1415.78	1420.91	55
56	1451.85	1457.04	1462.24	1467.45	1472.67	56
57	1504.17	1509.45	1514.74	1520.04	1525.35	57
58	1557.41	1562.78	1568.17	1573.56	1578.96	58
59	1611.57	1617.04	1622.52	1628.00	1633.50	59
60	1666.67	1672.23	1677.80	1683.37	1688.96	60
SUMS.	0	1	2	3	4	SUMS.

TABLE XV. Whole or Sub Sections.

SUMS.	5	6	7	8	9	SUMS.
1	1.04	1.19	1.34	1.50	1.67	1
2	2.89	3.13	3.38	3.63	3.89	2
3	5.67	6.00	6.34	6.69	7.04	3
4	9.38	9.80	10.23	10.67	11.12	4
5	14.00	14.52	15.04	15.57	16.12	5
6	19.56	20.17	20.78	21.41	22.04	6
7	26.04	26.74	27.45	28.17	28.89	7
8	33.45	34.24	35.04	35.85	36.67	8
9	41.78	42.67	43.56	44.46	45.38	9
10	51.04	52.02	53.00	54.00	55.00	10
11	61.23	62.30	63.38	64.46	65.56	11
12	72.34	73.50	74.67	75.85	77.04	12
13	84.38	85.63	86.89	88.17	89.45	13
14	97.34	98.69	100.04	101.41	102.78	14
15	111.23	112.67	114.12	115.57	117.04	15
16	126.04	127.57	129.12	130.67	132.23	16
17	141.78	143.41	145.04	146.69	148.34	17
18	158.45	160.17	161.89	163.63	165.37	18
19	176.04	177.85	179.67	181.50	183.34	19
20	194.56	196.46	198.37	200.30	202.23	20
21	214.00	216.00	218.00	220.02	222.04	21
22	234.38	236.46	238.56	240.67	242.78	22
23	255.67	257.85	260.04	262.24	264.45	23
24	277.89	280.17	282.45	284.74	287.04	24
25	301.04	303.41	305.78	308.17	310.56	25
26	325.12	327.57	330.04	332.52	335.00	26
27	350.12	352.67	355.23	357.80	360.37	27
28	376.04	378.69	381.34	384.00	386.67	28
29	402.89	405.63	408.37	411.13	413.89	29
30	430.67	433.50	436.34	439.19	442.04	30
31	459.38	462.30	465.23	468.17	471.12	31
32	489.00	492.02	495.04	498.07	501.12	32
33	519.56	522.67	525.78	528.91	532.04	33
34	551.04	554.24	557.45	560.67	563.89	34
35	583.45	586.74	590.04	593.35	596.67	35
36	616.78	620.17	623.56	626.96	630.38	36
37	651.04	654.52	658.00	661.50	665.00	37
38	686.23	689.80	693.38	696.96	700.56	38
39	722.34	726.00	729.67	733.35	737.04	39
40	759.37	763.13	766.89	770.67	774.45	40
41	797.34	801.19	805.04	808.91	812.78	41
42	836.23	840.17	844.12	848.07	852.04	42
43	876.04	880.07	884.12	888.17	892.23	43
44	916.78	920.91	925.04	929.19	933.34	44
45	958.45	962.67	966.89	971.13	975.38	45
46	1001.04	1005.35	1009.67	1014.00	1018.34	46
47	1044.56	1048.96	1053.37	1057.80	1062.23	47
48	1089.00	1093.50	1098.00	1102.52	1107.04	48
49	1134.38	1138.96	1143.56	1148.17	1152.78	49
50	1180.67	1185.35	1190.04	1194.74	1199.45	50
51	1227.89	1232.67	1237.45	1242.24	1247.04	51
52	1276.04	1280.91	1285.78	1290.67	1295.56	52
53	1325.12	1330.07	1335.04	1340.02	1345.00	53
54	1375.12	1380.17	1385.23	1390.30	1395.37	54
55	1426.04	1431.19	1436.34	1441.50	1446.67	55
56	1477.89	1483.13	1488.37	1493.63	1498.89	56
57	1530.67	1536.00	1541.34	1546.69	1552.04	57
58	1584.37	1589.80	1595.23	1600.67	1606.12	58
59	1639.00	1644.52	1650.04	1655.57	1661.12	59
60	1694.56	1700.17	1705.78	1711.41	1717.04	60
SUMS.	5	6	7	8	9	SUMS.

TABLE XV. Whole or Sub Sections.

SUMS.	0	1	2	3	4	SUMS.
61	1722.69	1728.34	1734.00	1739.67	1745.35	**61**
62	1779.63	1785.38	1791.13	1796.89	1802.67	**62**
63	1837.50	1843.34	1849.19	1855.04	1860.91	**63**
64	1896.30	1902.23	1908.17	1914.12	1920.07	**64**
65	1956.02	1962.04	1968.07	1974.12	1980.17	**65**
66	2016.67	2022.78	2028.91	2035.04	2041.19	**66**
67	2078.24	2084.45	2090.67	2096.89	2103.13	**67**
68	2140.74	2147.04	2153.35	2159.67	2166.00	**68**
69	2204.17	2210.56	2216.96	2223.37	2229.80	**69**
70	2268.52	2275.00	2281.50	2288.00	2294.52	**70**
71	2333.80	2340.37	2346.96	2353.56	2360.17	**71**
72	2400.00	2406.67	2413.35	2420.04	2426.74	**72**
73	2467.13	2473.89	2480.67	2487.45	2494.24	**73**
74	2535.19	2542.04	2548.91	2555.78	2562.67	**74**
75	2604.17	2611.12	2618.07	2625.04	2632.02	**75**
76	2674.07	2681.12	2688.17	2695.23	2702.30	**76**
77	2744.91	2752.04	2759.19	2766.34	2773.50	**77**
78	2816.67	2823.89	2831.13	2838.38	2845.63	**78**
79	2889.35	2896.67	2904.00	2911.34	2918.69	**79**
80	2962.96	2970.37	2977.80	2985.23	2992.67	**80**
81	3037.50	3045.00	3052.52	3060.04	3067.57	**81**
82	3112.96	3120.56	3128.17	3135.78	3143.41	**82**
83	3189.35	3197.04	3204.74	3212.45	3220.17	**83**
84	3266.67	3274.45	3282.24	3290.04	3297.85	**84**
85	3344.91	3352.78	3360.67	3368.56	3376.46	**85**
86	3424.07	3432.04	3440.02	3448.00	3456.00	**86**
87	3504.17	3512.23	3520.30	3528.37	3536.46	**87**
88	3585.19	3593.34	3601.50	3609.67	3617.85	**88**
89	3667.13	3675.37	3683.63	3691.89	3700.17	**89**
90	3750.00	3758.34	3766.69	3775.04	3783.41	**90**
91	3833.80	3842.23	3850.67	3859.12	3867.57	**91**
92	3918.52	3927.04	3935.57	3944.12	3952.67	**92**
93	4004.17	4012.78	4021.41	4030.04	4038.69	**93**
94	4090.74	4099.45	4108.17	4116.89	4125.63	**94**
95	4178.24	4187.04	4195.85	4204.67	4213.50	**95**
96	4266.67	4275.56	4284.46	4293.38	4302.30	**96**
97	4356.02	4365.00	4374.00	4383.00	4392.02	**97**
98	4446.30	4455.37	4464.46	4473.56	4482.67	**98**
99	4537.50	4546.67	4555.85	4565.04	4574.24	**99**
100	4629.63	4638.89	4648.17	4657.45	4666.74	**100**
101	4722.69	4732.04	4741.41	4750.78	4760.17	**101**
102	4816.67	4826.12	4835.57	4845.04	4854.52	**102**
103	4911.57	4921.12	4930.67	4940.23	4949.80	**103**
104	5007.41	5017.04	5026.69	5036.34	5046.00	**104**
105	5104.17	5113.89	5123.63	5133.38	5143.13	**105**
106	5201.85	5211.67	5221.50	5231.34	5241.19	**106**
107	5300.46	5310.38	5320.30	5330.23	5340.17	**107**
108	5400.00	5410.00	5420.02	5430.04	5440.07	**108**
109	5500.46	5510.56	5520.67	5530.78	5540.91	**109**
110	5601.85	5612.04	5622.24	5632.45	5642.67	**110**
111	5704.17	5714.45	5724.74	5735.04	5745.35	**111**
112	5807.41	5817.78	5828.17	5838.56	5848.96	**112**
113	5911.57	5922.04	5932.52	5943.00	5953.50	**113**
114	6016.67	6027.23	6037.80	6048.38	6058.96	**114**
115	6122.69	6133.34	6144.00	6154.67	6165.35	**115**
116	6229.63	6240.37	6251.13	6261.89	6272.67	**116**
117	6337.50	6348.34	6359.19	6370.04	6380.91	**117**
118	6446.30	6457.23	6468.17	6479.12	6490.07	**118**
119	6556.02	6567.04	6578.07	6589.12	6600.17	**119**
120	6666.67	6677.78	6688.91	6700.04	6711.19	**120**
SUMS.	0	1	2	3	4	SUMS.

TABLE XV. Whole or Sub Sections.

SUMS.	5	6	7	8	9	SUMS.
61	1751.04	1756.74	1762.45	1768.17	1773.89	61
62	1808.45	1814.24	1820.04	1825.85	1831.67	62
63	1866.78	1872.67	1878.56	1884.46	1890.37	63
64	1926.04	1932.02	1938.00	1944.00	1950.00	64
65	1986.23	1992.30	1998.37	2004.46	2010.56	65
66	2047.34	2053.50	2059.67	2065.85	2072.04	66
67	2109.37	2115.63	2121.89	2128.17	2134.45	67
68	2172.34	2178.69	2185.04	2191.41	2197.78	68
69	2236.23	2242.67	2249.12	2255.57	2262.04	69
70	2301.04	2307.57	2314.12	2320.67	2327.23	70
71	2366.78	2373.41	2380.04	2386.69	2393.34	71
72	2433.45	2440.17	2446.89	2453.63	2460.37	72
73	2501.04	2507.85	2514.67	2521.50	2528.34	73
74	2569.56	2576.46	2583.37	2590.30	2597.23	74
75	2639.00	2646.00	2653.00	2660.02	2667.04	75
76	2709.37	2716.46	2723.56	2730.67	2737.78	76
77	2780.67	2787.85	2795.04	2802.24	2809.45	77
78	2852.89	2860.17	2867.45	2874.74	2882.04	78
79	2926.04	2933.41	2940.78	2948.17	2955.56	79
80	3000.12	3007.57	3015.04	3022.52	3030.00	80
81	3075.12	3082.67	3090.23	3097.80	3105.37	81
82	3151.04	3158.69	3166.34	3174.00	3181.67	82
83	3227.89	3235.63	3243.38	3251.13	3258.89	83
84	3305.67	3313.50	3321.34	3329.19	3337.04	84
85	3384.37	3392.30	3400.23	3408.17	3416.12	85
86	3464.00	3472.02	3480.04	3488.07	3496.12	86
87	3544.56	3552.67	3560.78	3568.91	3577.04	87
88	3626.04	3634.24	3642.45	3650.67	3658.89	88
89	3708.45	3716.74	3725.04	3733.35	3741.67	89
90	3791.78	3800.17	3808.56	3816.96	3825.37	90
91	3876.04	3884.52	3893.00	3901.50	3910.00	91
92	3961.23	3969.80	3978.37	3986.96	3995.56	92
93	4047.34	4056.00	4064.67	4073.35	4082.04	93
94	4134.37	4143.13	4151.89	4160.67	4169.45	94
95	4222.34	4231.19	4240.04	4248.91	4257.78	95
96	4311.23	4320.17	4329.12	4338.07	4347.04	96
97	4401.04	4410.07	4419.12	4428.17	4437.23	97
98	4491.78	4500.91	4510.04	4519.19	4528.34	98
99	4583.45	4592.67	4601.89	4611.13	4620.37	99
100	4676.04	4685.35	4694.67	4704.00	4713.34	100
101	4769.56	4778.96	4788.37	4797.80	4807.23	101
102	4864.00	4873.50	4883.00	4892.52	4902.04	102
103	4959.37	4968.96	4978.56	4988.17	4997.78	103
104	5055.67	5065.35	5075.04	5084.74	5094.45	104
105	5152.89	5162.67	5172.45	5182.24	5192.04	105
106	5251.04	5260.91	5270.78	5280.67	5290.56	106
107	5350.12	5360.07	5370.04	5380.02	5390.00	107
108	5450.12	5460.17	5470.23	5480.30	5490.38	108
109	5551.04	5561.19	5571.34	5581.50	5591.67	109
110	5652.89	5663.13	5673.37	5683.63	5693.89	110
111	5755.67	5766.00	5776.34	5786.69	5797.04	111
112	5859.37	5869.80	5880.23	5890.67	5901.12	112
113	5964.00	5974.52	5985.04	5995.57	6006.12	113
114	6069.56	6080.17	6090.78	6101.41	6112.04	114
115	6176.04	6186.74	6197.45	6208.17	6218.89	115
116	6283.45	6294.24	6305.04	6315.85	6326.67	116
117	6391.78	6402.67	6413.56	6424.46	6435.37	117
118	6501.04	6512.02	6523.00	6534.00	6545.00	118
119	6611.23	6622.30	6633.38	6644.46	6655.56	119
120	6722.34	6733.50	6744.67	6755.85	6767.04	120
SUMS.	5	6	7	8	9	SUMS.

TABLE XV. Whole or Sub Sections.

SUMS.	0	1	2	3	4	SUMS.
121	6778.24	6789.45	6800.67	6811.89	6823.13	121
122	6890.74	6902.04	6913.35	6924.67	6936.00	122
123	7004.17	7015.56	7026.96	7038.37	7049.80	123
124	7118.52	7130.00	7141.50	7153.00	7164.52	124
125	7233.80	7245.37	7256.96	7268.56	7280.17	125
126	7350.00	7361.67	7373.35	7385.04	7396.74	126
127	7467.13	7478.89	7490.67	7502.45	7514.24	127
128	7585.19	7597.04	7608.91	7620.78	7632.67	128
129	7704.17	7716.12	7728.07	7740.04	7752.02	129
130	7824.07	7836.12	7848.17	7860.23	7872.30	130
131	7944.91	7957.04	7969.19	7981.34	7993.50	131
132	8066.67	8078.89	8091.13	8103.37	8115.63	132
133	8189.35	8201.67	8214.00	8226.34	8238.69	133
134	8312.96	8325.38	8337.80	8350.23	8362.67	134
135	8437.50	8450.00	8462.52	8475.04	8487.57	135
136	8562.96	8575.56	8588.17	8600.78	8613.41	136
137	8689.35	8702.04	8714.74	8727.45	8740.17	137
138	8816.67	8829.45	8842.24	8855.04	8867.85	138
139	8944.91	8957.78	8970.67	8983.56	8996.46	139
140	9074.07	9087.04	9100.02	9113.00	9126.00	140
141	9204.17	9217.23	9230.30	9243.38	9256.46	141
142	9335.19	9348.34	9361.50	9374.67	9387.85	142
143	9467.13	9480.37	9493.63	9506.89	9520.17	143
144	9600.00	9613.34	9626.69	9640.04	9653.41	144
145	9733.80	9747.23	9760.67	9774.12	9787.57	145
146	9868.52	9882.04	9895.57	9909.12	9922.67	146
147	10004.17	10017.78	10031.41	10045.04	10058.69	147
148	10140.74	10154.45	10168.17	10181.89	10195.63	148
149	10278.24	10292.04	10305.85	10319.67	10333.50	149
150	10416.67	10430.56	10444.46	10458.37	10472.30	150
151	10556.02	10570.00	10584.00	10598.00	10612.02	151
152	10696.30	10710.37	10724.46	10738.56	10752.67	152
153	10837.50	10851.67	10865.85	10880.04	10894.24	153
154	10979.63	10993.89	11008.17	11022.45	11036.74	154
155	11122.69	11137.04	11151.41	11165.78	11180.17	155
156	11266.67	11281.12	11295.57	11310.04	11324.52	156
157	11411.57	11426.12	11440.67	11455.23	11469.80	157
158	11557.41	11572.04	11586.69	11601.34	11616.00	158
159	11704.17	11718.89	11733.63	11748.38	11763.13	159
160	11851.85	11866.67	11881.50	11896.34	11911.19	160
161	12000.46	12015.37	12030.30	12045.23	12060.17	161
162	12150.00	12165.00	12180.02	12195.04	12210.07	162
163	12300.46	12315.56	12330.67	12345.78	12360.91	163
164	12451.85	12467.04	12482.24	12497.45	12512.67	164
165	12604.17	12619.45	12634.74	12650.04	12665.35	165
166	12757.41	12772.78	12788.17	12803.56	12818.96	166
167	12911.57	12927.04	12942.52	12958.00	12973.50	167
168	13066.67	13082.23	13097.80	13113.37	13128.96	168
169	13222.69	13238.34	13254.00	13269.67	13285.35	169
170	13379.63	13395.37	13411.13	13426.89	13442.67	170
171	13537.50	13553.34	13569.19	13585.04	13600.91	171
172	13696.30	13712.23	13728.17	13744.12	13760.07	172
173	13856.02	13872.04	13888.07	13904.12	13920.17	173
174	14016.67	14032.78	14048.91	14065.04	14081.19	174
175	14178.24	14194.45	14210.67	14226.89	14243.13	175
176	14340.74	14357.04	14373.35	14389.67	14406.00	176
177	14504.17	14520.56	14536.96	14553.38	14569.80	177
178	14668.52	14685.00	14701.50	14718.00	14734.52	178
179	14833.80	14850.38	14866.96	14883.56	14900.17	179
180	15000.00	15016.67	15033.35	15050.04	15066.74	180
SUMS.	0	1	2	3	4	SUMS.

TABLE XV. Whole or Sub Sections.

SUMS.	5	6	7	8	9	SUMS.
121	6834.37	6845.63	6856.89	6868.17	6879.45	121
122	6947.34	6958.69	6970.04	6981.41	6992.78	122
123	7061.23	7072.67	7084.12	7095.57	7107.04	123
124	7176.04	7187.57	7199.12	7210.67	7222.23	124
125	7291.78	7303.41	7315.04	7326.69	7338.34	125
126	7408.45	7420.17	7431.89	7443.63	7455.37	126
127	7526.04	7537.85	7549.67	7561.50	7573.34	127
128	7644.56	7656.46	7668.37	7680.30	7692.23	128
129	7764.00	7776.00	7788.00	7800.02	7812.04	129
130	7884.37	7896.46	7908.56	7920.67	7932.78	130
131	8005.67	8017.85	8030.04	8042.24	8054.45	131
132	8127.89	8140.17	8152.45	8164.74	8177.04	132
133	8251.04	8263.41	8275.78	8288.17	8300.56	133
134	8375.12	8387.57	8400.04	8412.52	8425.00	134
135	8500.12	8512.67	8525.23	8537.80	8550.38	135
136	8626.04	8638.69	8651.34	8664.00	8676.67	136
137	8752.89	8765.63	8778.37	8791.13	8803.89	137
138	8880.67	8893.50	8906.34	8919.19	8932.04	138
139	9009.37	9022.30	9035.23	9048.17	9061.12	139
140	9139.00	9152.02	9165.04	9178.07	9191.12	140
141	9269.56	9282.67	9295.78	9308.91	9322.04	141
142	9401.04	9414.24	9427.45	9440.67	9453.89	142
143	9533.45	9546.74	9560.04	9573.35	9586.67	143
144	9666.78	9680.17	9693.56	9706.96	9720.38	144
145	9801.04	9814.52	9828.00	9841.50	9855.00	145
146	9936.23	9949.80	9963.37	9976.96	9990.56	146
147	10072.34	10086.00	10099.67	10113.35	10127.04	147
148	10209.38	10223.13	10236.89	10250.67	10264.45	148
149	10347.34	10361.19	10375.04	10388.91	10402.78	149
150	10486.23	10500.17	10514.12	10528.07	10542.04	150
151	10626.04	10640.07	10654.12	10668.17	10682.23	151
152	10766.78	10780.91	10795.04	10809.19	10823.34	152
153	10908.45	10922.67	10936.89	10951.13	10965.37	153
154	11051.04	11065.35	11079.67	11094.00	11108.34	154
155	11194.56	11208.96	11223.37	11237.80	11252.23	155
156	11339.00	11353.50	11368.00	11382.52	11397.04	156
157	11484.38	11498.96	11513.56	11528.17	11542.78	157
158	11630.67	11645.35	11660.04	11674.74	11689.45	158
159	11777.89	11792.67	11807.45	11822.24	11837.04	159
160	11926.04	11940.91	11955.78	11970.67	11985.56	160
161	12075.12	12090.07	12105.04	12120.02	12135.00	161
162	12225.12	12240.17	12255.23	12270.30	12285.38	162
163	12376.04	12391.19	12406.34	12421.50	12436.67	163
164	12527.89	12543.13	12558.37	12573.63	12588.89	164
165	12680.67	12696.00	12711.34	12726.69	12742.04	165
166	12834.38	12849.80	12865.23	12880.67	12896.12	166
167	12989.00	13004.52	13020.04	13035.57	13051.12	167
168	13144.56	13160.17	13175.78	13191.41	13207.04	168
169	13301.04	13316.74	13332.45	13348.17	13363.89	169
170	13458.45	13474.24	13490.04	13505.85	13521.67	170
171	13616.78	13632.67	13648.56	13664.46	13680.37	171
172	13776.04	13792.02	13808.00	13824.00	13840.00	172
173	13936.23	13952.30	13968.37	13984.46	14000.56	173
174	14097.34	14113.50	14129.67	14145.85	14162.04	174
175	14259.37	14275.63	14291.89	14308.17	14324.45	175
176	14422.34	14438.69	14455.04	14471.41	14487.78	176
177	14586.23	14602.67	14619.12	14635.57	14652.04	177
178	14751.04	14767.57	14784.12	14800.67	14817.23	178
179	14916.78	14933.41	14950.04	14966.69	14983.34	179
180	15083.45	15100.17	15116.89	15133.63	15150.37	180
SUMS	5	6	7	8	9	SUMS.

TABLE XV. Whole or Sub Sections.

SUMS.	0	1	2	3	4	SUMS.
181	15167.13	15183.89	15200.67	15217.45	15234.24	181
182	15335.19	15352.04	15368.91	15385.78	15402.67	182
183	15504.17	15521.12	15538.07	15555.04	15572.02	183
184	15674.07	15691.12	15708.17	15725.23	15742.30	184
185	15844.91	15862.04	15879.19	15896.34	15913.50	185
186	16016.67	16033.89	16051.13	16068.38	16085.63	186
187	16189.35	16206.67	16224.00	16241.34	16258.69	187
188	16362.96	16380.38	16397.80	16415.23	16432.67	188
189	16537.50	16555.00	16572.52	16590.04	16607.57	189
190	16712.96	16730.56	16748.17	16765.78	16783.41	190
191	16889.35	16907.04	16924.74	16942.45	16960.17	191
192	17066.67	17084.45	17102.24	17120.04	17137.85	192
193	17244.91	17262.78	17280.67	17298.56	17316.46	193
194	17424.07	17442.04	17460.02	17478.00	17496.00	194
195	17604.17	17622.23	17640.30	17658.38	17676.46	195
196	17785.19	17803.34	17821.50	17839.67	17857.85	196
197	17967.13	17985.38	18003.63	18021.89	18040.17	197
198	18150.00	18168.34	18186.69	18205.04	18223.41	198
199	18333.80	18352.23	18370.67	18389.12	18407.57	199
200	18518.52	18537.04	18555.57	18574.12	18592.67	200
201	18704.17	18722.78	18741.41	18760.04	18778.69	201
202	18890.74	18909.45	18928.17	18946.89	18965.63	202
203	19078.24	19097.04	19115.85	19134.67	19153.50	203
204	19266.67	19285.56	19304.46	19323.38	19342.30	204
205	19456.02	19475.00	19494.00	19513.00	19532.02	205
206	19646.30	19665.38	19684.46	19703.56	19722.67	206
207	19837.50	19856.67	19875.85	19895.04	19914.24	207
208	20029.63	20048.89	20068.17	20087.45	20106.74	208
209	20222.69	20242.04	20261.41	20280.78	20300.17	209
210	20416.67	20436.12	20455.57	20475.04	20494.52	210
211	20611.57	20631.12	20650.67	20670.23	20689.80	211
212	20807.41	20827.04	20846.69	20866.34	20886.00	212
213	21004.17	21023.89	21043.63	21063.38	21083.13	213
214	21201.85	21221.67	21241.50	21261.34	21281.19	214
215	21400.46	21420.38	21440.30	21460.23	21480.17	215
216	21600.00	21620.00	21640.02	21660.04	21680.07	216
217	21800.46	21820.56	21840.67	21860.78	21880.91	217
218	22001.85	22022.04	22042.24	22062.45	22082.67	218
219	22204.17	22224.45	22244.74	22265.04	22285.35	219
220	22407.41	22427.78	22448.17	22468.56	22488.96	220
221	22611.57	22632.04	22652.52	22673.00	22693.50	221
222	22816.67	22837.23	22857.80	22878.37	22898.96	222
223	23022.69	23043.34	23064.00	23084.67	23105.35	223
224	23229.63	23250.38	23271.13	23291.89	23312.67	224
225	23437.50	23458.34	23479.19	23500.04	23520.91	225
226	23646.30	23667.23	23688.17	23709.12	23730.07	226
227	23856.02	23877.04	23898.07	23919.12	23940.17	227
228	24066.67	24087.78	24108.91	24130.04	24151.19	228
229	24278.24	24299.45	24320.67	24341.89	24363.13	229
230	24490.74	24512.04	24533.35	24554.67	24576.00	230
231	24704.17	24725.56	24746.96	24768.38	24789.80	231
232	24918.52	24940.00	24961.50	24983.00	25004.52	232
233	25133.80	25155.38	25176.96	25198.56	25220.17	233
234	25350.00	25371.67	25393.35	25415.04	25436.74	234
235	25567.13	25588.89	25610.67	25632.45	25654.24	235
236	25785.19	25807.04	25828.91	25850.78	25872.67	236
237	26004.17	26026.12	26048.07	26070.04	26092.02	237
238	26224.07	26246.12	26268.17	26290.23	26312.30	238
239	26444.91	26467.04	26489.19	26511.34	26533.50	239
240	26666.67	26688.89	26711.13	26733.38	26755.63	240
SUMS.	0	1	2	3	4	SUMS.

TABLE XV. Whole or Sub Sections.

SUMS.	5	6	7	8	9	SUMS.
181	15251.04	15267.85	15284.67	15301.50	15318.34	**181**
182	15419.56	15436.46	15453.37	15470.30	15487.23	**182**
183	15589.00	15606.00	15623.00	15640.02	15657.04	**183**
184	15759.38	15776.46	15793.56	15810.67	15827.78	**184**
185	15930.67	15947.85	15965.04	15982.24	15999.45	**185**
186	16102.89	16120.17	16137.45	16154.74	16172.04	**186**
187	16276.04	16293.41	16310.78	16328.17	16345.56	**187**
188	16450.12	16467.57	16485.04	16502.52	16520.00	**188**
189	16625.12	16642.67	16660.23	16677.80	16695.38	**189**
190	16801.04	16818.69	16836.34	16854.00	16871.67	**190**
191	16977.89	16995.63	17013.38	17031.13	17048.89	**191**
192	17155.67	17173.50	17191.34	17209.19	17227.04	**192**
193	17334.38	17352.30	17370.23	17388.17	17406.12	**193**
194	17514.00	17532.02	17550.04	17568.07	17586.12	**194**
195	17694.56	17712.67	17730.78	17748.91	17767.04	**195**
196	17876.04	17894.24	17912.45	17930.67	17948.89	**196**
197	18058.45	18076.74	18095.04	18113.35	18131.67	**197**
198	18241.78	18260.17	18278.56	18296.96	18315.37	**198**
199	18426.04	18444.52	18463.00	18481.50	18500.00	**199**
200	18611.23	18629.80	18648.38	18666.96	18685.56	**200**
201	18797.34	18816.00	18834.67	18853.35	18872.04	**201**
202	18984.38	19003.13	19021.89	19040.67	19059.45	**202**
203	19172.34	19191.19	19210.04	19228.91	19247.78	**203**
204	19361.23	19380.17	19399.12	19418.07	19437.04	**204**
205	19551.04	19570.07	19589.12	19608.17	19627.23	**205**
206	19741.78	19760.91	19780.04	19799.19	19818.34	**206**
207	19933.45	19952.67	19971.89	19991.13	20010.37	**207**
208	20126.04	20145.35	20164.67	20184.00	20203.34	**208**
209	20319.56	20338.96	20358.38	20377.80	20397.23	**209**
210	20514.00	20533.50	20553.00	20572.52	20592.04	**210**
211	20709.38	20728.96	20748.56	20768.17	20787.78	**211**
212	20905.67	20925.35	20945.04	20964.74	20984.45	**212**
213	21102.89	21122.67	21142.45	21162.24	21182.04	**213**
214	21301.04	21320.91	21340.78	21360.67	21380.56	**214**
215	21500.12	21520.07	21540.04	21560.02	21580.00	**215**
216	21700.12	21720.17	21740.23	21760.30	21780.38	**216**
217	21901.04	21921.19	21941.34	21961.50	21981.67	**217**
218	22102.89	22123.13	22143.38	22163.63	22183.89	**218**
219	22305.67	22326.00	22346.34	22366.69	22387.04	**219**
220	22509.38	22529.80	22550.23	22570.67	22591.12	**220**
221	22714.00	22734.52	22755.04	22775.57	22796.12	**221**
222	22919.56	22940.17	22960.78	22981.41	23002.04	**222**
223	23126.04	23146.74	23167.45	23188.17	23208.89	**223**
224	23333.45	23354.24	23375.04	23395.85	23416.67	**224**
225	23541.78	23562.67	23583.56	23604.46	23625.37	**225**
226	23751.04	23772.02	23793.00	23814.00	23835.00	**226**
227	23961.23	23982.30	24003.38	24024.46	24045.56	**227**
228	24172.34	24193.50	24214.67	24235.85	24257.04	**228**
229	24384.37	24405.63	24426.89	24448.17	24469.45	**229**
230	24597.34	24618.69	24640.04	24661.41	24682.78	**230**
231	24811.23	24832.67	24854.12	24875.57	24897.04	**231**
232	25026.04	25047.57	25069.12	25090.67	25112.23	**232**
233	25241.78	25263.41	25285.04	25306.69	25328.34	**233**
234	25458.45	25480.17	25501.89	25523.63	25545.37	**234**
235	25676.04	25697.85	25719.67	25741.50	25763.34	**235**
236	25894.56	25916.46	25938.37	25960.30	25982.23	**236**
237	26114.00	26136.00	26158.00	26180.02	26202.04	**237**
238	26334.38	26356.46	26378.56	26400.67	26422.78	**238**
239	26555.67	26577.85	26600.04	26622.24	26644.45	**239**
240	26777.89	26800.17	26822.45	26844.74	26867.04	**240**
SUMS.	5	6	7	8	9	SUMS.

SECOND PART.

DIFF.	0	1	2	3	4	DIFF.
0	.00	.00	.01	.01	.02	0
1	.15	.19	.22	.26	.30	1
2	.62	.68	.75	.82	.89	2
3	1.39	1.48	1.58	1.68	1.78	3
4	2.47	2.59	2.72	2.85	2.99	4
5	3.86	4.01	4.17	4.33	4.50	5
6	5.56	5.74	5.93	6.13	6.32	6
7	7.56	7.78	8.00	8.22	8.45	7
8	9.88	10.13	10.38	10.63	10.89	8
9	12.50	12.78	13.06	13.35	13.64	9
10	15.43	15.74	16.06	16.37	16.69	10
11	18.67	19.01	19.36	19.71	20.06	11
12	22.22	22.59	22.97	23.35	23.73	12
13	26.08	26.48	26.89	27.30	27.71	13
14	30.25	30.68	31.12	31.56	32.00	14
15	34.72	35.19	35.65	36.12	36.60	15
16	39.51	40.00	40.50	41.00	41.51	16
17	44.60	45.12	45.65	46.19	46.72	17
18	50.00	50.56	51.12	51.68	52.25	18
19	55.71	56.30	56.89	57.48	58.08	19
20	61.73	62.35	62.97	63.59	64.22	20
21	68.06	68.71	69.36	70.01	70.67	21
22	74.69	75.37	76.06	76.74	77.43	22
23	81.64	82.35	83.06	83.78	84.50	23
24	88.89	89.63	90.38	91.13	91.88	24
25	96.45	97.22	98.00	98.78	99.56	25
26	104.32	105.13	105.93	106.74	107.56	26
27	112.50	113.33	114.17	115.01	115.86	27
28	120.99	121.85	122.72	123.59	124.47	28
29	129.78	130.68	131.58	132.48	133.39	29
30	138.89	139.82	140.75	141.68	142.62	30
31	148.30	149.26	150.22	151.19	152.15	31
32	158.02	159.01	160.01	161.00	162.00	32
33	168.06	169.08	170.10	171.12	172.15	33
34	178.40	179.45	180.50	181.56	182.62	34
35	189.04	190.12	191.21	192.30	193.39	35
36	200.00	201.11	202.23	203.35	204.47	36
37	211.27	212.41	213.56	214.71	215.86	37
38	222.84	224.01	225.19	226.37	227.56	38
39	234.72	235.93	237.14	238.35	239.56	39
40	246.91	248.15	249.39	250.63	251.88	40
41	259.41	260.68	261.95	263.22	264.50	41
42	272.22	273.52	274.82	276.13	277.43	42
43	285.34	286.67	288.00	289.33	290.67	43
44	298.77	300.12	301.49	302.85	304.22	44
45	312.50	313.89	315.28	316.68	318.08	45
46	326.54	327.96	329.39	330.82	332.25	46
47	340.90	342.35	343.80	345.26	346.72	47
48	355.56	357.04	358.52	360.01	361.51	48
49	370.52	372.04	373.56	375.08	376.60	49
50	385.80	387.35	388.89	390.45	392.00	50
DIFF.	0	1	2	3	4	DIFF.

SECOND PART.

DIFF.	5	6	7	8	9	DIFF.
0	.04	.06	.08	.10	.13	0
1	.35	.40	.45	.50	.56	1
2	.96	1.04	1.13	1.21	1.30	2
3	1.89	2.00	2.11	2.23	2.35	3
4	3.13	3.27	3.41	3.56	3.71	4
5	4.67	4.84	5.01	5.19	5.37	5
6	6.52	6.72	6.93	7.14	7.35	6
7	8.68	8.91	9.15	9.39	9.63	7
8	11.15	11.41	11.68	11.95	12.22	8
9	13.93	14.22	14.52	14.82	15.13	9
10	17.01	17.34	17.67	18.00	18.33	10
11	20.41	20.77	21.13	21.49	21.85	11
12	24.11	24.50	24.89	25.28	25.68	12
13	28.13	28.54	28.96	29.39	29.82	13
14	32.45	32.90	33.35	33.80	34.26	14
15	37.08	37.56	38.04	38.52	39.01	15
16	42.01	42.52	43.04	43.56	44.08	16
17	47.26	47.80	48.35	48.90	49.45	17
18	52.82	53.39	53.96	54.54	55.12	18
19	58.68	59.28	59.89	60.50	61.11	19
20	64.85	65.49	66.13	66.77	67.41	20
21	71.33	72.00	72.67	73.34	74.01	21
22	78.13	78.82	79.52	80.22	80.93	22
23	85.22	85.95	86.68	87.41	88.15	23
24	92.63	93.39	94.15	94.91	95.68	24
25	100.35	101.14	101.93	102.72	103.52	25
26	108.37	109.19	110.01	110.84	111.67	26
27	116.71	117.56	118.41	119.27	120.12	27
28	125.35	126.23	127.11	128.00	128.89	28
29	134.30	135.21	136.12	137.04	137.96	29
30	143.56	144.50	145.45	146.40	147.35	30
31	153.13	154.10	155.08	156.06	157.04	31
32	163.00	164.01	165.01	166.02	167.04	32
33	173.19	174.22	175.26	176.30	177.35	33
34	183.68	184.75	185.82	186.89	187.96	34
35	194.48	195.58	196.68	197.78	198.89	35
36	205.59	206.72	207.85	208.99	210.13	36
37	217.01	218.17	219.33	220.50	221.67	37
38	228.74	229.93	231.13	232.32	233.52	38
39	240.78	242.00	243.22	244.45	245.68	39
40	253.12	254.38	255.63	256.89	258.15	40
41	265.78	267.06	268.35	269.64	270.93	41
42	278.74	280.06	281.37	282.69	284.01	42
43	292.01	293.36	294.71	296.06	297.41	43
44	305.59	306.97	308.35	309.73	311.11	44
45	319.48	320.89	322.30	323.71	325.13	45
46	333.68	335.12	336.56	338.00	339.45	46
47	348.19	349.65	351.12	352.60	354.08	47
48	363.00	364.50	366.00	367.51	369.01	48
49	378.13	379.65	381.19	382.72	384.26	49
50	393.56	395.12	396.68	398.25	399.82	50
DIFF.	5	6	7	8	9	DIFF.

Surface Slope.	SIDE SLOPE					
	2¾ to 1.	**2½ to 1.**	**2¼ to 1.**	**2 to 1.**	**1¾ to 1.**	**1½ to 1.**
0°	0.740 3627	0.698 9700	0.653 2125	0.602 0600	0.544 0680	0.477 1213
1°	0.741 3643	0.699 7975	0.653 8823	0.602 5895	0.544 4732	0.477 4192
2°	0.744 3864	0.702 2927	0.655 9017	0.604 1836	0.545 6929	0.478 3149
3°	0.749 4782	0.706 4897	0.659 2931	0.606 8577	0.547 7364	0.479 8137
4°	0.756 7266	0.712 4494	0.664 0982	0.610 6386	0.550 6206	0.481 9261
5°	0.766 2588	0.720 2594	0.670 3756	0.615 5645	0.554 3694	0.484 6661
6°	0.778 2500	0.730 0402	0.678 2054	0.621 6871	0.559 0148	0.488 0525
7°	0.792 9350	0.741 9497	0.687 6917	0.629 0727	0.564 5970	0.492 1090
8°	0.810 6231	0.756 1924	0.698 9662	0.637 8036	0.571 1664	0.496 8644
9°	0.831 7219	0.773 0316	0.712 1957	0.647 9826	0.578 7836	0.502 3533
10°	0.856 7733	0.792 8073	0.727 5903	0.659 7369	0.587 5234	0.508 6179
11°	0.886 5056	0.815 9608	0.745 4139	0.673 2213	0.597 4744	0.515 7068
12°	0.921 9229	0.843 0734	0.766 0028	0.688 6281	0.608 7443	0.523 6788
13°	0.964 4480	0.874 9258	0.789 7901	0.706 1957	0.621 4625	0.532 6021
14°	1.016 1842	0.912 5930	0.817 3359	0.726 2220	0.635 7858	0.542 5574
15°	1.080 4115	0.957 6051	0.849 3939	0.749 0843	0.651 9051	0.553 6408
16°	1.162 6537	1.012 2380	0.886 9878	0.775 2671	0.670 0545	0.565 9649
17°	1.273 3121	1.080 0806	0.931 5648	0.805 4057	0.690 5251	0.579 6652
18°	1.435 8601	1.167 2740	0.985 2575	0.840 3508	0.713 6824	0.594 9040
19°	1.725 9332	1.285 6858	1.051 3890	0.881 2773	0.739 9929	0.611 8778
20°	....	1.463 3516	1.135 5566	0.929 8669	0.770 0640	0.630 8262
21°	....	1.801 0535	1.248 3232	0.988 6477	0.804 7044	0.652 0470
22°	....	....	1.413 6337	1.061 6664	0.845 0230	0.675 9128
23°	....	....	1.709 4990	1.156 0135	0.892 5939	0.702 8988
24°	....	....	....	1.285 9102	0.949 7579	0.733 6235
25°	....	....	....	1.487 3538	1.020 2157	0.768 9105
26°	....	....	....	1.916 6080	1.110 3247	0.809 8896
27°	....	....	....	....	1.232 4715	0.858 1714
28°	....	....	....	....	1.416 3611	0.916 1505
29°	....	....	....	....	1.773 0612	0.987 6305
30°	....	....	....	....	....	1.079 1810
31°	....	....	....	....	....	1.203 7155
32°	....	....	....	....	....	1.392 6836
33°	....	....	....	....	....	1.768 6400
34°	....	....	....	....	....	....
35°	....	....	....	....	....	....
36°	....	....	....	....	....	....
37°	....	....	....	....	....	....
38°	....	....	....	....	....	....
39°	....	....	....	....	....	....
40°	....	....	....	....	....	....
Surface Slope.	**2¾ to 1.**	**2½ to 1.**	**2¼ to 1.**	**2 to 1.**	**1¾ to 1.**	**1½ to 1.**

TABLE XVI. Whole Sections. Logarithms of Multipliers.

Surface Slope.	SIDE SLOPE					
	1¼ to 1.	1 to 1.	¾ to 1.	½ to 1.	⅓ to 1.	¼ to 1.
0°	0.397 9400	0.301 0300	0.176 0913	0.000 0000	—1.823 9087	—1.698 9700
1°	0.398 1467	0.301 1622	0.176 1653	0.000 0331	—1.823 9232	—1.698 9783
2°	0.398 7684	0.301 5600	0.176 3890	0.000 1326	—1.823 9677	—1.699 0034
3°	0.399 8078	0.302 2244	0.176 7625	0.000 2985	—1.824 0413	—1.699 0448
4°	0.401 2709	0.303 1588	0.177 2872	0.000 5315	—1.824 1447	—1.699 1028
5°	0.403 1654	0.304 3669	0.177 9648	0.000 8320	—1.824 2781	—1.699 1779
6°	0.405 5016	0.305 8542	0.178 7981	0.001 2010	—1.824 4419	—1.699 2700
7°	0.408 2930	0.307 6273	0.179 7896	0.001 6401	—1.824 6368	—1.699 3794
8°	0.411 5546	0.309 6940	0.180 9433	0.002 1500	—1.824 8630	—1.699 5068
9°	0.415 3054	0.312 0635	0.182 2628	0.002 7323	—1.825 1209	—1.699 6515
10°	0.419 5679	0.314 7472	0.183 7537	0.003 3891	—1.825 4116	—1.699 8150
11°	0.424 3676	0.317 7573	0.185 4208	0.004 1220	—1.825 7358	—1.699 9970
12°	0.429 7348	0.321 1086	0.187 2709	0.004 9335	—1.826 0944	—1.700 1983
13°	0.435 7040	0.324 8176	0.189 3109	0.005 8260	—1.826 4888	—1.700 4192
14°	0.442 3158	0.328 9033	0.191 5490	0.006 8025	—1.826 9188	—1.700 6608
15°	0.449 6164	0.333 3870	0.193 9943	0.007 8663	—1.827 3872	—1.700 9235
16°	0.457 6592	0.338 2927	0.196 6565	0.009 0203	—1.827 8945	—1.701 2077
17°	0.466 5069	0.343 6484	0.199 5474	0.010 2691	—1.828 4427	—1.701 5148
18°	0.476 2314	0.349 4849	0.202 6789	0.011 6166	—1.829 0331	—1.701 8452
19°	0.486 9170	0.355 8380	0.206 0655	0.013 0675	—1.829 6679	—1.702 2004
20°	0.498 6620	0.362 7476	0.209 7224	0.014 6269	—1.830 3486	—1.702 5810
21°	0.511 5829	0.370 2599	0.213 6673	0.016 3007	—1.831 0779	—1.702 9883
22°	0.525 8178	0.378 4277	0.217 9195	0.018 0953	—1.831 8580	—1.703 4239
23°	0.541 5312	0.387 3109	0.222 5008	0.020 0171	—1.832 6913	—1.703 8884
24°	0.558 9226	0.396 9795	0.227 4354	0.022 0743	—1.833 5811	—1.704 3844
25°	0.578 2346	0.407 5139	0.232 7507	0.024 2746	—1.834 5302	—1.704 9128
26°	0.599 7678	0.419 0084	0.238 4775	0.026 6278	—1.835 5422	—1.705 4756
27°	0.623 8981	0.431 5731	0.244 6504	0.029 1440	—1.836 6210	—1.706 0749
28°	0.651 1052	0.445 3382	0.251 3089	0.031 8342	—1.837 7699	—1.706 7126
29°	0.682 0133	0.460 4589	0.258 4978	0.034 7113	—1.838 9944	—1.707 3915
30°	0.717 4534	0.477 1213	0.266 2674	0.037 7887	—1.840 2990	—1.708 1135
31°	0.758 5682	0.495 5519	0.274 6771	0.041 0821	—1.841 6894	—1.708 8821
32°	0.806 9832	0.516 0291	0.283 7930	0.044 6086	—1.843 1713	—1.709 7001
33°	0.865 1266	0.538 8995	0.293 6934	0.048 3870	—1.844 7514	—1.710 5709
34°	0.936 8584	0.564 6030	0.304 4690	0.052 4392	—1.846 4371	—1.711 4984
35°	1.028 8709	0.593 7073	0.316 2255	0.056 7889	—1.848 2364	—1.712 4864
36°	1.154 3755	0.626 9628	0.329 0882	0.061 4634	—1.850 1580	—1.713 5398
37°	1.345 8459	0.665 3891	0.343 2066	0.066 4931	—1.852 2124	—1.714 6635
38°	1.732 9342	0.710 4190	0.358 7598	0.071 9126	—1.854 4102	—1.715 8628
39°	....	0.764 1563	0.375 9651	0.077 7614	—1.856 7637	—1.717 1446
40°	....	0.829 8678	0.395 0901	0.084 0846	—1.859 2871	—1.718 5148
Surface Slope.	1¼ to 1.	1 to 1.	¾ to 1.	½ to 1.	⅓ to 1.	¼ to 1.

Surface Slope.	SIDE SLOPE					
	2¾ to 1.	2½ to 1.	2¼ to 1.	2 to 1.	1¾ to 1.	1½ to 1.
0°	Infinite.	Infinite.	Infinite.	Infinite.	Infinite.	Infinite.
1°	1.779 4422	1.777 4559	1.775 4788	1.773 5108	1.771 5514	1.769 6009
2°	1.500 7632	1.496 5891	1.492 4547	1.488 3593	1.484 3021	1.480 2826
3°	1.348 1919	1.341 5941	1.335 0949	1.328 6917	1.322 3814	1.316 1616
4°	1.248 1054	1.238 8060	1.229 7016	1.220 7840	1.212 0457	1.203 4800
5°	1.177 5740	1.165 2423	1.153 2512	1.141 5823	1.130 2186	1.119 1449
6°	1.126 5824	1.110 7711	1.095 5617	1.080 8672	1.066 6585	1.052 8904
7°	1.089 7735	1.070 0987	1.051 2767	1.033 2368	1.015 9162	0.999 2603
8°	1.064 3739	1.040 1884	1.017 2790	0.995 5180	0.974 7954	0.955 0168
9°	1.048 6673	1.019 2225	0.991 6477	0.965 7198	0.941 2529	0.918 0915
10°	1.041 7889	1.006 1276	0.973 1736	0.942 5449	0.913 9344	0.887 0933
11°	1.043 4710	1.000 3430	0.961 1140	0.925 1375	0.891 9130	0.861 0512
12°	1.053 9861	1.001 7151	0.955 0647	0.912 9430	0.874 5478	0.839 2732
13°	1.074 2088	1.010 4704	0.954 9002	0.905 6408	0.861 4036	0.821 2591
14°	1.105 8180	1.027 2561	0.960 7523	0.903 0929	0.852 1992	0.806 6491
15°	1.151 7609	1.053 2662	0.973 0317	0.905 3344	0.846 7803	0.795 1913
16°	1.217 2956	1.090 5071	0.992 4914	0.912 5749	0.845 1033	0.786 7188
17°	1.312 6073	1.142 3506	1.020 3589	0.925 2266	0.847 2347	0.781 1398
18°	1.460 9936	1.214 7578	1.058 5837	0.943 9564	0.853 3532	0.778 4282
19°	1.737 9416	1.319 4483	1.110 3389	0.969 7865	0.863 7710	0.778 6243
20°	....	1.484 3322	1.181 0951	1.004 2699	0.878 9649	0.781 8358
21°	....	1.810 0868	1.281 3080	1.049 8259	0.899 6335	0.788 2481
22°	....	....	1.434 8311	1.110 4081	0.926 7907	0.798 1380
23°	....	....	1.719 5958	1.193 0266	0.961 9293	0.811 8978
24°	....	....	....	1.311 8341	1.007 3196	0.830 0741
25°	....	....	....	1.502 7667	1.066 6002	0.853 4278
26°	....	....	....	1.922 0356	1.146 0751	0.883 0346
27°	....	....	....	....	1.258 0829	0.920 4536
28°	....	....	....	....	1.432 2867	0.968 0379
29°	....	....	....	....	1.779 7162	1.029 5541
30°	....	....	....	....	....	1.111 5378
31°	....	....	....	....	....	1.226 8689
32°	....	....	....	....	....	1.406 9707
33°	....	....	....	....	....	1.774 3725
34°	....	....	....	....	....	....
35°	....	....	....	....	....	....
36°	....	....	....	....	....	....
37°	....	....	....	....	....	....
38°	....	....	....	....	....	....
39°	....	....	....	....	....	....
40°	....	....	....	....	....	....
Surface Slope.	2¾ to 1.	2½ to 1.	2¼ to 1.	2 to 1.	1¾ to 1.	1½ to 1.

TABLE XVII. Sub-Sections. Logarithms of Multipliers.

Surface Slope.	SIDE SLOPE					
	$1\frac{1}{4}$ to 1.	1 to 1.	$\frac{3}{4}$ to 1.	$\frac{1}{2}$ to 1.	$\frac{1}{3}$ to 1.	$\frac{1}{4}$ to 1.
0°	Infinite.	Infinite.	Infinite.	Infinite.	Infinite.	Infinite.
1°	1.767 6591	1.765 7260	1.763 8015	1.761 8854	1.760 6126	1.759 9778
2°	1.476 2998	1.472 3533	1.468 4423	1.464 5662	1.462 0012	1.460 7244
3°	1.310 0294	1.303 9827	1.298 0191	1.292 1362	1.288 2580	1.286 3319
4°	1.195 0799	1.186 8392	1.178 7520	1.170 8127	1.165 5990	1.163 0156
5°	1.108 3464	1.097 8099	1.087 5230	1.077 4742	1.070 9017	1.067 6525
6°	1.039 5499	1.026 6072	1.014 0391	1.001 8243	0.993 8679	0.989 9438
7°	0.983 2194	0.967 7499	0.952 8127	0.938 3721	0.929 0050	0.924 3962
8°	0.936 0996	0.917 9723	0.900 5715	0.883 8409	0.873 0349	0.867 7311
9°	0.896 1026	0.875 1737	0.855 2073	0.836 1186	0.823 8434	0.817 8335
10°	0.861 8144	0.837 9265	0.815 2844	0.793 7644	0.779 9881	0.773 2606
11°	0.832 2378	0.805 2177	0.779 7808	0.755 7516	0.740 4402	0.732 9824
12°	0.806 6495	0.776 3061	0.747 9452	0.721 3233	0.704 4407	0.696 2394
13°	0.784 5130	0.750 6351	0.719 2098	0.689 9057	0.671 4134	0.662 4545
14°	0.765 4259	0.727 7787	0.693 1362	0.661 0541	0.640 9113	0.631 1798
15°	0.749 0845	0.707 4064	0.669 3801	0.634 4171	0.612 5800	0.602 0601
16°	0.735 2605	0.689 2589	0.647 6665	0.609 7116	0.586 1341	0.574 8087
17°	0.723 7873	0.673 1330	0.627 7746	0.586 7086	0.561 3412	0.549 1925
18°	0.714 5468	0.658 8684	0.609 5239	0.565 2183	0.538 0082	0.525 0170
19°	0.707 4655	0.646 3413	0.592 7682	0.545 0838	0.515 9749	0.502 1210
20°	0.702 5080	0.635 4566	0.577 3863	0.526 1729	0.495 1049	0.480 3667
21°	0.699 6772	0.626 1459	0.563 2803	0.508 3746	0.475 2833	0.459 6377
22°	0.699 0142	0.618 3634	0.550 3700	0.491 5949	0.456 4114	0.439 8341
23°	0.700 5991	0.612 0838	0.538 5906	0.475 7528	0.438 4034	0.420 8683
24°	0.704 5585	0.607 3029	0.527 8915	0.460 7805	0.421 1860	0.402 6652
25°	0.711 0712	0.604 0364	0.518 2842	0.446 6192	0.404 6947	0.385 1587
26°	0.720 3816	0.602 3215	0.509 5916	0.433 2196	0.388 8735	0.368 2906
27°	0.732 8161	0.602 2176	0.501 9469	0.420 5396	0.373 6732	0.352 0097
28°	0.748 8103	0.603 8102	0.495 2936	0.408 5436	0.359 0505	0.336 2701
29°	0.768 9491	0.607 2143	0.489 6358	0.397 2027	0.344 9677	0.321 0319
30°	0.794 0285	0.612 5800	0.484 9871	0.386 4926	0.331 3911	0.306 2581
31°	0.825 1594	0.620 1017	0.481 3736	0.376 3954	0.318 2920	0.291 9173
32°	0.863 9390	0.630 0283	0.478 8317	0.366 8969	0.305 6444	0.277 9802
33°	0.912 7697	0.642 6801	0.477 4123	0.357 9883	0.293 4264	0.264 4210
34°	0.975 4882	0.658 4729	0.477 1812	0.349 6656	0.281 6189	0.251 2167
35°	1.058 7654	0.677 9525	0.478 2219	0.341 9292	0.270 2057	0.238 3465
36°	1.175 7933	0.701 8491	0.480 6385	0.334 7845	0.259 1731	0.225 7922
37°	1.359 0278	0.731 1639	0.484 5615	0.328 2422	0.248 5107	0.213 5374
38°	1.738 1046	0.767 8127	0.490 1523	0.322 3182	0.238 2098	0.201 5675
39°	....	0.812 3838	0.497 6121	0.317 0351	0.228 2649	0.189 8708
40°	....	0.869 6295	0.507 1932	0.312 4216	0.218 6729	0.178 4357
Surface Slope.	$1\frac{1}{4}$ to 1.	1 to 1.	$\frac{3}{4}$ to 1.	$\frac{1}{2}$ to 1.	$\frac{1}{3}$ to 1.	$\frac{1}{4}$ to 1.

Surface Slope.	AUGMENTED CENTRE HEIGHT.									
	1	2	3	4	5	6	7	8	9	10
0°	1.00	2.00	3.00	4.00	5.00	6.00	7.00	8.00	9.00	10.00
1°	1.02	2.04	3.05	4.07	5.09	6.11	7.13	8.14	9.16	10.18
2°	1.04	2.07	3.11	4.15	5.18	6.22	7.26	8.29	9.33	10.37
3°	1.06	2.11	3.17	4.23	5.28	6.34	7.40	8.45	9.51	10.57
4°	1.08	2.16	3.23	4.31	5.39	6.47	7.54	8.62	9.70	10.78
5°	1.10	2.20	3.30	4.40	5.50	6.60	7.70	8.80	9.90	11.00
6°	1.12	2.25	3.37	4.49	5.62	6.74	7.87	8.99	10.11	11.24
7°	1.15	2.30	3.45	4.59	5.74	6.89	8.04	9.19	10.34	11.49
8°	1.17	2.35	3.52	4.70	5.87	7.05	8.22	9.40	10.57	11.75
9°	1.20	2.41	3.61	4.81	6.02	7.22	8.42	9.62	10.83	12.03
10°	1.23	2.47	3.70	4.93	6.16	7.40	8.63	9.86	11.10	12.33
11°	1.26	2.53	3.79	5.06	6.32	7.59	8.85	10.12	11.38	12.65
12°	1.30	2.60	3.89	5.19	6.49	7.79	9.09	10.39	11.68	12.98
13°	1.33	2.67	4.00	5.34	6.67	8.01	9.34	10.67	12.01	13.34
14°	1.37	2.75	4.12	5.49	6.86	8.24	9.61	10.98	12.36	13.73
15°	1.41	2.83	4.24	5.66	7.07	8.49	9.90	11.31	12.73	14.14
16°	1.46	2.92	4.38	5.83	7.29	8.75	10.21	11.67	13.13	14.59
17°	1.51	3.01	4.52	6.02	7.53	9.04	10.54	12.05	13.56	15.06
18°	1.56	3.12	4.67	6.23	7.79	9.35	10.90	12.46	14.02	15.58
19°	1.61	3.23	4.84	6.45	8.07	9.68	11.29	12.90	14.52	16.13
20°	1.67	3.35	5.02	6.69	8.37	10.04	11.71	13.39	15.06	16.73
21°	1.74	3.48	5.22	6.95	8.69	10.43	12.17	13.91	15.65	17.38
22°	1.81	3.62	5.43	7.24	9.05	10.86	12.67	14.48	16.29	18.10
23°	1.89	3.78	5.66	7.55	9.44	11.33	13.21	15.10	16.99	18.88
24°	1.97	3.95	5.92	7.89	9.87	11.84	13.81	15.78	17.76	19.73
25°	2.07	4.13	6.20	8.27	10.34	12.40	14.47	16.54	18.61	20.67
26°	2.17	4.34	6.52	8.69	10.86	13.03	15.20	17.38	19.55	21.72
27°	2.29	4.58	6.86	9.15	11.44	13.73	16.02	18.31	20.59	22.88
28°	2.42	4.84	7.26	9.67	12.09	14.51	16.93	19.35	21.76	24.18
29°	2.57	5.13	7.70	10.26	12.83	15.39	17.96	20.52	23.09	25.65
30°	2.73	5.46	8.20	10.93	13.66	16.39	19.12	21.86	24.59	27.32
31°	2.92	5.85	8.77	11.69	14.61	17.54	20.46	23.38	26.31	29.23
32°	3.14	6.29	9.43	12.57	15.72	18.86	22.00	25.15	28.29	31.43
33°	3.40	6.80	10.20	13.60	17.00	20.41	23.81	27.21	30.61	34.01
34°	3.71	7.41	11.12	14.82	18.53	22.23	25.94	29.65	33.35	37.06
35°	4.07	8.14	12.22	16.29	20.36	24.43	28.50	32.58	36.65	40.72
Surface Slope.	1	2	3	4	5	6	7	8	9	10

TABLE XVIII. **Short Slope Distances.** **Side Slope 1 to 1.**

Surface Slope.	AUGMENTED CENTRE HEIGHT.									
	1	2	3	4	5	6	7	8	9	10
0°	1.00	2.00	3.00	4.00	5.00	6.00	7.00	8.00	9.00	10.00
1°	.98	1.97	2.95	3.93	4.92	5.90	6.88	7.86	8.85	9.83
2°	.97	1.93	2.90	3.87	4.83	5.80	6.77	7.73	8.70	9.67
3°	.95	1.90	2.85	3.81	4.76	5.71	6.66	7.61	8.56	9.52
4°	.94	1.87	2.81	3.75	4.68	5.62	6.56	7.50	8.43	9.37
5°	.92	1.85	2.77	3.69	4.62	5.54	6.46	7.38	8.31	9.23
6°	.91	1.82	2.73	3.64	4.55	5.46	6.37	7.28	8.19	9.10
7°	.90	1.79	2.69	3.59	4.49	5.38	6.28	7.18	8.08	8.97
8°	.89	1.77	2.66	3.54	4.43	5.31	6.20	7.08	7.97	8.85
9°	.87	1.75	2.62	3.50	4.37	5.24	6.12	6.99	7.87	8.74
10°	.86	1.73	2.59	3.45	4.32	5.18	6.04	6.91	7.77	8.63
11°	.85	1.71	2.56	3.41	4.26	5.12	5.97	6.82	7.68	8.53
12°	.84	1.69	2.53	3.37	4.22	5.06	5.90	6.75	7.59	8.43
13°	.83	1.67	2.50	3.34	4.17	5.00	5.84	6.67	7.50	8.34
14°	.82	1.65	2.47	3.30	4.12	4.95	5.77	6.60	7.42	8.25
15°	.82	1.63	2.45	3.27	4.08	4.90	5.72	6.53	7.35	8.17
16°	.81	1.62	2.43	3.23	4.04	4.85	5.66	6.47	7.28	8.08
17°	.80	1.60	2.40	3.20	4.00	4.81	5.61	6.41	7.21	8.01
18°	.79	1.59	2.38	3.17	3.97	4.76	5.56	6.35	7.14	7.94
19°	.79	1.57	2.36	3.15	3.93	4.72	5.51	6.29	7.08	7.87
20°	.78	1.56	2.34	3.12	3.90	4.68	5.46	6.24	7.02	7.80
21°	.77	1.55	2.32	3.10	3.87	4.64	5.42	6.19	6.97	7.74
22°	.77	1.54	2.30	3.07	3.84	4.61	5.38	6.15	6.91	7.68
23°	.76	1.53	2.29	3.05	3.81	4.58	5.34	6.10	6.86	7.63
24°	.76	1.51	2.27	3.03	3.79	4.54	5.30	6.06	6.82	7.57
25°	.75	1.50	2.26	3.01	3.76	4.51	5.27	6.02	6.77	7.52
26°	.75	1.50	2.24	2.99	3.74	4.49	5.24	5.98	6.73	7.48
27°	.74	1.49	2.23	2.97	3.72	4.46	5.20	5.95	6.69	7.44
28°	.74	1.48	2.22	2.96	3.70	4.44	5.18	5.92	6.65	7.39
29°	.74	1.47	2.21	2.94	3.68	4.41	5.15	5.88	6.62	7.36
30°	.73	1.46	2.20	2.93	3.66	4.39	5.12	5.86	6.59	7.32
31°	.73	1.46	2.19	2.92	3.64	4.37	5.10	5.83	6.56	7.29
32°	.73	1.45	2.18	2.90	3.63	4.35	5.08	5.81	6.53	7.26
33°	.72	1.45	2.17	2.89	3.61	4.34	5.06	5.78	6.51	7.23
34°	.72	1.44	2.16	2.88	3.60	4.32	5.04	5.76	6.48	7.20
35°	.72	1.44	2.15	2.87	3.59	4.31	5.03	5.74	6.46	7.18
Surface Slope.	1	2	3	4	5	6	7	8	9	10

Surface Slope.	SIDE SLOPE						
	LEVEL.	1½ to 1.	1¼ to 1.	1 to 1.	¾ to 1.	½ to 1.	¼ to 1.
0°	Infinite.	—1.87506	—1.79588	—1.69897	—1.57403	—1.39794	—1.09691
1°	1.45705	—1.88658	—1.80546	—1.70662	—1.57975	—1.40175	—1.09881
2°	1.15589	—1.89843	—1.81526	—1.71441	—1.58556	—1.40559	—1.10072
3°	0.97957	—1.91062	—1.82531	—1.72235	—1.59145	—1.40947	—1.10264
4°	0.85433	—1.92318	—1.83560	—1.73045	—1.59743	—1.41340	—1.10457
5°	0.75702	—1.93616	—1.84618	—1.73873	—1.60351	—1.41737	—1.10651
6°	0.67735	—1.94957	—1.85705	—1.74720	—1.60969	—1.42188	—1.10847
7°	0.60983	—1.96347	—1.86824	—1.75586	—1.61599	—1.42546	—1.11045
8°	0.55117	—1.97788	—1.87978	—1.76474	—1.62241	—1.42958	—1.11244
9°	0.49926	—1.99287	—1.89170	—1.77386	—1.62895	—1.43377	—1.11446
10°	0.45265	0.00847	—1.90401	—1.78322	—1.63563	—1.43802	—1.11649
11°	0.41032	0.02476	—1.91677	—1.79284	—1.64246	—1.44234	—1.11854
12°	0.37150	0.04181	—1.93000	—1.80275	—1.64945	—1.44674	—1.12062
13°	0.33561	0.05968	—1.94376	—1.81297	—1.65661	—1.45121	—1.12273
14°	0.30220	0.07848	—1.95808	—1.82352	—1.66394	—1.45577	—1.12486
15°	0.27092	0.09830	—1.97302	—1.83443	—1.67146	—1.46041	—1.12702
16°	0.24147	0.11928	—1.98864	—1.84573	—1.67919	—1.46515	—1.12922
17°	0.21363	0.14154	0.00501	—1.85744	—1.68714	—1.46999	—1.13144
18°	0.18719	0.16527	0.02220	—1.86961	—1.69533	—1.47493	—1.13370
19°	0.16200	0.19066	0.04032	—1.88228	—1.70377	—1.48000	—1.13600
20°	0.13790	0.21796	0.05945	—1.89549	—1.71248	—1.48518	—1.13834
21°	0.11479	0.24749	0.07973	—1.90929	—1.72149	—1.49049	—1.14073
22°	0.09256	0.27961	0.10130	—1.92374	—1.73081	—1.49594	—1.14315
23°	0.07112	0.31481	0.12433	—1.93890	—1.74047	—1.50154	—1.14563
24°	0.05039	0.35372	0.14902	—1.95486	—1.75051	—1.50730	—1.14816
25°	0.03030	0.39716	0.17562	—1.97168	—1.76094	—1.51323	—1.15074
26°	0.01079	0.44628	0.20444	—1.98947	—1.77180	—1.51934	—1.15338
27°	—1.99180	0.50268	0.23586	0.00835	—1.78314	—1.52565	—1.15609
28°	—1.97330	0.56877	0.27036	0.02845	—1.79500	—1.53216	—1.15885
29°	—1.95522	0.64837	0.30858	0.04994	—1.80742	—1.53889	—1.16169
30°	—1.93753	0.74804	0.35135	0.07299	—1.82046	—1.54587	—1.16461
31°	—1.92020	0.88070	0.39981	0.09785	—1.83418	—1.55311	—1.16760
32°	—1.90318	1.07782	0.45561	0.12479	—1.84865	—1.56063	—1.17068
33°	—1.88645	1.46195	0.52117	0.15417	—1.86396	—1.56845	—1.17385
34°	—1.86998	....	0.60036	0.18643	—1.88020	—1.57659	—1.17711
35°	—1.85374	....	0.69987	0.22215	—1.89748	—1.58510	—1.18048
36°	—1.83771	....	0.83293	0.26208	—1.91593	—1.59399	—1.18396
37°	—1.82186	....	1.03202	0.30725	—1.93571	—1.60330	—1.18756
38°	—1.80616	....	1.42679	0.35909	—1.95699	—1.61307	—1.19129
39°	—1.79060	....	....	0.41972	—1.98001	—1.62334	—1.19515
40°	—1.77516	....	....	0.49241	0.00504	—1.63418	—1.19916
Surface Slope.	LEVEL.	1½ to 1.	1¼ to 1.	1 to 1.	¾ to 1.	½ to 1.	¼ to 1.

Surface Slope.	SIDE SLOPE						
	LEVEL.	1½ to 1.	1¼ to 1.	1 to 1.	¾ to 1.	½ to 1.	¼ to 1.
0°	Infinite.	—1.87506	—1.79588	—1.69897	—1.57403	—1.39794	—1.09691
1°	1.45705	—1.86384	—1.78651	—1.69145	—1.56838	—1.39417	—1.09502
2°	1.15589	—1.85289	—1.77732	—1.68406	—1.56280	—1.39042	—1.09314
3°	0.97957	—1.84220	—1.76832	—1.67679	—1.55729	—1.38671	—1.09126
4°	0.85433	—1.83174	—1.75949	—1.66962	—1.55183	—1.38302	—1.08938
5°	0.75702	—1.82151	—1.75081	—1.66255	—1.54643	—1.37935	—1.08751
6°	0.67735	—1.81148	—1.74227	—1.65557	—1.54108	—1.37570	—1.08565
7°	0.60983	—1.80164	—1.73387	—1.64867	—1.53577	—1.37206	—1.08378
8°	0.55117	—1.79198	—1.72559	—1.64186	—1.53051	—1.36845	—1.08191
9°	0.49926	—1.78249	—1.71743	—1.63512	—1.52528	—1.36484	—1.08005
10°	0.45265	—1.77315	—1.70937	—1.62844	—1.52009	—1.36125	—1.07818
11°	0.41032	—1.76394	—1.70142	—1.62188	—1.51493	—1.35766	—1.07630
12°	0.37150	—1.75487	—1.69355	—1.61527	—1.50979	—1.35408	—1.07442
13°	0.33561	—1.74592	—1.68577	—1.60876	—1.50468	—1.35050	—1.07254
14°	0.30220	—1.73708	—1.67806	—1.60229	—1.49958	—1.34692	—1.07065
15°	0.27092	—1.72834	—1.67042	—1.59587	—1.49450	—1.34334	—1.06875
16°	0.24147	—1.71969	—1.66284	—1.58948	—1.48943	—1.33975	—1.06684
17°	0.21363	—1.71113	—1.65532	—1.58312	—1.48437	—1.33616	—1.06492
18°	0.18719	—1.70264	—1.64785	—1.57678	—1.47932	—1.33256	—1.06299
19°	0.16200	—1.69422	—1.64042	—1.57046	—1.47427	—1.32895	—1.06105
20°	0.13790	—1.68586	—1.63303	—1.56417	—1.46921	—1.32533	—1.05909
21°	0.11479	—1.67756	—1.62567	—1.55788	—1.46415	—1.32169	—1.05711
22°	0.09256	—1.66931	—1.61833	—1.55159	—1.45908	—1.31803	—1.05512
23°	0.07112	—1.66109	—1.61102	—1.54532	—1.45400	—1.31435	—1.05311
24°	0.05039	—1.65291	—1.60372	—1.53903	—1.44890	—1.31065	—1.05108
25°	0.03030	—1.64475	—1.59643	—1.53274	—1.44378	—1.30692	—1.04902
26°	0.01079	—1.63661	—1.58914	—1.52645	—1.43864	—1.30317	—1.04694
27°	—1.99180	—1.62849	—1.58186	—1.52013	—1.43348	—1.29938	—1.04484
28°	—1.97330	—1.62038	—1.57456	—1.51379	—1.42828	—1.29556	—1.04271
29°	—1.95522	—1.61226	—1.56725	—1.50743	—1.42305	—1.29170	—1.04055
30°	—1.93753	—1.60414	—1.55993	—1.50104	—1.41778	—1.28780	—1.03836
31°	—1.92020	—1.59601	—1.55258	—1.49462	—1.41247	—1.28385	—1.03613
32°	—1.90318	—1.58786	—1.54519	—1.48815	—1.40711	—1.27986	—1.03387
33°	—1.88645	—1.57969	—1.53778	—1.48164	—1.40170	—1.27582	—1.03157
34°	—1.86998	....	—1.53032	—1.47508	—1.39624	—1.27173	—1.02923
35°	—1.85374	....	—1.52282	—1.46847	—1.39072	—1.26757	—1.02685
36°	—1.83771	....	—1.51526	—1.46179	—1.38513	—1.26336	—1.02443
37°	—1.82186	....	—1.50764	—1.45505	—1.37947	—1.25908	—1.02195
38°	—1.80616	....	—1.49996	—1.44824	—1.37374	—1.25472	—1.01943
39°	—1.79060	....	....	—1.44134	—1.36792	—1.25030	—1.01684
40°	—1.77516	....	....	—1.43436	—1.36202	—1.24579	—1.01421
Surface Slope.	LEVEL.	1½ to 1.	1¼ to 1.	1 to 1.	¾ to 1.	½ to 1.	¼ to 1.

TABLE XX. Logarithms for Long Slope Distance.

Surface Slope.	SIDE SLOPE						
	LEVEL.	1½ to 1.	1¼ to 1.	1 to 1.	¾ to 1.	½ to 1.	¼ to 1.
0°	Infinite.	—1.87506	—1.79588	—1.69897	—1.57403	—1.39794	—1.09691
1°	1.45711	—1.88665	—1.80553	—1.70668	—1.57982	—1.40181	—1.09888
2°	1.15615	—1.89869	—1.81553	—1.71467	—1.58582	—1.40585	—1.10098
3°	0.98017	—1.91121	—1.82590	—1.72294	—1.59204	—1.41007	—1.10323
4°	0.85539	—1.92424	—1.83666	—1.73151	—1.59849	—1.41446	—1.10563
5°	0.75867	—1.93781	—1.84783	—1.74039	—1.60516	—1.41902	—1.10817
6°	0.67974	—1.95196	—1.85944	—1.74958	—1.61208	—1.42377	—1.11086
7°	0.61308	—1.96671	—1.87149	—1.75911	—1.61924	—1.42871	—1.11370
8°	0.55541	—1.98213	—1.88403	—1.76899	—1.62665	—1.43383	—1.11669
9°	0.50464	—1.99825	—1.89708	—1.77924	—1.63433	—1.43915	—1.11984
10°	0.45930	0.01512	—1.91066	—1.78986	—1.64228	—1.44467	—1.12314
11°	0.41837	0.03282	—1.92482	—1.80089	—1.65052	—1.45040	—1.12660
12°	0.38109	0.05140	—1.93960	—1.81235	—1.65905	—1.45633	—1.13022
13°	0.34688	0.07096	—1.95503	—1.82425	—1.66788	—1.46249	—1.13400
14°	0.31529	0.09158	—1.97117	—1.83662	—1.67703	—1.46886	—1.13796
15°	0.28597	0.11336	—1.98807	—1.84949	—1.68652	—1.47547	—1.14208
16°	0.25863	0.13644	0.00580	—1.86288	—1.69635	—1.48231	—1.14637
17°	0.23303	0.16094	0.02441	—1.87685	—1.70655	—1.48939	—1.15085
18°	0.20899	0.18706	0.04400	—1.89141	—1.71712	—1.49673	—1.15550
19°	0.18633	0.21499	0.06465	—1.90661	—1.72810	—1.50433	—1.16033
20°	0.16492	0.24498	0.08647	—1.92251	—1.73950	—1.51219	—1.16536
21°	0.14464	0.27734	0.10958	—1.93914	—1.75134	—1.52034	—1.17057
22°	0.12539	0.31244	0.13414	—1.95658	—1.76364	—1.52878	—1.17599
23°	0.10709	0.35078	0.16030	—1.97488	—1.77645	—1.53752	—1.18160
24°	0.08966	0.39299	0.18829	—1.99413	—1.78978	—1.54657	—1.18743
25°	0.07302	0.43989	0.21835	0.01440	—1.80366	—1.55596	—1.19347
26°	0.05713	0.49262	0.25078	0.03581	—1.81814	—1.56568	—1.19972
27°	0.04192	0.55280	0.28598	0.05847	—1.83326	—1.57576	—1.20620
28°	0.02736	0.62283	0.32443	0.08252	—1.84906	—1.58622	—1.21292
29°	0.01340	0.70655	0.36676	0.10812	—1.86560	—1.59708	—1.21987
30°	0.00000	0.81051	0.41382	0.13546	—1.88293	—1.60834	—1.22708
31°	—1.98713	0.94764	0.46675	0.16478	—1.90111	—1.62004	—1.23454
32°	—1.97476	1.14940	0.52719	0.19637	—1.92023	—1.63221	—1.24226
33°	—1.96286	1.53836	0.59758	0.23058	—1.94037	—1.64485	—1.25026
34°	—1.95141	....	0.68178	0.26786	—1.96163	—1.65802	—1.25854
35°	—1.94038	....	0.78651	0.30878	—1.98412	—1.67173	—1.26712
36°	—1.92975	....	0.92498	0.35412	0.00797	—1.68603	—1.27601
37°	—1.91951	....	1.12967	0.40490	0.03336	—1.70095	—1.28521
38°	—1.90963	....	1.53026	0.46256	0.06046	—1.71654	—1.29476
39°	—1.90010	....	....	0.52922	0.08951	—1.73284	—1.30465
40°	—1.89090	....	....	0.60816	0.12078	—1.74992	—1.31491
Surface Slope.	LEVEL.	1½ to 1.	1¼ to 1.	1 to 1.	¾ to 1.	½ to 1.	¼ to 1.

Surface Slope.	SIDE SLOPE						
	LEVEL.	1½ to 1.	1¼ to 1.	1 to 1.	¾ to 1.	½ to 1.	¼ to 1.
0°	Infinite.	—1.87506	—1.79588	—1.69897	—1.57403	—1.39794	—1.09691
1°	1.45711	—1.86390	—1.78657	—1.69152	—1.56845	—1.39423	—1.09509
2°	1.15615	—1.85315	—1.77759	—1.68433	—1.56307	—1.39069	—1.09340
3°	0.98017	—1.84279	—1.76892	—1.67738	—1.55788	—1.38730	—1.09185
4°	0.85539	—1.83280	—1.76055	—1.67068	—1.55289	—1.38407	—1.09044
5°	0.75867	—1.82316	—1.75246	—1.66420	—1.54809	—1.38100	—1.08917
6°	0.67974	—1.81387	—1.74466	—1.65795	—1.54346	—1.37808	—1.08803
7°	0.61308	—1.80489	—1.73712	—1.65192	—1.53902	—1.37531	—1.08703
8°	0.55541	—1.79623	—1.72984	—1.64611	—1.53476	—1.37269	—1.08616
9°	0.50464	—1.78787	—1.72281	—1.64050	—1.53066	—1.37022	—1.08543
10°	0.45930	—1.77979	—1.71602	—1.63509	—1.52674	—1.36789	—1.08482
11°	0.41837	—1.77200	—1.70947	—1.62988	—1.52298	—1.36571	—1.08436
12°	0.38109	—1.76447	—1.70315	—1.62486	—1.51939	—1.36367	—1.08402
13°	0.34688	—1.75719	—1.69704	—1.62003	—1.51595	—1.36177	—1.08382
14°	0.31529	—1.75017	—1.69115	—1.61539	—1.51268	—1.36001	—1.08375
15°	0.28597	—1.74339	—1.68548	—1.61092	—1.50956	—1.35839	—1.08381
16°	0.25863	—1.73685	—1.68000	—1.60664	—1.50659	—1.35691	—1.08400
17°	0.23303	—1.73053	—1.67472	—1.60252	—1.50378	—1.35557	—1.08433
18°	0.20899	—1.72443	—1.66964	—1.59857	—1.50111	—1.35436	—1.08479
19°	0.18633	—1.71855	—1.66475	—1.59479	—1.49860	—1.35328	—1.08538
20°	0.16492	—1.71288	—1.66004	—1.59118	—1.49622	—1.35234	—1.08610
21°	0.14464	—1.70741	—1.65552	—1.58772	—1.49400	—1.35154	—1.08696
22°	0.12539	—1.70214	—1.65117	—1.58443	—1.49191	—1.35086	—1.08795
23°	0.10709	—1.69706	—1.64699	—1.58129	—1.48997	—1.35033	—1.08908
24°	0.08966	—1.69218	—1.64299	—1.57830	—1.48817	—1.34992	—1.09035
25°	0.07302	—1.68747	—1.63916	—1.57547	—1.48651	—1.34965	—1.09175
26°	0.05713	—1.68295	—1.63548	—1.57278	—1.48498	—1.34951	—1.09328
27°	0.04192	—1.67861	—1.63198	—1.57025	—1.48360	—1.34950	—1.09496
28°	0.02736	—1.67444	—1.62863	—1.56786	—1.48235	—1.34962	—1.09677
29°	0.01340	—1.67044	—1.62543	—1.56561	—1.48123	—1.34988	—1.09873
30°	0.00000	—1.66661	—1.62239	—1.56351	—1.48025	—1.35027	—1.10083
31°	—1.98713	—1.66295	—1.61951	—1.56155	—1.47940	—1.35079	—1.10307
32°	—1.97476	—1.65944	—1.61677	—1.55973	—1.47869	—1.35144	—1.10545
33°	—1.96286	—1.65610	—1.61419	—1.55805	—1.47811	—1.35223	—1.10798
34°	—1.95141	....	—1.61175	—1.55651	—1.47767	—1.35315	—1.11066
35°	—1.94038	....	—1.60945	—1.55510	—1.47735	—1.35421	—1.11349
36°	—1.92975	....	—1.60730	—1.55384	—1.47717	—1.35540	—1.11647
37°	—1.91951	....	—1.60530	—1.55270	—1.47712	—1.35673	—1.11960
38°	—1.90963	....	—1.60348	—1.55170	—1.47721	—1.35819	—1.12289
39°	—1.90010	....	....	—1.55084	—1.47742	—1.35979	—1.12634
40°	—1.89090	....	....	—1.55011	—1.47777	—1.36154	—1.12995
Surface Slope.	LEVEL.	1½ to 1.	1¼ to 1.	1 to 1.	¾ to 1.	½ to 1.	¼ to 1.

TABLE XXI. **Eighth Parts of Rectangular Prisms.**

H. or B.	1	2	3	4	5	6	7	8	9
0.1	0.046	0.093	0.139	0.185	0.231	0.278	0.324	0.370	0.417
0.2	0.093	0.185	0.278	0.370	0.463	0.556	0.648	0.741	0.833
0.3	0.139	0.278	0.417	0.556	0.694	0.833	0.972	1.111	1.250
0.4	0.185	0.370	0.556	0.741	0.926	1.111	1.296	1.481	1.667
0.5	0.231	0.463	0.694	0.926	1.157	1.389	1.620	1.852	2.083
0.6	0.278	0.556	0.833	1.111	1.389	1.667	1.944	2.222	2.500
0.7	0.324	0.648	0.972	1.296	1.620	1.944	2.269	2.593	2.917
0.8	0.370	0.741	1.111	1.481	1.852	2.222	2.593	2.963	3.333
0.9	0.417	0.833	1.250	1.667	2.083	2.500	2.917	3.333	3.750
1.0	0.463	0.926	1.389	1.852	2.315	2.778	3.241	3.704	4.167
1.1	0.509	1.019	1.528	2.037	2.546	3.056	3.565	4.074	4.583
1.2	0.556	1.111	1.667	2.222	2.778	3.333	3.889	4.444	5.000
1.3	0.602	1.204	1.806	2.407	3.009	3.611	4.213	4.815	5.417
1.4	0.648	1.296	1.944	2.593	3.241	3.889	4.537	5.185	5.833
1.5	0.694	1.389	2.083	2.778	3.472	4.167	4.861	5.556	6.250
1.6	0.741	1.481	2.222	2.963	3.704	4.444	5.185	5.926	6.667
1.7	0.787	1.574	2.361	3.148	3.935	4.722	5.509	6.296	7.083
1.8	0.833	1.667	2.500	3.333	4.167	5.000	5.833	6.667	7.500
1.9	0.880	1.759	2.639	3.519	4.398	5.278	6.157	7.037	7.917
2.0	0.926	1.852	2.778	3.704	4.630	5.556	6.481	7.407	8.333
2.1	0.972	1.944	2.917	3.889	4.861	5.833	6.806	7.778	8.750
2.2	1.019	2.037	3.056	4.074	5.093	6.111	7.130	8.148	9.167
2.3	1.065	2.130	3.194	4.259	5.324	6.389	7.454	8.519	9.583
2.4	1.111	2.222	3.333	4.444	5.556	6.667	7.778	8.889	10.000
2.5	1.157	2.315	3.472	4.630	5.787	6.944	8.102	9.259	10.417
2.6	1.204	2.407	3.611	4.815	6.019	7.222	8.426	9.630	10.833
2.7	1.250	2.500	3.750	5.000	6.250	7.500	8.750	10.000	11.250
2.8	1.296	2.593	3.889	5.185	6.481	7.778	9.074	10.370	11.667
2.9	1.343	2.685	4.028	5.370	6.713	8.056	9.398	10.741	12.083
3.0	1.389	2.778	4.167	5.556	6.944	8.333	9.722	11.111	12.500
3.1	1.435	2.870	4.306	5.741	7.176	8.611	10.046	11.481	12.917
3.2	1.481	2.963	4.444	5.926	7.407	8.889	10.370	11.852	13.333
3.3	1.528	3.056	4.583	6.111	7.639	9.167	10.694	12.222	13.750
3.4	1.574	3.148	4.722	6.296	7.870	9.444	11.019	12.593	14.167
3.5	1.620	3.241	4.861	6.481	8.102	9.722	11.343	12.963	14.583
3.6	1.667	3.333	5.000	6.667	8.333	10.000	11.667	13.333	15.000
3.7	1.713	3.426	5.139	6.852	8.565	10.278	11.991	13.704	15.417
3.8	1.759	3.519	5.278	7.037	8.796	10.556	12.315	14.074	15.833
3.9	1.806	3.611	5.417	7.222	9.028	10.833	12.639	14.444	16.250
4.0	1.852	3.704	5.556	7.407	9.259	11.111	12.963	14.815	16.667
4.1	1.898	3.796	5.694	7.593	9.491	11.389	13.287	15.185	17.083
4.2	1.944	3.889	5.833	7.778	9.722	11.667	13.611	15.556	17.500
4.3	1.991	3.981	5.972	7.963	9.954	11.944	13.935	15.926	17.917
4.4	2.037	4.074	6.111	8.148	10.185	12.222	14.259	16.296	18.333
4.5	2.083	4.167	6.250	8.333	10.417	12.500	14.583	16.667	18.750
4.6	2.130	4.259	6.389	8.519	10.648	12.778	14.907	17.037	19.167
4.7	2.176	4.352	6.528	8.704	10.880	13.056	15.231	17.407	19.583
4.8	2.222	4.444	6.667	8.889	11.111	13.333	15.556	17.778	20.000
4.9	2.269	4.537	6.806	9.074	11.343	13.611	15.880	18.148	20.417
5.0	2.315	4.630	6.944	9.259	11.574	13.889	16.204	18.519	20.833
5.1	2.361	4.722	7.083	9.444	11.806	14.167	16.528	18.889	21.250
5.2	2.407	4.815	7.222	9.630	12.037	14.444	16.852	19.259	21.667
5.3	2.454	4.907	7.361	9.815	12.269	14.722	17.176	19.630	22.083
5.4	2.500	5.000	7.500	10.000	12.500	15.000	17.500	20.000	22.500
5.5	2.546	5.093	7.639	10.185	12.731	15.278	17.824	20.370	22.917
5.6	2.593	5.185	7.778	10.370	12.963	15.556	18.148	20.741	23.333
5.7	2.639	5.278	7.917	10.556	13.194	15.833	18.472	21.111	23.750
5.8	2.685	5.370	8.056	10.741	13.426	16.111	18.796	21.481	24.167
5.9	2.731	5.463	8.194	10.926	13.657	16.389	19.120	21.852	24.583
6.0	2.778	5.556	8.333	11.111	13.889	16.667	19.444	22.222	25.000
H. or B.	1	2	3	4	5	6	7	8	9

TABLE XXI. **Eighth Parts of Rectangular Prisms.**

H. or B.	1	2	3	4	5	6	7	8	9
6.1	2.824	5.648	8.472	11.296	14.120	16.944	19.769	22.593	25.417
6.2	2.870	5.741	8.611	11.481	14.352	17.222	20.093	22.963	25.833
6.3	2.917	5.833	8.750	11.667	14.583	17.500	20.417	23.333	26.250
6.4	2.963	5.926	8.889	11.852	14.815	17.778	20.741	23.704	26.667
6.5	3.009	6.019	9.028	12.037	15.046	18.056	21.065	24.074	27.083
6.6	3.056	6.111	9.167	12.222	15.278	18.333	21.389	24.444	27.500
6.7	3.102	6.204	9.306	12.407	15.509	18.611	21.713	24.815	27.917
6.8	3.148	6.296	9.444	12.593	15.741	18.889	22.037	25.185	28.333
6.9	3.194	6.389	9.583	12.778	15.972	19.167	22.361	25.556	28.750
7.0	3.241	6.481	9.722	12.963	16.204	19.444	22.685	25.926	29.167
7.1	3.287	6.574	9.861	13.148	16.435	19.722	23.009	26.296	29.583
7.2	3.333	6.667	10.000	13.333	16.667	20.000	23.333	26.667	30.000
7.3	3.380	6.759	10.139	13.519	16.898	20.278	23.657	27.037	30.417
7.4	3.426	6.852	10.278	13.704	17.130	20.556	23.981	27.407	30.833
7.5	3.472	6.944	10.417	13.889	17.361	20.833	24.306	27.778	31.250
7.6	3.519	7.037	10.556	14.074	17.593	21.111	24.630	28.148	31.667
7.7	3.565	7.130	10.694	14.259	17.824	21.389	24.954	28.519	32.083
7.8	3.611	7.222	10.833	14.444	18.056	21.667	25.278	28.889	32.500
7.9	3.657	7.315	10.972	14.630	18.287	21.944	25.602	29.259	32.917
8.0	3.704	7.407	11.111	14.815	18.519	22.222	25.926	29.630	33.333
8.1	3.750	7.500	11.250	15.000	18.750	22.500	26.250	30.000	33.750
8.2	3.796	7.593	11.389	15.185	18.981	22.778	26.574	30.370	34.167
8.3	3.843	7.685	11.528	15.370	19.213	23.056	26.898	30.741	34.583
8.4	3.889	7.778	11.667	15.556	19.444	23.333	27.222	31.111	35.000
8.5	3.935	7.870	11.806	15.741	19.676	23.611	27.546	31.481	35.417
8.6	3.981	7.963	11.944	15.926	19.907	23.889	27.870	31.852	35.833
8.7	4.028	8.056	12.083	16.111	20.139	24.167	28.194	32.222	36.250
8.8	4.074	8.148	12.222	16.296	20.370	24.444	28.519	32.593	36.667
8.9	4.120	8.241	12.361	16.481	20.602	24.722	28.843	32.963	37.083
9.0	4.167	8.333	12.500	16.667	20.833	25.000	29.167	33.333	37.500
9.1	4.213	8.426	12.639	16.852	21.065	25.278	29.491	33.704	37.917
9.2	4.259	8.519	12.778	17.037	21.296	25.556	29.815	34.074	38.333
9.3	4.306	8.611	12.917	17.222	21.528	25.833	30.139	34.444	38.750
9.4	4.352	8.704	13.056	17.407	21.759	26.111	30.463	34.815	39.167
9.5	4.398	8.796	13.194	17.593	21.991	26.389	30.787	35.185	39.583
9.6	4.444	8.889	13.333	17.778	22.222	26.667	31.111	35.556	40.000
9.7	4.491	8.981	13.472	17.963	22.454	26.944	31.435	35.926	40.417
9.8	4.537	9.074	13.611	18.148	22.685	27.222	31.759	36.296	40.833
9.9	4.583	9.167	13.750	18.333	22.917	27.500	32.083	36.667	41.250
10.0	4.630	9.259	13.889	18.519	23.148	27.778	32.407	37.037	41.667
10.1	4.676	9.352	14.028	18.704	23.380	28.056	32.731	37.407	42.083
10.2	4.722	9.444	14.167	18.889	23.611	28.333	33.056	37.778	42.500
10.3	4.769	9.537	14.306	19.074	23.843	28.611	33.380	38.148	42.917
10.4	4.815	9.630	14.444	19.259	24.074	28.889	33.704	38.519	43.333
10.5	4.861	9.722	14.583	19.444	24.306	29.167	34.028	38.889	43.750
10.6	4.907	9.815	14.722	19.630	24.537	29.444	34.352	39.259	44.167
10.7	4.954	9.907	14.861	19.815	24.769	29.722	34.676	39.630	44.583
10.8	5.000	10.000	15.000	20.000	25.000	30.000	35.000	40.000	45.000
10.9	5.046	10.093	15.139	20.185	25.231	30.278	35.324	40.370	45.417
11.0	5.093	10.185	15.278	20.370	25.463	30.556	35.648	40.741	45.833
11.1	5.139	10.278	15.417	20.556	25.694	30.833	35.972	41.111	46.250
11.2	5.185	10.370	15.556	20.741	25.926	31.111	36.296	41.481	46.667
11.3	5.231	10.463	15.694	20.926	26.157	31.389	36.620	41.852	47.083
11.4	5.278	10.556	15.833	21.111	26.389	31.667	36.944	42.222	47.500
11.5	5.324	10.648	15.972	21.296	26.620	31.944	37.269	42.593	47.917
11.6	5.370	10.741	16.111	21.481	26.852	32.222	37.593	42.963	48.333
11.7	5.417	10.833	16.250	21.667	27.083	32.500	37.917	43.333	48.750
11.8	5.463	10.926	16.389	21.852	27.315	32.778	38.241	43.704	49.167
11.9	5.509	11.019	16.528	22.037	27.546	33.056	38.565	44.074	49.583
12.0	5.556	11.111	16.667	22.222	27.778	33.333	38.889	44.444	50.000
H. or B.	1	2	3	4	5	6	7	8	9

H. or B.	1	2	3	4	5	6	7	8	9
12.1	5.602	11.204	16.806	22.407	28.009	33.611	39.213	44.815	50.417
12.2	5.648	11.296	16.944	22.593	28.241	33.889	39.537	45.185	50.833
12.3	5.694	11.389	17.083	22.778	28.472	34.167	39.861	45.556	51.250
12.4	5.741	11.481	17.222	22.963	28.704	34.444	40.185	45.926	51.667
12.5	5.787	11.574	17.361	23.148	28.935	34.722	40.509	46.296	52.083
12.6	5.833	11.667	17.500	23.333	29.167	35.000	40.833	46.667	52.500
12.7	5.880	11.759	17.639	23.519	29.398	35.278	41.157	47.037	52.917
12.8	5.926	11.852	17.778	23.704	29.630	35.556	41.481	47.407	53.333
12.9	5.972	11.944	17.917	23.889	29.861	35.833	41.806	47.778	53.750
13.0	6.019	12.037	18.056	24.074	30.093	36.111	42.130	48.148	54.167
13.1	6.065	12.130	18.194	24.259	30.324	36.389	42.454	48.519	54.583
13.2	6.111	12.222	18.333	24.444	30.556	36.667	42.778	48.889	55.000
13.3	6.157	12.315	18.472	24.630	30.787	36.944	43.102	49.259	55.417
13.4	6.204	12.407	18.611	24.815	31.019	37.222	43.426	49.630	55.833
13.5	6.250	12.500	18.750	25.000	31.250	37.500	43.750	50.000	56.250
13.6	6.296	12.593	18.889	25.185	31.481	37.778	44.074	50.370	56.667
13.7	6.343	12.685	19.028	25.370	31.713	38.056	44.398	50.741	57.083
13.8	6.389	12.778	19.167	25.556	31.944	38.333	44.722	51.111	57.500
13.9	6.435	12.870	19.306	25.741	32.176	38.611	45.046	51.481	57.917
14.0	6.481	12.963	19.444	25.926	32.407	38.889	45.370	51.852	58.333
14.1	6.528	13.056	19.583	26.111	32.639	39.167	45.694	52.222	58.750
14.2	6.574	13.148	19.722	26.296	32.870	39.444	46.019	52.593	59.167
14.3	6.620	13.241	19.861	26.481	33.102	39.722	46.343	52.963	59.583
14.4	6.667	13.333	20.000	26.667	33.333	40.000	46.667	53.333	60.000
14.5	6.713	13.426	20.139	26.852	33.565	40.278	46.991	53.704	60.417
14.6	6.759	13.519	20.278	27.037	33.796	40.556	47.315	54.074	60.833
14.7	6.806	13.611	20.417	27.222	34.028	40.833	47.639	54.444	61.250
14.8	6.852	13.704	20.556	27.407	34.259	41.111	47.963	54.815	61.667
14.9	6.898	13.796	20.694	27.593	34.491	41.389	48.287	55.185	62.083
15.0	6.944	13.889	20.833	27.778	34.722	41.667	48.611	55.556	62.500
15.1	6.991	13.981	20.972	27.963	34.954	41.944	48.935	55.926	62.917
15.2	7.037	14.074	21.111	28.148	35.185	42.222	49.259	56.296	63.333
15.3	7.083	14.167	21.250	28.333	35.417	42.500	49.583	56.667	63.750
15.4	7.130	14.259	21.389	28.519	35.648	42.778	49.907	57.037	64.167
15.5	7.176	14.352	21.528	28.704	35.880	43.056	50.231	57.407	64.583
15.6	7.222	14.444	21.667	28.889	36.111	43.333	50.556	57.778	65.000
15.7	7.269	14.537	21.806	29.074	36.343	43.611	50.880	58.148	65.417
15.8	7.315	14.630	21.944	29.259	36.574	43.889	51.204	58.519	65.833
15.9	7.361	14.722	22.083	29.444	36.806	44.167	51.528	58.889	66.250
16.0	7.407	14.815	22.222	29.630	37.037	44.444	51.852	59.259	66.667
16.1	7.454	14.907	22.361	29.815	37.269	44.722	52.176	59.630	67.083
16.2	7.500	15.000	22.500	30.000	37.500	45.000	52.500	60.000	67.500
16.3	7.546	15.093	22.639	30.185	37.731	45.278	52.824	60.370	67.917
16.4	7.593	15.185	22.778	30.370	37.963	45.556	53.148	60.741	68.333
16.5	7.639	15.278	22.917	30.556	38.194	45.833	53.472	61.111	68.750
16.6	7.685	15.370	23.056	30.741	38.426	46.111	53.796	61.481	69.167
16.7	7.731	15.463	23.194	30.926	38.657	46.389	54.120	61.852	69.583
16.8	7.778	15.556	23.333	31.111	38.889	46.667	54.444	62.222	70.000
16.9	7.824	15.648	23.472	31.296	39.120	46.944	54.769	62.593	70.417
17.0	7.870	15.741	23.611	31.481	39.352	47.222	55.093	62.963	70.833
17.1	7.917	15.833	23.750	31.667	39.583	47.500	55.417	63.333	71.250
17.2	7.963	15.926	23.889	31.852	39.815	47.778	55.741	63.704	71.667
17.3	8.009	16.019	24.028	32.037	40.046	48.056	56.065	64.074	72.083
17.4	8.056	16.111	24.167	32.222	40.278	48.333	56.389	64.444	72.500
17.5	8.102	16.204	24.306	32.407	40.509	48.611	56.713	64.815	72.917
17.6	8.148	16.296	24.444	32.593	40.741	48.889	57.037	65.185	73.333
17.7	8.194	16.389	24.583	32.778	40.972	49.167	57.361	65.556	73.750
17.8	8.241	16.481	24.722	32.963	41.204	49.444	57.685	65.926	74.167
17.9	8.287	16.574	24.861	33.148	41.435	49.722	58.009	66.296	74.583
18.0	8.333	16.667	25.000	33.333	41.667	50.000	58.333	66.667	75.000
H. or B.	1	2	3	4	5	6	7	8	9

H. or B.	1	2	3	4	5	6	7	8	9
18.1	8.380	16.759	25.139	33.519	41.898	50.278	58.657	67.037	75.417
18.2	8.426	16.852	25.278	33.704	42.130	50.556	58.981	67.407	75.833
18.3	8.472	16.944	25.417	33.889	42.361	50.833	59.306	67.778	76.250
18.4	8.519	17.037	25.556	34.074	42.593	51.111	59.630	68.148	76.667
18.5	8.565	17.130	25.694	34.259	42.824	51.389	59.954	68.519	77.083
18.6	8.611	17.222	25.833	34.444	43.056	51.667	60.278	68.889	77.500
18.7	8.657	17.315	25.972	34.630	43.287	51.944	60.602	69.259	77.917
18.8	8.704	17.407	26.111	34.815	43.519	52.222	60.926	69.630	78.333
18.9	8.750	17.500	26.250	35.000	43.750	52.500	61.250	70.000	78.750
19.0	8.796	17.593	26.389	35.185	43.981	52.778	61.574	70.370	79.167
19.1	8.843	17.685	26.528	35.370	44.213	53.056	61.898	70.741	79.583
19.2	8.889	17.778	26.667	35.556	44.444	53.333	62.222	71.111	80.000
19.3	8.935	17.870	26.806	35.741	44.676	53.611	62.546	71.481	80.417
19.4	8.981	17.963	26.944	35.926	44.907	53.889	62.870	71.852	80.833
19.5	9.028	18.056	27.083	36.111	45.139	54.167	63.194	72.222	81.250
19.6	9.074	18.148	27.222	36.296	45.370	54.444	63.519	72.593	81.667
19.7	9.120	18.241	27.361	36.481	45.602	54.722	63.843	72.963	82.083
19.8	9.167	18.333	27.500	36.667	45.833	55.000	64.167	73.333	82.500
19.9	9.213	18.426	27.639	36.852	46.065	55.278	64.491	73.704	82.917
20.0	9.259	18.519	27.778	37.037	46.296	55.556	64.815	74.074	83.333
20.1	9.306	18.611	27.917	37.222	46.528	55.833	65.139	74.444	83.750
20.2	9.352	18.704	28.056	37.407	46.759	56.111	65.463	74.815	84.167
20.3	9.398	18.796	28.194	37.593	46.991	56.389	65.787	75.185	84.583
20.4	9.444	18.889	28.333	37.778	47.222	56.667	66.111	75.556	85.000
20.5	9.491	18.981	28.472	37.963	47.454	56.944	66.435	75.926	85.417
20.6	9.537	19.074	28.611	38.148	47.685	57.222	66.759	76.296	85.833
20.7	9.583	19.167	28.750	38.333	47.917	57.500	67.083	76.667	86.250
20.8	9.630	19.259	28.889	38.519	48.148	57.778	67.407	77.037	86.667
20.9	9.676	19.352	29.028	38.704	48.380	58.056	67.731	77.407	87.083
21.0	9.722	19.444	29.167	38.889	48.611	58.333	68.056	77.778	87.500
21.1	9.769	19.537	29.306	39.074	48.843	58.611	68.380	78.148	87.917
21.2	9.815	19.630	29.444	39.259	49.074	58.889	68.704	78.519	88.333
21.3	9.861	19.722	29.583	39.444	49.306	59.167	69.028	78.889	88.750
21.4	9.907	19.815	29.722	39.630	49.537	59.444	69.352	79.259	89.167
21.5	9.954	19.907	29.861	39.815	49.769	59.722	69.676	79.630	89.583
21.6	10.000	20.000	30.000	40.000	50.000	60.000	70.000	80.000	90.000
21.7	10.046	20.093	30.139	40.185	50.231	60.278	70.324	80.370	90.417
21.8	10.093	20.185	30.278	40.370	50.463	60.556	70.648	80.741	90.833
21.9	10.139	20.278	30.417	40.556	50.694	60.833	70.972	81.111	91.250
22.0	10.185	20.370	30.556	40.741	50.926	61.111	71.296	81.481	91.667
22.1	10.231	20.463	30.694	40.926	51.157	61.389	71.620	81.852	92.083
22.2	10.278	20.556	30.833	41.111	51.389	61.667	71.944	82.222	92.500
22.3	10.324	20.648	30.972	41.296	51.620	61.944	72.269	82.593	92.917
22.4	10.370	20.741	31.111	41.481	51.852	62.222	72.593	82.963	93.333
22.5	10.417	20.833	31.250	41.667	52.083	62.500	72.917	83.333	93.750
22.6	10,463	20.926	31.389	41.852	52.315	62.778	73.241	83.704	94.167
22.7	10.509	21.019	31.528	42.037	52.546	63.056	73.565	84.074	94.583
22.8	10.556	21.111	31.667	42.222	52.778	63.333	73.889	84.444	95.000
22.9	10.602	21.204	31.806	42.407	53.009	63.611	74.213	84.815	95.417
23.0	10.648	21.296	31.944	42.593	53.241	63.889	74.537	85.185	95.833
23.1	10.694	21.389	32.083	42.778	53.472	64.167	74.861	85.556	96.250
23.2	10.741	21.481	32.222	42.963	53.704	64.444	75.185	85.926	96.667
23.3	10.787	21.574	32.361	43.148	53.935	64.722	75.509	86.296	97.083
23.4	10.833	21.667	32.500	43.333	54.167	65.000	75.833	86.667	97.500
23.5	10.880	21.759	32.639	43.519	54.398	65.278	76.157	87.037	97.917
23.6	10.926	21.852	32.778	43.704	54.630	65.556	76.481	87.407	98.333
23.7	10.972	21.944	32.917	43.889	54.861	65.833	76.806	87.778	98.750
23.8	11.019	22.037	33.056	44.074	55.093	66.111	77.130	88.148	99.167
23.9	11.065	22.130	33.194	44.259	55.324	66.389	77.454	88 519	99.583
24.0	11.111	22.222	33.333	44.444	55.556	66.667	77.778	88.889	100.000
H. or B.	1	2	3	4	5	6	7	8	9

TABLE XXI. Eighth Parts of Rectangular Prisms.

H. or B.	1	2	3	4	5	6	7	8	9
24.1	11.157	22.315	33.472	44.630	55.787	66.944	78.102	89.259	100.417
24.2	11.204	22.407	33.611	44.815	56.019	67.222	78.426	89.630	100.833
24.3	11.250	22.500	33.750	45.000	56.250	67.500	78.750	90.000	101.250
24.4	11.296	22.593	33.889	45.185	56.481	67.778	79.074	90.370	101.667
24.5	11.343	22.685	34.028	45.370	56.713	68.056	79.398	90.741	102.083
24.6	11.389	22.778	34.167	45.556	56.944	68.333	79.722	91.111	102.500
24.7	11.435	22.870	34.306	45.741	57.176	68.611	80.046	91.481	102.917
24.8	11.481	22.963	34.444	45.926	57.407	68.889	80.370	91.852	103.333
24.9	11.528	23.056	34.583	46.111	57.639	69.167	80.694	92.222	103.750
25.0	11.574	23.148	34.722	46.296	57.870	69.444	81.019	92.593	104.167
25.1	11.620	23.241	34.861	46.481	58.102	69.722	81.343	92.963	104.583
25.2	11.667	23.333	35.000	46.667	58.333	70.000	81.667	93.333	105.000
25.3	11.713	23.426	35.139	46.852	58.565	70.278	81.991	93.704	105.417
25.4	11.759	23.519	35.278	47.037	58.796	70.556	82.315	94.074	105.833
25.5	11.806	23.611	35.417	47.222	59.028	70.833	82.639	94.444	106.250
25.6	11.852	23.704	35.556	47.407	59.259	71.111	82.963	94.815	106.667
25.7	11.898	23.796	35.694	47.593	59.491	71.389	83.287	95.185	107.083
25.8	11.944	23.889	35.833	47.778	59.722	71.667	83.611	95.556	107.500
25.9	11.991	23.981	35.972	47.963	59.954	71.944	83.935	95.926	107.917
26.0	12.037	24.074	36.111	48.148	60.185	72.222	84.259	96.296	108.333
26.1	12.083	24.167	36.250	48.333	60.417	72.500	84.583	96.667	108.750
26.2	12.130	24.259	36.389	48.519	60.648	72.778	84.907	97.037	109.167
26.3	12.176	24.352	36.528	48.704	60.880	73.056	85.231	97.407	109.583
26.4	12.222	24.444	36.667	48.889	61.111	73.333	85.556	97.778	110.000
26.5	12.269	24.537	36.806	49.074	61.343	73.611	85.880	98.148	110.417
26.6	12.315	24.630	36.944	49.259	61.574	73.889	86.204	98.519	110.833
26.7	12.361	24.722	37.083	49.444	61.806	74.167	86.528	98.889	111.250
26.8	12.407	24.815	37.222	49.630	62.037	74.444	86.852	99.259	111.667
26.9	12.454	24.907	37.361	49.815	62.269	74.722	87.176	99.630	112.083
27.0	12.500	25.000	37.500	50.000	62.500	75.000	87.500	100.000	112.500
27.1	12.546	25.093	37.639	50.185	62.731	75.278	87.824	100.370	112.917
27.2	12.593	25.185	37.778	50.370	62.963	75.556	88.148	100.741	113.333
27.3	12.639	25.278	37.917	50.556	63.194	75.833	88.472	101.111	113.750
27.4	12.685	25.370	38.056	50.741	63.426	76.111	88.796	101.481	114.167
27.5	12.731	25.463	38.194	50.926	63.657	76.389	89.120	101.852	114.583
27.6	12.778	25.556	38.333	51.111	63.889	76.667	89.444	102.222	115.000
27.7	12.824	25.648	38.472	51.296	64.120	76.944	89.769	102.593	115.417
27.8	12.870	25.741	38.611	51.481	64.352	77.222	90.093	102.963	115.833
27.9	12.917	25.833	38.750	51.667	64.583	77.500	90.417	103.333	116.250
28.0	12.963	25.926	38.889	51.852	64.815	77.778	90.741	103.704	116.667
28.1	13.009	26.019	39.028	52.037	65.046	78.056	91.065	104.074	117.083
28.2	13.056	26.111	39.167	52.222	65.278	78.333	91.389	104.444	117.500
28.3	13.102	26.204	39.306	52.407	65.509	78.611	91.713	104.815	117.917
28.4	13.148	26.296	39.444	52.593	65.741	78.889	92.037	105.185	118.333
28.5	13.194	26.389	39.583	52.778	65.972	79.167	92.361	105.556	118.750
28.6	13.241	26.481	39.722	52.963	66.204	79.444	92.685	105.926	119.167
28.7	13.287	26.574	39.861	53.148	66.435	79.722	93.009	106.296	119.583
28.8	13.333	26.667	40.000	53.333	66.667	80.000	93.333	106.667	120.000
28.9	13.380	26.759	40.139	53.519	66.898	80.278	93.657	107.037	120.417
29.0	13.426	26.852	40.278	53.704	67.130	80.556	93.981	107.407	120.833
29.1	13.472	26.944	40.417	53.889	67.361	80.833	94.306	107.778	121.250
29.2	13.519	27.037	40.556	54.074	67.593	81.111	94.630	108.148	121.667
29.3	13.565	27.130	40.694	54.259	67.824	81.389	94.954	108.519	122.083
29.4	13.611	27.222	40.833	54.444	68.056	81.667	95.278	108.889	122.500
29.5	13.657	27.315	40.972	54.630	68.287	81.944	95.602	109.259	122.917
29.6	13.704	27.407	41.111	54.815	68.519	82.222	95.926	109.630	123.333
29.7	13.750	27.500	41.250	55.000	68.750	82.500	96.250	110.000	123.750
29.8	13.796	27.593	41.389	55.185	68.981	82.778	96.574	110.370	124.167
29.9	13.843	27.685	41.528	55.370	69.213	83.056	96.898	110.741	124.583
30.0	13.889	27.778	41.667	55.556	69.444	83.333	97.222	111.111	125.000
H. or B.	1	2	3	4	5	6	7	8	9

TABLE XXI. **Eighth Parts of Rectangular Prisms.**

H. or B.	1	2	3	4	5	6	7	8	9
30.1	13.935	27.870	41.806	55.741	69.676	83.611	97.546	111.481	125.417
30.2	13.981	27.963	41.944	55.926	69.907	83.889	97.870	111.852	125.833
30.3	14.028	28.056	42.083	56.111	70.139	84.167	98.194	112.222	126.250
30.4	14.074	28.148	42.222	56.296	70.370	84.444	98.519	112.593	126.667
30.5	14.120	28.241	42.361	56.481	70.602	84.722	98.843	112.963	127.083
30.6	14.167	28.333	42.500	56.667	70.833	85.000	99.167	113.333	127.500
30.7	14.213	28.426	42.639	56.852	71.065	85.278	99.491	113.704	127.917
30.8	14.259	28.519	42.778	57.037	71.296	85.556	99.815	114.074	128.333
30.9	14.306	28.611	42.917	57.222	71.528	85.833	100.139	114.444	128.750
31.0	14.352	28.704	43.056	57.407	71.759	86.111	100.463	114.815	129.167
31.1	14.398	28.796	43.194	57.593	71.991	86.389	100.787	115.185	129.583
31.2	14.444	28.889	43.333	57.778	72.222	86.667	101.111	115.556	130.000
31.3	14.491	28.981	43.472	57.963	72.454	86.944	101.435	115.926	130.417
31.4	14.537	29.074	43.611	58.148	72.685	87.222	101.759	116.296	130.833
31.5	14.583	29.167	43.750	58.333	72.917	87.500	102.083	116.667	131.250
31.6	14.630	29.259	43.889	58.519	73.148	87.778	102.407	117.037	131.667
31.7	14.676	29.352	44.028	58.704	73.380	88.056	102.731	117.407	132.083
31.8	14.722	29.444	44.167	58.889	73.611	88.333	103.056	117.778	132.500
31.9	14.769	29.537	44.306	59.074	73.843	88.611	103.380	118.148	132.917
32.0	14.815	29.630	44.444	59.259	74.074	88.889	103.704	118.519	133.333
32.1	14.861	29.722	44.583	59.444	74.306	89.167	104.028	118.889	133.750
32.2	14.907	29.815	44.722	59.630	74.537	89.444	104.352	119.259	134.167
32.3	14.954	29.907	44.861	59.815	74.769	89.722	104.676	119.630	134.583
32.4	15.000	30.000	45.000	60.000	75.000	90.000	105.000	120.000	135.000
32.5	15.046	30.093	45.139	60.185	75.231	90.278	105.324	120.370	135.417
32.6	15.093	30.185	45.278	60.370	75.463	90.556	105.648	120.741	135.833
32.7	15.139	30.278	45.417	60.556	75.694	90.833	105.972	121.111	136.250
32.8	15.185	30.370	45.556	60.741	75.926	91.111	106.296	121.481	136.667
32.9	15.231	30.463	45.694	60.926	76.157	91.389	106.620	121.852	137.083
33.0	15.278	30.556	45.833	61.111	76.389	91.667	106.944	122.222	137.500
33.1	15.324	30.648	45.972	61.296	76.620	91.944	107.269	122.593	137.917
33.2	15.370	30.741	46.111	61.481	76.852	92.222	107.593	122.963	138.333
33.3	15.417	30.833	46.250	61.667	77.083	92.500	107.917	123.333	138.750
33.4	15.463	30.926	46.389	61.852	77.315	92.778	108.241	123.704	139.167
33.5	15.509	31.019	46.528	62.037	77.546	93.056	108.565	124.074	139.583
33.6	15.556	31.111	46.667	62.222	77.778	93.333	108.889	124.444	140.000
33.7	15.602	31.204	46.806	62.407	78.009	93.611	109.213	124.815	140.417
33.8	15.648	31.296	46.944	62.593	78.241	93.889	109.537	125.185	140.833
33.9	15.694	31.389	47.083	62.778	78.472	94.167	109.861	125.556	141.250
34.0	15.741	31.481	47.222	62.963	78.704	94.444	110.185	125.926	141.667
34.1	15.787	31.574	47.361	63.148	78.935	94.722	110.509	126.296	142.083
34.2	15.833	31.667	47.500	63.333	79.167	95.000	110.833	126.667	142.500
34.3	15.880	31.759	47.639	63.519	79.398	95.278	111.157	127.037	142.917
34.4	15.926	31.852	47.778	63.704	79.630	95.556	111.481	127.407	143.333
34.5	15.972	31.944	47.917	63.889	79.861	95.833	111.806	127.778	143.750
34.6	16.019	32.037	48.056	64.074	80.093	96.111	112.130	128.148	144.167
34.7	16.065	32.130	48.194	64.259	80.324	96.389	112.454	128.519	144.583
34.8	16.111	32.222	48.333	64.444	80.556	96.667	112.778	128.889	145.000
34.9	16.157	32.315	48.472	64.630	80.787	96.944	113.102	129.259	145.417
35.0	16.204	32.407	48.611	64.815	81.019	97.222	113.426	129.630	145.833
35.1	16.250	32.500	48.750	65.000	81.250	97.500	113.750	130.000	146.250
35.2	16.296	32.593	48.889	65.185	81.481	97.778	114.074	130.370	146.667
35.3	16.343	32.685	49.028	65.370	81.713	98.056	114.398	130.741	147.083
35.4	16.389	32.778	49.167	65.556	81.944	98.333	114.722	131.111	147.500
35.5	16.435	32.870	49.306	65.741	82.176	98.611	115.046	131.481	147.917
35.6	16.481	32.963	49.444	65.926	82.407	98.889	115.370	131.852	148.333
35.7	16.528	33.056	49.583	66.111	82.639	99.167	115.694	132.222	148.750
35.8	16.574	33.148	49.722	66.296	82.870	99.444	116.019	132.593	149.167
35.9	16.620	33.241	49.861	66.481	83.102	99.722	116.343	132.963	149.583
36.0	16.667	33.333	50.000	66.667	83.333	100.000	116.667	133.333	150.000
H. or B.	1	2	3	4	5	6	7	8	9

H. or B.	1	2	3	4	5	6	7	8	9
36.1	16.713	33.426	50.139	66.852	83.565	100.278	116.991	133.704	150.417
36.2	16.759	33.519	50.278	67.037	83.796	100.556	117.315	134.074	150.833
36.3	16.806	33.611	50.417	67.222	84.028	100.833	117.639	134.444	151.250
36.4	16.852	33.704	50.556	67.407	84.259	101.111	117.963	134.815	151.667
36.5	16.898	33.796	50.694	67.593	84.491	101.389	118.287	135.185	152.083
36.6	16.944	33.889	50.833	67.778	84.722	101.667	118.611	135.556	152.500
36.7	16.991	33.981	50.972	67.963	84.954	101.944	118.935	135.926	152.917
36.8	17.037	34.074	51.111	68.148	85.185	102.222	119.259	136.296	153.333
36.9	17.083	34.167	51.250	68.333	85.417	102.500	119.583	136.667	153.750
37.0	17.130	34.259	51.389	68.519	85.648	102.778	119.907	137.037	154.167
37.1	17.176	34.352	51.528	68.704	85.880	103.056	120.231	137.407	154.583
37.2	17.222	34.444	51.667	68.889	86.111	103.333	120.556	137.778	155.000
37.3	17.269	34.537	51.806	69.074	86.343	103.611	120.880	138.148	155.417
37.4	17.315	34.630	51.944	69.259	86.574	103.889	121.204	138.519	155.833
37.5	17.361	34.722	52.083	69.444	86.806	104.167	121.528	138.889	156.250
37.6	17.407	34.815	52.222	69.630	87.037	104.444	121.852	139.259	156.667
37.7	17.454	34.907	52.361	69.815	87.269	104.722	122.176	139.630	157.083
37.8	17.500	35.000	52.500	70.000	87.500	105.000	122.500	140.000	157.500
37.9	17.546	35.093	52.639	70.185	87.731	105.278	122.824	140.370	157.917
38.0	17.593	35.185	52.778	70.370	87.963	105.556	123.148	140.741	158.333
38.1	17.639	35.278	52.917	70.556	88.194	105.833	123.472	141.111	158.750
38.2	17.685	35.370	53.056	70.741	88.426	106.111	123.796	141.481	159.167
38.3	17.731	35.463	53.194	70.926	88.657	106.389	124.120	141.852	159.583
38.4	17.778	35.556	53.333	71.111	88.889	106.667	124.444	142.222	160.000
38.5	17.824	35.648	53.472	71.296	89.120	106.944	124.769	142.593	160.417
38.6	17.870	35.741	53.611	71.481	89.352	107.222	125.093	142.963	160.833
38.7	17.917	35.833	53.750	71.667	89.583	107.500	125.417	143.333	161.250
38.8	17.963	35.926	53.889	71.852	89.815	107.778	125.741	143.704	161.667
38.9	18.009	36.019	54.028	72.037	90.046	108.056	126.065	144.074	162.083
39.0	18.056	36.111	54.167	72.222	90.278	108.333	126.389	144.444	162.500
39.1	18.102	36.204	54.306	72.407	90.509	108.611	126.713	144.815	162.917
39.2	18.148	36.296	54.444	72.593	90.741	108.889	127.037	145.185	163.333
39.3	18.194	36.389	54.583	72.778	90.972	109.167	127.361	145.556	163.750
39.4	18.241	36.481	54.722	72.963	91.204	109.444	127.685	145.926	164.167
39.5	18.287	36.574	54.861	73.148	91.435	109.722	128.009	146.296	164.583
39.6	18.333	36.667	55.000	73.333	91.667	110.000	128.333	146.667	165.000
39.7	18.380	36.759	55.139	73.519	91.898	110.278	128.657	147.037	165.417
39.8	18.426	36.852	55.278	73.704	92.130	110.556	128.981	147.407	165.833
39.9	18.472	36.944	55.417	73.889	92.361	110.833	129.306	147.778	166.250
40.0	18.519	37.037	55.556	74.074	92.593	111.111	129.630	148.148	166.667
40.1	18.565	37.130	55.694	74.259	92.824	111.389	129.954	148.519	167.083
40.2	18.611	37.222	55.833	74.444	93.056	111.667	130.278	148.889	167.500
40.3	18.657	37.315	55.972	74.630	93.287	111.944	130.602	149.259	167.917
40.4	18.704	37.407	56.111	74.815	93.519	112.222	130.926	149.630	168.333
40.5	18.750	37.500	56.250	75.000	93.750	112.500	131.250	150.000	168.750
40.6	18.796	37.593	56.389	75.185	93.981	112.778	131.574	150.370	169.167
40.7	18.843	37.685	56.528	75.370	94.213	113.056	131.898	150.741	169.583
40.8	18.889	37.778	56.667	75.556	94.444	113.333	132.222	151.111	170.000
40.9	18.935	37.870	56.806	75.741	94.676	113.611	132.546	151.481	170.417
41.0	18.981	37.963	56.944	75.926	94.907	113.889	132.870	151.852	170.833
41.1	19.028	38.056	57.083	76.111	95.139	114.167	133.194	152.222	171.250
41.2	19.074	38.148	57.222	76.296	95.370	114.444	133.519	152.593	171.667
41.3	19.120	38.241	57.361	76.481	95.602	114.722	133.843	152.963	172.083
41.4	19.167	38.333	57.500	76.667	95.833	115.000	134.167	153.333	172.500
41.5	19.213	38.426	57.639	76.852	96.065	115.278	134.491	153.704	172.917
41.6	19.259	38.519	57.778	77.037	96.296	115.556	134.815	154.074	173.333
41.7	19.306	38.611	57.917	77.222	96.528	115.833	135.139	154.444	173.750
41.8	19.352	38.704	58.056	77.407	96.759	116.111	135.463	154.815	174.167
41.9	19.398	38.796	58.194	77.593	96.991	116.389	135.787	155.185	174.583
42.0	19.444	38.889	58.333	77.778	97.222	116.667	136.111	155.556	175.000
H. or B.	1	2	3	4	5	6	7	8	9

H. or B.	1	2	3	4	5	6	7	8	9
42.1	19.491	38.981	58.472	77.963	97.454	116.944	136.435	155.926	175.417
42.2	19.537	39.074	58.611	78.148	97.685	117.222	136.759	156.296	175.833
42.3	19.583	39.167	58.750	78.333	97.917	117.500	137.083	156.667	176.250
42.4	19.630	39.259	58.889	78.519	98.148	117.778	137.407	157.037	176.667
42.5	19.676	39.352	59.028	78.704	98.380	118.056	137.731	157.407	177.083
42.6	19.722	39.444	59.167	78.889	98.611	118.333	138.056	157.778	177.500
42.7	19.769	39.537	59.306	79.074	98.843	118.611	138.380	158.148	177.917
42.8	19.815	39.630	59.444	79.259	99.074	118.889	138.704	158.519	178.333
42.9	19.861	39.722	59.583	79.444	99.306	119.167	139.028	158.889	178.750
43.0	19.907	39.815	59.722	79.630	99.537	119.444	139.352	159.259	179.167
43.1	19.954	39.907	59.861	79.815	99.769	119.722	139.676	159.630	179.583
43.2	20.000	40.000	60.000	80.000	100.000	120.000	140.000	160.000	180.000
43.3	20.046	40.093	60.139	80.185	100.231	120.278	140.324	160.370	180.417
43.4	20.093	40.185	60.278	80.370	100.463	120.556	140.648	160.741	180.833
43.5	20.139	40.278	60.417	80.556	100.694	120.833	140.972	161.111	181.250
43.6	20.185	40.370	60.556	80.741	100.926	121.111	141.296	161.481	181.667
43.7	20.231	40.463	60.694	80.926	101.157	121.389	141.620	161.852	182.083
43.8	20.278	40.556	60.833	81.111	101.389	121.667	141.944	162.222	182.500
43.9	20.324	40.648	60.972	81.296	101.620	121.944	142.269	162.593	182.917
44.0	20.370	40.741	61.111	81.481	101.852	122.222	142.593	162.963	183.333
44.1	20.417	40.833	61.250	81.667	102.083	122.500	142.917	163.333	183.750
44.2	20.463	40.926	61.389	81.852	102.315	122.778	143.241	163.704	184.167
44.3	20.509	41.019	61.528	82.037	102.546	123.056	143.565	164.074	184.583
44.4	20.556	41.111	61.667	82.222	102.778	123.333	143.889	164.444	185.000
44.5	20.602	41.204	61.806	82.407	103.009	123.611	144.213	164.815	185.417
44.6	20.648	41.296	61.944	82.593	103.241	123.889	144.537	165.185	185.833
44.7	20.694	41.389	62.083	82.778	103.472	124.167	144.861	165.556	186.250
44.8	20.741	41.481	62.222	82.963	103.704	124.444	145.185	165.926	186.667
44.9	20.787	41.574	62.361	83.148	103.935	124.722	145.509	166.296	187.083
45.0	20.833	41.667	62.500	83.333	104.167	125.000	145.833	166.667	187.500
45.1	20.880	41.759	62.639	83.519	104.398	125.278	146.157	167.037	187.917
45.2	20.926	41.852	62.778	83.704	104.630	125.556	146.481	167.407	188.333
45.3	20.972	41.944	62.917	83.889	104.861	125.833	146.806	167.778	188.750
45.4	21.019	42.037	63.056	84.074	105.093	126.111	147.130	168.148	189.167
45.5	21.065	42.130	63.194	84.259	105.324	126.389	147.454	168.519	189.583
45.6	21.111	42.222	63.333	84.444	105.556	126.667	147.778	168.889	190.000
45.7	21.157	42.315	63.472	84.630	105.787	126.944	148.102	169.259	190.417
45.8	21.204	42.407	63.611	84.815	106.019	127.222	148.426	169.630	190.833
45.9	21.250	42.500	63.750	85.000	106.250	127.500	148.750	170.000	191.250
46.0	21.296	42.593	63.889	85.185	106.481	127.778	149.074	170.370	191.667
46.1	21.343	42.685	64.028	85.370	106.713	128.056	149.398	170.741	192.083
46.2	21.389	42.778	64.167	85.556	106.944	128.333	149.722	171.111	192.500
46.3	21.435	42.870	64.306	85.741	107.176	128.611	150.046	171.481	192.917
46.4	21.481	42.963	64.444	85.926	107.407	128.889	150.370	171.852	193.333
46.5	21.528	43.056	64.583	86.111	107.639	129.167	150.694	172.222	193.750
46.6	21.574	43.148	64.722	86.296	107.870	129.444	151.019	172.593	194.167
46.7	21.620	43.241	64.861	86.481	108.102	129.722	151.343	172.963	194.583
46.8	21.667	43.333	65.000	86.667	108.333	130.000	151.667	173.333	195.000
46.9	21.713	43.426	65.139	86.852	108.565	130.278	151.991	173.704	195.417
47.0	21.759	43.519	65.278	87.037	108.796	130.556	152.315	174.074	195.833
47.1	21.806	43.611	65.417	87.222	109.028	130.833	152.639	174.444	196.250
47.2	21.852	43.704	65.556	87.407	109.259	131.111	152.963	174.815	196.667
47.3	21.898	43.796	65.694	87.593	109.491	131.389	153.287	175.185	197.083
47.4	21.944	43.889	65.833	87.778	109.722	131.667	153.611	175.556	197.500
47.5	21.991	43.981	65.972	87.963	109.954	131.944	153.935	175.926	197.917
47.6	22.037	44.074	66.111	88.148	110.185	132.222	154.259	176.296	198.333
47.7	22.083	44.167	66.250	88.333	110.417	132.500	154.583	176.667	198.750
47.8	22.130	44.259	66.389	88.519	110.648	132.778	154.907	177.037	199.167
47.9	22.176	44.352	66.528	88.704	110.880	133.056	155.231	177.407	199.583
48.0	22.222	44.444	66.667	88.889	111.111	133.333	155.556	177.778	200.000
H. or B.	1	2	3	4	5	6	7	8	9

TABLE XXI. Eighth Parts of Rectangular Prisms.

H. or B.	1	2	3	4	5	6	7	8	9
48.1	22.269	44.537	66.806	89.074	111.343	133.611	155.880	178.148	200.417
48.2	22.315	44.630	66.944	89.259	111.574	133.889	156.204	178.519	200.833
48.3	22 361	44.722	67.083	89.444	111.806	134.167	156.528	178.889	201.250
48.4	22.407	44.815	67.222	89.630	112.037	134.444	156.852	179.259	201.667
48.5	22.454	44.907	67.361	89.815	112.269	134.722	157.176	179.630	202.083
48.6	22.500	45.000	67.500	90.000	112.500	135.000	157.500	180.000	202.500
48.7	22.546	45.093	67.639	90.185	112.731	135.278	157.824	180.370	202.917
48.8	22.593	45.185	67.778	90.370	112.963	135.556	158.148	180.741	203.333
48.9	22.639	45.278	67.917	90.556	113.194	135.833	158.472	181.111	203.750
49.0	22.685	45.370	68.056	90.741	113.426	136.111	158.796	181.481	204.167
49.1	22.731	45.463	68.194	90.926	113.657	136.389	159.120	181.852	204.583
49.2	22.778	45.556	68.333	91.111	113.889	136.667	159.444	182.222	205.000
49.3	22.824	45.648	68.472	91.296	114.120	136.944	159.769	182.593	205.417
49.4	22.870	45.741	68.611	91.481	114.352	137.222	160.093	182.963	205.833
49.5	22.917	45.833	68.750	91.667	114.583	137.500	160.417	183.333	206.250
49.6	22.963	45.926	68.889	91.852	114.815	137.778	160.741	183.704	206.667
49.7	23.009	46.019	69.028	92.037	115.046	138.056	161.065	184.074	207.083
49.8	23.056	46.111	69.167	92.222	115.278	138.333	161.389	184.444	207.500
49.9	23.102	46.204	69.306	92.407	115.509	138.611	161.713	184.815	207.917
50.0	23.148	46.296	69.444	92.593	115.741	138.889	162.037	185.185	208.333
50.1	23.194	46.389	69.583	92.778	115.972	139.167	162.361	185.556	208.750
50.2	23.241	46.481	69.722	92.963	116.204	139.444	162.685	185.926	209.167
50.3	23.287	46.574	69.861	93.148	116.435	139.722	163.009	186.296	209.583
50.4	23.333	46.667	70.000	93.333	116.667	140.000	163.333	186.667	210.000
50.5	23.380	46.759	70.139	93.519	116.898	140.278	163.657	187.037	210.417
50.6	23.426	46.852	70.278	93.704	117.130	140.556	163.981	187.407	210.833
50.7	23.472	46.944	70.417	93.889	117.361	140.833	164.306	187.778	211.250
50.8	23.519	47.037	70.556	94.074	117.593	141.111	164.630	188.148	211.667
50.9	23.565	47.130	70.694	94.259	117.824	141.389	164.954	188.519	212.083
51.0	23.611	47.222	70.833	94.444	118.056	141.667	165.278	188.889	212.500
51.1	23.657	47.315	70.972	94.630	118.287	141.944	165.602	189.259	212.917
51.2	23.704	47.407	71.111	94.815	118.519	142.222	165.926	189.630	213.333
51.3	23.750	47.500	71.250	95.000	118.750	142.500	166.250	190.000	213.750
51.4	23.796	47.593	71.389	95.185	118.981	142.778	166.574	190.370	214.167
51.5	23.843	47.685	71.528	95.370	119.213	143.056	166.898	190.741	214.583
51.6	23.889	47.778	71.667	95.556	119.444	143.333	167.222	191.111	215.000
51.7	23.935	47.870	71.806	95.741	119.676	143.611	167.546	191.481	215.417
51.8	23.981	47.963	71.944	95.926	119.907	143.889	167.870	191.852	215.833
51.9	24.028	48.056	72.083	96.111	120.139	144.167	168.194	192.222	216.250
52.0	24.074	48.148	72.222	96.296	120.370	144.444	168.519	192.593	216.667
52.1	24.120	48.241	72.361	96.481	120.602	144.722	168.843	192.963	217.083
52.2	24.167	48.333	72.500	96.667	120.833	145.000	169.167	193.333	217.500
52.3	24.213	48.426	72.639	96.852	121.065	145.278	169.491	193.704	217.917
52.4	24.259	48.519	72.778	97.037	121.296	145.556	169.815	194.074	218.333
52.5	24.306	48.611	72.917	97.222	121.528	145.833	170.139	194.444	218.750
52.6	24.352	48.704	73.056	97.407	121.759	146.111	170.463	194.815	219.167
52.7	24.398	48.796	73.194	97.593	121.991	146.389	170.787	195.185	219.583
52.8	24.444	48.889	73.333	97.778	122.222	146.667	171.111	195.556	220.000
52.9	24.491	48.981	73.472	97.963	122.454	146.944	171.435	195.926	220.417
53.0	24.537	49.074	73.611	98.148	122.685	147.222	171.759	196.296	220.833
53.1	24.583	49.167	73.750	98.333	122.917	147.500	172.083	196.667	221.250
53.2	24.630	49.259	73.889	98.519	123.148	147.778	172.407	197.037	221.667
53.3	24.676	49.352	74.028	98.704	123.380	148.056	172.731	197.407	222.083
53.4	24.722	49.444	74.167	98.889	123.611	148.333	173.056	197.778	222.500
53.5	24.769	49.537	74.306	99.074	123.843	148.611	173.380	198.148	222.917
53.6	24.815	49.630	74.444	99.259	124.074	148.889	173.704	198.519	223.333
53.7	24.861	49.722	74.583	99.444	124.306	149.167	174.028	198.889	223.750
53.8	24.907	49.815	74.722	99.630	124.537	149.444	174.352	199.259	224.167
53.9	24.954	49.907	74.861	99.815	124.769	149.722	174.676	199.630	224.583
54.0	25.000	50.000	75.000	100.000	125.000	150.000	175.000	200.000	225.000
H. or B.	1	2	3	4	5	6	7	8	9

H. or B.	1	2	3	4	5	6	7	8	9
54.1	25.046	50.093	75.139	100.185	125.231	150.278	175.324	200.370	225.417
54.2	25.093	50.185	75.278	100.370	125.463	150.556	175.648	200.741	225.833
54.3	25.139	50.278	75.417	100.556	125.694	150.833	175.972	201.111	226.250
54.4	25.185	50.370	75.556	100.741	125.926	151.111	176.296	201.481	226.667
54.5	25.231	50.463	75.694	100.926	126.157	151.389	176.620	201.852	227.083
54.6	25.278	50.556	75.833	101.111	126.389	151.667	176.944	202.222	227.500
54.7	25.324	50.648	75.972	101.296	126.620	151.944	177.269	202.593	227.917
54.8	25.370	50.741	76.111	101.481	126.852	152.222	177.593	202.963	228.333
54.9	25.417	50.833	76.250	101.667	127.083	152.500	177.917	203.333	228.750
55.0	25.463	50.926	76.389	101.852	127.315	152.778	178.241	203.704	229.167
55.1	25.509	51.019	76.528	102.037	127.546	153.056	178.565	204.074	229.583
55.2	25.556	51.111	76.667	102.222	127.778	153.333	178.889	204.444	230.000
55.3	25.602	51.204	76.806	102.407	128.009	153.611	179.213	204.815	230.417
55.4	25.648	51.296	76.944	102.593	128.241	153.889	179.537	205.185	230.833
55.5	25.694	51.389	77.083	102.778	128.472	154.167	179.861	205.556	231.250
55.6	25.741	51.481	77.222	102.963	128.704	154.444	180.185	205.926	231.667
55.7	25.787	51.574	77.361	103.148	128.935	154.722	180.509	206.296	232.083
55.8	25.833	51.667	77.500	103.333	129.167	155.000	180.833	206.667	232.500
55.9	25.880	51.759	77.639	103.519	129.398	155.278	181.157	207.037	232.917
56.0	25.926	51.852	77.778	103.704	129.630	155.556	181.481	207.407	233.333
56.1	25.972	51.944	77.917	103.889	129.861	155.833	181.806	207.778	233.750
56.2	26.019	52.037	78.056	104.074	130.093	156.111	182.130	208.148	234.167
56.3	26.065	52.130	78.194	104.259	130.324	156.389	182.454	208.519	234.583
56.4	26.111	52.222	78.333	104.444	130.556	156.667	182.778	208.889	235.000
56.5	26.157	52.315	78.472	104.630	130.787	156.944	183.102	209.259	235.417
56.6	26.204	52.407	78.611	104.815	131.019	157.222	183.426	209.630	235.833
56.7	26.250	52.500	78.750	105.000	131.250	157.500	183.750	210.000	236.250
56.8	26.296	52.593	78.889	105.185	131.481	157.778	184.074	210.370	236.667
56.9	26.343	52.685	79.028	105.370	131.713	158.056	184.398	210.741	237.083
57.0	26.389	52.778	79.167	105.556	131.944	158.333	184.722	211.111	237.500
57.1	26.435	52.870	79.306	105.741	132.176	158.611	185.046	211.481	237.917
57.2	26.481	52.963	79.444	105.926	132.407	158.889	185.370	211.852	238.333
57.3	26.528	53.056	79.583	106.111	132.639	159.167	185.694	212.222	238.750
57.4	26.574	53.148	79.722	106.296	132.870	159.444	186.019	212.593	239.167
57.5	26.620	53.241	79.861	106.481	133.102	159.722	186.343	212.963	239.583
57.6	26.667	53.333	80.000	106.667	133.333	160.000	186.667	213.333	240.000
57.7	26.713	53.426	80.139	106.852	133.565	160.278	186.991	213.704	240.417
57.8	26.759	53.519	80.278	107.037	133.796	160.556	187.315	214.074	240.833
57.9	26.806	53.611	80.417	107.222	134.028	160.833	187.639	214.444	241.250
58.0	26.852	53.704	80.556	107.407	134.259	161.111	187.963	214.815	241.667
58.1	26.898	53.796	80.694	107.593	134.491	161.389	188.287	215.185	242.083
58.2	26.944	53.889	80.833	107.778	134.722	161.667	188.611	215.556	242.500
58.3	26.991	53.981	80.972	107.963	134.954	161.944	188.935	215.926	242.917
58.4	27.037	54.074	81.111	108.148	135.185	162.222	189.259	216.296	243.333
58.5	27.083	54.167	81.250	108.333	135.417	162.500	189.583	216.667	243.750
58.6	27.130	54.259	81.389	108.519	135.648	162.778	189.907	217.037	244.167
58.7	27.176	54.352	81.528	108.704	135.880	163.056	190.231	217.407	244.583
58.8	27.222	54.444	81.667	108.889	136.111	163.333	190.556	217.778	245.000
58.9	27.269	54.537	81.806	109.074	136.343	163.611	190.880	218.148	245.417
59.0	27.315	54.630	81.944	109.259	136.574	163.889	191.204	218.519	245.833
59.1	27.361	54.722	82.083	109.444	136.806	164.167	191.528	218.889	246.250
59.2	27.407	54.815	82.222	109.630	137.037	164.444	191.852	219.259	246.667
59.3	27.454	54.907	82.361	109.815	137.269	164.722	192.176	219.630	247.083
59.4	27.500	55.000	82.500	110.000	137.500	165.000	192.500	220.000	247.500
59.5	27.546	55.093	82.639	110.185	137.731	165.278	192.824	220.370	247.917
59.6	27.593	55.185	82.778	110.370	137.963	165.556	193.148	220.741	248.333
59.7	27.639	55.278	82.917	110.556	138.194	165.833	193.472	221.111	248.750
59.8	27.685	55.370	83.056	110.741	138.426	166.111	193.796	221.481	249.167
59.9	27.731	55.463	83.194	110.926	138.657	166.389	194.120	221.852	249.583
60.0	27.778	55.556	83.333	111.111	138.889	166.667	194.444	222.222	250.000
H. or B.	1	2	3	4	5	6	7	8	9

H. or B.	1	2	3	4	5	6	7	8	9
60.1	27.824	55.648	83.472	111.296	139.120	166.944	194.769	222.593	250.417
60.2	27.870	55.741	83.611	111.481	139.352	167.222	195.093	222.963	250.833
60.3	27.917	55.833	83.750	111.667	139.583	167.500	195.417	223.333	251.250
60.4	27.963	55.926	83.889	111.852	139.815	167.778	195.741	223.704	251.667
60.5	28.009	56.019	84.028	112.037	140.046	168.056	196.065	224.074	252.083
60.6	28.056	56.111	84.167	112.222	140.278	168.333	196.389	224.444	252.500
60.7	28.102	56.204	84.306	112.407	140.509	168.611	196.713	224.815	252.917
60.8	28.148	56.296	84.444	112.593	140.741	168.889	197.037	225.185	253.333
60.9	28.194	56.389	84.583	112.778	140.972	169.167	197.361	225.556	253.750
61.0	28.241	56.481	84.722	112.963	141.204	169.444	197.685	225.926	254.167
61.1	28.287	56.574	84.861	113.148	141.435	169.722	198.009	226.296	254.583
61.2	28.333	56.667	85.000	113.333	141.667	170.000	198.333	226.667	255.000
61.3	28.380	56.759	85.139	113.519	141.898	170.278	198.657	227.037	255.417
61.4	28.426	56.852	85.278	113.704	142.130	170.556	198.981	227.407	255.833
61.5	28.472	56.944	85.417	113.889	142.361	170.833	199.306	227.778	256.250
61.6	28.519	57.037	85.556	114.074	142.593	171.111	199.630	228.148	256.667
61.7	28.565	57.130	85.694	114.259	142.824	171.389	199.954	228.519	257.083
61.8	28.611	57.222	85.833	114.444	143.056	171.667	200.278	228.889	257.500
61.9	28.657	57.315	85.972	114.630	143.287	171.944	200.602	229.259	257.917
62.0	28.704	57.407	86.111	114.815	143.519	172.222	200.926	229.630	258.333
62.1	28.750	57.500	86.250	115.000	143.750	172.500	201.250	230.000	258.750
62.2	28.796	57.593	86.389	115.185	143.981	172.778	201.574	230.370	259.167
62.3	28.843	57.685	86.528	115.370	144.213	173.056	201.898	230.741	259.583
62.4	28.889	57.778	86.667	115.556	144.444	173.333	202.222	231.111	260.000
62.5	28.935	57.870	86.806	115.741	144.676	173.611	202.546	231.481	260.417
62.6	28.981	57.963	86.944	115.926	144.907	173.889	202.870	231.852	260.833
62.7	29.028	58.056	87.083	116.111	145.139	174.167	203.194	232.222	261.250
62.8	29.074	58.148	87.222	116.296	145.370	174.444	203.519	232.593	261.667
62.9	29.120	58.241	87.361	116.481	145.602	174.722	203.843	232.963	262.083
63.0	29.167	58.333	87.500	116.667	145.833	175.000	204.167	233.333	262.500
63.1	29.213	58.426	87.639	116.852	146.065	175.278	204.491	233.704	262.917
63.2	29.259	58.519	87.778	117.037	146.296	175.556	204.815	234.074	263.333
63.3	29.306	58.611	87.917	117.222	146.528	175.833	205.139	234.444	263.750
63.4	29.352	58.704	88.056	117.407	146.759	176.111	205.463	234.815	264.167
63.5	29.398	58.796	88.194	117.593	146.991	176.389	205.787	235.185	264.583
63.6	29.444	58.889	88.333	117.778	147.222	176.667	206.111	235.556	265.000
63.7	29.491	58.981	88.472	117.963	147.454	176.944	206.435	235.926	265.417
63.8	29.537	59.074	88.611	118.148	147.685	177.222	206.759	236.296	265.833
63.9	29.583	59.167	88.750	118.333	147.917	177.500	207.083	236.667	266.250
64.0	29.630	59.259	88.889	118.519	148.148	177.778	207.407	237.037	266.667
64.1	29.676	59.352	89.028	118.704	148.380	178.056	207.731	237.407	267.083
64.2	29.722	59.444	89.167	118.889	148.611	178.333	208.056	237.778	267.500
64.3	29.769	59.537	89.306	119.074	148.843	178.611	208.380	238.148	267.917
64.4	29.815	59.630	89.444	119.259	149.074	178.889	208.704	238.519	268.333
64.5	29.861	59.722	89.583	119.444	149.306	179.167	209.028	238.889	268.750
64.6	29.907	59.815	89.722	119.630	149.537	179.444	209.352	239.259	269.167
64.7	29.954	59.907	89.861	119.815	149.769	179.722	209.676	239.630	269.583
64.8	30.000	60.000	90.000	120.000	150.000	180.000	210.000	240.000	270.000
64.9	30.046	60.093	90.139	120.185	150.231	180.278	210.324	240.370	270.417
65.0	30.093	60.185	90.278	120.370	150.463	180.556	210.648	240.741	270.833
65.1	30.139	60.278	90.417	120.556	150.694	180.833	210.972	241.111	271.250
65.2	30.185	60.370	90.556	120.741	150.926	181.111	211.296	241.481	271.667
65.3	30.231	60.463	90.694	120.926	151.157	181.389	211.620	241.852	272.083
65.4	30.278	60.556	90.833	121.111	151.389	181.667	211.944	242.222	272.500
65.5	30.324	60.648	90.972	121.296	151.620	181.944	212.269	242.593	272.917
65.6	30.370	60.741	91.111	121.481	151.852	182.222	212.593	242.963	273.333
65.7	30.417	60.833	91.250	121.667	152.083	182.500	212.917	243.333	273.750
65.8	30.463	60.926	91.389	121.852	152.315	182.778	213.241	243.704	274.167
65.9	30.509	61.019	91.528	122.037	152.546	183.056	213.565	244.074	274.583
66.0	30.556	61.111	91.667	122.222	152.778	183.333	213.889	244.444	275.000
H. or B.	1	2	3	4	5	6	7	8	9

H. or B.	1	2	3	4	5	6	7	8	9
66.1	30.602	61.204	91.806	122.407	153.009	183.611	214.213	244.815	275.417
66.2	30.648	61.296	91.944	122.593	153.241	183.889	214.537	245.185	275.833
66.3	30.694	61.389	92.083	122.778	153.472	184.167	214.861	245.556	276.250
66.4	30.741	61.481	92.222	122.963	153.704	184.444	215.185	245.926	276.667
66.5	30.787	61.574	92.361	123.148	153.935	184.722	215.509	246.296	277.083
66.6	30.833	61.667	92.500	123.333	154.167	185.000	215.833	246.667	277.500
66.7	30.880	61.759	92.639	123.519	154.398	185.278	216.157	247.037	277.917
66.8	30.926	61.852	92.778	123.704	154.630	185.556	216.481	247.407	278.333
66.9	30.972	61.944	92.917	123.889	154.861	185.833	216.806	247.778	278.750
67.0	31.019	62.037	93.056	124.074	155.093	186.111	217.130	248.148	279.167
67.1	31.065	62.130	93.194	124.259	155.324	186.389	217.454	248.519	279.583
67.2	31.111	62.222	93.333	124.444	155.556	186.667	217.778	248.889	280.000
67.3	31.157	62.315	93.472	124.630	155.787	186.944	218.102	249.259	280.417
67.4	31.204	62.407	93.611	124.815	156.019	187.222	218.426	249.630	280.833
67.5	31.250	62.500	93.750	125.000	156.250	187.500	218.750	250.000	281.250
67.6	31.296	62.593	93.889	125.185	156.481	187.778	219.074	250.370	281.667
67.7	31.343	62.685	94.028	125.370	156.713	188.056	219.398	250.741	282.083
67.8	31.389	62.778	94.167	125.556	156.944	188.333	219.722	251.111	282.500
67.9	31.435	62.870	94.306	125.741	157.176	188.611	220.046	251.481	282.917
68.0	31.481	62.963	94.444	125.926	157.407	188.889	220.370	251.852	283.333
68.1	31.528	63.056	94.583	126.111	157.639	189.167	220.694	252.222	283.750
68.2	31.574	63.148	94.722	126.296	157.870	189.444	221.019	252.593	284.167
68.3	31.620	63.241	94.861	126.481	158.102	189.722	221.343	252.963	284.583
68.4	31.667	63.333	95.000	126.667	158.333	190.000	221.667	253.333	285.000
68.5	31.713	63.426	95.139	126.852	158.565	190.278	221.991	253.704	285.417
68.6	31.759	63.519	95.278	127.037	158.796	190.556	222.315	254.074	285.833
68.7	31.806	63.611	95.417	127.222	159.028	190.833	222.639	254.444	286.250
68.8	31.852	63.704	95.556	127.407	159.259	191.111	222.963	254.815	286.667
68.9	31.898	63.796	95.694	127.593	159.491	191.389	223.287	255.185	287.083
69.0	31.944	63.889	95.833	127.778	159.722	191.667	223.611	255.556	287.500
69.1	31.991	63.981	95.972	127.963	159.954	191.944	223.935	255.926	287.917
69.2	32.037	64.074	96.111	128.148	160.185	192.222	224.259	256.296	288.333
69.3	32.083	64.167	96.250	128.333	160.417	192.500	224.583	256.667	288.750
69.4	32.130	64.259	96.389	128.519	160.648	192.778	224.907	257.037	289.167
69.5	32.176	64.352	96.528	128.704	160.880	193.056	225.231	257.407	289.583
69.6	32.222	64.444	96.667	128.889	161.111	193.333	225.556	257.778	290.000
69.7	32.269	64.537	96.806	129.074	161.343	193.611	225.880	258.148	290.417
69.8	32.315	64.630	96.944	129.259	161.574	193.889	226.204	258.519	290.833
69.9	32.361	64.722	97.083	129.444	161.806	194.167	226.528	258.889	291.250
70.0	32.407	64.815	97.222	129.630	162.037	194.444	226.852	259.259	291.667
70.1	32.454	64.907	97.361	129.815	162.269	194.722	227.176	259.630	292.083
70.2	32.500	65.000	97.500	130.000	162.500	195.000	227.500	260.000	292.500
70.3	32.546	65.093	97.639	130.185	162.731	195.278	227.824	260.370	292.917
70.4	32.593	65.185	97.778	130.370	162.963	195.556	228.148	260.741	293.333
70.5	32.639	65.278	97.917	130.556	163.194	195.833	228.472	261.111	293.750
70.6	32.685	65.370	98.056	130.741	163.426	196.111	228.796	261.481	294.167
70.7	32.731	65.463	98.194	130.926	163.657	196.389	229.120	261.852	294.583
70.8	32.778	65.556	98.333	131.111	163.889	196.667	229.444	262.222	295.000
70.9	32.824	65.648	98.472	131.296	164.120	196.944	229.769	262.593	295.417
71.0	32.870	65.741	98.611	131.481	164.352	197.222	230.093	262.963	295.833
71.1	32.917	65.833	98.750	131.667	164.583	197.500	230.417	263.333	296.250
71.2	32.963	65.926	98.889	131.852	164.815	197.778	230.741	263.704	296.667
71.3	33.009	66.019	99.028	132.037	165.046	198.056	231.065	264.074	297.083
71.4	33.056	66.111	99.167	132.222	165.278	198.333	231.389	264.444	297.500
71.5	33.102	66.204	99.306	132.407	165.509	198.611	231.713	264.815	297.917
71.6	33.148	66.296	99.444	132.593	165.741	198.889	232.037	265.185	298.333
71.7	33.194	66.389	99.583	132.778	165.972	199.167	232.361	265.556	298.750
71.8	33.241	66.481	99.722	132.963	166.204	199.444	232.685	265.926	299.167
71.9	33.287	66.574	99.861	133.148	166.435	199.722	233.009	266.296	299.583
72.0	33.333	66.667	100.000	133.333	166.667	200.000	233.333	266.667	300.000
H. or B.	1	2	3	4	5	6	7	8	9

H. or B.	1	2	3	4	5	6	7	8	9
72.1	33.380	66.759	100.139	133.519	166.898	200.278	233.657	267.037	300.417
72.2	33.426	66.852	100.278	133.704	167.130	200.556	233.981	267.407	300.833
72.3	33.472	66.944	100.417	133.889	167.361	200.833	234.306	267.778	301.250
72.4	33.519	67.037	100.556	134.074	167.593	201.111	234.630	268.148	301.667
72.5	33.565	67.130	100.694	134.259	167.824	201.389	234.954	268.519	302.083
72.6	33.611	67.222	100.833	134.444	168.056	201.667	235.278	268.889	302.500
72.7	33.657	67.315	100.972	134.630	168.287	201.944	235.602	269.259	302.917
72.8	33.704	67.407	101.111	134.815	168.519	202.222	235.926	269.630	303.333
72.9	33.750	67.500	101.250	135.000	168.750	202.500	236.250	270.000	303.750
73.0	33.796	67.593	101.389	135.185	168.981	202.778	236.574	270.370	304.167
73.1	33.843	67.685	101.528	135.370	169.213	203.056	236.898	270.741	304.583
73.2	33.889	67.778	101.667	135.556	169.444	203.333	237.222	271.111	305.000
73.3	33.935	67.870	101.806	135.741	169.676	203.611	237.546	271.481	305.417
73.4	33.981	67.963	101.944	135.926	169.907	203.889	237.870	271.852	305.833
73.5	34.028	68.056	102.083	136.111	170.139	204.167	238.194	272.222	306.250
73.6	34.074	68.148	102.222	136.296	170.370	204.444	238.519	272.593	306.667
73.7	34.120	68.241	102.361	136.481	170.602	204.722	238.843	272.963	307.083
73.8	34.167	68.333	102.500	136.667	170.833	205.000	239.167	273.333	307.500
73.9	34.213	68.426	102.639	136.852	171.065	205.278	239.491	273.704	307.917
74.0	34.259	68.519	102.778	137.037	171.296	205.556	239.815	274.074	308.333
74.1	34.306	68.611	102.917	137.222	171.528	205.833	240.139	274.444	308.750
74.2	34.352	68.704	103.056	137.407	171.759	206.111	240.463	274.815	309.167
74.3	34.398	68.796	103.194	137.593	171.991	206.389	240.787	275.185	309.583
74.4	34.444	68.889	103.333	137.778	172.222	206.667	241.111	275.556	310.000
74.5	34.491	68.981	103.472	137.963	172.454	206.944	241.435	275.926	310.417
74.6	34.537	69.074	103.611	138.148	172.685	207.222	241.759	276.296	310.833
74.7	34.583	69.167	103.750	138.333	172.917	207.500	242.083	276.667	311.250
74.8	34.630	69.259	103.889	138.519	173.148	207.778	242.407	277.037	311.667
74.9	34.676	69.352	104.028	138.704	173.380	208.056	242.731	277.407	312.083
75.0	34.722	69.444	104.167	138.889	173.611	208.333	243.056	277.778	312.500
75.1	34.769	69.537	104.306	139.074	173.843	208.611	243.380	278.148	312.917
75.2	34.815	69.630	104.444	139.259	174.074	208.889	243.704	278.519	313.333
75.3	34.861	69.722	104.583	139.444	174.306	209.167	244.028	278.889	313.750
75.4	34.907	69.815	104.722	139.630	174.537	209.444	244.352	279.259	314.167
75.5	34.954	69.907	104.861	139.815	174.769	209.722	244.676	279.630	314.583
75.6	35.000	70.000	105.000	140.000	175.000	210.000	245.000	280.000	315.000
75.7	35.046	70.093	105.139	140.185	175.231	210.278	245.324	280.370	315.417
75.8	35.093	70.185	105.278	140.370	175.463	210.556	245.648	280.741	315.833
75.9	35.139	70.278	105.417	140.556	175.694	210.833	245.972	281.111	316.250
76.0	35.185	70.370	105.556	140.741	175.926	211.111	246.296	281.481	316.667
76.1	35.231	70.463	105.694	140.926	176.157	211.389	246.620	281.852	317.083
76.2	35.278	70.556	105.833	141.111	176.389	211.667	246.944	282.222	317.500
76.3	35.324	70.648	105.972	141.296	176.620	211.944	247.269	282.593	317.917
76.4	35.370	70.741	106.111	141.481	176.852	212.222	247.593	282.963	318.333
76.5	35.417	70.833	106.250	141.667	177.083	212.500	247.917	283.333	318.750
76.6	35.463	70.926	106.389	141.852	177.315	212.778	248.241	283.704	319.167
76.7	35.509	71.019	106.528	142.037	177.546	213.056	248.565	284.074	319.583
76.8	35.556	71.111	106.667	142.222	177.778	213.333	248.889	284.444	320.000
76.9	35.602	71.204	106.806	142.407	178.009	213.611	249.213	284.815	320.417
77.0	35.648	71.296	106.944	142.593	178.241	213.889	249.537	285.185	320.833
77.1	35.694	71.389	107.083	142.778	178.472	214.167	249.861	285.556	321.250
77.2	35.741	71.481	107.222	142.963	178.704	214.444	250.185	285.926	321.667
77.3	35.787	71.574	107.361	143.148	178.935	214.722	250.509	286.296	322.083
77.4	35.833	71.667	107.500	143.333	179.167	215.000	250.833	286.667	322.500
77.5	35.880	71.759	107.639	143.519	179.398	215.278	251.157	287.037	322.917
77.6	35.926	71.852	107.778	143.704	179.630	215.556	251.481	287.407	323.333
77.7	35.972	71.944	107.917	143.889	179.861	215.833	251.806	287.778	323.750
77.8	36.019	72.037	108.056	144.074	180.093	216.111	252.130	288.148	324.167
77.9	36.065	72.130	108.194	144.259	180.324	216.389	252.454	288.519	324.583
78.0	36.111	72.222	108.333	144.444	180.556	216.667	252.778	288.889	325.000
H. or B.	1	2	3	4	5	6	7	8	9

H. or B.	1	2	3	4	5	6	7	8	9
78.1	36.157	72.315	108.472	144.630	180.787	216.944	253.102	289.259	325.417
78.2	36.204	72.407	108.611	144.815	181.019	217.222	253.426	289.630	325.833
78.3	36.250	72.500	108.750	145.000	181.250	217.500	253.750	290.000	326.250
78.4	36.296	72.593	108.889	145.185	181.481	217.778	254.074	290.370	326.667
78.5	36.343	72.685	109.028	145.370	181.713	218.056	254.398	290.741	327.083
78.6	36.389	72.778	109.167	145.556	181.944	218.333	254.722	291.111	327.500
78.7	36.435	72.870	109.306	145.741	182.176	218.611	255.046	291.481	327.917
78.8	36.481	72.963	109.444	145.926	182.407	218.889	255.370	291.852	328.333
78.9	36.528	73.056	109.583	146.111	182.639	219.167	255.694	292.222	328.750
79.0	36.574	73.148	109.722	146.296	182.870	219.444	256.019	292.593	329.167
79.1	36.620	73.241	109.861	146.481	183.102	219.722	256.343	292.963	329.583
79.2	36.667	73.333	110.000	146.667	183.333	220.000	256.667	293.333	330.000
79.3	36.713	73.426	110.139	146.852	183.565	220.278	256.991	293.704	330.417
79.4	36.759	73.519	110.278	147.037	183.796	220.556	257.315	294.074	330.833
79.5	36.806	73.611	110.417	147.222	184.028	220.833	257.639	294.444	331.250
79.6	36.852	73.704	110.556	147.407	184.259	221.111	257.963	294.815	331.667
79.7	36.898	73.796	110.694	147.593	184.491	221.389	258.287	295.185	332.083
79.8	36.944	73.889	110.833	147.778	184.722	221.667	258.611	295.556	332.500
79.9	36.991	73.981	110.972	147.963	184.954	221.944	258.935	295.926	332.917
80.0	37.037	74.074	111.111	148.148	185.185	222.222	259.259	296.296	333.333
80.1	37.083	74.167	111.250	148.333	185.417	222.500	259.583	296.667	333.750
80.2	37.130	74.259	111.389	148.519	185.648	222.778	259.907	297.037	334.167
80.3	37.176	74.352	111.528	148.704	185.880	223.056	260.231	297.407	334.583
80.4	37.222	74.444	111.667	148.889	186.111	223.333	260.556	297.778	335.000
80.5	37.269	74.537	111.806	149.074	186.343	223.611	260.880	298.148	335.417
80.6	37.315	74.630	111.944	149.259	186.574	223.889	261.204	298.519	335.833
80.7	37.361	74.722	112.083	149.444	186.806	224.167	261.528	298.889	336.250
80.8	37.407	74.815	112.222	149.630	187.037	224.444	261.852	299.259	336.667
80.9	37.454	74.907	112.361	149.815	187.269	224.722	262.176	299.630	337.083
81.0	37.500	75.000	112.500	150.000	187.500	225.000	262.500	300.000	337.500
81.1	37.546	75.093	112.639	150.185	187.731	225.278	262.824	300.370	337.917
81.2	37.593	75.185	112.778	150.370	187.963	225.556	263.148	300.741	338.333
81.3	37.639	75.278	112.917	150.556	188.194	225.833	263.472	301.111	338.750
81.4	37.685	75.370	113.056	150.741	188.426	226.111	263.796	301.481	339.167
81.5	37.731	75.463	113.194	150.926	188.657	226.389	264.120	301.852	339.583
81.6	37.778	75.556	113.333	151.111	188.889	226.667	264.444	302.222	340.000
81.7	37.824	75.648	113.472	151.296	189.120	226.944	264.769	302.593	340.417
81.8	37.870	75.741	113.611	151.481	189.352	227.222	265.093	302.963	340.833
81.9	37.917	75.833	113.750	151.667	189.583	227.500	265.417	303.333	341.250
82.0	37.963	75.926	113.889	151.852	189.815	227.778	265.741	303.704	341.667
82.1	38.009	76.019	114.028	152.037	190.046	228.056	266.065	304.074	342.083
82.2	38.056	76.111	114.167	152.222	190.278	228.333	266.389	304.444	342.500
82.3	38.102	76.204	114.306	152.407	190.509	228.611	266.713	304.815	342.917
82.4	38.148	76.296	114.444	152.593	190.741	228.889	267.037	305.185	343.333
82.5	38.194	76.389	114.583	152.778	190.972	229.167	267.361	305.556	343.750
82.6	38.241	76.481	114.722	152.963	191.204	229.444	267.685	305.926	344.167
82.7	38.287	76.574	114.861	153.148	191.435	229.722	268.009	306.296	344.583
82.8	38.333	76.667	115.000	153.333	191.667	230.000	268.333	306.667	345.000
82.9	38.380	76.759	115.139	153.519	191.898	230.278	268.657	307.037	345.417
83.0	38.426	76.852	115.278	153.704	192.130	230.556	268.981	307.407	345.833
83.1	38.472	76.944	115.417	153.889	192.361	230.833	269.306	307.778	346.250
83.2	38.519	77.037	115.556	154.074	192.593	231.111	269.630	308.148	346.667
83.3	38.565	77.130	115.694	154.259	192.824	231.389	269.954	308.519	347.083
83.4	38.611	77.222	115.833	154.444	193.056	231.667	270.278	308.889	347.500
83.5	38.657	77.315	115.972	154.630	193.287	231.944	270.602	309.259	347.917
83.6	38.704	77.407	116.111	154.815	193.519	232.222	270.926	309.630	348.333
83.7	38.750	77.500	116.250	155.000	193.750	232.500	271.250	310.000	348.750
83.8	38.796	77.593	116.389	155.185	193.981	232.778	271.574	310.370	349.167
83.9	38.843	77.685	116.528	155.370	194.213	233.056	271.898	310.741	349.583
84.0	38.889	77.778	116.667	155.556	194.444	233.333	272.222	311.111	350.000
H. or B.	1	2	3	4	5	6	7	8	9

H. or B.	1	2	3	4	5	6	7	8	9
84.1	38.935	77.870	116.806	155.741	194.676	233.611	272.546	311.481	350.417
84.2	38.981	77.963	116.944	155.926	194.907	233.889	272.870	311.852	350.833
84.3	39.028	78.056	117.083	156.111	195.139	234.167	273.194	312.222	351.250
84.4	39.074	78.148	117.222	156.296	195.370	234.444	273.519	312.593	351.667
84.5	39.120	78.241	117.361	156.481	195.602	234.722	273.843	312.963	352.083
84.6	39.167	78.333	117.500	156.667	195.833	235.000	274.167	313.333	352.500
84.7	39.213	78.426	117.639	156.852	196.065	235.278	274.491	313.704	352.917
84.8	39.259	78.519	117.778	157.037	196.296	235.556	274.815	314.074	353.333
84.9	39.306	78.611	117.917	157.222	196.528	235.833	275.139	314.444	353.750
85.0	39.352	78.704	118.056	157.407	196.759	236.111	275.463	314.815	354.167
85.1	39.398	78.796	118.194	157.593	196.991	236.389	275.787	315.185	354.583
85.2	39.444	78.889	118.333	157.778	197.222	236.667	276.111	315.556	355.000
85.3	39.491	78.981	118.472	157.963	197.454	236.944	276.435	315.926	355.417
85.4	39.537	79.074	118.611	158.148	197.685	237.222	276.759	316.296	355.833
85.5	39.583	79.167	118.750	158.333	197.917	237.500	277.083	316.667	356.250
85.6	39.630	79.259	118.889	158.519	198.148	237.778	277.407	317.037	356.667
85.7	39.676	79.352	119.028	158.704	198.380	238.056	277.731	317.407	357.083
85.8	39.722	79.444	119.167	158.889	198.611	238.333	278.056	317.778	357.500
85.9	39.769	79.537	119.306	159.074	198.843	238.611	278.380	318.148	357.917
86.0	39.815	79.630	119.444	159.259	199.074	238.889	278.704	318.519	358.333
86.1	39.861	79.722	119.583	159.444	199.306	239.167	279.028	318.889	358.750
86.2	39.907	79.815	119.722	159.630	199.537	239.444	279.352	319.259	359.167
86.3	39.954	79.907	119.861	159.815	199.769	239.722	279.676	319.630	359.583
86.4	40.000	80.000	120.000	160.000	200.000	240.000	280.000	320.000	360.000
86.5	40.046	80.093	120.139	160.185	200.231	240.278	280.324	320.370	360.417
86.6	40.093	80.185	120.278	160.370	200.463	240.556	280.648	320.741	360.833
86.7	40.139	80.278	120.417	160.556	200.694	240.833	280.972	321.111	361.250
86.8	40.185	80.370	120.556	160.741	200.926	241.111	281.296	321.481	361.667
86.9	40.231	80.463	120.694	160.926	201.157	241.389	281.620	321.852	362.083
87.0	40.278	80.556	120.833	161.111	201.389	241.667	281.944	322.222	362.500
87.1	40.324	80.648	120.972	161.296	201.620	241.944	282.269	322.593	362.917
87.2	40.370	80.741	121.111	161.481	201.852	242.222	282.593	322.963	363.333
87.3	40.417	80.833	121.250	161.667	202.083	242.500	282.917	323.333	363.750
87.4	40.463	80.926	121.389	161.852	202.315	242.778	283.241	323.704	364.167
87.5	40.509	81.019	121.528	162.037	202.546	243.056	283.565	324.074	364.583
87.6	40.556	81.111	121.667	162.222	202.778	243.333	283.889	324.444	365.000
87.7	40.602	81.204	121.806	162.407	203.009	243.611	284.213	324.815	365.417
87.8	40.648	81.296	121.944	162.593	203.241	243.889	284.537	325.185	365.833
87.9	40.694	81.389	122.083	162.778	203.472	244.167	284.861	325.556	366.250
88.0	40.741	81.481	122.222	162.963	203.704	244.444	285.185	325.926	366.667
88.1	40.787	81.574	122.361	163.148	203.935	244.722	285.509	326.296	367.083
88.2	40.833	81.667	122.500	163.333	204.167	245.000	285.833	326.667	367.500
88.3	40.880	81.759	122.639	163.519	204.398	245.278	286.157	327.037	367.917
88.4	40.926	81.852	122.778	163.704	204.630	245.556	286.481	327.407	368.333
88.5	40.972	81.944	122.917	163.889	204.861	245.833	286.806	327.778	368.750
88.6	41.019	82.037	123.056	164.074	205.093	246.111	287.130	328.148	369.167
88.7	41.065	82.130	123.194	164.259	205.324	246.389	287.454	328.519	369.583
88.8	41.111	82.222	123.333	164.444	205.556	246.667	287.778	328.889	370.000
88.9	41.157	82.315	123.472	164.630	205.787	246.944	288.102	329.259	370.417
89.0	41.204	82.407	123.611	164.815	206.019	247.222	288.426	329.630	370.833
89.1	41.250	82.500	123.750	165.000	206.250	247.500	288.750	330.000	371.250
89.2	41.296	82.593	123.889	165.185	206.481	247.778	289.074	330.370	371.667
89.3	41.343	82.685	124.028	165.370	206.713	248.056	289.398	330.741	372.083
89.4	41.389	82.778	124.167	165.556	206.944	248.333	289.722	331.111	372.500
89.5	41.435	82.870	124.306	165.741	207.176	248.611	290.046	331.481	372.917
89.6	41.481	82.963	124.444	165.926	207.407	248.889	290.370	331.852	373.333
89.7	41.528	83.056	124.583	166.111	207.639	249.167	290.694	332.222	373.750
89.8	41.574	83.148	124.722	166.296	207.870	249.444	291.019	332.593	374.167
89.9	41.620	83.241	124.861	166.481	208.102	249.722	291.343	332.963	374.583
90.0	41.667	83.333	125.000	166.667	208.333	250.000	291.667	333.333	375.000
H. or B.	1	2	3	4	5	6	7	8	9

H. or B.	1	2	3	4	5	6	7	8	9
90.1	41.713	83.426	125.139	166.852	208.565	250.278	291.991	333.704	375.417
90.2	41.759	83.519	125.278	167.037	208.796	250.556	292.315	334.074	375.833
90.3	41.806	83.611	125.417	167.222	209.028	250.833	292.639	334.444	376.250
90.4	41.852	83.704	125.556	167.407	209.259	251.111	292.963	334.815	376.667
90.5	41.898	83.796	125.694	167.593	209.491	251.389	293.287	335.185	377.083
90.6	41.944	83.889	125.833	167.778	209.722	251.667	293.611	335.556	377.500
90.7	41.991	83.981	125.972	167.963	209.954	251.944	293.935	335.926	377.917
90.8	42.037	84.074	126.111	168.148	210.185	252.222	294.259	336.296	378.333
90.9	42.083	84.167	126.250	168.333	210.417	252.500	294.583	336.667	378.750
91.0	42.130	84.259	126.389	168.519	210.648	252.778	294.907	337.037	379.167
91.1	42.176	84.352	126.528	168.704	210.880	253.056	295.231	337.407	379.583
91.2	42.222	84.444	126.667	168.889	211.111	253.333	295.556	337.778	380.000
91.3	42.269	84.537	126.806	169.074	211.343	253.611	295.880	338.148	380.417
91.4	42.315	84.630	126.944	169.259	211.574	253.889	296.204	338.519	380.833
91.5	42.361	84.722	127.083	169.444	211.806	254.167	296.528	338.889	381.250
91.6	42.407	84.815	127.222	169.630	212.037	254.444	296.852	339.259	381.667
91.7	42.454	84.907	127.361	169.815	212.269	254.722	297.176	339.630	382.083
91.8	42.500	85.000	127.500	170.000	212.500	255.000	297.500	340.000	382.500
91.9	42.546	85.093	127.639	170.185	212.731	255.278	297.824	340.370	382.917
92.0	42.593	85.185	127.778	170.370	212.963	255.556	298.148	340.741	383.333
92.1	42.639	85.278	127.917	170.556	213.194	255.833	298.472	341.111	383.750
92.2	42.685	85.370	128.056	170.741	213.426	256.111	298.796	341.481	384.167
92.3	42.731	85.463	128.194	170.926	213.657	256.389	299.120	341.852	384.583
92.4	42.778	85.556	128.333	171.111	213.889	256.667	299.444	342.222	385.000
92.5	42.824	85.648	128.472	171.296	214.120	256.944	299.769	342.593	385.417
92.6	42.870	85.741	128.611	171.481	214.352	257.222	300.093	342.963	385.833
92.7	42.917	85.833	128.750	171.667	214.583	257.500	300.417	343.333	386.250
92.8	42.963	85.926	128.889	171.852	214.815	257.778	300.741	343.704	386.667
92.9	43.009	86.019	129.028	172.037	215.046	258.056	301.065	344.074	387.083
93.0	43.056	86.111	129.167	172.222	215.278	258.333	301.389	344.444	387.500
93.1	43.102	86.204	129.306	172.407	215.509	258.611	301.713	344.815	387.917
93.2	43.148	86.296	129.444	172.593	215.741	258.889	302.037	345.185	388.333
93.3	43.194	86.389	129.583	172.778	215.972	259.167	302.361	345.556	388.750
93.4	43.241	86.481	129.722	172.963	216.204	259.444	302.685	345.926	389.167
93.5	43.287	86.574	129.861	173.148	216.435	259.722	303.009	346.296	389.583
93.6	43.333	86.667	130.000	173.333	216.667	260.000	303.333	346.667	390.000
93.7	43.380	86.759	130.139	173.519	216.898	260.278	303.657	347.037	390.417
93.8	43.426	86.852	130.278	173.704	217.130	260.556	303.981	347.407	390.833
93.9	43.472	86.944	130.417	173.889	217.361	260.833	304.306	347.778	391.250
94.0	43.519	87.037	130.556	174.074	217.593	261.111	304.630	348.148	391.667
94.1	43.565	87.130	130.694	174.259	217.824	261.389	304.954	348.519	392.083
94.2	43.611	87.222	130.833	174.444	218.056	261.667	305.278	348.889	392.500
94.3	43.657	87.315	130.972	174.630	218.287	261.944	305.602	349.259	392.917
94.4	43.704	87.407	131.111	174.815	218.519	262.222	305.926	349.630	393.333
94.5	43.750	87.500	131.250	175.000	218.750	262.500	306.250	350.000	393.750
94.6	43.796	87.593	131.389	175.185	218.981	262.778	306.574	350.370	394.167
94.7	43.843	87.685	131.528	175.370	219.213	263.056	306.898	350.741	394.583
94.8	43.889	87.778	131.667	175.556	219.444	263.333	307.222	351.111	395.000
94.9	43.935	87.870	131.806	175.741	219.676	263.611	307.546	351.481	395.417
95.0	43.981	87.963	131.944	175.926	219.907	263.889	307.870	351.852	395.833
95.1	44.028	88.056	132.083	176.111	220.139	264.167	308.194	352.222	396.250
95.2	44.074	88.148	132.222	176.296	220.370	264.444	308.519	352.593	396.667
95.3	44.120	88.241	132.361	176.481	220.602	264.722	308.843	352.963	397.083
95.4	44.167	88.333	132.500	176.667	220.833	265.000	309.167	353.333	397.500
95.5	44.213	88.426	132.639	176.852	221.065	265.278	309.491	353.704	397.917
95.6	44.259	88.519	132.778	177.037	221.296	265.556	309.815	354.074	398.333
95.7	44.306	88.611	132.917	177.222	221.528	265.833	310.139	354.444	398.750
95.8	44.352	88.704	133.056	177.407	221.759	266.111	310.463	354.815	399.167
95.9	44.398	88.796	133.194	177.593	221.991	266.389	310.787	355.185	399.583
96.0	44.444	88.889	133.333	177.778	222.222	266.667	311.111	355.556	400.000
H. or B.	1	2	3	4	5	6	7	8	9

H. or B.	1	2	3	4	5	6	7	8	9
96.1	44.491	88.981	133.472	177.963	222.454	266.944	311.435	355.926	400.417
96.2	44.537	89.074	133.611	178.148	222.685	267.222	311.759	356.296	400.833
96.3	44.583	89.167	133.750	178.333	222.917	267.500	312.083	356.667	401.250
96.4	44.630	89.259	133.889	178.519	223.148	267.778	312.407	357.037	401.667
96.5	44.676	89.352	134.028	178.704	223.380	268.056	312.731	357.407	402.083
96.6	44.722	89.444	134.167	178.889	223.611	268.333	313.056	357.778	402.500
96.7	44.769	89.537	134.306	179.074	223.843	268.611	313.380	358.148	402.917
96.8	44.815	89.630	134.444	179.259	224.074	268.889	313.704	358.519	403.333
96.9	44.861	89.722	134.583	179.444	224.306	269.167	314.028	358.889	403.750
97.0	44.907	89.815	134.722	179.630	224.537	269.444	314.352	359.259	404.167
97.1	44.954	89.907	134.861	179.815	224.769	269.722	314.676	359.630	404.583
97.2	45.000	90.000	135.000	180.000	225.000	270.000	315.000	360.000	405.000
97.3	45.046	90.093	135.139	180.185	225.231	270.278	315.324	360.370	405.417
97.4	45.093	90.185	135.278	180.370	225.463	270.556	315.648	360.741	405.833
97.5	45.139	90.278	135.417	180.556	225.694	270.833	315.972	361.111	406.250
97.6	45.185	90.370	135.556	180.741	225.926	271.111	316.296	361.481	406.667
97.7	45.231	90.463	135.694	180.926	226.157	271.389	316.620	361.852	407.083
97.8	45.278	90.556	135.833	181.111	226.389	271.667	316.944	362.222	407.500
97.9	45.324	90.648	135.972	181.296	226.620	271.944	317.269	362.593	407.917
98.0	45.370	90.741	136.111	181.481	226.852	272.222	317.593	362.963	408.333
98.1	45.417	90.833	136.250	181.667	227.083	272.500	317.917	363.333	408.750
98.2	45.463	90.926	136.389	181.852	227.315	272.778	318.241	363.704	409.167
98.3	45.509	91.019	136.528	182.037	227.546	273.056	318.565	364.074	409.583
98.4	45.556	91.111	136.667	182.222	227.778	273.333	318.889	364.444	410.000
98.5	45.602	91.204	136.806	182.407	228.009	273.611	319.213	364.815	410.417
98.6	45.648	91.296	136.944	182.593	228.241	273.889	319.537	365.185	410.833
98.7	45.694	91.389	137.083	182.778	228.472	274.167	319.861	365.556	411.250
98.8	45.741	91.481	137.222	182.963	228.704	274.444	320.185	365.926	411.667
98.9	45.787	91.574	137.361	183.148	228.935	274.722	320.509	366.296	412.083
99.0	45.833	91.667	137.500	183.333	229.167	275.000	320.833	366.667	412.500
99.1	45.880	91.759	137.639	183.519	229.398	275.278	321.157	367.037	412.917
99.2	45.926	91.852	137.778	183.704	229.630	275.556	321.481	367.407	413.333
99.3	45.972	91.944	137.917	183.889	229.861	275.833	321.806	367.778	413.750
99.4	46.019	92.037	138.056	184.074	230.093	276.111	322.130	368.148	414.167
99.5	46.065	92.130	138.194	184.259	230.324	276.389	322.454	368.519	414.583
99.6	46.111	92.222	138.333	184.444	230.556	276.667	322.778	368.889	415.000
99.7	46.157	92.315	138.472	184.630	230.787	276.944	323.102	369.259	415.417
99.8	46.204	92.407	138.611	184.815	231.019	277.222	323.426	369.630	415.833
99.9	46.250	92.500	138.750	185.000	231.250	277.500	323.750	370.000	416.250
100.0	46.296	92.593	138.889	185.185	231.481	277.778	324.074	370.370	416.667
100.1	46.343	92.685	139.028	185.370	231.713	278.056	324.398	370.741	417.083
100.2	46.389	92.778	139.167	185.556	231.944	278.333	324.722	371.111	417.500
100.3	46.435	92.870	139.306	185.741	232.176	278.611	325.046	371.481	417.917
100.4	46.481	92.963	139.444	185.926	232.407	278.889	325.370	371.852	418.333
100.5	46.528	93.056	139.583	186.111	232.639	279.167	325.694	372.222	418.750
100.6	46.574	93.148	139.722	186.296	232.870	279.444	326.019	372.593	419.167
100.7	46.620	93.241	139.861	186.481	233.102	279.722	326.343	372.963	419.583
100.8	46.667	93.333	140.000	186.667	233.333	280.000	326.667	373.333	420.000
100.9	46.713	93.426	140.139	186.852	233.565	280.278	326.991	373.704	420.417
101.0	46.759	93.519	140.278	187.037	233.796	280.556	327.315	374.074	420.833
101.1	46.806	93.611	140.417	187.222	234.028	280.833	327.639	374.444	421.250
101.2	46.852	93.704	140.556	187.407	234.259	281.111	327.963	374.815	421.667
101.3	46.898	93.796	140.694	187.593	234.491	281.389	328.287	375.185	422.083
101.4	46.944	93.889	140.833	187.778	234.722	281.667	328.611	375.556	422.500
101.5	46.991	93.981	140.972	187.963	234.954	281.944	328.935	375.926	422.917
101.6	47.037	94.074	141.111	188.148	235.185	282.222	329.259	376.296	423.333
101.7	47.083	94.167	141.250	188.333	235.417	282.500	329.583	376.667	423.750
101.8	47.130	94.259	141.389	188.519	235.648	282.778	329.907	377.037	424.167
101.9	47.176	94.352	141.528	188.704	235.880	283.056	330.231	377.407	424.583
102.0	47.222	94.444	141.667	188.889	236.111	283.333	330.556	377.778	425.000
H. or B.	1	2	3	4	5	6	7	8	9

H. or B.	1	2	3	4	5	6	7	8	9
102.1	47.269	94.537	141.806	189.074	236.843	283.611	330.880	378.148	425.417
102.2	47.315	94.630	141.944	189.259	236.574	283.889	331.204	378.519	425.833
102.3	47.361	94.722	142.083	189.444	236.806	284.167	331.528	378.889	426.250
102.4	47.407	94.815	142.222	189.630	237.037	284.444	331.852	379.259	426.667
102.5	47.454	94.907	142.361	189.815	237.269	284.722	332.176	379.630	427.083
102.6	47.500	95.000	142.500	190.000	237.500	285.000	332.500	380.000	427.500
102.7	47.546	95.093	142.639	190.185	237.731	285.278	332.824	380.370	427.917
102.8	47.593	95.185	142.778	190.370	237.963	285.556	333.148	380.741	428.333
102.9	47.639	95.278	142.917	190.556	238.194	285.833	333.472	381.111	428.750
103.0	47.685	95.370	143.056	190.741	238.426	286.111	333.796	381.481	429.167
103.1	47.731	95.463	143.194	190.926	238.657	286.389	334.120	381.852	429.583
103.2	47.778	95.556	143.333	191.111	238.889	286.667	334.444	382.222	430.000
103.3	47.824	95.648	143.472	191.296	239.120	286.944	334.769	382.593	430.417
103.4	47.870	95.741	143.611	191.481	239.352	287.222	335.093	382.963	430.833
103.5	47.917	95.833	143.750	191.667	239.583	287.500	335.417	383.333	431.250
103.6	47.963	95.926	143.889	191.852	239.815	287.778	335.741	383.704	431.667
103.7	48.009	96.019	144.028	192.037	240.046	288.056	336.065	384.074	432.083
103.8	48.056	96.111	144.167	192.222	240.278	288.333	336.389	384.444	432.500
103.9	48.102	96.204	144.306	192.407	240.509	288.611	336.713	384.815	432.917
104.0	48.148	96.296	144.444	192.593	240.741	288.889	337.037	385.185	433.333
104.1	48.194	96.389	144.583	192.778	240.972	289.167	337.361	385.556	433.750
104.2	48.241	96.481	144.722	192.963	241.204	289.444	337.685	385.926	434.167
104.3	48.287	96.574	144.861	193.148	241.435	289.722	338.009	386.296	434.583
104.4	48.333	96.667	145.000	193.333	241.667	290.000	338.333	386.667	435.000
104.5	48.380	96.759	145.139	193.519	241.898	290.278	338.657	387.037	435.417
104.6	48.426	96.852	145.278	193.704	242.130	290.556	338.981	387.407	435.833
104.7	48.472	96.944	145.417	193.889	242.361	290.833	339.306	387.778	436.250
104.8	48.519	97.037	145.556	194.074	242.593	291.111	339.630	388.148	436.667
104.9	48.565	97.130	145.694	194.259	242.824	291.389	339.954	388.519	437.083
105.0	48.611	97.222	145.833	194.444	243.056	291.667	340.278	388.889	437.500
105.1	48.657	97.315	145.972	194.630	243.287	291.944	340.602	389.259	437.917
105.2	48.704	97.407	146.111	194.815	243.519	292.222	340.926	389.630	438.333
105.3	48.750	97.500	146.250	195.000	243.750	292.500	341.250	390.000	438.750
105.4	48.796	97.593	146.389	195.185	243.981	292.778	341.574	390.370	439.167
105.5	48.843	97.685	146.528	195.370	244.213	293.056	341.898	390.741	439.583
105.6	48.889	97.778	146.667	195.556	244.444	293.333	342.222	391.111	440.000
105.7	48.935	97.870	146.806	195.741	244.676	293.611	342.546	391.481	440.417
105.8	48.981	97.963	146.944	195.926	244.907	293.889	342.870	391.852	440.833
105.9	49.028	98.056	147.083	196.111	245.139	294.167	343.194	392.222	441.250
106.0	49.074	98.148	147.222	196.296	245.370	294.444	343.519	392.593	441.667
106.1	49.120	98.241	147.361	196.481	245.602	294.722	343.843	392.963	442.083
106.2	49.167	98.333	147.500	196.667	245.833	295.000	344.167	393.333	442.500
106.3	49.213	98.426	147.639	196.852	246.065	295.278	344.491	393.704	442.917
106.4	49.259	98.519	147.778	197.037	246.296	295.556	344.815	394.074	443.333
106.5	49.306	98.611	147.917	197.222	246.528	295.833	345.139	394.444	443.750
106.6	49.352	98.704	148.056	197.407	246.759	296.111	345.463	394.815	444.167
106.7	49.398	98.796	148.194	197.593	246.991	296.389	345.787	395.185	444.583
106.8	49.444	98.889	148.333	197.778	247.222	296.667	346.111	395.556	445.000
106.9	49.491	98.981	148.472	197.963	247.454	296.944	346.435	395.926	445.417
107.0	49.537	99.074	148.611	198.148	247.685	297.222	346.759	396.296	445.833
107.1	49.583	99.167	148.750	198.333	247.917	297.500	347.083	396.667	446.250
107.2	49.630	99.259	148.889	198.519	248.148	297.778	347.407	397.037	446.667
107.3	49.676	99.352	149.028	198.704	248.380	298.056	347.731	397.407	447.083
107.4	49.722	99.444	149.167	198.889	248.611	298.333	348.056	397.778	447.500
107.5	49.769	99.537	149.306	199.074	248.843	298.611	348.380	398.148	447.917
107.6	49.815	99.630	149.444	199.259	249.074	298.889	348.704	398.519	448.333
107.7	49.861	99.722	149.583	199.444	249.306	299.167	349.028	398.889	448.750
107.8	49.907	99.815	149.722	199.630	249.537	299.444	349.352	399.259	449.167
107.9	49.954	99.907	149.861	199.815	249.769	299.722	349.676	399.630	449.583
108.0	50.000	100.000	150.000	200.000	250.000	300.000	350.000	400.000	450.000
H. or B.	1	2	3	4	5	6	7	8	9

H. or B.	1	2	3	4	5	6	7	8	9
108.1	50.046	100.093	150.139	200.185	250.231	300.278	350.324	400.370	450.417
108.2	50.093	100.185	150.278	200.370	250.463	300.556	350.648	400.741	450.833
108.3	50.139	100.278	150.417	200.556	250.694	300.833	350.972	401.111	451.250
108.4	50.185	100.370	150.556	200.741	250.926	301.111	351.296	401.481	451.667
108.5	50.231	100.463	150.694	200.926	251.157	301.389	351.620	401.852	452.083
108.6	50.278	100.556	150.833	201.111	251.389	301.667	351.944	402.222	452.500
108.7	50.324	100.648	150.972	201.296	251.620	301.944	352.269	402.593	452.917
108.8	50.370	100.741	151.111	201.481	251.852	302.222	352.593	402.963	453.333
108.9	50.417	100.833	151.250	201.667	252.083	302.500	352.917	403.333	453.750
109.0	50.463	100.926	151.389	201.852	252.315	302.778	353.241	403.704	454.167
109.1	50.509	101.019	151.528	202.037	252.546	303.056	353.565	404.074	454.583
109.2	50.556	101.111	151.667	202.222	252.778	303.333	353.889	404.444	455.000
109.3	50.602	101.204	151.806	202.407	253.009	303.611	354.213	404.815	455.417
109.4	50.648	101.296	151.944	202.593	253.241	303.889	354.537	405.185	455.833
109.5	50.694	101.389	152.083	202.778	253.472	304.167	354.861	405.556	456.250
109.6	50.741	101.481	152.222	202.963	253.704	304.444	355.185	405.926	456.667
109.7	50.787	101.574	152.361	203.148	253.935	304.722	355.509	406.296	457.083
109.8	50.833	101.667	152.500	203.333	254.167	305.000	355.833	406.667	457.500
109.9	50.880	101.759	152.639	203.519	254.398	305.278	356.157	407.037	457.917
110.0	50.926	101.852	152.778	203.704	254.630	305.556	356.481	407.407	458.333
110.1	50.972	101.944	152.917	203.889	254.861	305.833	356.806	407.778	458.750
110.2	51.019	102.037	153.056	204.074	255.093	306.111	357.130	408.148	459.167
110.3	51.065	102.130	153.194	204.259	255.324	306.389	357.454	408.519	459.583
110.4	51.111	102.222	153.333	204.444	255.556	306.667	357.778	408.889	460.000
110.5	51.157	102.315	153.472	204.630	255.787	306.944	358.102	409.259	460.417
110.6	51.204	102.407	153.611	204.815	256.019	307.222	358.426	409.630	460.833
110.7	51.250	102.500	153.750	205.000	256.250	307.500	358.750	410.000	461.250
110.8	51.296	102.593	153.889	205.185	256.481	307.778	359.074	410.370	461.667
110.9	51.343	102.685	154.028	205.370	256.713	308.056	359.398	410.741	462.083
111.0	51.389	102.778	154.167	205.556	256.944	308.333	359.722	411.111	462.500
111.1	51.435	102.870	154.306	205.741	257.176	308.611	360.046	411.481	462.917
111.2	51.481	102.963	154.444	205.926	257.407	308.889	360.370	411.852	463.333
111.3	51.528	103.056	154.583	206.111	257.639	309.167	360.694	412.222	463.750
111.4	51.574	103.148	154.722	206.296	257.870	309.444	361.019	412.593	464.167
111.5	51.620	103.241	154.861	206.481	258.102	309.722	361.343	412.963	464.583
111.6	51.667	103.333	155.000	206.667	258.333	310.000	361.667	413.333	465.000
111.7	51.713	103.426	155.139	206.852	258.565	310.278	361.991	413.704	465.417
111.8	51.759	103.519	155.278	207.037	258.796	310.556	362.315	414.074	465.833
111.9	51.806	103.611	155.417	207.222	259.028	310.833	362.639	414.444	466.250
112.0	51.852	103.704	155.556	207.407	259.259	311.111	362.963	414.815	466.667
112.1	51.898	103.796	155.694	207.593	259.491	311.389	363.287	415.185	467.083
112.2	51.944	103.889	155.833	207.778	259.722	311.667	363.611	415.556	467.500
112.3	51.991	103.981	155.972	207.963	259.954	311.944	363.935	415.926	467.917
112.4	52.037	104.074	156.111	208.148	260.185	312.222	364.259	416.296	468.333
112.5	52.083	104.167	156.250	208.333	260.417	312.500	364.583	416.667	468.750
112.6	52.130	104.259	156.389	208.519	260.648	312.778	364.907	417.037	469.167
112.7	52.176	104.352	156.528	208.704	260.880	313.056	365.231	417.407	469.583
112.8	52.222	104.444	156.667	208.889	261.111	313.333	365.556	417.778	470.000
112.9	52.269	104.537	156.806	209.074	261.343	313.611	365.880	418.148	470.417
113.0	52.315	104.630	156.944	209.259	261.574	313.889	366.204	418.519	470.833
113.1	52.361	104.722	157.083	209.444	261.806	314.167	366.528	418.889	471.250
113.2	52.407	104.815	157.222	209.630	262.037	314.444	366.852	419.259	471.667
113.3	52.454	104.907	157.361	209.815	262.269	314.722	367.176	419.630	472.083
113.4	52.500	105.000	157.500	210.000	262.500	315.000	367.500	420.000	472.500
113.5	52.546	105.093	157.639	210.185	262.731	315.278	367.824	420.370	472.917
113.6	52.593	105.185	157.778	210.370	262.963	315.556	368.148	420.741	473.333
113.7	52.639	105.278	157.917	210.556	263.194	315.833	368.472	421.111	473.750
113.8	52.685	105.370	158.056	210.741	263.426	316.111	368.796	421.481	474.167
113.9	52.731	105.463	158.194	210.926	263.657	316.389	369.120	421.852	474.583
114.0	52.778	105.556	158.333	211.111	263.889	316.667	369.444	422.222	475.000
H. or B.	1	2	3	4	5	6	7	8	9

H. or B.	1	2	3	4	5	6	7	8	9
114.1	52.824	105.648	158.472	211.296	264.120	316.944	369.769	422.593	475.417
114.2	52.870	105.741	158.611	211.481	264.352	317.222	370.093	422.963	475.833
114.3	52.917	105.833	158.750	211.667	264.583	317.500	370.417	423.333	476.250
114.4	52.963	105.926	158.889	211.852	264.815	317.778	370.741	423.704	476.667
114.5	53.009	106.019	159.028	212.037	265.046	318.056	371.065	424.074	477.083
114.6	53.056	106.111	159.167	212.222	265.278	318.333	371.389	424.444	477.500
114.7	53.102	106.204	159.306	212.407	265.509	318.611	371.713	424.815	477.917
114.8	53.148	106.296	159.444	212.593	265.741	318.889	372.037	425.185	478.333
114.9	53.194	106.389	159.583	212.778	265.972	319.167	372.361	425.556	478.750
115.0	53.241	106.481	159.722	212.963	266.204	319.444	372.685	425.926	479.167
115.1	53.287	106.574	159.861	213.148	266.435	319.722	373.009	426.296	479.583
115.2	53.333	106.667	160.000	213.333	266.667	320.000	373.333	426.667	480.000
115.3	53.380	106.759	160.139	213.519	266.898	320.278	373.657	427.037	480.417
115.4	53.426	106.852	160.278	213.704	267.130	320.556	373.981	427.407	480.833
115.5	53.472	106.944	160.417	213.889	267.361	320.833	374.306	427.778	481.250
115.6	53.519	107.037	160.556	214.074	267.593	321.111	374.630	428.148	481.667
115.7	53.565	107.130	160.694	214.259	267.824	321.389	374.954	428.519	482.083
115.8	53.611	107.222	160.833	214.444	268.056	321.667	375.278	428.889	482.500
115.9	53.657	107.315	160.972	214.630	268.287	321.944	375.602	429.259	482.917
116.0	53.704	107.407	161.111	214.815	268.519	322.222	375.926	429.630	483.333
116.1	53.750	107.500	161.250	215.000	268.750	322.500	376.250	430.000	483.750
116.2	53.796	107.593	161.389	215.185	268.981	322.778	376.574	430.370	484.167
116.3	53.843	107.685	161.528	215.370	269.213	323.056	376.898	430.741	484.583
116.4	53.889	107.778	161.667	215.556	269.444	323.333	377.222	431.111	485.000
116.5	53.935	107.870	161.806	215.741	269.676	323.611	377.546	431.481	485.417
116.6	53.981	107.963	161.944	215.926	269.907	323.889	377.870	431.852	485.833
116.7	54.028	108.056	162.083	216.111	270.139	324.167	378.194	432.222	486.250
116.8	54.074	108.148	162.222	216.296	270.370	324.444	378.519	432.593	486.667
116.9	54.120	108.241	162.361	216.481	270.602	324.722	378.843	432.963	487.083
117.0	54.167	108.333	162.500	216.667	270.833	325.000	379.167	433.333	487.500
117.1	54.213	108.426	162.639	216.852	271.065	325.278	379.491	433.704	487.917
117.2	54.259	108.519	162.778	217.037	271.296	325.556	379.815	434.074	488.333
117.3	54.306	108.611	162.917	217.222	271.528	325.833	380.139	434.444	488.750
117.4	54.352	108.704	163.056	217.407	271.759	326.111	380.463	434.815	489.167
117.5	54.398	108.796	163.194	217.593	271.991	326.389	380.787	435.185	489.583
117.6	54.444	108.889	163.333	217.778	272.222	326.667	381.111	435.556	490.000
117.7	54.491	108.981	163.472	217.963	272.454	326.944	381.435	435.926	490.417
117.8	54.537	109.074	163.611	218.148	272.685	327.222	381.759	436.296	490.833
117.9	54.583	109.167	163.750	218.333	272.917	327.500	382.083	436.667	491.250
118.0	54.630	109.259	163.889	218.519	273.148	327.778	382.407	437.037	491.667
118.1	54.676	109.352	164.028	218.704	273.380	328.056	382.731	437.407	492.083
118.2	54.722	109.444	164.167	218.889	273.611	328.333	383.056	437.778	492.500
118.3	54.769	109.537	164.306	219.074	273.843	328.611	383.380	438.148	492.917
118.4	54.815	109.630	164.444	219.259	274.074	328.889	383.704	438.519	493.333
118.5	54.861	109.722	164.583	219.444	274.306	329.167	384.028	438.889	493.750
118.6	54.907	109.815	164.722	219.630	274.537	329.444	384.352	439.259	494.167
118.7	54.954	109.907	164.861	219.815	274.769	329.722	384.676	439.630	494.583
118.8	55.000	110.000	165.000	220.000	275.000	330.000	385.000	440.000	495.000
118.9	55.046	110.093	165.139	220.185	275.231	330.278	385.324	440.370	495.417
119.0	55.093	110.185	165.278	220.370	275.463	330.556	385.648	440.741	495.833
119.1	55.139	110.278	165.417	220.556	275.694	330.833	385.972	441.111	496.250
119.2	55.185	110.370	165.556	220.741	275.926	331.111	386.296	441.481	496.667
119.3	55.231	110.463	165.694	220.926	276.157	331.389	386.620	441.852	497.083
119.4	55.278	110.556	165.833	221.111	276.389	331.667	386.944	442.222	497.500
119.5	55.324	110.648	165.972	221.296	276.620	331.944	387.269	442.593	497.917
119.6	55.370	110.741	166.111	221.481	276.852	332.222	387.593	442.963	498.333
119.7	55.417	110.833	166.250	221.667	277.083	332.500	387.917	443.333	498.750
119.8	55.463	110.926	166.389	221.852	277.315	332.778	388.241	443.704	499.167
119.9	55.509	111.019	166.528	222.037	277.546	333.056	388.565	444.074	499.583
120.0	55.556	111.111	166.667	222.222	277.778	333.333	388.889	444.444	500.000
H. or B.	1	2	3	4	5	6	7	8	9

TABLE XXII. Rectangular Prisms.

H. or B.	1	2	3	4	5	6	7	8	9
0.1	0.37	0.74	1.11	1.48	1.85	2.22	2.59	2.96	3.33
0.2	0.74	1.48	2.22	2.96	3.70	4.44	5.19	5.93	6.67
0.3	1.11	2.22	3.33	4.44	5.56	6.67	7.78	8.89	10.00
0.4	1.48	2.96	4.44	5.93	7.41	8.89	10.37	11.85	13.33
0.5	1.85	3.70	5.56	7.41	9.26	11.11	12.96	14.81	16.67
0.6	2.22	4.44	6.67	8.89	11.11	13.33	15.56	17.78	20.00
0.7	2.59	5.19	7.78	10.37	12.96	15.56	18.15	20.74	23.33
0.8	2.96	5.93	8.89	11.85	14.81	17.78	20.74	23.70	26.67
0.9	3.33	6.67	10.00	13.33	16.67	20.00	23.33	26.67	30.00
1.0	3.70	7.41	11.11	14.81	18.52	22.22	25.93	29.63	33.33
1.1	4.07	8.15	12.22	16.30	20.37	24.44	28.52	32.59	36.67
1.2	4.44	8.89	13.33	17.78	22.22	26.67	31.11	35.56	40.00
1.3	4.81	9.63	14.44	19.26	24.07	28.89	33.70	38.52	43.33
1.4	5.19	10.37	15.56	20.74	25.93	31.11	36.30	41.48	46.67
1.5	5.56	11.11	16.67	22.22	27.78	33.33	38.89	44.44	50.00
1.6	5.93	11.85	17.78	23.70	29.63	35.56	41.48	47.41	53.33
1.7	6.30	12.59	18.89	25.19	31.48	37.78	44.07	50.37	56.67
1.8	6.67	13.33	20.00	26.67	33.33	40.00	46.67	53.33	60.00
1.9	7.04	14.07	21.11	28.15	35.19	42.22	49.26	56.30	63.33
2.0	7.41	14.81	22.22	29.63	37.04	44.44	51.85	59.26	66.67
2.1	7.78	15.56	23.33	31.11	38.89	46.67	54.44	62.22	70.00
2.2	8.15	16.30	24.44	32.59	40.74	48.89	57.04	65.19	73.33
2.3	8.52	17.04	25.56	34.07	42.59	51.11	59.63	68.15	76.67
2.4	8.89	17.78	26.67	35.56	44.44	53.33	62.22	71.11	80.00
2.5	9.26	18.52	27.78	37.04	46.30	55.56	64.81	74.07	83.33
2.6	9.63	19.26	28.89	38.52	48.15	57.78	67.41	77.04	86.67
2.7	10.00	20.00	30.00	40.00	50.00	60.00	70.00	80.00	90.00
2.8	10.37	20.74	31.11	41.48	51.85	62.22	72.59	82.96	93.33
2.9	10.74	21.48	32.22	42.96	53.70	64.44	75.19	85.93	96.67
3.0	11.11	22.22	33.33	44.44	55.56	66.67	77.78	88.89	100.00
3.1	11.48	22.96	34.44	45.93	57.41	68.89	80.37	91.85	103.33
3.2	11.85	23.70	35.56	47.41	59.26	71.11	82.96	94.81	106.67
3.3	12.22	24.44	36.67	48.89	61.11	73.33	85.56	97.78	110.00
3.4	12.59	25.19	37.78	50.37	62.96	75.56	88.15	100.74	113.33
3.5	12.96	25.93	38.89	51.85	64.81	77.78	90.74	103.70	116.67
3.6	13.33	26.67	40.00	53.33	66.67	80.00	93.33	106.67	120.00
3.7	13.70	27.41	41.11	54.81	68.52	82.22	95.93	109.63	123.33
3.8	14.07	28.15	42.22	56.30	70.37	84.44	98.52	112.59	126.67
3.9	14.44	28.89	43.33	57.78	72.22	86.67	101.11	115.56	130.00
4.0	14.81	29.63	44.44	59.26	74.07	88.89	103.70	118.52	133.33
4.1	15.19	30.37	45.56	60.74	75.93	91.11	106.30	121.48	136.67
4.2	15.56	31.11	46.67	62.22	77.78	93.33	108.89	124.44	140.00
4.3	15.93	31.85	47.78	63.70	79.63	95.56	111.48	127.41	143.33
4.4	16.30	32.59	48.89	65.19	81.48	97.78	114.07	130.37	146.67
4.5	16.67	33.33	50.00	66.67	83.33	100.00	116.67	133.33	150.00
4.6	17.04	34.07	51.11	68.15	85.19	102.22	119.26	136.30	153.33
4.7	17.41	34.81	52.22	69.63	87.04	104.44	121.85	139.26	156.67
4.8	17.78	35.56	53.33	71.11	88.89	106.67	124.44	142.22	160.00
4.9	18.15	36.30	54.44	72.59	90.74	108.89	127.04	145.19	163.33
5.0	18.52	37.04	55.56	74.07	92.59	111.11	129.63	148.15	166.67
5.1	18.89	37.78	56.67	75.56	94.44	113.33	132.22	151.11	170.00
5.2	19.26	38.52	57.78	77.04	96.30	115.56	134.81	154.07	173.33
5.3	19.63	39.26	58.89	78.52	98.15	117.78	137.41	157.04	176.67
5.4	20.00	40.00	60.00	80.00	100.00	120.00	140.00	160.00	180.00
5.5	20.37	40.74	61.11	81.48	101.85	122.22	142.59	162.96	183.33
5.6	20.74	41.48	62.22	82.96	103.70	124.44	145.19	165.93	186.67
5.7	21.11	42.22	63.33	84.44	105.56	126.67	147.78	168.89	190.00
5.8	21.48	42.96	64.44	85.93	107.41	128.89	150.37	171.85	193.33
5.9	21.85	43.70	65.56	87.41	109.26	131.11	152.96	174.81	196.67
6.0	22.22	44.44	66.67	88.89	111.11	133.33	155.56	177.78	200.00
H. or B.	1	2	3	4	5	6	7	8	9

TABLE XXII. Rectangular Prisms.

H. or B.	1	2	3	4	5	6	7	8	9
6.1	22.59	45.19	67.78	90.37	112.96	135.56	158.15	180.74	203.33
6.2	22.96	45.93	68.89	91.85	114.81	137.78	160.74	183.70	206.67
6.3	23.33	46.67	70.00	93.33	116.67	140.00	163.33	186.67	210.00
6.4	23.70	47.41	71.11	94.81	118.52	142.22	165.93	189.63	213.33
6.5	24.07	48.15	72.22	96.30	120.37	144.44	168.52	192.59	216.67
6.6	24.44	48.89	73.33	97.78	122.22	146.67	171.11	195.56	220.00
6.7	24.81	49.63	74.44	99.26	124.07	148.89	173.70	198.52	223.33
6.8	25.19	50.37	75.56	100.74	125.93	151.11	176.30	201.48	226.67
6.9	25.56	51.11	76.67	102.22	127.78	153.33	178.89	204.44	230.00
7.0	25.93	51.85	77.78	103.70	129.63	155.56	181.48	207.41	233.33
7.1	26.30	52.59	78.89	105.19	131.48	157.78	184.07	210.37	236.67
7.2	26.67	53.33	80.00	106.67	133.33	160.00	186.67	213.33	240.00
7.3	27.04	54.07	81.11	108.15	135.19	162.22	189.26	216.30	243.33
7.4	27.41	54.81	82.22	109.63	137.04	164.44	191.85	219.26	246.67
7.5	27.78	55.56	83.33	111.11	138.89	166.67	194.44	222.22	250.00
7.6	28.15	56.30	84.44	112.59	140.74	168.89	197.04	225.19	253.33
7.7	28.52	57.04	85.56	114.07	142.59	171.11	199.63	228.15	256.67
7.8	28.89	57.78	86.67	115.56	144.44	173.33	202.22	231.11	260.00
7.9	29.26	58.52	87.78	117.04	146.30	175.56	204.81	234.07	263.33
8.0	29.63	59.26	88.89	118.52	148.15	177.78	207.41	237.04	266.67
8.1	30.00	60.00	90.00	120.00	150.00	180.00	210.00	240.00	270.00
8.2	30.37	60.74	91.11	121.48	151.85	182.22	212.59	242.96	273.33
8.3	30.74	61.48	92.22	122.96	153.70	184.44	215.19	245.93	276.67
8.4	31.11	62.22	93.33	124.44	155.56	186.67	217.78	248.89	280.00
8.5	31.48	62.96	94.44	125.93	157.41	188.89	220.37	251.85	283.33
8.6	31.85	63.70	95.56	127.41	159.26	191.11	222.96	254.81	286.67
8.7	32.22	64.44	96.67	128.89	161.11	193.33	225.56	257.78	290.00
8.8	32.59	65.19	97.78	130.37	162.96	195.56	228.15	260.74	293.33
8.9	32.96	65.93	98.89	131.85	164.81	197.78	230.74	263.70	296.67
9.0	33.33	66.67	100.00	133.33	166.67	200.00	233.33	266.67	300.00
9.1	33.70	67.41	101.11	134.81	168.52	202.22	235.93	269.63	303.33
9.2	34.07	68.15	102.22	136.30	170.37	204.44	238.52	272.59	306.67
9.3	34.44	68.89	103.33	137.78	172.22	206.67	241.11	275.56	310.00
9.4	34.81	69.63	104.44	139.26	174.07	208.89	243.70	278.52	313.33
9.5	35.19	70.37	105.56	140.74	175.93	211.11	246.30	281.48	316.67
9.6	35.56	71.11	106.67	142.22	177.78	213.33	248.89	284.44	320.00
9.7	35.93	71.85	107.78	143.70	179.63	215.56	251.48	287.41	323.33
9.8	36.30	72.59	108.89	145.19	181.48	217.78	254.07	290.37	326.67
9.9	36.67	73.33	110.00	146.67	183.33	220.00	256.67	293.33	330.00
10.0	37.04	74.07	111.11	148.15	185.19	222.22	259.26	296.30	333.33
10.1	37.41	74.81	112.22	149.63	187.04	224.44	261.85	299.26	336.67
10.2	37.78	75.56	113.33	151.11	188.89	226.67	264.44	302.22	340.00
10.3	38.15	76.30	114.44	152.59	190.74	228.89	267.04	305.19	343.33
10.4	38.52	77.04	115.56	154.07	192.59	231.11	269.63	308.15	346.67
10.5	38.89	77.78	116.67	155.56	194.44	233.33	272.22	311.11	350.00
10.6	39.26	78.52	117.78	157.04	196.30	235.56	274.81	314.07	353.33
10.7	39.63	79.26	118.89	158.52	198.15	237.78	277.41	317.04	356.67
10.8	40.00	80.00	120.00	160.00	200.00	240.00	280.00	320.00	360.00
10.9	40.37	80.74	121.11	161.48	201.85	242.22	282.59	322.96	363.33
11.0	40.74	81.48	122.22	162.96	203.70	244.44	285.19	325.93	366.67
11.1	41.11	82.22	123.33	164.44	205.56	246.67	287.78	328.89	370.00
11.2	41.48	82.96	124.44	165.93	207.41	248.89	290.37	331.85	373.33
11.3	41.85	83.70	125.56	167.41	209.26	251.11	292.96	334.81	376.67
11.4	42.22	84.44	126.67	168.89	211.11	253.33	295.56	337.78	380.00
11.5	42.59	85.19	127.78	170.37	212.96	255.56	298.15	340.74	383.33
11.6	42.96	85.93	128.89	171.85	214.81	257.78	300.74	343.70	386.67
11.7	43.33	86.67	130.00	173.33	216.67	260.00	303.33	346.67	390.00
11.8	43.70	87.41	131.11	174.81	218.52	262.22	305.93	349.63	393.33
11.9	44.07	88.15	132.22	176.30	220.37	264.44	308.52	352.59	396.67
12.0	44.44	88.89	133.33	177.78	222.22	266.67	311.11	355.56	400.00
H. or B.	1	2	3	4	5	6	7	8	9

H. or B.	1	2	3	4	5	6	7	8	9
12.1	44.81	89.63	134.44	179.26	224.07	268.89	313.70	358.52	403.33
12.2	45.19	90.37	135.56	180.74	225.93	271.11	316.30	361.48	406.67
12.3	45.56	91.11	136.67	182.22	227.78	273.33	318.89	364.44	410.00
12.4	45.93	91.85	137.78	183.70	229.63	275.56	321.48	367.41	413.33
12.5	46.30	92.59	138.89	185.19	231.48	277.78	324.07	370.37	416.67
12.6	46.67	93.33	140.00	186.67	233.33	280.00	326.67	373.33	420.00
12.7	47.04	94.07	141.11	188.15	235.19	282.22	329.26	376.30	423.33
12.8	47.41	94.81	142.22	189.63	237.04	284.44	331.85	379.26	426.67
12.9	47.78	95.56	143.33	191.11	238.89	286.67	334.44	382.22	430.00
13.0	48.15	96.30	144.44	192.59	240.74	288.89	337.04	385.19	433.33
13.1	48.52	97.04	145.56	194.07	242.59	291.11	339.63	388.15	436.67
13.2	48.89	97.78	146.67	195.56	244.44	293.33	342.22	391.11	440.00
13.3	49.26	98.52	147.78	197.04	246.30	295.56	344.81	394.07	443.33
13.4	49.63	99.26	148.89	198.52	248.15	297.78	347.41	397.04	446.67
13.5	50.00	100.00	150.00	200.00	250.00	300.00	350.00	400.00	450.00
13.6	50.37	100.74	151.11	201.48	251.85	302.22	352.59	402.96	453.33
13.7	50.74	101.48	152.22	202.96	253.70	304.44	355.19	405.93	456.67
13.8	51.11	102.22	153.33	204.44	255.56	306.67	357.78	408.89	460.00
13.9	51.48	102.96	154.44	205.93	257.41	308.89	360.37	411.85	463.33
14.0	51.85	103.70	155.56	207.41	259.26	311.11	362.96	414.81	466.67
14.1	52.22	104.44	156.67	208.89	261.11	313.33	365.56	417.78	470.00
14.2	52.59	105.19	157.78	210.37	262.96	315.56	368.15	420.74	473.33
14.3	52.96	105.93	158.89	211.85	264.81	317.78	370.74	423.70	476.67
14.4	53.33	106.67	160.00	213.33	266.67	320.00	373.33	426.67	480.00
14.5	53.70	107.41	161.11	214.81	268.52	322.22	375.93	429.63	483.33
14.6	54.07	108.15	162.22	216.30	270.37	324.44	378.52	432.59	486.67
14.7	54.44	108.89	163.33	217.78	272.22	326.67	381.11	435.56	490.00
14.8	54.81	109.63	164.44	219.26	274.07	328.89	383.70	438.52	493.33
14.9	55.19	110.37	165.56	220.74	275.93	331.11	386.30	441.48	496.67
15.0	55.56	111.11	166.67	222.22	277.78	333.33	388.89	444.44	500.00
15.1	55.93	111.85	167.78	223.70	279.63	335.56	391.48	447.41	503.33
15.2	56.30	112.59	168.89	225.19	281.48	337.78	394.07	450.37	506.67
15.3	56.67	113.33	170.00	226.67	283.33	340.00	396.67	453.33	510.00
15.4	57.04	114.07	171.11	228.15	285.19	342.22	399.26	456.30	513.33
15.5	57.41	114.81	172.22	229.63	287.04	344.44	401.85	459.26	516.67
15.6	57.78	115.56	173.33	231.11	288.89	346.67	404.44	462.22	520.00
15.7	58.15	116.30	174.44	232.59	290.74	348.89	407.04	465.19	523.33
15.8	58.52	117.04	175.56	234.07	292.59	351.11	409.63	468.15	526.67
15.9	58.89	117.78	176.67	235.56	294.44	353.33	412.22	471.11	530.00
16.0	59.26	118.52	177.78	237.04	296.30	355.56	414.81	474.07	533.33
16.1	59.63	119.26	178.89	238.52	298.15	357.78	417.41	477.04	536.67
16.2	60.00	120.00	180.00	240.00	300.00	360.00	420.00	480.00	540.00
16.3	60.37	120.74	181.11	241.48	301.85	362.22	422.59	482.96	543.33
16.4	60.74	121.48	182.22	242.96	303.70	364.44	425.19	485.93	546.67
16.5	61.11	122.22	183.33	244.44	305.56	366.67	427.78	488.89	550.00
16.6	61.48	122.96	184.44	245.93	307.41	368.89	430.37	491.85	553.33
16.7	61.85	123.70	185.56	247.41	309.26	371.11	432.96	494.81	556.67
16.8	62.22	124.44	186.67	248.89	311.11	373.33	435.56	497.78	560.00
16.9	62.59	125.19	187.78	250.37	312.96	375.56	438.15	500.74	563.33
17.0	62.96	125.93	188.89	251.85	314.81	377.78	440.74	503.70	566.67
17.1	63.33	126.67	190.00	253.33	316.67	380.00	443.33	506.67	570.00
17.2	63.70	127.41	191.11	254.81	318.52	382.22	445.93	509.63	573.33
17.3	64.07	128.15	192.22	256.30	320.37	384.44	448.52	512.59	576.67
17.4	64.44	128.89	193.33	257.78	322.22	386.67	451.11	515.56	580.00
17.5	64.81	129.63	194.44	259.26	324.07	388.89	453.70	518.52	583.33
17.6	65.19	130.37	195.56	260.74	325.93	391.11	456.30	521.48	586.67
17.7	65.56	131.11	196.67	262.22	327.78	393.33	458.89	524.44	590.00
17.8	65.93	131.85	197.78	263.70	329.63	395.56	461.48	527.41	593.33
17.9	66.30	132.59	198.89	265.19	331.48	397.78	464.07	530.37	596.67
18.0	66.67	133.33	200.00	266.67	333.33	400.00	466.67	533.33	600.00
H. or B.	1	2	3	4	5	6	7	8	9

TABLE XXII. Rectangular Prisms.

H. or B.	1	2	3	4	5	6	7	8	9
18.1	67.04	134.07	201.11	268.15	335.19	402.22	469.26	536.30	603.33
18.2	67.41	134.81	202.22	269.63	337.04	404.44	471.85	539.26	606.67
18.3	67.78	135.56	203.33	271.11	338.89	406.67	474.44	542.22	610.00
18.4	68.15	136.30	204.44	272.59	340.74	408.89	477.04	545.19	613.33
18.5	68.52	137.04	205.56	274.07	342.59	411.11	479.63	548.15	616.67
18.6	68.89	137.78	206.67	275.56	344.44	413.33	482.22	551.11	620.00
18.7	69.26	138.52	207.78	277.04	346.30	415.56	484.81	554.07	623.33
18.8	69.63	139.26	208.89	278.52	348.15	417.78	487.41	557.04	626.67
18.9	70.00	140.00	210.00	280.00	350.00	420.00	490.00	560.00	630.00
19.0	70.37	140.74	211.11	281.48	351.85	422.22	492.59	562.96	633.33
19.1	70.74	141.48	212.22	282.96	353.70	424.44	495.19	565.93	636.67
19.2	71.11	142.22	213.33	284.44	355.56	426.67	497.78	568.89	640.00
19.3	71.48	142.96	214.44	285.93	357.41	428.89	500.37	571.85	643.33
19.4	71.85	143.70	215.56	287.41	359.26	431.11	502.96	574.81	646.67
19.5	72.22	144.44	216.67	288.89	361.11	433.33	505.56	577.78	650.00
19.6	72.59	145.19	217.78	290.37	362.96	435.56	508.15	580.74	653.33
19.7	72.96	145.93	218.89	291.85	364.81	437.78	510.74	583.70	656.67
19.8	73.33	146.67	220.00	293.33	366.67	440.00	513.33	586.67	660.00
19.9	73.70	147.41	221.11	294.81	368.52	442.22	515.93	589.63	663.33
20.0	74.07	148.15	222.22	296.30	370.37	444.44	518.52	592.59	666.67
20.1	74.44	148.89	223.33	297.78	372.22	446.67	521.11	595.56	670.00
20.2	74.81	149.63	224.44	299.26	374.07	448.89	523.70	598.52	673.33
20.3	75.19	150.37	225.56	300.74	375.93	451.11	526.30	601.48	676.67
20.4	75.56	151.11	226.67	302.22	377.78	453.33	528.89	604.44	680.00
20.5	75.93	151.85	227.78	303.70	379.63	455.56	531.48	607.41	683.33
20.6	76.30	152.59	228.89	305.19	381.48	457.78	534.07	610.37	686.67
20.7	76.67	153.33	230.00	306.67	383.33	460.00	536.67	613.33	690.00
20.8	77.04	154.07	231.11	308.15	385.19	462.22	539.26	616.30	693.33
20.9	77.41	154.81	232.22	309.63	387.04	464.44	541.85	619.26	696.67
21.0	77.78	155.56	233.33	311.11	388.89	466.67	544.44	622.22	700.00
21.1	78.15	156.30	234.44	312.59	390.74	468.89	547.04	625.19	703.33
21.2	78.52	157.04	235.56	314.07	392.59	471.11	549.63	628.15	706.67
21.3	78.89	157.78	236.67	315.56	394.44	473.33	552.22	631.11	710.00
21.4	79.26	158.52	237.78	317.04	396.30	475.56	554.81	634.07	713.33
21.5	79.63	159.26	238.89	318.52	398.15	477.78	557.41	637.04	716.67
21.6	80.00	160.00	240.00	320.00	400.00	480.00	560.00	640.00	720.00
21.7	80.37	160.74	241.11	321.48	401.85	482.22	562.59	642.96	723.33
21.8	80.74	161.48	242.22	322.96	403.70	484.44	565.19	645.93	726.67
21.9	81.11	162.22	243.33	324.44	405.56	486.67	567.78	648.89	730.00
22.0	81.48	162.96	244.44	325.93	407.41	488.89	570.37	651.85	733.33
22.1	81.85	163.70	245.56	327.41	409.26	491.11	572.96	654.81	736.67
22.2	82.22	164.44	246.67	328.89	411.11	493.33	575.56	657.78	740.00
22.3	82.59	165.19	247.78	330.37	412.96	495.56	578.15	660.74	743.33
22.4	82.96	165.93	248.89	331.85	414.81	497.78	580.74	663.70	746.67
22.5	83.33	166.67	250.00	333.33	416.67	500.00	583.33	666.67	750.00
22.6	83.70	167.41	251.11	334.81	418.52	502.22	585.93	669.63	753.33
22.7	84.07	168.15	252.22	336.30	420.37	504.44	588.52	672.59	756.67
22.8	84.44	168.89	253.33	337.78	422.22	506.67	591.11	675.56	760.00
22.9	84.81	169.63	254.44	339.26	424.07	508.89	593.70	678.52	763.33
23.0	85.19	170.37	255.56	340.74	425.93	511.11	596.30	681.48	766.67
23.1	85.56	171.11	256.67	342.22	427.78	513.33	598.89	684.44	770.00
23.2	85.93	171.85	257.78	343.70	429.63	515.56	601.48	687.41	773.33
23.3	86.30	172.59	258.89	345.19	431.48	517.78	604.07	690.37	776.67
23.4	86.67	173.33	260.00	346.67	433.33	520.00	606.67	693.33	780.00
23.5	87.04	174.07	261.11	348.15	435.19	522.22	609.26	696.30	783.33
23.6	87.41	174.81	262.22	349.63	437.04	524.44	611.85	699.26	786.67
23.7	87.78	175.56	263.33	351.11	438.89	526.67	614.44	702.22	790.00
23.8	88.15	176.30	264.44	352.59	440.74	528.89	617.04	705.19	793.33
23.9	88.52	177.04	265.56	354.07	442.59	531.11	619.63	708.15	796.67
24.0	88.89	177.78	266.67	355.56	444.44	533.33	622.22	711.11	800.00
H. or B.	1	2	3	4	5	6	7	8	9

TABLE XXII. Rectangular Prisms.

H. or B.	1	2	3	4	5	6	7	8	9
24.1	89.26	178.52	267.78	357.04	446.30	535.56	624.81	714.07	803.33
24.2	89.63	179.26	268.89	358.52	448.15	537.78	627.41	717.04	806.67
24.3	90.00	180.00	270.00	360.00	450.00	540.00	630.00	720.00	810.00
24.4	90.37	180.74	271.11	361.48	451.85	542.22	632.59	722.96	813.33
24.5	90.74	181.48	272.22	362.96	453.70	544.44	635.19	725.93	816.67
24.6	91.11	182.22	273.33	364.44	455.56	546.67	637.78	728.89	820.00
24.7	91.48	182.96	274.44	365.93	457.41	548.89	640.37	731.85	823.33
24.8	91.85	183.70	275.56	367.41	459.26	551.11	642.96	734.81	826.67
24.9	92.22	184.44	276.67	368.89	461.11	553.33	645.56	737.78	830.00
25.0	92.59	185.19	277.78	370.37	462.96	555.56	648.15	740.74	833.33
25.1	92.96	185.93	278.89	371.85	464.81	557.78	650.74	743.70	836.67
25.2	93.33	186.67	280.00	373.33	466.67	560.00	653.33	746.67	840.00
25.3	93.70	187.41	281.11	374.81	468.52	562.22	655.93	749.63	843.33
25.4	94.07	188.15	282.22	376.30	470.37	564.44	658.52	752.59	846.67
25.5	94.44	188.89	283.33	377.78	472.22	566.67	661.11	755.56	850.00
25.6	94.81	189.63	284.44	379.26	474.07	568.89	663.70	758.52	853.33
25.7	95.19	190.37	285.56	380.74	475.93	571.11	666.30	761.48	856.67
25.8	95.56	191.11	286.67	382.22	477.78	573.33	668.89	764.44	860.00
25.9	95.93	191.85	287.78	383.70	479.63	575.56	671.48	767.41	863.33
26.0	96.30	192.59	288.89	385.19	481.48	577.78	674.07	770.37	866.67
26.1	96.67	193.33	290.00	386.67	483.33	580.00	676.67	773.33	870.00
26.2	97.04	194.07	291.11	388.15	485.19	582.22	679.26	776.30	873.33
26.3	97.41	194.81	292.22	389.63	487.04	584.44	681.85	779.26	876.67
26.4	97.78	195.56	293.33	391.11	488.89	586.67	684.44	782.22	880.00
26.5	98.15	196.30	294.44	392.59	490.74	588.89	687.04	785.19	883.33
26.6	98.52	197.04	295.56	394.07	492.59	591.11	689.63	788.15	886.67
26.7	98.89	197.78	296.67	395.56	494.44	593.33	692.22	791.11	890.00
26.8	99.26	198.52	297.78	397.04	496.30	595.56	694.81	794.07	893.33
26.9	99.63	199.26	298.89	398.52	498.15	597.78	697.41	797.04	896.67
27.0	100.00	200.00	300.00	400.00	500.00	600.00	700.00	800.00	900.00
27.1	100.37	200.74	301.11	401.48	501.85	602.22	702.59	802.96	903.33
27.2	100.74	201.48	302.22	402.96	503.70	604.44	705.19	805.93	906.67
27.3	101.11	202.22	303.33	404.44	505.56	606.67	707.78	808.89	910.00
27.4	101.48	202.96	304.44	405.93	507.41	608.89	710.37	811.85	913.33
27.5	101.85	203.70	305.56	407.41	509.26	611.11	712.96	814.81	916.67
27.6	102.22	204.44	306.67	408.89	511.11	613.33	715.56	817.78	920.00
27.7	102.59	205.19	307.78	410.37	512.96	615.56	718.15	820.74	923.33
27.8	102.96	205.93	308.89	411.85	514.81	617.78	720.74	823.70	926.67
27.9	103.33	206.67	310.00	413.33	516.67	620.00	723.33	826.67	930.00
28.0	103.70	207.41	311.11	414.81	518.52	622.22	725.93	829.63	933.33
28.1	104.07	208.15	312.22	416.30	520.37	624.44	728.52	832.59	936.67
28.2	104.44	208.89	313.33	417.78	522.22	626.67	731.11	835.56	940.00
28.3	104.81	209.63	314.44	419.26	524.07	628.89	733.70	838.52	943.33
28.4	105.19	210.37	315.56	420.74	525.93	631.11	736.30	841.48	946.67
28.5	105.56	211.11	316.67	422.22	527.78	633.33	738.89	844.44	950.00
28.6	105.93	211.85	317.78	423.70	529.63	635.56	741.48	847.41	953.33
28.7	106.30	212.59	318.89	425.19	531.48	637.78	744.07	850.37	956.67
28.8	106.67	213.33	320.00	426.67	533.33	640.00	746.67	853.33	960.00
28.9	107.04	214.07	321.11	428.15	535.19	642.22	749.26	856.30	963.33
29.0	107.41	214.81	322.22	429.63	537.04	644.44	751.85	859.26	966.67
29.1	107.78	215.56	323.33	431.11	538.89	646.67	754.44	862.22	970.00
29.2	108.15	216.30	324.44	432.59	540.74	648.89	757.04	865.19	973.33
29.3	108.52	217.04	325.56	434.07	542.59	651.11	759.63	868.15	976.67
29.4	108.89	217.78	326.67	435.56	544.44	653.33	762.22	871.11	980.00
29.5	109.26	218.52	327.78	437.04	546.30	655.56	764.81	874.07	983.33
29.6	109.63	219.26	328.89	438.52	548.15	657.78	767.41	877.04	986.67
29.7	110.00	220.00	330.00	440.00	550.00	660.00	770.00	880.00	990.00
29.8	110.37	220.74	331.11	441.48	551.85	662.22	772.59	882.96	993.33
29.9	110.74	221.48	332.22	442.96	553.70	664.44	775.19	885.93	996.67
30.0	111.11	222.22	333.33	444.44	555.56	666.67	777.78	888.89	1000.00
H. or B.	1	2	3	4	5	6	7	8	9

TABLE XXII. **Rectangular Prisms.**

H. or B.	1	2	3	4	5	6	7	8	9
30.1	111.48	222.96	334.44	445.93	557.41	668.89	780.37	891.85	1003.33
30.2	111.85	223.70	335.56	447.41	559.26	671.11	782.96	894.81	1006.67
30.3	112.22	224.44	336.67	448.89	561.11	673.33	785.56	897.78	1010.00
30.4	112.59	225.19	337.78	450.37	562.96	675.56	788.15	900.74	1013.33
30.5	112.96	225.93	338.89	451.85	564.81	677.78	790.74	903.70	1016.67
30.6	113.33	226.67	340.00	453.33	566.67	680.00	793.33	906.67	1020.00
30.7	113.70	227.41	341.11	454.81	568.52	682.22	795.93	909.63	1023.33
30.8	114.07	228.15	342.22	456.30	570.37	684.44	798.52	912.59	1026.67
30.9	114.44	228.89	343.33	457.78	572.22	686.67	801.11	915.56	1030.00
31.0	114.81	229.63	344.44	459.26	574.07	688.89	803.70	918.52	1033.33
31.1	115.19	230.37	345.56	460.74	575.93	691.11	806.30	921.48	1036.67
31.2	115.56	231.11	346.67	462.22	577.78	693.33	808.89	924.44	1040.00
31.3	115.93	231.85	347.78	463.70	579.63	695.56	811.48	927.41	1043.33
31.4	116.30	232.59	348.89	465.19	581.48	697.78	814.07	930.37	1046.67
31.5	116.67	233.33	350.00	466.67	583.33	700.00	816.67	933.33	1050.00
31.6	117.04	234.07	351.11	468.15	585.19	702.22	819.26	936.30	1053.33
31.7	117.41	234.81	352.22	469.63	587.04	704.44	821.85	939.26	1056.67
31.8	117.78	235.56	353.33	471.11	588.89	706.67	824.44	942.22	1060.00
31.9	118.15	236.30	354.44	472.59	590.74	708.89	827.04	945.19	1063.33
32.0	118.52	237.04	355.56	474.07	592.59	711.11	829.63	948.15	1066.67
32.1	118.89	237.78	356.67	475.56	594.44	713.33	832.22	951.11	1070.00
32.2	119.26	238.52	357.78	477.04	596.30	715.56	834.81	954.07	1073.33
32.3	119.63	239.26	358.89	478.52	598.15	717.78	837.41	957.04	1076.67
32.4	120.00	240.00	360.00	480.00	600.00	720.00	840.00	960.00	1080.00
32.5	120.37	240.74	361.11	481.48	601.85	722.22	842.59	962.96	1083.33
32.6	120.74	241.48	362.22	482.96	603.70	724.44	845.19	965.93	1086.67
32.7	121.11	242.22	363.33	484.44	605.56	726.67	847.78	968.89	1090.00
32.8	121.48	242.96	364.44	485.93	607.41	728.89	850.37	971.85	1093.33
32.9	121.85	243.70	365.56	487.41	609.26	731.11	852.96	974.81	1096.67
33.0	122.22	244.44	366.67	488.89	611.11	733.33	855.56	977.78	1100.00
33.1	122.59	245.19	367.78	490.37	612.96	735.56	858.15	980.74	1103.33
33.2	122.96	245.93	368.89	491.85	614.81	737.78	860.74	983.70	1106.67
33.3	123.33	246.67	370.00	493.33	616.67	740.00	863.33	986.67	1110.00
33.4	123.70	247.41	371.11	494.81	618.52	742.22	865.93	989.63	1113.33
33.5	124.07	248.15	372.22	496.30	620.37	744.44	868.52	992.59	1116.67
33.6	124.44	248.89	373.33	497.78	622.22	746.67	871.11	995.56	1120.00
33.7	124.81	249.63	374.44	499.26	624.07	748.89	873.70	998.52	1123.33
33.8	125.19	250.37	375.56	500.74	625.93	751.11	876.30	1001.48	1126.67
33.9	125.56	251.11	376.67	502.22	627.78	753.33	878.89	1004.44	1130.00
34.0	125.93	251.85	377.78	503.70	629.63	755.56	881.48	1007.41	1133.33
34.1	126.30	252.59	378.89	505.19	631.48	757.78	884.07	1010.37	1136.67
34.2	126.67	253.33	380.00	506.67	633.33	760.00	886.67	1013.33	1140.00
34.3	127.04	254.07	381.11	508.15	635.19	762.22	889.26	1016.30	1143.33
34.4	127.41	254.81	382.22	509.63	637.04	764.44	891.85	1019.26	1146.67
34.5	127.78	255.56	383.33	511.11	638.89	766.67	894.44	1022.22	1150.00
34.6	128.15	256.30	384.44	512.59	640.74	768.89	897.04	1025.19	1153.33
34.7	128.52	257.04	385.56	514.07	642.59	771.11	899.63	1028.15	1156.67
34.8	128.89	257.78	386.67	515.56	644.44	773.33	902.22	1031.11	1160.00
34.9	129.26	258.52	387.78	517.04	646.30	775.56	904.81	1034.07	1163.33
35.0	129.63	259.26	388.89	518.52	648.15	777.78	907.41	1037.04	1166.67
35.1	130.00	260.00	390.00	520.00	650.00	780.00	910.00	1040.00	1170.00
35.2	130.37	260.74	391.11	521.48	651.85	782.22	912.59	1042.96	1173.33
35.3	130.74	261.48	392.22	522.96	653.70	784.44	915.19	1045.93	1176.67
35.4	131.11	262.22	393.33	524.44	655.56	786.67	917.78	1048.89	1180.00
35.5	131.48	262.96	394.44	525.93	657.41	788.89	920.37	1051.85	1183.33
35.6	131.85	263.70	395.56	527.41	659.26	791.11	922.96	1054.81	1186.67
35.7	132.22	264.44	396.67	528.89	661.11	793.33	925.56	1057.78	1190.00
35.8	132.59	265.19	397.78	530.37	662.96	795.56	928.15	1060.74	1193.33
35.9	132.96	265.93	398.89	531.85	664.81	797.78	930.74	1063.70	1196.67
36.0	133.33	266.67	400.00	533.33	666.67	800.00	933.33	1066.67	1200.00
H. or B.	1	2	3	4	5	6	7	8	9

TABLE XXII. Rectangular Prisms.

H. or B.	1	2	3	4	5	6	7	8	9
36.1	133.70	267.41	401.11	534.81	668.52	802.22	935.93	1069.63	1203.33
36.2	134.07	268.15	402.22	536.30	670.37	804.44	938.52	1072.59	1206.67
36.3	134.44	268.89	403.33	537.78	672.22	806.67	941.11	1075.56	1210.00
36.4	134.81	269.63	404.44	539.26	674.07	808.89	943.70	1078.52	1213.33
36.5	135.19	270.37	405.56	540.74	675.93	811.11	946.30	1081.48	1216.67
36.6	135.56	271.11	406.67	542.22	677.78	813.33	948.89	1084.44	1220.00
36.7	135.93	271.85	407.78	543.70	679.63	815.56	951.48	1087.41	1223.33
36.8	136.30	272.59	408.89	545.19	681.48	817.78	954.07	1090.37	1226.67
36.9	136.67	273.33	410.00	546.67	683.33	820.00	956.67	1093.33	1230.00
37.0	137.04	274.07	411.11	548.15	685.19	822.22	959.26	1096.30	1233.33
37.1	137.41	274.81	412.22	549.63	687.04	824.44	961.85	1099.26	1236.67
37.2	137.78	275.56	413.33	551.11	688.89	826.67	964.44	1102.22	1240.00
37.3	138.15	276.30	414.44	552.59	690.74	828.89	967.04	1105.19	1243.33
37.4	138.52	277.04	415.56	554.07	692.59	831.11	969.63	1108.15	1246.67
37.5	138.89	277.78	416.67	555.56	694.44	833.33	972.22	1111.11	1250.00
37.6	139.26	278.52	417.78	557.04	696.30	835.56	974.81	1114.07	1253.33
37.7	139.63	279.26	418.89	558.52	698.15	837.78	977.41	1117.04	1256.67
37.8	140.00	280.00	420.00	560.00	700.00	840.00	980.00	1120.00	1260.00
37.9	140.37	280.74	421.11	561.48	701.85	842.22	982.59	1122.96	1263.33
38.0	140.74	281.48	422.22	562.96	703.70	844.44	985.19	1125.93	1266.67
38.1	141.11	282.22	423.33	564.44	705.56	846.67	987.78	1128.89	1270.00
38.2	141.48	282.96	424.44	565.93	707.41	848.89	990.37	1131.85	1273.33
38.3	141.85	283.70	425.56	567.41	709.26	851.11	992.96	1134.81	1276.67
38.4	142.22	284.44	426.67	568.89	711.11	853.33	995.56	1137.78	1280.00
38.5	142.59	285.19	427.78	570.37	712.96	855.56	998.15	1140.74	1283.33
38.6	142.96	285.93	428.89	571.85	714.81	857.78	1000.74	1143.70	1286.67
38.7	143.33	286.67	430.00	573.33	716.67	860.00	1003.33	1146.67	1290.00
38.8	143.70	287.41	431.11	574.81	718.52	862.22	1005.93	1149.63	1293.33
38.9	144.07	288.15	432.22	576.30	720.37	864.44	1008.52	1152.59	1296.67
39.0	144.44	288.89	433.33	577.78	722.22	866.67	1011.11	1155.56	1300.00
39.1	144.81	289.63	434.44	579.26	724.07	868.89	1013.70	1158.52	1303.33
39.2	145.19	290.37	435.56	580.74	725.93	871.11	1016.30	1161.48	1306.67
39.3	145.56	291.11	436.67	582.22	727.78	873.33	1018.89	1164.44	1310.00
39.4	145.93	291.85	437.78	583.70	729.63	875.56	1021.48	1167.41	1313.33
39.5	146.30	292.59	438.89	585.19	731.48	877.78	1024.07	1170.37	1316.67
39.6	146.67	293.33	440.00	586.67	733.33	880.00	1026.67	1173.33	1320.00
39.7	147.04	294.07	441.11	588.15	735.19	882.22	1029.26	1176.30	1323.33
39.8	147.41	294.81	442.22	589.63	737.04	884.44	1031.85	1179.26	1326.67
39.9	147.78	295.56	443.33	591.11	738.89	886.67	1034.44	1182.22	1330.00
40.0	148.15	296.30	444.44	592.59	740.74	888.89	1037.04	1185.19	1333.33
40.1	148.52	297.04	445.56	594.07	742.59	891.11	1039.63	1188.15	1336.67
40.2	148.89	297.78	446.67	595.56	744.44	893.33	1042.22	1191.11	1340.00
40.3	149.26	298.52	447.78	597.04	746.30	895.56	1044.81	1194.07	1343.33
40.4	149.63	299.26	448.89	598.52	748.15	897.78	1047.41	1197.04	1346.67
40.5	150.00	300.00	450.00	600.00	750.00	900.00	1050.00	1200.00	1350.00
40.6	150.37	300.74	451.11	601.48	751.85	902.22	1052.59	1202.96	1353.33
40.7	150.74	301.48	452.22	602.96	753.70	904.44	1055.19	1205.93	1356.67
40.8	151.11	302.22	453.33	604.44	755.56	906.67	1057.78	1208.89	1360.00
40.9	151.48	302.96	454.44	605.93	757.41	908.89	1060.37	1211.85	1363.33
41.0	151.85	303.70	455.56	607.41	759.26	911.11	1062.96	1214.81	1366.67
41.1	152.22	304.44	456.67	608.89	761.11	913.33	1065.56	1217.78	1370.00
41.2	152.59	305.19	457.78	610.37	762.96	915.56	1068.15	1220.74	1373.33
41.3	152.96	305.93	458.89	611.85	764.81	917.78	1070.74	1223.70	1376.67
41.4	153.33	306.67	460.00	613.33	766.67	920.00	1073.33	1226.67	1380.00
41.5	153.70	307.41	461.11	614.81	768.52	922.22	1075.93	1229.63	1383.33
41.6	154.07	308.15	462.22	616.30	770.37	924.44	1078.52	1232.59	1386.67
41.7	154.44	308.89	463.33	617.78	772.22	926.67	1081.11	1235.56	1390.00
41.8	154.81	309.63	464.44	619.26	774.07	928.89	1083.70	1238.52	1393.33
41.9	155.19	310.37	465.56	620.74	775.93	931.11	1086.30	1241.48	1396.67
42.0	155.56	311.11	466.67	622.22	777.78	933.33	1088.89	1244.44	1400.00
H. or B.	1	2	3	4	5	6	7	8	9

H. or B.	1	2	3	4	5	6	7	8	9
42.1	155.93	311.85	467.78	623.70	779.63	935.56	1091.48	1247.41	1403.33
42.2	156.30	312.59	468.89	625.19	781.48	937.78	1094.07	1250.37	1406.67
42.3	156.67	313.33	470.00	626.67	783.33	940.00	1096.67	1253.33	1410.00
42.4	157.04	314.07	471.11	628.15	785.19	942.22	1099.26	1256.30	1413.33
42.5	157.41	314.81	472.22	629.63	787.04	944.44	1101.85	1259.26	1416.67
42.6	157.78	315.56	473.33	631.11	788.89	946.67	1104.44	1262.22	1420.00
42.7	158.15	316.30	474.44	632.59	790.74	948.89	1107.04	1265.19	1423.33
42.8	158.52	317.04	475.56	634.07	792.59	951.11	1109.63	1268.15	1426.67
42.9	158.89	317.78	476.67	635.56	794.44	953.33	1112.22	1271.11	1430.00
43.0	159.26	318.52	477.78	637.04	796.30	955.56	1114.81	1274.07	1433.33
43.1	159.63	319.26	478.89	638.52	798.15	957.78	1117.41	1277.04	1436.67
43.2	160.00	320.00	480.00	640.00	800.00	960.00	1120.00	1280.00	1440.00
43.3	160.37	320.74	481.11	641.48	801.85	962.22	1122.59	1282.96	1443.33
43.4	160.74	321.48	482.22	642.96	803.70	964.44	1125.19	1285.93	1446.67
43.5	161.11	322.22	483.33	644.44	805.56	966.67	1127.78	1288.89	1450.00
43.6	161.48	322.96	484.44	645.93	807.41	968.89	1130.37	1291.85	1453.33
43.7	161.85	323.70	485.56	647.41	809.26	971.11	1132.96	1294.81	1456.67
43.8	162.22	324.44	486.67	648.89	811.11	973.33	1135.56	1297.78	1460.00
43.9	162.59	325.19	487.78	650.37	812.96	975.56	1138.15	1300.74	1463.33
44.0	162.96	325.93	488.89	651.85	814.81	977.78	1140.74	1303.70	1466.67
44.1	163.33	326.67	490.00	653.33	816.67	980.00	1143.33	1306.67	1470.00
44.2	163.70	327.41	491.11	654.81	818.52	982.22	1145.93	1309.63	1473.33
44.3	164.07	328.15	492.22	656.30	820.37	984.44	1148.52	1312.59	1476.67
44.4	164.44	328.89	493.33	657.78	822.22	986.67	1151.11	1315.56	1480.00
44.5	164.81	329.63	494.44	659.26	824.07	988.89	1153.70	1318.52	1483.33
44.6	165.19	330.37	495.56	660.74	825.93	991.11	1156.30	1321.48	1486.67
44.7	165.56	331.11	496.67	662.22	827.78	993.33	1158.89	1324.44	1490.00
44.8	165.93	331.85	497.78	663.70	829.63	995.56	1161.48	1327.41	1493.33
44.9	166.30	332.59	498.89	665.19	831.48	997.78	1164.07	1330.37	1496.67
45.0	166.67	333.33	500.00	666.67	833.33	1000.00	1166.67	1333.33	1500.00
45.1	167.04	334.07	501.11	668.15	835.19	1002.22	1169.26	1336.30	1503.33
45.2	167.41	334.81	502.22	669.63	837.04	1004.44	1171.85	1339.26	1506.67
45.3	167.78	335.56	503.33	671.11	838.89	1006.67	1174.44	1342.22	1510.00
45.4	168.15	336.30	504.44	672.59	840.74	1008.89	1177.04	1345.19	1513.33
45.5	168.52	337.04	505.56	674.07	842.59	1011.11	1179.63	1348.15	1516.67
45.6	168.89	337.78	506.67	675.56	844.44	1013.33	1182.22	1351.11	1520.00
45.7	169.26	338.52	507.78	677.04	846.30	1015.56	1184.81	1354.07	1523.33
45.8	169.63	339.26	508.89	678.52	848.15	1017.78	1187.41	1357.04	1526.67
45.9	170.00	340.00	510.00	680.00	850.00	1020.00	1190.00	1360.00	1530.00
46.0	170.37	340.74	511.11	681.48	851.85	1022.22	1192.59	1362.96	1533.33
46.1	170.74	341.48	512.22	682.96	853.70	1024.44	1195.19	1365.93	1536.67
46.2	171.11	342.22	513.33	684.44	855.56	1026.67	1197.78	1368.89	1540.00
46.3	171.48	342.96	514.44	685.93	857.41	1028.89	1200.37	1371.85	1543.33
46.4	171.85	343.70	515.56	687.41	859.26	1031.11	1202.96	1374.81	1546.67
46.5	172.22	344.44	516.67	688.89	861.11	1033.33	1205.56	1377.78	1550.00
46.6	172.59	345.19	517.78	690.37	862.96	1035.56	1208.15	1380.74	1553.33
46.7	172.96	345.93	518.89	691.85	864.81	1037.78	1210.74	1383.70	1556.67
46.8	173.33	346.67	520.00	693.33	866.67	1040.00	1213.33	1386.67	1560.00
46.9	173.70	347.41	521.11	694.81	868.52	1042.22	1215.93	1389.63	1563.33
47.0	174.07	348.15	522.22	696.30	870.37	1044.44	1218.52	1392.59	1566.67
47.1	174.44	348.89	523.33	697.78	872.22	1046.67	1221.11	1395.56	1570.00
47.2	174.81	349.63	524.44	699.26	874.07	1048.89	1223.70	1398.52	1573.33
47.3	175.19	350.37	525.56	700.74	875.93	1051.11	1226.30	1401.48	1576.67
47.4	175.56	351.11	526.67	702.22	877.78	1053.33	1228.89	1404.44	1580.00
47.5	175.93	351.85	527.78	703.70	879.63	1055.56	1231.48	1407.41	1583.33
47.6	176.30	352.59	528.89	705.19	881.48	1057.78	1234.07	1410.37	1586.67
47.7	176.67	353.33	530.00	706.67	883.33	1060.00	1236.67	1413.33	1590.00
47.8	177.04	354.07	531.11	708.15	885.19	1062.22	1239.26	1416.30	1593.33
47.9	177.41	354.81	532.22	709.63	887.04	1064.44	1241.85	1419.26	1596.67
48.0	177.78	355.56	533.33	711.11	888.89	1066.67	1244.44	1422.22	1600.00
H. or B.	1	2	3	4	5	6	7	8	9

TABLE XXII. **Rectangular Prisms.**

H. or B.	1	2	3	4	5	6	7	8	9
48.1	178.15	356.30	534.44	712.59	890.74	1068.89	1247.04	1425.19	1603.33
48.2	178.52	357.04	535.56	714.07	892.59	1071.11	1249.63	1428.15	1606.67
48.3	178.89	357.78	536.67	715.56	894.44	1073.33	1252.22	1431.11	1610.00
48.4	179.26	358.52	537.78	717.04	896.30	1075.56	1254.81	1434.07	1613.33
48.5	179.63	359.26	538.89	718.52	898.15	1077.78	1257.41	1437.04	1616.67
48.6	180.00	360.00	540.00	720.00	900.00	1080.00	1260.00	1440.00	1620.00
48.7	180.37	360.74	541.11	721.48	901.85	1082.22	1262.59	1442.96	1623.33
48.8	180.74	361.48	542.22	722.96	903.70	1084.44	1265.19	1445.93	1626.67
48.9	181.11	362.22	543.33	724.44	905.56	1086.67	1267.78	1448.89	1630.00
49.0	181.48	362.96	544.44	725.93	907.41	1088.89	1270.37	1451.85	1633.33
49.1	181.85	363.70	545.56	727.41	909.26	1091.11	1272.96	1454.81	1636.67
49.2	182.22	364.44	546.67	728.89	911.11	1093.33	1275.56	1457.78	1640.00
49.3	182.59	365.19	547.78	730.37	912.96	1095.56	1278.15	1460.74	1643.33
49.4	182.96	365.93	548.89	731.85	914.81	1097.78	1280.74	1463.70	1646.67
49.5	183.33	366.67	550.00	733.33	916.67	1100.00	1283.33	1466.67	1650.00
49.6	183.70	367.41	551.11	734.81	918.52	1102.22	1285.93	1469.63	1653.33
49.7	184.07	368.15	552.22	736.30	920.37	1104.44	1288.52	1472.59	1656.67
49.8	184.44	368.89	553.33	737.78	922.22	1106.67	1291.11	1475.56	1660.00
49.9	184.81	369.63	554.44	739.26	924.07	1108.89	1293.70	1478.52	1663.33
50.0	185.19	370.37	555.56	740.74	925.93	1111.11	1296.30	1481.48	1666.67
50.1	185.56	371.11	556.67	742.22	927.78	1113.33	1298.89	1484.44	1670.00
50.2	185.93	371.85	557.78	743.70	929.63	1115.56	1301.48	1487.41	1673.33
50.3	186.30	372.59	558.89	745.19	931.48	1117.78	1304.07	1490.37	1676.67
50.4	186.67	373.33	560.00	746.67	933.33	1120.00	1306.67	1493.33	1680.00
50.5	187.04	374.07	561.11	748.15	935.19	1122.22	1309.26	1496.30	1683.33
50.6	187.41	374.81	562.22	749.63	937.04	1124.44	1311.85	1499.26	1686.67
50.7	187.78	375.56	563.33	751.11	938.89	1126.67	1314.44	1502.22	1690.00
50.8	188.15	376.30	564.44	752.59	940.74	1128.89	1317.04	1505.19	1693.33
50.9	188.52	377.04	565.56	754.07	942.59	1131.11	1319.63	1508.15	1696.67
51.0	188.89	377.78	566.67	755.56	944.44	1133.33	1322.22	1511.11	1700.00
51.1	189.26	378.52	567.78	757.04	946.30	1135.56	1324.81	1514.07	1703.33
51.2	189.63	379.26	568.89	758.52	948.15	1137.78	1327.41	1517.04	1706.67
51.3	190.00	380.00	570.00	760.00	950.00	1140.00	1330.00	1520.00	1710.00
51.4	190.37	380.74	571.11	761.48	951.85	1142.22	1332.59	1522.96	1713.33
51.5	190.74	381.48	572.22	762.96	953.70	1144.44	1335.19	1525.93	1716.67
51.6	191.11	382.22	573.33	764.44	955.56	1146.67	1337.78	1528.89	1720.00
51.7	191.48	382.96	574.44	765.93	957.41	1148.89	1340.37	1531.85	1723.33
51.8	191.85	383.70	575.56	767.41	959.26	1151.11	1342.96	1534.81	1726.67
51.9	192.22	384.44	576.67	768.89	961.11	1153.33	1345.56	1537.78	1730.00
52.0	192.59	385.19	577.78	770.37	962.96	1155.56	1348.15	1540.74	1733.33
52.1	192.96	385.93	578.89	771.85	964.81	1157.78	1350.74	1543.70	1736.67
52.2	193.33	386.67	580.00	773.33	966.67	1160.00	1353.33	1546.67	1740.00
52.3	193.70	387.41	581.11	774.81	968.52	1162.22	1355.93	1549.63	1743.33
52.4	194.07	388.15	582.22	776.30	970.37	1164.44	1358.52	1552.59	1746.67
52.5	194.44	388.89	583.33	777.78	972.22	1166.67	1361.11	1555.56	1750.00
52.6	194.81	389.63	584.44	779.26	974.07	1168.89	1363.70	1558.52	1753.33
52.7	195.19	390.37	585.56	780.74	975.93	1171.11	1366.30	1561.48	1756.67
52.8	195.56	391.11	586.67	782.22	977.78	1173.33	1368.89	1564.44	1760.00
52.9	195.93	391.85	587.78	783.70	979.63	1175.56	1371.48	1567.41	1763.33
53.0	196.30	392.59	588.89	785.19	981.48	1177.78	1374.07	1570.37	1766.67
53.1	196.67	393.33	590.00	786.67	983.33	1180.00	1376.67	1573.33	1770.00
53.2	197.04	394.07	591.11	788.15	985.19	1182.22	1379.26	1576.30	1773.33
53.3	197.41	394.81	592.22	789.63	987.04	1184.44	1381.85	1579.26	1776.67
53.4	197.78	395.56	593.33	791.11	988.89	1186.67	1384.44	1582.22	1780.00
53.5	198.15	396.30	594.44	792.59	990.74	1188.89	1387.04	1585.19	1783.33
53.6	198.52	397.04	595.56	794.07	992.59	1191.11	1389.63	1588.15	1786.67
53.7	198.89	397.78	596.67	795.56	994.44	1193.33	1392.22	1591.11	1790.00
53.8	199.26	398.52	597.78	797.04	996.30	1195.56	1394.81	1594.07	1793.33
53.9	199.63	399.26	598.89	798.52	998.15	1197.78	1397.41	1597.04	1796.67
54.0	200.00	400.00	600.00	800.00	1000.00	1200.00	1400.00	1600.00	1800.00
H. or B.	1	2	3	4	5	6	7	8	9

TABLE XXII. Rectangular Prisms.

H. or B.	1	2	3	4	5	6	7	8	9
54.1	200.37	400.74	601.11	801.48	1001.85	1202.22	1402.59	1602.96	1803.33
54.2	200.74	401.48	602.22	802.96	1003.70	1204.44	1405.19	1605.93	1806.67
54.3	201.11	402.22	603.33	804.44	1005.56	1206.67	1407.78	1608.89	1810.00
54.4	201.48	402.96	604.44	805.93	1007.41	1208.89	1410.37	1611.85	1813.33
54.5	201.85	403.70	605.56	807.41	1009.26	1211.11	1412.96	1614.81	1816.67
54.6	202.22	404.44	606.67	808.89	1011.11	1213.33	1415.56	1617.78	1820.00
54.7	202.59	405.19	607.78	810.37	1012.96	1215.56	1418.15	1620.74	1823.33
54.8	202.96	405.93	608.89	811.85	1014.81	1217.78	1420.74	1623.70	1826.67
54.9	203.33	406.67	610.00	813.33	1016.67	1220.00	1423.33	1626.67	1830.00
55.0	203.70	407.41	611.11	814.81	1018.52	1222.22	1425.93	1629.63	1833.33
55.1	204.07	408.15	612.22	816.30	1020.37	1224.44	1428.52	1632.59	1836.67
55.2	204.44	408.89	613.33	817.78	1022.22	1226.67	1431.11	1635.56	1840.00
55.3	204.81	409.63	614.44	819.26	1024.07	1228.89	1433.70	1638.52	1843.33
55.4	205.19	410.37	615.56	820.74	1025.93	1231.11	1436.30	1641.48	1846.67
55.5	205.56	411.11	616.67	822.22	1027.78	1233.33	1438.89	1644.44	1850.00
55.6	205.93	411.85	617.78	823.70	1029.63	1235.56	1441.48	1647.41	1853.33
55.7	206.30	412.59	618.89	825.19	1031.48	1237.78	1444.07	1650.37	1856.67
55.8	206.67	413.33	620.00	826.67	1033.33	1240.00	1446.67	1653.33	1860.00
55.9	207.04	414.07	621.11	828.15	1035.19	1242.22	1449.26	1656.30	1863.33
56.0	207.41	414.81	622.22	829.63	1037.04	1244.44	1451.85	1659.26	1866.67
56.1	207.78	415.56	623.33	831.11	1038.89	1246.67	1454.44	1662.22	1870.00
56.2	208.15	416.30	624.44	832.59	1040.74	1248.89	1457.04	1665.19	1873.33
56.3	208.52	417.04	625.56	834.07	1042.59	1251.11	1459.63	1668.15	1876.67
56.4	208.89	417.78	626.67	835.56	1044.44	1253.33	1462.22	1671.11	1880.00
56.5	209.26	418.52	627.78	837.04	1046.30	1255.56	1464.81	1674.07	1883.33
56.6	209.63	419.26	628.89	838.52	1048.15	1257.78	1467.41	1677.04	1886.67
56.7	210.00	420.00	630.00	840.00	1050.00	1260.00	1470.00	1680.00	1890.00
56.8	210.37	420.74	631.11	841.48	1051.85	1262.22	1472.59	1682.96	1893.33
56.9	210.74	421.48	632.22	842.96	1053.70	1264.44	1475.19	1685.93	1896.67
57.0	211.11	422.22	633.33	844.44	1055.56	1266.67	1477.78	1688.89	1900.00
57.1	211.48	422.96	634.44	845.93	1057.41	1268.89	1480.37	1691.85	1903.33
57.2	211.85	423.70	635.56	847.41	1059.26	1271.11	1482.96	1694.81	1906.67
57.3	212.22	424.44	636.67	848.89	1061.11	1273.33	1485.56	1697.78	1910.00
57.4	212.59	425.19	637.78	850.37	1062.96	1275.56	1488.15	1700.74	1913.33
57.5	212.96	425.93	638.89	851.85	1064.81	1277.78	1490.74	1703.70	1916.67
57.6	213.33	426.67	640.00	853.33	1066.67	1280.00	1493.33	1706.67	1920.00
57.7	213.70	427.41	641.11	854.81	1068.52	1282.22	1495.93	1709.63	1923.33
57.8	214.07	428.15	642.22	856.30	1070.37	1284.44	1498.52	1712.59	1926.67
57.9	214.44	428.89	643.33	857.78	1072.22	1286.67	1501.11	1715.56	1930.00
58.0	214.81	429.63	644.44	859.26	1074.07	1288.89	1503.70	1718.52	1933.33
58.1	215.19	430.37	645.56	860.74	1075.93	1291.11	1506.30	1721.48	1936.67
58.2	215.56	431.11	646.67	862.22	1077.78	1293.33	1508.89	1724.44	1940.00
58.3	215.93	431.85	647.78	863.70	1079.63	1295.56	1511.48	1727.41	1943.33
58.4	216.30	432.59	648.89	865.19	1081.48	1297.78	1514.07	1730.37	1946.67
58.5	216.67	433.33	650.00	866.67	1083.33	1300.00	1516.67	1733.33	1950.00
58.6	217.04	434.07	651.11	868.15	1085.19	1302.22	1519.26	1736.30	1953.33
58.7	217.41	434.81	652.22	869.63	1087.04	1304.44	1521.85	1739.26	1956.67
58.8	217.78	435.56	653.33	871.11	1088.89	1306.67	1524.44	1742.22	1960.00
58.9	218.15	436.30	654.44	872.59	1090.74	1308.89	1527.04	1745.19	1963.33
59.0	218.52	437.04	655.56	874.07	1092.59	1311.11	1529.63	1748.15	1966.67
59.1	218.89	437.78	656.67	875.56	1094.44	1313.33	1532.22	1751.11	1970.00
59.2	219.26	438.52	657.78	877.04	1096.30	1315.56	1534.81	1754.07	1973.33
59.3	219.63	439.26	658.89	878.52	1098.15	1317.78	1537.41	1757.04	1976.67
59.4	220.00	440.00	660.00	880.00	1100.00	1320.00	1540.00	1760.00	1980.00
59.5	220.37	440.74	661.11	881.48	1101.85	1322.22	1542.59	1762.96	1983.33
59.6	220.74	441.48	662.22	882.96	1103.70	1324.44	1545.19	1765.93	1986.67
59.7	221.11	442.22	663.33	884.44	1105.56	1326.67	1547.78	1768.89	1990.00
59.8	221.48	442.96	664.44	885.93	1107.41	1328.89	1550.37	1771.85	1993.33
59.9	221.85	443.70	665.56	887.41	1109.26	1331.11	1552.96	1774.81	1996.67
60.0	222.22	444.44	666.67	888.89	1111.11	1333.33	1555.56	1777.78	2000.00
H. or B.	1	2	3	4	5	6	7	8	9

TABLE XXII. Rectangular Prisms.

H. or B.	1	2	3	4	5	6	7	8	9
60.1	222.59	445.19	667.78	890.37	1112.96	1335.56	1558.15	1780.74	2003.33
60.2	222.96	445.93	668.89	891.85	1114.81	1337.78	1560.74	1783.70	2006.67
60.3	223.33	446.67	670.00	893.33	1116.67	1340.00	1563.33	1786.67	2010.00
60.4	223.70	447.41	671.11	894.81	1118.52	1342.22	1565.93	1789.63	2013.33
60.5	224.07	448.15	672.22	896.30	1120.37	1344.44	1568.52	1792.59	2016.67
60.6	224.44	448.89	673.33	897.78	1122.22	1346.67	1571.11	1795.56	2020.00
60.7	224.81	449.63	674.44	899.26	1124.07	1348.89	1573.70	1798.52	2023.33
60.8	225.19	450.37	675.56	900.74	1125.93	1351.11	1576.30	1801.48	2026.67
60.9	225.56	451.11	676.67	902.22	1127.78	1353.33	1578.89	1804.44	2030.00
61.0	225.93	451.85	677.78	903.70	1129.63	1355.56	1581.48	1807.41	2033.33
61.1	226.30	452.59	678.89	905.19	1131.48	1357.78	1584.07	1810.37	2036.67
61.2	226.67	453.33	680.00	906.67	1133.33	1360.00	1586.67	1813.33	2040.00
61.3	227.04	454.07	681.11	908.15	1135.19	1362.22	1589.26	1816.30	2043.33
61.4	227.41	454.81	682.22	909.63	1137.04	1364.44	1591.85	1819.26	2046.67
61.5	227.78	455.56	683.33	911.11	1138.89	1366.67	1594.44	1822.22	2050.00
61.6	228.15	456.30	684.44	912.59	1140.74	1368.89	1597.04	1825.19	2053.33
61.7	228.52	457.04	685.56	914.07	1142.59	1371.11	1599.63	1828.15	2056.67
61.8	228.89	457.78	686.67	915.56	1144.44	1373.33	1602.22	1831.11	2060.00
61.9	229.26	458.52	687.78	917.04	1146.30	1375.56	1604.81	1834.07	2063.33
62.0	229.63	459.26	688.89	918.52	1148.15	1377.78	1607.41	1837.04	2066.67
62.1	230.00	460.00	690.00	920.00	1150.00	1380.00	1610.00	1840.00	2070.00
62.2	230.37	460.74	691.11	921.48	1151.85	1382.22	1612.59	1842.96	2073.33
62.3	230.74	461.48	692.22	922.96	1153.70	1384.44	1615.19	1845.93	2076.67
62.4	231.11	462.22	693.33	924.44	1155.56	1386.67	1617.78	1848.89	2080.00
62.5	231.48	462.96	694.44	925.93	1157.41	1388.89	1620.37	1851.85	2083.33
62.6	231.85	463.70	695.56	927.41	1159.26	1391.11	1622.96	1854.81	2086.67
62.7	232.22	464.44	696.67	928.89	1161.11	1393.33	1625.56	1857.78	2090.00
62.8	232.59	465.19	697.78	930.37	1162.96	1395.56	1628.15	1860.74	2093.33
62.9	232.96	465.93	698.89	931.85	1164.81	1397.78	1630.74	1863.70	2096.67
63.0	233.33	466.67	700.00	933.33	1166.67	1400.00	1633.33	1866.67	2100.00
63.1	233.70	467.41	701.11	934.81	1168.52	1402.22	1635.93	1869.63	2103.33
63.2	234.07	468.15	702.22	936.30	1170.37	1404.44	1638.52	1872.59	2106.67
63.3	234.44	468.89	703.33	937.78	1172.22	1406.67	1641.11	1875.56	2110.00
63.4	234.81	469.63	704.44	939.26	1174.07	1408.89	1643.70	1878.52	2113.33
63.5	235.19	470.37	705.56	940.74	1175.93	1411.11	1646.30	1881.48	2116.67
63.6	235.56	471.11	706.67	942.22	1177.78	1413.33	1648.89	1884.44	2120.00
63.7	235.93	471.85	707.78	943.70	1179.63	1415.56	1651.48	1887.41	2123.33
63.8	236.30	472.59	708.89	945.19	1181.48	1417.78	1654.07	1890.37	2126.67
63.9	236.67	473.33	710.00	946.67	1183.33	1420.00	1656.67	1893.33	2130.00
64.0	237.04	474.07	711.11	948.15	1185.19	1422.22	1659.26	1896.30	2133.33
64.1	237.41	474.81	712.22	949.63	1187.04	1424.44	1661.85	1899.26	2136.67
64.2	237.78	475.56	713.33	951.11	1188.89	1426.67	1664.44	1902.22	2140.00
64.3	238.15	476.30	714.44	952.59	1190.74	1428.89	1667.04	1905.19	2143.33
64.4	238.52	477.04	715.56	954.07	1192.59	1431.11	1669.63	1908.15	2146.67
64.5	238.89	477.78	716.67	955.56	1194.44	1433.33	1672.22	1911.11	2150.00
64.6	239.26	478.52	717.78	957.04	1196.30	1435.56	1674.81	1914.07	2153.33
64.7	239.63	479.26	718.89	958.52	1198.15	1437.78	1677.41	1917.04	2156.67
64.8	240.00	480.00	720.00	960.00	1200.00	1440.00	1680.00	1920.00	2160.00
64.9	240.37	480.74	721.11	961.48	1201.85	1442.22	1682.59	1922.96	2163.33
65.0	240.74	481.48	722.22	962.96	1203.70	1444.44	1685.19	1925.93	2166.67
65.1	241.11	482.22	723.33	964.44	1205.56	1446.67	1687.78	1928.89	2170.00
65.2	241.48	482.96	724.44	965.93	1207.41	1448.89	1690.37	1931.85	2173.33
65.3	241.85	483.70	725.56	967.41	1209.26	1451.11	1692.96	1934.81	2176.67
65.4	242.22	484.44	726.67	968.89	1211.11	1453.33	1695.56	1937.78	2180.00
65.5	242.59	485.19	727.78	970.37	1212.96	1455.56	1698.15	1940.74	2183.33
65.6	242.96	485.93	728.89	971.85	1214.81	1457.78	1700.74	1943.70	2186.67
65.7	243.33	486.67	730.00	973.33	1216.67	1460.00	1703.33	1946.67	2190.00
65.8	243.70	487.41	731.11	974.81	1218.52	1462.22	1705.93	1949.63	2193.33
65.9	244.07	488.15	732.22	976.30	1220.37	1464.44	1708.52	1952.59	2196.67
66.0	244.44	488.89	733.33	977.78	1222.22	1466.67	1711.11	1955.56	2200.00
H. or B.	1	2	3	4	5	6	7	8	9

H. or B.	1	2	3	4	5	6	7	8	9
66.1	244.81	489.63	734.44	979.26	1224.07	1468.89	1713.70	1958.52	2203.33
66.2	245.19	490.37	735.56	980.74	1225.93	1471.11	1716.30	1961.48	2206.67
66.3	245.56	491.11	736.67	982.22	1227.78	1473.33	1718.89	1964.44	2210.00
66.4	245.93	491.85	737.78	983.70	1229.63	1475.56	1721.48	1967.41	2213.33
66.5	246.30	492.59	738.89	985.19	1231.48	1477.78	1724.07	1970.37	2216.67
66.6	246.67	493.33	740.00	986.67	1233.33	1480.00	1726.67	1973.33	2220.00
66.7	247.04	494.07	741.11	988.15	1235.19	1482.22	1729.26	1976.30	2223.33
66.8	247.41	494.81	742.22	989.63	1237.04	1484.44	1731.85	1979.26	2226.67
66.9	247.78	495.56	743.33	991.11	1238.89	1486.67	1734.44	1982.22	2230.00
67.0	248.15	496.30	744.44	992.59	1240.74	1488.89	1737.04	1985.19	2233.33
67.1	248.52	497.04	745.56	994.07	1242.59	1491.11	1739.63	1988.15	2236.67
67.2	248.89	497.78	746.67	995.56	1244.44	1493.33	1742.22	1991.11	2240.00
67.3	249.26	498.52	747.78	997.04	1246.30	1495.56	1744.81	1994.07	2243.33
67.4	249.63	499.26	748.89	998.52	1248.15	1497.78	1747.41	1997.04	2246.67
67.5	250.00	500.00	750.00	1000.00	1250.00	1500.00	1750.00	2000.00	2250.00
67.6	250.37	500.74	751.11	1001.48	1251.85	1502.22	1752.59	2002.96	2253.33
67.7	250.74	501.48	752.22	1002.96	1253.70	1504.44	1755.19	2005.93	2256.67
67.8	251.11	502.22	753.33	1004.44	1255.56	1506.67	1757.78	2008.89	2260.00
67.9	251.48	502.96	754.44	1005.93	1257.41	1508.89	1760.37	2011.85	2263.33
68.0	251.85	503.70	755.56	1007.41	1259.26	1511.11	1762.96	2014.81	2266.67
68.1	252.22	504.44	756.67	1008.89	1261.11	1513.33	1765.56	2017.78	2270.00
68.2	252.59	505.19	757.78	1010.37	1262.96	1515.56	1768.15	2020.74	2273.33
68.3	252.96	505.93	758.89	1011.85	1264.81	1517.78	1770.74	2023.70	2276.67
68.4	253.33	506.67	760.00	1013.33	1266.67	1520.00	1773.33	2026.67	2280.00
68.5	253.70	507.41	761.11	1014.81	1268.52	1522.22	1775.93	2029.63	2283.33
68.6	254.07	508.15	762.22	1016.30	1270.37	1524.44	1778.52	2032.59	2286.67
68.7	254.44	508.89	763.33	1017.78	1272.22	1526.67	1781.11	2035.56	2290.00
68.8	254.81	509.63	764.44	1019.26	1274.07	1528.89	1783.70	2038.52	2293.33
68.9	255.19	510.37	765.56	1020.74	1275.93	1531.11	1786.30	2041.48	2296.67
69.0	255.56	511.11	766.67	1022.22	1277.78	1533.33	1788.89	2044.44	2300.00
69.1	255.93	511.85	767.78	1023.70	1279.63	1535.56	1791.48	2047.41	2303.33
69.2	256.30	512.59	768.89	1025.19	1281.48	1537.78	1794.07	2050.37	2306.67
69.3	256.67	513.33	770.00	1026.67	1283.33	1540.00	1796.67	2053.33	2310.00
69.4	257.04	514.07	771.11	1028.15	1285.19	1542.22	1799.26	2056.30	2313.33
69.5	257.41	514.81	772.22	1029.63	1287.04	1544.44	1801.85	2059.26	2316.67
69.6	257.78	515.56	773.33	1031.11	1288.89	1546.67	1804.44	2062.22	2320.00
69.7	258.15	516.30	774.44	1032.59	1290.74	1548.89	1807.04	2065.19	2323.33
69.8	258.52	517.04	775.56	1034.07	1292.59	1551.11	1809.63	2068.15	2326.67
69.9	258.89	517.78	776.67	1035.56	1294.44	1553.33	1812.22	2071.11	2330.00
70.0	259.26	518.52	777.78	1037.04	1296.30	1555.56	1814.81	2074.07	2333.33
70.1	259.63	519.26	778.89	1038.52	1298.15	1557.78	1817.41	2077.04	2336.67
70.2	260.00	520.00	780.00	1040.00	1300.00	1560.00	1820.00	2080.00	2340.00
70.3	260.37	520.74	781.11	1041.48	1301.85	1562.22	1822.59	2082.96	2343.33
70.4	260.74	521.48	782.22	1042.96	1303.70	1564.44	1825.19	2085.93	2346.67
70.5	261.11	522.22	783.33	1044.44	1305.56	1566.67	1827.78	2088.89	2350.00
70.6	261.48	522.96	784.44	1045.93	1307.41	1568.89	1830.37	2091.85	2353.33
70.7	261.85	523.70	785.56	1047.41	1309.26	1571.11	1832.96	2094.81	2356.67
70.8	262.22	524.44	786.67	1048.89	1311.11	1573.33	1835.56	2097.78	2360.00
70.9	262.59	525.19	787.78	1050.37	1312.96	1575.56	1838.15	2100.74	2363.33
71.0	262.96	525.93	788.89	1051.85	1314.81	1577.78	1840.74	2103.70	2366.67
71.1	263.33	526.67	790.00	1053.33	1316.67	1580.00	1843.33	2106.67	2370.00
71.2	263.70	527.41	791.11	1054.81	1318.52	1582.22	1845.93	2109.63	2373.33
71.3	264.07	528.15	792.22	1056.30	1320.37	1584.44	1848.52	2112.59	2376.67
71.4	264.44	528.89	793.33	1057.78	1322.22	1586.67	1851.11	2115.56	2380.00
71.5	264.81	529.63	794.44	1059.26	1324.07	1588.89	1853.70	2118.52	2383.33
71.6	265.19	530.37	795.56	1060.74	1325.93	1591.11	1856.30	2121.48	2386.67
71.7	265.56	531.11	796.67	1062.22	1327.78	1593.33	1858.89	2124.44	2390.00
71.8	265.93	531.85	797.78	1063.70	1329.63	1595.56	1861.48	2127.41	2393.33
71.9	266.30	532.59	798.89	1065.19	1331.48	1597.78	1864.07	2130.37	2396.67
72.0	266.67	533.33	800.00	1066.67	1333.33	1600.00	1866.67	2133.33	2400.00
H. or B.	1	2	3	4	5	6	7	8	9

H. or B.	1	2	3	4	5	6	7	8	9
72.1	267.04	534.07	801.11	1068.15	1335.19	1602.22	1869.26	2136.30	2403.33
72.2	267.41	534.81	802.22	1069.63	1337.04	1604.44	1871.85	2139.26	2406.67
72.3	267.78	535.56	803.33	1071.11	1338.89	1606.67	1874.44	2142.22	2410.00
72.4	268.15	536.30	804.44	1072.59	1340.74	1608.89	1877.04	2145.19	2413.33
72.5	268.52	537.04	805.56	1074.07	1342.59	1611.11	1879.63	2148.15	2416.67
72.6	268.89	537.78	806.67	1075.56	1344.44	1613.33	1882.22	2151.11	2420.00
72.7	269.26	538.52	807.78	1077.04	1346.30	1615.56	1884.81	2154.07	2423.33
72.8	269.63	539.26	808.89	1078.52	1348.15	1617.78	1887.41	2157.04	2426.67
72.9	270.00	540.00	810.00	1080.00	1350.00	1620.00	1890.00	2160.00	2430.00
73.0	270.37	540.74	811.11	1081.48	1351.85	1622.22	1892.59	2162.96	2433.33
73.1	270.74	541.48	812.22	1082.96	1353.70	1624.44	1895.19	2165.93	2436.67
73.2	271.11	542.22	813.33	1084.44	1355.56	1626.67	1897.78	2168.89	2440.00
73.3	271.48	542.96	814.44	1085.93	1357.41	1628.89	1900.37	2171.85	2443.33
73.4	271.85	543.70	815.56	1087.41	1359.26	1631.11	1902.96	2174.81	2446.67
73.5	272.22	544.44	816.67	1088.89	1361.11	1633.33	1905.56	2177.78	2450.00
73.6	272.59	545.19	817.78	1090.37	1362.96	1635.56	1908.15	2180.74	2453.33
73.7	272.96	545.93	818.89	1091.85	1364.81	1637.78	1910.74	2183.70	2456.67
73.8	273.33	546.67	820.00	1093.33	1366.67	1640.00	1913.33	2186.67	2460.00
73.9	273.70	547.41	821.11	1094.81	1368.52	1642.22	1915.93	2189.63	2463.33
74.0	274.07	548.15	822.22	1096.30	1370.37	1644.44	1918.52	2192.59	2466.67
74.1	274.44	548.89	823.33	1097.78	1372.22	1646.67	1921.11	2195.56	2470.00
74.2	274.81	549.63	824.44	1099.26	1374.07	1648.89	1923.70	2198.52	2473.33
74.3	275.19	550.37	825.56	1100.74	1375.93	1651.11	1926.30	2201.48	2476.67
74.4	275.56	551.11	826.67	1102.22	1377.78	1653.33	1928.89	2204.44	2480.00
74.5	275.93	551.85	827.78	1103.70	1379.63	1655.56	1931.48	2207.41	2483.33
74.6	276.30	552.59	828.89	1105.19	1381.48	1657.78	1934.07	2210.37	2486.67
74.7	276.67	553.33	830.00	1106.67	1383.33	1660.00	1936.67	2213.33	2490.00
74.8	277.04	554.07	831.11	1108.15	1385.19	1662.22	1939.26	2216.30	2493.33
74.9	277.41	554.81	832.22	1109.63	1387.04	1664.44	1941.85	2219.26	2496.67
75.0	277.78	555.56	833.33	1111.11	1388.89	1666.67	1944.44	2222.22	2500.00
75.1	278.15	556.30	834.44	1112.59	1390.74	1668.89	1947.04	2225.19	2503.33
75.2	278.52	557.04	835.56	1114.07	1392.59	1671.11	1949.63	2228.15	2506.67
75.3	278.89	557.78	836.67	1115.56	1394.44	1673.33	1952.22	2231.11	2510.00
75.4	279.26	558.52	837.78	1117.04	1396.30	1675.56	1954.81	2234.07	2513.33
75.5	279.63	559.26	838.89	1118.52	1398.15	1677.78	1957.41	2237.04	2516.67
75.6	280.00	560.00	840.00	1120.00	1400.00	1680.00	1960.00	2240.00	2520.00
75.7	280.37	560.74	841.11	1121.48	1401.85	1682.22	1962.59	2242.96	2523.33
75.8	280.74	561.48	842.22	1122.96	1403.70	1684.44	1965.19	2245.93	2526.67
75.9	281.11	562.22	843.33	1124.44	1405.56	1686.67	1967.78	2248.89	2530.00
76.0	281.48	562.96	844.44	1125.93	1407.41	1688.89	1970.37	2251.85	2533.33
76.1	281.85	563.70	845.56	1127.41	1409.26	1691.11	1972.96	2254.81	2536.67
76.2	282.22	564.44	846.67	1128.89	1411.11	1693.33	1975.56	2257.78	2540.00
76.3	282.59	565.19	847.78	1130.37	1412.96	1695.56	1978.15	2260.74	2543.33
76.4	282.96	565.93	848.89	1131.85	1414.81	1697.78	1980.74	2263.70	2546.67
76.5	283.33	566.67	850.00	1133.33	1416.67	1700.00	1983.33	2266.67	2550.00
76.6	283.70	567.41	851.11	1134.81	1418.52	1702.22	1985.93	2269.63	2553.33
76.7	284.07	568.15	852.22	1136.30	1420.37	1704.44	1988.52	2272.59	2556.67
76.8	284.44	568.89	853.33	1137.78	1422.22	1706.67	1991.11	2275.56	2560.00
76.9	284.81	569.63	854.44	1139.26	1424.07	1708.89	1993.70	2278.52	2563.33
77.0	285.19	570.37	855.56	1140.74	1425.93	1711.11	1996.30	2281.48	2566.67
77.1	285.56	571.11	856.67	1142.22	1427.78	1713.33	1998.89	2284.44	2570.00
77.2	285.93	571.85	857.78	1143.70	1429.63	1715.56	2001.48	2287.41	2573.33
77.3	286.30	572.59	858.89	1145.19	1431.48	1717.78	2004.07	2290.37	2576.67
77.4	286.67	573.33	860.00	1146.67	1433.33	1720.00	2006.67	2293.33	2580.00
77.5	287.04	574.07	861.11	1148.15	1435.19	1722.22	2009.26	2296.30	2583.33
77.6	287.41	574.81	862.22	1149.63	1437.04	1724.44	2011.85	2299.26	2586.67
77.7	287.78	575.56	863.33	1151.11	1438.89	1726.67	2014.44	2302.22	2590.00
77.8	288.15	576.30	864.44	1152.59	1440.74	1728.89	2017.04	2305.19	2593.33
77.9	288.52	577.04	865.56	1154.07	1442.59	1731.11	2019.63	2308.15	2596.67
78.0	288.89	577.78	866.67	1155.56	1444.44	1733.33	2022.22	2311.11	2600.00
H. or B.	1	2	3	4	5	6	7	8	9

TABLE XXII. Rectangular Prisms.

H. or B.	1	2	3	4	5	6	7	8	9
78.1	289.26	578.52	867.78	1157.04	1446.30	1735.56	2024.81	2314.07	2603.33
78.2	289.63	579.26	868.89	1158.52	1448.15	1737.78	2027.41	2317.04	2606.67
78.3	290.00	580.00	870.00	1160.00	1450.00	1740.00	2030.00	2320.00	2610.00
78.4	290.37	580.74	871.11	1161.48	1451.85	1742.22	2032.59	2322.96	2613.33
78.5	290.74	581.48	872.22	1162.96	1453.70	1744.44	2035.19	2325.93	2616.67
78.6	291.11	582.22	873.33	1164.44	1455.56	1746.67	2037.78	2328.89	2620.00
78.7	291.48	582.96	874.44	1165.93	1457.41	1748.89	2040.37	2331.85	2623.33
78.8	291.85	583.70	875.56	1167.41	1459.26	1751.11	2042.96	2334.81	2626.67
78.9	292.22	584.44	876.67	1168.89	1461.11	1753.33	2045.56	2337.78	2630.00
79.0	292.59	585.19	877.78	1170.37	1462.96	1755.56	2048.15	2340.74	2633.33
79.1	292.96	585.93	878.89	1171.85	1464.81	1757.78	2050.74	2343.70	2636.67
79.2	293.33	586.67	880.00	1173.33	1466.67	1760.00	2053.33	2346.67	2640.00
79.3	293.70	587.41	881.11	1174.81	1468.52	1762.22	2055.93	2349.63	2643.33
79.4	294.07	588.15	882.22	1176.30	1470.37	1764.44	2058.52	2352.59	2646.67
79.5	294.44	588.89	883.33	1177.78	1472.22	1766.67	2061.11	2355.56	2650.00
79.6	294.81	589.63	884.44	1179.26	1474.07	1768.89	2063.70	2358.52	2653.33
79.7	295.19	590.37	885.56	1180.74	1475.93	1771.11	2066.30	2361.48	2656.67
79.8	295.56	591.11	886.67	1182.22	1477.78	1773.33	2068.89	2364.44	2660.00
79.9	295.93	591.85	887.78	1183.70	1479.63	1775.56	2071.48	2367.41	2663.33
80.0	296.30	592.59	888.89	1185.19	1481.48	1777.78	2074.07	2370.37	2666.67
80.1	296.67	593.33	890.00	1186.67	1483.33	1780.00	2076.67	2373.33	2670.00
80.2	297.04	594.07	891.11	1188.15	1485.19	1782.22	2079.26	2376.30	2673.33
80.3	297.41	594.81	892.22	1189.63	1487.04	1784.44	2081.85	2379.26	2676.67
80.4	297.78	595.56	893.33	1191.11	1488.89	1786.67	2084.44	2382.22	2680.00
80.5	298.15	596.30	894.44	1192.59	1490.74	1788.89	2087.04	2385.19	2683.33
80.6	298.52	597.04	895.56	1194.07	1492.59	1791.11	2089.63	2388.15	2686.67
80.7	298.89	597.78	896.67	1195.56	1494.44	1793.33	2092.22	2391.11	2690.00
80.8	299.26	598.52	897.78	1197.04	1496.30	1795.56	2094.81	2394.07	2693.33
80.9	299.63	599.26	898.89	1198.52	1498.15	1797.78	2097.41	2397.04	2696.67
81.0	300.00	600.00	900.00	1200.00	1500.00	1800.00	2100.00	2400.00	2700.00
81.1	300.37	600.74	901.11	1201.48	1501.85	1802.22	2102.59	2402.96	2703.33
81.2	300.74	601.48	902.22	1202.96	1503.70	1804.44	2105.19	2405.93	2706.67
81.3	301.11	602.22	903.33	1204.44	1505.56	1806.67	2107.78	2408.89	2710.00
81.4	301.48	602.96	904.44	1205.93	1507.41	1808.89	2110.37	2411.85	2713.33
81.5	301.85	603.70	905.56	1207.41	1509.26	1811.11	2112.96	2414.81	2716.67
81.6	302.22	604.44	906.67	1208.89	1511.11	1813.33	2115.56	2417.78	2720.00
81.7	302.59	605.19	907.78	1210.37	1512.96	1815.56	2118.15	2420.74	2723.33
81.8	302.96	605.93	908.89	1211.85	1514.81	1817.78	2120.74	2423.70	2726.67
81.9	303.33	606.67	910.00	1213.33	1516.67	1820.00	2123.33	2426.67	2730.00
82.0	303.70	607.41	911.11	1214.81	1518.52	1822.22	2125.93	2429.63	2733.33
82.1	304.07	608.15	912.22	1216.30	1520.37	1824.44	2128.52	2432.59	2736.67
82.2	304.44	608.89	913.33	1217.78	1522.22	1826.67	2131.11	2435.56	2740.00
82.3	304.81	609.63	914.44	1219.26	1524.07	1828.89	2133.70	2438.52	2743.33
82.4	305.19	610.37	915.56	1220.74	1525.93	1831.11	2136.30	2441.48	2746.67
82.5	305.56	611.11	916.67	1222.22	1527.78	1833.33	2138.89	2444.44	2750.00
82.6	305.93	611.85	917.78	1223.70	1529.63	1835.56	2141.48	2447.41	2753.33
82.7	306.30	612.59	918.89	1225.19	1531.48	1837.78	2144.07	2450.37	2756.67
82.8	306.67	613.33	920.00	1226.67	1533.33	1840.00	2146.67	2453.33	2760.00
82.9	307.04	614.07	921.11	1228.15	1535.19	1842.22	2149.26	2456.30	2763.33
83.0	307.41	614.81	922.22	1229.63	1537.04	1844.44	2151.85	2459.26	2766.67
83.1	307.78	615.56	923.33	1231.11	1538.89	1846.67	2154.44	2462.22	2770.00
83.2	308.15	616.30	924.44	1232.59	1540.74	1848.89	2157.04	2465.19	2773.33
83.3	308.52	617.04	925.56	1234.07	1542.59	1851.11	2159.63	2468.15	2776.67
83.4	308.89	617.78	926.67	1235.56	1544.44	1853.33	2162.22	2471.11	2780.00
83.5	309.26	618.52	927.78	1237.04	1546.30	1855.56	2164.81	2474.07	2783.33
83.6	309.63	619.26	928.89	1238.52	1548.15	1857.78	2167.41	2477.04	2786.67
83.7	310.00	620.00	930.00	1240.00	1550.00	1860.00	2170.00	2480.00	2790.00
83.8	310.37	620.74	931.11	1241.48	1551.85	1862.22	2172.59	2482.96	2793.33
83.9	310.74	621.48	932.22	1242.96	1553.70	1864.44	2175.19	2485.93	2796.67
84.0	311.11	622.22	933.33	1244.44	1555.56	1866.67	2177.78	2488.89	2800.00
H. or B.	1	2	3	4	5	6	7	8	9

TABLE XXII. Rectangular Prisms.

H. or B.	1	2	3	4	5	6	7	8	9
84.1	311.48	622.96	934.44	1245.93	1557.41	1868.89	2180.37	2491.85	2803.33
84.2	311.85	623.70	935.56	1247.41	1559.26	1871.11	2182.96	2494.81	2806.67
84.3	312.22	624.44	936.67	1248.89	1561.11	1873.33	2185.56	2497.78	2810.00
84.4	312.59	625.19	937.78	1250.37	1562.96	1875.56	2188.15	2500.74	2813.33
84.5	312.96	625.93	938.89	1251.85	1564.81	1877.78	2190.74	2503.70	2816.67
84.6	313.33	626.67	940.00	1253.33	1566.67	1880.00	2193.33	2506.67	2820.00
84.7	313.70	627.41	941.11	1254.81	1568.52	1882.22	2195.93	2509.63	2823.33
84.8	314.07	628.15	942.22	1256.30	1570.37	1884.44	2198.52	2512.59	2826.67
84.9	314.44	628.89	943.33	1257.78	1572.22	1886.67	2201.11	2515.56	2830.00
85.0	314.81	629.63	944.44	1259.26	1574.07	1888.89	2203.70	2518.52	2833.33
85.1	315.19	630.37	945.56	1260.74	1575.93	1891.11	2206.30	2521.48	2836.67
85.2	315.56	631.11	946.67	1262.22	1577.78	1893.33	2208.89	2524.44	2840.00
85.3	315.93	631.85	947.78	1263.70	1579.63	1895.56	2211.48	2527.41	2843.33
85.4	316.30	632.59	948.89	1265.19	1581.48	1897.78	2214.07	2530.37	2846.67
85.5	316.67	633.33	950.00	1266.67	1583.33	1900.00	2216.67	2533.33	2850.00
85.6	317.04	634.07	951.11	1268.15	1585.19	1902.22	2219.26	2536.30	2853.33
85.7	317.41	634.81	952.22	1269.63	1587.04	1904.44	2221.85	2539.26	2856.67
85.8	317.78	635.56	953.33	1271.11	1588.89	1906.67	2224.44	2542.22	2860.00
85.9	318.15	636.30	954.44	1272.59	1590.74	1908.89	2227.04	2545.19	2863.33
86.0	318.52	637.04	955.56	1274.07	1592.59	1911.11	2229.63	2548.15	2866.67
86.1	318.89	637.78	956.67	1275.56	1594.44	1913.33	2232.22	2551.11	2870.00
86.2	319.26	638.52	957.78	1277.04	1596.30	1915.56	2234.81	2554.07	2873.33
86.3	319.63	639.26	958.89	1278.52	1598.15	1917.78	2237.41	2557.04	2876.67
86.4	320.00	640.00	960.00	1280.00	1600.00	1920.00	2240.00	2560.00	2880.00
86.5	320.37	640.74	961.11	1281.48	1601.85	1922.22	2242.59	2562.96	2883.33
86.6	320.74	641.48	962.22	1282.96	1603.70	1924.44	2245.19	2565.93	2886.67
86.7	321.11	642.22	963.33	1284.44	1605.56	1926.67	2247.78	2568.89	2890.00
86.8	321.48	642.96	964.44	1285.93	1607.41	1928.89	2250.37	2571.85	2893.33
86.9	321.85	643.70	965.56	1287.41	1609.26	1931.11	2252.96	2574.81	2896.67
87.0	322.22	644.44	966.67	1288.89	1611.11	1933.33	2255.56	2577.78	2900.00
87.1	322.59	645.19	967.78	1290.37	1612.96	1935.56	2258.15	2580.74	2903.33
87.2	322.96	645.93	968.89	1291.85	1614.81	1937.78	2260.74	2583.70	2906.67
87.3	323.33	646.67	970.00	1293.33	1616.67	1940.00	2263.33	2586.67	2910.00
87.4	323.70	647.41	971.11	1294.81	1618.52	1942.22	2265.93	2589.63	2913.33
87.5	324.07	648.15	972.22	1296.30	1620.37	1944.44	2268.52	2592.59	2916.67
87.6	324.44	648.89	973.33	1297.78	1622.22	1946.67	2271.11	2595.56	2920.00
87.7	324.81	649.63	974.44	1299.26	1624.07	1948.89	2273.70	2598.52	2923.33
87.8	325.19	650.37	975.56	1300.74	1625.93	1951.11	2276.30	2601.48	2926.67
87.9	325.56	651.11	976.67	1302.22	1627.78	1953.33	2278.89	2604.44	2930.00
88.0	325.93	651.85	977.78	1303.70	1629.63	1955.56	2281.48	2607.41	2933.33
88.1	326.30	652.59	978.89	1305.19	1631.48	1957.78	2284.07	2610.37	2936.67
88.2	326.67	653.33	980.00	1306.67	1633.33	1960.00	2286.67	2613.33	2940.00
88.3	327.04	654.07	981.11	1308.15	1635.19	1962.22	2289.26	2616.30	2943.33
88.4	327.41	654.81	982.22	1309.63	1637.04	1964.44	2291.85	2619.26	2946.67
88.5	327.78	655.56	983.33	1311.11	1638.89	1966.67	2294.44	2622.22	2950.00
88.6	328.15	656.30	984.44	1312.59	1640.74	1968.89	2297.04	2625.19	2953.33
88.7	328.52	657.04	985.56	1314.07	1642.59	1971.11	2299.63	2628.15	2956.67
88.8	328.89	657.78	986.67	1315.56	1644.44	1973.33	2302.22	2631.11	2960.00
88.9	329.26	658.52	987.78	1317.04	1646.30	1975.56	2304.81	2634.07	2963.33
89.0	329.63	659.26	988.89	1318.52	1648.15	1977.78	2307.41	2637.04	2966.67
89.1	330.00	660.00	990.00	1320.00	1650.00	1980.00	2310.00	2640.00	2970.00
89.2	330.37	660.74	991.11	1321.48	1651.85	1982.22	2312.59	2642.96	2973.33
89.3	330.74	661.48	992.22	1322.96	1653.70	1984.44	2315.19	2645.93	2976.67
89.4	331.11	662.22	993.33	1324.44	1655.56	1986.67	2317.78	2648.89	2980.00
89.5	331.48	662.96	994.44	1325.93	1657.41	1988.89	2320.37	2651.85	2983.33
89.6	331.85	663.70	995.56	1327.41	1659.26	1991.11	2322.96	2654.81	2986.67
89.7	332.22	664.44	996.67	1328.89	1661.11	1993.33	2325.56	2657.78	2990.00
89.8	332.59	665.19	997.78	1330.37	1662.96	1995.56	2328.15	2660.74	2993.33
89.9	332.96	665.93	998.89	1331.85	1664.81	1997.78	2330.74	2663.70	2996.67
90.0	333.33	666.67	1000.00	1333.33	1666.67	2000.00	2333.33	2666.67	3000.00
H. or B.	1	2	3	4	5	6	7	8	9

TABLE XXII. Rectangular Prisms.

H. or B.	1	2	3	4	5	6	7	8	9
90.1	333.70	667.41	1001.11	1334.81	1668.52	2002.22	2335.93	2669.63	3003.33
90.2	334.07	668.15	1002.22	1336.30	1670.37	2004.44	2338.52	2672.59	3006.67
90.3	334.44	668.89	1003.33	1337.78	1672.22	2006.67	2341.11	2675.56	3010.00
90.4	334.81	669.63	1004.44	1339.26	1674.07	2008.89	2343.70	2678.52	3013.33
90.5	335.19	670.37	1005.56	1340.74	1675.93	2011.11	2346.30	2681.48	3016.67
90.6	335.56	671.11	1006.67	1342.22	1677.78	2013.33	2348.89	2684.44	3020.00
90.7	335.93	671.85	1007.78	1343.70	1679.63	2015.56	2351.48	2687.41	3023.33
90.8	336.30	672.59	1008.89	1345.19	1681.48	2017.78	2354.07	2690.37	3026.67
90.9	336.67	673.33	1010.00	1346.67	1683.33	2020.00	2356.67	2693.33	3030.00
91.0	337.04	674.07	1011.11	1348.15	1685.19	2022.22	2359.26	2696.30	3033.33
91.1	337.41	674.81	1012.22	1349.63	1687.04	2024.44	2361.85	2699.26	3036.67
91.2	337.78	675.56	1013.33	1351.11	1688.89	2026.67	2364.44	2702.22	3040.00
91.3	338.15	676.30	1014.44	1352.59	1690.74	2028.89	2367.04	2705.19	3043.33
91.4	338.52	677.04	1015.56	1354.07	1692.59	2031.11	2369.63	2708.15	3046.67
91.5	338.89	677.78	1016.67	1355.56	1694.44	2033.33	2372.22	2711.11	3050.00
91.6	339.26	678.52	1017.78	1357.04	1696.30	2035.56	2374.81	2714.07	3053.33
91.7	339.63	679.26	1018.89	1358.52	1698.15	2037.78	2377.41	2717.04	3056.67
91.8	340.00	680.00	1020.00	1360.00	1700.00	2040.00	2380.00	2720.00	3060.00
91.9	340.37	680.74	1021.11	1361.48	1701.85	2042.22	2382.59	2722.96	3063.33
92.0	340.74	681.48	1022.22	1362.96	1703.70	2044.44	2385.19	2725.93	3066.67
92.1	341.11	682.22	1023.33	1364.44	1705.56	2046.67	2387.78	2728.89	3070.00
92.2	341.48	682.96	1024.44	1365.93	1707.41	2048.89	2390.37	2731.85	3073.33
92.3	341.85	683.70	1025.56	1367.41	1709.26	2051.11	2392.96	2734.81	3076.67
92.4	342.22	684.44	1026.67	1368.89	1711.11	2053.33	2395.56	2737.78	3080.00
92.5	342.59	685.19	1027.78	1370.37	1712.96	2055.56	2398.15	2740.74	3083.33
92.6	342.96	685.93	1028.89	1371.85	1714.81	2057.78	2400.74	2743.70	3086.67
92.7	343.33	686.67	1030.00	1373.33	1716.67	2060.00	2403.33	2746.67	3090.00
92.8	343.70	687.41	1031.11	1374.81	1718.52	2062.22	2405.93	2749.63	3093.33
92.9	344.07	688.15	1032.22	1376.30	1720.37	2064.44	2408.52	2752.59	3096.67
93.0	344.44	688.89	1033.33	1377.78	1722.22	2066.67	2411.11	2755.56	3100.00
93.1	344.81	689.63	1034.44	1379.26	1724.07	2068.89	2413.70	2758.52	3103.33
93.2	345.19	690.37	1035.56	1380.74	1725.93	2071.11	2416.30	2761.48	3106.67
93.3	345.56	691.11	1036.67	1382.22	1727.78	2073.33	2418.89	2764.44	3110.00
93.4	345.93	691.85	1037.78	1383.70	1729.63	2075.56	2421.48	2767.41	3113.33
93.5	346.30	692.59	1038.89	1385.19	1731.48	2077.78	2424.07	2770.37	3116.67
93.6	346.67	693.33	1040.00	1386.67	1733.33	2080.00	2426.67	2773.33	3120.00
93.7	347.04	694.07	1041.11	1388.15	1735.19	2082.22	2429.26	2776.30	3123.33
93.8	347.41	694.81	1042.22	1389.63	1737.04	2084.44	2431.85	2779.26	3126.67
93.9	347.78	695.56	1043.33	1391.11	1738.89	2086.67	2434.44	2782.22	3130.00
94.0	348.15	696.30	1044.44	1392.59	1740.74	2088.89	2437.04	2785.19	3133.33
94.1	348.52	697.04	1045.56	1394.07	1742.59	2091.11	2439.63	2788.15	3136.67
94.2	348.89	697.78	1046.67	1395.56	1744.44	2093.33	2442.22	2791.11	3140.00
94.3	349.26	698.52	1047.78	1397.04	1746.30	2095.56	2444.81	2794.07	3143.33
94.4	349.63	699.26	1048.89	1398.52	1748.15	2097.78	2447.41	2797.04	3146.67
94.5	350.00	700.00	1050.00	1400.00	1750.00	2100.00	2450.00	2800.00	3150.00
94.6	350.37	700.74	1051.11	1401.48	1751.85	2102.22	2452.59	2802.96	3153.33
94.7	350.74	701.48	1052.22	1402.96	1753.70	2104.44	2455.19	2805.93	3156.67
94.8	351.11	702.22	1053.33	1404.44	1755.56	2106.67	2457.78	2808.89	3160.00
94.9	351.48	702.96	1054.44	1405.93	1757.41	2108.89	2460.37	2811.85	3163.33
95.0	351.85	703.70	1055.56	1407.41	1759.26	2111.11	2462.96	2814.81	3166.67
95.1	352.22	704.44	1056.67	1408.89	1761.11	2113.33	2465.56	2817.78	3170.00
95.2	352.59	705.19	1057.78	1410.37	1762.96	2115.56	2468.15	2820.74	3173.33
95.3	352.96	705.93	1058.89	1411.85	1764.81	2117.78	2470.74	2823.70	3176.67
95.4	353.33	706.67	1060.00	1413.33	1766.67	2120.00	2473.33	2826.67	3180.00
95.5	353.70	707.41	1061.11	1414.81	1768.52	2122.22	2475.93	2829.63	3183.33
95.6	354.07	708.15	1062.22	1416.30	1770.37	2124.44	2478.52	2832.59	3186.67
95.7	354.44	708.89	1063.33	1417.78	1772.22	2126.67	2481.11	2835.56	3190.00
95.8	354.81	709.63	1064.44	1419.26	1774.07	2128.89	2483.70	2838.52	3193.33
95.9	355.19	710.37	1065.56	1420.74	1775.93	2131.11	2486.30	2841.48	3196.67
96.0	355.56	711.11	1066.67	1422.22	1777.78	2133.33	2488.89	2844.44	3200.00
H. or B.	1	2	3	4	5	6	7	8	9

H. or B.	1	2	3	4	5	6	7	8	9
96.1	355.93	711.85	1067.78	1423.70	1779.63	2135.56	2491.48	2847.41	3203.33
96.2	356.30	712.59	1068.89	1425.19	1781.48	2137.78	2494.07	2850.37	3206.67
96.3	356.67	713.33	1070.00	1426.67	1783.33	2140.00	2496.67	2853.33	3210.00
96.4	357.04	714.07	1071.11	1428.15	1785.19	2142.22	2499.26	2856.30	3213.33
96.5	357.41	714.81	1072.22	1429.63	1787.04	2144.44	2501.85	2859.26	3216.67
96.6	357.78	715.56	1073.33	1431.11	1788.89	2146.67	2504.44	2862.22	3220.00
96.7	358.15	716.30	1074.44	1432.59	1790.74	2148.89	2507.04	2865.19	3223.33
96.8	358.52	717.04	1075.56	1434.07	1792.59	2151.11	2509.63	2868.15	3226.67
96.9	358.89	717.78	1076.67	1435.56	1794.44	2153.33	2512.22	2871.11	3230.00
97.0	359.26	718.52	1077.78	1437.04	1796.30	2155.56	2514.81	2874.07	3233.33
97.1	359.63	719.26	1078.89	1438.52	1798.15	2157.78	2517.41	2877.04	3236.67
97.2	360.00	720.00	1080.00	1440.00	1800.00	2160.00	2520.00	2880.00	3240.00
97.3	360.37	720.74	1081.11	1441.48	1801.85	2162.22	2522.59	2882.96	3243.33
97.4	360.74	721.48	1082.22	1442.96	1803.70	2164.44	2525.19	2885.93	3246.67
97.5	361.11	722.22	1083.33	1444.44	1805.56	2166.67	2527.78	2888.89	3250.00
97.6	361.48	722.96	1084.44	1445.93	1807.41	2168.89	2530.37	2891.85	3253.33
97.7	361.85	723.70	1085.56	1447.41	1809.26	2171.11	2532.96	2894.81	3256.67
97.8	362.22	724.44	1086.67	1448.89	1811.11	2173.33	2535.56	2897.78	3260.00
97.9	362.59	725.19	1087.78	1450.37	1812.96	2175.56	2538.15	2900.74	3263.33
98.0	362.96	725.93	1088.89	1451.85	1814.81	2177.78	2540.74	2903.70	3266.67
98.1	363.33	726.67	1090.00	1453.33	1816.67	2180.00	2543.33	2906.67	3270.00
98.2	363.70	727.41	1091.11	1454.81	1818.52	2182.22	2545.93	2909.63	3273.33
98.3	364.07	728.15	1092.22	1456.30	1820.37	2184.44	2548.52	2912.59	3276.67
98.4	364.44	728.89	1093.33	1457.78	1822.22	2186.67	2551.11	2915.56	3280.00
98.5	364.81	729.63	1094.44	1459.26	1824.07	2188.89	2553.70	2918.52	3283.33
98.6	365.19	730.37	1095.56	1460.74	1825.93	2191.11	2556.30	2921.48	3286.67
98.7	365.56	731.11	1096.67	1462.22	1827.78	2193.33	2558.89	2924.44	3290.00
98.8	365.93	731.85	1097.78	1463.70	1829.63	2195.56	2561.48	2927.41	3293.33
98.9	366.30	732.59	1098.89	1465.19	1831.48	2197.78	2564.07	2930.37	3296.67
99.0	366.67	733.33	1100.00	1466.67	1833.33	2200.00	2566.67	2933.33	3300.00
99.1	367.04	734.07	1101.11	1468.15	1835.19	2202.22	2569.26	2936.30	3303.33
99.2	367.41	734.81	1102.22	1469.63	1837.04	2204.44	2571.85	2939.26	3306.67
99.3	367.78	735.56	1103.33	1471.11	1838.89	2206.67	2574.44	2942.22	3310.00
99.4	368.15	736.30	1104.44	1472.59	1840.74	2208.89	2577.04	2945.19	3313.33
99.5	368.52	737.04	1105.56	1474.07	1842.59	2211.11	2579.63	2948.15	3316.67
99.6	368.89	737.78	1106.67	1475.56	1844.44	2213.33	2582.22	2951.11	3320.00
99.7	369.26	738.52	1107.78	1477.04	1846.30	2215.56	2584.81	2954.07	3323.33
99.8	369.63	739.26	1108.89	1478.52	1848.15	2217.78	2587.41	2957.04	3326.67
99.9	370.00	740.00	1110.00	1480.00	1850.00	2220.00	2590.00	2960.00	3330.00
100.0	370.37	740.74	1111.11	1481.48	1851.85	2222.22	2592.59	2962.96	3333.33
100.1	370.74	741.48	1112.22	1482.96	1853.70	2224.44	2595.19	2965.93	3336.67
100.2	371.11	742.22	1113.33	1484.44	1855.56	2226.67	2597.78	2968.89	3340.00
100.3	371.48	742.96	1114.44	1485.93	1857.41	2228.89	2600.37	2971.85	3343.33
100.4	371.85	743.70	1115.56	1487.41	1859.26	2231.11	2602.96	2974.81	3346.67
100.5	372.22	744.44	1116.67	1488.89	1861.11	2233.33	2605.56	2977.78	3350.00
100.6	372.59	745.19	1117.78	1490.37	1862.96	2235.56	2608.15	2980.74	3353.33
100.7	372.96	745.93	1118.89	1491.85	1864.81	2237.78	2610.74	2983.70	3356.67
100.8	373.33	746.67	1120.00	1493.33	1866.67	2240.00	2613.33	2986.67	3360.00
100.9	373.70	747.41	1121.11	1494.81	1868.52	2242.22	2615.93	2989.63	3363.33
101.0	374.07	748.15	1122.22	1496.30	1870.37	2244.44	2618.52	2992.59	3366.67
101.1	374.44	748.89	1123.33	1497.78	1872.22	2246.67	2621.11	2995.56	3370.00
101.2	374.81	749.63	1124.44	1499.26	1874.07	2248.89	2623.70	2998.52	3373.33
101.3	375.19	750.37	1125.56	1500.74	1875.93	2251.11	2626.30	3001.48	3376.67
101.4	375.56	751.11	1126.67	1502.22	1877.78	2253.33	2628.89	3004.44	3380.00
101.5	375.93	751.85	1127.78	1503.70	1879.63	2255.56	2631.48	3007.41	3383.33
101.6	376.30	752.59	1128.89	1505.19	1881.48	2257.78	2634.07	3010.37	3386.67
101.7	376.67	753.33	1130.00	1506.67	1883.33	2260.00	2636.67	3013.33	3390.00
101.8	377.04	754.07	1131.11	1508.15	1885.19	2262.22	2639.26	3016.30	3393.33
101.9	377.41	754.81	1132.22	1509.63	1887.04	2264.44	2641.85	3019.26	3396.67
102.0	377.78	755.56	1133.33	1511.11	1888.89	2266.67	2644.44	3022.22	3400.00
H. or B.	1	2	3	4	5	6	7	8	9

H. or B.	1	2	3	4	5	6	7	8	9
102.1	378.15	756.30	1134.44	1512.59	1890.74	2268.89	2647.04	3025.19	3403.33
102.2	378.52	757.04	1135.56	1514.07	1892.59	2271.11	2649.63	3028.15	3406.67
102.3	378.89	757.78	1136.67	1515.56	1894.44	2273.33	2652.22	3031.11	3410.00
102.4	379.26	758.52	1137.78	1517.04	1896.30	2275.56	2654.81	3034.07	3413.33
102.5	379.63	759.26	1138.89	1518.52	1898.15	2277.78	2657.41	3037.04	3416.67
102.6	380.00	760.00	1140.00	1520.00	1900.00	2280.00	2660.00	3040.00	3420.00
102.7	380.37	760.74	1141.11	1521.48	1901.85	2282.22	2662.59	3042.96	3423.33
102.8	380.74	761.48	1142.22	1522.96	1903.70	2284.44	2665.19	3045.93	3426.67
102.9	381.11	762.22	1143.33	1524.44	1905.56	2286.67	2667.78	3048.89	3430.00
103.0	381.48	762.96	1144.44	1525.93	1907.41	2288.89	2670.37	3051.85	3433.33
103.1	381.85	763.70	1145.56	1527.41	1909.26	2291.11	2672.96	3054.81	3436.67
103.2	382.22	764.44	1146.67	1528.89	1911.11	2293.33	2675.56	3057.78	3440.00
103.3	382.59	765.19	1147.78	1530.37	1912.96	2295.56	2678.15	3060.74	3443.33
103.4	382.96	765.93	1148.89	1531.85	1914.81	2297.78	2680.74	3063.70	3446.67
103.5	383.33	766.67	1150.00	1533.33	1916.67	2300.00	2683.33	3066.67	3450.00
103.6	383.70	767.41	1151.11	1534.81	1918.52	2302.22	2685.93	3069.63	3453.33
103.7	384.07	768.15	1152.22	1536.30	1920.37	2304.44	2688.52	3072.59	3456.67
103.8	384.44	768.89	1153.33	1537.78	1922.22	2306.67	2691.11	3075.56	3460.00
103.9	384.81	769.63	1154.44	1539.26	1924.07	2308.89	2693.70	3078.52	3463.33
104.0	385.19	770.37	1155.56	1540.74	1925.93	2311.11	2696.30	3081.48	3466.67
104.1	385.56	771.11	1156.67	1542.22	1927.78	2313.33	2698.89	3084.44	3470.00
104.2	385.93	771.85	1157.78	1543.70	1929.63	2315.56	2701.48	3087.41	3473.33
104.3	386.30	772.59	1158.89	1545.19	1931.48	2317.78	2704.07	3090.37	3476.67
104.4	386.67	773.33	1160.00	1546.67	1933.33	2320.00	2706.67	3093.33	3480.00
104.5	387.04	774.07	1161.11	1548.15	1935.19	2322.22	2709.26	3096.30	3483.33
104.6	387.41	774.81	1162.22	1549.63	1937.04	2324.44	2711.85	3099.26	3486.67
104.7	387.78	775.56	1163.33	1551.11	1938.89	2326.67	2714.44	3102.22	3490.00
104.8	388.15	776.30	1164.44	1552.59	1940.74	2328.89	2717.04	3105.19	3493.33
104.9	388.52	777.04	1165.56	1554.07	1942.59	2331.11	2719.63	3108.15	3496.67
105.0	388.89	777.78	1166.67	1555.56	1944.44	2333.33	2722.22	3111.11	3500.00
105.1	389.26	778.52	1167.78	1557.04	1946.30	2335.56	2724.81	3114.07	3503.33
105.2	389.63	779.26	1168.89	1558.52	1948.15	2337.78	2727.41	3117.04	3506.67
105.3	390.00	780.00	1170.00	1560.00	1950.00	2340.00	2730.00	3120.00	3510.00
105.4	390.37	780.74	1171.11	1561.48	1951.85	2342.22	2732.59	3122.96	3513.33
105.5	390.74	781.48	1172.22	1562.96	1953.70	2344.44	2735.19	3125.93	3516.67
105.6	391.11	782.22	1173.33	1564.44	1955.56	2346.67	2737.78	3128.89	3520.00
105.7	391.48	782.96	1174.44	1565.93	1957.41	2348.89	2740.37	3131.85	3523.33
105.8	391.85	783.70	1175.56	1567.41	1959.26	2351.11	2742.96	3134.81	3526.67
105.9	392.22	784.44	1176.67	1568.89	1961.11	2353.33	2745.56	3137.78	3530.00
106.0	392.59	785.19	1177.78	1570.37	1962.96	2355.56	2748.15	3140.74	3533.33
106.1	392.96	785.93	1178.89	1571.85	1964.81	2357.78	2750.74	3143.70	3536.67
106.2	393.33	786.67	1180.00	1573.33	1966.67	2360.00	2753.33	3146.67	3540.00
106.3	393.70	787.41	1181.11	1574.81	1968.52	2362.22	2755.93	3149.63	3543.33
106.4	394.07	788.15	1182.22	1576.30	1970.37	2364.44	2758.52	3152.59	3546.67
106.5	394.44	788.89	1183.33	1577.78	1972.22	2366.67	2761.11	3155.56	3550.00
106.6	394.81	789.63	1184.44	1579.26	1974.07	2368.89	2763.70	3158.52	3553.33
106.7	395.19	790.37	1185.56	1580.74	1975.93	2371.11	2766.30	3161.48	3556.67
106.8	395.56	791.11	1186.67	1582.22	1977.78	2373.33	2768.89	3164.44	3560.00
106.9	395.93	791.85	1187.78	1583.70	1979.63	2375.56	2771.48	3167.41	3563.33
107.0	396.30	792.59	1188.89	1585.19	1981.48	2377.78	2774.07	3170.37	3566.67
107.1	396.67	793.33	1190.00	1586.67	1983.33	2380.00	2776.67	3173.33	3570.00
107.2	397.04	794.07	1191.11	1588.15	1985.19	2382.22	2779.26	3176.30	3573.33
107.3	397.41	794.81	1192.22	1589.63	1987.04	2384.44	2781.85	3179.26	3576.67
107.4	397.78	795.56	1193.33	1591.11	1988.89	2386.67	2784.44	3182.22	3580.00
107.5	398.15	796.30	1194.44	1592.59	1990.74	2388.89	2787.04	3185.19	3583.33
107.6	398.52	797.04	1195.56	1594.07	1992.59	2391.11	2789.63	3188.15	3586.67
107.7	398.89	797.78	1196.67	1595.56	1994.44	2393.33	2792.22	3191.11	3590.00
107.8	399.26	798.52	1197.78	1597.04	1996.30	2395.56	2794.81	3194.07	3593.33
107.9	399.63	799.26	1198.89	1598.52	1998.15	2397.78	2797.41	3197.04	3596.67
108.0	400.00	800.00	1200.00	1600.00	2000.00	2400.00	2800.00	3200.00	3600.00
H. or B.	1	2	3	4	5	6	7	8	9

TABLE XXII. Rectangular Prisms.

H. or B.	1	2	3	4	5	6	7	8	9
108.1	400.37	800.74	1201.11	1601.48	2001.85	2402.22	2802.59	3202.96	3603.33
108.2	400.74	801.48	1202.22	1602.96	2003.70	2404.44	2805.19	3205.93	3606.67
108.3	401.11	802.22	1203.33	1604.44	2005.56	2406.67	2807.78	3208.89	3610.00
108.4	401.48	802.96	1204.44	1605.93	2007.41	2408.89	2810.37	3211.85	3613.33
108.5	401.85	803.70	1205.56	1607.41	2009.26	2411.11	2812.96	3214.81	3616.67
108.6	402.22	804.44	1206.67	1608.89	2011.11	2413.33	2815.56	3217.78	3620.00
108.7	402.59	805.19	1207.78	1610.37	2012.96	2415.56	2818.15	3220.74	3623.33
108.8	402.96	805.93	1208.89	1611.85	2014.81	2417.78	2820.74	3223.70	3626.67
108.9	403.33	806.67	1210.00	1613.33	2016.67	2420.00	2823.33	3226.67	3630.00
109.0	403.70	807.41	1211.11	1614.81	2018.52	2422.22	2825.93	3229.63	3633.33
109.1	404.07	808.15	1212.22	1616.30	2020.37	2424.44	2828.52	3232.59	3636.67
109.2	404.44	808.89	1213.33	1617.78	2022.22	2426.67	2831.11	3235.56	3640.00
109.3	404.81	809.63	1214.44	1619.26	2024.07	2428.89	2833.70	3238.52	3643.33
109.4	405.19	810.37	1215.56	1620.74	2025.93	2431.11	2836.30	3241.48	3646.67
109.5	405.56	811.11	1216.67	1622.22	2027.78	2433.33	2838.89	3244.44	3650.00
109.6	405.93	811.85	1217.78	1623.70	2029.63	2435.56	2841.48	3247.41	3653.33
109.7	406.30	812.59	1218.89	1625.19	2031.48	2437.78	2844.07	3250.37	3656.67
109.8	406.67	813.33	1220.00	1626.67	2033.33	2440.00	2846.67	3253.33	3660.00
109.9	407.04	814.07	1221.11	1628.15	2035.19	2442.22	2849.26	3256.30	3663.33
110.0	407.41	814.81	1222.22	1629.63	2037.04	2444.44	2851.85	3259.26	3666.67
110.1	407.78	815.56	1223.33	1631.11	2038.89	2446.67	2854.44	3262.22	3670.00
110.2	408.15	816.30	1224.44	1632.59	2040.74	2448.89	2857.04	3265.19	3673.33
110.3	408.52	817.04	1225.56	1634.07	2042.59	2451.11	2859.63	3268.15	3676.67
110.4	408.89	817.78	1226.67	1635.56	2044.44	2453.33	2862.22	3271.11	3680.00
110.5	409.26	818.52	1227.78	1637.04	2046.30	2455.56	2864.81	3274.07	3683.33
110.6	409.63	819.26	1228.89	1638.52	2048.15	2457.78	2867.41	3277.04	3686.67
110.7	410.00	820.00	1230.00	1640.00	2050.00	2460.00	2870.00	3280.00	3690.00
110.8	410.37	820.74	1231.11	1641.48	2051.85	2462.22	2872.59	3282.96	3693.33
110.9	410.74	821.48	1232.22	1642.96	2053.70	2464.44	2875.19	3285.93	3696.67
111.0	411.11	822.22	1233.33	1644.44	2055.56	2466.67	2877.78	3288.89	3700.00
111.1	411.48	822.96	1234.44	1645.93	2057.41	2468.89	2880.37	3291.85	3703.33
111.2	411.85	823.70	1235.56	1647.41	2059.26	2471.11	2882.96	3294.81	3706.67
111.3	412.22	824.44	1236.67	1648.89	2061.11	2473.33	2885.56	3297.78	3710.00
111.4	412.59	825.19	1237.78	1650.37	2062.96	2475.56	2888.15	3300.74	3713.33
111.5	412.96	825.93	1238.89	1651.85	2064.81	2477.78	2890.74	3303.70	3716.67
111.6	413.33	826.67	1240.00	1653.33	2066.67	2480.00	2893.33	3306.67	3720.00
111.7	413.70	827.41	1241.11	1654.81	2068.52	2482.22	2895.93	3309.63	3723.33
111.8	414.07	828.15	1242.22	1656.30	2070.37	2484.44	2898.52	3312.59	3726.67
111.9	414.44	828.89	1243.33	1657.78	2072.22	2486.67	2901.11	3315.56	3730.00
112.0	414.81	829.63	1244.44	1659.26	2074.07	2488.89	2903.70	3318.52	3733.33
112.1	415.19	830.37	1245.56	1660.74	2075.93	2491.11	2906.30	3321.48	3736.67
112.2	415.56	831.11	1246.67	1662.22	2077.78	2493.33	2908.89	3324.44	3740.00
112.3	415.93	831.85	1247.78	1663.70	2079.63	2495.56	2911.48	3327.41	3743.33
112.4	416.30	832.59	1248.89	1665.19	2081.48	2497.78	2914.07	3330.37	3746.67
112.5	416.67	833.33	1250.00	1666.67	2083.33	2500.00	2916.67	3333.33	3750.00
112.6	417.04	834.07	1251.11	1668.15	2085.19	2502.22	2919.26	3336.30	3753.33
112.7	417.41	834.81	1252.22	1669.63	2087.04	2504.44	2921.85	3339.26	3756.67
112.8	417.78	835.56	1253.33	1671.11	2088.89	2506.67	2924.44	3342.22	3760.00
112.9	418.15	836.30	1254.44	1672.59	2090.74	2508.89	2927.04	3345.19	3763.33
113.0	418.52	837.04	1255.56	1674.07	2092.59	2511.11	2929.63	3348.15	3766.67
113.1	418.89	837.78	1256.67	1675.56	2094.44	2513.33	2932.22	3351.11	3770.00
113.2	419.26	838.52	1257.78	1677.04	2096.30	2515.56	2934.81	3354.07	3773.33
113.3	419.63	839.26	1258.89	1678.52	2098.15	2517.78	2937.41	3357.04	3776.67
113.4	420.00	840.00	1260.00	1680.00	2100.00	2520.00	2940.00	3360.00	3780.00
113.5	420.37	840.74	1261.11	1681.48	2101.85	2522.22	2942.59	3362.96	3783.33
113.6	420.74	841.48	1262.22	1682.96	2103.70	2524.44	2945.19	3365.93	3786.67
113.7	421.11	842.22	1263.33	1684.44	2105.56	2526.67	2947.78	3368.89	3790.00
113.8	421.48	842.96	1264.44	1685.93	2107.41	2528.89	2950.37	3371.85	3793.33
113.9	421.85	843.70	1265.56	1687.41	2109.26	2531.11	2952.96	3374.81	3796.67
114.0	422.22	844.44	1266.67	1688.89	2111.11	2533.33	2955.56	3377.78	3800.00
H. or B.	1	2	3	4	5	6	7	8	9

TABLE XXII. Rectangular Prisms.

H. or B.	1	2	3	4	5	6	7	8	9
114.1	422.59	845.19	1267.78	1690.37	2112.96	2535.56	2958.15	3380.74	3803.33
114.2	422.96	845.93	1268.89	1691.85	2114.81	2537.78	2960.74	3383.70	3806.67
114.3	423.33	846.67	1270.00	1693.33	2116.67	2540.00	2963.33	3386.67	3810.00
114.4	423.70	847.41	1271.11	1694.81	2118.52	2542.22	2965.93	3389.63	3813.33
114.5	424.07	848.15	1272.22	1696.30	2120.37	2544.44	2968.52	3392.59	3816.67
114.6	424.44	848.89	1273.33	1697.78	2122.22	2546.67	2971.11	3395.56	3820.00
114.7	424.81	849.63	1274.44	1699.26	2124.07	2548.89	2973.70	3398.52	3823.33
114.8	425.19	850.37	1275.56	1700.74	2125.93	2551.11	2976.30	3401.48	3826.67
114.9	425.56	851.11	1276.67	1702.22	2127.78	2553.33	2978.89	3404.44	3830.00
115.0	425.93	851.85	1277.78	1703.70	2129.63	2555.56	2981.48	3407.41	3833.33
115.1	426.30	852.59	1278.89	1705.19	2131.48	2557.78	2984.07	3410.37	3836.67
115.2	426.67	853.33	1280.00	1706.67	2133.33	2560.00	2986.67	3413.33	3840.00
115.3	427.04	854.07	1281.11	1708.15	2135.19	2562.22	2989.26	3416.30	3843.33
115.4	427.41	854.81	1282.22	1709.63	2137.04	2564.44	2991.85	3419.26	3846.67
115.5	427.78	855.56	1283.33	1711.11	2138.89	2566.67	2994.44	3422.22	3850.00
115.6	428.15	856.30	1284.44	1712.59	2140.74	2568.89	2997.04	3425.19	3853.33
115.7	428.52	857.04	1285.56	1714.07	2142.59	2571.11	2999.63	3428.15	3856.67
115.8	428.89	857.78	1286.67	1715.56	2144.44	2573.33	3002.22	3431.11	3860.00
115.9	429.26	858.52	1287.78	1717.04	2146.30	2575.56	3004.81	3434.07	3863.33
116.0	429.63	859.26	1288.89	1718.52	2148.15	2577.78	3007.41	3437.04	3866.67
116.1	430.00	860.00	1290.00	1720.00	2150.00	2580.00	3010.00	3440.00	3870.00
116.2	430.37	860.74	1291.11	1721.48	2151.85	2582.22	3012.59	3442.96	3873.33
116.3	430.74	861.48	1292.22	1722.96	2153.70	2584.44	3015.19	3445.93	3876.67
116.4	431.11	862.22	1293.33	1724.44	2155.56	2586.67	3017.78	3448.89	3880.00
116.5	431.48	862.96	1294.44	1725.93	2157.41	2588.89	3020.37	3451.85	3883.33
116.6	431.85	863.70	1295.56	1727.41	2159.26	2591.11	3022.96	3454.81	3886.67
116.7	432.22	864.44	1296.67	1728.89	2161.11	2593.33	3025.56	3457.78	3890.00
116.8	432.59	865.19	1297.78	1730.37	2162.96	2595.56	3028.15	3460.74	3893.33
116.9	432.96	865.93	1298.89	1731.85	2164.81	2597.78	3030.74	3463.70	3896.67
117.0	433.33	866.67	1300.00	1733.33	2166.67	2600.00	3033.33	3466.67	3900.00
117.1	433.70	867.41	1301.11	1734.81	2168.52	2602.22	3035.93	3469.63	3903.33
117.2	434.07	868.15	1302.22	1736.30	2170.37	2604.44	3038.52	3472.59	3906.67
117.3	434.44	868.89	1303.33	1737.78	2172.22	2606.67	3041.11	3475.56	3910.00
117.4	434.81	869.63	1304.44	1739.26	2174.07	2608.89	3043.70	3478.52	3913.33
117.5	435.19	870.37	1305.56	1740.74	2175.93	2611.11	3046.30	3481.48	3916.67
117.6	435.56	871.11	1306.67	1742.22	2177.78	2613.33	3048.89	3484.44	3920.00
117.7	435.93	871.85	1307.78	1743.70	2179.63	2615.56	3051.48	3487.41	3923.33
117.8	436.30	872.59	1308.89	1745.19	2181.48	2617.78	3054.07	3490.37	3926.67
117.9	436.67	873.33	1310.00	1746.67	2183.33	2620.00	3056.67	3493.33	3930.00
118.0	437.04	874.07	1311.11	1748.15	2185.19	2622.22	3059.26	3496.30	3933.33
118.1	437.41	874.81	1312.22	1749.63	2187.04	2624.44	3061.85	3499.26	3936.67
118.2	437.78	875.56	1313.33	1751.11	2188.89	2626.67	3064.44	3502.22	3940.00
118.3	438.15	876.30	1314.44	1752.59	2190.74	2628.89	3067.04	3505.19	3943.33
118.4	438.52	877.04	1315.56	1754.07	2192.59	2631.11	3069.63	3508.15	3946.67
118.5	438.89	877.78	1316.67	1755.56	2194.44	2633.33	3072.22	3511.11	3950.00
118.6	439.26	878.52	1317.78	1757.04	2196.30	2635.56	3074.81	3514.07	3953.33
118.7	439.63	879.26	1318.89	1758.52	2198.15	2637.78	3077.41	3517.04	3956.67
118.8	440.00	880.00	1320.00	1760.00	2200.00	2640.00	3080.00	3520.00	3960.00
118.9	440.37	880.74	1321.11	1761.48	2201.85	2642.22	3082.59	3522.96	3963.33
119.0	440.74	881.48	1322.22	1762.96	2203.70	2644.44	3085.19	3525.93	3966.67
119.1	441.11	882.22	1323.33	1764.44	2205.56	2646.67	3087.78	3528.89	3970.00
119.2	441.48	882.96	1324.44	1765.93	2207.41	2648.89	3090.37	3531.85	3973.33
119.3	441.85	883.70	1325.56	1767.41	2209.26	2651.11	3092.96	3534.81	3976.67
119.4	442.22	884.44	1326.67	1768.89	2211.11	2653.33	3095.56	3537.78	3980.00
119.5	442.59	885.19	1327.78	1770.37	2212.96	2655.56	3098.15	3540.74	3983.33
119.6	442.96	885.93	1328.89	1771.85	2214.81	2657.78	3100.74	3543.70	3986.67
119.7	443.33	886.67	1330.00	1773.33	2216.67	2660.00	3103.33	3546.67	3990.00
119.8	443.70	887.41	1331.11	1774.81	2218.52	2662.22	3105.93	3549.63	3993.33
119.9	444.07	888.15	1332.22	1776.30	2220.37	2664.44	3108.52	3552.59	3996.67
120.0	444.44	888.89	1333.33	1777.78	2222.22	2666.67	3111.11	3555.56	4000.00
H. or B.	1	2	3	4	5	6	7	8	9

TABLE XXIII. Logarithms for Eighth Parts of Rectangular Prisms.

H. or B.	0	1	2	3	4	5	6	7	8	9
0	Inf. neg	—2.83277	—1.13380	—1.30989	—1.43483	—1.53174	—1.61092	—1.67787	—1.73586	—1.78701
1	—1.83277	—1.87416	—1.91195	—1.94671	—1.97890	0.00886	0.03689	0.06322	0.08804	0.11152
2	0.13380	0.15499	0.17519	0.19450	0.21298	0.23071	0.24774	0.26413	0.27993	0.29517
3	0.30989	0.32413	0.33792	0.35128	0.36425	0.37684	0.38907	0.40097	0.41255	0.42383
4	0.43483	0.44555	0.45602	0.46624	0.47622	0.48598	0.49553	0.50487	0.51401	0.52297
5	0.53174	0.54034	0.54877	0.55705	0.56516	0.57313	0.58096	0.58864	0.59620	0.60362
6	0.61092	0.61810	0.62516	0.63211	0.63895	0.64568	0.65231	0.65884	0.66528	0.67162
7	0.67787	0.68403	0.69010	0.69609	0.70200	0.70783	0.71358	0.71926	0.72486	0.73040
8	0.73586	0.74126	0.74658	0.75185	0.75705	0.76219	0.76727	0.77229	0.77725	0.78216
9	0.78701	0.79181	0.79656	0.80125	0.80590	0.81049	0.81504	0.81954	0.82400	0.82841
10	0.83277	0.83709	0.84137	0.84561	0.84980	0.85396	0.85808	0.86215	0.86619	0.87020
11	0.87416	0.87809	0.88199	0.88585	0.88967	0.89347	0.89723	0.90096	0.90465	0.90832
12	0.91195	0.91556	0.91913	0.92268	0.92619	0.92968	0.93314	0.93657	0.93998	0.94336
13	0.94671	0.95004	0.95334	0.95662	0.95987	0.96310	0.96631	0.96949	0.97265	0.97578
14	0.97890	0.98199	0.98506	0.98811	0.99113	0.99414	0.99712	1.00009	1.00303	1.00596
15	1.00886	1.01175	1.01461	1.01746	1.02029	1.02310	1.02589	1.02867	1.03143	1.03417
16	1.03689	1.03960	1.04229	1.04496	1.04761	1.05025	1.05288	1.05549	1.05808	1.06066
17	1.06322	1.06577	1.06830	1.07082	1.07332	1.07581	1.07828	1.08074	1.08319	1.08562
18	1.08804	1.09045	1.09284	1.09522	1.09759	1.09994	1.10228	1.10461	1.10693	1.10923
19	1.11152	1.11380	1.11607	1.11833	1.12057	1.12280	1.12503	1.12724	1.12944	1.13162
20	1.13380	1.13597	1.13812	1.14027	1.14240	1.14452	1.14664	1.14874	1.15083	1.15292
21	1.15499	1.15705	1.15911	1.16115	1.16318	1.16521	1.16722	1.16923	1.17123	1.17321
22	1.17519	1.17716	1.17912	1.18107	1.18302	1.18495	1.18688	1.18880	1.19070	1.19261
23	1.19450	1.19638	1.19826	1.20013	1.20199	1.20384	1.20568	1.20752	1.20935	1.21117
24	1.21298	1.21479	1.21659	1.21838	1.22016	1.22194	1.22371	1.22547	1.22722	1.22897
25	1.23071	1.23244	1.23417	1.23589	1.23760	1.23931	1.24101	1.24270	1.24439	1.24607
26	1.24774	1.24941	1.25107	1.25273	1.25437	1.25602	1.25765	1.25928	1.26090	1.26252
27	1.26413	1.26574	1.26734	1.26893	1.27052	1.27210	1.27368	1.27525	1.27681	1.27837
28	1.27993	1.28148	1.28302	1.28456	1.28609	1.28761	1.28914	1.29065	1.29216	1.29367
29	1.29517	1.29666	1.29815	1.29964	1.30112	1.30259	1.30406	1.30553	1.30699	1.30844
30	1.30989	1.31134	1.31278	1.31421	1.31564	1.31707	1.31849	1.31991	1.32132	1.32273
31	1.32413	1.32553	1.32692	1.32831	1.32970	1.33108	1.33246	1.33383	1.33520	1.33656
32	1.33792	1.33928	1.34063	1.34197	1.34332	1.34465	1.34599	1.34732	1.34864	1.34997
33	1.35128	1.35260	1.35391	1.35521	1.35652	1.35781	1.35911	1.36040	1.36169	1.36297
34	1.36425	1.36552	1.36680	1.36806	1.36933	1.37059	1.37185	1.37310	1.37435	1.37560
35	1.37684	1.37808	1.37931	1.38054	1.38177	1.38300	1.38422	1.38544	1.38665	1.38786
36	1.38907	1.39028	1.39148	1.39268	1.39387	1.39506	1.39625	1.39744	1.39862	1.39980
37	1.40097	1.40214	1.40331	1.40448	1.40564	1.40680	1.40796	1.40911	1.41026	1.41141
38	1.41255	1.41369	1.41483	1.41597	1.41710	1.41823	1.41936	1.42048	1.42160	1.42272
39	1.42383	1.42495	1.42606	1.42716	1.42827	1.42937	1.43047	1.43156	1.43265	1.43374
40	1.43483	1.43591	1.43700	1.43808	1.43915	1.44023	1.44130	1.44236	1.44343	1.44449
41	1.44555	1.44661	1.44767	1.44872	1.44977	1.45082	1.45186	1.45291	1.45395	1.45498
42	1.45602	1.45705	1.45808	1.45911	1.46014	1.46116	1.46218	1.46320	1.46421	1.46523
43	1.46624	1.46725	1.46825	1.46926	1.47026	1.47126	1.47226	1.47325	1.47424	1.47523
44	1.47622	1.47721	1.47819	1.47917	1.48015	1.48113	1.48210	1.48308	1.48405	1.48502
45	1.48598	1.48695	1.48791	1.48887	1.48983	1.49078	1.49173	1.49269	1.49364	1.49458
46	1.49553	1.49647	1.49741	1.49835	1.49929	1.50022	1.50116	1.50209	1.50302	1.50394
47	1.50487	1.50579	1.50671	1.50763	1.50855	1.50946	1.51038	1.51129	1.51220	1.51311
48	1.51401	1.51492	1.51582	1.51672	1.51762	1.51851	1.51941	1.52030	1.52119	1.52208
49	1.52297	1.52385	1.52474	1.52562	1.52650	1.52738	1.52825	1.52913	1.53000	1.53087
50	1.53174	1.53261	1.53347	1.53434	1.53520	1.53606	1.53692	1.53778	1.53863	1.53949
51	1.54034	1.54119	1.54204	1.54289	1.54373	1.54458	1.54542	1.54626	1.54710	1.54794
52	1.54877	1.54961	1.55044	1.55127	1.55210	1.55293	1.55376	1.55458	1.55540	1.55623
53	1.55705	1.55786	1.55868	1.55950	1.56031	1.56112	1 56193	1.56274	1.56355	1.56436
54	1.56516	1.56597	1.56677	1.56757	1.56837	1.56917	1.56996	1.57076	1.57155	1.57234
55	1.57313	1.57392	1.57471	1.57550	1.57628	1.57706	1.57784	1.57863	1.57940	1.58018
56	1.58096	1.58173	1.58251	1.58328	1.58405	1.58482	1.58559	1.58635	1.58712	1.58788
57	1.58864	1.58941	1.59017	1.59092	1.59168	1.59244	1.59319	1.59395	1.59470	1.59545
58	1.59620	1.59695	1.59769	1.59844	1.59918	1.59993	1.60067	1.60141	1.60215	1.60289
59	1.60362	1.60436	1.60509	1.60582	1.60656	1.60729	1.60802	1.60874	1.60947	1.61020
H. or B.	0	1	2	3	4	5	6	7	8	9

TABLE XXIII. Logarithms for Eighth Parts of Rectangular Prisms.

H. or B.	0	1	2	3	4	5	6	7	8	9
60	1.61092	1.61164	1.61237	1.61309	1.61381	1.61453	1.61524	1.61596	1.61667	1.61739
61	1.61810	1.61881	1.61952	1.62023	1.62094	1.62165	1.62235	1.62306	1.62376	1.62446
62	1.62516	1.62586	1.62656	1.62726	1.62795	1.62865	1.62934	1.63004	1.63073	1.63142
63	1.63211	1.63280	1.63349	1.63417	1.63486	1.63554	1.63623	1.63691	1.63759	1.63827
64	1.63895	1.63963	1.64031	1.64098	1.64166	1.64233	1.64300	1.64367	1.64435	1.64501
65	1.64568	1.64635	1.64702	1.64768	1.64835	1.64901	1.64967	1.65034	1.65100	1.65166
66	1.65231	1.65297	1.65363	1.65428	1.65494	1.65559	1.65624	1.65690	1.65755	1.65820
67	1.65884	1.65949	1.66014	1.66079	1.66143	1.66207	1.66272	1.66336	1.66400	1.66464
68	1.66528	1.66592	1.66655	1.66719	1.66783	1.66846	1.66909	1.66973	1.67036	1.67099
69	1.67162	1.67225	1.67288	1.67350	1.67413	1.67475	1.67538	1.67600	1.67663	1.67725
70	1.67787	1.67849	1.67911	1.67973	1.68034	1.68096	1.68157	1.68219	1.68280	1.68342
71	1.68403	1.68464	1.68525	1.68586	1.68647	1.68708	1.68768	1.68829	1.68889	1.68950
72	1.69010	1.69071	1.69131	1.69191	1.69251	1.69311	1.69371	1.69430	1.69490	1.69550
73	1.69609	1.69669	1.69728	1.69787	1.69847	1.69906	1.69965	1.70024	1.70083	1.70141
74	1.70200	1.70259	1.70317	1.70376	1.70434	1.70493	1.70551	1.70609	1.70667	1.70725
75	1.70783	1.70841	1.70899	1.70956	1.71014	1.71072	1.71129	1.71187	1.71244	1.71301
76	1.71358	1.71415	1.71472	1.71529	1.71586	1.71643	1.71700	1.71757	1.71813	1.71870
77	1.71926	1.71982	1.72039	1.72095	1.72151	1.72207	1.72263	1.72319	1.72375	1.72431
78	1.72486	1.72542	1.72598	1.72653	1.72709	1.72764	1.72819	1.72874	1.72930	1.72985
79	1.73040	1.73095	1.73150	1.73204	1.73259	1.73314	1.73368	1.73423	1.73477	1.73532
80	1.73586	1.73640	1.73694	1.73749	1.73803	1.73857	1.73911	1.73964	1.74018	1.74072
81	1.74126	1.74179	1.74233	1.74286	1.74339	1.74393	1.74446	1.74499	1.74552	1.74605
82	1.74658	1.74711	1.74764	1.74817	1.74870	1.74922	1.74975	1.75028	1.75080	1.75132
83	1.75185	1.75237	1.75289	1.75342	1.75394	1.75446	1.75498	1.75550	1.75601	1.75653
84	1.75705	1.75757	1.75808	1.75860	1.75911	1.75963	1.76014	1.76065	1.76117	1.76168
85	1.76219	1.76270	1.76321	1.76372	1.76423	1.76474	1.76524	1.76575	1.76626	1.76676
86	1.76727	1.76777	1.76828	1.76878	1.76928	1.76979	1.77029	1.77079	1.77129	1.77179
87	1.77229	1.77279	1.77329	1.77378	1.77428	1.77478	1.77527	1.77577	1.77626	1.77676
88	1.77725	1.77775	1.77824	1.77873	1.77922	1.77971	1.78020	1.78069	1.78118	1.78167
89	1.78216	1.78265	1.78313	1.78362	1.78411	1.78459	1.78508	1.78556	1.78605	1.78653
90	1.78701	1.78749	1.78798	1.78846	1.78894	1.78942	1.78990	1.79038	1.79086	1.79133
91	1.79181	1.79229	1.79276	1.79324	1.79372	1.79419	1.79467	1.79514	1.79561	1.79609
92	1.79656	1.79703	1.79750	1.79797	1.79844	1.79891	1.79938	1.79985	1.80032	1.80079
93	1.80125	1.80172	1.80219	1.80265	1.80312	1.80358	1.80405	1.80451	1.80497	1.80544
94	1.80590	1.80636	1.80682	1.80728	1.80774	1.80820	1.80866	1.80912	1.80958	1.81004
95	1.81049	1.81095	1.81141	1.81186	1.81232	1.81277	1.81323	1.81368	1.81414	1.81459
96	1.81504	1.81549	1.81595	1.81640	1.81685	1.81730	1.81775	1.81820	1.81865	1.81909
97	1.81954	1.81999	1.82044	1.82088	1.82133	1.82177	1.82222	1.82266	1.82311	1.82355
98	1.82400	1.82444	1.82488	1.82532	1.82577	1.82621	1.82665	1.82709	1.82753	1.82797
99	1.82841	1.82884	1.82928	1.82972	1.83016	1.83059	1.83103	1.83147	1.83190	1.83234
100	1.83277	1.83320	1.83364	1.83407	1.83450	1.83494	1.83537	1.83580	1.83623	1.83666
101	1.83709	1.83752	1.83795	1.83838	1.83881	1.83924	1.83966	1.84009	1.84052	1.84094
102	1.84137	1.84180	1.84222	1.84265	1.84307	1.84349	1.84392	1.84434	1.84476	1.84519
103	1.84561	1.84603	1.84645	1.84687	1.84729	1.84771	1.84813	1.84855	1.84897	1.84939
104	1.84980	1.85022	1.85064	1.85105	1.85147	1.85189	1.85230	1.85272	1.85313	1.85355
105	1.85396	1.85437	1.85479	1.85520	1.85561	1.85602	1.85643	1.85684	1.85726	1.85767
106	1.85808	1.85849	1.85889	1.85930	1.85971	1.86012	1.86053	1.86093	1.86134	1.86175
107	1.86215	1.86256	1.86296	1.86337	1.86377	1.86418	1.86458	1.86499	1.86539	1.86579
108	1.86619	1.86660	1.86700	1.86740	1.86780	1.86820	1.86860	1.86900	1.86940	1.86980
109	1.87020	1.87059	1.87099	1.87139	1.87179	1.87218	1.87258	1.87298	1.87337	1.87377
110	1.87416	1.87456	1.87495	1.87535	1.87574	1.87613	1.87653	1.87692	1.87731	1.87770
111	1.87809	1.87848	1.87887	1.87927	1.87966	1.88004	1.88043	1.88082	1.88121	1.88160
112	1.88199	1.88238	1.88276	1.88315	1.88354	1.88392	1.88431	1.88469	1.88508	1.88546
113	1.88585	1.88623	1.88662	1.88700	1.88738	1.88777	1.88815	1.88853	1.88891	1.88929
114	1.88967	1.89006	1.89044	1.89082	1.89120	1.89158	1.89195	1.89233	1.89271	1.89309
115	1.89347	1.89385	1.89422	1.89460	1.89498	1.89535	1.89573	1.89610	1.89648	1.89685
116	1.89723	1.89760	1.89798	1.89835	1.89872	1.89910	1.89947	1.89984	1.90021	1.90058
117	1.90096	1.90133	1.90170	1.90207	1.90244	1.90281	1.90318	1.90355	1.90392	1.90428
118	1.90465	1.90502	1.90539	1.90575	1.90612	1.90649	1.90685	1.90722	1.90759	1.90795
119	1.90832	1.90868	1.90905	1.90941	1.90977	1.91014	1.91050	1.91086	1.91123	1.91159
H. or B.	0	1	2	3	4	5	6	7	8	9

H. or B.	0	1	2	3	4	5	6	7	8	9
0	Inf. neg	—1.28432	—1.58535	—1.76144	—1.88638	—1.98329	0.06247	0.12942	0.18741	0.23856
1	0.28432	0.32571	0.36350	0.39826	0.43045	0.46041	0.48844	0.51477	0.53959	0.56307
2	0.58535	0.60654	0.62674	0.64605	0.66453	0.68226	0.69929	0.71568	0.73148	0.74672
3	0.76144	0.77568	0.78947	0.80283	0.81580	0.82839	0.84062	0.85252	0.86410	0.87538
4	0.88638	0.89710	0.90757	0.91779	0.92777	0.93753	0.94708	0.95642	0.96556	0.97452
5	0.98329	0.99189	1.00032	1.00860	1.01671	1.02468	1.03251	1.04019	1.04775	1.05517
6	1.06247	1.06965	1.07671	1.08366	1.09050	1.09723	1.10386	1.11039	1.11683	1.12317
7	1.12942	1.13558	1.14165	1.14764	1.15355	1.15938	1.16513	1.17081	1.17641	1.18195
8	1.18741	1.19281	1.19813	1.20340	1.20860	1.21374	1.21882	1.22384	1.22880	1.23371
9	1.23856	1.24336	1.24811	1.25280	1.25745	1.26204	1.26659	1.27109	1.27555	1.27996
10	1.28432	1.28864	1.29292	1.29716	1.30135	1.30551	1.30963	1.31370	1.31774	1.32175
11	1.32571	1.32964	1.33354	1.33740	1.34122	1.34502	1.34878	1.35251	1.35620	1.35987
12	1.36350	1.36711	1.37068	1.37423	1.37774	1.38123	1.38469	1.38812	1.39153	1.39491
13	1.39826	1.40159	1.40489	1.40817	1.41142	1.41465	1.41786	1.42104	1.42420	1.42733
14	1.43045	1.43354	1.43661	1.43966	1.44268	1.44569	1.44867	1.45164	1.45458	1.45751
15	1.46041	1.46330	1.46616	1.46901	1.47184	1.47465	1.47744	1.48022	1.48298	1.48572
16	1.48844	1.49115	1.49384	1.49651	1.49916	1.50180	1.50443	1.50704	1.50963	1.51221
17	1.51477	1.51732	1.51985	1.52237	1.52487	1.52736	1.52983	1.53229	1.53474	1.53717
18	1.53959	1.54200	1.54439	1.54677	1.54914	1.55149	1.55383	1.55616	1.55848	1.56078
19	1.56307	1.56535	1.56762	1.56988	1.57212	1.57435	1.57658	1.57879	1.58099	1.58317
20	1.58535	1.58752	1.58967	1.59182	1.59395	1.59607	1.59819	1.60029	1.60238	1.60447
21	1.60654	1.60860	1.61066	1.61270	1.61473	1.61676	1.61877	1.62078	1.62278	1.62476
22	1.62674	1.62871	1.63067	1.63262	1.63457	1.63650	1.63843	1.64035	1.64225	1.64416
23	1.64605	1.64793	1.64981	1.65168	1.65354	1.65539	1.65723	1.65907	1.66090	1.66272
24	1.66453	1.66634	1.66814	1.66993	1.67171	1.67349	1.67526	1.67702	1.67877	1.68052
25	1.68226	1.68399	1.68572	1.68744	1.68915	1.69086	1.69256	1.69425	1.69594	1.69762
26	1.69929	1.70096	1.70262	1.70428	1.70592	1.70757	1.70920	1.71083	1.71245	1.71407
27	1.71568	1.71729	1.71889	1.72048	1.72207	1.72365	1.72523	1.72680	1.72836	1.72992
28	1.73148	1.73303	1.73457	1.73611	1.73764	1.73916	1.74069	1.74220	1.74371	1.74522
29	1.74672	1.74821	1.74970	1.75119	1.75267	1.75414	1.75561	1.75708	1.75854	1.75999
30	1.76144	1.76289	1.76433	1.76576	1.76719	1.76862	1.77004	1.77146	1.77287	1.77428
31	1.77568	1.77708	1.77847	1.77986	1.78125	1.78263	1.78401	1.78538	1.78675	1.78811
32	1.78947	1.79083	1.79218	1.79352	1.79487	1.79620	1.79754	1.79887	1.80019	1.80152
33	1.80283	1.80415	1.80546	1.80676	1.80807	1.80936	1.81066	1.81195	1.81324	1.81452
34	1.81580	1.81707	1.81835	1.81961	1.82088	1.82214	1.82340	1.82465	1.82590	1.82715
35	1.82839	1.82963	1.83086	1.83209	1.83332	1.83455	1.83577	1.83699	1.83820	1.83941
36	1.84062	1.84183	1.84303	1.84423	1.84542	1.84661	1.84780	1.84899	1.85017	1.85135
37	1.85252	1.85369	1.85486	1.85603	1.85719	1.85835	1.85951	1.86066	1.86181	1.86296
38	1.86410	1.86524	1.86638	1.86752	1.86865	1.86978	1.87091	1.87203	1.87315	1.87427
39	1.87538	1.87650	1.87761	1.87871	1.87982	1.88092	1.88202	1.88311	1.88420	1.88529
40	1.88638	1.88746	1.88855	1.88963	1.89070	1.89178	1.89285	1.89391	1.89498	1.89604
41	1.89710	1.89816	1.89922	1.90027	1.90132	1.90237	1.90341	1.90446	1.90550	1.90653
42	1.90757	1.90860	1.90963	1.91066	1.91169	1.91271	1.91373	1.91475	1.91576	1.91678
43	1.91779	1.91880	1.91980	1.92081	1.92181	1.92281	1.92381	1.92480	1.92579	1.92678
44	1.92777	1.92876	1.92974	1.93072	1.93170	1.93268	1.93365	1.93463	1.93560	1.93657
45	1.93753	1.93850	1.93946	1.94042	1.94138	1.94233	1.94328	1.94424	1.94519	1.94613
46	1.94708	1.94802	1.94896	1.94990	1.95084	1.95177	1.95271	1.95364	1.95457	1.95549
47	1.95642	1.95734	1.95826	1.95918	1.96010	1.96101	1.96193	1.96284	1.96375	1.96466
48	1.96556	1.96647	1.96737	1.96827	1.96917	1.97006	1.97096	1.97185	1.97274	1.97363
49	1.97452	1.97540	1.97629	1.97717	1.97805	1.97893	1.97980	1.98068	1.98155	1.98242
50	1.98329	1.98416	1.98502	1.98589	1.98675	1.98761	1.98847	1.98933	1.99018	1.99104
51	1.99189	1.99274	1.99359	1.99444	1.99528	1.99613	1.99697	1.99781	1.99865	1.99949
52	2.00032	2.00116	2.00199	2.00282	2.00365	2.00448	2.00531	2.00613	2.00695	2.00778
53	2.00860	2.00941	2.01023	2.01105	2.01186	2.01267	2.01348	2.01429	2.01510	2.01591
54	2.01671	2.01752	2.01832	2.01912	2.01992	2.02072	2.02151	2.02231	2.02310	2.02389
55	2.02468	2.02547	2.02626	2.02705	2.02783	2.02861	2.02939	2.03018	2.03095	2.03173
56	2.03251	2.03328	2.03406	2.03483	2.03560	2.03637	2.03714	2.03790	2.03867	2.03943
57	2.04019	2.04096	2.04172	2.04247	2.04323	2.04399	2.04474	2.04550	2.04625	2.04700
58	2.04775	2.04850	2.04924	2.04999	2.05073	2.05148	2.05222	2.05296	2.05370	2.05444
59	2.05517	2.05591	2.05664	2.05737	2.05811	2.05884	2.05957	2.06029	2.06102	2.06175

H. or B. 0 1 2 3 4 5 6 7 8 9

H. or B.	0	1	2	3	4	5	6	7	8	9
60	2.06247	2.06319	2.06392	2.06464	2.06536	2.06608	2.06679	2.06751	2.06822	2.06894
61	2.06965	2.07036	2.07107	2.07178	2.07249	2.07320	2.07390	2.07461	2.07531	2.07601
62	2.07671	2.07741	2.07811	2.07881	2.07950	2.08020	2.08089	2.08159	2.08228	2.08297
63	2.08366	2.08435	2.08504	2.08572	2.08641	2.08709	2.08778	2.08846	2.08914	2.08982
64	2.09050	2.09118	2.09186	2.09253	2.09321	2.09388	2.09455	2.09522	2.09590	2.09656
65	2.09723	2.09790	2.09857	2.09923	2.09990	2.10056	2.10122	2.10189	2.10255	2.10321
66	2.10386	2.10452	2.10518	2.10583	2.10649	2.10714	2.10779	2.10845	2.10910	2.10975
67	2.11039	2.11104	2.11169	2.11234	2.11298	2.11362	2.11427	2.11491	2.11555	2.11619
68	2.11683	2.11747	2.11810	2.11874	2.11938	2.12001	2.12064	2.12128	2.12191	2.12254
69	2.12317	2.12380	2.12443	2.12505	2.12568	2.12630	2.12693	2.12755	2.12818	2.12880
70	2.12942	2.13004	2.13066	2.13128	2.13189	2.13251	2.13312	2.13374	2.13435	2.13497
71	2.13558	2.13619	2.13680	2.13741	2.13802	2.13863	2.13923	2.13984	2.14044	2.14105
72	2.14165	2.14226	2.14286	2.14346	2.14406	2.14466	2.14526	2.14585	2.14645	2.14705
73	2.14764	2.14824	2.14883	2.14942	2.15002	2.15061	2.15120	2.15179	2.15238	2.15296
74	2.15355	2.15414	2.15472	2.15531	2.15589	2.15648	2.15706	2.15764	2.15822	2.15880
75	2.15938	2.15996	2.16054	2.16111	2.16169	2.16227	2.16284	2.16342	2.16399	2.16456
76	2.16513	2.16570	2.16627	2.16684	2.16741	2.16798	2.16855	2.16912	2.16968	2.17025
77	2.17081	2.17137	2.17194	2.17250	2.17306	2.17362	2.17418	2.17474	2.17530	2.17586
78	2.17641	2.17697	2.17753	2.17808	2.17864	2.17919	2.17974	2.18029	2.18085	2.18140
79	2.18195	2.18250	2.18305	2.18359	2.18414	2.18469	2.18523	2.18578	2.18632	2.18687
80	2.18741	2.18795	2.18849	2.18904	2.18958	2.19012	2.19066	2.19119	2.19173	2.19227
81	2.19281	2.19334	2.19388	2.19441	2.19494	2.19548	2.19601	2.19654	2.19707	2.19760
82	2.19813	2.19866	2.19919	2.19972	2.20025	2.20077	2.20130	2.20183	2.20235	2.20287
83	2.20340	2.20392	2.20444	2.20497	2.20549	2.20601	2.20653	2.20705	2.20756	2.20808
84	2.20860	2.20912	2.20963	2.21015	2.21066	2.21118	2.21169	2.21220	2.21272	2.21323
85	2.21374	2.21425	2.21476	2.21527	2.21578	2.21629	2.21679	2.21730	2.21781	2.21831
86	2.21882	2.21932	2.21983	2.22033	2.22083	2.22134	2.22184	2.22234	2.22284	2.22334
87	2.22384	2.22434	2.22484	2.22533	2.22583	2.22633	2.22682	2.22732	2.22781	2.22831
88	2.22880	2.22930	2.22979	2.23028	2.23077	2.23126	2.23175	2.23224	2.23273	2.23322
89	2.23371	2.23420	2.23468	2.23517	2.23566	2.23614	2.23663	2.23711	2.23760	2.23808
90	2.23856	2.23904	2.23953	2.24001	2.24049	2.24097	2.24145	2.24193	2.24241	2.24288
91	2.24336	2.24384	2.24431	2.24479	2.24527	2.24574	2.24622	2.24669	2.24716	2.24764
92	2.24811	2.24858	2.24905	2.24952	2.24999	2.25046	2.25093	2.25140	2.25187	2.25234
93	2.25280	2.25327	2.25374	2.25420	2.25467	2.25513	2.25560	2.25606	2.25652	2.25699
94	2.25745	2.25791	2.25837	2.25883	2.25929	2.25975	2.26021	2.26067	2.26113	2.26159
95	2.26204	2.26250	2.26296	2.26341	2.26387	2.26432	2.26478	2.26523	2.26569	2.26614
96	2.26659	2.26704	2.26750	2.26795	2.26840	2.26885	2.26930	2.26975	2.27020	2.27064
97	2.27109	2.27154	2.27199	2.27243	2.27288	2.27332	2.27377	2.27421	2.27466	2.27510
98	2.27555	2.27599	2.27643	2.27687	2.27732	2.27776	2.27820	2.27864	2.27908	2.27952
99	2.27996	2.28039	2.28083	2.28127	2.28171	2.28214	2.28258	2.28302	2.28345	2.28389
100	2.28432	2.28475	2.28519	2.28562	2.28605	2.28649	2.28692	2.28735	2.28778	2.28821
101	2.28864	2.28907	2.28950	2.28993	2.29036	2.29079	2.29121	2.29164	2.29207	2.29249
102	2.29292	2.29335	2.29377	2.29420	2.29462	2.29504	2.29547	2.29589	2.29631	2.29674
103	2.29716	2.29758	2.29800	2.29842	2.29884	2.29926	2.29968	2.30010	2.30052	2.30094
104	2.30135	2.30177	2.30219	2.30260	2.30302	2.30344	2.30385	2.30427	2.30468	2.30510
105	2.30551	2.30592	2.30634	2.30675	2.30716	2.30757	2.30798	2.30839	2.30881	2.30922
106	2.30963	2.31004	2.31044	2.31085	2.31126	2.31167	2.31208	2.31248	2.31289	2.31330
107	2.31370	2.31411	2.31451	2.31492	2.31532	2.31573	2.31613	2.31654	2.31694	2.31734
108	2.31774	2.31815	2.31855	2.31895	2.31935	2.31975	2.32015	2.32055	2.32095	2.32135
109	2.32175	2.32214	2.32254	2.32294	2.32334	2.32373	2.32413	2.32453	2.32492	2.32532
110	2.32571	2.32611	2.32650	2.32690	2.32729	2.32768	2.32808	2.32847	2.32886	2.32925
111	2.32964	2.33003	2.33042	2.33082	2.33121	2.33159	2.33198	2.33237	2.33276	2.33315
112	2.33354	2.33393	2.33431	2.33470	2.33509	2.33547	2.33586	2.33624	2.33663	2.33701
113	2.33740	2.33778	2.33817	2.33855	2.33893	2.33932	2.33970	2.34008	2.34046	2.34084
114	2.34122	2.34161	2.34199	2.34237	2.34275	2.34313	2.34350	2.34388	2.34426	2.34464
115	2.34502	2.34540	2.34577	2.34615	2.34653	2.34690	2.34728	2.34765	2.34803	2.34840
116	2.34878	2.34915	2.34953	2.34990	2.35027	2.35065	2.35102	2.35139	2.35176	2.35213
117	2.35251	2.35288	2.35325	2.35362	2.35399	2.35436	2.35473	2.35510	2.35547	2.35583
118	2.35620	2.35657	2.35694	2.35730	2.35767	2.35804	2.35840	2.35877	2.35914	2.35950
119	2.35987	2.36023	2.36060	2.36096	2.36132	2.36169	2.36205	2.36241	2.36278	2.36314
H. or B.	0	1	2	3	4	5	6	7	8	9

TABLE XXV. Logarithms of Eighth Parts of Square Prisms.

SUMS.	0	1	2	3	4	SUMS.
1	—1.665 5463	—1.748 3315	—1.823 9090	—1.893 4327	—1.957 8022	1
2	0.267 6058	0.309 9855	0.350 3915	0.389 0012	0.425 9693	2
3	0.619 7891	0.648 2693	0.675 8461	0.702 5744	0.728 5040	3
4	0.869 6664	0.891 1141	0.912 0450	0.932 4834	0.952 4515	4
5	1.063 4873	1.080 6878	1.097 5523	1.114 0970	1.130 3338	5
6	1.221 8496	1.236 2072	1.250 8297	1.264 2273	1.277 9070	6
7	1.355 7426	1.368 0636	1.380 2112	1.392 1921	1.404 0105	7
8	1.471 7258	1.482 5163	1.493 1735	1.503 7022	1.514 1053	8
9	1.574 0313	1.583 6295	1.593 1221	1.602 5125	1.611 8018	9
10	1.665 5463	1.674 1895	1.682 7469	1.691 2203	1.699 6132	10
11	1.748 3315	1.756 1924	1.763 9825	1.771 7028	1.779 3562	11
12	1.823 9090	1.831 1170	1.838 2658	1.845 3566	1.852 3897	12
13	1.893 4327	1.900 0890	1.906 6943	1.913 2495	1.919 7557	13
14	1.957 8022	1.963 9846	1.970 1281	1.976 2184	1.982 2712	14
15	2.017 7301	2.023 4994	2.029 2336	2.034 9291	2.040 5865	15
16	2.073 7879	2.079 1993	2.084 5763	2.089 9227	2.095 2356	16
17	2.126 4431	2.131 5385	2.136 6032	2.141 6379	2.146 6458	17
18	2.176 0913	2.180 9026	2.185 6895	2.190 4494	2.195 1826	18
19	2.223 0544	2.227 6142	2.232 1496	2.236 6607	2.241 1504	19
20	2.267 6058	2.271 9391	2.276 2480	2.280 5374	2.284 8074	20
21	2.309 9855	2.314 1117	2.318 2178	2.322 3061	2.326 3748	21
22	2.350 3915	2.354 3313	2.358 2528	2.362 1562	2.366 0417	22
23	2.389 0012	2.392 7708	2.396 5219	2.400 2581	2.403 9780	23
24	2.425 9693	2.429 5811	2.433 1776	2.436 7588	2.440 3265	24
25	2.461 4265	2.464 8933	2.468 3473	2.471 7874	2.475 2134	25
26	2.495 4930	2.498 8273	2.502 1484	2.505 4580	2.508 7546	26
27	2.528 2738	2.531 4853	2.534 6846	2.537 8719	2.541 0473	27
28	2.559 8624	2.562 9587	2.566 0449	2.569 1186	2.572 1824	28
29	2.590 3424	2.593 3326	2.596 3122	2.599 2814	2.602 2413	29
30	2.619 7891	2.622 6792	2.625 5604	2.628 4318	2.631 2935	30
31	2.648 2693	2.651 0666	2.653 8557	2.656 6347	2.659 4056	31
32	2.675 8461	2.678 5566	2.681 2584	2.683 9516	2.686 6363	32
33	2.702 5744	2.705 2024	2.707 8222	2.710 4347	2.713 0392	33
34	2.728 5040	2.731 0551	2.733 5985	2.736 1343	2.738 6633	34
35	2.753 6826	2.756 1605	2.758 6319	2.761 0960	2.763 5531	35
36	2.778 1513	2.780 5607	2.782 9633	2.785 3597	2.787 7488	36
37	2.801 9495	2.804 2942	2.806 6324	2.808 9641	2.811 2894	37
38	2.825 1138	2.827 3964	2.829 6730	2.831 9439	2.834 2089	38
39	2.847 6757	2.849 8995	2.852 1182	2.854 3315	2.856 5386	39
40	2.869 6664	2.871 8349	2.873 9986	2.876 1566	2.878 3092	40
41	2.891 1141	2.893 2301	2.895 3408	2.897 4462	2.899 5469	41
42	2.912 0450	2.914 1103	2.916 1712	2.918 2270	2.920 2778	42
43	2.932 4834	2.934 5010	2.936 5137	2.938 5222	2.940 5259	43
44	2.952 4515	2.954 4234	2.956 3908	2.958 3536	2.960 3124	44
45	2.971 9713	2.973 8992	2.975 8232	2.977 7428	2.979 6581	45
46	2.991 0621	2.992 9483	2.994 8304	2.996 7082	2.998 5823	46
47	3.009 7440	3.011 5874	3.013 4313	3.015 2675	3.017 1043	47
48	3.028 0301	3.029 8381	3.031 6387	3.033 4399	3.035 2376	48
49	3.045 9368	3.047 7109	3.049 4777	3.051 2413	3.053 0016	49
50	3.063 4873	3.065 2211	3.066 9555	3.068 6830	3.070 4073	50
51	3.080 6878	3.082 3868	3.084 0863	3.085 7810	3.087 4726	51
52	3.097 5523	3.099 2213	3.100 8873	3.102 5503	3.104 2105	52
53	3.114 0970	3.115 7353	3.117 3707	3.119 0017	3.120 6298	53
54	3.130 3338	3.131 9393	3.133 5453	3.135 1454	3.136 7428	54
55	3.146 2707	3.147 8493	3.149 4255	3.150 9958	3.152 5666	55
56	3.161 9218	3.163 4715	3.165 0187	3.166 5633	3.168 1055	56
57	3.177 2969	3.178 8187	3.180 3381	3.181 8550	3.183 3695	57
58	3.192 4030	3.193 8978	3.195 3931	3.196 8833	3.198 3711	58
59	3.207 2492	3.208 7208	3.210 1901	3.211 6544	3.213 1191	59
60	3.221 8496	3.223 2960	3.224 7402	3.226 1808	3.227 6193	60
SUMS.	0	1	2	3	4	SUMS.

SUMS.	5	6	7	8	9	SUMS.
1	0.017 7302	0.073 7879	0.126 4431	0.176 0913	0.223 0544	1
2	0.461 4265	0.495 4930	0.528 2738	0.559 8624	0.590 3424	2
3	0.758 6826	0.778 1513	0.801 9495	0.825 1138	0.847 6757	3
4	0.971 9718	0.991 0621	1.009 7440	1.028 0301	1.045 9368	4
5	1.146 2707	1.161 9218	1.177 2969	1.192 4030	1.207 2492	5
6	1.291 3733	1.304 6349	1.317 6957	1.330 5639	1.343 2451	6
7	1.415 6693	1.427 1727	1.438 5281	1.449 7360	1.460 8002	7
8	1.524 3844	1.534 5426	1.544 5852	1.554 5122	1.564 3263	8
9	1.620 9934	1.630 0890	1.639 0899	1.647 9988	1.656 8166	9
10	1.707 9252	1.716 1579	1.724 3185	1.732 3938	1.740 3990	10
11	1.786 9423	1.794 4623	1.801 9180	1.809 3105	1.816 6402	11
12	1.859 3665	1.866 2873	1.873 1537	1.879 9664	1.886 7258	12
13	1.926 2138	1.932 6239	1.938 9873	1.945 3046	1.951 5760	13
14	1.988 2824	1.994 2520	2.000 1823	2.006 0680	2.011 9171	14
15	2.046 2102	2.051 7967	2.057 3466	2.062 8601	2.068 3417	15
16	2.100 5153	2.105 7622	2.110 9801	2.116 1659	2.121 3201	16
17	2.151 6211	2.156 5703	2.161 4938	2.166 3857	2.171 2524	17
18	2.199 8895	2.204 5731	2.209 2307	2.213 8629	2.218 4699	18
19	2.245 6163	2.250 0588	2.254 4780	2.258 8766	2.263 2525	19
20	2.289 0536	2.293 2807	2.297 4870	2.301 6723	2.305 8392	20
21	2.330 4240	2.334 4538	2.338 4665	2.342 4602	2.346 4351	21
22	2.369 9113	2.373 7632	2.377 5976	2.381 4166	2.385 2165	22
23	2.407 6815	2.411 3705	2.415 0435	2.418 7006	2.422 3420	23
24	2.443 8791	2.447 4170	2.450 9401	2.454 4500	2.457 9454	24
25	2.478 6271	2.482 0256	2.485 4119	2.488 7862	2.492 1455	25
26	2.512 0383	2.515 3094	2.518 5692	2.521 8165	2.525 0513	26
27	2.544 2119	2.547 3648	2.550 5059	2.553 6355	2.556 7547	27
28	2.575 2363	2.578 2781	2.581 3101	2.584 3312	2.587 3416	28
29	2.605 1908	2.608 1301	2.611 0592	2.613 9792	2.616 8891	29
30	2.634 1456	2.636 9891	2.639 8230	2.642 6475	2.645 4636	30
31	2.662 1674	2.664 9201	2.667 6649	2.670 4008	2.673 1278	31
32	2.689 3133	2.691 9819	2.694 6421	2.697 2939	2.699 9383	32
33	2.715 6357	2.718 2251	2.720 8057	2.723 3793	2.725 9459	33
34	2.741 1847	2.743 6987	2.746 2051	2.748 7050	2.751 1975	34
35	2.766 0029	2.768 4464	2.770 8830	2.773 3124	2.775 7349	35
36	2.790 1317	2.792 5087	2.794 8782	2.797 2419	2.799 5990	36
37	2.813 6090	2.815 9222	2.818 2292	2.820 5298	2.822 8249	37
38	2.836 4678	2.838 7207	2.840 9682	2.843 2098	2.845 4453	38
39	2.858 7405	2.860 9366	2.863 1271	2.865 3125	2.867 4923	39
40	2.880 4563	2.882 5985	2.884 7353	2.886 8668	2.888 9928	40
41	2.901 6425	2.903 7328	2.905 8186	2.907 8986	2.909 9741	41
42	2.922 3242	2.924 3656	2.926 4021	2.928 4337	2.930 4610	42
43	2.942 5249	2.944 5192	2.946 5092	2.948 4946	2.950 4754	43
44	2.962 2661	2.964 2158	2.966 1614	2.968 1022	2.970 0390	44
45	2.981 5690	2.983 4761	2.985 3789	2.987 2774	2.989 1716	45
46	3.000 4514	3.002 3173	3.004 1794	3.006 0380	3.007 8927	46
47	3.018 9334	3.020 7589	3.022 5830	3.024 4036	3.026 2186	47
48	3.037 0279	3.038 8188	3.040 6023	3.042 3865	3.044 1633	48
49	3.054 7566	3.056 5085	3.058 2589	3.060 0062	3.061 7464	49
50	3.072 1286	3.073 8466	3.075 5616	3.077 2734	3.078 9822	50
51	3.089 1595	3.090 8468	3.092 5276	3.094 2055	3.095 8805	51
52	3.105 8643	3.107 5186	3.109 1666	3.110 8152	3.112 4575	52
53	3.122 2552	3.123 8745	3.125 4943	3.127 1113	3.128 7223	53
54	3.138 8406	3.139 9826	3.141 5219	3.143 1085	3.144 6908	54
55	3.154 1317	3.155 6973	3.157 2573	3.158 8146	3.160 3695	55
56	3.169 6421	3.171 1792	3.172 7124	3.174 2430	3.175 7698	56
57	3.184 8816	3.186 3912	3.187 8985	3.189 4033	3.190 9029	57
58	3.199 8580	3.201 3425	3.202 8233	3.204 3018	3.205 7780	58
59	3.214 5790	3.216 0892	3.217 4945	3.218 9475	3.220 4010	59
60	3.229 0570	3.230 4924	3.231 9230	3.233 3540	3.234 7804	60
SUMS.	5	6	7	8	9	SUMS.

TABLE XXV. Logarithms of Eighth Parts of Square Prisms.

SUMS.	0	1	2	3	4	SUMS.
61	3.236 2072	3.237 6292	3.239 0491	3.240 4669	3.241 8826	61
62	3.250 3297	3.251 7294	3.253 1271	3.254 5215	3.255 9163	62
63	3.264 2273	3.265 6054	3.266 9816	3.268 3533	3.269 7253	63
64	3.277 9070	3.279 2630	3.280 6171	3.281 9691	3.283 3170	64
65	3.291 3783	3.292 7078	3.294 0406	3.295 3735	3.296 7025	65
66	3.304 6349	3.305 9486	3.307 2627	3.308 5730	3.309 8835	66
67	3.317 6957	3.318 9915	3.320 2855	3.321 5756	3.322 8661	67
68	3.330 5639	3.331 8401	3.333 1146	3.334 3874	3.335 6585	68
69	3.343 2451	3.344 5023	3.345 7579	3.347 0128	3.348 2659	69
70	3.355 7426	3.356 9814	3.358 2205	3.359 4560	3.360 6919	70
71	3.368 0636	3.369 2854	3.370 5057	3.371 7253	3.372 9433	71
72	3.380 2112	3.381 4166	3.382 6208	3.383 8226	3.385 0233	72
73	3.392 1921	3.393 3804	3.394 5690	3.395 7544	3.396 9383	73
74	3.404 0105	3.405 1823	3.406 3545	3.407 5235	3.408 6927	74
75	3.415 6693	3.416 8268	3.417 9812	3.419 1359	3.420 2892	75
76	3.427 1727	3.428 3162	3.429 4567	3.430 5958	3.431 7336	76
77	3.438 5281	3.439 6547	3.440 7816	3.441 9056	3.443 0282	77
78	3.449 7360	3.450 8478	3.451 9598	3.453 0698	3.454 1785	78
79	3.460 8002	3.461 8990	3.462 9966	3.464 0930	3.465 1880	79
80	3.471 7258	3.472 8113	3.473 8955	3.474 9778	3.476 0589	80
81	3.482 5163	3.483 5873	3.484 6585	3.485 7271	3.486 7945	81
82	3.493 1735	3.494 2325	3.495 2903	3.496 3456	3.497 4010	82
83	3.503 7022	3.504 7480	3.505 7928	3.506 8364	3.507 8788	83
84	3.514 1053	3.515 1384	3.516 1708	3.517 2012	3.518 2309	84
85	3.524 3844	3.525 4050	3.526 4258	3.527 4443	3.528 4616	85
86	3.534 5426	3.535 5523	3.536 5609	3.537 5673	3.538 5737	86
87	3.544 5852	3.545 5829	3.546 5797	3.547 5747	3.548 5688	87
88	3.554 5122	3.555 4983	3.556 4834	3.557 4676	3.558 4506	88
89	3.564 3263	3.565 3016	3.566 2760	3.567 2487	3.568 2217	89
90	3.574 0318	3.574 9960	3.575 9599	3.576 9216	3.577 8834	90
91	3.583 6295	3.584 5834	3.585 5363	3.586 4883	3.587 4382	91
92	3.593 1221	3.594 0653	3.595 0077	3.595 9501	3.596 8906	92
93	3.602 5125	3.603 4453	3.604 3784	3.605 3093	3.606 2405	93
94	3.611 8018	3.612 7256	3.613 6484	3.614 5693	3.615 4903	94
95	3.620 9934	3.621 9071	3.622 8200	3.623 7319	3.624 6430	95
96	3.630 0890	3.630 9930	3.631 8961	3.632 7988	3.633 7007	96
97	3.639 0899	3.639 9842	3.640 8788	3.641 7715	3.642 6643	97
98	3.647 9988	3.648 8843	3.649 7689	3.650 6532	3.651 5368	98
99	3.656 8166	3.657 6934	3.658 5695	3.659 4446	3.660 3189	99
100	3.665 5463	3.666 4141	3.667 2820	3.668 1482	3.669 0136	100
101	3.674 1895	3.675 0484	3.675 9075	3.676 7649	3.677 6225	101
102	3.682 7469	3.683 5981	3.684 4477	3.685 2974	3.686 1463	102
103	3.691 2203	3.692 0640	3.692 9060	3.693 7471	3.694 5877	103
104	3.699 6132	3.700 4476	3.701 2821	3.702 1150	3.702 9472	104
105	3.707 9252	3.708 7514	3.709 5778	3.710 4030	3.711 2275	105
106	3.716 1579	3.716 9769	3.717 7953	3.718 6129	3.719 4299	106
107	3.724 3135	3.725 1252	3.725 9361	3.726 7460	3.727 5551	107
108	3.732 3938	3.733 1978	3.734 0009	3.734 8030	3.735 6045	108
109	3.740 3990	3.741 1957	3.741 9918	3.742 7864	3.743 5811	109
110	3.748 3315	3.749 1208	3.749 9094	3.750 6974	3.751 4847	110
111	3.756 1924	3.756 9744	3.757 7557	3.758 5364	3.759 3165	111
112	3.763 9825	3.764 7573	3.765 5322	3.766 3057	3.767 0786	112
113	3.771 7028	3.772 4713	3.773 2392	3.774 0057	3.774 7724	113
114	3.779 3562	3.780 1178	3.780 8787	3.781 6387	3.782 3981	114
115	3.786 9423	3.787 6970	3.788 4512	3.789 2048	3.789 9578	115
116	3.794 4623	3.795 2106	3.795 9585	3.796 7054	3.797 4524	116
117	3.801 9180	3.802 6602	3.803 4018	3.804 1421	3.804 8826	117
118	3.809 3105	3.810 0462	3.810 7814	3.811 5160	3.812 2494	118
119	3.816 6402	3.817 3696	3.818 0985	3.818 8274	3.819 5551	119
120	3.823 9090	3.824 6321	3.825 3554	3.826 0774	3.826 7996	120
SUMS.	0	1	2	3	4	SUMS.

SUMS.	5	6	7	8	9	SUMS.
61	3.243 2960	3.244 7075	3.246 1168	3.247 5240	3.248 9267	61
62	3.257 3065	3.258 6948	3.260 0809	3.261 4651	3.262 8472	62
63	3.271 0931	3.272 4612	3.273 8251	3.275 1869	3.276 5480	63
64	3.284 6653	3.286 0116	3.287 3538	3.288 6963	3.290 0346	64
65	3.298 0295	3.299 3547	3.300 6770	3.301 9974	3.303 3171	65
66	3.311 1900	3.312 4947	3.313 7977	3.315 0988	3.316 3982	66
67	3.324 1538	3.325 4398	3.326 7229	3.328 0063	3 329 2860	67
68	3.336 9278	3.338 1954	3.339 4594	3.340 7237	3.341 9842	68
69	3.349 5165	3.350 7654	3.352 0127	3.353 2563	3.354 5003	69
70	3.361 9242	3.363 1549	3.364 3859	3.365 6134	3.366 8393	70
71	3.374 1579	3.375 3727	3.376 5843	3.377 7960	3.379 0044	71
72	3.386 2225	3.387 .4201	3.388 6144	3.389 8091	3.391 0013	72
73	3.398 1207	3.399 3016	3.400 4810	3.401 6590	3.402 8355	73
74	3.409 8587	3.411 0234	3.412 1874	3.413 3501	3.414 5104	74
75	3.421 4394	3.422 5898	3.423 7372	3.424 8849	3.426 0295	75
76	3.432 8691	3.434 0033	3.435 1369	3.436 2692	3.437 3985	76
77	3.444 1494	3.445 2694	3.446 3880	3.447 5053	3.448 6213	77
78	3.455 2850	3.456 3918	3.457 4959	3.458 5985	3.459 7000	78
79	3.466 2803	3.467 3728	3.468 4625	3.469 5525	3.470 6398	79
80	3.477 1386	3.478 2158	3.479 2931	3.480 3692	3.481 4426	80
81	3.487 8620	3.488 9271	3.489 9908	3.491 0534	3.492 1140	81
82	3.498 4539	3.499 5070	3.500 5576	3.501 6069	3.502 6551	82
83.	3.508 9188	3.509 9588	3.510 9971	3.512 0343	3.513 0697	83
84	3.519 2595	3.520 2870	3.521 3133	3.522 3386	3.523 3614	84
85	3.529 4785	3.530 4943	3.531 5083	3.532 5213	3.533 5331	85
86	3.539 5779	3.540 5822	3.541 5842	3.542 5852	3.543 5863	86
87	3.549 5623	3.550 5548	3.551 5452	3.552 5356	3.553 5238	87
88	3.559 4326	3.560 4136	3.561 3936	3.562 3725	3.563 3493	88
89	3.569 1925	3.570 1622	3.571 1309	3.572 0987	3.573 0655	89
90	3.578 8431	3.579 8031	3.580 7608	3.581 7176	3.582 6740	90
91	3.588 3883	3.589 3373	3.590 2844	3.591 2316	3.592 1768	91
92	3.597 8301	3.598 7686	3.599 7056	3.600 6418	3.601 5776	92
93	3.607 1697	3.608 0979	3.609 0253	3.609 9518	3.610 8772	93
94	3.616 4099	3.617 3286	3.618 2459	3.619 1633	3.620 0788	94
95	3.625 5532	3.626 4626	3.627 3700	3.628 2775	3.629 1833	95
96	3.634 6012	3.635 5009	3.636 3996	3.637 2966	3.638 1936	96
97	3.643 5553	3.644 4455	3.645 3358	3.646 2243	3.647 1119	97
98	3.652 4185	3.653 3004	3.654 1804	3.655 0606	3.655 9390	98
99	3.661 1925	3.662 0653	3.662 9363	3.663 8074	3.664 6773	99
100	3.669 8782	3.670 7421	3.671 6050	3.672 4673	3.673 3288	100
101	3.678 4784	3.679 3334	3.680 1882	3.681 0421	3.681 8949	101
102	3.686 9936	3.687 8410	3.688 6867	3.689 5326	3.690 3769	102
103	3.695 4270	3.696 2655	3.697 1037	3.697 9413	3.698 7772	103
104	3.703 7787	3.704 6095	3.705 4394	3.706 2687	3.707 0973	104
105	3.712 0509	3.712 8744	3.713 6963	3.714 5176	3.715 3380	105
106	3.720 2453	3.721 0608	3.721 8749	3.722 6890	3.723 5016	106
107	3.728 3635	3.729 1705	3.729 9775	3.730 7839	3.731 5888	107
108	3.736 4061	3.737 2062	3.738 0056	3.738 8043	3.739 6020	108
109	3.744 3744	3.745 1677	3.745 9596	3.746 7509	3.747 5416	109
110	3.752 2705	3.753 0565	3.753 8415	3.754 6258	3.755 4090	110
111	3.760 0959	3.760 8746	3.761 6527	3.762 4303	3.763 2063	111
112	3.767 8512	3.768 6233	3.769 3943	3.770 1647	3.770 9345	112
113	3.775 5376	3.776 3030	3.777 0671	3.777 8305	3.778 5940	113
114	3.783 1572	3.783 9157	3.784 6729	3.785 4302	3.786 1862	114
115	3.790 7101	3.791 4619	3.792 2130	3.792 9636	3.793 7129	115
116	3.798 1982	3.798 9433	3.799 6879	3.800 4318	3.801 1752	116
117	3.805 6218	3.806 3612	3.807 0992	3.807 8366	3.808 5738	117
118	3.812 9828	3.813 7157	3.814 4474	3.815 1791	3.815 9097	118
119	3.820 2823	3.821 0089	3.821 7346	3.822 4597	3.823 1846	119
120	3.827 5205	3.828 2409	3.828 9607	3.829 6800	3.830 3988	120
SUMS.	5	6	7	8	9	SUMS.

LOGARITHMS OF NUMBERS

FROM 1 TO 10,000.

Note. The index of the logarithm of every integer number consisting of only one figure is 0, of two figures 1, of three figures 2, of four figures 3; being always a unit less than the number of figures contained in the integer number. In this table, as is generally the case, the index to the logarithm of every number above 100 is omitted; yet in the operation must be prefixed according to this remark; so the logarithm of 700 is 2.84510, and of 7000 is 3,84510, and so of the rest.

No.	Log.	No.	Log.	No.	Log.	No.	Log.	No.	Log.
1	0.00000	21	1.32222	41	1.61278	61	1.78533	81	1.90849
2	0.30103	22	1.34242	42	1.62325	62	1.79239	82	1.91381
3	0.47712	23	1.36173	43	1.63347	63	1.79934	83	1.91908
4	0.60206	24	1.38021	44	1.64345	64	1.80618	84	1.92428
5	0.69897	25	1.39794	45	1.65321	65	1.81291	85	1.92942
6	0.77815	26	1.41497	46	1.66276	66	1.81954	86	1.93450
7	0.84510	27	1.43136	47	1.67210	67	1.82607	87	1.93952
8	0.90309	28	1.44716	48	1.68124	68	1.83251	88	1.94448
9	0.95424	29	1.46240	49	1.69020	69	1.83885	89	1.94939
10	1.00000	30	1.47712	50	1.69897	70	1.84510	90	1.95424
11	1.04139	31	1.49136	51	1.70757	71	1.85126	91	1.95904
12	1.07918	32	1.50515	52	1.71600	72	1.85733	92	1 96379
13	1.11394	33	1.51851	53	1.72428	73	1.86332	93	1.96848
14	1.14613	34	1.53148	54	1.73239	74	1.86923	94	1.97313
15	1.17609	35	1.54407	55	1.74036	75	1.87506	95	1.97772
16	1.20412	36	1.55630	56	1.74819	76	1.88081	96	1.98227
17	1.23045	37	1.56820	57	1.75587	77	1.88649	97	1.98677
18	1.25527	38	1.57978	58	1.76343	78	1.89209	98	1.99123
19	1.27875	39	1.59106	59	1.77085	79	1.89763	99	1.99564
20	1.30103	40	1.60206	60	1.77815	80	1.90309	100	2.00000

TABLE XXVI. Logarithms of Numbers from 1 to 10,000.

No.	0	1	2	3	4	5	6	7	8	9
100	00000	00043	00087	00130	00173	00217	00260	00303	00346	00389
101	00432	00475	00518	00561	00604	00647	00689	00732	00775	00817
102	00860	00903	00945	00988	01030	01072	01115	01157	01199	01242
103	01284	01326	01368	01410	01452	01494	01536	01578	01620	01662
104	01703	01745	01787	01828	01870	01912	01953	01995	02036	02078
105	02119	02160	02202	02243	02284	02325	02366	02407	02449	02490
106	02531	02572	02612	02653	02694	02735	02776	02816	02857	02898
107	02938	02979	03019	03060	03100	03141	03181	03222	03262	03302
108	03342	03383	03423	03463	03503	03543	03583	03623	03663	03703
109	03743	03782	03822	03862	03902	03941	03981	04021	04060	04100
110	04139	04179	04218	04258	04297	04336	04376	04415	04454	04493
111	04532	04571	04610	04650	04689	04727	04766	04805	04844	04883
112	04922	04961	04999	05038	05077	05115	05154	05192	05231	05269
113	05308	05346	05385	05423	05461	05500	05538	05576	05614	05652
114	05690	05729	05767	05805	05843	05881	05918	05956	05994	06032
115	06070	06108	06145	06183	06221	06258	06296	06333	06371	06408
116	06446	06483	06521	06558	06595	06633	06670	06707	06744	06781
117	06819	06856	06893	06930	06967	07004	07041	07078	07115	07151
118	07188	07225	07262	07298	07335	07372	07408	07445	07482	07518
119	07555	07591	07628	07664	07700	07737	07773	07809	07846	07882
120	07918	07954	07990	08027	08063	08099	08135	08171	08207	08243
121	08279	08314	08350	08386	08422	08458	08493	08529	08565	08600
122	08636	08672	08707	08743	08778	08814	08849	08884	08920	08955
123	08991	09026	09061	09096	09132	09167	09202	09237	09272	09307
124	09342	09377	09412	09447	09482	09517	09552	09587	09621	09656
125	09691	09726	09760	09795	09830	09864	09899	09934	09968	10003
126	10037	10072	10106	10140	10175	10209	10243	10278	10312	10346
127	10380	10415	10449	10483	10517	10551	10585	10619	10653	10687
128	10721	10755	10789	10823	10857	10890	10924	10958	10992	11025
129	11059	11093	11126	11160	11193	11227	11261	11294	11327	11361
130	11394	11428	11461	11494	11528	11561	11594	11628	11661	11694
131	11727	11760	11793	11826	11860	11893	11926	11959	11992	12024
132	12057	12090	12123	12156	12189	12222	12254	12287	12320	12352
133	12385	12418	12450	12483	12516	12548	12581	12613	12646	12678
134	12710	12743	12775	12808	12840	12872	12905	12937	12969	13001
135	13033	13066	13098	13130	13162	13194	13226	13258	13290	13322
136	13354	13386	13418	13450	13481	13513	13545	13577	13609	13640
137	13672	13704	13735	13767	13799	13830	13862	13893	13925	13956
138	13988	14019	14051	14082	14114	14145	14176	14208	14239	14270
139	14301	14333	14364	14395	14426	14457	14489	14520	14551	14582
140	14613	14644	14675	14706	14737	14768	14799	14829	14860	14891
141	14922	14953	14983	15014	15045	15076	15106	15137	15168	15198
142	15229	15259	15290	15320	15351	15381	15412	15442	15473	15503
143	15534	15564	15594	15625	15655	15685	15715	15746	15776	15806
144	15836	15866	15897	15927	15957	15987	16017	16047	16077	16107
145	16137	16167	16197	16227	16256	16286	16316	16346	16376	16406
146	16435	16465	16495	16524	16554	16584	16613	16643	16673	16702
147	16732	16761	16791	16820	16850	16879	16909	16938	16967	16997
148	17026	17056	17085	17114	17143	17173	17202	17231	17260	17289
149	17319	17348	17377	17406	17435	17464	17493	17522	17551	17580
150	17609	17638	17667	17696	17725	17754	17782	17811	17840	17869
151	17898	17926	17955	17984	18013	18041	18070	18099	18127	18156
152	18184	18213	18241	18270	18298	18327	18355	18384	18412	18441
153	18469	18498	18526	18554	18583	18611	18639	18667	18696	18724
154	18752	18780	18808	18837	18865	18893	18921	18949	18977	19005
155	19033	19061	19089	19117	19145	19173	19201	19229	19257	19285
156	19312	19340	19368	19396	19424	19451	19479	19507	19535	19562
157	19590	19618	19645	19673	19700	19728	19756	19783	19811	19838
158	19866	19893	19921	19948	19976	20003	20030	20058	20085	20112
159	20140	20167	20194	20222	20249	20276	20303	20330	20358	20385

No.	0	1	2	3	4	5	6	7	8	9
160	20412	20439	20466	20493	20520	20548	20575	20602	20629	20656
161	20683	20710	20737	20763	20790	20817	20844	20871	20898	20925
162	20952	20978	21005	21032	21059	21085	21112	21139	21165	21192
163	21219	21245	21272	21299	21325	21352	21378	21405	21431	21458
164	21484	21511	21537	21564	21590	21617	21643	21669	21696	21722
165	21748	21775	21801	21827	21854	21880	21906	21932	21958	21985
166	22011	22037	22063	22089	22115	22141	22167	22194	22220	22246
167	22272	22298	22324	22350	22376	22401	22427	22453	22479	22505
168	22531	22557	22583	22608	22634	22660	22686	22712	22737	22763
169	22789	22814	22840	22866	22891	22917	22943	22968	22994	23019
170	23045	23070	23096	23121	23147	23172	23198	23223	23249	23274
171	23300	23325	23350	23376	23401	23426	23452	23477	23502	23528
172	23553	23578	23603	23629	23654	23679	23704	23729	23754	23779
173	23805	23830	23855	23880	23905	23930	23955	23980	24005	24030
174	24055	24080	24105	24130	24155	24180	24204	24229	24254	24279
175	24304	24329	24353	24378	24403	24428	24452	24477	24502	24527
176	24551	24576	24601	24625	24650	24674	24699	24724	24748	24773
177	24797	24822	24846	24871	24895	24920	24944	24969	24993	25018
178	25042	25066	25091	25115	25139	25164	25188	25212	25237	25261
179	25285	25310	25334	25358	25382	25406	25431	25455	25479	25503
180	25527	25551	25575	25600	25624	25648	25672	25696	25720	25744
181	25768	25792	25816	25840	25864	25888	25912	25935	25959	25983
182	26007	26031	26055	26079	26102	26126	26150	26174	26198	26221
183	26245	26269	26293	26316	26340	26364	26387	26411	26435	26458
184	26482	26505	26529	26553	26576	26600	26623	26647	26670	26694
185	26717	26741	26764	26788	26811	26834	26858	26881	26905	26928
186	26951	26975	26998	27021	27045	27068	27091	27114	27138	27161
187	27184	27207	27231	27254	27277	27300	27323	27346	27370	27393
188	27416	27439	27462	27485	27508	27531	27554	27577	27600	27623
189	27646	27669	27692	27715	27738	27761	27784	27807	27830	27852
190	27875	27898	27921	27944	27967	27989	28012	28035	28058	28081
191	28103	28126	28149	28171	28194	28217	28240	28262	28285	28307
192	28330	28353	28375	28398	28421	28443	28466	28488	28511	28533
193	28556	28578	28601	28623	28646	28668	28691	28713	28735	28758
194	28780	28803	28825	28847	28870	28892	28914	28937	28959	28981
195	29003	29026	29048	29070	29092	29115	29137	29159	29181	29203
196	29226	29248	29270	29292	29314	29336	29358	29380	29403	29425
197	29447	29469	29491	29513	29535	29557	29579	29601	29623	29645
198	29667	29688	29710	29732	29754	29776	29798	29820	29842	29863
199	29885	29907	29929	29951	29973	29994	30016	30038	30060	30081
200	30103	30125	30146	30168	30190	30211	30233	30255	30276	30298
201	30320	30341	30363	30384	30406	30428	30449	30471	30492	30514
202	30535	30557	30578	30600	30621	30643	30664	30685	30707	30728
203	30750	30771	30792	30814	30835	30856	30878	30899	30920	30942
204	30963	30984	31006	31027	31048	31069	31091	31112	31133	31154
205	31175	31197	31218	31239	31260	31281	31302	31323	31345	31366
206	31387	31408	31429	31450	31471	31492	31513	31534	31555	31576
207	31597	31618	31639	31660	31681	31702	31723	31744	31765	31785
208	31806	31827	31848	31869	31890	31911	31931	31952	31973	31994
209	32015	32035	32056	32077	32098	32118	32139	32160	32181	32201
210	32222	32243	32263	32284	32305	32325	32346	32366	32387	32408
211	32428	32449	32469	32490	32510	32531	32552	32572	32593	32613
212	32634	32654	32675	32695	32715	32736	32756	32777	32797	32818
213	32838	32858	32879	32899	32919	32940	32960	32980	33001	33021
214	33041	33062	33082	33102	33122	33143	33163	33183	33203	33224
215	33244	33264	33284	33304	33325	33345	33365	33385	33405	33425
216	33445	33465	33486	33506	33526	33546	33566	33586	33606	33626
217	33646	33666	33686	33706	33726	33746	33766	33786	33806	33826
218	33846	33866	33885	33905	33925	33945	33965	33985	34005	34025
219	34044	34064	34084	34104	34124	34143	34163	34183	34203	34223

TABLE XXVI. Logarithms of Numbers from 1 to 10,000.

No.	0	1	2	3	4	5	6	7	8	9
220	34242	34262	34282	34301	34321	34341	34361	34380	34400	34420
221	34439	34459	34479	34498	34518	34537	34557	34577	34596	34616
222	34635	34655	34674	34694	34713	34733	34753	34772	34792	34811
223	34830	34850	34869	34889	34908	34928	34947	34967	34986	35005
224	35025	35044	35064	35083	35102	35122	35141	35160	35180	35199
225	35218	35238	35257	35276	35295	35315	35334	35353	35372	35392
226	35411	35430	35449	35468	35488	35507	35526	35545	35564	35583
227	35603	35622	35641	35660	35679	35698	35717	35736	35755	35774
228	35793	35813	35832	35851	35870	35889	35908	35927	35946	35965
229	35984	36003	36021	36040	36059	36078	36097	36116	36135	36154
230	36173	36192	36211	36229	36248	36267	36286	36305	36324	36342
231	36361	36380	36399	36418	36436	36455	36474	36493	36511	36530
232	36549	36568	36586	36605	36624	36642	36661	36680	36698	36717
233	36736	36754	36773	36791	36810	36829	36847	36866	36884	36903
234	36922	36940	36959	36977	36996	37014	37033	37051	37070	37088
235	37107	37125	37144	37162	37181	37199	37218	37236	37254	37273
236	37291	37310	37328	37346	37365	37383	37401	37420	37438	37457
237	37475	37493	37511	37530	37548	37566	37585	37603	37621	37639
238	37658	37676	37694	37712	37731	37749	37767	37785	37803	37822
239	37840	37858	37876	37894	37912	37931	37949	37967	37985	38003
240	38021	38039	38057	38075	38093	38112	38130	38148	38166	38184
241	38202	38220	38238	38256	38274	38292	38310	38328	38346	38364
242	38382	38399	38417	38435	38453	38471	38489	38507	38525	38543
243	38561	38578	38596	38614	38632	38650	38668	38686	38703	38721
244	38739	38757	38775	38792	38810	38828	38846	38863	38881	38899
245	38917	38934	38952	38970	38987	39005	39023	39041	39058	39076
246	39094	39111	39129	39146	39164	39182	39199	39217	39235	39252
247	39270	39287	39305	39322	39340	39358	39375	39393	39410	39428
248	39445	39463	39480	39498	39515	39533	39550	39568	39585	39602
249	39620	39637	39655	39672	39690	39707	39724	39742	39759	39777
250	39794	39811	39829	39846	39863	39881	39898	39915	39933	39950
251	39967	39985	40002	40019	40037	40054	40071	40088	40106	40123
252	40140	40157	40175	40192	40209	40226	40243	40261	40278	40295
253	40312	40329	40346	40364	40381	40398	40415	40432	40449	40466
254	40483	40500	40518	40535	40552	40569	40586	40603	40620	40637
255	40654	40671	40688	40705	40722	40739	40756	40773	40790	40807
256	40824	40841	40858	40875	40892	40909	40926	40943	40960	40976
257	40993	41010	41027	41044	41061	41078	41095	41111	41128	41145
258	41162	41179	41196	41212	41229	41246	41263	41280	41296	41313
259	41330	41347	41363	41380	41397	41414	41430	41447	41464	41481
260	41497	41514	41531	41547	41564	41581	41597	41614	41631	41647
261	41664	41681	41697	41714	41731	41747	41764	41780	41797	41814
262	41830	41847	41863	41880	41896	41913	41929	41946	41963	41979
263	41996	42012	42029	42045	42062	42078	42095	42111	42127	42144
264	42160	42177	42193	42210	42226	42243	42259	42275	42292	42308
265	42325	42341	42357	42374	42390	42406	42423	42439	42455	42472
266	42488	42504	42521	42537	42553	42570	42586	42602	42619	42635
267	42651	42667	42684	42700	42716	42732	42749	42765	42781	42797
268	42813	42830	42846	42862	42878	42894	42911	42927	42943	42959
269	42975	42991	43008	43024	43040	43056	43072	43088	43104	43120
270	43136	43152	43169	43185	43201	43217	43233	43249	43265	43281
271	43297	43313	43329	43345	43361	43377	43393	43409	43425	43441
272	43457	43473	43489	43505	43521	43537	43553	43569	43584	43600
273	43616	43632	43648	43664	43680	43696	43712	43727	43743	43759
274	43775	43791	43807	43823	43838	43854	43870	43886	43902	43917
275	43933	43949	43965	43981	43996	44012	44028	44044	44059	44075
276	44091	44107	44122	44138	44154	44170	44185	44201	44217	44232
277	44248	44264	44279	44295	44311	44326	44342	44358	44373	44389
278	44404	44420	44436	44451	44467	44483	44498	44514	44529	44545
279	44560	44576	44592	44607	44623	44638	44654	44669	44685	44700

No.	0	1	2	3	4	5	6	7	8	9
280	44716	44731	44747	44762	44778	44793	44809	44824	44840	44855
281	44871	44886	44902	44917	44932	44948	44963	44979	44994	45010
282	45025	45040	45056	45071	45086	45102	45117	45133	45148	45163
283	45179	45194	45209	45225	45240	45255	45271	45286	45301	45317
284	45332	45347	45362	45378	45393	45408	45423	45439	45454	45469
285	45484	45500	45515	45530	45545	45561	45576	45591	45606	45621
286	45637	45652	45667	45682	45697	45712	45728	45743	45758	45773
287	45788	45803	45818	45834	45849	45864	45879	45894	45909	45924
288	45939	45954	45969	45984	46000	46015	46030	46045	46060	46075
289	46090	46105	46120	46135	46150	46165	46180	46195	46210	46225
290	46240	46255	46270	46285	46300	46315	46330	46345	46359	46374
291	46389	46404	46419	46434	46449	46464	46479	46494	46509	46523
292	46538	46553	46568	46583	46598	46613	46627	46642	46657	46672
293	46687	46702	46716	46731	46746	46761	46776	46790	46805	46820
294	46835	46850	46864	46879	46894	46909	46923	46938	46953	46967
295	46982	46997	47012	47026	47041	47056	47070	47085	47100	47114
296	47129	47144	47159	47173	47188	47202	47217	47232	47246	47261
297	47276	47290	47305	47319	47334	47349	47363	47378	47392	47407
298	47422	47436	47451	47465	47480	47494	47509	47524	47538	47553
299	47567	47582	47596	47611	47625	47640	47654	47669	47683	47698
300	47712	47727	47741	47756	47770	47784	47799	47813	47828	47842
301	47857	47871	47885	47900	47914	47929	47943	47958	47972	47986
302	48001	48015	48029	48044	48058	48073	48087	48101	48116	48130
303	48144	48159	48173	48187	48202	48216	48230	48244	48259	48273
304	48287	48302	48316	48330	48344	48359	48373	48387	48401	48416
305	48430	48444	48458	48473	48487	48501	48515	48530	48544	48558
306	48572	48586	48601	48615	48629	48643	48657	48671	48686	48700
307	48714	48728	48742	48756	48770	48785	48799	48813	48827	48841
308	48855	48869	48883	48897	48911	48926	48940	48954	48968	48982
309	48996	49010	49024	49038	49052	49066	49080	49094	49108	49122
310	49136	49150	49164	49178	49192	49206	49220	49234	49248	49262
311	49276	49290	49304	49318	49332	49346	49360	49374	49388	49402
312	49415	49429	49443	49457	49471	49485	49499	49513	49527	49541
313	49554	49568	49582	49596	49610	49624	49638	49651	49665	49679
314	49693	49707	49721	49734	49748	49762	49776	49790	49803	49817
315	49831	49845	49859	49872	49886	49900	49914	49927	49941	49955
316	49969	49982	49996	50010	50024	50037	50051	50065	50079	50092
317	50106	50120	50133	50147	50161	50174	50188	50202	50215	50229
318	50243	50256	50270	50284	50297	50311	50325	50338	50352	50365
319	50379	50393	50406	50420	50433	50447	50461	50474	50488	50501
320	50515	50529	50542	50556	50569	50583	50596	50610	50623	50637
321	50651	50664	50678	50691	50705	50718	50732	50745	50759	50772
322	50786	50799	50813	50826	50840	50853	50866	50880	50893	50907
323	50920	50934	50947	50961	50974	50987	51001	51014	51028	51041
324	51055	51068	51081	51095	51108	51121	51135	51148	51162	51175
325	51188	51202	51215	51228	51242	51255	51268	51282	51295	51308
326	51322	51335	51348	51362	51375	51388	51402	51415	51428	51441
327	51455	51468	51481	51495	51508	51521	51534	51548	51561	51574
328	51587	51601	51614	51627	51640	51654	51667	51680	51693	51706
329	51720	51733	51746	51759	51772	51786	51799	51812	51825	51838
330	51851	51865	51878	51891	51904	51917	51930	51943	51957	51970
331	51983	51996	52009	52022	52035	52048	52061	52075	52088	52101
332	52114	52127	52140	52153	52166	52179	52192	52205	52218	52231
333	52244	52257	52270	52284	52297	52310	52323	52336	52349	52362
334	52375	52388	52401	52414	52427	52440	52453	52466	52479	52492
335	52504	52517	52530	52543	52556	52569	52582	52595	52608	52621
336	52634	52647	52660	52673	52686	52699	52711	52724	52737	52750
337	52763	52776	52789	52802	52815	52827	52840	52853	52866	52879
338	52892	52905	52917	52930	52943	52956	52969	52982	52994	53007
339	53020	53033	53046	53058	53071	53084	53097	53110	53122	53135

TABLE XXVI. Logarithms of Numbers from 1 to 10,000.

No.	0	1	2	3	4	5	6	7	8	9
340	53148	53161	53173	53186	53199	53212	53224	53237	53250	53263
341	53275	53288	53301	53314	53326	53339	53352	53364	53377	53390
342	53403	53415	53428	53441	53453	53466	53479	53491	53504	53517
343	53529	53542	53555	53567	53580	53593	53605	53618	53631	53643
344	53656	53668	53681	53694	53706	53719	53732	53744	53757	53769
345	53782	53794	53807	53820	53832	53845	53857	53870	53882	53895
346	53908	53920	53933	53945	53958	53970	53983	53995	54008	54020
347	54033	54045	54058	54070	54083	54095	54108	54120	54133	54145
348	54158	54170	54183	54195	54208	54220	54233	54245	54258	54270
349	54283	54295	54307	54320	54332	54345	54357	54370	54382	54394
350	54407	54419	54432	54444	54456	54469	54481	54494	54506	54518
351	54531	54543	54555	54568	54580	54593	54605	54617	54630	54642
352	54654	54667	54679	54691	54704	54716	54728	54741	54753	54765
353	54777	54790	54802	54814	54827	54839	54851	54864	54876	54888
354	54900	54913	54925	54937	54949	54962	54974	54986	54998	55011
355	55023	55035	55047	55060	55072	55084	55096	55108	55121	55133
356	55145	55157	55169	55182	55194	55206	55218	55230	55242	55255
357	55267	55279	55291	55303	55315	55328	55340	55352	55364	55376
358	55388	55400	55413	55425	55437	55449	55461	55473	55485	55497
359	55509	55522	55534	55546	55558	55570	55582	55594	55606	55618
360	55630	55642	55654	55666	55678	55691	55703	55715	55727	55739
361	55751	55763	55775	55787	55799	55811	55823	55835	55847	55859
362	55871	55883	55895	55907	55919	55931	55943	55955	55967	55979
363	55991	56003	56015	56027	56038	56050	56062	56074	56086	56098
364	56110	56122	56134	56146	56158	56170	56182	56194	56205	56217
365	56229	56241	56253	56265	56277	56289	56301	56312	56324	56336
366	56348	56360	56372	56384	56396	56407	56419	56431	56443	56455
367	56467	56478	56490	56502	56514	56526	56538	56549	56561	56573
368	56585	56597	56608	56620	56632	56644	56656	56667	56679	56691
369	56703	56714	56726	56738	56750	56761	56773	56785	56797	56808
370	56820	56832	56844	56855	56867	56879	56891	56902	56914	56926
371	56937	56949	56961	56972	56984	56996	57008	57019	57031	57043
372	57054	57066	57078	57089	57101	57113	57124	57136	57148	57159
373	57171	57183	57194	57206	57217	57229	57241	57252	57264	57276
374	57287	57299	57310	57322	57334	57345	57357	57368	57380	57392
375	57403	57415	57426	57438	57449	57461	57473	57484	57496	57507
376	57519	57530	57542	57553	57565	57576	57588	57600	57611	57623
377	57634	57646	57657	57669	57680	57692	57703	57715	57726	57738
378	57749	57761	57772	57784	57795	57807	57818	57830	57841	57852
379	57864	57875	57887	57898	57910	57921	57933	57944	57955	57967
380	57978	57990	58001	58013	58024	58035	58047	58058	58070	58081
381	58092	58104	58115	58127	58138	58149	58161	58172	58184	58195
382	58206	58218	58229	58240	58252	58263	58274	58286	58297	58309
383	58320	58331	58343	58354	58365	58377	58388	58399	58410	58422
384	58433	58444	58456	58467	58478	58490	58501	58512	58524	58535
385	58546	58557	58569	58580	58591	58602	58614	58625	58636	58647
386	58659	58670	58681	58692	58704	58715	58726	58737	58749	58760
387	58771	58782	58794	58805	58816	58827	58838	58850	58861	58872
388	58883	58894	58906	58917	58928	58939	58950	58961	58973	58984
389	58995	59006	59017	59028	59040	59051	59062	59073	59084	59095
390	59106	59118	59129	59140	59151	59162	59173	59184	59195	59207
391	59218	59229	59240	59251	59262	59273	59284	59295	59306	59318
392	59329	59340	59351	59362	59373	59384	59395	59406	59417	59428
393	59439	59450	59461	59472	59483	59494	59506	59517	59528	59539
394	59550	59561	59572	59583	59594	59605	59616	59627	59638	59649
395	59660	59671	59682	59693	59704	59715	59726	59737	59748	59759
396	59770	59780	59791	59802	59813	59824	59835	59846	59857	59868
397	59879	59890	59901	59912	59923	59934	59945	59956	59966	59977
398	59988	59999	60010	60021	60032	60043	60054	60065	60076	60086
399	60097	60108	60119	60130	60141	60152	60163	60173	60184	60195

No.	0	1	2	3	4	5	6	7	8	9
400	60206	60217	60228	60239	60249	60260	60271	60282	60293	60304
401	60314	60325	60336	60347	60358	60369	60379	60390	60401	60412
402	60423	60433	60444	60455	60466	60477	60487	60498	60509	60520
403	60531	60541	60552	60563	60574	60584	60595	60606	60617	60627
404	60638	60649	60660	60670	60681	60692	60703	60713	60724	60735
405	60746	60756	60767	60778	60788	60799	60810	60821	60831	60842
406	60853	60863	60874	60885	60895	60906	60917	60927	60938	60949
407	60959	60970	60981	60991	61002	61013	61023	61034	61045	61055
408	61066	61077	61087	61098	61109	61119	61130	61140	61151	61162
409	61172	61183	61194	61204	61215	61225	61236	61247	61257	61268
410	61278	61289	61300	61310	61321	61331	61342	61352	61363	61374
411	61384	61395	61405	61416	61426	61437	61448	61458	61469	61479
412	61490	61500	61511	61521	61532	61542	61553	61563	61574	61584
413	61595	61606	61616	61627	61637	61648	61658	61669	61679	61690
414	61700	61711	61721	61731	61742	61752	61763	61773	61784	61794
415	61805	61815	61826	61836	61847	61857	61868	61878	61888	61899
416	61909	61920	61930	61941	61951	61962	61972	61982	61993	62003
417	62014	62024	62034	62045	62055	62066	62076	62086	62097	62107
418	62118	62128	62138	62149	62159	62170	62180	62190	62201	62211
419	62221	62232	62242	62252	62263	62273	62284	62294	62304	62315
420	62325	62335	62346	62356	62366	62377	62387	62397	62408	62418
421	62428	62439	62449	62459	62469	62480	62490	62500	62511	62521
422	62531	62542	62552	62562	62572	62583	62593	62603	62613	62624
423	62634	62644	62655	62665	62675	62685	62696	62706	62716	62726
424	62737	62747	62757	62767	62778	62788	62798	62808	62818	62829
425	62839	62849	62859	62870	62880	62890	62900	62910	62921	62931
426	62941	62951	62961	62972	62982	62992	63002	63012	63022	63033
427	63043	63053	63063	63073	63083	63094	63104	63114	63124	63134
428	63144	63155	63165	63175	63185	63195	63205	63215	63225	63236
429	63246	63256	63266	63276	63286	63296	63306	63317	63327	63337
430	63347	63357	63367	63377	63387	63397	63407	63417	63428	63438
431	63448	63458	63468	63478	63488	63498	63508	63518	63528	63538
432	63548	63558	63568	63579	63589	63599	63609	63619	63629	63639
433	63649	63659	63669	63679	63689	63699	63709	63719	63729	63739
434	63749	63759	63769	63779	63789	63799	63809	63819	63829	63839
435	63849	63859	63869	63879	63889	63899	63909	63919	63929	63939
436	63949	63959	63969	63979	63988	63998	64008	64018	64028	64038
437	64048	64058	64068	64078	64088	64098	64108	64118	64128	64137
438	64147	64157	64167	64177	64187	64197	64207	64217	64227	64237
439	64246	64256	64266	64276	64286	64296	64306	64316	64326	64335
440	64345	64355	64365	64375	64385	64395	64404	64414	64424	64434
441	64444	64454	64464	64473	64483	64493	64503	64513	64523	64532
442	64542	64552	64562	64572	64582	64591	64601	64611	64621	64631
443	64640	64650	64660	64670	64680	64689	64699	64709	64719	64729
444	64738	64748	64758	64768	64777	64787	64797	64807	64816	64826
445	64836	64846	64856	64865	64875	64885	64895	64904	64914	64924
446	64933	64943	64953	64963	64972	64982	64992	65002	65011	65021
447	65031	65040	65050	65060	65070	65079	65089	65099	65108	65118
448	65128	65137	65147	65157	65167	65176	65186	65196	65205	65215
449	65225	65234	65244	65254	65263	65273	65283	65292	65302	65312
450	65321	65331	65341	65350	65360	65369	65379	65389	65398	65408
451	65418	65427	65437	65447	65456	65466	65475	65485	65495	65504
452	65514	65523	65533	65543	65552	65562	65571	65581	65591	65600
453	65610	65619	65629	65639	65648	65658	65667	65677	65686	65696
454	65706	65715	65725	65734	65744	65753	65763	65772	65782	65792
455	65801	65811	65820	65830	65839	65849	65858	65868	65877	65887
456	65896	65906	65916	65925	65935	65944	65954	65963	65973	65982
457	65992	66001	66011	66020	66030	66039	66049	66058	66068	66077
458	66087	66096	66106	66115	66124	66134	66143	66153	66162	66172
459	66181	66191	66200	66210	66219	66229	66238	66247	66257	66266

No.	0	1	2	3	4	5	6	7	8	9
460	66276	66285	66295	66304	66314	66323	66332	66342	66351	66361
461	66370	66380	66389	66398	66408	66417	66427	66436	66445	66455
462	66464	66474	66483	66492	66502	66511	66521	66530	66539	66549
463	66558	66567	66577	66586	66596	66605	66614	66624	66633	66642
464	66652	66661	66671	66680	66689	66699	66708	66717	66727	66736
465	66745	66755	66764	66773	66783	66792	66801	66811	66820	66829
466	66839	66848	66857	66867	66876	66885	66894	66904	66913	66922
467	66932	66941	66950	66960	66969	66978	66987	66997	67006	67015
468	67025	67034	67043	67052	67062	67071	67080	67089	67099	67108
469	67117	67127	67136	67145	67154	67164	67173	67182	67191	67201
470	67210	67219	67228	67237	67247	67256	67265	67274	67284	67293
471	67302	67311	67321	67330	67339	67348	67357	67367	67376	67385
472	67394	67403	67413	67422	67431	67440	67449	67459	67468	67477
473	67486	67495	67504	67514	67523	67532	67541	67550	67560	67569
474	67578	67587	67596	67605	67614	67624	67633	67642	67651	67660
475	67669	67679	67688	67697	67706	67715	67724	67733	67742	67752
476	67761	67770	67779	67788	67797	67806	67815	67825	67834	67843
477	67852	67861	67870	67879	67888	67897	67906	67916	67925	67934
478	67943	67952	67961	67970	67979	67988	67997	68006	68015	68024
479	68034	68043	68052	68061	68070	68079	68088	68097	68106	68115
480	68124	68133	68142	68151	68160	68169	68178	68187	68196	68205
481	68215	68224	68233	68242	68251	68260	68269	68278	68287	68296
482	68305	68314	68323	68332	68341	68350	68359	68368	68377	68386
483	68395	68404	68413	68422	68431	68440	68449	68458	68467	68476
484	68485	68494	68502	68511	68520	68529	68538	68547	68556	68565
485	68574	68583	68592	68601	68610	68619	68628	68637	68646	68655
486	68664	68673	68681	68690	68699	68708	68717	68726	68735	68744
487	68753	68762	68771	68780	68789	68797	68806	68815	68824	68833
488	68842	68851	68860	68869	68878	68886	68895	68904	68913	68922
489	68931	68940	68949	68958	68966	68975	68984	68993	69002	69011
490	69020	69028	69037	69046	69055	69064	69073	69082	69090	69099
491	69108	69117	69126	69135	69144	69152	69161	69170	69179	69188
492	69197	69205	69214	69223	69232	69241	69249	69258	69267	69276
493	69285	69294	69302	69311	69320	69329	69338	69346	69355	69364
494	69373	69381	69390	69399	69408	69417	69425	69434	69443	69452
495	69461	69469	69478	69487	69496	69504	69513	69522	69531	69539
496	69548	69557	69566	69574	69583	69592	69601	69609	69618	69627
497	69636	69644	69653	69662	69671	69679	69688	69697	69705	69714
498	69723	69732	69740	69749	69758	69767	69775	69784	69793	69801
499	69810	69819	69827	69836	69845	69854	69862	69871	69880	69888
500	69897	69906	69914	69923	69932	69940	69949	69958	69966	69975
501	69984	69992	70001	70010	70018	70027	70036	70044	70053	70062
502	70070	70079	70088	70096	70105	70114	70122	70131	70140	70148
503	70157	70165	70174	70183	70191	70200	70209	70217	70226	70234
504	70243	70252	70260	70269	70278	70286	70295	70303	70312	70321
505	70329	70338	70346	70355	70364	70372	70381	70389	70398	70406
506	70415	70424	70432	70441	70449	70458	70467	70475	70484	70492
507	70501	70509	70518	70526	70535	70544	70552	70561	70569	70578
508	70586	70595	70603	70612	70621	70629	70638	70646	70655	70663
509	70672	70680	70689	70697	70706	70714	70723	70731	70740	70749
510	70757	70766	70774	70783	70791	70800	70808	70817	70825	70834
511	70842	70851	70859	70868	70876	70885	70893	70902	70910	70919
512	70927	70935	70944	70952	70961	70969	70978	70986	70995	71003
513	71012	71020	71029	71037	71046	71054	71063	71071	71079	71088
514	71096	71105	71113	71122	71130	71139	71147	71155	71164	71172
515	71181	71189	71198	71206	71214	71223	71231	71240	71248	71257
516	71265	71273	71282	71290	71299	71307	71315	71324	71332	71341
517	71349	71357	71366	71374	71383	71391	71399	71408	71416	71425
518	71433	71441	71450	71458	71466	71475	71483	71492	71500	71508
519	71517	71525	71533	71542	71550	71559	71567	71575	71584	71592

TABLE XXVI. Logarithms of Numbers from 1 to 10,000.

No.	0	1	2	3	4	5	6	7	8	9
520	71600	71609	71617	71625	71634	71642	71650	71659	71667	71675
521	71684	71692	71700	71709	71717	71725	71734	71742	71750	71759
522	71767	71775	71784	71792	71800	71809	71817	71825	71834	71842
523	71850	71858	71867	71875	71883	71892	71900	71908	71917	71925
524	71933	71941	71950	71958	71966	71975	71983	71991	71999	72008
525	72016	72024	72032	72041	72049	72057	72066	72074	72082	72090
526	72099	72107	72115	72123	72132	72140	72148	72156	72165	72173
527	72181	72189	72198	72206	72214	72222	72230	72239	72247	72255
528	72263	72272	72280	72288	72296	72304	72313	72321	72329	72337
529	72346	72354	72362	72370	72378	72387	72395	72403	72411	72419
530	72428	72436	72444	72452	72460	72469	72477	72485	72493	72501
531	72509	72518	72526	72534	72542	72550	72558	72567	72575	72583
532	72591	72599	72607	72616	72624	72632	72640	72648	72656	72665
533	72673	72681	72689	72697	72705	72713	72722	72730	72738	72746
534	72754	72762	72770	72779	72787	72795	72803	72811	72819	72827
535	72835	72843	72852	72860	72868	72876	72884	72892	72900	72908
536	72916	72925	72933	72941	72949	72957	72965	72973	72981	72989
537	72997	73006	73014	73022	73030	73038	73046	73054	73062	73070
538	73078	73086	73094	73102	73111	73119	73127	73135	73143	73151
539	73159	73167	73175	73183	73191	73199	73207	73215	73223	73231
540	73239	73247	73255	73263	73272	73280	73288	73296	73304	73312
541	73320	73328	73336	73344	73352	73360	73368	73376	73384	73392
542	73400	73408	73416	73424	73432	73440	73448	73456	73464	73472
543	73480	73488	73496	73504	73512	73520	73528	73536	73544	73552
544	73560	73568	73576	73584	73592	73600	73608	73616	73624	73632
545	73640	73648	73656	73664	73672	73679	73687	73695	73703	73711
546	73719	73727	73735	73743	73751	73759	73767	73775	73783	73791
547	73799	73807	73815	73823	73830	73838	73846	73854	73862	73870
548	73878	73886	73894	73902	73910	73918	73926	73933	73941	73949
549	73957	73965	73973	73981	73989	73997	74005	74013	74020	74028
550	74036	74044	74052	74060	74068	74076	74084	74092	74099	74107
551	74115	74123	74131	74139	74147	74155	74162	74170	74178	74186
552	74194	74202	74210	74218	74225	74233	74241	74249	74257	74265
553	74273	74280	74288	74296	74304	74312	74320	74327	74335	74343
554	74351	74359	74367	74374	74382	74390	74398	74406	74414	74421
555	74429	74437	74445	74453	74461	74468	74476	74484	74492	74500
556	74507	74515	74523	74531	74539	74547	74554	74562	74570	74578
557	74586	74593	74601	74609	74617	74624	74632	74640	74648	74656
558	74663	74671	74679	74687	74695	74702	74710	74718	74726	74733
559	74741	74749	74757	74764	74772	74780	74788	74796	74803	74811
560	74819	74827	74834	74842	74850	74858	74865	74873	74881	74889
561	74896	74904	74912	74920	74927	74935	74943	74950	74958	74966
562	74974	74981	74989	74997	75005	75012	75020	75028	75035	75043
563	75051	75059	75066	75074	75082	75089	75097	75105	75113	75120
564	75128	75136	75143	75151	75159	75166	75174	75182	75189	75197
565	75205	75213	75220	75228	75236	75243	75251	75259	75266	75274
566	75282	75289	75297	75305	75312	75320	75328	75335	75343	75351
567	75358	75366	75374	75381	75389	75397	75404	75412	75420	75427
568	75435	75442	75450	75458	75465	75473	75481	75488	75496	75504
569	75511	75519	75526	75534	75542	75549	75557	75565	75572	75580
570	75587	75595	75603	75610	75618	75626	75633	75641	75648	75656
571	75664	75671	75679	75686	75694	75702	75709	75717	75724	75732
572	75740	75747	75755	75762	75770	75778	75785	75793	75800	75808
573	75815	75823	75831	75838	75846	75853	75861	75868	75876	75884
574	75891	75899	75906	75914	75921	75929	75937	75944	75952	75959
575	75967	75974	75982	75989	75997	76005	76012	76020	76027	76035
576	76042	76050	76057	76065	76072	76080	76087	76095	76103	76110
577	76118	76125	76133	76140	76148	76155	76163	76170	76178	76185
578	76193	76200	76208	76215	76223	76230	76238	76245	76253	76260
579	76268	76275	76283	76290	76298	76305	76313	76320	76328	76335

No.	0	1	2	3	4	5	6	7	8	9
580	76343	76350	76358	76365	76373	76380	76388	76395	76403	76410
581	76418	76425	76433	76440	76448	76455	76462	76470	76477	76485
582	76492	76500	76507	76515	76522	76530	76537	76545	76552	76559
583	76567	76574	76582	76589	76597	76604	76612	76619	76626	76634
584	76641	76649	76656	76664	76671	76678	76686	76693	76701	76708
585	76716	76723	76730	76738	76745	76753	76760	76768	76775	76782
586	76790	76797	76805	76812	76819	76827	76834	76842	76849	76856
587	76864	76871	76879	76886	76893	76901	76908	76916	76923	76930
588	76938	76945	76953	76960	76967	76975	76982	76989	76997	77004
589	77012	77019	77026	77034	77041	77048	77056	77063	77070	77078
590	77085	77093	77100	77107	77115	77122	77129	77137	77144	77151
591	77159	77166	77173	77181	77188	77195	77203	77210	77217	77225
592	77232	77240	77247	77254	77262	77269	77276	77283	77291	77298
593	77305	77313	77320	77327	77335	77342	77349	77357	77364	77371
594	77379	77386	77393	77401	77408	77415	77422	77430	77437	77444
595	77452	77459	77466	77474	77481	77488	77495	77503	77510	77517
596	77525	77532	77539	77546	77554	77561	77568	77576	77583	77590
597	77597	77605	77612	77619	77627	77634	77641	77648	77656	77663
598	77670	77677	77685	77692	77699	77706	77714	77721	77728	77735
599	77743	77750	77757	77764	77772	77779	77786	77793	77801	77808
600	77815	77822	77830	77837	77844	77851	77859	77866	77873	77880
601	77887	77895	77902	77909	77916	77924	77931	77938	77945	77952
602	77960	77967	77974	77981	77988	77996	78003	78010	78017	78025
603	78032	78039	78046	78053	78061	78068	78075	78082	78089	78097
604	78104	78111	78118	78125	78132	78140	78147	78154	78161	78168
605	78176	78183	78190	78197	78204	78211	78219	78226	78233	78240
606	78247	78254	78262	78269	78276	78283	78290	78297	78305	78312
607	78319	78326	78333	78340	78347	78355	78362	78369	78376	78383
608	78390	78398	78405	78412	78419	78426	78433	78440	78447	78455
609	78462	78469	78476	78483	78490	78497	78504	78512	78519	78526
610	78533	78540	78547	78554	78561	78569	78576	78583	78590	78597
611	78604	78611	78618	78625	78633	78640	78647	78654	78661	78668
612	78675	78682	78689	78696	78704	78711	78718	78725	78732	78739
613	78746	78753	78760	78767	78774	78781	78789	78796	78803	78810
614	78817	78824	78831	78838	78845	78852	78859	78866	78873	78880
615	78888	78895	78902	78909	78916	78923	78930	78937	78944	78951
616	78958	78965	78972	78979	78986	78993	79000	79007	79014	79021
617	79029	79036	79043	79050	79057	79064	79071	79078	79085	79092
618	79099	79106	79113	79120	79127	79134	79141	79148	79155	79162
619	79169	79176	79183	79190	79197	79204	79211	79218	79225	79232
620	79239	79246	79253	79260	79267	79274	79281	79288	79295	79302
621	79309	79316	79323	79330	79337	79344	79351	79358	79365	79372
622	79379	79386	79393	79400	79407	79414	79421	79428	79435	79442
623	79449	79456	79463	79470	79477	79484	79491	79498	79505	79511
624	79518	79525	79532	79539	79546	79553	79560	79567	79574	79581
625	79588	79595	79602	79609	79616	79623	79630	79637	79644	79650
626	79657	79664	79671	79678	79685	79692	79699	79706	79713	79720
627	79727	79734	79741	79748	79754	79761	79768	79775	79782	79789
628	79796	79803	79810	79817	79824	79831	79837	79844	79851	79858
629	79865	79872	79879	79886	79893	79900	79906	79913	79920	79927
630	79934	79941	79948	79955	79962	79969	79975	79982	79989	79996
631	80003	80010	80017	80024	80030	80037	80044	80051	80058	80065
632	80072	80079	80085	80092	80099	80106	80113	80120	80127	80134
633	80140	80147	80154	80161	80168	80175	80182	80188	80195	80202
634	80209	80216	80223	80229	80236	80243	80250	80257	80264	80271
635	80277	80284	80291	80298	80305	80312	80318	80325	80332	80339
636	80346	80353	80359	80366	80373	80380	80387	80393	80400	80407
637	80414	80421	80428	80434	80441	80448	80455	80462	80468	80475
638	80482	80489	80496	80502	80509	80516	80523	80530	80536	80543
639	80550	80557	80564	80570	80577	80584	80591	80598	80604	80611

No.	0	1	2	3	4	5	6	7	8	9
640	80618	80625	80632	80638	80645	80652	80659	80665	80672	80679
641	80686	80693	80699	80706	80713	80720	80726	80733	80740	80747
642	80754	80760	80767	80774	80781	80787	80794	80801	80808	80814
643	80821	80828	80835	80841	80848	80855	80862	80868	80875	80882
644	80889	80895	80902	80909	80916	80922	80929	80936	80943	80949
645	80956	80963	80969	80976	80983	80990	80996	81003	81010	81017
646	81023	81030	81037	81043	81050	81057	81064	81070	81077	81084
647	81090	81097	81104	81111	81117	81124	81131	81137	81144	81151
648	81158	81164	81171	81178	81184	81191	81198	81204	81211	81218
649	81224	81231	81238	81245	81251	81258	81265	81271	81278	81285
650	81291	81298	81305	81311	81318	81325	81331	81338	81345	81351
651	81358	81365	81371	81378	81385	81391	81398	81405	81411	81418
652	81425	81431	81438	81445	81451	81458	81465	81471	81478	81485
653	81491	81498	81505	81511	81518	81525	81531	81538	81544	81551
654	81558	81564	81571	81578	81584	81591	81598	81604	81611	81617
655	81624	81631	81637	81644	81651	81657	81664	81671	81677	81684
656	81690	81697	81704	81710	81717	81723	81730	81737	81743	81750
657	81757	81763	81770	81776	81783	81790	81796	81803	81809	81816
658	81823	81829	81836	81842	81849	81856	81862	81869	81875	81882
659	81889	81895	81902	81908	81915	81921	81928	81935	81941	81948
660	81954	81961	81968	81974	81981	81987	81994	82000	82007	82014
661	82020	82027	82033	82040	82046	82053	82060	82066	82073	82079
662	82086	82092	82099	82105	82112	82119	82125	82132	82138	82145
663	82151	82158	82164	82171	82178	82184	82191	82197	82204	82210
664	82217	82223	82230	82236	82243	82249	82256	82263	82269	82276
665	82282	82289	82295	82302	82308	82315	82321	82328	82334	82341
666	82347	82354	82360	82367	82373	82380	82387	82393	82400	82406
667	82413	82419	82426	82432	82439	82445	82452	82458	82465	82471
668	82478	82484	82491	82497	82504	82510	82517	82523	82530	82536
669	82543	82549	82556	82562	82569	82575	82582	82588	82595	82601
670	82607	82614	82620	82627	82633	82640	82646	82653	82659	82666
671	82672	82679	82685	82692	82698	82705	82711	82718	82724	82730
672	82737	82743	82750	82756	82763	82769	82776	82782	82789	82795
673	82802	82808	82814	82821	82827	82834	82840	82847	82853	82860
674	82866	82872	82879	82885	82892	82898	82905	82911	82918	82924
675	82930	82937	82943	82950	82956	82963	82969	82975	82982	82988
676	82995	83001	83008	83014	83020	83027	83033	83040	83046	83052
677	83059	83065	83072	83078	83085	83091	83097	83104	83110	83117
678	83123	83129	83136	83142	83149	83155	83161	83168	83174	83181
679	83187	83193	83200	83206	83213	83219	83225	83232	83238	83245
680	83251	83257	83264	83270	83276	83283	83289	83296	83302	83308
681	83315	83321	83327	83334	83340	83347	83353	83359	83366	83372
682	83378	83385	83391	83398	83404	83410	83417	83423	83429	83436
683	83442	83448	83455	83461	83467	83474	83480	83487	83493	83499
684	83506	83512	83518	83525	83531	83537	83544	83550	83556	83563
685	83569	83575	83582	83588	83594	83601	83607	83613	83620	83626
686	83632	83639	83645	83651	83658	83664	83670	83677	83683	83689
687	83696	83702	83708	83715	83721	83727	83734	83740	83746	83753
688	83759	83765	83771	83778	83784	83790	83797	83803	83809	83816
689	83822	83828	83835	83841	83847	83853	83860	83866	83872	83879
690	83885	83891	83897	83904	83910	83916	83923	83929	83935	83942
691	83948	83954	83960	83967	83973	83979	83985	83992	83998	84004
692	84011	84017	84023	84029	84036	84042	84048	84055	84061	84067
693	84073	84080	84086	84092	84098	84105	84111	84117	84123	84130
694	84136	84142	84148	84155	84161	84167	84173	84180	84186	84192
695	84198	84205	84211	84217	84223	84230	84236	84242	84248	84255
696	84261	84267	84273	84280	84286	84292	84298	84305	84311	84317
697	84323	84330	84336	84342	84348	84354	84361	84367	84373	84379
698	84386	84392	84398	84404	84410	84417	84423	84429	84435	84442
699	84448	84454	84460	84466	84473	84479	84485	84491	84497	84504

TABLE XXVI. Logarithms of Numbers from 1 to 10,000.

No.	0	1	2	3	4	5	6	7	8	9
700	84510	84516	84522	84528	84535	84541	84547	84553	84559	84566
701	84572	84578	84584	84590	84597	84603	84609	84615	84621	84628
702	84634	84640	84646	84652	84658	84665	84671	84677	84683	84689
703	84696	84702	84708	84714	84720	84726	84733	84739	84745	84751
704	84757	84763	84770	84776	84782	84788	84794	84800	84807	84813
705	84819	84825	84831	84837	84844	84850	84856	84862	84868	84874
706	84880	84887	84893	84899	84905	84911	84917	84924	84930	84936
707	84942	84948	84954	84960	84967	84973	84979	84985	84991	84997
708	85003	85009	85016	85022	85028	85034	85040	85046	85052	85058
709	85065	85071	85077	85083	85089	85095	85101	85107	85114	85120
710	85126	85132	85138	85144	85150	85156	85163	85169	85175	85181
711	85187	85193	85199	85205	85211	85217	85224	85230	85236	85242
712	85248	85254	85260	85266	85272	85278	85285	85291	85297	85303
713	85309	85315	85321	85327	85333	85339	85345	85352	85358	85364
714	85370	85376	85382	85388	85394	85400	85406	85412	85418	85425
715	85431	85437	85443	85449	85455	85461	85467	85473	85479	85485
716	85491	85497	85503	85509	85516	85522	85528	85534	85540	85546
717	85552	85558	85564	85570	85576	85582	85588	85594	85600	85606
718	85612	85618	85625	85631	85637	85643	85649	85655	85661	85667
719	85673	85679	85685	85691	85697	85703	85709	85715	85721	85727
720	85733	85739	85745	85751	85757	85763	85769	85775	85781	85788
721	85794	85800	85806	85812	85818	85824	85830	85836	85842	85848
722	85854	85860	85866	85872	85878	85884	85890	85896	85902	85908
723	85914	85920	85926	85932	85938	85944	85950	85956	85962	85968
724	85974	85980	85986	85992	85998	86004	86010	86016	86022	86028
725	86034	86040	86046	86052	86058	86064	86070	86076	86082	86088
726	86094	86100	86106	86112	86118	86124	86130	86136	86141	86147
727	86153	86159	86165	86171	86177	86183	86189	86195	86201	86207
728	86213	86219	86225	86231	86237	86243	86249	86255	86261	86267
729	86273	86279	86285	86291	86297	86303	86308	86314	86320	86326
730	86332	86338	86344	86350	86356	86362	86368	86374	86380	86386
731	86392	86398	86404	86410	86415	86421	86427	86433	86439	86445
732	86451	86457	86463	86469	86475	86481	86487	86493	86499	86504
733	86510	86516	86522	86528	86534	86540	86546	86552	86558	86564
734	86570	86576	86581	86587	86593	86599	86605	86611	86617	86623
735	86629	86635	86641	86646	86652	86658	86664	86670	86676	86682
736	86688	86694	86700	86705	86711	86717	86723	86729	86735	86741
737	86747	86753	86759	86764	86770	86776	86782	86788	86794	86800
738	86806	86812	86817	86823	86829	86835	86841	86847	86853	86859
739	86864	86870	86876	86882	86888	86894	86900	86906	86911	86917
740	86923	86929	86935	86941	86947	86953	86958	86964	86970	86976
741	86982	86988	86994	86999	87005	87011	87017	87023	87029	87035
742	87040	87046	87052	87058	87064	87070	87075	87081	87087	87093
743	87099	87105	87111	87116	87122	87128	87134	87140	87146	87151
744	87157	87163	87169	87175	87181	87186	87192	87198	87204	87210
745	87216	87221	87227	87233	87239	87245	87251	87256	87262	87268
746	87274	87280	87286	87291	87297	87303	87309	87315	87320	87326
747	87332	87338	87344	87349	87355	87361	87367	87373	87379	87384
748	87390	87396	87402	87408	87413	87419	87425	87431	87437	87442
749	87448	87454	87460	87466	87471	87477	87483	87489	87495	87500
750	87506	87512	87518	87523	87529	87535	87541	87547	87552	87558
751	87564	87570	87576	87581	87587	87593	87599	87604	87610	87616
752	87622	87628	87633	87639	87645	87651	87656	87662	87668	87674
753	87679	87685	87691	87697	87703	87708	87714	87720	87726	87731
754	87737	87743	87749	87754	87760	87766	87772	87777	87783	87789
755	87795	87800	87806	87812	87818	87823	87829	87835	87841	87846
756	87852	87858	87864	87869	87875	87881	87887	87892	87898	87904
757	87910	87915	87921	87927	87933	87938	87944	87950	87955	87961
758	87967	87973	87978	87984	87990	87996	88001	88007	88013	83018
759	88024	88030	88036	88041	88047	88053	88058	88064	88070	88076

No.	0	1	2	3	4	5	6	7	8	9
760	88081	88087	88093	88098	88104	88110	88116	88121	88127	88133
761	88138	88144	88150	88156	88161	88167	88173	88178	88184	88190
762	88195	88201	88207	88213	88218	88224	88230	88235	88241	88247
763	88252	88258	88264	88270	88275	88281	88287	88292	88298	88304
764	88309	88315	88321	88326	88332	88338	88343	88349	88355	88360
765	88366	88372	88377	88383	88389	88395	88400	88406	88412	88417
766	88423	88429	88434	88440	88446	88451	88457	88463	88468	88474
767	88480	88485	88491	88497	88502	88508	88513	88519	88525	88530
768	88536	88542	88547	88553	88559	88564	88570	88576	88581	88587
769	88593	88598	88604	88610	88615	88621	88627	88632	88638	88643
770	88649	88655	88660	88666	88672	88677	88683	88689	88694	88700
771	88705	88711	88717	88722	88728	88734	88739	88745	88750	88756
772	88762	88767	88773	88779	88784	88790	88795	88801	88807	88812
773	88818	88824	88829	88835	88840	88846	88852	88857	88863	88868
774	88874	88880	88885	88891	88897	88902	88908	88913	88919	88925
775	88930	88936	88941	88947	88953	88958	88964	88969	88975	88981
776	88986	88992	88997	89003	89009	89014	89020	89025	89031	89037
777	89042	89048	89053	89059	89064	89070	89076	89081	89087	89092
778	89098	89104	89109	89115	89120	89126	89131	89137	89143	89148
779	89154	89159	89165	89170	89176	89182	89187	89193	89198	89204
780	89209	89215	89221	89226	89232	89237	89243	89248	89254	89260
781	89265	89271	89276	89282	89287	89293	89298	89304	89310	89315
782	89321	89326	89332	89337	89343	89348	89354	89360	89365	89371
783	89376	89382	89387	89393	89398	89404	89409	89415	89421	89426
784	89432	89437	89443	89448	89454	89459	89465	89470	89476	89481
785	89487	89492	89498	89504	89509	89515	89520	89526	89531	89537
786	89542	89548	89553	89559	89564	89570	89575	89581	89586	89592
787	89597	89603	89609	89614	89620	89625	89631	89636	89642	89647
788	89653	89658	89664	89669	89675	89680	89686	89691	89697	89702
789	89708	89713	89719	89724	89730	89735	89741	89746	89752	89757
790	89763	89768	89774	89779	89785	89790	89796	89801	89807	89812
791	89818	89823	89829	89834	89840	89845	89851	89856	89862	89867
792	89873	89878	89883	89889	89894	89900	89905	89911	89916	89922
793	89927	89933	89938	89944	89949	89955	89960	89966	89971	89977
794	89982	89988	89993	89998	90004	90009	90015	90020	90026	90031
795	90037	90042	90048	90053	90059	90064	90069	90075	90080	90086
796	90091	90097	90102	90108	90113	90119	90124	90129	90135	90140
797	90146	90151	90157	90162	90168	90173	90179	90184	90189	90195
798	90200	90206	90211	90217	90222	90227	90233	90238	90244	90249
799	90255	90260	90266	90271	90276	90282	90287	90293	90298	90304
800	90309	90314	90320	90325	90331	90336	90342	90347	90352	90358
801	90363	90369	90374	90380	90385	90390	90396	90401	90407	90412
802	90417	90423	90428	90434	90439	90445	90450	90455	90461	90466
803	90472	90477	90482	90488	90493	90499	90504	90509	90515	90520
804	90526	90531	90536	90542	90547	90553	90558	90563	90569	90574
805	90580	90585	90590	90596	90601	90607	90612	90617	90623	90628
806	90634	90639	90644	90650	90655	90660	90666	90671	90677	90682
807	90687	90693	90698	90703	90709	90714	90720	90725	90730	90736
808	90741	90747	90752	90757	90763	90768	90773	90779	90784	90789
809	90795	90800	90806	90811	90816	90822	90827	90832	90838	90843
810	90849	90854	90859	90865	90870	90875	90881	90886	90891	90897
811	90902	90907	90913	90918	90924	90929	90934	90940	90945	90950
812	90956	90961	90966	90972	90977	90982	90988	90993	90998	91004
813	91009	91014	91020	91025	91030	91036	91041	91046	91052	91057
814	91062	91068	91073	91078	91084	91089	91094	91100	91105	91110
815	91116	91121	91126	91132	91137	91142	91148	91153	91158	91164
816	91169	91174	91180	91185	91190	91196	91201	91206	91212	91217
817	91222	91228	91233	91238	91243	91249	91254	91259	91265	91270
818	91275	91281	91286	91291	91297	91302	91307	91312	91318	91323
819	91328	91334	91339	91344	91350	91355	91360	91365	91371	91376

No.	0	1	2	3	4	5	6	7	8	9
820	91381	91387	91392	91397	91403	91408	91413	91418	91424	91429
821	91434	91440	91445	91450	91455	91461	91466	91471	91477	91482
822	91487	91492	91498	91503	91508	91514	91519	91524	91529	91535
823	91540	91545	91551	91556	91561	91566	91572	91577	91582	91587
824	91593	91598	91603	91609	91614	91619	91624	91630	91635	91640
825	91645	91651	91656	91661	91666	91672	91677	91682	91687	91693
826	91698	91703	91709	91714	91719	91724	91730	91735	91740	91745
827	91751	91756	91761	91766	91772	91777	91782	91787	91793	91798
828	91803	91808	91814	91819	91824	91829	91834	91840	91845	91850
829	91855	91861	91866	91871	91876	91882	91887	91892	91897	91903
830	91908	91913	91918	91924	91929	91934	91939	91944	91950	91955
831	91960	91965	91971	91976	91981	91986	91991	91997	92002	92007
832	92012	92018	92023	92028	92033	92038	92044	92049	92054	92059
833	92065	92070	92075	92080	92085	92091	92096	92101	92106	92111
834	92117	92122	92127	92132	92137	92143	92148	92153	92158	92163
835	92169	92174	92179	92184	92189	92195	92200	92205	92210	92215
836	92221	92226	92231	92236	92241	92247	92252	92257	92262	92267
837	92273	92278	92283	92288	92293	92298	92304	92309	92314	92319
838	92324	92330	92335	92340	92345	92350	92355	92361	92366	92371
839	92376	92381	92387	92392	92397	92402	92407	92412	92418	92423
840	92428	92433	92438	92443	92449	92454	92459	92464	92469	92474
841	92480	92485	92490	92495	92500	92505	92511	92516	92521	92526
842	92531	92536	92542	92547	92552	92557	92562	92567	92572	92578
843	92583	92588	92593	92598	92603	92609	92614	92619	92624	92629
844	92634	92639	92645	92650	92655	92660	92665	92670	92675	92681
845	92686	92691	92696	92701	92706	92711	92716	92722	92727	92732
846	92737	92742	92747	92752	92758	92763	92768	92773	92778	92783
847	92788	92793	92799	92804	92809	92814	92819	92824	92829	92834
848	92840	92845	92850	92855	92860	92865	92870	92875	92881	92886
849	92891	92896	92901	92906	92911	92916	92921	92927	92932	92937
850	92942	92947	92952	92957	92962	92967	92973	92978	92983	92988
851	92993	92998	93003	93008	93013	93018	93024	93029	93034	93039
852	93044	93049	93054	93059	93064	93069	93075	93080	93085	93090
853	93095	93100	93105	93110	93115	93120	93125	93131	93136	93141
854	93146	93151	93156	93161	93166	93171	93176	93181	93186	93192
855	93197	93202	93207	93212	93217	93222	93227	93232	93237	93242
856	93247	93252	93258	93263	93268	93273	93278	93283	93288	93293
857	93298	93303	93308	93313	93318	93323	93328	93334	93339	93344
858	93349	93354	93359	93364	93369	93374	93379	93384	93389	93394
859	93399	93404	93409	93414	93420	93425	93430	93435	93440	93445
860	93450	93455	93460	93465	93470	93475	93480	93485	93490	93495
861	93500	93505	93510	93515	93520	93526	93531	93536	93541	93546
862	93551	93556	93561	93566	93571	93576	93581	93586	93591	93596
863	93601	93606	93611	93616	93621	93626	93631	93636	93641	93646
864	93651	93656	93661	93666	93671	93676	93682	93687	93692	93697
865	93702	93707	93712	93717	93722	93727	93732	93737	93742	93747
866	93752	93757	93762	93767	93772	93777	93782	93787	93792	93797
867	93802	93807	93812	93817	93822	93827	93832	93837	93842	93847
868	93852	93857	93862	93867	93872	93877	93882	93887	93892	93897
869	93902	93907	93912	93917	93922	93927	93932	93937	93942	93947
870	93952	93957	93962	93967	93972	93977	93982	93987	93992	93997
871	94002	94007	94012	94017	94022	94027	94032	94037	94042	94047
872	94052	94057	94062	94067	94072	94077	94082	94086	94091	94096
873	94101	94106	94111	94116	94121	94126	94131	94136	94141	94146
874	94151	94156	94161	94166	94171	94176	94181	94186	94191	94196
875	94201	94206	94211	94216	94221	94226	94231	94236	94240	94245
876	94250	94255	94260	94265	94270	94275	94280	94285	94290	94295
877	94300	94305	94310	94315	94320	94325	94330	94335	94340	94345
878	94349	94354	94359	94364	94369	94374	94379	94384	94389	94394
879	94399	94404	94409	94414	94419	94424	94429	94433	94438	94443

No.	0	1	2	3	4	5	6	7	8	9
880	94448	94453	94458	94463	94468	94473	94478	94483	94488	94493
881	94498	94503	94507	94512	94517	94522	94527	94532	94537	94542
882	94547	94552	94557	94562	94567	94571	94576	94581	94586	94591
883	94596	94601	94606	94611	94616	94621	94626	94630	94635	94640
884	94645	94650	94655	94660	94665	94670	94675	94680	94685	94689
885	94694	94699	94704	94709	94714	94719	94724	94729	94734	94738
886	94743	94748	94753	94758	94763	94768	94773	94778	94783	94787
887	94792	94797	94802	94807	94812	94817	94822	94827	94832	94836
888	94841	94846	94851	94856	94861	94866	94871	94876	94880	94885
889	94890	94895	94900	94905	94910	94915	94919	94924	94929	94934
890	94939	94944	94949	94954	94959	94963	94968	94973	94978	94983
891	94988	94993	94998	95002	95007	95012	95017	95022	95027	95032
892	95036	95041	95046	95051	95056	95061	95066	95071	95075	95080
893	95085	95090	95095	95100	95105	95109	95114	95119	95124	95129
894	95134	95139	95143	95148	95153	95158	95163	95168	95173	95177
895	95182	95187	95192	95197	95202	95207	95211	95216	95221	95226
896	95231	95236	95240	95245	95250	95255	95260	95265	95270	95274
897	95279	95284	95289	95294	95299	95303	95308	95313	95318	95323
898	95328	95332	95337	95342	95347	95352	95357	95361	95366	95371
899	95376	95381	95386	95390	95395	95400	95405	95410	95415	95419
900	95424	95429	95434	95439	95444	95448	95453	95458	95463	95468
901	95472	95477	95482	95487	95492	95497	95501	95506	95511	95516
902	95521	95525	95530	95535	95540	95545	95550	95554	95559	95564
903	95569	95574	95578	95583	95588	95593	95598	95602	95607	95612
904	95617	95622	95626	95631	95636	95641	95646	95650	95655	95660
905	95665	95670	95674	95679	95684	95689	95694	95698	95703	95708
906	95713	95718	95722	95727	95732	95737	95742	95746	95751	95756
907	95761	95766	95770	95775	95780	95785	95789	95794	95799	95804
908	95809	95813	95818	95823	95828	95832	95837	95842	95847	95852
909	95856	95861	95866	95871	95875	95880	95885	95890	95895	95899
910	95904	95909	95914	95918	95923	95928	95933	95938	95942	95947
911	95952	95957	95961	95966	95971	95976	95980	95985	95990	95995
912	95999	96004	96009	96014	96019	96023	96028	96033	96038	96042
913	96047	96052	96057	96061	96066	96071	96076	96080	96085	96090
914	96095	96099	96104	96109	96114	96118	96123	96128	96133	96137
915	96142	96147	96152	96156	96161	96166	96171	96175	96180	96185
916	96190	96194	96199	96204	96209	96213	96218	96223	96227	96232
917	96237	96242	96246	96251	96256	96261	96265	96270	96275	96280
918	96284	96289	96294	96298	96303	96308	96313	96317	96322	96327
919	96332	96336	96341	96346	96350	96355	96360	96365	96369	96374
920	96379	96384	96388	96393	96398	96402	96407	96412	96417	96421
921	96426	96431	96435	96440	96445	96450	96454	96459	96464	96468
922	96473	96478	96483	96487	96492	96497	96501	96506	96511	96515
923	96520	96525	96530	96534	96539	96544	96548	96553	96558	96562
924	96567	96572	96577	96581	96586	96591	96595	96600	96605	96609
925	96614	96619	96624	96628	96633	96638	96642	96647	96652	96656
926	96661	96666	96670	96675	96680	96685	96689	96694	96699	96703
927	96708	96713	96717	96722	96727	96731	96736	96741	96745	96750
928	96755	96759	96764	96769	96774	96778	96783	96788	96792	96797
929	96802	96806	96811	96816	96820	96825	96830	96834	96839	96844
930	96848	96853	96858	96862	96867	96872	96876	96881	96886	96890
931	96895	96900	96904	96909	96914	96918	96923	96928	96932	96937
932	96942	96946	96951	96956	96960	96965	96970	96974	96979	96984
933	96988	96993	96997	97002	97007	97011	97016	97021	97025	97030
934	97035	97039	97044	97049	97053	97058	97063	97067	97072	97077
935	97081	97086	97090	97095	97100	97104	97109	97114	97118	97123
936	97128	97132	97137	97142	97146	97151	97155	97160	97165	97169
937	97174	97179	97183	97188	97192	97197	97202	97206	97211	97216
938	97220	97225	97230	97234	97239	97243	97248	97253	97257	97262
939	97267	97271	97276	97280	97285	97290	97294	97299	97304	97308

No.	0	1	2	3	4	5	6	7	8	9
940	97313	97317	97322	97327	97331	97336	97340	97345	97350	97354
941	97359	97364	97368	97373	97377	97382	97387	97391	97396	97400
942	97405	97410	97414	97419	97424	97428	97433	97437	97442	97447
943	97451	97456	97460	97465	97470	97474	97479	97483	97488	97493
944	97497	97502	97506	97511	97516	97520	97525	97529	97534	97539
945	97543	97548	97552	97557	97562	97566	97571	97575	97580	97585
946	97589	97594	97598	97603	97607	97612	97617	97621	97626	97630
947	97635	97640	97644	97649	97653	97658	97663	97667	97672	97676
948	97681	97685	97690	97695	97699	97704	97708	97713	97717	97722
949	97727	97731	97736	97740	97745	97749	97754	97759	97763	97768
950	97772	97777	97782	97786	97791	97795	97800	97804	97809	97813
951	97818	97823	97827	97832	97836	97841	97845	97850	97855	97859
952	97864	97868	97873	97877	97882	97886	97891	97896	97900	97905
953	97909	97914	97918	97923	97928	97932	97937	97941	97946	97950
954	97955	97959	97964	97968	97973	97978	97982	97987	97991	97996
955	98000	98005	98009	98014	98019	98023	98028	98032	98037	98041
956	98046	98050	98055	98059	98064	98068	98073	98078	98082	98087
957	98091	98096	98100	98105	98109	98114	98118	98123	98127	98132
958	98137	98141	98146	98150	98155	98159	98164	98168	98173	98177
959	98182	98186	98191	98195	98200	98204	98209	98214	98218	98223
960	98227	98232	98236	98241	98245	98250	98254	98259	98263	98268
961	98272	98277	98281	98286	98290	98295	98299	98304	98308	98313
962	98318	98322	98327	98331	98336	98340	98345	98349	98354	98358
963	98363	98367	98372	98376	98381	98385	98390	98394	98399	98403
964	98408	98412	98417	98421	98426	98430	98435	98439	98444	98448
965	98453	98457	98462	98466	98471	98475	98480	98484	98489	98493
966	98498	98502	98507	98511	98516	98520	98525	98529	98534	98538
967	98543	98547	98552	98556	98561	98565	98570	98574	98579	98583
968	98588	98592	98597	98601	98605	98610	98614	98619	98623	98628
969	98632	98637	98641	98646	98650	98655	98659	98664	98668	98673
970	98677	98682	98686	98691	98695	98700	98704	98709	98713	98717
971	98722	98726	98731	98735	98740	98744	98749	98753	98758	98762
972	98767	98771	98776	98780	98784	98789	98793	98798	98802	98807
973	98811	98816	98820	98825	98829	98834	98838	98843	98847	98851
974	98856	98860	98865	98869	98874	98878	98883	98887	98892	98896
975	98900	98905	98909	98914	98918	98923	98927	98932	98936	98941
976	98945	98949	98954	98958	98963	98967	98972	98976	98981	98985
977	98989	98994	98998	99003	99007	99012	99016	99021	99025	99029
978	99034	99038	99043	99047	99052	99056	99061	99065	99069	99074
979	99078	99083	99087	99092	99096	99100	99105	99109	99114	99118
980	99123	99127	99131	99136	99140	99145	99149	99154	99158	99162
981	99167	99171	99176	99180	99185	99189	99193	99198	99202	99207
982	99211	99216	99220	99224	99229	99233	99238	99242	99247	99251
983	99255	99260	99264	99269	99273	99277	99282	99286	99291	99295
984	99300	99304	99308	99313	99317	99322	99326	99330	99335	99339
985	99344	99348	99352	99357	99361	99366	99370	99374	99379	99383
986	99388	99392	99396	99401	99405	99410	99414	99419	99423	99427
987	99432	99436	99441	99445	99449	99454	99458	99463	99467	99471
988	99476	99480	99484	99489	99493	99498	99502	99506	99511	99515
989	99520	99524	99528	99533	99537	99542	99546	99550	99555	99559
990	99564	99568	99572	99577	99581	99585	99590	99594	99599	99603
991	99607	99612	99616	99621	99625	99629	99634	99638	99642	99647
992	99651	99656	99660	99664	99669	99673	99677	99682	99686	99691
993	99695	99699	99704	99708	99712	99717	99721	99726	99730	99734
994	99739	99743	99747	99752	99756	99760	99765	99769	99774	99778
995	99782	99787	99791	99795	99800	99804	99808	99813	99817	99822
996	99826	99830	99835	99839	99843	99848	99852	99856	99861	99865
997	99870	99874	99878	99883	99887	99891	99896	99900	99904	99909
998	99913	99917	99922	99926	99930	99935	99939	99944	99948	99952
999	99957	99961	99965	99970	99974	99978	99983	99987	99991	99996

INDEX TO THE TABLES.

PART II.—THEORETICAL TREATISE.

AUXILIARY CONSTRUCTIONS AND CALCULATIONS.

1. PROFILES. (See Art. 38, Part I.) (1.) *Straight Profiles.*—Let A C (Fig. 39) represent the trace of the roadbed upon any plane, and let A B, C D, parallel to each other upon that plane, make any convenient angle with A C. Let A B and C D be respectively equal or in the same ratio to the marginal or the centre heights at A and C measured upon the plane of the profile. Let h be the height at A and h' the height at C. Make $\text{A B} = m\,h$ and $\text{C D} = m\,h'$. It is required to find the abscissa $\text{A P} = x$. Put $\text{A C} = \text{L}$. The similar triangles

Fig. 39.

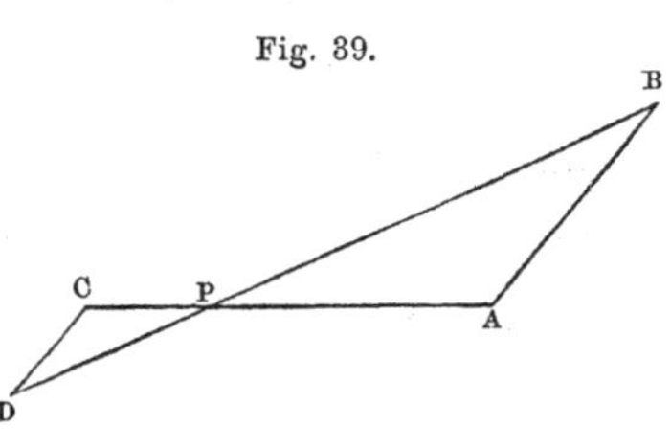

A P B, C P D give $\frac{\text{P A}}{\text{P C}} = \frac{\text{A B}}{\text{C D}}$; or $\frac{x}{x - \text{L}} = \frac{m\,h}{m\,h'}$; whence $x = \frac{\text{L}\,h}{h - h'}$ . . . . 1.

(2.) *Curved Profile of the Median Plane.* (See Art. 38, Part I.)—Let A B C (Fig. 41) be the cross-section from the surface to the meeting of the side-slopes. Let $\text{A B} = \text{M}$ and $\text{A C} = \text{N}$, for any given cross-section at the origin A; the intersection of the side-slopes is the axis of x; $\text{A F} = y$; $\text{C A N} = \text{B A M} = \sigma$. The values of AB and A C, at a distance x from the origin, may be expressed by $\text{A B} = \text{M} + p\,x$, $\text{A C} = \text{N} + q\,x$. Also, $\tan\gamma = \tan \text{F B O} = \frac{\text{C N} - \text{B M}}{\text{A M} + \text{A N}}$; wherein $\text{C N} = (\text{N} + q\,x)\sin\sigma$, $\text{B M} = (\text{M} + p\,x)\sin\sigma$, $\text{A M} = (\text{M} + p\,x)\cos\sigma$, $\text{A N} = (\text{N} + q\,x)\cos\sigma$. Substituting these values in the above expression for $\tan\gamma$,

$\tan\gamma = \frac{\sin\sigma}{\cos\sigma} \times \frac{\text{N} - \text{M} + (q - p)\,x}{\text{M} + \text{N} + (p + q)\,x}$. . . 2. Also, $\text{F O} = \text{B O}\tan\gamma = \text{A M}\tan\gamma$ $= (\text{M} + p\,x)\cos\sigma\tan\gamma = \sin\sigma\,(\text{M} + p\,x)\,\frac{\text{N} - \text{M} + (q - p)\,x}{\text{M} + \text{N} + (p + q)\,x}$. Then $\text{A F} = y$ $= \text{B M} + \text{F O} = \sin\sigma\,(\text{M} + p\,x)\left\{1 + \frac{\text{N} - \text{M} + (q - p)\,x}{\text{M} + \text{N} + (p + q)\,x}\right\}$

$$\text{Or, } y = \sin\sigma\,(\text{M} + p\,x)\,\frac{2\,(\text{N} + q\,x)}{\text{M} + \text{N} + (p + q)\,x}. \quad . . . 3.$$

The equation being cleared of fractions, the product of the variables will be present with the square of only one of them: the curve is therefore an hyperbola. Making $y = 0$, we have the two equations $M + p\,x = 0$, $N + q\,x = 0$, whence the two values, $x = -\frac{M}{p}$ and $x = -\frac{N}{q}$ are the abscissas of the points of intersection of the curve with the axis of x. The line of intersection of the side-slopes is, therefore, a secant of the curve.

The only finite value of x which being substituted in equation 3 will render y infinite, is $x = -\frac{M + N}{p + q}$. The ordinate corresponding to this abscissa is an asymptote. Substituting this last value of x in equation 2, we have $\tan \gamma = \frac{\sin \sigma}{\cos \sigma} \times \frac{2\,(p\,N - q\,M)}{0} = \infty$. Which shows that when the ordinate becomes an asymptote, the generatrix BC of the surface is perpendicular to the horizontal plane, that is, parallel to the median plane.

The augmented centre-height of a cross-section may be found by formula 3. Making $x = 0$, we have

$$y = \sin \sigma \frac{2\,M\,N}{M + N}.$$

Calling the distances out d and d', we may put $M = d \sec \sigma$, $N = d' \sec \sigma$; when the value of y becomes $y = \sin \sigma \frac{2\,d\,d' \sec \sigma}{d + d'} = \tan \sigma \frac{2\,d\,d'}{d + d'} = \frac{2\,d\,d'}{\cot \sigma\,(d + d')}$. (See Art. 76, Part I.)

Let S be the sum of all the distances out at the ends of a section. The sum of the distances out of the mid-section is then $d + d' = \frac{1}{2}$ S. Further, let s and s' be the sums of the end distances out on the sides d, d' respectively; so that $d = \frac{1}{2}\,s$ and $d' = \frac{1}{2}\,s'$. The last expression for y becomes

$$y = \frac{\frac{1}{2}\,s\,s'}{\cot \sigma\, \frac{1}{2}\,S} = \frac{s\,s'}{\cot \sigma\, S}. \quad \text{(See Art. 75, Part I.)}$$

2. Tabulation of Cross-Sections and of Marginal and Median Profiles.

Fig. 40.

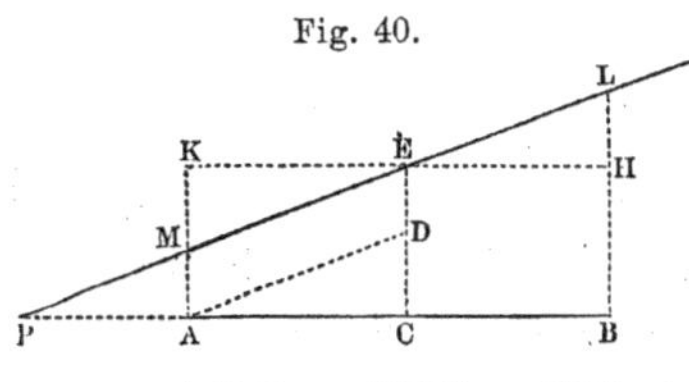

(1.) *Marginal Heights.* (See Articles 61 and 66, Part I.)—Let AB = B (Fig. 40) be the mean roadbed, ML the surface-line, AM and BL the marginal heights. Draw KH parallel to AB. HL and KM are of opposite sign, but each equal to the height CD of the neutral cross-section; whence

BL = (BH or CE) + CD, and AM = (AK or CE) — CD.

Let t be the tangent of the surface-slope at this end of the section, and t' the tangent at the other end: then (CE or h) + $\frac{1}{2}$ Bt = BL, and $h - \frac{1}{2}$ Bt = AM. In the same way the marginal heights are found at the other end, observing to make t' negative when the slope which it designates is opposed to the slope of ML. We may then derive the marginal heights, for both ends of the section, as follows, putting h' for the centre-height of the other end, and a, a' for the tabular augments corresponding to each end respectively.

Difference.	Marginal Height.	Augment.	Centre-Height.	Augment.	Marginal Height.	Difference.
$h - h' + a' - a$	$h - a$	$-a$	h	$+a$	$h + a$	$h - h' + a - a'$
	$h' - a'$	$-a'$	h'	$+a'$	$h' + a'$	

The several quantities are here arranged as in the table. (See Art. 66, Part I.) The abscissas are found from Table IV., according to formula 1.

(2.) *Sum and Difference of Bases for Sub-Sections.* (See Art. 70, Part I.)—It is obvious that the distance C P, called the distance out of the grade-point, $=$ C E cot E P C. Hence the base B P $= \frac{1}{2}$ B $+ h \cot \gamma$. If h be negative, P will fall between C and B. If h and h' represent the heights at the ends of a section, and the surface be a plane, the sum of the end-bases will be B $+ (h + h') \cot \gamma$, and their difference will be $(h - h') \cot \gamma$, which is independent of B. The end-heights are here taken positively when they are on the same side of the roadbed as the work for which the sum of the bases is to be found.

3. Trace of the Ground-Surface upon the Plane of the Roadbed. (See Art. 50 and following, Part I.)—Let L P B $= \gamma$ (Fig. 40) be the surface-slope; h, h', t, t', as before in Art. 2. Let A M $=$ M, B L $=$ N, at the first end of the section, and let C be the origin. Then the straight median surface-line through E gives for the value of C E at a distance x from the origin, C E $= h + n\,x$. And the straight directrices through M and L give, in like manner, A M $=$ M $+ p\,x$, B L $=$ N $+ q\,x$. But the values of M and N at the first end of the section are, by Art. 2, M $= h - \frac{1}{2}$ B t, N $= h + \frac{1}{2}$ B t. Also, $\tan \gamma =$

$$\frac{\mathrm{BL} - \mathrm{AM}}{\mathrm{AB}} = \frac{\mathrm{N} - \mathrm{M} + (q - p)\,x}{\mathrm{B}} = \frac{\mathrm{B}\,t + (q - p)\,x}{\mathrm{B}} = t + \frac{(q - p)\,x}{\mathrm{B}}.$$

Then $\mathrm{C\,P} = y = \mathrm{C\,E} \cot \gamma = (h + n\,x) \cot \gamma = \dfrac{h + n\,x}{t + \dfrac{q - p}{\mathrm{B}}\,x}$ . . . . 4.

To find the values of n, p, q in this equation, we have, by putting for x the length L of the section, $h + n\,\mathrm{L} = h'$; whence $n = \dfrac{h' - h}{\mathrm{L}}$:

$$h + \tfrac{1}{2}\,\mathrm{B}\,t + q\,\mathrm{L} = h' + \tfrac{1}{2}\,\mathrm{B}\,t'; \text{ whence } q = \frac{h' - h + \frac{1}{2}\,\mathrm{B}\,(t' - t)}{\mathrm{L}}:$$

$$h - \tfrac{1}{2}\,\mathrm{B}\,t + p\,\mathrm{L} = h' - \tfrac{1}{2}\,\mathrm{B}\,t'; \text{ whence } p = \frac{h' - h - \frac{1}{2}\,\mathrm{B}\,(t' - t)}{\mathrm{L}}:$$

and from these values of p and q, $q - p = \mathrm{B}\,\dfrac{t' - t}{\mathrm{L}}$.

Substituting these values of n and $q - p$ in equation 4, there results

$$y = \frac{h + \dfrac{h' - h}{\mathrm{L}}\,x}{t + \dfrac{t' - t}{\mathrm{L}}\,x} \quad . \; . \; . \; . \; 5.$$

The equation being cleared of fractions, the squares of the variables w absent, and their product present: the curve is therefore an hyperbola.

The value $x = \mathrm{L}\,\dfrac{t}{t - t'}$ will be the only value of x which can ren infinite; the ordinate corresponding to this value is therefore an asymptote.

From equation 5 may be derived for x,

$$x = \frac{t\,y - h}{\dfrac{h' - h}{\mathrm{L}} - \dfrac{t' - t}{\mathrm{L}}\,y} \quad . \; . \; . \; 6.$$

In which $\frac{h' - h}{t' - t}$ will be the only value of y which can render x infinite: the line parallel to the axis of abscissas, that is, parallel to the centre-line of the roadbed, whose ordinate is $\frac{h' - h}{t' - t}$, is therefore the other asymptote. As the asymptotes are at right angles, the hyperbola is equilateral.

When $y = 0$, equation 6 gives for the abscissa, $x = \text{L} \frac{h}{h - h'}$.

$$\text{When } y = \tfrac{1}{2} \text{B}, x = \text{L} \frac{h - \frac{1}{2} \text{B} t}{h - h' - \frac{1}{2} \text{B} (t - t')}.$$

$$\text{When } y = - \tfrac{1}{2} \text{B}, x = \text{L} \frac{h + \frac{1}{2} \text{B} t}{h - h' + \frac{1}{2} \text{B} (t - t')}.$$

If the surface be a plane, $t = t'$, and both these expressions for x may be included in the form

$$x = \text{L} \frac{h \pm \frac{1}{2} \text{B} t}{h - h'} \quad . \; . \; . \; . \quad 7,$$

wherein the sign $+ \frac{1}{2}$ B corresponds to the negative value of y, or to the higher side of the cross-section. When $y = \pm \frac{1}{2}$ B, x is equal to the marginal abscissa, (Art. 65, Part I.;) and when $y = 0$, x is the median abscissa. The abscissas, and hence the equation of the curve, may also be obtained from equation 1, where, if the marginal abscissas be sought, $h - t y$ and $h' - t' y$ must be put for the marginal heights.

COMPUTATION OF SOLIDITY.

4. Whole-Section or Full Work. (1.) *Solidity in Terms of the Sides of the Triangular Cross-Section. Curved Surface.* (See Articles 8 and 28, Part I.)—Let BCED (Fig. 41) represent the cross-section of an excavation or embankment. DE is the roadbed, BC the surface-slope. It is required to find the content of the solid generated by the motion of ABC in a direction perpendicular to the plane of the figure, this plane always being parallel to its first position. It is further supposed that each of the points A, B, C moves upon a straight directrix. B and C follow the external surface-lines, and A follows the intersection of the side-planes. The side-slopes BDH, CEQ are equal.

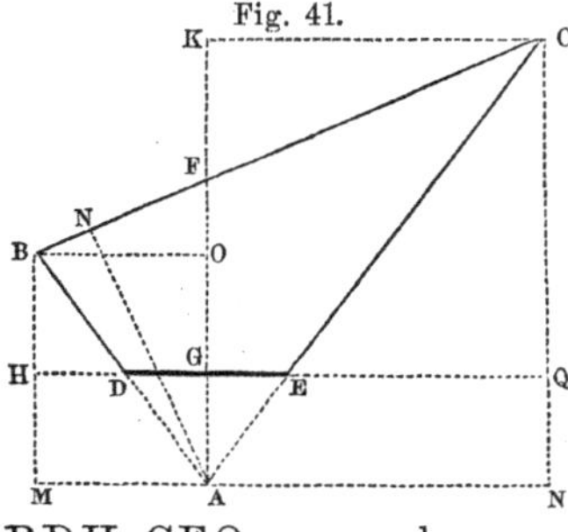

Fig. 41.

In a given position of the generating plane, let AB = M, AC = N; and let BDH $= \sigma$.

Because the points B and C move upon straight lines respectively in the planes of AB and AC, the value of the variable side AB, for any position of the generating plane BAC at a distance x from the origin, may be expressed by M $+ p x$; and, in like manner, AC = N $+ q x$; p and q being constants.

We have, by Trigonometry, for the area A of any cross-section ABC,

$$\text{A} = \tfrac{1}{2} \sin \text{BAC} . \text{AB} \times \text{AC} = \tfrac{1}{2} \sin 2 \sigma (\text{M} + p x)(\text{N} + q x) \; . \; . \; . \; . \; 8.$$

Whence the volume V of the solid included between two cross-sections B A C at the distances respectively of $x = -\frac{1}{2}$ L and $x = +\frac{1}{2}$ L from the origin is,

$$V = \tfrac{1}{2}\sin 2\,\sigma\int_{-\frac{1}{2}L}^{+\frac{1}{2}L}(M + p\,x)\,(N + q\,x)\,d\,x = \tfrac{1}{2}\sin 2\,\sigma\,L\,(MN + \tfrac{1}{12}\,p\,q\,L^2)\;\ldots\;9.$$

$$= \tfrac{1}{2}\sin 2\,\sigma\,\tfrac{1}{6}\,L\,(6\,M\,N + \tfrac{1}{2}\,p\,q\,L^2)\;\ldots\;.\;10.$$

(2.) *Prismoidal Formula.**—By this formula, if A be the area of the mid cross-section of any solid to which the formula applies, and A′ and A″ the areas of the ends, the volume V is

$$V = \tfrac{1}{6}\,L\,(4\,A + A' + A'')\;\ldots\;.\;11.$$

To show that this is equivalent to formula 10, it will only be necessary to express the areas of the cross-sections according to formula 8, and to perform the addition of the quantities within the parenthesis of equation 11. Making in this operation the sides A B, A C of the ends respectively $M \pm \frac{1}{2}\,p\,L$, and $N \pm \frac{1}{2}\,q\,L$. We have

$$4\,A = \tfrac{1}{2}\sin 2\,\sigma\,4\,M\,N.$$

$$A' = \tfrac{1}{2}\sin 2\,\sigma\left\{M\,N + \tfrac{1}{2}\,L\,(M\,q + N\,p) + \tfrac{1}{4}\,p\,q\,L^2\right\}$$

$$A'' = \tfrac{1}{2}\sin 2\,\sigma\left\{M\,N - \tfrac{1}{2}\,L\,(M\,q + N\,p) + \tfrac{1}{4}\,p\,q\,L^2\right\}$$

which, by adding together the three equations and multiplying by $\frac{1}{6}$ L, gives

$$V = \tfrac{1}{6}\,L\,(4\,A + A' + A'') = \tfrac{1}{2}\sin 2\,\sigma\,\tfrac{1}{6}\,L\,(6\,M\,N + \tfrac{1}{2}\,p\,q\,L^2)\;\ldots\;.\;12.$$

If the side-slopes are plane, D and E follow straight directrices: the same things are true of the solid generated by D A E, and the prismoidal formula will hold for the solid generated by B C E D, the difference of B A C and D A E.

(3.) *Solidity by Transverse Ground-Slopes. Plane Surface.*—We shall now inquire the volume of the solid on B A C, under a plane ground-surface, in terms of the end-heights A F and the surface-slope F C K. C K is parallel to D E, and A F bisects the angle B A C; that is, D E is supposed to be horizontal and A F vertical. Let the width of roadbed D E = B, the end-heights A F = H and H′ at the respective ends, $F\,C\,K = \gamma$. Make H + H′ = S and H — H′ = D; the rest as before. The height at the mid-section will then be $\frac{1}{2}$ S. $F\,C\,A = K\,C\,A - F\,C\,K = \sigma - \gamma$: $F\,B\,A = O\,B\,A + F\,B\,O = \sigma + \gamma$. Sin A F C = sin B F A = cos γ. We have then, by Trigonometry, $A\,B = A\,F\,\dfrac{\cos\gamma}{\sin(\sigma + \gamma)}$, and $A\,C = A\,F\,\dfrac{\cos\gamma}{\sin(\sigma - \gamma)}$. Also, the heights A F at the end cross-sections are $\frac{1}{2}$ (S + D) and $\frac{1}{2}$ (S — D). The values of A B and A C at the mid cross-section will be

$$A\,B = M = \tfrac{1}{2}\,S\,\frac{\cos\gamma}{\sin(\sigma + \gamma)},\quad A\,C = N = \tfrac{1}{2}\,S\,\frac{\cos\gamma}{\sin(\sigma - \gamma)}.$$

The values of A B at the two ends will, also, be

$\frac{1}{2}\,(S + D)\,\dfrac{\cos\gamma}{\sin(\sigma + \gamma)}$, and $\frac{1}{2}\,(S - D)\,\dfrac{\cos\gamma}{\sin(\sigma + \gamma)}$; whence for the value of p we shall have $p = \frac{1}{2}\left\{(S + D) - (S - D)\right\}\dfrac{\cos\gamma}{\sin(\sigma + \gamma)} \div L = \dfrac{D}{L}\,\dfrac{\cos\gamma}{\sin(\sigma + \gamma)}$.

---

* See also, under Straight Solids of Revolution, page 290.

In like manner we shall find for q, on the side A C, $q = \frac{D}{L} \frac{\cos \gamma}{\sin (\sigma - \gamma)}$.

Substituting these values of M, N, p, q, in equation 9, there results

$$V = \tfrac{1}{8} L (S^2 + \frac{D^2}{3}) \frac{\sin 2 \sigma \cos^2 \gamma}{\sin (\sigma + \gamma) \sin (\sigma - \gamma)} \quad \ldots . 13.$$

This form is convenient for logarithmic computation of the factor outside of the parenthesis containing σ and γ. We have employed it for this purpose in constructing the tables. (See § 2, Art. 11, Appendix.)

By subtracting from this expression the value of the solid upon D A E, we should derive a formula for the solidity of the body upon B D E C.

The area of the triangle A B C, and hence the solidity of the work, may also be derived from the height A N and the base B C, which may both be found in terms of σ and γ. We shall, however, proceed as follows:—

Draw A N perpendicular to B C. $AFC = \frac{1}{2}\pi + \gamma$, and, because it is an external angle, is equal to $FNA + NAF$; therefore $NAF = \gamma$, and $AN = AF \cos \gamma$. Refer B C to A F as an axis, with A for the pole, and let φ be the polar angle.

The length of any radius vector A C will be $\rho = AN \sec NAC = AF \cos \gamma \sec (\varphi - \gamma)$. And the equation of D E will be $\rho' = AG \sec \varphi = \frac{1}{2} B \tan \sigma \sec \varphi$. Now, the general expression for the area A included between two curves and two radii common to both is

$$A = \tfrac{1}{2} \int (\rho^2 - \rho'^2)\, d\varphi$$

which in the present case, between the limits $\varphi = -(\frac{1}{2}\pi - \sigma)$ and $\varphi = +(\frac{1}{2}\pi - \sigma)$, becomes

$$A = \tfrac{1}{2} \int_{-(\frac{1}{2}\pi - \sigma)}^{+(\frac{1}{2}\pi - \sigma)} \left(\overline{AF}^2 \cos^2 \gamma \sec^2 (\varphi - \gamma) - \tfrac{1}{4} B^2 \tan^2 \sigma \sec^2 \varphi\right) d\varphi;$$

which integration being performed gives

$$A = \tfrac{1}{2} \overline{AF}^2 \cos^2 \gamma \left\{ \cot (\sigma + \gamma) + \cot (\sigma - \gamma) \right\} - \tfrac{1}{4} B^2 \tan \sigma \quad \ldots . 14.$$

A part of this expression may be transformed as follows: Making use of the formula $\cot (a \pm b) = \frac{1 \mp \tan a \tan b}{\tan a \pm \tan b}$, we have

$$\cos^2 \gamma \left\{ \cot (\sigma + \gamma) + \cot (\sigma - \gamma) \right\} = \cos^2 \gamma \left\{ \frac{1 - \tan \sigma \tan \gamma}{\tan \sigma + \tan \gamma} + \frac{1 + \tan \sigma \tan \gamma}{\tan \sigma - \tan \gamma} \right\}$$

$$= \cos^2 \gamma \left\{ \frac{2 \tan \sigma + 2 \tan \sigma \tan^2 \gamma}{\tan^2 \sigma - \tan^2 \gamma} \right\} = 2 \cos^2 \gamma \left\{ \frac{\tan \sigma (1 + \tan^2 \gamma)}{\tan^2 \sigma - \tan^2 \gamma} \right\}$$

$$= 2 \cos^2 \gamma \frac{\tan \sigma \sec^2 \gamma}{\tan^2 \sigma - \tan^2 \gamma} = \frac{2 \tan \sigma}{\tan^2 \sigma - \tan^2 \gamma}.$$

Substituting this last in equation 14, we have for the area of B D E C

$$A = \overline{AF}^2 \frac{\tan \sigma}{\tan^2 \sigma - \tan^2 \gamma} - \tfrac{1}{4} B^2 \tan \sigma = \frac{4 \overline{AF}^2 \tan \sigma - B^2 \tan^3 \sigma + B^2 \tan \sigma \tan^2 \gamma}{4 (\tan^2 \sigma - \tan^2 \gamma)},$$

$$\text{Or, } A = \tfrac{1}{4} (4 \overline{AF}^2 - B^2 \tan^2 \sigma + B^2 \tan^2 \gamma) \frac{\tan \sigma}{\tan^2 \sigma - \tan^2 \gamma} \quad \ldots . 15.$$

We had, however, $\frac{1}{2}$ S for the height of the mid-section, and D for the difference of the end-heights. The height A F at any distance x from the origin, will therefore be $\frac{1}{2} S + \frac{D}{L} x$. Substituting this in equation 15, we shall have for the volume V between the limits $x = -\frac{1}{2} L$ and $x = +\frac{1}{2} L$,

$$V = \frac{1}{4} \int_{-\frac{1}{2}L}^{+\frac{1}{2}L} \left\{ (S + 2 \frac{D}{L} x)^2 - B^2 \tan^2 \sigma + B^2 \tan^2 \gamma \right\} d\,x \frac{\tan \sigma}{\tan^2 \sigma - \tan^2 \gamma},$$

which gives for the solid upon B D E C between the surface and the roadbed,

$$V = \frac{1}{4} L \left(S^2 - B^2 \tan^2 \sigma + B^2 \tan^2 \gamma + \frac{D^2}{3}\right) \frac{\tan \sigma}{\tan^2 \sigma - \tan^2 \gamma} \quad \ldots . 16.$$

$$\text{Or, } V = \frac{1}{4} L \left(S^2 - B^2 \tan^2 \sigma + B^2 \tan^2 \gamma + \frac{D^2}{3}\right) \frac{\cot \sigma}{1 - \frac{\tan^2 \gamma}{\tan^2 \sigma}} \quad \ldots . 17.$$

If B be made = 0, that is, if D E vanish upon A, this last equation becomes

$$V = \frac{1}{4} L \left(S^2 + \frac{D^2}{3}\right) \frac{\cot \sigma}{1 - \frac{\tan^2 \gamma}{\tan^2 \sigma}} \quad \ldots . 18,$$

which is equivalent to equation 13. If, further, the end-heights be equal, D = 0 and we have

$$V = \frac{1}{4} L S^2 \frac{\cot \sigma}{1 - \frac{\tan^2 \gamma}{\tan^2 \sigma}} \quad \ldots . 19.$$

Hence, if this value of V be taken from a table with the argument S and under the degree of surface-slope γ, the solidity thus obtained is that of a prism erected upon the area of the mid-section. If to this prism the third part of another of similar base, and whose height is $\frac{1}{2}$ D and tabular argument D, be added, the solidity thus obtained is that of formula 18. (See Art. 85, Part I.)

If in formula 17 the quantity within the parenthesis be put $= S_1^2$, then S_1 is the tabular argument for the solidity of a prism erected on a base whose height is $\frac{1}{2} S_1$ and surface-slope γ. (See Art. 97, Part I.) We may also extract the square root of $S^2 + \frac{D^2}{3}$ in equation 18, and take V from the table with the argument $\sqrt{S^2 + \frac{D^2}{3}}$. (See Art. 96, Part I.)

5. SUB-SECTION OR PARTIAL WORK BY TRANSVERSE GROUND-SLOPES. (See Art. 85, Part I.) As the solidities in this kind of work are generally comparatively small, it will suffice for our purpose to consider the surface a plane. The solids in question will then be truncated pyramids and pyramids. We propose to include both in the same formula.

Fig. 42.

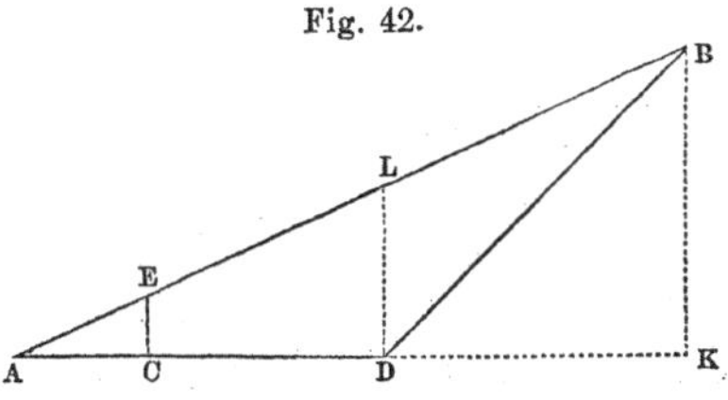

Let A D B (Fig. 42) represent the cross-section. A D is a portion of the roadbed, and C D = $\frac{1}{2}$ B is the half-width of the roadbed. Besides the angle B A C = γ, we have here given the centre-height C E. The area A of this triangle may be found by letting fall the perpendicular B K upon A D K. We have A = $\frac{1}{2}$ A D × B K. But now, as before, $ABD = \sigma - \gamma$; hence, by Trigonometry, in the triangle ABD, $BD = AD \frac{\sin\gamma}{\sin(\sigma-\gamma)}$, and, therefore, $BK = BD \sin\sigma = AD \frac{\sin\sigma\sin\gamma}{\sin(\sigma-\gamma)}$.

$$\text{And } A = \tfrac{1}{2} AD \times BK = \tfrac{1}{2} \overline{AD}^2 \frac{\sin\sigma\sin\gamma}{\sin(\sigma-\gamma)}.$$

Or, (by § 2, Art. 2,)

$$A = \tfrac{1}{2}(\tfrac{1}{2}B + h\cot\gamma)^2 \frac{\sin\sigma\sin\gamma}{\sin(\sigma-\gamma)} = \tfrac{1}{8}(B + 2h\cot\gamma)^2 \frac{\sin\sigma\sin\gamma}{\sin(\sigma-\gamma)} \quad \ldots\ldots 20,$$

wherein $B + 2h\cot\gamma$ = the sum of the end-bases, h being put for the height of the mid-section. Denote this sum by S, and let D be the difference of the end-bases; then the width of base at a distance x from the mid-section is $\tfrac{1}{2}S + \frac{D}{L}x$, whence we shall have for the volume

$$V = \tfrac{1}{8}\int_{-\frac{1}{2}L}^{+\frac{1}{2}L} (S + 2\tfrac{D}{L}x)^2\, dx \frac{\sin\sigma\sin\gamma}{\sin(\sigma-\gamma)} = \tfrac{1}{8}L\,(S^2 + \tfrac{D^2}{3}) \frac{\sin\sigma\sin\gamma}{\sin(\sigma-\gamma)} \quad \ldots\ldots 21.$$

This formula is proper for computing the solidity by means of the end-bases.

If, in equation 20, the right-hand member be multiplied within the parenthesis by $\tan\gamma$, and divided outside by $\tan^2\gamma$, that is, multiplied outside by $\frac{\cos^2\gamma}{\sin^2\gamma}$, there results

$$A = \tfrac{1}{8}(2h + B\tan\gamma)^2 \frac{\sin\sigma\cos^2\gamma}{\sin\gamma\sin(\sigma-\gamma)} \quad \ldots\ldots 22.$$

In which, if h represent the height of the mid-section, $2h + B\tan\gamma$ represents twice the marginal height DL = the sum of these heights at the ends. Put S for the sum of these heights, and D for their difference; then, in a manner similar to that employed for equation 21, we find for the volume

$$V = \tfrac{1}{8}L\,(S^2 + \tfrac{D^2}{3}) \frac{\sin\sigma\cos^2\gamma}{\sin\gamma\sin(\sigma-\gamma)} \quad \ldots\ldots 23.$$

This formula is proper for computing the solidity by means of the end-heights: S is the augmented sum, that is, of the heights which are augmented by $\tfrac{1}{2}B\tan\gamma$. (See § 1, Art. 2. For other forms, see Note 2, p. 315.)

Equivalence of Formulæ.—Full and partial work may merge into the same when the side BD (Fig. 41) vanishes at both ends of the work, or when the grade-point A (Fig. 42) falls at each end upon the edge of the roadbed. To show the equivalence, in this case, of formulæ 16 and 21, we may proceed thus. Making use of the formula $\cot a \pm \cot b = \pm \frac{\sin(a-b)}{\sin a \sin b}$, equation 21 becomes

$$V = \tfrac{1}{8}L\,(S^2 + \tfrac{D^2}{3}) \frac{1}{\cot'\gamma - \cot\sigma} \quad \ldots\ldots 24.$$

Multiplying this last form above and below by $\tan\sigma\tan\gamma$, we have

$$V = \tfrac{1}{8}L\,(S^2 + \tfrac{D^2}{3}) \frac{\tan\sigma\tan\gamma}{\tan\sigma - \tan\gamma} \quad \ldots\ldots 25.$$

In formula 16, the difference of the end-heights D, and in formula 21 the difference D of the bases, will vanish under the proposed conditions. Also, in equation 21, S becomes = 2 B, which being put for S in equation 25, and the equation multiplied above and below by tan σ + tan γ, there results

$$V = \tfrac{1}{2} L B^2 \frac{\tan^2 \sigma \tan \gamma + \tan \sigma \tan^2 \gamma}{\tan^2 \sigma - \tan^2 \gamma} \quad \ldots . 26.$$

In equation 16, S = 2 (A G + G F) (Fig. 41) becomes = B (tan σ + tan γ), which being there substituted, equation 26 is reproduced.

6. COMPUTATION OF SOLIDITY BY CENTRE AND SIDE HEIGHTS. (See Chapter IV., Part I.) Let DBFCE (Fig. 43) be the mid cross-section of the work, and ABFC the whole cross-section down to the intersection of the side-slopes. We shall inquire the volume of the solid generated by the whole cross-section. The centre-height AF and the distances out AM, AN are supposed to increase or diminish regularly in proportion to the distance passed over by the generating plane. The side-heights BM, CN are generally considered to be each in a constant ratio to its distance out; but we shall not assume them to be so necessarily.

Fig. 43.

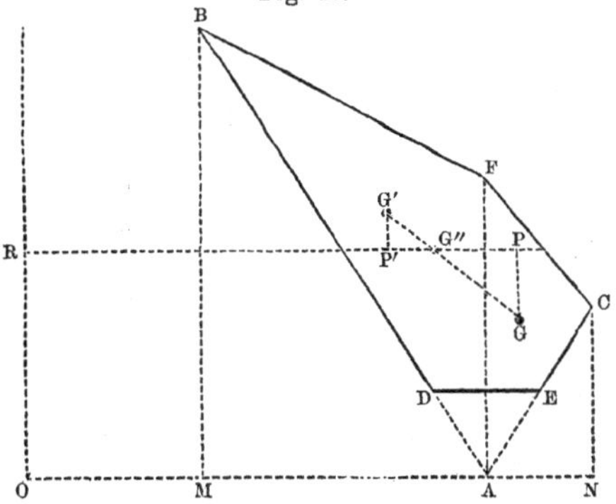

In Fig. 44, ABC is the cross-section. The height CN and the base AB are supposed to increase or diminish proportionally to the distance passed over by the generating plane. The centre-height KL is supposed to be known. AB is either given or is to be found by an auxiliary process.

Fig. 44.

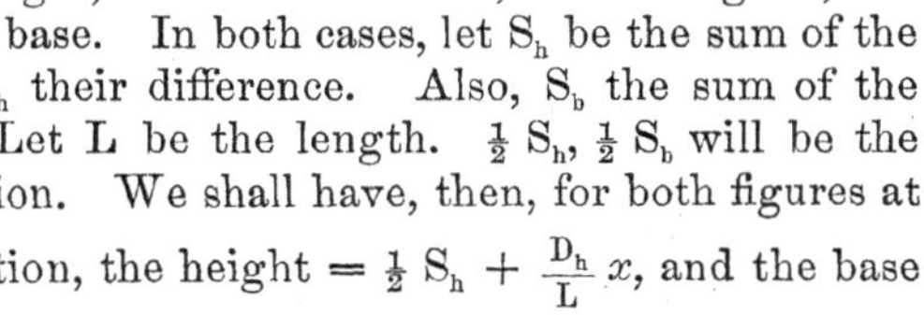

In Fig. 43, call AF the end-height, and MN the base; and in Fig. 44, call CN the end-height, and AB the base. In both cases, let S_h be the sum of the end-heights of the solid, and D_h their difference. Also, S_b the sum of the bases, and D_b their difference. Let L be the length. $\tfrac{1}{2} S_h$, $\tfrac{1}{2} S_b$ will be the dimensions of the mid cross-section. We shall have, then, for both figures at any distance x from the mid-section, the height $= \tfrac{1}{2} S_h + \frac{D_h}{L} x$, and the base $= \tfrac{1}{2} S_b + \frac{D_b}{L} x$. The area of the cross-section is, for both,

$$A = \tfrac{1}{2} \left(\tfrac{1}{2} S_h + \frac{D_h}{L} x\right) \left(\tfrac{1}{2} S_b + \frac{D_b}{L} x\right) = \tfrac{1}{8} \left(S_h + 2 \frac{D_h}{L} x\right) \left(S_b + 2 \frac{D_b}{L} x\right).$$

And the volume V will be

$$V = \tfrac{1}{8} \int_{-\frac{1}{2} L}^{+\frac{1}{2} L} \left(S_h + 2 \frac{D_h}{L} x\right) \left(S_b + 2 \frac{D_b}{L} x\right) d x = \tfrac{1}{8} L \left(S_h S_b + \frac{D_h D_b}{3}\right) \quad \ldots . 27,$$

where $\frac{D_h D_b}{3}$ will be positive if D_h and D_b be of like sign; that is, if the greater end-height correspond to the greater base.

Equidistant Level-Heights or Ordinates. (Art. 4, Appendix.) Let there be $n+1$ heights. The area A will now consist of n trapezoids, having the common width $\frac{1}{n}(\frac{1}{2}S_b+\frac{D_b}{L}x)$. Designate the heights taken in order across the section thus: $\frac{1}{2}S_{0h}+\frac{D_{0h}}{L}x$, $\frac{1}{2}S_{1h}+\frac{D_{1h}}{L}x$, &c., $\frac{1}{2}S_{nh}+\frac{D_{nh}}{L}x$; where S_h and D_h, according to the ordinals $_0$, $_1$, &c., represent the sum and difference of heights at opposite ends of the work. The area of each trapezoid is equal to the half-sum of its heights multiplied by the width. In summing the trapezoids the external heights will be taken once, and each of the others twice. Then

$$A=\tfrac{1}{2}(\tfrac{1}{2}S_{0h}+\tfrac{1}{2}S_{nh}+S_{1h}+\&c.+S_{n-1h}+\frac{D_{0h}+D_{nh}+2D_{1h}+\&c.+2D_{n-1h}}{L}x)\frac{1}{n}(\tfrac{1}{2}S_b+\frac{D_b}{L}x);$$

$$\text{Or, } A=\frac{1}{n}\times\tfrac{1}{2}(\tfrac{1}{2}S'_h+\frac{D'_h}{L}x)(\tfrac{1}{2}S_b+\frac{D_b}{L}x).$$

Wherein S'_h is the sum of *level-totals*, and D'_h their difference; and we shall have, by a process similar to that for equation 27,

$$V=\frac{L}{n}\times\tfrac{1}{8}(S'_h\,S_b+\frac{D'_h\,D_b}{3})\;.\;.\;.\;.\;.\;.\;28.$$

7. CURVES. (1.) *Whole Sections by Centre and Side Heights.* (See Art. 120, Part I.)—We propose to consider the curve-solid as a solid of revolution, and to employ Guldin's theorem. By this theorem, the volume is equal to the area of the cross-section multiplied by the distance passed over by the centre of gravity, in a direction perpendicular to the plane of the section.

D B F C E (Fig. 43) is the cross-section of the work, and A B F C the whole cross-section. We shall inquire the volume generated by the whole cross-section. R O is the vertical axis of revolution. The centre-height A F and the distances out A M, A N are supposed to increase or decrease regularly, each in a constant ratio to the distance described by the point A. The abscissa from A will be measured on the intersection of the horizontal plane M N with the cylindrical surface described by A F.

The whole cross-section is divided into two triangles A F C, A F B. Let G be the centre of gravity of A F C, and G′ that of A F B; also, let G″ be the centre of gravity of the whole cross-section. Make the area of A F B = B, and the area of A F C = C: then B = $\frac{1}{2}$ F A × A M, and C = $\frac{1}{2}$ F A × A N. But we shall have, because the areas of these triangles are respectively the measures of their weights,

$$B\times G'G''=C\times GG''; \text{ whence } \frac{GG''}{G'G''}=\frac{B}{C}=\frac{AM}{AN}.$$

Draw the verticals G P, G′ P′, then $\frac{GG''}{G'G''}=\frac{AM}{AN}=\frac{PG''}{P'G''}$, or AM : AN :: PG″ : P′ G″; whence P′ G″ + P G″ : P′ G″ :: A M + A N : A N; which gives

$$P'G''=\frac{(P'G''+PG'')\times AN}{AM+AN}\;.\;.\;.\;.\;29.$$

Let ρ be the distance of G and ρ' of G′ from the axis R O, and let ρ'' be the distance of G″. Also let x be the abscissa of revolution, as above described, of the point A. And let O A = R. Then the variable lengths A M, A N, at a distance x from A, may be expressed by $AM=M+q'x$, $AN=N+qx$.

We shall then have $P' G'' + P G'' = P' P = \rho - \rho'$; and equation 29 may be transformed into

$$P' G'' = \frac{(\rho - \rho')(N + q x)}{M + N + (q + q') x}.$$

But $\rho'' = \rho' + P' G''$; whence

$$\rho'' = \rho' + \frac{(\rho - \rho')(N + q x)}{M + N + (q + q') x}.$$

We have now to find the values of ρ and ρ' as functions of x, and substitute them in this equation. These are the abscissas of the centres of gravity of A F C and A F B reckoned from R O. The abscissa of the centre of gravity of a triangle is equal to one-third the sum of the abscissas of its angular points. The abscissa of the angular point is equal to R, for A and F; hence

$$\rho = R + \tfrac{1}{3}(N + q x),\ \rho' = R - \tfrac{1}{3}(M + q' x), \text{ and}$$

$$\rho - \rho' = \tfrac{1}{3}\left\{ M + N + (q + q') x \right\}.$$ Hence the value of ρ'' is

$$\rho'' = R + \frac{(N + q x) - (M + q' x)}{3} = R + \frac{N - M + (q - q') x}{3} \quad \ldots . 30.$$

Let A be the area of the whole cross-section, and φ the horizontal angle of revolution; then, if the cross-section revolve through the infinitely small arc $d\varphi$, the volume generated will be dV, the differential of the volume of the curved solid. But the distance passed over by the centre of gravity of the whole section in this revolution is $\rho'' d\varphi$; hence, by Guldin's theorem,

$$dV = \rho'' A\, d\varphi \quad \ldots . 31.$$

But we shall have $x = R\varphi$, whence $d\varphi = \frac{dx}{R}$. Putting this value of $d\varphi$ in the last equation, and substituting the value of ρ'' found in formula 30, there results

$$dV = \left(1 + \frac{N - M}{3R}\right) A\, dx + \frac{q - q'}{3R} A\, x\, dx \quad \ldots . 32.$$

Make now $A F = \frac{1}{2} S_h + p x$, and put $M + N = \frac{1}{2} S_b$; then (Fig. 43)

$$A = \tfrac{1}{2} A F \times M N = \tfrac{1}{2}\left(\tfrac{1}{2} S_h + p x\right)\left\{ M + N + (q + q') x \right\}$$

$$= \tfrac{1}{8}(S_h + 2 p x)\left\{ S_b + 2(q + q') x \right\} \quad \ldots . 33.$$

Substituting this value of A in the last term of equation 32, and integrating between the limits $x = -\frac{1}{2} L$, $x = +\frac{1}{2} L$, we shall have

$$\frac{q - q'}{24 R} \int_{-\frac{1}{2}L}^{+\frac{1}{2}L} (S_h + 2px)\left\{ S_b + 2(q + q') x \right\} x\, dx.$$

Call this C': then

$$C' = \frac{L^3}{144 R}(q - q')\left\{ S_h (q + q') + S_b\, p \right\},$$

which, by making $q + q' = \frac{D_b}{L}$, and $p = \frac{D_h}{L}$, becomes

$$C' = \frac{L^2}{144 R}(q - q')(S_h D_b + S_b D_h).$$

Denoting the difference of the end distances out by D'_m on the side A M, and by D'_n on the side A N, we have $\frac{D'_m}{L} = q'$, $\frac{D'_n}{L} = q$. Hence C' becomes

$$C' = \frac{L}{144 R} (D'_n - D'_m)(S_h D_b + S_b D_h).$$

In practical questions this term is generally small, and may be neglected.

Designating the approximate value of V by V′, we shall then have, by formula 32,

$$dV' = \left(1 + \frac{N - M}{3 R}\right) A\, dx.$$

$$\text{And } V' = \left(1 + \frac{N - M}{3 R}\right) \int A\, dx = \left(1 + \frac{N - M}{3 R}\right) V \ldots . 34.$$

Wherein V is the volume of the straight solid by formula 27, which is, in fact, derivable from 32 by making R infinite.

Let C be the correction required by the straight solid. The last equation gives $C = \frac{N - M}{3 R} V = \frac{2 (N - M)}{6 R} V$. (See Art. 122, Part I.)

(2.) *Sub-Sections by Centre and Side Heights.*—When the cross-section is triangular, the side A B may be supposed to coincide with A M, and the point A to represent the margin of the roadbed, as in Fig. 44. We desire, however, to employ the height C N and to have the radius R = O L, L being the centre of the roadbed. The investigation leads to formulæ similar to those already derived.

Let L B = M + $q' x$ and L N = N + $q x$. Make L A = $\frac{1}{2}$ B, and put $\frac{1}{2}$ B + N = N′. The radius ρ'' of the centre of gravity will now be

$$\rho'' = \tfrac{1}{3} \left\{ R + \tfrac{1}{2} B + R + (N + q x) + R - (M + q' x) \right\}$$

$$= R + \frac{\frac{1}{2} B + N - M + (q - q') x}{3} = R + \frac{N' - M + (q - q') x}{3}.$$

Substituting this in the value of dV, equation 31, and putting $\frac{dx}{R}$ for $d\varphi$, there results

$$dV = \left(1 + \frac{N' - M}{3 R}\right) A\, dx + \frac{q - q'}{3 R} A\, x\, dx,$$

$$\text{and } V = \left(1 + \frac{N' - M}{3 R}\right) \int A\, dx + \frac{q - q'}{3 R} \int A\, x\, dx.$$

The first term gives the same form for the approximate solidity as the previous expression, equation 34, for the solid of Fig. 43, namely,

$$V' = \left(1 + \frac{N' - M}{3 R}\right) V \ldots . 35;$$

where V is found as in formula 27. The correction is $C = \frac{2 (N' - M)}{6 R} V$. (See Article 122, Part I.)

In the second term, A has a form similar to the previous, by putting $C N = \frac{1}{2} S_h + p x$ and $A B = \frac{1}{2} B + M + q' x = \frac{1}{2} S_b + q' x$. In the value previously found for C′ must be substituted q' for $q + q'$.

(3.) *Whole Sections by Transverse Ground-Slopes.* (See Art. 105, Part I.)—The preceding discussion of triangular or partial cross-sections will suffice. The full-work solids present equations analogous to those obtained for centre and side heights. It is only necessary to introduce the constant co-efficients cos σ and sin B A C, which belong to the problem of the straight solid, by making the side-slopes constant and equal, as is done in Art. 4. Suppose B F C (Fig. 43) to be a straight line. Let A B = M, A C = N, at the mid-section. At a distance x from the origin these lines will be $M + q' x$, $N + q x$. The distance out A M = $(M + q' x) \cos \sigma$, A N = $(N + q x) \cos \sigma$. The radius of the centre of gravity will then be

$$\rho'' = R + \frac{\cos \sigma (N - M + (q - q') x)}{3}.$$

This being substituted in equation 31 gives, by putting as before $d \varphi = \frac{d x}{R}$,

$$d V = \left(1 + \frac{\cos \sigma (N - M)}{3 R}\right) A \, d x + \frac{\cos \sigma (q - q')}{3 R} A \, x \, d x \; . \; . \; . \; . \; 36.$$

The first term here represents, as before, the differential of a straight solid. By integrating this term, we shall find for the approximate volume V′

$$V' = \left(1 + \frac{\cos \sigma (N - M)}{3 R}\right) V \; . \; . \; . \; . \; 37,$$

where V is found as in formula 9.

The correction necessary to derive V′ from V, is $C = \frac{\cos \sigma (N - M)}{3 R} V$; wherein $\cos \sigma$ N and $\cos \sigma$ M are the distances out of the mid cross-section. (See Art. 107, Part I.)

For the value of A in the last term of equation 36, we have

$$A = \tfrac{1}{2} \sin 2 \sigma (M + q' x) (N + q x).$$

Therefore to find the value of the correction C′, which is equal to the last term, we have to integrate

$$\frac{\frac{1}{2} \sin 2 \sigma \cos \sigma (q - q')}{3 R} \int_{-\frac{1}{2} L}^{+\frac{1}{2} L} (M + q' x) (N + q x) \, x \, d x,$$

$$\text{which gives } C' = L^3 \frac{\sin 2 \sigma \cos \sigma (q - q')}{72 R} (M q + N q').$$

Put $2 \sin \sigma \cos \sigma$ for $\sin 2 \sigma$. Also call the sums of the sides A B, A C, at the ends of the solid, S_m on the side A M, and S_n on the side A N; making $M = \frac{1}{2} S_m$, $N = \frac{1}{2} S_n$. Designate, further, the differences of these sides by D_m, D_n, which gives $q' = \frac{D_m}{L}$, $q = \frac{D_n}{L}$. The above equation then becomes

$$C' = L \frac{\sin \sigma \cos^2 \sigma (D_n - D_m)}{72 R} (S_m D_n + S_n D_m).$$

The side-heights B M, C N upon any section are, respectively, B M = A B × $\sin \sigma$, C N = A C × $\sin \sigma$. Call the difference of the side-heights D''_m on the side A M, and D''_n on the side A N: then $D''_m = D_m \sin \sigma$, and $D''_n = D_n \sin \sigma$. Whence

$$C' = L \frac{\cos^2 \sigma (D''_n - D''_m)}{72 R} (S_m D_n + S_n D_m).$$

The distances out A M, A N are A M = A B × $\cos \sigma$, A N = A C × $\cos \sigma$. Call their sum, on the side AM, S'_m, and their difference D'_m; then $S'_m = S_m \cos \sigma$, $D'_m = D_m \cos \sigma$. On the side A N, call the sum S'_n, and the difference D'_n; then $S'_n = S_n \cos \sigma$, $D'_n = D_n \cos \sigma$, and we have

$$C' = \frac{L}{72 R} (D''_n - D''_m) (S'_m D'_n + S'_n D'_m).$$

8. Straight Work Considered as a Solid of Revolution. The method of Article 7 may be applied to the derivation of formulæ for straight work. In this manner rules may be found for obliquely truncated solids.*

(1.) *Prisms.*—Suppose a plane to revolve about a straight line drawn in the plane of a cross-section perpendicular to the axis of the prism. This line is the trace of the revolving plane upon the plane of the fixed cross-section. Through the centre of gravity of this cross-section, draw a perpendicular to the trace of the revolving plane. Let the length of this perpendicular be R, and let its intersection with the trace be the pole of the revolving cross-section. And let φ be the polar angle included between the two planes. Consider the axis of the prism to be the path of the centre of gravity of the oblique cross-section on the revolving plane. The radius vector of this centre will be $\rho'' = \mathrm{R} \sec \varphi$. Let A be the area of the perpendicular cross-section. The area of the oblique cross-section will be $\mathrm{A} \sec \varphi$. Hence, by formula 31, we shall have $d\mathrm{V} = \rho'' \mathrm{A} \sec \varphi \, d\varphi = \mathrm{A} \times \mathrm{R} \sec^2 \varphi \, d\varphi$; whence

$$\mathrm{V} = \mathrm{A} \times \mathrm{R} \int \sec^2 \varphi \, d\varphi = \mathrm{A} \times \mathrm{R} \tan \varphi \ldots\ldots 38,$$

in which $\mathrm{R} \tan \varphi$ is the length of the truncated prism, measured upon the axis.

By joining two prisms having the same perpendicular cross-section, the rule will apply to prisms obliquely truncated at both ends.

If the cross-section of the prism be a triangle or a parallelogram, the length required will be the average of the lengths of the corners of the prism. (See Articles 126 and 127, Part I.)

(2.) *Straight Solids generated by revolution of the Side-Plane.*—We shall suppose A B C D E K (Fig. 3, page 18) to be generated by the revolution of A C D K about the axis A K, which is perpendicular to the end-planes. C D is always straight, and slides upon the straight end-slopes C B, D E.

Imagine A C D K to be divided by a diagonal C K (not shown) into two triangles A C K, D C K. Put $\mathrm{AC} = \rho$, $\mathrm{KD} = \rho'$. The distance of the centre of gravity of A C K from A K is $\frac{\rho}{3}$; and for D C K, $\frac{\rho + \rho'}{3}$; and the distance ρ'' of the centre of gravity of A C D K will, by a formula of statics, then be

$$\rho'' = \frac{\text{Area ACK} \times \frac{\rho}{3} + \text{Area DCK} \times \frac{\rho + \rho'}{3}}{\text{Area ACDK}}.$$

But, since $\mathrm{AK} = \mathrm{L}$, Area $\mathrm{ACK} = \frac{\mathrm{L}}{2} \rho$, and Area $\mathrm{DCK} = \frac{\mathrm{L}}{2} \rho'$; also Area $\mathrm{ACDK} = \frac{\mathrm{L}}{2} (\rho + \rho')$: whence, after proper substitutions, we find by formula 31

$$\mathrm{V} = \frac{\mathrm{L}}{6} \int (\rho^2 + \rho \rho' + \rho'^2) \, d\varphi = \frac{\mathrm{L}}{3} \times \frac{1}{2} \int \rho \rho' \, d\varphi + \frac{\mathrm{L}}{3} \times \frac{1}{2} \int (\rho^2 + \rho'^2) \, d\varphi \quad . \quad . \quad 39,$$

in which $\frac{1}{2} \int (\rho^2 + \rho'^2) \, d\varphi$ represents the sum of the end-areas A B C, K E D.

* We shall not now pursue this at length. The combined prismoid and pyramid F and P (Fig. 8, Plate 1) may be tolerably well imitated by either of the methods in the text. We may here refer to Hutton's Mathematics, 1770, p. 469, and to Weisbach's Mechanics, London translation, 1848, vol. i. pp. 96 to 101.

These areas, or the prisms erected upon them, may be found by formula 8, or by Art. 85, page 41. It remains to find $\frac{L}{3} \times \frac{1}{2} \int \rho \rho' \, d\varphi$.

Let P Q, R S, (Fig. 15, p. 26,) be the respective projections of any end-slopes B C, E D, (Fig. 3,) upon the plane of the mid cross-section. H S is the trace of the revolving side-plane; $HQ = \rho$, $HS = \rho'$. Let the angle included between P Q and $RS = 2\delta$; and suppose T U to bisect it. Refer the surface-line of the mid cross-section to H as the pole, and to an axis perpendicular to T U. Also refer P Q and R S respectively to perpendiculars upon these lines from H, (as B C is referred to A N, Fig. 41, pp. 278 and 280.) Let the perpendicular upon $PQ = M$, and that upon $RS = N$. Then $HQ = \rho = M \sec(\varphi + \delta) = \frac{M}{\cos(\phi + \delta)}$, and $HS = \rho' = N \sec(\varphi - \delta) = \frac{N}{\cos(\phi - \delta)}$: whence

$$\frac{L}{3} \times \frac{1}{2} \int \rho \rho' \, d\varphi = \frac{L}{3} \times \frac{1}{2} \int \frac{MN}{\cos(\phi + \delta)\cos(\phi - \delta)} \, d\varphi = \frac{L}{3} \times \frac{1}{2} \int \frac{MN}{\cos^2\phi - \sin^2\delta} \, d\varphi$$

$$= \frac{L}{3} \times \frac{1}{2} \int \frac{MN}{\sin^2\delta} \times \frac{1}{\operatorname{cosec}^2\delta \cos^2\phi - 1} \, d\varphi = \frac{L}{3} \times \frac{1}{2} \int \frac{MN}{\sin^2\delta \cot^2\delta} \times \frac{\cot^2\delta}{\operatorname{cosec}^2\delta \cos^2\phi - 1} \, d\varphi$$

$$= \frac{L}{3} \times \frac{1}{2} \int \frac{MN}{\cos^2\delta} \times \frac{\operatorname{cosec}^2\delta - 1}{\operatorname{cosec}^2\delta \cos^2\phi - 1} \, d\varphi \quad \ldots\ldots\ldots\ldots \quad 40.$$

Assume $a = \sqrt{\frac{MN}{\cos^2\delta}}$, $e = \operatorname{cosec}\delta$, and $r^2 = \rho\rho'$: the preceding becomes

$$\frac{L}{3} \times \frac{1}{2} \int \rho\rho' \, d\varphi = \frac{L}{3} \times \frac{1}{2} \int r^2 \, d\varphi = \frac{L}{3} \times \frac{1}{2} \int \left(a \sqrt{\frac{e^2 - 1}{e^2 \cos^2\phi - 1}} \right)^2 d\varphi \quad \ldots\ldots \quad 41,$$

wherein $r = a \sqrt{\frac{e^2 - 1}{e^2 \cos^2\phi - 1}}$ is the radius-vector from the centre, of an hyperbola with semi-transverse axis a and eccentricity e; and the integral, excluding the factor $\frac{L}{3}$, is the area of the sector included by this radius. The integration of equation 41 gives

$$\frac{L}{3} \times \frac{1}{2} \int \rho\rho' \, d\varphi = \frac{L}{3} \times \frac{1}{2} a^2 \sqrt{e^2 - 1} \text{ hyp. log.} \left(\frac{\sqrt{e^2 - 1} \cos\phi + \sin\phi}{\sqrt{e^2 \cos^2\phi - 1}} \right) \quad \ldots\ldots \quad 42.$$

By restoring in this the values $\operatorname{cosec}\delta = e$, $\frac{MN}{\cos^2\delta} = a^2$, (which is equivalent to the integration of equation 40,) we shall find, by observing $\frac{MN}{\cos^2\delta}\sqrt{e^2 - 1} = \frac{MN}{\cos^2\delta} \cot\delta = \frac{MN}{\cos\delta \sin\delta} = \frac{2MN}{\sin 2\delta} = 2\,MN \operatorname{cosec} 2\delta$,

$$\frac{L}{3} \times \frac{1}{2} \int \rho\rho' \, d\varphi = \frac{L}{3} \times MN \operatorname{cosec} 2\delta \text{ hyp. log.} \left(\frac{\cot\delta \cos\phi + \sin\phi}{\sqrt{\operatorname{cosec}^2\delta \cos^2\phi - 1}} \right) \quad \ldots\ldots \quad 43.$$

If the end-slopes be γ' and γ'', we shall have $2\delta = \gamma' \sim \gamma''$; that is, the difference of similar or the sum of opposite slopes. Let $\frac{1}{2}(S \pm D)$ be the augmented centre-height for γ', and $\frac{1}{2}(S \mp D)$ the same for γ''; we shall find $MN = \frac{1}{4}(S^2 - D^2) \cos\gamma' \cos\gamma''$. (See the value of A N, Fig. 41, p. 280.) Equation 43 may then be transformed into

$$\frac{L}{3} \times \frac{1}{2} \int \rho\rho' \, d\varphi = \frac{L}{3} \times \frac{1}{4} (S^2 - D^2) \cos\gamma' \cos\gamma'' \operatorname{cosec}(\gamma' \sim \gamma'') \times$$
$$\text{hyp. log.} \left(\frac{\cot\frac{1}{2}(\gamma' \sim \gamma'') \cos\phi + \sin\phi}{\sqrt{\operatorname{cosec}^2\frac{1}{2}(\gamma' \sim \gamma'') \cos^2\phi - 1}} \right) \quad \ldots\ldots\ldots \quad 44.$$

We have assumed T U (Fig. 15) to be the mean slope, (as in Art. 53, p. 28.) Let the slope of T U $=\gamma$. We shall have to put successively in equation 44, $\varphi=\frac{1}{2}\pi-\sigma+\gamma$ and $\varphi=\frac{1}{2}\pi-\sigma-\gamma$, in order to find the areas of two sectors whose sum or difference is the whole area required. (Always the sum, if $\frac{1}{2}\pi-\sigma>\gamma$.) Call this whole hyperbolic area A_h, and let A′ and A″ be the end-areas: we shall have, by formula 39,

$$V=\frac{L}{3}(A_h+A'+A'') \quad . \; . \; . \; . \; 45.$$

Prismoidal Formula.—Let the area of the mid cross-section be A_H, and its radius-vector ρ'''. If U be now supposed to trace the surface-line, H U will always be a mean between H Q and H S; that is, $\rho'''=\frac{\rho+\rho'}{2}$: hence, the area between the limits φ', φ'' will be

$$A_H=\tfrac{1}{2}\int_{\phi'}^{\phi''}\left(\frac{\rho+\rho'}{2}\right)^2 d\varphi=\tfrac{1}{2}\int_{\phi'}^{\phi''}\left(\frac{\rho^2+2\rho\rho'+\rho'^2}{4}\right)d\varphi \quad . \; . \; . \; . \; 46,$$

$$\text{Or, } A_H=\tfrac{1}{2}\times\tfrac{1}{2}\int_{\phi'}^{\phi''}\rho\rho'\,d\varphi+\tfrac{1}{4}\times\tfrac{1}{2}\int_{\phi'}^{\phi''}(\rho^2+\rho'^2)\,d\varphi=\tfrac{1}{2}A_h+\tfrac{1}{4}(A'+A'') \quad . \; . \; 47,$$

whence $A_h=2A_H-\frac{1}{2}(A'+A'')$; and, therefore, by formula 45,

$$V=\frac{L}{3}(A_h+A'+A'')=\frac{L}{6}(4A_H+A'+A'') \quad . \; . \; . \; . \; . \; . \; 48,$$

The last member of which is the prismoidal formula. (See p. 279.) Equations 39, and 45 to 48, are not founded on any relation existing between ρ, ρ', and φ: hence, in order that these shall hold, it is not necessary that the directrices B C, E D, (Fig. 3,) be of any particular form. This tends to confirm the belief in the practical sufficiency of the prismoidal formula; but the choice of a ground-surface from among those surfaces to which the formula applies, is left to individual judgment. (Art. 8, Appendix.) The point U (Fig. 15) describes an hyperbolic arc with its convexity towards H.*

*Every cross-section gives an hyperbola, and the projections P Q, R S, of the end-slopes upon the cross-section are parallel to the asymptotes. This is because the parts Q U, U S, of the intercept Q S, are always in a constant ratio; that is, in the ratio of the lengths of the two parts into which the solid is divided by the cross-section. We omit the demonstration, intending to publish it elsewhere; but will here remark upon a simple and, we believe, new method of describing an hyperbola when the axes are given. Suppose H K to be the transverse axis; through one extremity, as K, draw straight lines through the ends of the conjugate axis; these will, therefore, be parallel to the asymptotes of the required hyperbola, and they will correspond to the projections of equal and opposite end-slopes having equal centre-heights. Bisect the intercept Q S constantly in U, and the locus of U will be an hyperbola with the given axes.

APPENDIX.

Notes to the Rules and Examples of Part I.

1. Further Examples in Whole and Sub Sections. (See Art. 88, Part I., and the Table, page 33.) *Sections* 1, 2, 4, *and* 9 exhibit all the varieties of Case II. In Nos. 1 and 4, the length of the pyramid is the same as that of the marginal abscissa,—viz.: for No. 1, 23 feet; for No. 4, 46 feet. The length of the reduced full-work solid, $\frac{1}{2}$ T + F,* will be, for these sections respectively, $\frac{23}{2} + 100 - 23 = 100 - \frac{23}{2} = 88.5$; and $\frac{46}{2} + 100 - 46 = 100 - \frac{46}{2} = 77$. In Nos. 2 and 9, the length of the abscissa is, for No. 2, 49 feet; for No. 9, 23 feet. The length of the reduced full-work solid F + $\frac{1}{2}$ T will be respectively, $49 + \frac{100 - 49}{2} = 74.5$, and $23 + \frac{100 - 23}{2} = 61.5$. The length of the pyramid will be, for No. 2, $100 - 49 = 51$; for No. 9, $100 - 23 = 77$. The lesser end-height of the full work, in all these sections, is the height of the neutral cross-section belonging to the work and to the mean slope. All these are not unusual forms.

Sections 3 *and* 11 are varieties of Case III. They represent forms of frequent occurrence,—viz., truncated pyramids running from station to station. The length is given by the length of the section. The bases are easily found by constructing the cross-sections, or by calculation.

Sections 5 *and* 8.—Two varieties of Case I. These forms will be met with on ground which rises or falls rapidly in the direction of the length. The work reduces to two full-work portions. The length of one part is the median abscissa; of the other, the length of the section less the abscissa. The lesser end-height, in each part, is the height of the neutral cross-section of that part, under the mean slope. We have, for No. 5, the median abscissa 43 feet; the length of the other part is therefore 57 feet. For No. 8, the median abscissa is 67 feet; the length of the remainder, 33 feet.

Sections 6 *and* 7.—The two other varieties of Case I. These are frequent forms. They are whole sections not requiring subdivision.

Sections 10 *and* 12.—The two remaining varieties of Case III. The work which runs entirely through is treated as a truncated pyramid similar to those of Sections 3 and 11, which also belong to this Case. The correction for the difference of the bases, however, is here omitted, as it is supposed the cubic content found from the sum of the bases will sufficiently well represent the whole solidity. To find the sum of the bases by calculation, proceed as directed in Art. 70, Part I., using a slope equal to the half-sum of the given slopes. The sum of the bases of the two pyramids will be found in the same way; but it is the half-sum, or mean base, which is required. In like manner, the rule (Art. 71, Part I.) may be applied to finding the augmented sum of the heights of the thorough work, and thence the mean height of the pyramids. In finding by construction the mean base or mean height of the pyramids, it will be sufficient to take the dimensions as they appear on the cross-sections drawn with the given slopes. The rule for these figures is only intended to give a running estimate.

2. Unusual Cases. *Calculation of the Elements for Unequal End-Widths.* (See Example, Art. 91, Part I.)—The elements may be thus found by calculation. The height of the redundant prismoid at each end, is evidently half the augment from Table II. for a roadbed equal to the given width A B or E F. The heights L V, R U are respectively the augments from Table III. for a roadbed equal to twice Q V, and twice N U; that is, for a roadbed = 2 ($\frac{1}{2}$ A B — K B) = A B —

---

* This is merely a designation intended to point out, by reference to the diagrams, the mode of combination of the reduced solids; and having no strict quantitative application to solidity.

$2\,KB = 33.4 - 28 = 5.4$; and for a roadbed $= 2\,(\frac{1}{2}\,EF - EM) = EF - 2\,EM = 40 - 31.8 = 8.2$. Hence

33.4 = A B gives half the augment from Table II. = O S . . .	16.7	3.3 difference.
40.0 = E F gives half the augment from Table II. = P T . . .	20.0	
Sum of the end-heights of the redundant prismoid	36.7	
2 Q V = 5.4, under 10°, in Table III., gives L V	—0.5	
K L, the given end-height	17.6	
S Q	17.1	
2 N U = 8.2, under 10°, in Table III., gives R U	+0.7	
M N, the given end-height	9.2	
T R	9.9	

$OQ = OS + SQ = 16.7 + 17.1 = 33.8$: $PR = PT + TR = 20 + 9.9 = 29.9$
$OQ + PR =$ Augmented sum of heights for the whole solid $= 33.8 + 29.9 = 63.7$
$OQ - PR =$ Difference of heights for the whole solid $= 33.8 - 29.9 = 3.9$

3. Unusual Cases by Equidistant Level-Heights. Each end cross-section is divided into the same number of spaces by equidistant level-heights,—as many as desirable. If the heights have not been taken on the field, they may be found after constructing the cross-sections.

Preparation of Elements. Form the sum and difference of total bases, as L M, (Fig. 30, p. 56, and Art. 111, Part I.) Form two *level-totals,*—one for each end,—by adding together the two external heights B M, D L, with *twice* the sum of all the intermediate heights. Take the sum and difference of the *level-totals.*

4. Rule for Computation of Solidity by Equidistant Level-Heights. Proceed as in Art. 112 or 113, Part I., retaining the sum and difference of *total bases,* and substituting the sum and difference of *level-totals* for the sum and difference of heights there employed. Observe that the second term is to be added if the greater *level-total* is at the same end of the work with the greater *total base,* and subtracted if otherwise. Divide the result by the number of spaces on the cross-section; that is, by the number of level-heights at either end, *less one.* The result is the whole solidity between the vertical side-planes B M, D L.

If the content upon a figure like B A E D K is required, the redundant solids upon B A M and D E L must be found, (by Art. 115 or 118,) and deducted. If B A or D E—one or both—were sloping opposite to the present direction, one or both of the external solids must then be added.

EXAMPLE.

First End. Outside heights, 16, 17; intermediate heights, 13, 15, 4, 5, 18, 14; interval of heights, 6. We find, Total Base $= 42$; Level-Total $= (16 + 17) + 2\,(13 + 15 + 4 + 5 + 18 + 14) = 171$.

Second End. Outside heights, 10, 13; intermediate heights, 11, 7, 8, 15, 14, 12; interval of heights, 10. We find, Total Base $= 70$; Level-Total $= (10 + 13) + 2\,(11 + 7 + 8 + 15 + 14 + 12) = 157$.

Then, Sum of Total Bases $= 112$; Difference $= 28$; Sum of Level-Totals $= 328$; Difference $= 14$.

Table XXI., opposite 112.0 under 3 (hundreds) 2 (tens) 8 (units) . . .	17007.4
" " " 28.0 take one-third for 1 (ten) 4 (units) . . .	—60.5
Divide by 7, the number of spaces	7)16946.9
Content between the vertical side-planes	2421.0

5. Curvature of the Median Profile of Whole Sections. (See Articles 103, Part I., and 1, Part II.) When the external surface-lines incline in different directions, they will, if produced, meet the intersection of the side-slopes in two points at opposite ends of the work. The line which passes through these points and through the ends of the centre-heights will obviously be curved, with the concave side towards the roadbed. When the points where the median surface-line meets the intersection of the side-slopes are both at the same end of the work, consider the point which is nearest to the work, and imagine a curve passing through this and through the ends of the centre-heights.

6. Correction for Curved Surface. (See Note, Art. 104, Part I.) The correction for all straight work included under surfaces generated according to the method of Art. 8, Part I., may be made in the same general manner. A plane surface is only a particular variety of the surface there described; but, when the surface is plane, the method of correction takes a simpler form than for curved surfaces, although the same in principle.

Let A B C (Fig. 45) represent one entire end cross-section of any piece of whole-section work, and A D E the other.

Fig. 45.

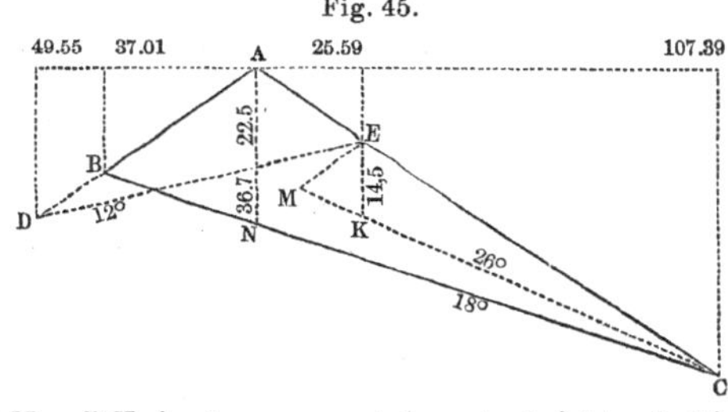

Through E, one of the points where A C, a side-slope of one of the end cross-sections, ABC, is cut by the surface-slope of the other, A D E, draw a line E M parallel to the other side-slope; and make E M equal to B D, the distance cut off by the surface-slope of ABC from the side-slope of A D E. Join M with the external angle C of A B C. The correction is equal to one-twelfth part of a prism erected upon the triangle C M E as a base, and of the same length as the work. Draw E K parallel to the centre-height A N. E K is the augmented centre-height of this prism.

If we should enter the tables with double the height E K, under the surface-slope of C M, (which can be measured as in Art. 43, Part I.,) the tabular quantity would be equal to the content of a prism 100 feet long, standing on the base C M E. But it is one-twelfth of this tabular quantity which is required. Now, the tabular quantities are as the squares of the arguments in the side column; hence, if we enter the tables with the height E K, the tabular quantity is one-fourth the solidity of the prism upon C M E. One-third of this is the twelfth part required for the correction. The correction is to be *added* if both external surface-lines rise or fall together towards the same end of the section, and *subtracted* if one of them rises whilst the other falls towards the same end.

Fig. 46.

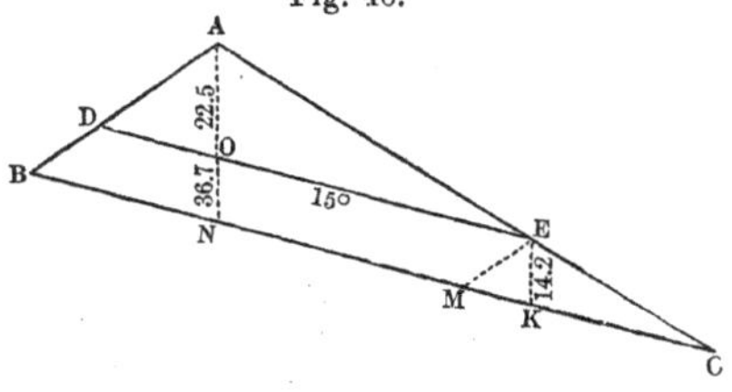

When the ground becomes a plane, as in Fig. 46, the surface-slopes B C, D E are parallel; hence E K becomes equal to O N, which is the difference of the end-heights: the slope of C M is the original surface-slope. These things being known, it is unnecessary to find E K and the surface-slope, by construction.

Explanation.—By formula 9, page 279, it appears that the term which is neglected, in the Rule, Art. 104, Part I., is $\frac{1}{24} \sin 2\,\sigma\, p\, q\, L^3$. Put the lengths of the side-slopes (Fig. 45) respectively, $AD = M$, $AB = M'$, $AC = N$, $AE = N'$: then $p = \frac{M - M'}{L}$ and $q = \frac{N - N'}{L}$. Hence the neglected term $= \frac{1}{12} \times \frac{1}{2} \sin 2\,\sigma\, L\, L^2\, p\, q = \frac{1}{12} \times \frac{1}{2} \times \sin 2\,\sigma\, (M - M')\,(N - N')\, L$. This represents the twelfth part of a prism whose length is L, and whose triangular base has an angle $= \frac{1}{2}\pi - 2\,\sigma$, with the sides about this angle respectively equal to $M - M'$ and $N - N'$. But C E M is, by construction, such a triangular base. The correction is additive if p and q are of the same sign,—that is, if the directrices are inclined in the same direction,—and subtractive otherwise. If $AB = AD$, M E and the base C E M both vanish.

Fig. 46, where the slope is the half-sum of the slopes of Fig. 45, may represent the end cross-sections of Example 1, Art. 86, Part I., and Fig. 45 those of Examples 1 and 2, Articles 72 and 104, Part I. These references for Fig. 45 will be useful in studying the following examples:—

Example 1.—Take Example 1, Art. 104, Part I. E K is found = 12.7, and the surface-slope C M = 24°.

Opposite 12.7, under 24°, in Table VII.	3)404.9—
Correction additive	134.9
Opposite 59.68, under 16°, in Table VII.	6070.1
Whole content corrected	6205.0
Redundant prism	355.6
Corrected residual prismoid	5849.4

The error in working according to the rule (Art. 104, Part I.) is 134.9, or about 2 per cent., in defect on the whole content, 6205.

Example 2.—Take Example 2, Art. 104, Part I. E K is found =14.5, and the surface-slope C M = 26°.

Opposite 14.5, under 26°, in Table VII.	3)629.1
Correction subtractive	209.7
Opposite 69.9, under 8°, in Table VII.	7101.8
Whole content corrected	6892.1
Redundant prism	355.6
Corrected residual prismoid	6536.5

The error in working according to the rule (Art. 104, Part I.) is 209.7, or about 3 per cent., in excess on the whole content, 6892.1.

7. Secondary Dimensions found by Calculation. The dimensions of the base C M E (Fig. 45) of the secondary prism may be found by calculation. Call the side-heights and distances out of the whole work *primary*, and those of the base C M E *secondary*, dimensions; also, call those heights and distances which lie on the same side of the work homogeneous. The side-heights of the base of the secondary prism are equal respectively to the difference of the homogeneous primary side-heights: the same for the distances out.

Secondary Distances Out.—In the above examples, we find, for No. 1, the distances out 57.84 and 11.42; for No. 2, 81.80 and 12.54. (See Art. 72, Part I., for the primary distances out.)

Secondary Centre-Height.—Then (see Examples 1 and 2, Art. 76, Part I.) the heights are found, for No. 1, =12.7; and for No. 2, =14.5.

Difference of Secondary Side-Heights.—This is required in order to find the secondary surface-slope. The mode of proceeding is evident from Art. 78, Part I. The division by the rate of side-slope directed in Art. 78 may be deferred until after the division by the sum of distances out directed in Art. 79, Part I.

Secondary Surface-Slope. (See Art. 79, Part I.)—The difference of secondary distances out is, for No. 1, = 46.42, and the sum of the same, 69.26. Then 46.42 divided by 69.26, and again by the rate of side-slope, 1½, gives .447 = tan 24°, the secondary surface-slope. For No. 2, difference, = 69.26; sum, = 94.34. Then, 69.26 divided by 94.34, and again by the rate of side-slope, 1½, gives .489 = tan 26°, the secondary surface-slope.

8. Comparison of the Methods by Transverse Slopes and by Centre and Side Heights. The rule of Art. 112, Part I. is founded on a very usual supposition concerning the nature of the surface,—viz., that the median and external surface-lines are straight; also, that the surface-line of the cross-section is straight on each side, from the centre out. Computation upon this hypothesis has generally been considered more accurate than by transverse ground-slopes, supposing each method to be correctly carried out. Having, then, by the method of transverse slopes, determined the points B, C, D, E on the end cross-sections, (Fig. 45,) these points ought to be adopted, as if they had been observed upon the field; but their adoption is not a sufficient reason for giving up the supposition of a straight median surface-line. This supposition is, however, violated by assuming the surface to be generated as in Art. 8, Part I. (See Art. 5.) In Example 1, Art. 104, Part I., the centre-height of the mid cross-section was found = 29.84; but, on the supposition of a straight median line, that height would have been 29.6. In Example 2 of the same article, the mid-height was found = 34.96. With a straight median line, the mid-height would have been 29.6, the same as before; for the difference between these examples is only in the direction of the surface-slope of the ends. To show in what degree this increase of centre-height affects the result, if the method by centre and side-heights be taken as a standard, we shall compute the above examples by that method. One computation will suffice, because none of the elements for this computation are changed by reversing the direction of the slopes. The distances out are given in Art. 72, Part I.

We have, for the elements, augmented sum of heights, 59.2; difference of heights, 14.2; sum of total bases, 219.6; difference of total bases, 69.3.

Opposite 59.2, under 200, in Table XXI.	5481.5
" " " 10, " "	274.1
" " " 9, " "	246.7
" " " .6, " "	16.4
" 69.3, " 10, (add one-third of tabular quantity,)	106.9
" " " 4, " " " "	42.8
" " " .2, " " " "	2.1
Content of whole ground by centre and side heights	6170.5
Redundant prism	355.6
Residual prismoid, by centre and side heights	5814.9

Assuming this result (6170.5 yards) to be the true content of the whole ground, we have the following comparison with the results obtained in Article 6.

Example 1.

True whole content by centre and side heights	6170.5
Corrected whole content by transverse slopes	6205.0
Error in excess (about $\frac{6}{10}$ per cent. on 6170.5)	34.5

Example 2.

True whole content by centre and side heights	6170.5
Corrected whole content by transverse slopes	6892.1
Error in excess (about 12 per cent. on 6170.5)	721.6

The error committed in working according to the approximate rule is thus shown.

Example 1.

True whole content by centre and side heights	6170.5
Approximate whole content by Art. 104, Part I.	6070.1
Error in defect (about $1\frac{3}{4}$ per cent. on 6170.5)	100.4

Example 2.

True whole content by centre and side heights	6170.5
Approximate whole content by Art. 104, Part I.	7101.8
Error in excess (about 15 per cent. on 6170.5)	931.3

The above per centages of error on the whole ground become more important as the width of roadbed is increased; that is, as the amount of work to be done is lessened, whilst the absolute error of computation remains the same.

It will be observed that the error in the corrected result by transverse slopes, for the second example, is 721.6, whilst the content of the secondary prism, (see Art. 6,) which is the correction for the approximate rule, is 209.7; that is, the error of approximate calculation under the rule, for the paraboloidal surface adopted, (209.7,) is here considerably less than the absolute error (721.6) caused by the adoption of that surface. This surface has, we believe, been recommended by high professional authority. Whether or not it is the proper one, its adoption appears to us to be in contradiction to the hypothesis made in the method by centre and side heights,—viz., that the median surface-line between observed points should be considered straight. This difficulty is avoided by adopting the surface proposed in § 2, Art. 8, Part II., whilst straightness of outline and longitudinal straightness are preserved. The solidity is less than by either of the above methods. Formula 45 gives for the whole ground,—say, Example 1, 6150 yds., Example 2, 5952 yds. The straight cross-surface of the paraboloid may be entitled to some preference, because of the tendency to straightness of hill-side surfaces from natural and artificial causes.

Conclusions.—The use of the method by transverse slopes is generally for preliminary estimates. We are not prepared to decide what amount of error is permissible in computation by this method, nor what standard of comparison should be adopted in estimating it. It is well to run the risk of making preliminary estimates too high, rather than too low. On the whole, we are inclined to think that the rule of Article 104, Part I., may be adopted in practice. Taking the mid-section slope in whole degrees, and the allowance of a tenth or two in the sum of augmented centre-heights, present means either of empirically approximating the paraboloid more nearly, or of finding an intermediate solidity between that and the solid of revolution.

9. Application of Tables to Various Formulæ.—Several formulæ in use for earthwork computations embrace terms containing a multiple or submultiple of the square of a given linear dimension, or of the product of two such dimensions. It may be useful to indicate how our tables can sometimes be employed in such cases.

Let a and b represent heights, widths, or other linear dimensions in feet. Let l be the length of work $=100$; and let $q = 27\,Q$ be the number of cubic feet in the term in question. Q is the tabular quantity of cubic yards.

For Table XV.—For the First Part, $q = \frac{1}{8}\,l\,a^2$; for the Second Part, $q = \frac{1}{24}\,l\,a^2$. Make $a = 2\,a'$; then, for the First Part, $q = \frac{1}{8}\,l\,4\,a'^2 = \frac{1}{2}\,l\,a'^2$; for the Second Part, $q = \frac{1}{24}\,l\,4\,a'^2 = \frac{1}{6}\,l\,a'^2$. Table XXV. contains logarithms proper for the same computations.

For Table XXI.—Here, $q = \frac{1}{8}\,l\,a\,b$. If $a = 2\,a'$ and $b = 2\,b'$, $q = \frac{1}{8}\,l\,4\,a'\,b' = \frac{1}{2}\,l\,a'\,b'$. Table XXIII. contains logarithms proper for the same computations.

For Table XXII.—Here, $q = l\,a\,b$; whence any multiple or submultiple of this term may be found. Table XXIV. contains logarithms proper for the same computations.

Catalogue of Formulæ and Construction of the Tables.

10. Catalogue of Formulæ. This contains formulæ for the computation of the several tables. By attending to the references of the catalogue, and by consulting Chapter V., Part I., the rules for the application of the tables will be understood. The following notation has been employed: Q = tabular quantity, B = width of roadbed, L = length of the section, S_h = sum of heights, S_b = sum of bases, D_h = difference of heights, σ = angle of side-slope, γ = angle of surface-slope. The tabular length of the section is 100 feet; the tabular solidities are in cubic yards.

Table I. $27\,Q = \frac{1}{4}\,L\,B^2 \tan\sigma$. See formula 14, page 280, where $\frac{1}{4}\,B^2 \tan\sigma$ represents the area of the cross-section of the redundant prism.

Table II. $Q = B \tan\sigma = 2\,A\,G$. See Fig. 41, page 278.

Table III. $Q = \frac{1}{2}\,B \tan\gamma = C\,D$. See Fig. 40, page 276.

Table IV. $Q = L\frac{h}{h - h'}$. See formula 1, page 275, wherein h = either the marginal or the centre height at the origin, and h' = the corresponding height at the other end of the section.

Table V. $Q = h \cot\gamma = C\,P$. See Fig. 40, page 276, wherein h = centre-height, C E.

Table VI. $Q = h \cot\sigma = D\,H$, A M, E Q, or A N. See Fig. 41, page 278, wherein h = the side-height, augmented or unaugmented; that is, B H, B M, C Q, or C N.

Table VII. $27\,Q = \frac{1}{8} L S_h^2 \times \frac{\sin 2\sigma \cos^2 \gamma}{\sin(\sigma+\gamma)\sin(\sigma-\gamma)}$. . . . . See formula 13, page 280.

Table VIII. $27\,Q = \frac{1}{8} L S_b^2 \times \frac{\sin\sigma \sin\gamma}{\sin(\sigma-\gamma)}$. . . . . See formula 21, page 282.

Table IX. $27\,Q = \frac{1}{8} L S_h^2 \times \frac{\sin 2\sigma \cos^2 \gamma}{\sin(\sigma+\gamma)\sin(\sigma-\gamma)}$. . . . . See formula 13, page 280.

Table X. $27\,Q = \frac{1}{8} L S_b^2 \times \frac{\sin\sigma \sin\gamma}{\sin(\sigma-\gamma)}$. . . . . See formula 21, page 282.

Table XI. $27\,Q = \frac{1}{8} L S_h^2 \times \frac{\sin 2\sigma \cos^2 \gamma}{\sin(\sigma+\gamma)\sin(\sigma-\gamma)}$. . . . . See formula 13, page 280.

Table XII. $27\,Q = \frac{1}{8} L S_h^2 \times \frac{\sin\sigma \cos^2\gamma}{\sin\gamma \sin(\sigma-\gamma)}$. . . . . . . See formula 23, page 282.

Table XIII. $27\,Q = \frac{1}{8} L S^2_h \times \frac{\sin\sigma \cos^2\gamma}{\sin\gamma \sin(\sigma-\gamma)}$. . . . . . See formula 23, page 282.

Table XIV. $27\,Q = \frac{1}{8} L\left(S_h^2 - B^2 \tan^2\sigma + B^2 \tan^2\gamma + \frac{D_h^2}{3}\right) \times \frac{\sin 2\sigma \cos^2\gamma}{\sin(\sigma+\gamma)\sin(\sigma-\gamma)}$. See formulæ 16 and 18, page 281, and 13, page 280.

Table XV. $27\,Q = \frac{1}{8} L S_h^2$. For the Second Part, $27\,Q = \frac{1}{24} L D_h^2$. See formula 13, page 280.

Table XVI. $Q = \log. \frac{\sin 2\sigma \cos^2\gamma}{\sin(\sigma+\gamma)\sin(\sigma-\gamma)}$. . . . . See formula 13, page 280.*

Table XVII. $Q = \log. \frac{\sin\sigma \cos^2\gamma}{\sin\gamma \sin(\sigma-\gamma)}$. . . . . See formula 23, page 282.*

Table XVIII. $Q = \frac{h\cos\sigma}{\sin(\sigma-\gamma)}$, or $Q = \frac{h\cos\sigma}{\sin(\sigma+\gamma)}$; wherein $h = AF$. (Fig. 41, page 278.) In the triangles AFB, AFC, we have, by Trigonometry,

$$FC = AF \times \frac{\sin FAC}{\sin FCA} = \frac{h\cos\sigma}{\sin(\sigma-\gamma)};\quad FB = AF \times \frac{\sin FAB}{\sin FBA} = \frac{h\cos\sigma}{\sin(\sigma+\gamma)}.$$

Table XIX. $Q = \log. \frac{1}{2}\frac{\cos\sigma\cos\gamma}{\sin(\sigma-\gamma)}$, or $Q = \log. \frac{1}{2}\frac{\cos\sigma\cos\gamma}{\sin(\sigma+\gamma)}$. Employing the same notation, and referring to the same figure as before, we have

$$CK = FC \times \cos\gamma = \frac{h\cos\sigma\cos\gamma}{\sin(\sigma-\gamma)};\quad OB = FB\cos\gamma = \frac{h\cos\sigma\cos\gamma}{\sin(\sigma+\gamma)}: \text{whence}$$

$$\log. CK = \log. 2h + \log. \frac{1}{2}\frac{\cos\sigma\cos\gamma}{\sin(\sigma-\gamma)}, \text{ and } \log. OB = \log. 2h + \log. \frac{1}{2}\frac{\cos\sigma\cos\gamma}{\sin(\sigma+\gamma)}.*$$

Table XX. $Q = \log. \frac{1}{2}\frac{\cos\sigma}{\sin(\sigma-\gamma)}$, or $Q = \log. \frac{1}{2}\frac{\cos\sigma}{\sin(\sigma+\gamma)}$. By Table XVIII., we have

$$\log. FC = \log. 2h + \log. \frac{1}{2}\frac{\cos\sigma}{\sin(\sigma-\gamma)};\quad \log. FB = \log. 2h + \log. \frac{1}{2}\frac{\cos\sigma}{\sin(\sigma+\gamma)}.*$$

Table XXI. $27\,Q = \frac{1}{8} L S_h S_b$. . . . . See formula 27, page 283.

Table XXII. $27\,Q = L S_h S_b$. . . . . See Art. 126, Part I., and Art. 9.

Table XXIII. $Q = \log. (S_h \text{ or } S_b) + \log. 10 - \frac{1}{2}\log. 216$. See formula 27, page 283.†

Table XXIV. $Q = \log. (S_h \text{ or } S_b) + \log. 10 - \frac{1}{2}\log. 27$. See Art. 126, Part I., and Art. 9.†

Table XXV. $Q = \log. \frac{1}{216} L S^2_h$. . . . . See formula 13, page 280.

Tables XXVI., A and B. Tables XXVI. and A are well known. For Table B, see Note, Art. 25.

11. Construction of the Tables. (1.) *Tables proceeding in the direct ratio of the argument.*—The method of continued addition was employed in the construction of Tables II., III., IV., V., VI., XVIII., XXI., XXII. These proceed regularly, either downwards or across, and, in some tables, in both ways, with the tabular number in direct proportion to the argument. Tables thus constructed admit of proof at the end of every interval of ten lines or of ten columns, beginning with the first line or column. At the end of every such interval, divide both the argument and

* See Note 1, page 314.

† See, also, page 300, § 4, Art. 11.

tabular number by ten. The resulting argument and number should, respectively, equal an argument and its number found above.

(2.) *Tables proceeding as the square of the argument.*—Tables I., VII., VIII., IX., X., XI., XII., XIII., XV. proceed with the tabular number proportional to the square of the argument in the side column. They admit of proof at intervals of ten lines, nearly as the tables previously mentioned. When the argument is divided by ten, the tabular number must be divided by one hundred. This mode of proof applies only partially in Table XV.

Table XIV. is properly classed among the tables here enumerated. (See the formula, Art. 10. Also, Art. 89, Part I.)

Such tables can be accurately, and probably most readily, computed by a method of continued addition in two columns simultaneously formed. In the equation of Table IX., for example, put $F = \frac{100}{216} \frac{\sin 2\sigma \cos^2 \gamma}{\sin(\sigma + \gamma)\sin(\sigma - \gamma)}$; then $Q = S_h^2 F$. Let $Q, Q_1, Q_2, Q_3, \ldots Q_{n-1}, Q_n$ be successive tabular numbers of the same column, corresponding to the successive values of the argument $S_h, S_h + 1, S_h + 2, S_h + 3$, down to $S_h + n - 1$ and $S_h + n$. We have, by the formula,

$$S_h^2 F = \ldots\ldots\ldots Q$$

$$(S_h + 1)^2 F = S_h^2 F + (2 S_h + 1) F = \ldots\ldots Q_1 = Q + (2 S_h + 1) F.$$

$$\left\{(S_h + 1) + 1\right\}^2 F = (S_h + 1)^2 F + \left\{2(S_h + 1) + 1\right\} F = \ldots Q_2 = Q_1 + (2 S_h + 3) F.$$

$$\left[\left\{(S_h + 1) + 1\right\} + 1\right]^2 F = \left\{(S_h + 1) + 1\right\}^2 F + \left[2\left\{(S_h + 1) + 1\right\} + 1\right] F =$$

$$Q_3 = Q_2 + (2 S_h + 5) F.$$

The law of this series being such that

$$\left\{S_h + (n - 1)\right\}^2 F = \left\{S_h^2 + 2 S_h (n - 1) + (n - 1)^2\right\} F = (S_h^2 + 2 S_h n + n^2 - 2 S_h - 2n + 1) F = Q_{n-1}, \text{ and}$$

$$\left\{S_h + (n - 1) + 1\right\}^2 F = (S_h + n)^2 F = (S_h^2 + 2 S_h n + n^2) F = Q_n = Q_{n-1} + (2 S_h + 2n - 1) F.$$

	Sums.	9°	
$S_h =$	0	.00 .95	.95 = $(2 S_h + 1) F =$ 1 F 1.90 = 2 F
$S_h + 1 =$	1	.95 2.85	2.85 = $(2 S_h + 3) F =$ 3 F 1.90 = 2 F
$S_h + 2 =$	2	3.80 4.75	4.75 = $(2 S_h + 5) F =$ 5 F 1.90 = 2 F
$S_h + 3 =$	3	8.55 6.65	6.65 = $(2 S_h + 7) F =$ 7 F 1.90 = 2 F
$S_h + 4 =$	4	15.20 8.55	8.55 = $(2 S_h + 9) F =$ 9 F 1.90 = 2 F
$S_h + 5 =$	5	23.75 10.45	10.45 = $(2 S_h + 11) F =$ 11 F 1.90 = 2 F
$S_h + 6 =$	6	34.20 12.35	12.35 = $(2 S_h + 13) F =$ 13 F 1.90 = 2 F
$S_h + 7 =$	7	46.55 14.25	14.25 = $(2 S_h + 15) F =$ 15 F 1.90 = 2 F
$S_h + 8 =$	8	60.80 16.15	16.15 = $(2 S_h + 17) F =$ 17 F 1.90 = 2 F
$S_h + 9 =$	9	76.95 18.05	18.05 = $(2 S_h + 19) F =$ 19 F 1.90 = 2 F
$S_h + 10 =$	10	95.00	19.95 = $(2 S_h + 21) F =$ 21 F

The increment to be added to any tabular quantity Q_{n-1}, in order to produce the next Q_n, is, therefore, $Q_n - Q_{n-1} = (2\ S_h + 2\,n - 1)$ F. The increments are formed on the right-hand side of the annexed scheme by the continued addition of 2 F to the first increment. Take the 9° column of Table IX. Let $S_h = 0$, and suppose F = .95; then $Q = S^2_h\ F = 0$. Take n successively = 1, 2, 3, &c.: the first increment is $(2\ S_h + 2 - 1)\ F = (2\ S_h + 1)\ F = F$. The differences for one-tenth of a foot are formed by dividing the increments by 10. In actual computation we have taken F to five or six decimals. The following examples show the methods of proof:—The argument 10 gives the tabular quantity 95.00; one-tenth of the argument is 1, opposite to which is .95, the one-hundredth of 95.00. For the increments, we have $21\ F = 20\ F + F = 2\ F \times 10 + F = 19.00 + .95 = 19.95$. The increments should be proved when an error occurs in the tabular quantities.*

(3.) *Correct Interpolation for Heights in Tables proceeding as the Square of the Argument.*

As before, let S_h, $S_h + 1$, be two consecutive side numbers: Q, Q_1 their respective tabular quantities. Further, let $S_h + \frac{t}{10}$ be a side number, for whose number t of odd tenths interpolation is required; and let the tabular quantity Q_t correspond to the argument $S_h + \frac{t}{10}$. Also, let x be the true quantity to be interpolated for the odd tenths, $\frac{t}{10}$, so that $Q_t = Q + x$. Make p = the quantity which would be interpolated for $\frac{t}{10}$ by proportional parts; and assume $\varepsilon = p - x$. It is required to find the correction ε, which must be applied after proportional interpolation. We have

$$x = Q_t - Q = \left\{ (S_h + \tfrac{t}{10})^2 - S_h^2 \right\} F = (\tfrac{2\,S_h}{10} + \tfrac{t}{100})\ F\ t;\ \text{and}$$

$$p = \frac{Q_1 - Q}{10}\,t = \left\{ (S_h + 1)^2 - S_h^2 \right\} F\ \frac{t}{10} = \frac{2\,S_h + 1}{10}\ F\ t.$$

Therefore, substituting these values of x and p in $\varepsilon = p - x$, we find

$$\varepsilon = p - x = \frac{2\,S_h + 1}{10}\ F\ t - (\tfrac{2\,S_h}{10} + \tfrac{t}{100})\ F\ t = (\tfrac{1}{10} - \tfrac{t}{100})\ F\ t = t\,\frac{10 - t}{100}\ F.$$

The maximum value of ε is when $t = 5$, in which case $t\,\frac{10-t}{100} = .25$. Hence the error by proportional interpolation cannot exceed one-fourth the first tabular number in the given column. ε is positive; that is, p is greater than x, because t is always less than 10. Hence the following

RULE.

Interpolate by proportional parts, and reserve the tabular quantity thus found for subsequent correction.

Multiply the tabular quantity for the side number *one foot*, by *ten less the number of odd tenths*, and again by the *number of odd tenths itself*. Divide the product by one hundred, and subtract this result from the tabular number reserved for correction.

Example.—What is the tabular quantity for 45.6, under 15°, in Table VII.?

---

* *Another Demonstration.*—(See Art. 130, Part I.)—Let x be the argument, k its increment, and $\psi\,x = Q_{n-1}$, the tabular quantity for x; also, let $\psi\,(x + k) = Q_n$ be the tabular quantity for the argument $x + k$. By Taylor's theorem, $\psi\,(x + k) - \psi\,x = k\,\frac{d\,\psi\,x}{d\,x} + \frac{k^2}{2}\,\frac{d^2\,\psi\,x}{d\,x^2} + \&c.$ We have here $\psi\,x = x^2$ F; whence $\frac{d\,\psi\,x}{d\,x} = 2\,x$ F, $\frac{d^2\,\psi\,x}{d\,x^2} = 2$ F. Hence, $Q_n - Q_{n-1} = 2\ k\,x\ F + k^2\ F$, which, if $x = S_h + n - 1$, and $k = 1$, becomes $= (2\ S_h + 2\,n - 1)$ F. And this is the increment of the above scheme: also, if x be any argument, and $k = 1$, the increment $= (2\,x + 1)$ F; which is evident from the scheme. If $\psi\,x = x$ F, and $k = 1$, then $\frac{d\,\psi\,x}{d\,x} = F$, $\frac{d^2\,\psi\,x}{d\,x^2} = 0$, and the increment is $Q_n - Q_{n-1} = F$; which gives the rule of §1 for computation by continued addition.

The Table of Pythagoras, or common Multiplication Table, may be thus formed. The *Tabulæ Arithmeticæ* of Herwart (1610) are an extension of the Pythagorean Table for factors from 1 to 1000. By proceeding in a manner somewhat similar to that explained for our Tables XXI. and XXII. (page 81), Herwart converts the multiplication of larger factors than 1000, into addition. He also performs division by inspection of the tables, or by the aid of subtraction. Montucla has reviewed this work, (*Histoire des Math.*, tom. ii. p. 18,) and gives as reasons for its falling into disuse, the invention of logarithms, and the unwieldiness of the work in plan and dimensions, being a large folio of 1000 pages. It may be seen in the Astor Library.

Opposite 45, under 15°	. 3354.4
Opposite 45, under 15°, take six times the difference	90.4
Quantity by proportional interpolation	. 3444.8
Ten less *six*, the number of odd tenths, is 4.	
The tabular number for one foot, under 15°, is	1.7
Multiply by 4	4
	6.8
And again by 6, the number of odd tenths, and divide by 100	6
Correction	.408
Quantity by proportional interpolation, as above	3444.8
Corrected tabular quantity	3444.4

(4.) *Logarithmic Tables.*—The inspection of the proper formula will generally explain sufficiently the construction of these tables.

Table XXIII. contains the logarithm of one of the factors of Table XXI. If, in this latter,

$$L = 100, Q = \frac{100}{216} S_h S_b = \frac{10 S_h}{\sqrt{216}} \times \frac{10 S_b}{\sqrt{216}}.$$

The logarithm of one of these factors may be thus expressed:—

$$\log. \frac{10 S_h}{\sqrt{216}} = \log. S_h + \log. 10 - \tfrac{1}{2} \log. 216 = \log. S_h - 1.83277.$$

Table XXIV. contains the logarithm of one of the factors of Table XXII. If in this latter

$$L = 100, Q = \frac{100}{27} S_h S_b = \frac{10 S_h}{\sqrt{27}} \times \frac{10 S_b}{\sqrt{27}}.$$

The logarithm of one of these factors may be thus expressed:—

$$\log. \frac{10 S_h}{\sqrt{27}} = \log. S_h + \log. 10 - \tfrac{1}{2} \log. 27 = \log. S_h + 0.28432.$$

By adding $\frac{1}{2}$ log. 8 = 0.45155 to the logarithm of Table XXIII., the logarithm of Table XXIV. is produced. In this way the correctness of both tables may be tested.

Discussion of Graphical Processes.

CONSTRUCTION OF SCALES.

12. CONSTRUCTION OF GENERAL AND SPECIAL SCALES. (1.) *Sub-Section Diagram*, Plate VII., and *Mid-Section Diagram*, Plate VIII.—The explanation of these figures is sufficiently obvious from Articles 43, 45, 50, 52, and others, Part I.

(2.) *General Stereometric Scale for Whole and Sub Sections. First Form.*—This scale may be exhibited in two forms. We shall first take the most simple, which is not given on the plate. The object of the scale is to find an augmented sum of heights, or a sum of bases, which, in the table, under the given surface-slope, shall contain the same quantity as would be derived by adding together the quantities corresponding to the sum and to the difference, according to the General Rule, Art. 85, Part I.

By formula 13, page 280, and 21 and 23, page 282, the solidity of the whole ground in whole sections, and of the work in sub-sections, may be put under the general form

$$V = (S^2 + \tfrac{D^2}{3})\, F : \ldots . \; 1,$$

wherein S is the augmented sum of heights or sum of bases, and D the difference of heights or bases. F is a factor depending upon the side-slope and surface-slope. We have only to find a new sum of heights or bases, S_1; such that $S_1{}^2 = S^2 + \frac{D^2}{3}$ or $S_1 = \sqrt{S^2 + \frac{D^2}{3}}$: that is, to extract the square root of $S^2 + \frac{D^2}{3}$ by construction. The extraction of the square root is performed, in

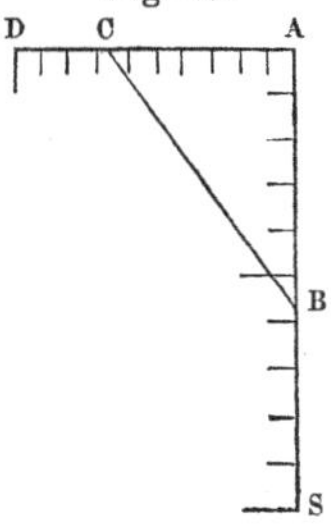

Geometry, by means of a right-angled triangle. Let S A D (Fig. 47) be a right-angle. Take any desirable length A S, and divide it into equal parts, each of which represents one foot. Take A D to A S in the same proportion as $\frac{1}{\sqrt{3}}$ to 1, and divide A D into a like number of equal parts with A S. Take A B = S and A C = D, according to the respective scales. Then, taking the unit of A S as a standard, $AC = \frac{D}{\sqrt{3}}$. By the property of right-angled triangles, $\overline{BC}^2 = \overline{AB}^2 + \overline{AC}^2$, and

$$BC = \sqrt{\overline{AB}^2 + \overline{AC}^2} = \sqrt{S^2 + \tfrac{D^2}{3}} = S_1, \quad \ldots . \; 1,$$

the new sum of heights or bases which was required.

Fig. 47.

Second Form, Plate VIII.—Equation 1 may be modified so as to allow the use of two right-angled triangles. By this means, the operation upon the scale is made similar to the operation upon the special scales, Plate IX.; and the divisions upon the scales for differences may be enlarged. We have

$$\sqrt{S^2 + \tfrac{D^2}{3}} = \sqrt{S^2 + (n^2+1)\tfrac{D^2}{3} - n^2\tfrac{D^2}{3}} = \sqrt{S^2 + \left(\sqrt{\tfrac{n^2+1}{3}}\right)^2 D^2 - \left(\tfrac{n}{\sqrt{3}}\right)^2 D^2};$$

wherein n is a number taken at pleasure.

Take, therefore, (Fig. 48,) $AD : AS :: \sqrt{\frac{n^2+1}{3}} : 1$; and divide each scale into the same number of equal parts. Take A B = S and A C = D, according to the respective scales: then $\overline{BC}^2 = S^2 + (n^2+1)\frac{D^2}{3}$.

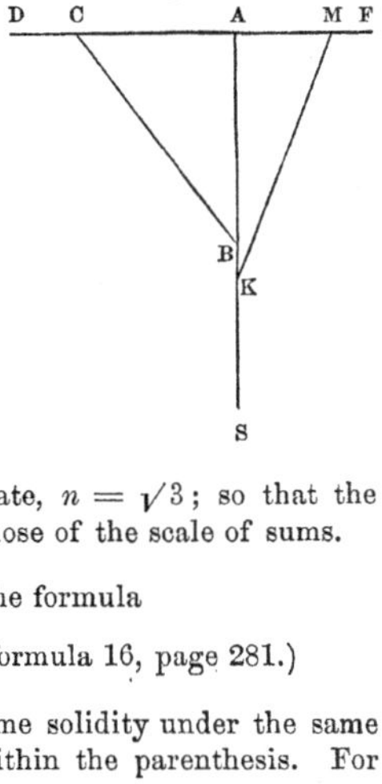

Make now $AF : AS :: \frac{n}{\sqrt{3}} : 1$; and divide A F into a like number of equal parts with A S. Take A M = D, according to the scale A F. Then $AM = n\frac{D}{\sqrt{3}}$. Make M K = B C. We have

Fig. 48.

$$\overline{AK}^2 = \overline{MK}^2 - \overline{AM}^2; \text{ that is,}$$

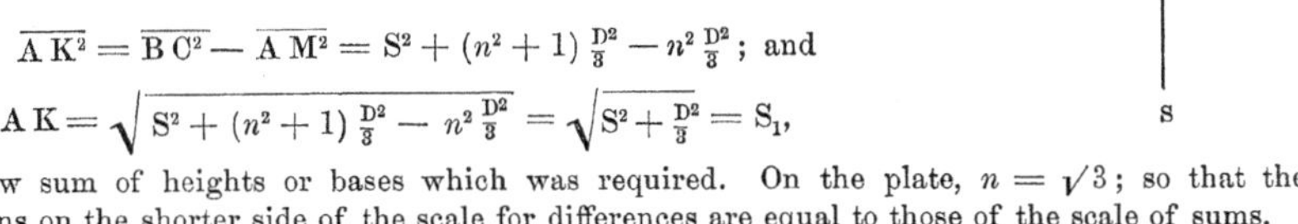

$$\overline{AK}^2 = \overline{BC}^2 - \overline{AM}^2 = S^2 + (n^2+1)\tfrac{D^2}{3} - n^2\tfrac{D^2}{3}; \text{ and}$$

$$AK = \sqrt{S^2 + (n^2+1)\tfrac{D^2}{3} - n^2\tfrac{D^2}{3}} = \sqrt{S^2 + \tfrac{D^2}{3}} = S_1,$$

the new sum of heights or bases which was required. On the plate, $n = \sqrt{3}$; so that the divisions on the shorter side of the scale for differences are equal to those of the scale of sums.

(3.) *Special Scales, Plate IX.*—These scales are constructed upon the formula

$$V = \tfrac{1}{4} L \left(S^2 - B^2 \tan^2\sigma + B^2 \tan^2\gamma + \tfrac{D^2}{3}\right) \frac{\tan\sigma}{\tan^2\sigma - \tan^2\gamma}. \text{ (See formula 16, page 281.)}$$

We have to find a new sum of heights which shall contain the same solidity under the same slope; that is, we have to extract the square root of the quantity within the parenthesis. For this purpose, we may transform that quantity into $S^2 + \frac{D^2}{3} - (B^2\tan^2\sigma - B^2\tan^2\gamma)$. We shall first construct $\sqrt{B^2\tan^2\sigma - B^2\tan^2\gamma}$.

Upon the diameter $AB = B\tan\sigma$ (Fig. 49) describe a semicircle. Make A C = B, and draw C D, making $DCA = \gamma$: then $AD = B\tan\gamma$. From A as a centre describe the arc D K: join A K and B K. A K B, being in a semicircle, is, by Geometry, a right-angled triangle, and $\overline{BK}^2 = \overline{AB}^2 - \overline{AK}^2 = \overline{AB}^2 - \overline{AD}^2 = B^2\tan^2\sigma - B^2\tan^2\gamma$; hence, $BK = \sqrt{B^2\tan^2\sigma - B^2\tan^2\gamma}$.

Fig. 49.

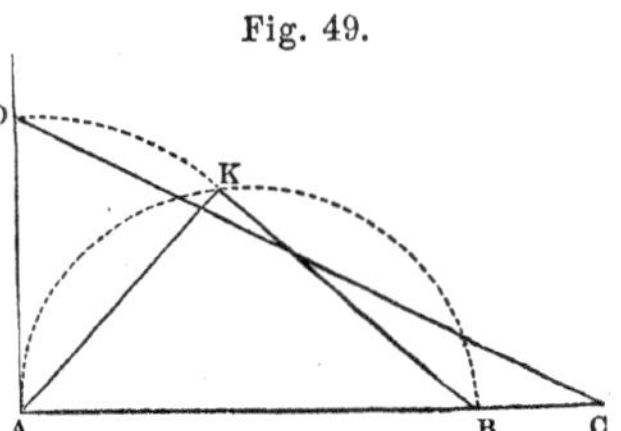

Draw and divide A S and A D (Fig. 50) as in Fig. 47, and take, as before, A B = S, A C = D:

Fig. 50.

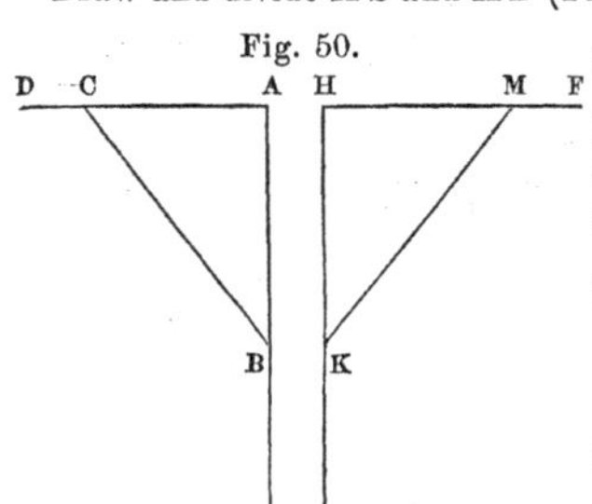

then $\overline{BC}^2 = S^2 + \frac{D^2}{3}$. Make T H F a right angle, and let H T be a scale like A S. On H F take H M = B K, (of Fig. 49, which is supposed of the same scale as A S, Fig. 50,) and make M K = B C (of the present figure.) Then,

$$\overline{HK}^2 = \overline{MK}^2 - \overline{HM}^2 = S^2 + \tfrac{D^2}{3} - (B^2 \tan^2 \sigma - B^2 \tan^2 \gamma);$$

$$\text{and } HK = \sqrt{S^2 - B^2 \tan^2 \sigma + B^2 \tan^2 \gamma + \tfrac{D^2}{3}} = S_1,$$

the new sum of heights which was required.

On the scales, Plate IX., this construction is only modified by leaving, between the zero-point of the scale A S and the side A D, a blank space equal to the tabular augment, from Table II., for the sum of the heights. The distance A B is not altered by this arrangement.

13. Given Dimensions.—Application of the Diagrams. In the following discussions, the given sum of heights for whole-section work may be either the augmented sum, which gives an approximate content for the whole ground, (see Art. 85, Part I., and Formula 13, page 280;) or the sum found by General Scale, (see Art. 96, Part I.,) which gives the true content of the whole ground; or the sum found by Special Scale, (see Art. 97, Part I., and Formula 16, page 281,) which gives the content of the residual prismoid.

For sub-sections, the given sum may be either the sum of the bases, or the augmented sum of the end-heights. These may be employed to find the approximate content. For the true content, the sum must be found by General Scale. (See Art. 96, Part I.)

The rules and diagrams apply to straight work and plane ground, or to all work after reduction to this form. The length of work in the examples is understood to be 100 feet.

BASES OF EQUIVALENT SQUARE PRISMS.

14.—To find the Base of an Equivalent Square Prism by Mean Proportionals. We shall not, at present, actually exhibit this base, but will find the value of the base multiplied by $\sqrt{8}$. This quantity is proper for entering Table XV.

(1.) *Whole Sections.*—On the plane of the cross-section, draw the horizontal line R O L, (Plate X.,) the vertical centre-line O H, and the side-slopes O A, O B. Also draw O P, of indefinite length, perpendicular to O A; and, parallel to O P, draw M N through any point T on the side-slope O B. Divide O A, O H, O B, O R according to the same scale of equal parts. Make N K = N T, and N I = O T. On I K describe a semicircle cutting N T in M. Then N T = O T $\times$ sin A O T. Also, by Geometry, N M is a mean proportional between N K and N I, that is, between N T and O T; and $NM = \sqrt{OT \times NT} = \sqrt{\overline{OT}^2 \times \sin AOT} = OT \times \sqrt{\sin AOT}$. Make O Q = O T, and O G = N M. Join G Q, and draw T P parallel to G Q. Then, by similar triangles, O P : O Q :: O T : O G; whence $OP = \frac{OQ \times OT}{OG} = \frac{\overline{OT}^2}{NM} = \frac{\overline{OT}^2}{OT \times \sqrt{\sin AOT}} = \frac{OT}{\sqrt{\sin AOT}}$. Hence, if O P be divided into the same number of equal parts as O T, the length of the unit on O P will be $\frac{1}{\sqrt{\sin AOT}}$; the unit on O T being the standard. And the reading of any length l, transferred from the scale O T to the scale O P, will be $l\,\sqrt{\sin AOT}$. Let O D = 2 H be the sum of the augmented end-heights. Then the triangle A O B, having a given surface-slope A B, is four times as great in area as the similar triangle, having the height H, which latter triangle is that of the mid cross-section. Therefore, putting the area of A O B = A′, and that of the mid cross-section = A, $A' = \frac{1}{2} \sin AOT \times OA \times OB = 4A$; whence $A = \frac{1}{8} \sin AOT \times OA \times OB$. Put $\sqrt{\sin AOT \times OA \times OB} = S$; then $A = \frac{1}{8} S^2$. From what precedes, we know that if $\sqrt{OA \times OB}$, measured on O A or O B, be transferred to O P, the reading will be $\sqrt{OA \times OB}\,\sqrt{\sin AOT}$; that is, the reading will give the value of S. It remains to find $\sqrt{OA \times OB}$. This is a mean proportional between O A and O B, and may be found by taking O U = O B; then describing a semicircle on A U, cutting O P in S. O S is the mean proportional required, and is transferred to the scale O P. Hence, upon the scale O P, O S = S, and $A = \frac{1}{8} OS^2$.

It will not be necessary actually to lay off O U, or to describe the whole semicircle. We may add the reading of O B to the reading of O A, and set off the half-sum of the readings from A to Y. Then from the centre Y, with radius YA find the point S.

(2.) *Sub-Sections.*—A similar construction applies. It may either be made separately, or may be exhibited on the same diagram in the following manner:—

Having the sum of heights or of bases and the surface-slope given, draw F V, observing to take the sum of heights, or of bases, for the marginal height or the base of the triangle; and let fall the perpendicular F C. The area of F O V is equal to four times the area of the mid cross-section; hence, calling the area of F O V A′, and the area of the mid-section A, $4A = A' = \frac{1}{2} OV \times FC$, and $A = \frac{1}{8} OV \times FC$. A mean proportional is now to be found between O V and F C. Graduate O L so that the reading may give $OC = OF \times \sin AOL = FC$ as read upon the scale O R or O H. Add the reading of O C to the reading of O V. The half-sum of these readings is the radius, which set off from V to X. With the centre X and radius X V find the point Z on the scale O H. $OZ = \sqrt{OV \times FC}$; whence $A = \frac{1}{8} OZ^2$.

Since Table XV. contains the eighth part of a square prism, the side of whose base is the argument, it is obvious the solidity will be found by entering this table with O S or O Z. If B be the base of an equivalent square prism, then $A = \frac{1}{8} (OS \text{ or } OZ)^2 = B^2$, and O S or $OZ = \sqrt{8}\, B$.

Because the distance O S (not the reading) $= \sqrt{OA \times OB}$; if O S be laid off from O on O A and O B, an isosceles triangle may be formed, the product of whose two equal sides is equal to $OA \times OB$; and, consequently, the area of the triangle equal to the area of A O B. Hence, the height of the isosceles triangle will be the equivalent sum of heights under level ground.

15. To find the Content by Diagram. (Plates X. and XI.)

RULE.

(1.) *For Whole Sections.*—On the scale O H, take O D, equal to the given sum of centre-heights. By aid of the graduated arc, whose centre is O, draw A D B with the given surface-slope. Read O A and A B on their scales, and add the readings together. Lay off the half-sum of the readings from A to Y. From Y as a centre, with radius Y A describe an arc cutting O P in S. With the number shown by O S on its scale, enter Table XV. and take out the content, which will correspond to the given sum of heights.

Note.—In Plate XI., the lines O P and O T fall together.

(2.) *For Sub-Sections.*—Take O V equal to the sum of bases, or take the augmented sum of the centre-heights on the scale O H; and draw the surface-slope F V. Draw F C parallel to O H. Add together the readings of O V and O C. Measure the half-sum of the readings by the scale O R, and lay it off from V to X. From the centre X, with radius X V describe an arc cutting O H in Z. With the number shown by O Z on its scale, enter Table XV. and take out the required content.

Example 1.—The augmented sum of heights for a piece of whole-section work is 30, the surface-slope 15°, the side-slope 1½ to 1. What is the content of the whole ground?

On Plate X., make O D equal to 30. Draw A D B with the surface-slope of 15°. O A reads 90.4; O B reads 39.0. The half-sum of these readings is 64.7. Make A Y equal to 64.7, and with the centre Y and radius 64.7 find O S equal to 56.8. Then, in Table XV., opposite 56 and under 8, find 1493.6, which is the whole content nearly.

Example 2.—The sum of the bases of a piece of sub-section work is 50, the surface-slope 10°, the side-slope 1½ to 1. What is the content?

The example is drawn and lettered on Plate X. O V is 50; the reading of O C is 12.0. The radius V X is therefore 31. From the centre X, with this radius find O Z, equal to 24.5. Then, in Table XV., with 24.5 take out 277.9, which is the content nearly.

Two other examples are drawn on Plate XI. In regard to this diagram, it is only necessary to remark that O S is to be taken upon the side-slope.

Example 3.—The augmented sum of heights for a piece of whole-section work is 40, the surface-slope 25°, the side-slope 1 to 1. What is the whole content between the surface and the intersection of the side-slopes? O S is found to be 63.9, which, in Table XV., gives 1890.4.

Example 4.—The sum of the bases of a piece of sub-section work is 30, the surface-slope 20°, the side-slope 1 to 1. What is the content? O Z is found to be 22.7, which, in Table XV., gives 238.6.

16. BASES OF EQUIVALENT SQUARE PRISMS AND EQUIVALENT HEIGHTS FOUND BY GEOMETRIC LOCI.

(1.) *Investigation of Formulæ for Whole Sections.*—Let the solidity be $V = \frac{1}{4} L S^2 \times \frac{\tan\sigma}{\tan^2\sigma - \tan^2\gamma}$. (See formulæ 16 and 19, page 281.) As we propose to find the square cross-section of a prism which is equal to the solid represented by this equation, and whose length is L, we need only seek the side of this square base, and may treat the equation $A' = \frac{1}{4} S^2 \times \frac{\tan\sigma}{\tan^2\sigma - \tan^2\gamma}$; wherein A′ is the area of the square. In order to transform this expression, we have

$$\frac{\tan\sigma}{\tan^2\sigma - \tan^2\gamma} = \frac{\tan\sigma}{\sec^2\sigma - 1 - \tan^2\gamma} = \frac{\tan\sigma}{\sec^2\sigma - (1+\tan^2\gamma)} = \frac{\tan\sigma}{\sec^2\sigma - \sec^2\gamma} = \frac{\tan\sigma}{\sec^2\sigma - \frac{1}{\cos^2\gamma}} = \frac{\tan\sigma}{\frac{\sec^2\sigma\cos^2\gamma - 1}{\cos^2\gamma}}$$

$$= \frac{\tan\sigma}{\sec^2\sigma\cos^2\gamma - 1} \times \cos^2\gamma = \cot\sigma \times \frac{\tan^2\sigma}{\sec^2\sigma\cos^2\gamma - 1} \times \cos^2\gamma = \cot\sigma \times \frac{\sec^2\sigma - 1}{\sec^2\sigma\cos^2\gamma - 1} \times \cos^2\gamma.$$

$$\text{Whence } A' = \tfrac{1}{4} S^2 \cot\sigma \times \frac{\sec^2\sigma - 1}{\sec^2\sigma\cos^2\gamma - 1} \times \cos^2\gamma$$

$$= \left\{\sqrt{\tfrac{1}{4} S^2 \cot\sigma}\right\}^2 \times \left\{\sqrt{\frac{\sec^2\sigma - 1}{\sec^2\sigma\cos^2\gamma - 1}} \times \cos\gamma\right\}^2 \quad \ldots\ldots 1.$$

If A be the semi-transverse axis of an hyperbola whose eccentricity is e and polar angle γ, the polar equation of the curve referred to the centre as a pole is

$$\rho = A\sqrt{\frac{e^2 - 1}{e^2\cos^2\gamma - 1}}.$$

Therefore, making $A = \sqrt{\frac{1}{4} S^2 \cot\sigma}$ and $e = \sec\sigma$, equation 1 becomes $A' = (\rho\cos\gamma)^2$. When $\gamma = \sigma$, $\rho = \infty$; whence the asymptotes make an angle $= \sigma$ with the polar axis. When $\sigma = 45°$, or when the side-slope is 1 to 1, the hyperbola is equilateral.

It now remains to find $\rho\cos\gamma$, which is the required side of the square.

(2.) *To construct a Diagram for finding the bases of Equivalent Square Prisms for Whole Sections.*—Let A O B (Plate XII.) be a horizontal line upon the mid cross-section, and passing through the intersection O of the side-slopes. O Y is the vertical centre-line; O S and O T the side-slopes. Upon O Y take any convenient length O H, and draw H D parallel to O B. $HD = OH \times \cot SOB = OH \times \cot\sigma$. Upon O H produced make $OC = HD$, and describe the semicircle H B C. By Geometry, $OB = \sqrt{OH \times OC} = \sqrt{OH \times HD} = \sqrt{\overline{OH}^2 \times \cot\sigma}$.

Draw B K parallel to O H, and from the centre O describe through K an arc K F′ cutting O B in F′. Make $OA = OB$ and $OF = OF'$. Put $OK = OF' = c$, $OB = A$; and make

$$\frac{c}{A} = e: \text{ then } e = \frac{OK}{OB} = \sec SOB = \sec\sigma : BK = \sqrt{c^2 - A^2}.$$

By the property of the hyperbola, if $e = \sec\sigma$ be the eccentricity, $A = OB = OA$ is the semi-transverse axis, $B = BK$, the semi-conjugate; F and F′ are the foci, and O S and O T the asymptotes. Construct the hyperbola; draw any radius vector $O\gamma = \rho$, making the polar angle $PO\gamma = \gamma$; and draw the ordinate $P\gamma$: then $OP = \rho\cos\gamma$.

If $OH = \frac{1}{2} S$, O P is the line required whose square $= A'$. For we have found above, $OB = A = \sqrt{\overline{OH}^2 \times \cot\sigma}$; whence, if $OH = \frac{1}{2} S$, $A = \sqrt{\frac{1}{4} S^2 \cot\sigma}$; also, we have made, by construction, $e = \sec\sigma$: but $A = \sqrt{\frac{1}{4} S^2 \cot\sigma}$ and $e = \sec\sigma$ are the conditions required by the previous investigation, in order that $A' = (\rho\cos\gamma)^2 = \overline{OP}^2$. (See also § 5, Art. 25.)

The areas of similar plane figures are proportional to the squares of their homologous lines. Hence we infer that for given values of σ and γ, the area of the whole cross-section will be, for different values of S, proportional to S^2, and hence, also, to $\frac{1}{4}S^2$. The side of the equivalent square base will then be proportional to $\frac{1}{2}S$: this is also evident from equation 1, § 1.

It is, therefore, not necessary to make O H = the half-sum of heights in order to find the side of the base. For, let $OH = \frac{1}{2}S$ = the augmented centre-height of a cross-section similar to the one proposed, of which latter let the augmented centre-height be $\frac{1}{2}S'$. It is now required to find O N, the side of the square base equal in area to the proposed cross-section. For any sum S and surface-slope γ, find O P, as before; we shall then evidently have

$$OP : ON :: \tfrac{1}{2}S : \tfrac{1}{2}S' :: S : S'.$$

The same conclusion may be reached by considering that, whilst S O B is constant, the hyperbolas corresponding to different values of O H will all be similar; and, therefore, with $PO\gamma = \gamma$ constant, the abscissas O P will be to each other as the respective values of O H. But these values of O H are to each other as the respective sums of heights. The above proportion will then be obtained, by regarding O N as the abscissa corresponding to the surface-slope γ, for an hyperbola in which O H has been made equal to the half-sum of augmented heights.

To satisfy this proportion, take, upon the scale O T, O H′ equal or in a given ratio to $OH = \frac{1}{2}S$; also take O M in the same ratio to $\frac{1}{2}S'$. Draw H′ P, and parallel to it draw M N. The similar triangles O M N, O H′ P give the required proportion.

To avoid the necessity of finding $\frac{1}{2}S'$ when S′ is given, we may make $OR = 2\,OH = S$: then make $OV = S'$; join R P, and draw V N parallel to R P.

The First Part of Table XV. contains the eighth parts of prisms 100 feet long, upon a square base. If the scale O P be so graduated that its divisions are to those of O T as 1 to $\sqrt{8}$, we may enter Table XV. with O N as read upon its own scale, and may take out the required content for 100 feet. The necessity of this graduation of O P might be avoided by preparing a Table similar to XV., but containing the whole solidities of square prisms.

(3.) *Equivalent Heights for New Surface-Slopes.*—If it be required to find a new sum of heights which, with a new surface-slope, shall contain the original solidity, let P O L be the new surface-slope. Find O P, and thence O N, as before, for the original sum of heights and slope; then find O U for the new slope P O L, as O P was found for the original slope. Draw U R, and N W parallel to it, cutting off from the scale O T the distance O W, equal to the required new sum of heights.

It is evident, from the construction shown in section 2, that P O L may be regarded as the surface-slope of a cross-section for which O N is the side of the equivalent base, and in which O W = the sum of heights. By joining U H′ and drawing through N a line parallel to U H′, we should find the half-sum of the new heights.

(4.) *Equivalent Level-Heights.*—If the new surface-slope be level, or = 0°, L and U fall upon A. Therefore, after finding O P, and thence O N, for the original cross-section, join A R, and through N draw a line parallel to A R, cutting off from O T the required new sum of heights. To find the half-sum, or augmented height of the new cross-section, join A H′, and draw a parallel to it through N.

(5.) *Geometrical Basis of these Constructions.*—Since $\cot\sigma = \frac{OB}{BK} = \frac{A}{B}$, we have, (§ 2,)

$$A = \sqrt{\overline{OH}^2 \times \cot\sigma} = \sqrt{\overline{OH}^2 \times \frac{A}{B}};$$

whence $\overline{OH}^2 = A \times B$; that is, O H is a mean proportional between the semi-axes. Hence these constructions depend on the following property of the hyperbola.

Take from the centre O, upon the line of the conjugate axis, O H a mean proportional between the semi-axes. The area of any triangle included between the asymptotes and a third side drawn through H, is equal to the square of the abscissa O P subtended by the radius $O\gamma$ drawn parallel to this third side.

17. Examples in finding the Content of Whole Sections by the Diagram. (See Plate XII.) The diagram is adapted to the side-slope $1\frac{1}{2}$ to 1.

Example 1. *Equivalent Square Bases.*—The augmented sum of heights is 45; surface-slope, 25°; side-slope, $1\frac{1}{2}$ to 1. Required the side of the equivalent square base, and the content of the section.

Draw Oγ, making the angle POγ equal to 25°, the given surface-slope.* Mark the point of intersection γ with the curved line ALγ. Draw Pγ parallel to OH, and join PR. Make OV equal to 45, the given sum of heights, and through V draw VN parallel to PR. Read the number (say 109.1) indicated by N upon the scale ON. Then,

Opposite 109, under 1, in Table XV., First Part, find the solidity . . . 5510.6

Example 2. *Equivalent Heights for New Surface-Slopes.*—If, in Example 1, the surface-slope were changed to 15°, what must be the augmented sum of heights to contain the same solidity?

Find the point N, as before, for the given sum 45 and surface-slope 25°. Make POL equal to 15°, the new surface-slope, and draw LU parallel to OH. Draw UR, and parallel to it draw NW. Read the number (say 55.7) equal to the required sum, indicated by W upon the scale OT. Then,

Opposite 57.7, under 15°, in Table VII., find the solidity 5515.3

Example 3. *Equivalent Level-Heights.*—If, in Example 1, the surface-slope were made level, what must be the augmented sum of heights to contain the same solidity?

Proceed, as in Examples 1 and 2, to find P and N for the given sum 45 and surface-slope 25°; the point U will now fall upon A. Join AR, and through N draw a parallel to AR, cutting the scale OT in a point indicating, say 63.0, the new sum required. Then,

Opposite 63.0, under 0°, in Table VII., find the solidity 5512.5

18. Bases of Equivalent Square Prisms found by Geometric Loci. (1.) *Investigation of Formulæ for Sub-Sections.*—The solidity for sub-sections (see formula 24, page 282) is

$$V = \tfrac{1}{8}\,L\,S_b^2 \times \frac{1}{\cot\gamma - \cot\sigma};$$

wherein S_b is put for the sum of the bases. Leaving out of consideration the length, and proceeding as before to find the side of a square equal in area to A, the area of the triangle, we have

$$A = \tfrac{1}{8}\,S_b^2 \times \frac{1}{\cot\gamma - \cot\sigma} = \tfrac{1}{8}\,S_b \tan\gamma \times \frac{S_b}{1 - \frac{\cot\sigma}{\cot\gamma}}.$$

Because γ is always less than σ, we may put $\frac{\cot\sigma}{\cot\gamma} = \cot\sigma\tan\gamma = \cos\phi$, which gives, by substitution,

$$A = \tfrac{1}{8}\,S_b \tan\gamma \times \frac{S_b}{1 - \cos\phi}, \quad \dots\ 1.$$

In which $\frac{S_b}{1-\cos\phi}$ is the radius vector of a parabola whose semi-parameter is S_b.

If this equation be first multiplied and then divided by $\tan^2\gamma$, the term $S_b^2\tan^2\gamma$ applies to computation by the augmented sum of centre-heights. (See equations 21, 22, 23, page 282.) Therefore, designating the sum of the augmented centre-heights by S_h, we have

$$A = \tfrac{1}{8}\,S_h \cot\gamma\,\frac{S_h}{1-\cos\phi}, \quad \dots\ 2.$$

If ρ' be the radius vector of the parabola in this last equation, and ρ in the previous, and if the side of the square which is equal to A be put, respectively, $= S_b'$, S_h', we shall have

$$S_b' = \sqrt{\tfrac{1}{8}} \times \sqrt{\rho\,S_b\tan\gamma}; \text{ and } S_h' = \sqrt{\tfrac{1}{8}} \times \sqrt{\rho'\,S_h\cot\gamma}.$$

As we propose to enter Table XV., we shall proceed to construct, not S_b' and S_h', but $S_b'\sqrt{8}$ and $S_h'\sqrt{8}$, equal, respectively, to $\sqrt{\rho\,S_b\tan\gamma}$ and $\sqrt{\rho'\,S_h\cot\gamma}$.

(2.) *To construct a Diagram for finding the Bases of Equivalent Square Prisms for Sub-Sections.*—About the focus O and axis OX, (Fig. 1, Plate XIII.,) construct a parabola Pϕ, having the semi-parameter OP of any convenient length. Upon the line of the parameter, make OM = unity, and describe a circular quadrant MQ. Make the angle YO$\gamma = \gamma$, and take OY = cot σ. Draw Yγ parallel to OX, and γN parallel to OY, cutting the circular quadrant in N; also,

* If desirable, a graduated arc may be added to the diagram, in order to facilitate the drawing of slopes; or, the requisite number of slopes may be permanently indicated by radii.

through N draw $O\phi N$, cutting the parabola in ϕ: then $XO\phi = \phi$, because cos $XO\phi = Y\gamma =$ cot σ tan γ.

$$\text{The radius vector } O\phi = \frac{OP}{1-\cos\phi}\text{; whence } \frac{O\phi}{OP} = \frac{1}{1-\cos\phi}$$

Upon OX construct a scale of equal parts, and, according to this scale, take $OB = S_b$. Draw $P\phi$ and BK parallel to it, cutting $O\phi$ in K: then, by similar triangles,

$$\frac{OK}{OB} = \frac{O\phi}{OP}, \text{ or } \frac{OK}{S_b} = \frac{O\phi}{OP}\text{; whence } OK = S_b \times \frac{O\phi}{OP} = \frac{S_b}{1-\cos\phi}.$$

Draw BT parallel to OX, and TH parallel to OY: then $BT = OH = OB \tan\gamma = S_b \tan\gamma$. Make $OL = OH$ and $OX = OK = \frac{S_b}{1-\cos\phi}$. On LX describe a semicircle cutting OY in F: then

$$OF = \sqrt{OL \times OX} = \sqrt{S_b \tan\gamma \times \frac{S_b}{1-\cos\phi}};$$

which is the quantity sought $= \sqrt{8\,S_b'} = \sqrt{A}$. (See equation 1, § 1.)

If S_h be given instead of S_b, let $OH = S_h$, instead of taking $OB = S_b$. Draw HT parallel to OB, and TB parallel to OX; then $HT = OB = S_h \cot\gamma$. Make $OS = OH = S_h$, and draw SR parallel to $P\phi$, which is found as before: then, by similar triangles,

$$OR = OS \times \frac{O\phi}{OP} = S_h \times \frac{O\phi}{OP} = \frac{S_h}{1-\cos\phi}.$$

Make $OU = OR$, and describe the semicircle BVU, cutting OX in V: then

$$OV = \sqrt{OB \times OU} = \sqrt{S_h \cot\gamma \times \frac{S_h}{1-\cos\phi}},$$

which is the quantity sought, $= \sqrt{8\,S_h'} = \sqrt{A}$. (See equation 2, § 1.)

By making permanent the parabola and various radii $P\phi$ for the different surface-slopes required, there would remain the other parts of the construction to be performed in particular cases.

19. Examples in finding the Content of Sub-Sections by the Diagram. (See Fig. 1, Plate XIII.) If radii be drawn similarly to OK for the requisite number of surface-slopes, the diagram will apply to a particular rate of side-slope. But if no such radii have been drawn, and the diagram contains only the curved line, the curved line will apply to all side-slopes. For the method of drawing such radii, see § 2, Art. 18. In the following examples the radius OK is supposed to correspond to a surface-slope of 20°, and to be one of a series adapted to the side-slope 1½ to 1.

Example 1.—The sum of the end-bases is 40, the surface-slope 20°, and the side-slope 1½ to 1. Required the argument for Table XV., and the corresponding content.

Make OB equal to 40, the sum of the bases, according to the scale upon OX; and draw OT, making the angle TOB equal to 20°, the given surface-slope. Draw, also, BT parallel to OX. Draw BK parallel to $P\phi$, and make OX equal to OK; also make OL equal to BT. On LX describe a semicircle cutting OB in F. Measure OF on the scale OX, and find the required argument, say 35.8: then

Opposite 35, under 8, in Table XV., find the solidity 593.4

Example 2.—The augmented sum of heights is 14.6, the surface-slope 20°, and the side-slope 1½ to 1. Required the argument for Table XV. and the corresponding content.

Make OH equal to the sum of the heights, upon the scale OX; and draw OT, making the angle TOB equal to 20°, the given surface-slope. Draw, also, HT parallel to OY. Make OS equal to OH, and draw SR parallel to $P\phi$. Make OU equal to OR, and OB equal to HT. On BU describe a semicircle cutting OX in V. OV read upon the scale OX is the required augment, say 35.8: then,

Opposite 35, under 8, in Table XV., find the solidity 593.4

CONVERSION OF SLOPES.

20. Conversion of Slopes is changing one or both slopes of a cross-section, whilst the area either remains unchanged, or is made equal to another given area. There are two cases,—viz., *single conversion*, when only one slope is changed, and *double conversion*, when both slopes are changed. This problem requires the finding a new sum of heights or bases, by which the solidity may be obtained from the tables under new slopes. The practical application of this method has generally been confined to changing the surface to a level one. The conversion of slopes has already been referred to. (See Art. 98, Part I., Art. 14, § 2, Art. 16, § 3, and Art. 17.) We propose, in the following articles, to consider further the conversion of slopes.

21. Nature of the Problem of Conversion of Slopes. The problem is as follows:—
Having given a triangle A O B, (Fig. 50,) to find another triangle L O M, (Fig. 51,) equal in area to A O B, and similar to a third triangle H O K. A O B is the given base of a prism containing the solidity of the work, and L O M is the required base of another prism containing the same solidity.

22. General Construction by Mean Proportionals. This applies both to whole and sub sections; the use of mean proportionals has also been shown in Art. 14.

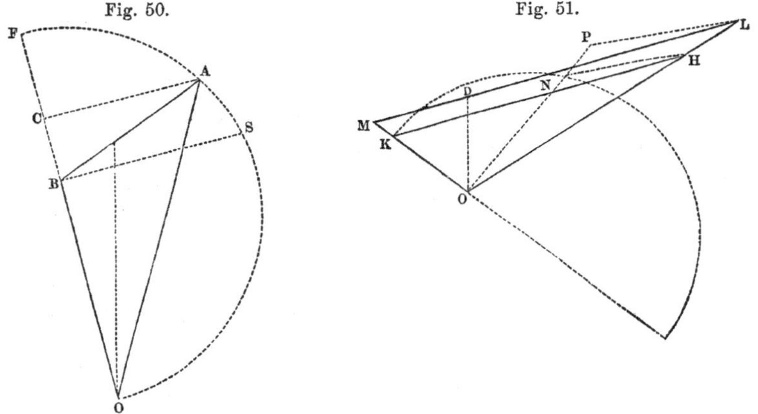

From one of the angles B of the given cross-section A O B, draw B S perpendicular to O B, one of the sides adjacent to B. Make B F equal to A C, the altitude of the triangle. On O F describe the semicircle F S O, cutting B S in S. B S is a mean proportional between B O and A C; that is, the square of B S is equal to the rectangle of B O and A C, or equal to twice the area of A O B. In a similar manner find (Fig. 51) O N, the side of a square equal to twice the area of H O K, the triangle which exhibits the new slope or slopes. Upon the line of O N, take O P, equal to B S. Join N H, and draw P L parallel to N H; then, by the similar triangles O L P, O H N,

$$\frac{OL}{OH} = \frac{OP}{ON}, \text{ whence } \frac{\overline{OL}^2}{\overline{OH}^2} = \frac{\overline{OP}^2}{\overline{ON}^2} = \frac{\overline{BS}^2}{\overline{ON}^2}.$$

$$\text{But } \frac{\overline{OL}^2}{\overline{OH}^2} = \frac{\text{Area LOM}}{\text{Area HOK}} = \frac{\overline{BS}^2}{\overline{ON}^2} = \frac{\text{Area AOB}}{\text{Area HOK}};$$

whence, Area L O M = Area A O B, which was required. The length of the new centre-height O D can now be measured.

If it be required to find the area L O M = Area A O B $\times$ m, the construction may be varied by making O P = B S $\times \sqrt{m}$.

23. Investigation of Formulæ by Auxiliary Angles. The following articles on this subject apply to whole sections only: the method of auxiliary angles has been partially discussed in Art. 18.

(1.) *For Construction.*—We have for the solidity of whole sections, (see formula 19, page 281,)

$$V = \tfrac{1}{4} L S^2 \times \frac{\cot \sigma}{1 - \frac{\tan^2 \gamma}{\tan^2 \sigma}}.$$

Because σ is always greater than γ, we may replace $\frac{\tan \gamma}{\tan \sigma}$ by the sine of an auxiliary angle. Putting $\frac{\tan \gamma}{\tan \sigma} = \sin \phi$, the above equation becomes

$$V = \tfrac{1}{4} L S^2 \times \frac{\cot \sigma}{1 - \sin^2 \phi} = \tfrac{1}{4} L S^2 \times \frac{\cot \sigma}{\cos^2 \phi} = \tfrac{1}{4} L S^2 \cot \sigma \sec^2 \phi.$$

Let σ' and γ' be new slopes; and let S_1 be the new sum of heights which, with these slopes, contains the original volume V. Put $\frac{\tan \gamma'}{\tan \sigma'} = \sin \phi'$. We have, by the previous reasoning and by equating the two expressions for V,

$$\tfrac{1}{4} L S_1^2 \times \cot \sigma' \sec^2 \phi' = \tfrac{1}{4} L S^2 \times \cot \sigma \sec^2 \phi. \quad \text{Whence}$$

$$S_1 = S \sqrt{\cot \sigma \tan \sigma'} \times \frac{\sec \phi}{\sec \phi'} \ldots\ldots 1.$$

This formula is applicable either to single or double conversion. If the side-slope is unchanged, the equation takes the form

$$S_1 = S \times \frac{\sec \phi}{\sec \phi'} \ldots\ldots 2.$$

If the new surface-slope be level, that is, if $\gamma' = 0$, then $\phi' = 0$, and $\sec \phi' = 1$: equation 1 becomes

$$S_1 = S \sqrt{\cot \sigma \tan \sigma'} \times \sec \phi \ldots\ldots 3.$$

And equation 2 becomes $S_1 = S \sec \phi \ldots\ldots\ldots\ldots\ldots\ldots 4.$

We have, then, the following cases of conversion, of which the number designates the formula:—

1. General Form: change of one or both slopes.
2. Side-slope unchanged; surface-slope changed arbitrarily.
3. Side-slope changed arbitrarily; surface-slope made level.
4. Side-slope unchanged; surface-slope made level.

The finding of the new sum S_1 is then reduced to the construction or the numerical solution of these equations. For numerical solution, it will be convenient to have formulæ adapted to logarithmic computation.

(2.) *Logarithmic Formulæ.*—Since $\sin \phi = \frac{\tan \gamma}{\tan \sigma}$ and $\sin \phi' = \frac{\tan \gamma'}{\tan \sigma'}$, we have $\sin \phi = \tan \gamma \cot \sigma$ and $\sin \phi' = \tan \gamma' \cot \sigma'$; whence

$$\log. \sin \phi = \log. \tan \gamma + \log. \cot \sigma; \text{ and } \log. \sin \phi' = \log. \tan \gamma' + \log. \cot \sigma'.$$

By these last formulæ we may find ϕ and ϕ'; when log. $\cos \phi$ and log. $\cos \phi'$ can be readily found. Now,

$$\frac{\sec \phi}{\sec \phi'} = \frac{\cos \phi'}{\cos \phi}; \text{ and, therefore, } \log. \frac{\sec \phi}{\sec \phi'} = \log. \cos \phi' - \log. \cos \phi.$$

Hence, by substituting successively in formulæ 1, 2, 3, and 4, § 1 the required logarithms, we have

$$\log. S_1 = \log. S + \tfrac{1}{2} \log. \cot \sigma + \tfrac{1}{2} \log. \tan \sigma' + \log. \cos \phi' - \log. \cos \phi.\ 1.$$
$$\log. S_1 = \log. S + \log. \cos \phi' - \log. \cos \phi \ldots\ldots\ldots\ldots\ldots 2.$$
$$\log. S_1 = \log. S + \tfrac{1}{2} \log. \cot \sigma + \tfrac{1}{2} \log. \tan \sigma' - \log. \cos \phi \ldots\ldots 3.$$
$$\log. S_1 = \log. S - \log. \cos \phi \ldots\ldots\ldots\ldots\ldots\ldots\ldots 4.$$

(3.) *Interpolation for Parts of a Degree* in tables similar to Table VII. may be made by auxiliary tables constructed from the formula for conversion. The side-slope remains unchanged.

Let γ' indicate the angle in whole degrees for a given surface-slope γ which contains a fraction. By means of Formula 2, an auxiliary table might be constructed containing the values of S_1, or of an increment for S, for a limited series of values of S and for consecutive values of γ with intervals of one degree. It would, however, probably be better at once to extend the principal table.

(4.) *Auxiliary Tables for Equivalent Level-Heights.**—By means of Formula 4, an auxiliary table might be formed containing the equivalent sum of level-heights S_1 for a series of values of S.

The heights thus obtained might be employed with a table adapted to particular side-slopes. (See § 1, Art. 25.) These latter might be made to contain tenths of feet in the argument, in a manner similar to that of Table XV. Or, Table XV., or one constructed on a similar plan suitable for all side-slopes, might be adopted. (See § 2, Art. 25.) Instead of adapting the table of cubical content to odd tenths of height, we might employ its several columns for graduated lengths of work.

24. Construction by Auxiliary Angles. (1.) *General Construction for Double Conversion.* (See Formula 1, § 1, Art. 23.)—From any convenient scale take $CA = 1$, (Fig. 2, Plate XIII.,) and with centre C describe an arc A B. Make $AC\gamma = \gamma$, the original surface-slope, and produce $C\gamma$. On the same scale take $CE = \cot\sigma$, and perpendicular to C A draw $EH = \cot\sigma \tan\gamma = \sin\phi$, cutting $C\gamma$ in H. Draw H I parallel to C A, cutting the arc A B in I; and through I draw $CI\phi$. $ICA = \phi$, because the sine of this angle to radius $CI = CA = 1$ is equal to $EH = \sin\phi$.

In the same manner, make $AC\gamma' = \gamma'$ the new surface-slope. Make $CE' = \cot\sigma'$. Draw E′H′, H I′, and $CI'\phi'$, making $I'CA = \phi'$. Draw the tangent A M M′; and draw I′ P parallel to A M M′. Then, from the similar triangles C M M′, C P I′; $\frac{CP}{CI'} = \frac{CM}{CM'}$; whence, because

$$CI' = CA = 1,\ CP = \frac{\sec\phi}{\sec\phi'}.$$

Draw N C O perpendicular to C A. On any scale, make $CO = S\cot\sigma$, and $CN = S\tan\sigma'$. Upon N O describe a semicircle cutting C A in R. C R is a mean proportional between C N and C O; that is,

$$CR = \sqrt{CO \times CN} = \sqrt{S\cot\sigma\, S\tan\sigma'} = S\sqrt{\cot\sigma\tan\sigma'}.$$

Draw R I, and P T parallel to it. Because of the similar triangles C R I, C T P; $\frac{CT}{CP} = \frac{CR}{CI}$; but

$$CI = 1,\ CP = \frac{\sec\phi}{\sec\phi'},\ \text{and}\ CR = S\sqrt{\cot\sigma\tan\sigma'}:\ \text{hence,}$$

$$CT = S\sqrt{\cot\sigma\tan\sigma'} \times \frac{\sec\phi}{\sec\phi'} = S_1.$$

In the example represented upon the diagram, the augmented end-heights are 95 and 64; the surface-slope 35°; side-slope ¼ to 1. The sum of end-heights containing the same solidity is found by Art. 96, Part I.; say 160. It is required to find a sum of heights which will contain the same solidity under a surface-slope of 18° and side-slope 1½ to 1. The construction gives the equivalent sum, say 57.9. For the same by computation, see Example 1, Art. 26.

(2.) *Single Conversion of Surface-Slope.* (See Formula 2, § 1, Art. 23.)—Find $CP = \frac{\sec\phi}{\sec\phi'}$ as before, observing that $CE' = CE$ when the side-slope is unchanged. No construction is necessary to find C R, which may be at once taken $= S$. We then have

$$CT = CR \times \frac{\sec\phi}{\sec\phi'} = S_1.$$

(3.) *Double Conversion with Surface-Slope made Level.* (See Formula 3, § 1, Art. 23.)—Omit that part of the construction pertaining to the finding of ϕ', which is now $= 0$. The point I′ will fall upon A, and P will coincide with M. Through M draw a parallel to I R cutting C A in a new point T′, (not marked on the figure:) then

$$CT' = CR \times \frac{CM}{CI} = CR \times \sec\phi = S\sqrt{\cot\sigma\tan\sigma'} \times \sec\phi = S_1.$$

(4.) *Single Conversion with Surface-Slope made Level.* (See Formula 4, § 1, Art. 23.)—Omit that part of the construction pertaining to the finding of ϕ', which is now $= 0$. The point I′

* The writer has not had the advantage of consulting the work of Macneil, cited on this subject by Mr. Morris, to whose paper and to the work of Mr. Lyons we have referred. (See Introduction.)

will fall upon A, and P will coincide with M. Take C R = S, and through M draw a parallel to I R cutting C A in T′: then

$$C\,T' = C\,R \times \frac{C\,M}{C\,I} = C\,R \times \sec\phi = S \sec\phi = S_1.$$

This construction may be simplified and applied to drawing a diagram for finding equivalent level-heights.

(5.) *To construct a Diagram for finding Equivalent Level-Heights.*—Upon any convenient scale take C A = 1. (Plate XIV.) With centre C and radius C A describe an arc A B. Make the angle $A\,C\,\gamma = \gamma$, the original surface-slope, and prolong $C\,\gamma$ as far as required. Take C E = the number denoting the rate of side-slope; that is, = 1½ for 1½ to 1; and for other side-slopes in the same manner. Draw E H perpendicular and H I parallel to C E. Through I draw $C\,I\,\phi$: then $A\,C\,I = \phi$. On any suitable scale make C K = S; draw $K\,\phi$ perpendicular to C K: then

$$C\,\phi = C\,K \times \sec\phi = S \sec\phi = S_1.$$

To complete the diagram, find the radius $C\,I\,\phi$ for each degree of surface-slope, from 0° upwards as far as required; and, in some convenient part, mark each of these radii with the degree of original surface-slope to which it corresponds. Also, graduate the scale C E, and through the points of division, at suitable regular intervals, draw perpendiculars to C E. The radius for a given sum of heights and given surface-slope may be measured by applying a scale from C. Or the scale may be hinged at C as a movable radius, upon a tablet; and the radii omitted.

25. To find the Solidity by a Diagram of Equivalent Level-Heights. (1.) *With Tables adapted to particular Side-Slopes.*—Tables VII., IX., and XI. are of this kind. Upon the diagram (Plate XIV.) find the radius marked with the given degree of surface-slope. Apply a scale, graduated like the scale C E, along the radius; and measure the distance intercepted between C and a line, perpendicular to C E, which passes through that division of the scale C E indicating the given sum of augmented heights. The distance measured upon the radius is the equivalent sum of level heights. If the distance upon C E be taken equal to the augmented height of a cross-section, the length measured upon the radius will be the equivalent level-height of the cross-section.

If there is a fraction in the number of degrees indicating the surface-slope, the space between the two adjacent radii containing the slope may be divided, by estimation, by the edge of the scale applied from C in the direction of the radii. The spaces between the perpendiculars to the scale C E may also be divided by estimation.

After finding the equivalent sum of level-heights, enter the proper table, under 0°, with this sum, and take out the tabular quantity.

Example 1.—The augmented end-heights are 38.5 and 20.6; surface-slope, 23°; side-slope, 1½ to 1. Required the equivalent sum of level-heights and the content of the whole ground.

The sum of heights containing the same solidity is found by Art. 96, Part I.; say 60. With 60 on the scale C E and the radius of 23°, find $C\,\phi$ upon the diagram equal to, say 77.8 +; then

Opposite 77.8 +, under 0°, in Table VII., find the solidity . . . 8406.9 +

Example 2.—The first end-height, from the roadbed, is 28.7; surface-slope, 18° to the right. Second end-height, 14.5; surface-slope, 12° to the right. The side-slope is 1½ to 1; roadbed, 24. Required the equivalent sum of level-heights and the content.

The surface is here curved, because the surface-slopes at the ends are different. The solidity of the whole ground may be approximately found (see Example 1, Art. 104, Part I.) by an augmented sum of heights 59.68 and a surface-slope of 16°.

(2.) *With Table XV., adapted to all Side-Slopes.*—Find the equivalent sum of level-heights as directed in section 1. With this equivalent sum take the tabular quantity from the First Part of Table XV., and multiply the quantity thus found by twice the rate of the given side-slope.

Note.—Twice the rate of side-slope may be taken from the auxiliary table B, page 179. The radial scale may, however, be so divided that no multiplier is required. (See § 5, page 312.)

Example 1.—Take Example 1, § 1. The equivalent sum of level-heights is found as before, 77.8 +; then

Opposite 77, under 8 +, in Table XV., say	2802.96
Multiplier equal to twice the rate of side-slope	3
Content of the whole ground	8408.88

Example 2.—Take Example 2, § 1. For the operation, see Example 1, Art. 104, Part I.

Explanation.—The tabular quantity of the First Part of Table XV. is $\frac{1}{6}$ L S^2. If this be multiplied by twice the rate of side-slope = 2 cot σ, there results $\frac{1}{4}$ L S^2 cot σ, which is the solidity when the end-heights are equal and the surface-slope level. (See Formula 19, page 281.)

The Redundant Prism may obviously be found by the above method, as it is contained under a level surface-slope. The sum of the end-heights is the tabular number from Table II.

(3.) *Depths of Equivalent Prisms found by Construction.*—Let S_1 be the equivalent sum of level-heights, and S the sum of heights for the redundant prism. It is required to find the depth of a prism equal to the solidity contained between the surface and roadbed. The solidity of the whole ground is $\frac{1}{4}$ L S_1^2 cot σ, and of the redundant prism $\frac{1}{4}$ L S^2 cot σ. The difference is $\frac{1}{4}$ L $(S_1^2 - S^2)$ cot σ. Put $S_2 = \sqrt{S_1^2 - S^2}$; then the solidity of the residual prismoid is $\frac{1}{4}$ L $S_2^2 \times$ cot σ. It is obvious that S_2 may be found by the construction of § 3, Art. 12, after obtaining S_1 and S. Having found S_2, we may proceed as above directed to find the content. We may, however, proceed at once (Art. 97, Part I.) to find an equivalent depth under the original surface-slope, and then work as above directed. (See Art. 13.)

(4.) *Remarks on the Method of Equivalent Level-Heights.*—The facility of constructing a diagram for any required side-slope, together with the use of Table XV. as above shown, make this a method of general application. As a purely tabular method, such as indicated in § 4, Art. 23, it has advantages in the compendiousness of the tables of cubical content. To make it satisfactory, however, the auxiliary tables would require to be as extensive as a series constructed on the plan of Table VII. and others similar, embracing the same number of side-slopes.

(5.) *Bases of Equivalent Square Prisms found by Auxiliary Angles.*—From the equation V = $\frac{1}{4}$ L S^2 cot σ $\sec^2 \phi$, (§ 1, Art. 23,) we have for the side of the square base A′, $\sqrt{A'} = \sqrt{\frac{1}{4} S^2 \cot \sigma} \times \sec \phi$. If $\sqrt{\frac{1}{4} S^2 \cot \sigma}$ be found as in Art. 16, and then put for S in the formula of section 4, Art. 24, the construction according to section 5 will give the side of the Equivalent Square Base instead of the sum of Equivalent Level Heights.

The argument required for Table XV. is $\sqrt{A'} \times \sqrt{8} = S \sec \phi \times \sqrt{\frac{1}{4} \cot \sigma} \times \sqrt{8} = S \sec \phi \times \sqrt{2 \cot \sigma}$. Hence, to find the content, enter Table XV. with S sec ϕ, and multiply the result by 2 cot σ, which is the rule above given in Sect. 2. (See also the Explanation, page 312.)

Or if (as indicated in the Note to § 2) the radial scale (§ 5, Art. 24) be so graduated that its unit is to the unit of C K (Plate XIV.) as $\frac{1}{\sqrt{2 \cot \sigma}}$ to 1, the reading of the radial scale will be S sec $\phi \times \sqrt{2 \cot \sigma}$, and the quantity taken from Table XV. with this argument will be the required content; and the method of equivalent square bases is substituted for that of equivalent level heights. We have already employed a similar method of graduation. (See the Scale O P, Arts. 14 and 16.)

The Second Part of Table XV. might be used in a similar manner to find the second term or correction, (Art. 85, Part I.,) when the sum employed for the First Part is the augmented sum of heights. Observe that the Redundant Prism is to be subtracted when the content obtained is that of the whole ground, (Art. 13.)

Example.—Take Example 1, § 1. The radial scale must here be graduated so as to read S sec $\phi \times \sqrt{2 \times 1\frac{1}{2}}$ = S sec $\phi \sqrt{3}$. With this scale measure the radius corresponding to 60 on the scale C K and to 23°, and find, say 134.8—.

Then opposite 134, under 8— in Table XV., find the whole content, say.................... 8408.88

If, as suggested in Art. 16, a table similar to XV. were made to contain the term L S^2, the multiplier (§ 2, Art. 25) would become $\frac{1}{4}$ cot σ; which would not, in general, be more convenient than 2 cot σ which we have employed. Were it desired to dispense with the multiplier by the method here explained, the unit of the radial scale should, for the proposed table, bear to that of C K the proportion $\frac{1}{\sqrt{\frac{1}{4}\cot\sigma}}$ to $1 = \frac{2}{\sqrt{\cot\sigma}}$ to 1; which would increase the size of the divisions of the radial scale.

A table of the kind mentioned would frequently be convenient, (Art. 9; and Arts. 126, 127, Part I.) On a future occasion we may perhaps supply it.

By bisecting the angle of surface-slope on a partial cross-section, a median line may be found homologous with the augmented centre-height of a full cross-section. This line might be obtained by construction, or by the aid of auxiliary tables. Thus both whole and sub sections may, theoretically, be included under one method; but the practical application of this idea would perhaps be too complex.

26. Examples in Conversion of Slopes by Logarithmic Formulæ. The formulæ for the following examples will be found in § 2, Art. 23.

Example 1. *Double Conversion.* (See Formula 1.)—The augmented end-heights are 95 and 64; surface-slope, 35°; side-slope, $\frac{1}{4}$ to 1. The sum of end-heights containing the same solidity is found by Art. 96, Part I.; say 160. It is required to find a sum of heights which will contain the same solidity under a surface-slope of 18° and side-slope $1\frac{1}{2}$ to 1. The construction for this example is shown in Fig. 2, Plate XIII. (See § 1, Art. 26.)

We have first to find log. cos ϕ and log. cos ϕ'.

Log. tan γ, 35°	9.8452268
Log. cot σ = log. $\frac{1}{4}$	—1.3979400
Log. sin ϕ, (say 10° 4′ 54″)	9.2431668

Whence log. cos ϕ = 9.9932419.

Log. tan γ', 18°	9.5117760
Log. cot σ' = log. $1\frac{1}{2}$	0.1760913
Log. sin ϕ', (say 29° 10′ 7″)	9.6878673

Whence log. cos ϕ' = 9.9411084.

Having now log. cos ϕ and log. cos ϕ', we proceed to find those logarithms which are yet wanting, and to subtract log. cos ϕ from the sum of all the others.

Log. S = log. 160	2.2041200
$\frac{1}{2}$ log. cot σ = $\frac{1}{2}$ log. $\frac{1}{4}$	—1.6989700
$\frac{1}{2}$ log. tan σ' = $\frac{1}{2}$ log. $\frac{2}{3}$	—1.9119544
Log. cos ϕ'	9.9411084
	11.7561528
Log. cos ϕ	9.9932419
Log. S_1, the required sum, 57.93	1.7629109
160, under 35°, in Table XI., gives	6113.3
57.93, under 18°, in Table VII., gives	6113.1

Example 2. *Single Conversion*. (See Formula 4.)—The augmented end-heights are 38.5 and 20.6; surface-slope, 23°; side-slope, $1\frac{1}{2}$ to 1. Required the equivalent sum of level-heights and the content. The sum of heights containing the same solidity is found by Art. 96, Part I., or by computation; say 60.

The construction for this example is shown on the diagram, Plate XIV. (See Example 1, § 1, Art. 25.)

We have to find log. cos ϕ, and to add to it log. S.

Log. tan γ, 23°	. 9.6278519
Log. cot σ = log. $1\frac{1}{2}$	. 0.1760913
Log. sin ϕ 39° 32′ 49″.4	. 9.8039432
Whence log. cos ϕ = 9.8871118.	
Log. S = log. 60	. 1.7781513
Log. cos ϕ (= tabular log. — 10)	—1.8871118
Log. S_1, the required sum, 77.81	. 1.8910395
60, under 23°, in Table VII., gives	8409.1
77.81, under 0°, in Table VII., gives	8409.1

NOTES.

We here record some formulæ which have been omitted in the text. Those of Note 1, although early known to us, we had not actually employed until, when too late for convenient insertion, they were used to verify some of the tabular computations. Those of Note 2 were at one time embodied, at greater length, in the text to which they refer; but were afterwards rejected as not entirely appropriate.

In closing the work we have finally decided to preserve them all in the following form:—

(1.) *Article* 10, *page* 296.—From $V = \frac{1}{4}\, L\, S^2 \times \frac{\cot \sigma}{\cos^2 \phi}$ (page 309,) we find for the logarithm of Table XVI., log. $\frac{2 \cot \sigma}{\cos^2 \phi} = \text{log. } 2 \cot \sigma - 2 \text{ log. } \cos \phi$.

The formulæ of the catalogue, for the computation of Tables XVI., XVII., XIX., and XX., are frequently less expeditious than the following, in which tan σ and cot σ are derivable from the rate of side-slope, and where tan γ and cot γ may be taken from a table of natural tangents and cotangents.

For Table XVI.—The logarithm required is log. $\frac{2 \tan \sigma}{\tan^2 \sigma - \tan^2 \gamma} = \text{log. } \frac{2 \tan \sigma}{(\tan \sigma + \tan \gamma)\,(\tan \sigma - \tan \gamma)} =$ log. $2 \tan \sigma - \left\{ \text{log. } (\tan \sigma + \tan \gamma) + \text{log. } (\tan \sigma - \tan \gamma) \right\}$.

For Table XVII.—The logarithm required is (by the formulæ of Art. 18) log. $\frac{\cot^2 \gamma}{\cot \gamma - \cot \sigma} =$ 2 log. $\cot \gamma$ — log. $(\cot \gamma - \cot \sigma)$. A similar form for computation by bases, derived from the same formulæ, would give log. $\frac{1}{\cot \gamma - \cot \sigma} =$ log. 1 — log. $(\cot \gamma - \cot \sigma)$. See note, page 49.

For Tables XIX. and XX.—By aid of the formula $\tan a \pm \tan b = \frac{\sin (a \pm b)}{\cos a \cos b}$, the expression log. $\frac{1}{2} \frac{\cos \sigma \cos \gamma}{\sin (\sigma \pm \gamma)}$ may be transformed to log. $\frac{1}{2}$ — log. $(\tan \sigma \pm \tan \gamma)$; which serves for Table XIX. In a similar manner log. $\frac{1}{2} \frac{\cos \gamma}{\sin (\sigma \pm \gamma)}$, becomes log. $\frac{1}{2}$ — log. $(\tan \sigma \pm \tan \gamma)$ — log. $\cos \gamma$; which serves for Table XX. If the logarithm for Table XIX. be denoted by log. XIX., and that for Table XX. by log. XX., we have log. XX. = log. XIX. — log. cos. γ.

(2.) *Surface-Slope not given in Degrees*, (pp. 281, 282.)—If the surface-slope were given by its rate similarly to the side-slope, we might determine the tangent, and find the degree of surface-slope by Table A; and then proceed, by any suitable mode of construction or computation, to the solution of any problems embraced by our rules. The following substitutions, which directly employ the rate of surface-slope, may, however, be noted.

Let r denote the rate of side-slope, and r′ the rate of surface-slope; that is, let $r = \cot \sigma$, and $r' = \cot \gamma$: we shall find $\frac{\tan \sigma}{\tan^2 \sigma - \tan^2 \gamma} = \frac{r r'^2}{r'^2 - r^2}$. (Formula 16.) Also $\frac{1}{\cot \gamma - \cot \sigma} = \frac{1}{r' - r}$, (Formulæ 21, 24;) and this divided by $\tan^2 \gamma$ gives $\frac{\cot^2 \gamma}{\cot \gamma - \cot \sigma} = \frac{r'^2}{r' - r}$, (Formula 22.)

DESCRIPTION OF THE PLATES.

In order to view Plates I., II., and III., turn the top of the volume towards the left, (or direct the sight across the page,) so as to bring the right-hand margin of the plate upwards.

Plates I., II., III., and IV.—These represent the warped surfaces of Art. 9, page 17, and also the solid forms to be considered in excavation and embankment upon such surfaces. The drawings are from models made of rectangular blocks, the blocks being formed of veneers piled together. The veneers represent horizontal strata, and the surface of the ground is shown by curved bands which represent the outcroppings of the strata. The curved lines of division between the strata are called by topographers *Contour Lines.* That contour line which extends on to the roadbed is the *Ground-Trace,* (Art. 16, page 17.) The ends of the models are presented towards the spectator, and are numbered.

Plates I., II., and III. represent excavation and embankment upon the same (or mean) width of roadbed. The numbers designate the *Varieties* of the General Scheme, page 21. Nos. 1 and 2 give a satisfactory (though not strict) illustration of the surfaces described in Art. 8, page 16.

The lines drawn across the roadbed and continued on the side of the excavation or embankment denote the place of *neutral cross-sections.* Attention to these lines will aid the study of Art. 32, page 21, by supposing, when necessary, the neutral cross-section to be at the end of the work.

Plate IV. represents earthwork as it is really made; viz. with extra width in excavation, to permit drainage. No. 13 belongs to Variety 3 of the General Scheme, and shows a plane surface with straight ground-trace. No. 14 belongs to Variety 4 of the General Scheme.

The remarks of Art. 20, page 18, should be remembered in viewing these plates.

Plate V. See Art. 54, page 29; and Art. 88, page 44.
Plate VI. See Art. 57, page 31; and Art. 88, page 44.
Plate VII. See Art. 58, page 31; and Art. 12, page 300.
Plate VIII. See Art. 55, page 30, for the Mid-Section Diagram; and Arts. 96, page 47, and 12, page 301, for the General Scale.
Plate IX. See Art. 97, page 48; and Art. 12, page 301.
Plate X. See Art. 14, page 302; and Art. 15, page 303.
Plate XI. See Art. 14, page 302; and Art. 15, page 303.
Plate XII. See Art. 16, page 304; and Art. 17, page 305.
Plate XIII. See Art. 18, § 2, page 306, for Fig. 1; and Art. 24, page 310, for Fig. 2.
Plate XIV. See Art. 24, § 5, page 311; and Art. 25, § 5, page 312.

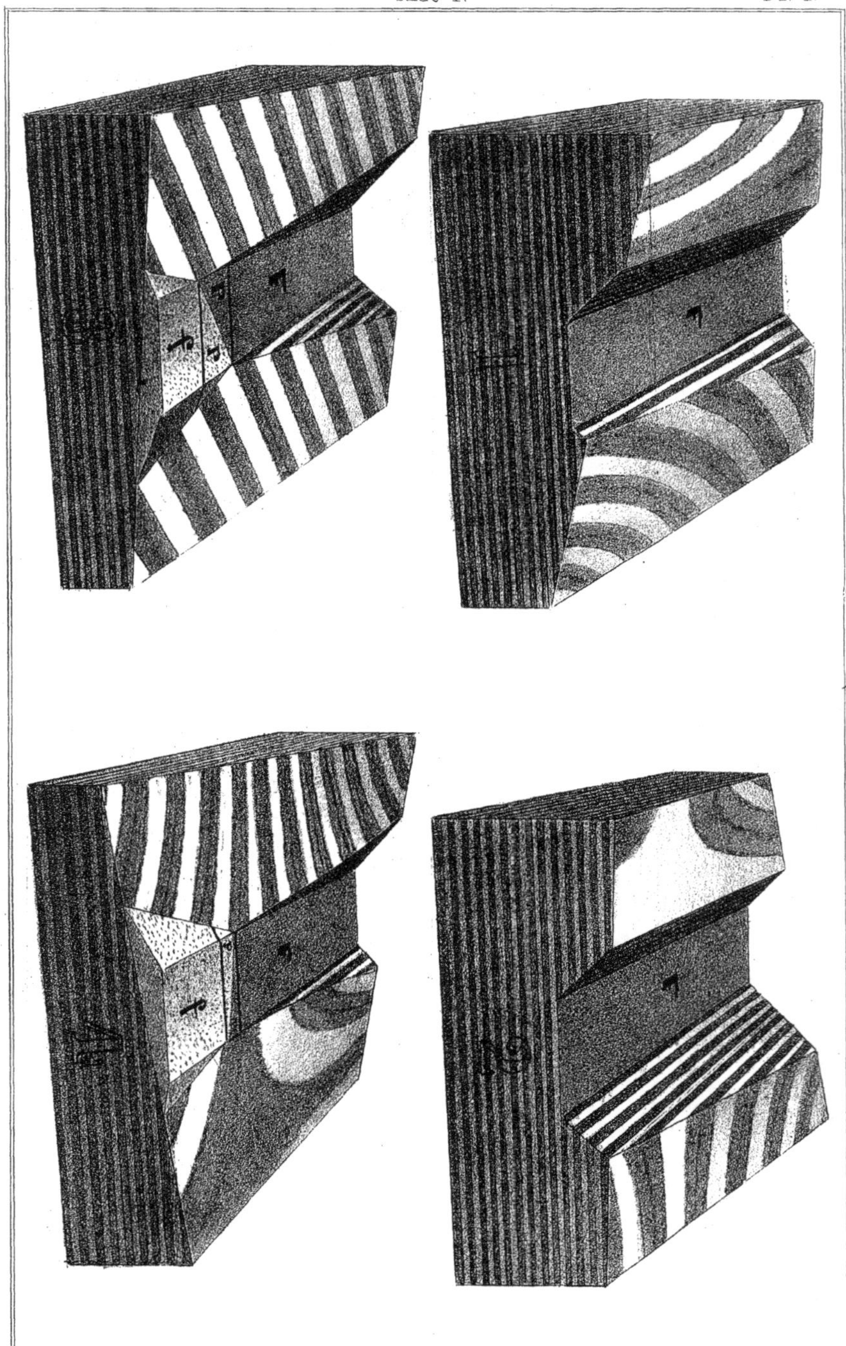

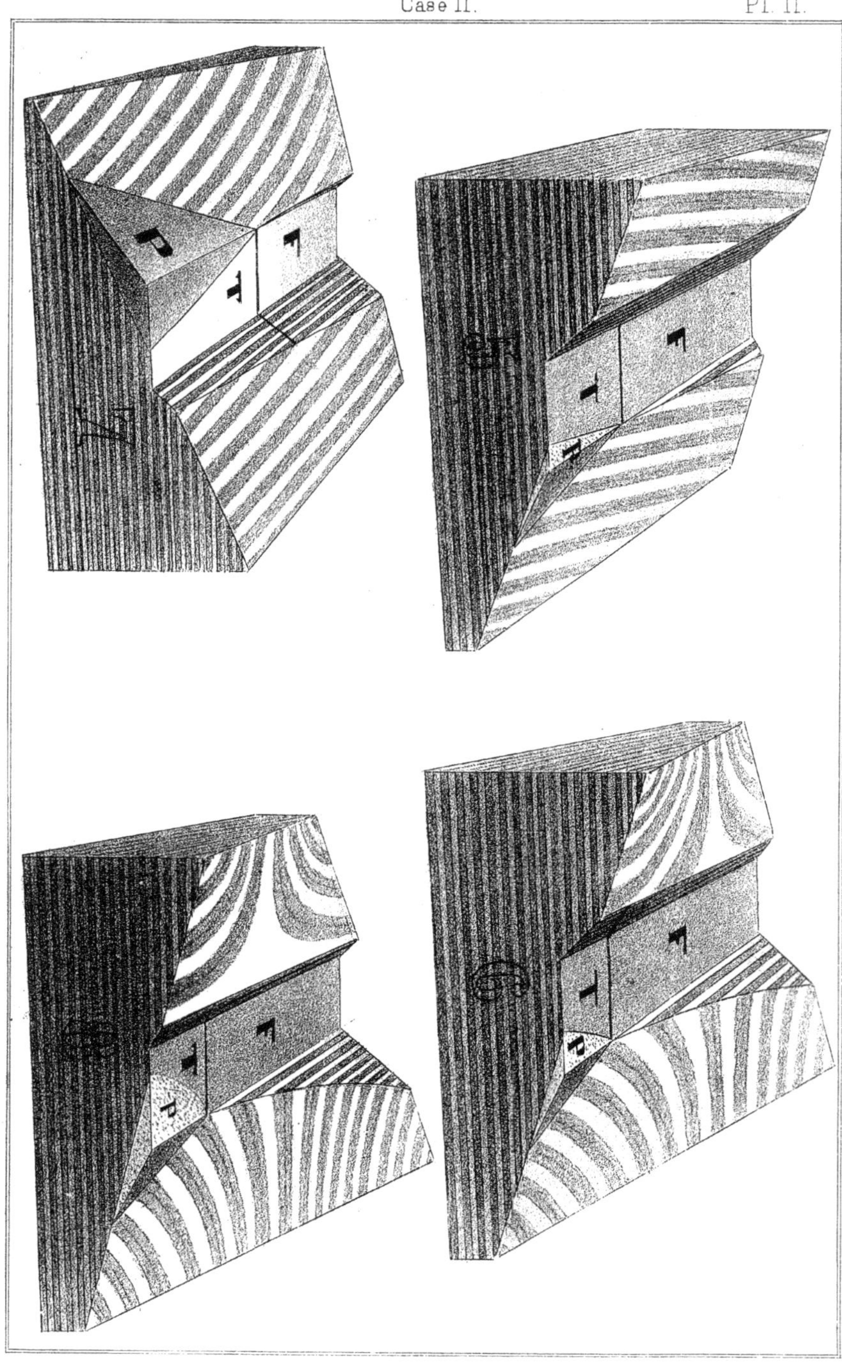
P
T
F
T
F
P
T
F
P
T
F
P

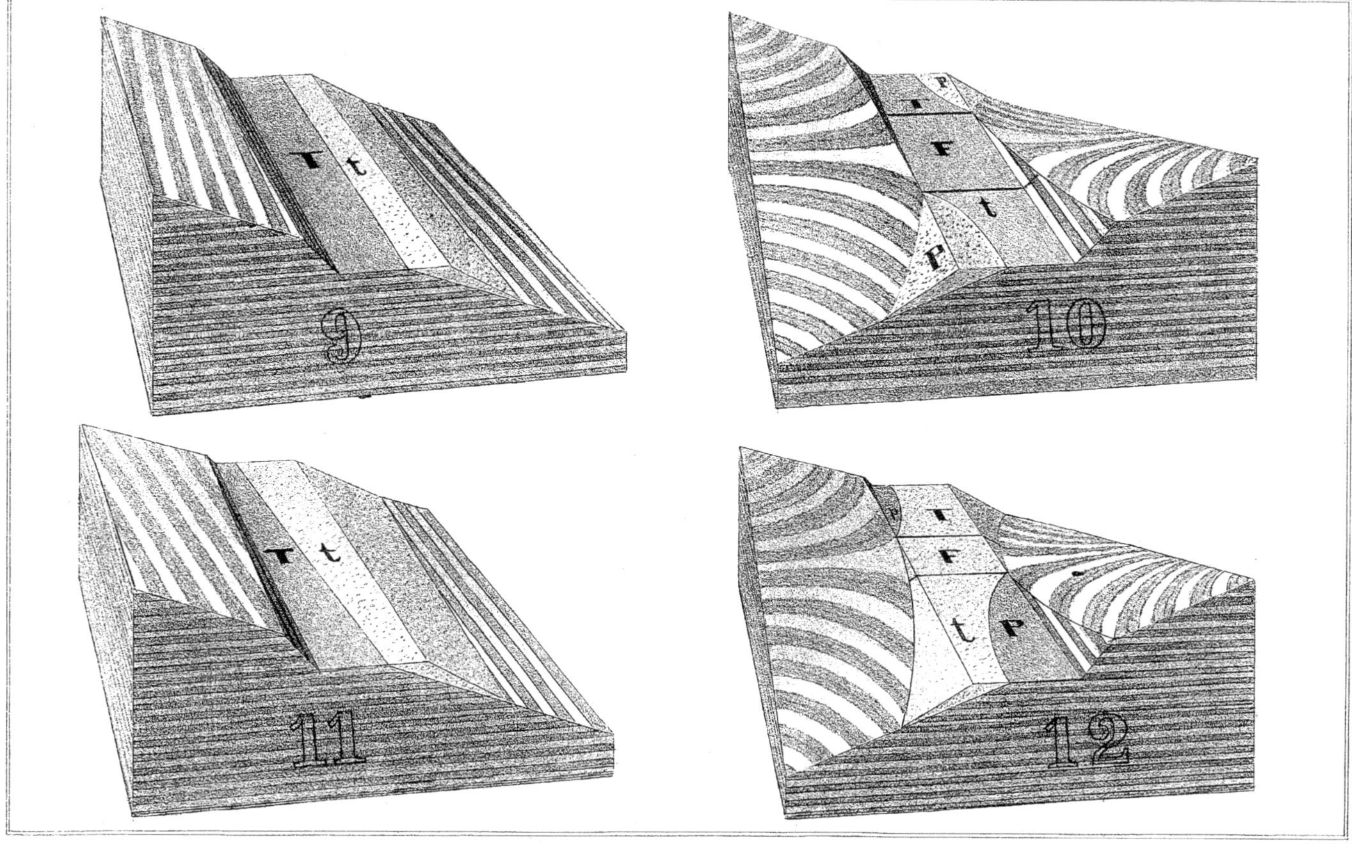
T t
9
P
T
F
t
P
10
T t
11
P T
F
t P
12

Pl IV

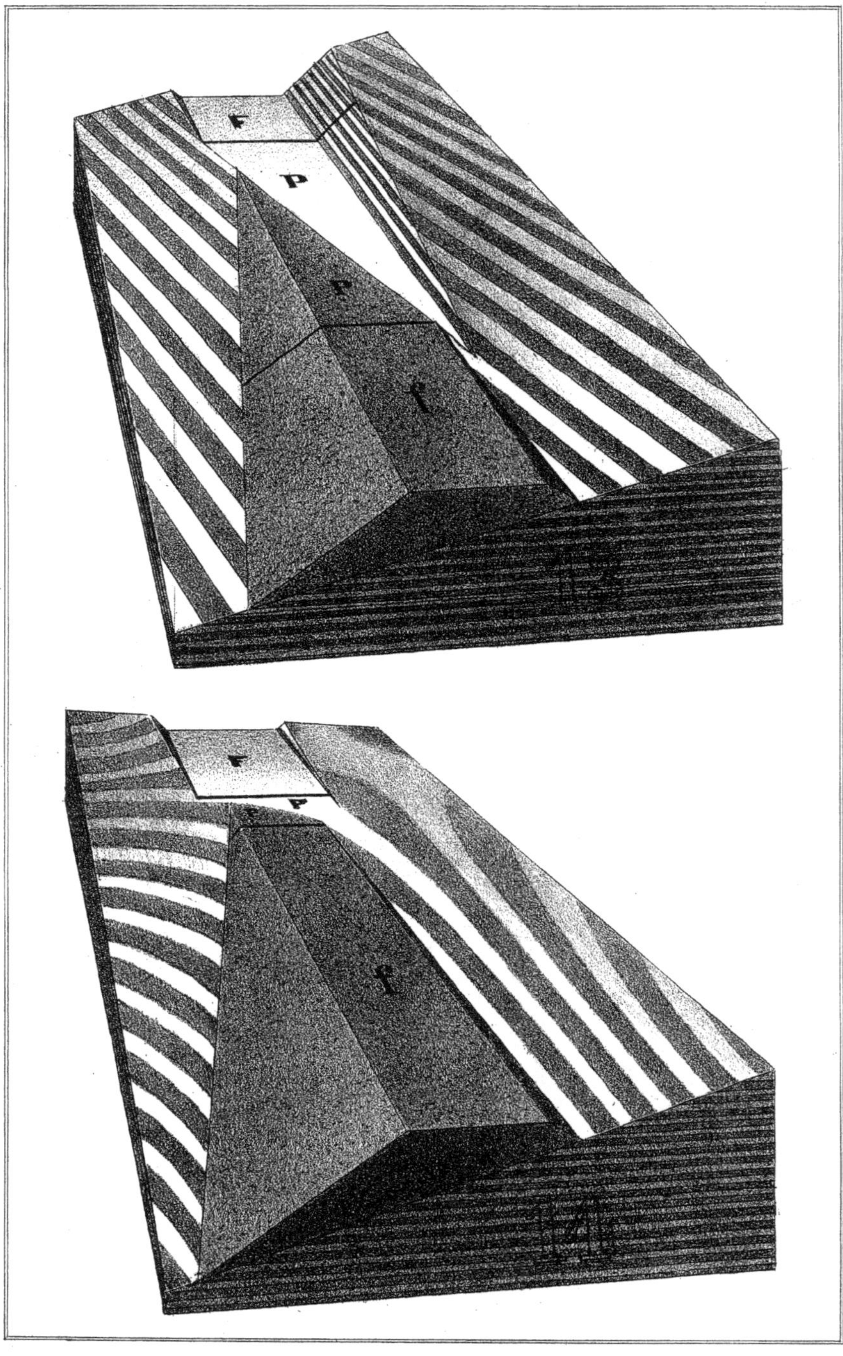

CROSS SECTIONS

For twelve consecutive Sections
Scale of the cross sections, 20ft to 1 inch.

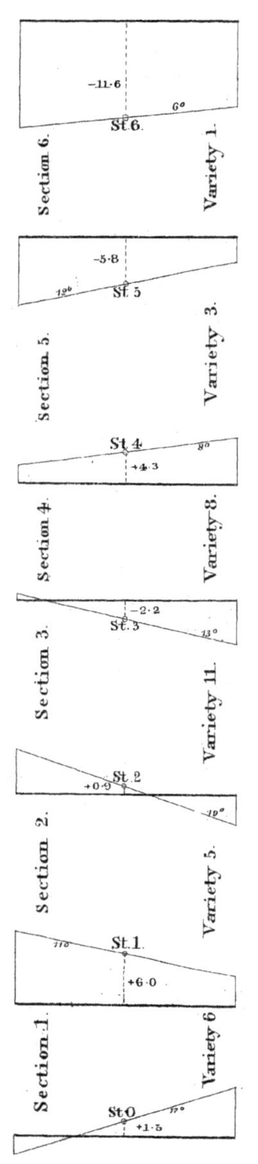

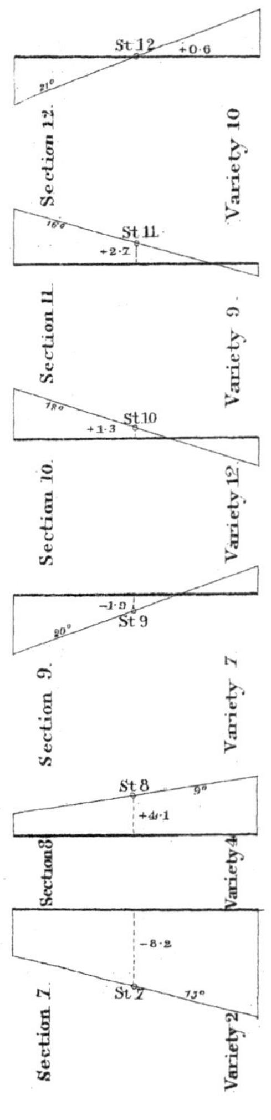

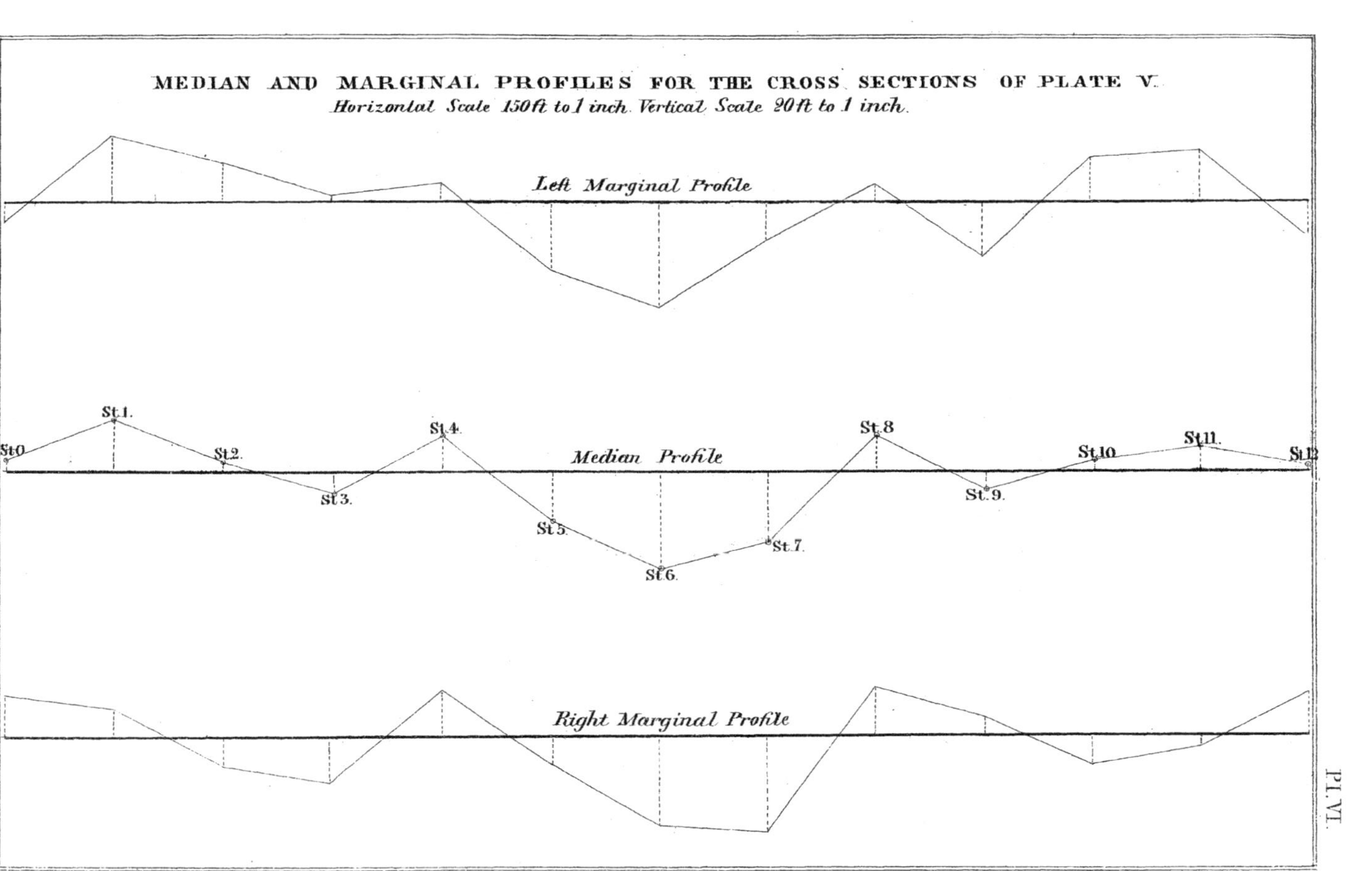
MEDIAN AND MARGINAL PROFILES FOR THE CROSS SECTIONS OF PLATE V.
Horizontal Scale 150 ft to 1 inch. Vertical Scale 20 ft to 1 inch.
Left Marginal Profile
St.0
St.1.
St.2.
St.3.
St.4.
St.5.
St.6.
St.7.
St.8
St.9.
St.10
St.11.
St.12
Median Profile
Right Marginal Profile

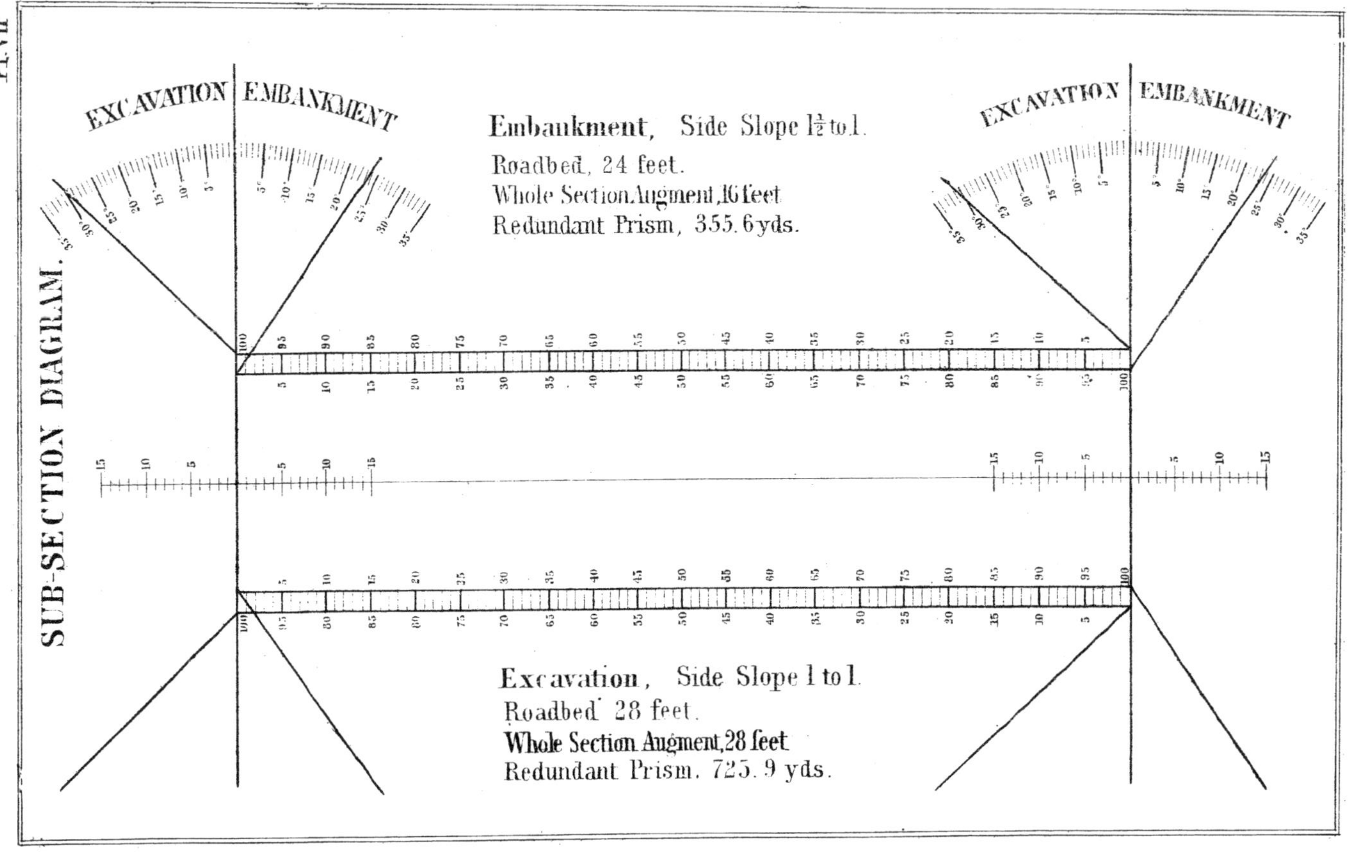
SUB-SECTION DIAGRAM.
EXCAVATION
EMBANKMENT
EXCAVATION
EMBANKMENT
Embankment, Side Slope 1½ to 1.
Roadbed, 24 feet.
Whole Section Augment, 16 feet
Redundant Prism, 355.6 yds.
Excavation, Side Slope 1 to 1.
Roadbed 28 feet.
Whole Section Augment, 28 feet
Redundant Prism. 725.9 yds.

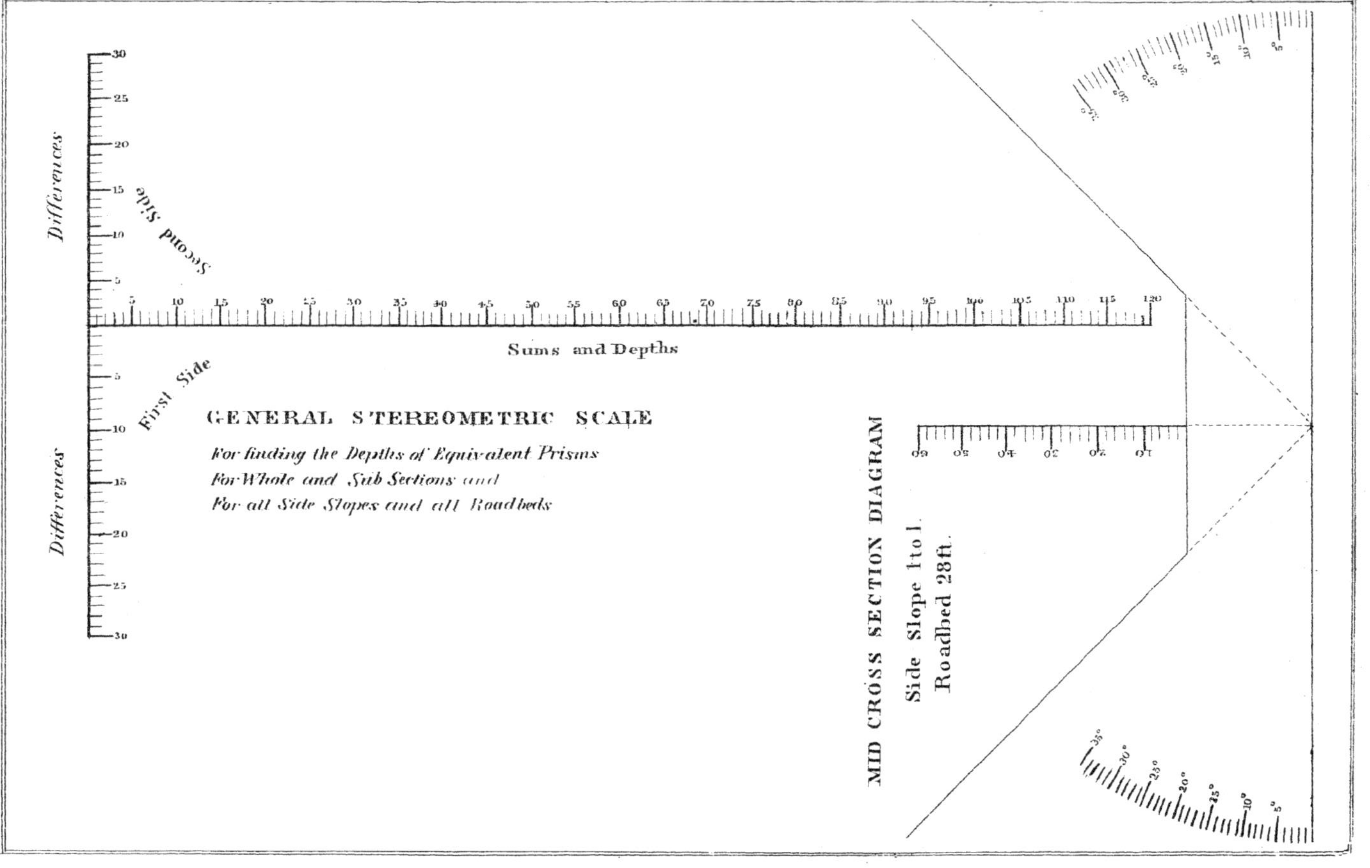
Differences
Second Side
Sums and Depths
First Side
Differences
GENERAL STEREOMETRIC SCALE
For finding the Depths of Equivalent Prisms
For Whole and Sub Sections and
For all Side Slopes and all Roadbeds
MID CROSS SECTION DIAGRAM
Side Slope 1 to 1.
Roadbed 28 ft.

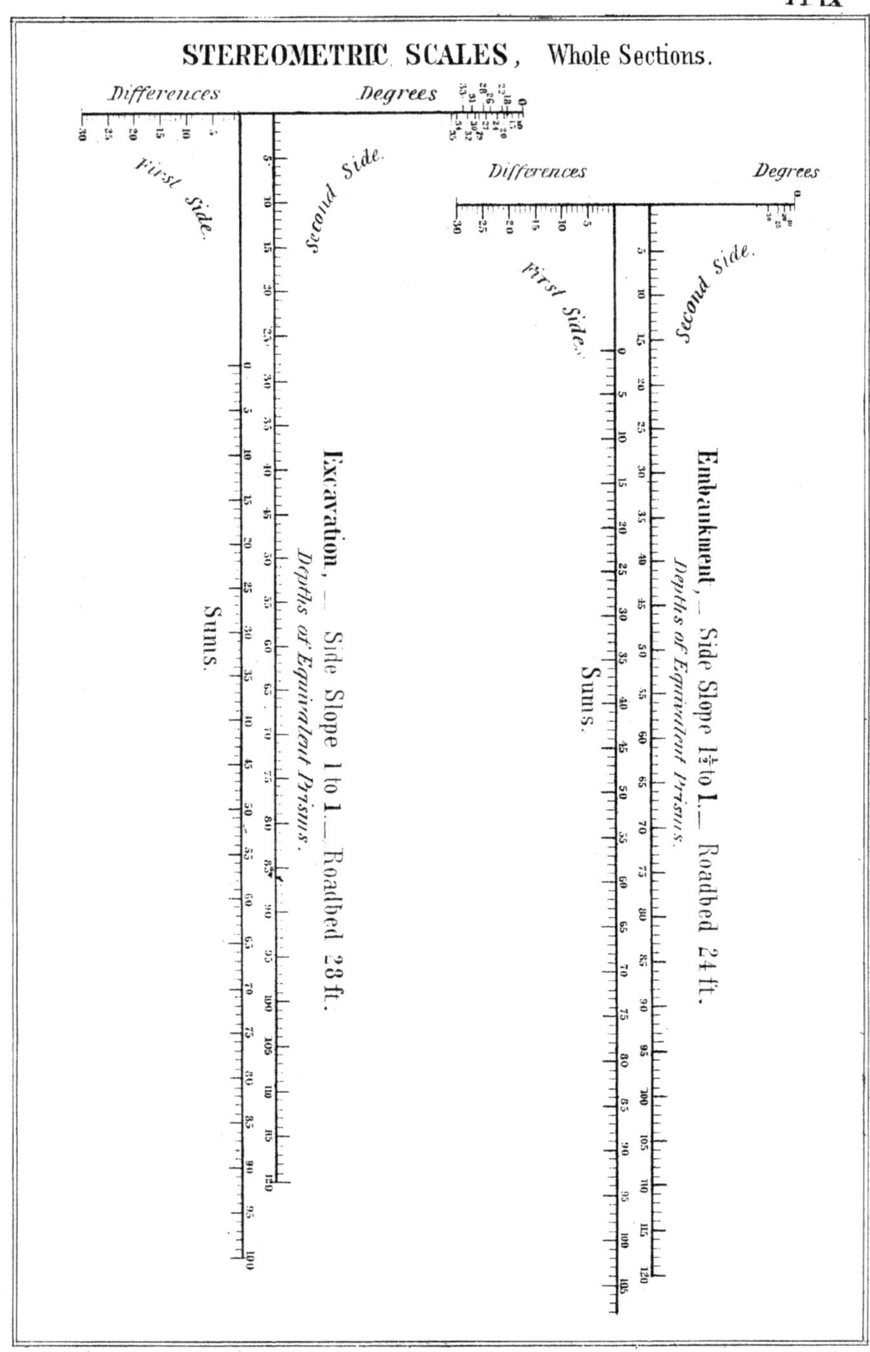
STEREOMETRIC SCALES, Whole Sections.
Differences
Degrees
First Side.
Second Side.
Sums.
Excavation, — Side Slope 1 to 1. — Roadbed 28 ft.
Depths of Equivalent Prisms.
Differences
Degrees
First Side.
Second Side.
Sums.
Embankment, — Side Slope 1½ to 1. — Roadbed 24 ft.
Depths of Equivalent Prisms.

Pl. X.

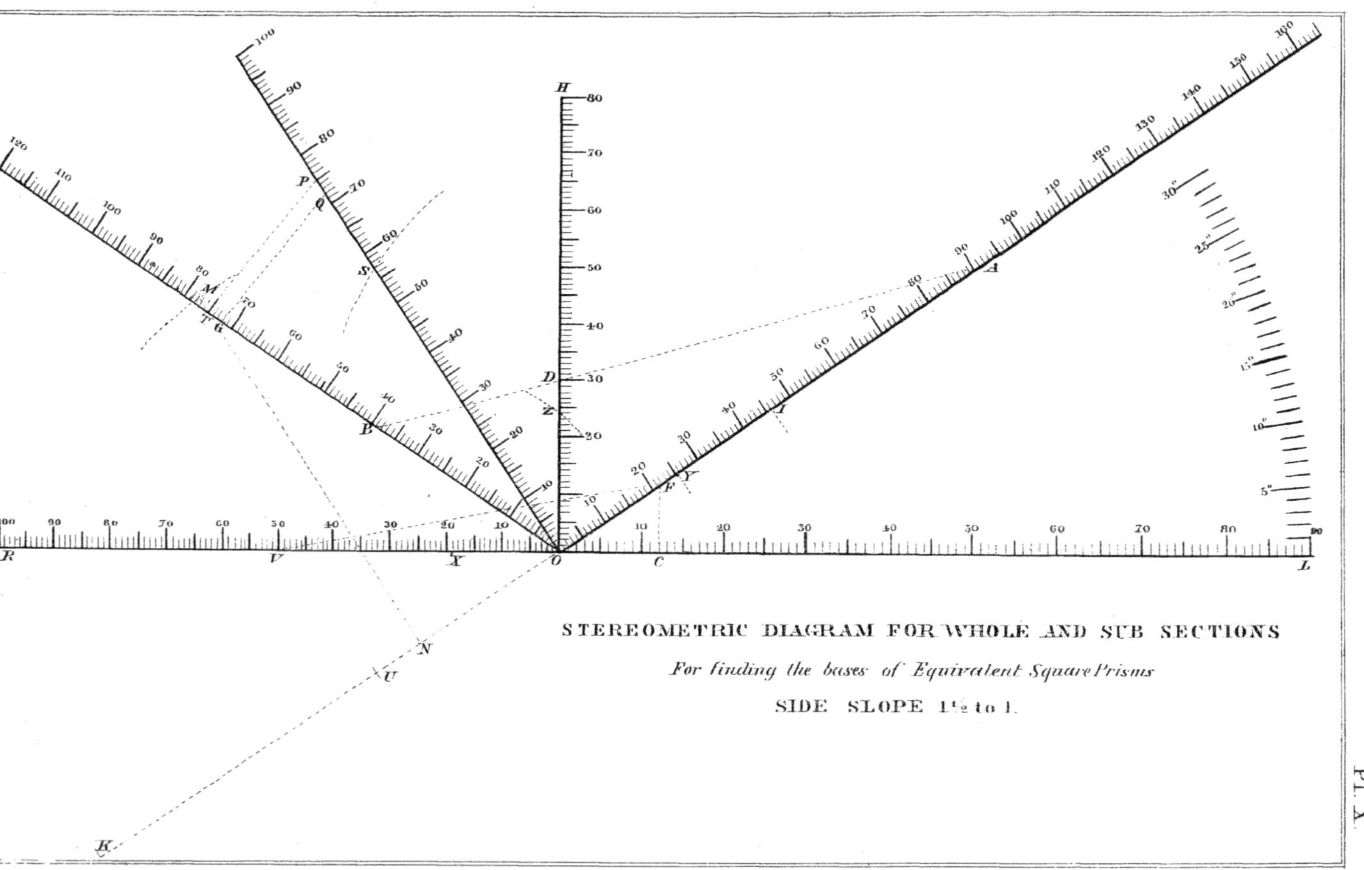

STEREOMETRIC DIAGRAM FOR WHOLE AND SUB SECTIONS

For finding the bases of Equivalent Square Prisms

SIDE SLOPE 1½ to 1.

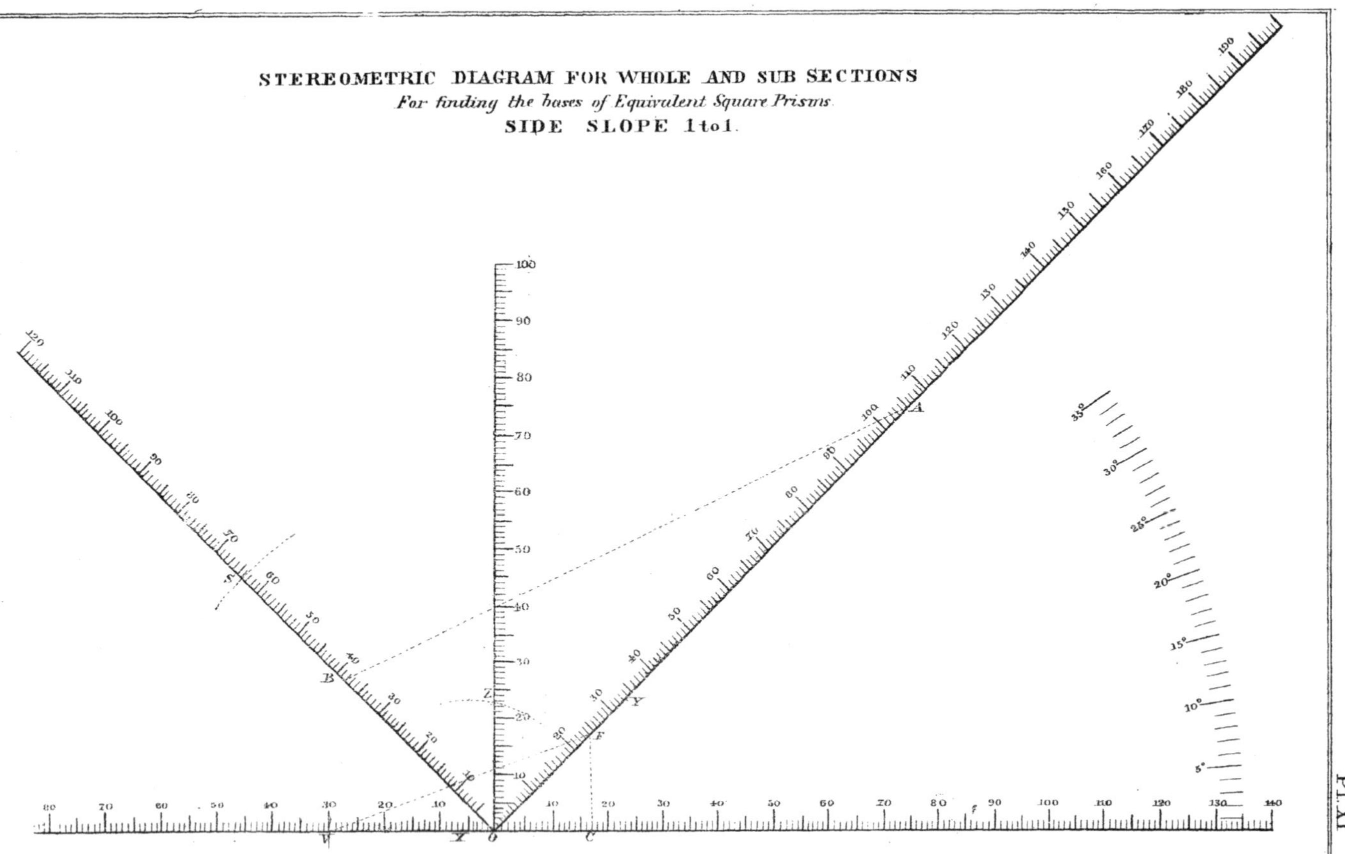

STEREOMETRIC DIAGRAM FOR WHOLE AND SUB SECTIONS
For finding the bases of Equivalent Square Prisms.
SIDE SLOPE 1 to 1.

Pl. XI

Pl. XII

Pl. XIII

Fig. 1.
X
80
70
60
50
Q
40
V
30
20
10
H
K
N
R
T
Y
M
B
F
P
S
O
U
L
Fig. 2
110
N
B
100
90
80
70
60
50
40
30
20
10
C
E
T
R
A
E'
H
I
M
P
L'
M'
H'
0

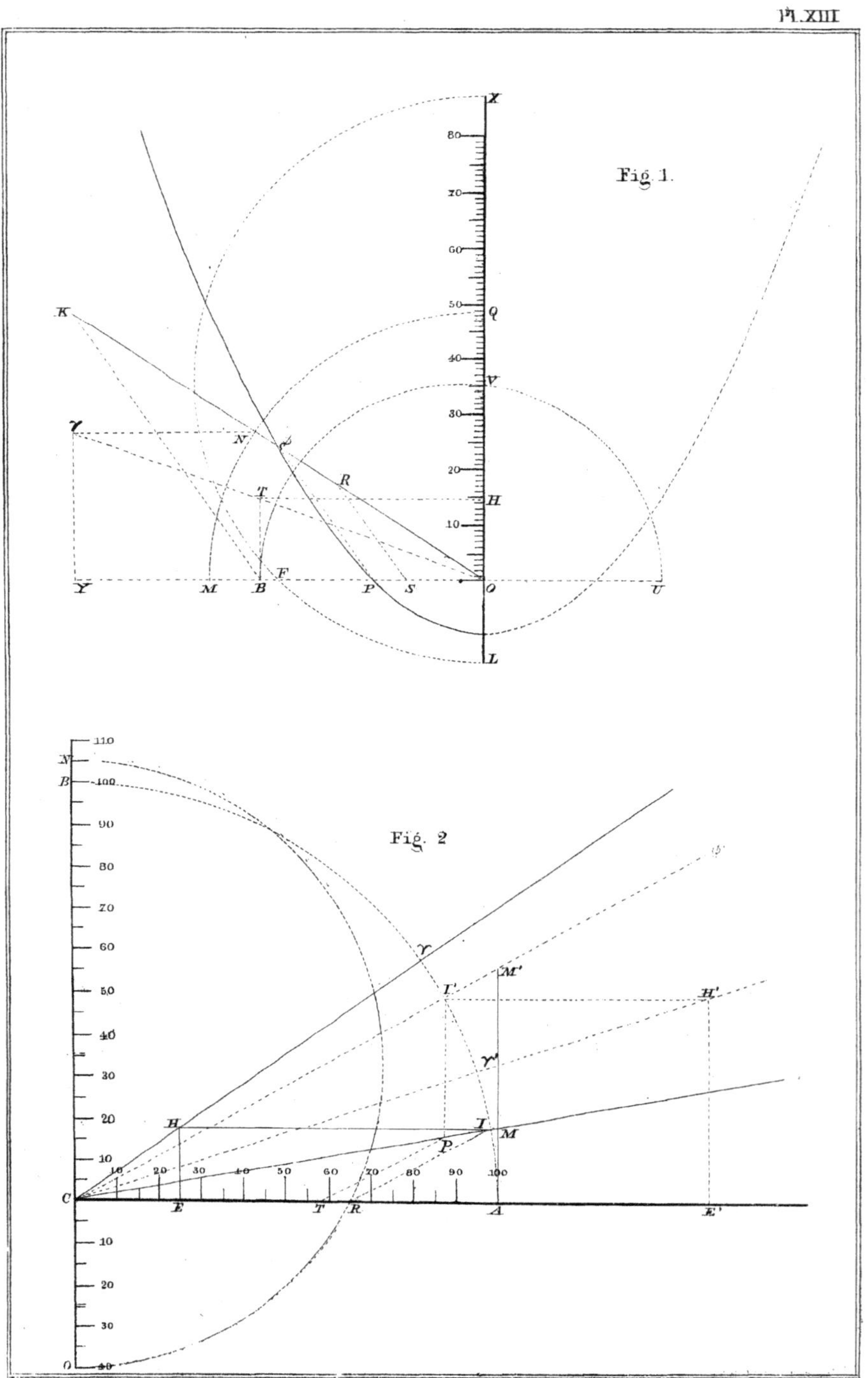

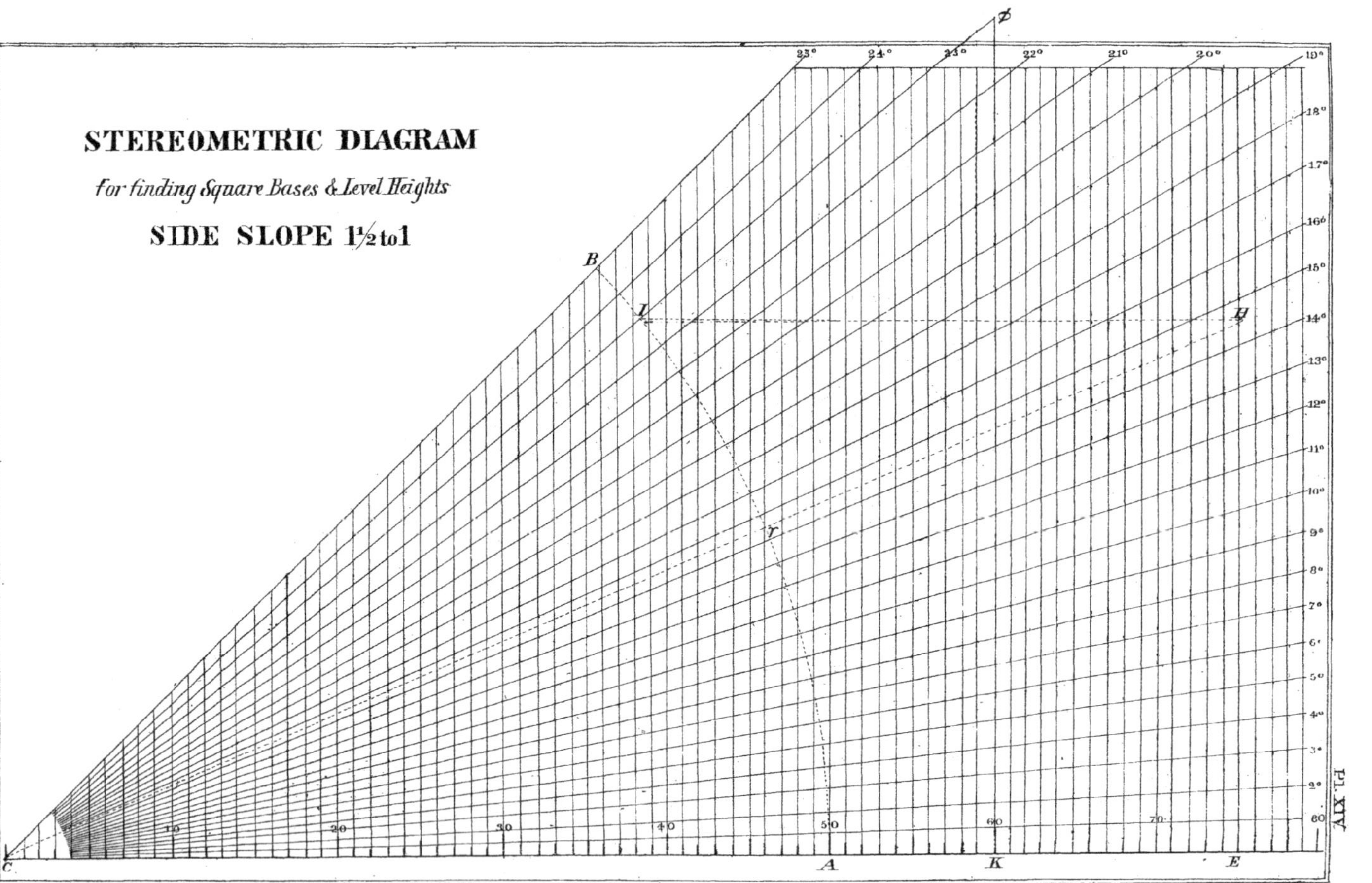

Pl. XIV.
STEREOMETRIC DIAGRAM
for finding Square Bases & Level Heights
SIDE SLOPE 1½ to 1
25° 24° 23° 22° 21° 20° 19°
18° 17° 16° 15° 14° 13° 12° 11° 10° 9° 8° 7° 6° 5° 4° 3° 2°
10 20 30 40 50 60 70 80
B
L
H
D
Y
C
A
K
E